# AN INTRODUCTION TO CHRISTIAN EDUCATION

Marvin J. Taylor

Editor

ABINGDON PRESS

NASHVILLE    NEW YORK

AN INTRODUCTION TO CHRISTIAN EDUCATION

*Copyright © 1966 by Abingdon Press*

*Library of Congress Catalog Card Number: 66-11452*

Scripture quotations unless otherwise noted are from
the Revised Standard Version of the Bible, copyrighted
1946 and 1952 by the Division of Christian Education, National Council of Churches, and are used by
permission.

SET UP, PRINTED, AND BOUND BY THE
PARTHENON PRESS, AT NASHVILLE,
TENNESSEE, UNITED STATES OF AMERICA

# INTRODUCTION

ONE OF THE MOST SIGNIFICANT CHARACTERISTICS OF THE CONTEMPORARY
Christian education movement is change. Very little appears to be static or
beyond question. Curriculum theory and materials, age group ministries, religion and the public schools, and even the whole matter of Protestant strategies
for Christian education are undergoing searching analysis and evaluation. These
and many other comparable evidences of change have called forth this book,
still another in this series of Abingdon Press publications.

The first volume, *Studies in Religious Education,* appeared in 1931 and
served the churches well until after World War II. *Orientation in Religious
Education* followed in 1950. It was succeeded by *Religious Education: A
Comprehensive Survey* in early 1960. Thus, this *Introduction to Christian
Education* has a considerable history, all of which points rather emphatically
to the continuing forward movement evident in Christian education today.

In conversations and correspondence while planning the book, the question
of authorship was repeatedly raised. A few advised that I write the entire
book, while others preferred a symposium. Upon reflection, however, it was
concluded that only a symposium could do justice to this broad field. For
Christian education is really a collective discipline, catching up much of its
substance from other areas (biblical and theological studies, learning theory,
psychology, educational philosophy, etc.). In fact, its very diversity is so
great that some even question whether it has any central unity. And this
variety of interests is so wide, and the depth being achieved within each so
significant, that I doubt if any one author can any longer do justice to *all* of
Christian education. There is now simply too much for one person to master
thoroughly.

It is readily acknowledged that the decision regarding multiple authorship
is made at the sacrifice of a single theoretical viewpoint. The several contributors
bring their different approaches to bear on the segment of the discipline within
which they write. But I view this as an asset rather than a liability! The
primary audiences to which this book is addressed, college and seminary classes,
all have instructors who are quite competent to develop such a theoretical
framework. A symposium then provides data from a variety of viewpoints
which can be considered and interpreted in the light of this educational
philosophy. Thus, a symposium makes available a whole range of insights which
may be discussed as a group is building its own philosophy of Christian
education.

The reader will have already noticed that the three previous volumes all
used *religious* education in their titles. In this one we have turned to *Christian*

education. I believe that this is one of the significant changes which has been taking place. A profound new respect for the Christian heritage has developed among church educators. Biblical and theological foundations for Christian education have assumed a renewed prominence in the church's educational thinking. Hence, the change in title has been made to reflect this fundamental emphasis which is now apparent almost everywhere within the discipline.

The attention of the reader is also called to the fact that this is an *introductory* volume. It does not pretend to be encyclopedic at any point, and some may find this brevity inadequate. As many will already know, every chapter is the subject of numerous other books. But it seemed wise to introduce the reader to these several phases of Christian education in a brief, survey fashion. I recognize that many will want more information on some topics. And it is for these persons that two types of bibliographic resource are included. Each chapter concludes with a "For Additional Reading" section, and the book contains an extensive "Selected Bibliography" of several hundred supplemental publications (see pp. 383-98). Thus, it has been the expectation that these essays will not only introduce one to the subject under consideration but also point the way for more thorough study whenever this is desired.

This volume has been planned primarily to serve as an introductory survey of all that we call Christian education. As such, it will be particularly useful in the classrooms and libraries of colleges and seminaries, especially those providing professional training for church workers. But the book's value should not be limited to this group. Also considered in the planning were local church leaders—pastors, ministers and directors of Christian education, lay church school personnel, and so forth. It is my expectation that they will also find it a useful reference work. And it is to all of these persons, those upon whom Christian education ultimately depends for its effectiveness, that it is hopefully offered.

The contents of the book have been arranged in logical order. Part I considers "foundations," those elements from which one's Christian education theory is composed. Part II describes "administration"—local church structures, lay and professional leadership, research, and evaluation. Part III examines the local church's "programs, methods, and materials." The last section, Part IV, is devoted to various "agencies and organizations" which are supportive of and important to religious nurture. It also includes chapters on Roman Catholic and Jewish education.

As editor I am especially grateful to two different groups of persons who have assisted in the work. The more than seventy professors who responded to my request for advice on format and content were most helpful in the initial planning stages. While sharing none of the responsibility for its weaknesses, they have contributed much to its strengths. And secondly I am also much appreciative of the cooperation and efforts of the thirty-one contributors who found time in their busy lives to write chapters. Each is a specialist in his field, and I am grateful for the values which they have brought to the book. The reader will find biographical information about each in the index pages 399-404.

MARVIN J. TAYLOR

# CONTENTS

## I. FOUNDATIONS FOR CHRISTIAN EDUCATION

## II. THE ADMINISTRATION OF CHRISTIAN EDUCATION

7

## III. PROGRAMS, METHODS, AND MATERIALS FOR CHRISTIAN EDUCATION

## IV. AGENCIES AND ORGANIZATIONS

# CONTENTS

*Part I*

# FOUNDATIONS FOR CHRISTIAN EDUCATION

*Chapter 1*

## THE EDUCATIONAL MINISTRY OF THE CHURCH

### *Roger L. Shinn*

THE CHRISTIAN CHURCH HAS ONE MINISTRY, NOT MANY. THE NEW TESTAment describes it as the "ministry of reconciliation." Paul writes to the Corinthians that it is the doing of God, "who through Christ reconciled us to himself and gave us the ministry of reconciliation" (II Cor. 5:18). Curiously it sometimes provokes strife, because exposure of disease may be a stage in its healing.

This ministry is many-faceted. It includes the telling of the gospel to mankind, the cultivation of worship, deeds of mercy and works of love, efforts of Christians to live as citizens of God's kingdom while they are citizens of the kingdoms of this world, the education of the faithful and of humanity to the meaning of God's activity in the world.

No part of the ministry can be isolated from the whole. We can single out some one aspect for definition and understanding, as we are here doing with the educational ministry. But this facet, like all the others, is integral to the whole ministry. When people isolate it—either to make grandiose claims for it or to dismiss it as the task of somebody else—they distort its meaning. From the beginning educational work has been a vital part of the church's entire ministry. Education has taken place in homes and marketplaces, in the coliseum where Christians faced lions, in monasteries and in prisons, in church buildings and on battle fields, in nursery schools and universities.

A turbulent history brings new possibilities and problems to new generations, certainly to our own. The meaning and methods of Christian education will always show recognizable continuity with the past, from biblical times through the centuries, because the ministry of reconciliation is constant. Yet we can never simply repeat the thoughts or practices of the past, because Christian faith requires fresh response to God in every era.

11

# AN INTRODUCTION TO CHRISTIAN EDUCATION
## The Central Thrust of Christian Education

To understand the educational ministry of the church we must realize that Christianity is the faith of a community living in history. Christianity is not a package of ideas and beliefs that once descended from the clouds. Nor is it a philosophy that any intelligent individual might think up for himself. It is the life of a community of people responding to God's deed in Christ and to God's continuing activity in the world.

This basic fact determines the nature of Christian education. Such education has always been willing to borrow ideas and techniques from pagan or secular sources, as today it may learn from new developments in psychology and public education. (After all, in God's world all truth and experience should have some meaning for Christians.) But Christian education brings to such new knowledge its own purposes and sensitivities; it appropriates, evaluates, and appreciates experience and information in the light of its own faith.

Because Christianity is the life of a community, its educational ministry is the work of that community. Its aim is not the promotion of the community but the reconciling mission to which the community is called. Hence Christian education may be described as the effort "to introduce persons into the life and mission of the community of Christian faith." [1] This conception of Christian education, I suggest, is consistent both with the biblical understanding of the church and with the findings of recent educational psychology about the learning process.

The New Testament uses the figure of adoption to describe what happens to persons in Christian faith (Rom. 8:23, Gal. 4:5). In adoption a child enters a family; the family becomes *his* family, and he becomes *its* child. He adopts the style of life of the family, its practices and ideas, its precious symbols, and its family jokes. The family, adopting him, receives him in warmth, makes its resources his, transmits to him its habits and values. In this educational process deliberate instruction plays an important part, but it is less significant than the teaching and learning that inevitably go with life. Thus adoption is a suggestive metaphor for the educational ministry of the church.

Likewise contemporary educational psychology emphasizes the importance of the human relationships in which education takes place. Freud and his many followers have shown that human development involves far more than intellectual forces. American educators from Dewey to Conant have given convincing evidence that learning gets much of its significance from the social context in which it takes place. The Supreme Court, striking down the "separate but equal" doctrine in 1954, made clear that the social structure of schools and communities is itself a major factor in the educational process.

For both biblical and contemporary reasons, therefore, it makes sense to understand Christian education as the effort to introduce persons into the life

[1] I have used this phraseology earlier in my book, *The Educational Mission of Our Church* (Philadelphia: United Church Press, 1962). This chapter has a different purpose from that book, and I hope that I have gained some wisdom in the interval; but occasionally ideas and language have filtered from the book into this chapter.

and mission of the Christian community. This conception calls for three immediate comments, then for a more detailed exposition.

The first comment concerns the word "introduce." I use this with no implication that Christian education is for children or for those who are just getting acquainted with Christian faith and life. In a profound sense the Christian life is a perennial beginning. "Unless you turn and become like children, you will never enter the kingdom of heaven." (Matt. 18:3.) Education into the Christian life is not a matter of attaining progressive stages of achievement. As Kierkegaard saw it, the issue is not so much that of "being a Christian" as it is that of "becoming a Christian." Because Christian possibilities are always new, because Christian life calls for continuous decision, because sinners can be priests to saints, and because sophisticated Christians can constantly learn from simple believers, Christian education is ceaseless introduction.

A second comment concerns the educator in Christian education. In the last analysis God is the educator. He may reach men in the most unexpected ways and places. It is not for us to prescribe his ways of operation. "The wind blows where it wills, and you hear the sound of it, but you do not know whence it comes or whither it goes; so it is with every one who is born of the Spirit." (John 3:8.) Even so, the church has a specific educational ministry, which it may not evade by pious talk about God's ways of working. And here the church faces the portentous truth that the church itself is the chief human agent of Christian education.

Most of us, if we should investigate the educational ministry of a local church, would probably begin by asking about the church school, the facilities, the curricular materials, the teachers, and the program. We might better look at the total life and impact of the church upon its members and those whose life it touches. The unintended educational influence of the church may enhance or frustrate its purposive educational efforts. A church whose members bear one another's burdens and accept some responsibility for the world can overcome considerable technical ineptitude in education. And a snobbish, segregated church can undo all the concepts of brotherhood and all the carefully designed pictures of interracial groups in the curricular literature.

A third comment concerns an appropriate modesty and ambition in Christian education. A modesty is necessary because education cannot do everything that wistful people expect of it. No educational process can assure that persons will become Christians or that they will experience the riches of Christ. Education cannot even guarantee the far different—and more popular—goal that children will keep out of trouble and grow up to be law-abiding citizens. Freedom and sin are part of human life, and any educator who thinks that he can always manipulate students or direct their lives is dealing in pretentious nonsense. In fact, such surreptitious coercion is the direct opposite of the purpose of Christian freedom.

On the other hand the Christian educator has a right to claim high purposes. He is doing far more than giving information about religion or selling a religious product. The Supreme Court has suggested that certain types of instruction about religion may be a valid part of secular education. Increasingly state universities are offering such instruction, and the public schools may

13

take up the opportunity. But Christian education, although it includes the study of Christianity, is more than that. Likewise it is more than promoting religion, a cause that is popular enough these days. Christian education introduces persons into the life and mission of the community of faith. Persons, offered that introduction, may then decide whether they will adopt that life and mission.

Thus the educational ministry of the church, to summarize, is a process of continuous "introduction"; it is a work of the entire church in all its life; and it brings to persons the opportunity and demand for decision. We may now investigate the further meaning and practice of this ministry.

## The Major Processes Within the Educational Ministry

For the purposes of understanding Christian education we may distinguish three major components in it: (1) learning to participate in the Christian community and its way of life; (2) appropriating the Christian heritage; (3) training for mission. Although we shall see that these three are inseparable, it will be convenient to consider them in turn.

1. *The educational ministry of the church invites and incorporates persons into the life of the Christian community. It engages them in the characteristic acts by which this community responds to God.*

Christian education starts with the present. It is concerned with the past as that past impinges upon the present. It reaches into the future to whatever extent the future influences present purpose and expectation. Past and future are part of Christian education only as they enter into present reality and experience.

Therefore, it makes sense to look first at the educating community to see how it lives and what it does. It is a unique community, whether we see it in its majesty or its mediocrity. Across the centuries and around the world it has taken on many historical and cultural colorations; thus the contemporary American Christian might feel alarmed or bored if he could visit an ancient Greek or a modern Chinese church. Yet always there would be signs to tell him that this is a Christian church.

Let us quickly grant that this community, concrete and historical as it is, has resemblances to other types of human community. For example, every community has ties that hold it together. For better or for worse, these help it to know itself and to define its identity. The uniting forces may be highly articulated in concepts, purposes, constitutions; or they may work subconsciously in some dimly sensed notion of kinship. Race, color, common language, common enemies, shared symbols, memories of hardship and struggle, feelings of superiority or inferiority to rivals—any of these may function to maintain community consciousness. Christian churches have from time to time relied upon all of them, sometimes in shameful ways.

Nevertheless the one continuous tie that has united the church has been its faith. This is not to say that the faith has always been pure and strong; usually it has been diluted or distorted by other influences. But it has, from time to time across the centuries, transcended the many barriers that often divide men.

14

This central significance of faith raises one of the issues that has haunted Christian education. Can faith be taught? The arguments that have raged about that question will never entirely be resolved, because they rest in the basic mystery of freedom and selfhood. But some of the issues can be clarified by a verbal distinction. Faith cannot be *imposed*; when the effort is made, whatever is imposed is not faith. But faith can—sometimes—be *evoked*, and it can be *shared* in the community of faith. This community finds modes of expression that communicate and evoke faith. All such expressions are part of the educational ministry of the church. We may enumerate a few.

One is *worship*. Perhaps worship in some form or other is so indigenous to human life that people would worship in any event. But probably they would worship badly without education. Certainly Christian worship takes place only when there has been some education that transforms the raw reverence of life into Christian reverence. Such reverence expresses itself in prayer, hymnody, sacraments, individual and common acts of thanksgiving and repentance. By participation in the community of faith people learn to enter into Christian worship.

If people need education in order to worship, it is equally true that worship educates. Worship needs no purpose extraneous to itself; and to regard it as a means to anything else, even something so good as education, is to be irreverent. But though worship is not designed for the purpose of education, it has the consequence of education. A person can hardly learn what reverence is except by participating in acts of reverence. Traditionally the worship of the church has taught people Christian traditions and ideas, and it has communicated Christian attitudes and awareness.

Another expression of faith is *Christian thought*. Although faith is not identical with belief or doctrine, faith expresses itself in beliefs and doctrines. Christianity is not a shapeless emotionalism or a chaotic flux of passion; it has an intellectual content.

Obviously not all Christians are intellectuals. The faithful include illiterates and men of modest intelligence. But in a highly literate culture, where even the poorly educated have inherited at least some scraps of learning wrought out of centuries of intellectual struggle, faith has no right to thrive on ignorance and stupidity. It deserves and requires intellectualization. Hence, Christian education must educate the mind.

An intellectual faith inevitably has its vocabulary. Usually such a vocabulary need not be complex or abstruse. So simple a word as "cross" has a peculiarly Christian meaning—a meaning not communicated by words such as "gallows," "guillotine," or "electric chair." Although few Christians can articulate the meaning in an intelligible doctrine of the atonement, Christians respond to the Cross because they know—intellectually as well as emotionally—that Jesus Christ died on a cross. Faith in Christ inevitably demands elements of belief about Christ.

Still another expression of faith is *ethos* and *ethic*. Ethos is the spirit of the community, displayed in its architecture and art, its organization and government, its use of its resources, its sense of purpose. Ethos in action, particularly in human relations, is ethic.

Christian education has always been education in the Christian ethic. Such education has been least effective when the ethic became detached from ethos and authorities taught it as an imposed code. It has been most effective when the ethos was so communicated that it led learners to their own discovery of the ethic—a discovery not always anticipated by the teachers. Thus the early church lived with an ethos in which the slave was welcomed as a brother, but only after many centuries did the church discover the ethical consequence that human slavery is an intolerable wrong. Each generation of Christians depends upon a past that has communicated the Christian ethos, but each generation has the responsibility for rediscovering or discovering afresh the ethical implications of that ethos.

In describing the educational ministry as it touches upon worship, thought, and ethos-ethic, I have assumed that these are present aspects of Christian experience and education. But they are constantly interfused with past and future through the memory and mission of the church. These further implications must also be considered.

2. *The educational ministry of the church is the appropriation of a heritage. It involves men in a past that significantly constitutes their present.*

I have said earlier that Christianity is not an abstract creed or philosophy of religion. Rather, it is the life of a community living in history. The community is what it is because of its history.

All persons and institutions, of course, are influenced by history. Often history is a burden. The American race problem, for example, is so hard to solve because of a bitter history that haunts society yet today. Men have often felt like James Joyce's Stephen Dedalus, who says in *Ulysses:* "History is a nightmare from which I am trying to awake." But history can also be liberating. It can free us from the limited vision and the mores of our own time by showing us how we became what we are and by opening up new vistas upon experience. History can help us unlock the secret of our own identity—both our common identity and our various personal identities.

It is in exactly these terms that the Old Testament—long before people discussed methodologies of religious education—described a pattern of education in the Hebrew faith. The setting is a family within the Jewish community of faith. The son sees the worship, the beliefs, and the ethic of the family, and he asks his father the meaning of it all. The father replies by telling of the history of Israel. The book of Deuteronomy describes the process: "When your son asks you in time to come, 'What is the meaning of the testimonies and the statutes and the ordinances which the Lord our God has commanded you?' then you shall say to your son, 'We were Pharaoh's slaves in Egypt; and the Lord brought us out of Egypt with a mighty hand' " (6:20-21).

Here is a paradigm of all later Christian education: The person confronts the issues of faith in contemporary life, and in order to understand them he is driven to the history of the community of faith.

The Christian faith has a *specific* historical heritage. This faith is not generated from experience in general—even though it can never be separated from all such experience. Hence, Christian education must include some factual information—specifically, information concerning Jesus Christ and the biblical history. Instruction—the telling of the story set forth in Scripture—is an inherent part of the educational ministry of the church. Whenever Christian education has omitted instruction, with the aim of developing its processes solely out of the life of the individual or the dynamics of the group, it has missed something fundamental.

Yet instruction is in itself far less than Christian education. No quantity of drill in the facts of the Bible amounts to Christian education, unless the learning is part of the appropriation of a heritage. Christian education requires the internalizing of a meaningful history.

Adoption, I have suggested, is a clue to the educational ministry of the church. An adopted child, entering into a family, becomes its heir. His inheritance usually includes both material assets and a tradition of meaning. Eagerly or reluctantly, he appropriates a new ancestry, mediated to him through the thousands of acts and attitudes, some of them barely noticed, that constitute family life. Similarly, entrance into the Christian community means the appropriation of an inheritance. Christians adopt new ancestors—ancient Jewish patriarchs, prophets, apostles—who become more important for the Christian's contemporary identity than his "blood ancestors" of the same period, about whom he probably knows nothing at all.

In one striking respect the biblical heritage is different from the many other human inheritances that we cultivate. Usually the appropriation of a heritage adds to our self-esteem. It enriches life on *our* terms. When we choose the ancestors whom we want to remember (or to ritualize in some of the modern forms of ancestor-worship), we select those who nourish our pride. The biblical inheritance does not fit this usual pattern.

The Bible is a record of God's dealings with men. There are no heroes in it. Every time the documents may seem to start building up a hero (e.g., David in the Old Testament or Peter in the New Testament), the turn of events unmasks him at his worst. The great figures of biblical history are magnificent portrayals of persons in conflict—not models of character. To appropriate the biblical heritage is to accept an inheritance of guilt as truly as of comfort. The heritage does not simply establish and confirm the identity of the community; it constantly corrects, stimulates, and transforms the community. Thus the Bible becomes, in Christian faith, the searing and healing Word of God.

Here is the answer to the great danger in describing Christian education as the work of a community in introducing persons into its own life. Churches, like all human communities, are tempted to exalt themselves, to ignore the world while they cultivate their own prosperity, to engage in self-idolatry. But the heritage of the church does not flatter the church. The biblical record centers in God, above all in his deed in Jesus Christ. It reminds mankind of guilt. It calls for repentance, pronounces a good news of forgiveness, and engages the church in a mission to mankind. This mission constitutes the third component in Christian education.

3. *The educational ministry of the church is training in mission. It requires learning by service and for service of God in his world.*

The church is by nature a missionary community, called into being to carry on the reconciling ministry of Christ. Just as Jesus' education of his disciples was in considerable part an introduction into mission, so authentic Christian education requires this missionary impulse.

Perhaps the greatest weakness of the familiar patterns of Christian education is at exactly this point. They have too often been introverted, concerned to develop Christian character and Christian institutions by protecting persons and church from the world. They have valued gentility over toughness of character, good manners over resolute purpose, devotion to religious organizations over service of mankind. They have organized the educational process itself so as to draw persons from life in the world instead of driving them into the world, where Christian witness and service are most meaningful.

But faith in Jesus Christ means a belief that God himself is not willing to stand aloof from the world he has created. He exposes himself to the world, risks its scorn and cruelty, enters into its life for the purpose of reconciliation. He calls his church to engage in his divine work. A Christian educational ministry that is unconcerned for mission is a contradiction in terms.

Hence, Christian education includes study of the world, understanding of life in the world, training for Christian action. A major part of it must be the interpretation of lay vocations as responsible activities in which the Christian makes his witness and obeys his God. Thus the campus ministry has increasingly become less a program alongside the educational program of college and university, and more an effort to help young men and women understand their vocations as students. Adult education puts less and less of its emphasis on the traditional rut-bound "Men's Bible Class," and gives more and more attention to vocational and intervocational groups that search for the meaning of mission in urban, industrialized society.

There will always be resistance to Christian education that is directed toward mission. Some of the pious, for example, resent those units of the church school curriculum that mean study of the local community, of problems of poverty and race, of Christian responsibility in sex, of obedience to God in the relationships between nations. The common objection is that such studies are (1) not biblical and (2) controversial. Such criticism raises the obvious question: How can education possibly be biblical without entering into controversy? We may quickly grant that not all controversy is wise and Christian; it is easy to work off hostilities by trying righteously to pummel sinners. And the aim of Christian controversy—even with communists, predatory criminals, and segregationists— is faithful witness to God and reconciliation among God and men. But faithful witness and reconciliation, as Scripture shows, do not come about by evasion of controversy.

If Bible study is simply the passing on of received truths, such Bible study is itself unbiblical; for the Bible is constantly concerned with its contemporary world. Indeed, if Bible study never goes beyond study, it is unbiblical; for the Bible is a record of action. Christian education takes place before action, during action, and after action. There are appropriate times for withdrawing from action in order to seek fresh perspectives and consider the meaning of one's action. But there are no appropriate times to abandon mission and the action that mission demands. Christian education is missionary education, and mission is engagement in the world.

## Conclusion and Forecast

As a matter of convenience and for the sake of clarity I have distinguished three components in the educational ministry of the church: incorporation in the life of the community, appropriation of a heritage, and training in mission. More important than their mutual distinction is their interpenetration. Isolation and undue emphasis on any one may falsify Christian faith. Concentration on the life of the community may turn into mere chumminess or organizational aggrandizement; cultivation of a heritage may become a luxurious fascination with antiquities; involvement in mission may degenerate into superficial activism. But within the ministry of reconciliation these three tasks mutually reinforce and correct each other.

Christian education is a perennial work that constantly changes its tactics. In the swift-paced history of our time it is especially important to understand the basic meaning of the educational ministry, in order that we may realize that meaning in the midst of forms that are sure to change. From time to time the church has focused on various social organisms to carry out its educational ministry: on homes, monasteries, colleges, Sunday schools, camps and conferences, lay academies, and all the rest. No one can say what the appropriate institutions of the future will be.

As society becomes more urbanized, as machines take over many jobs and men gain new leisure, as patterns of family life and weekend living change, as mobility modifies the forms of human associations, the church will seek new forms of Christian education. Some of these may be as different from the best modern church schools as these church schools are different from a medieval monastery. Certainly experimentation and new techniques are in order.

Even more important, much of the content of Christian education will change. No church today teaches exactly the doctrines of Augustine or Calvin, and churches tomorrow will not teach exactly the doctrines of today. Ethical decisions, too, will take new forms. I have already mentioned that the church needed centuries to discover that the ethic of the New Testament called for the abolition of slavery. Future generations of Christian educators and students will discover meanings in the Christian ethic that are now hidden from us. Certainly some of our beliefs and practices will seem as irrelevant to them as much of medievalism seems to us.

The church, because it is a living church, will learn to adapt to new situations. There is nothing shameful in this fact; the church has always learned to adapt. But some adaptations mean fidelity and some adaptations mean apostasy. Christian education, like Christian theology, will have trouble knowing the difference.

There are no assured devices for determining the pathways of fidelity. Least of all does adherence to time-honored practices and procedures guarantee faithfulness. Experimentation, with all its risks, will be required. We can say, however, that the educational ministry of the church will be most authentic when the church understands God and itself in the light of Jesus Christ and his ministry of reconciliation.

19

## FOR ADDITIONAL READING

Gilkey, Langdon. *How the Church Can Minister to the World Without Losing Itself*. New York: Harper & Row, 1964.

Hunter, David. *Christian Education as Engagement*. New York: The Seabury Press, 1963.

Miller, Randolph Crump. *Christian Nurture and the Church*. New York: Charles Scribner's Sons, 1961.

Niebuhr, H. Richard. *The Meaning of Revelation*. New York: The Macmillan Company, 1946.

Shinn, Roger L. *The Educational Mission of Our Church*. Philadelphia: United Church Press, 1962.

Tillich, Paul. *The Dynamics of Faith*. New York: Harper & Row, 1957.

*Chapter 2*

# CHRISTIAN EDUCATION
# THROUGH HISTORY

*William Bean Kennedy*

EDUCATION DEPENDS UPON WHAT BERNARD BAILYN CALLS "THE GREAT AXLES of society—family, church, community, and the economy." [1] As those fundamental social institutions shift over the generations the forms of education also shift. Through the major epochs of history the church has developed different agencies and instruments by which it has sought to fulfill its educational task. Surveying Christian education through history should provide insight for the church today as it strives to carry out its teaching function.

## In the Biblical Period

There are at least three major biblical periods in which conscious education took place: before and after the Old Testament Exile and in New Testament times.

Before the Exile, as the familiar passage in Deuteronomy 6 suggests, the strong clan or family pattern of life provided the major setting for nurture. A Hebrew child grew up absorbing the meaning of life in his society. Family ritual, interpretation, and discussion helped him unconsciously and consciously to sense the religious reference for life, and the particular Exodus orientation for their unique way of life. Other cultic practices arose, but probably the major traditioning took place as the child shared the life and worship of his extended family. In the absence of written records oral tradition, developed to a high degree, became the medium by which the heritage came into the life of each new generation.

The Exile ushered in a long period during which the earlier, more stable patterns were shattered. The children of Israel were scattered across the Mediterranean world, chiefly in urban centers. Dispersed in alien cultures, where their native tongue was not spoken, the Jews had to turn to more conscious cultic and educational institutions to communicate the heritage to the new generations. The synagogue developed as a local center of worship and instruction, where the adult Jewish community learned the Law (Torah) and its interpretation for their lives. Trained in the synagogue, the parents expected to nurture their children in the homes. Later the rabbis or teachers added schools to the synagogues, where they taught the boys the Hebrew language and great amounts of the oral tradition as well as their written Scriptures. Today's "Hebrew schools" for Jewish boys came from these developments dur-

[1] *Education in the Forming of American Society* (New York: Vintage Books, 1960), p. 45.

21

ing centuries of dispersion before Christ. In the schools the children learned more formally what the family earlier had taught: a distinctive way of life for God's people under God's law, and the interpretation of their heritage from Abraham and Moses and David to that day. As a Jewish boy, Jesus grew up under such a system of schooling.

As the followers of Jesus began to gather regularly amidst the Jewish culture of Jerusalem, they followed the same general patterns of worship and learning. At the beginning, because of the excitement of newness, the eschatological expectations of the imminent return of Christ, and the resulting time-foreshortened perspective, the earlier parts of the New Testament had relatively little to say about education as such. The later books give evidence of the use of many different types of education, most of which reflected earlier Jewish customs. Some persons learned their Christian faith in family settings (e.g., Timothy), others needed instruction before or after responding to the good news about Jesus (e.g., the Ethiopian eunuch), while others assimilated their new faith into well-trained backgrounds from pagan and Jewish schools (e.g., Paul). Gradually education, as reflected in the New Testament, came to emphasize a distinctive way of life for God's chosen people, the teachings about and by Jesus, and the Old Testament background for interpreting the meaning of his Lordship to Gentile converts. The creedal summaries which reflect the early preaching and the extensive didactic material of the New Testament both suggest elements that the early Christians felt important for converts to learn. Gradually there arose certain official teachers after the rabbinic pattern, although church offices in the New Testament seem to have remained fluid.[2]

Thus these three biblical periods show how God's people used various patterns of education to maintain the historical continuity and distinctiveness of their way of life and its interpretation through many generations.

## In the Patristic Period

Again the general cultural settings influenced the major forms of education. As the church grew, it faced the serious problem of teaching the new members what their conversion meant so that the faith would not be endangered in their hands. But how could this be done now that the Christians were scattered all over the Roman world in many kinds of cultural situations? One of the major forms was training for church membership. In varying degrees church-men required new converts to learn the meaning of Christian faith and to practice its teachings in their lives before they could become full members. The early important documents of the church speak of long periods of instruction in the faith, lasting from three months to three years. Only those who were trained could share the church's mysteries (its sacraments). During persecutions such testing helped safeguard the community of faith. In the widespread dispersion the lack of clear order and authoritative creeds and scriptures also demanded firm teaching. So, by special classes for catechumens

---

[2] E.g., Eduard Schweizer, *Church Order in the New Testament* (Naperville, Ill.: Alec R. Allenson, 1961).

as well as by home training and worship services, the church taught its new converts and nurtured its members and their children.

In the sophisticated world of the early centuries, Christianity soon found itself also needing highly educated apologists in order to interpret the faith in the Hellenistic ways of thinking and to defend it against cultured attackers. Alongside pagan centers of learning the church established catechetical schools, such as the one in which Clement and Origen taught, by the university at Alexandria. There future leaders of Christian thought were trained in the philosophies and disciplines of classic Hellenistic culture. Some thought that to use the language of Greek philosophy to express the gospel was very dangerous (e.g., Tertullian); others believed it essential and sought to develop Christian belief as clearly as possible in contemporary terms (e.g., Origen). At such centers emerged Christian schools similar to church institutions of higher education of more recent times.

## In the Medieval Period

With the establishment of Christianity under Constantine the problem of Christian education changed drastically; now the church could no longer require intensive preparation by those who became members. Rather it had to find ways to nurture and lead to deeper faith the hordes of persons who now were baptized into membership. Actually, in the declining years of the Empire and the early years of what has been called the "Dark Ages," the task was too great for much measurable success. Under the strain much of church life shifted. Some sought to escape the tension by forming monastic bands whose discipline made of them highly intensive Christians. In the hands of these monks, living often in isolated monasteries, much of the heritage of learning continued. There they copied the Scriptures and preserved the content of Christian study. Elsewhere rational understanding of the faith declined as learning slumped in society generally. Churchmen worked out new ways of teaching rude Christians the way of life fitting for them, and of interpreting God's revelation in the stories of the Bible and especially in Jesus Christ. As teaching had to become simpler, it tended to crystallize and become more authoritative. It was communicated through drama and sacraments, through architecture, through pictures of mosaic and stained glass, and through the confessional where sacramental developments led believers to seek priestly guidance. Thus in the absence of formal schooling and literate culture, liturgy, drama, and architecture became more important educative instruments.

As the centuries passed, the centers where learning survived became more and more important since out of them came the leaders who could maintain the educational processes by which the populace learned the faith. Charlemagne's chief educator, Alcuin, rightly emphasized that an ignorant leadership seriously threatened the integrity of the faith. Their efforts to revive learning resulted in significant advances. Schools grew up around cathedrals and monasteries. As towns began to develop, the early universities began to take shape in the form of guilds of scholars who resided in Paris, Bologna, Oxford, and elsewhere. Because the church remained the major custodian of the religious heritage and of general culture, these early schools united Christianity and classical studies. Thus at the very beginning of the European development of humanistic scholarship the church was closely involved.

The pattern of education developed on a double track: for the few leaders, formal schooling; for the great majority, informal appropriation of the faith through participation in medieval life and worship. Because the culture was generally stable, however, and was permeated with the symbols and meanings of Christianity, people absorbed much of the meaning of faith merely by growing up in such communities. Paul Tillich characterizes this age as a prime example of "inductive" education, because of the unconscious absorption of the meaning of life through ordinary living where the symbols of meaning were always present.[3] At the higher levels by the eleventh century onward a quite advanced order of schools had arisen, enough, in fact, to help give the later period the title "High Middle Ages." That period led on into the Renaissance of the fourteenth and later centuries when learning became dramatically important. From the rebirth of culture and learning came a higher level of education. Erasmus, Luther, Melanchthon, and Calvin represent that advanced scholarship.

## In the Period of the Reformation

The patterns from the preceding period continued on past the schism of the church into Protestant and Roman Catholic divisions, for both utilized the same forms: home training, worship, pastoral teaching, and guidance. But the newer climate of controversy and religious wars demanded a much higher level of rational definition. In order to ensure correct belief, lengthy statements of faith were developed and taught to the people, along with shorter catechisms for the children. In reaction to Roman Catholic formalism, Protestants emphasized the direct relationship of the believer to God and sought to develop ways of intensifying the meaning of that relationship. Believing that each Christian should read his Bible himself, the reformers translated it into the vernacular languages. Taking advantage of recent advances in printing, they set out to teach all men to read. The major Protestant movements developed various patterns by which they nurtured their own into some maturity of faith and knowledge. The sermon once again became more central in worship, recalling the synagogue stress on exposition and minimizing the dramatic liturgical predominance of the intervening centuries. In order to enable congregations to think doctrinally and participate intelligently in worship and life, the reformers set up schools to teach literacy. Thus a strong religious impulse to teach the people to read was joined to the humanistic trend to encourage what was to become universal compulsory education. Usually the new schools were joint ventures of church and government, for the two still were closely tied. As the major educated person in the community, the minister became the chief teacher or school supervisor, and the importance of right doctrine demanded that he put teaching high among his priorities. Thus the office of teacher, often

[3] "The Theology of Education," in *Theology of Culture* (New York: Oxford University Press, 1959), pp. 146-57.

one with that of preacher, became a predominant form of church office in the period.[4]

The pattern that developed during the sixteenth and seventeenth centuries continued into the later period. Essentially it was a two-level educational system. On the upper level Latin grammar schools taught those with the background or promise to become future societal and church leaders and prepared them for the university; on the lower level vernacular schools taught children to read. But wars and other factors prevented any universal application of this hope for centuries. Meanwhile most people continued to learn the faith through the ordinary activities of parish life: Protestants, through preaching, catechisms, and moral guidance by church leaders and parents; Roman Catholics, through the liturgy, catechisms, home training, and guidance through the confessional.

But the development of newer forms was under way. Jesuits, Moravians, Puritans, and others began to intensify their educational efforts and to increase the effectiveness of their teaching processes. Education for the sake of the community of faith, for its protection, its enhancement or extension, began to share primacy with education for the development of the individual, first for his religious response but increasingly for the fulfillment of his individual potential and personality. The great predominance of the church over all formal learning, which had characterized western education for over a millenium, was beginning to decline.

## In the Seventeenth and Eighteenth Centuries

As western Europe moved into the period from 1600 to 1800, major forces that were to affect education were gathering strength. The industrial revolution contributed to urbanization and the mobility and dislocation of life. The great social institutions upon which the inductive education of medieval society had depended—the extended family pattern of living, the close-knit systems of labor, the close tie of life with worship in the midst of permeating symbols —all began to change. As Bailyn points out, by the latter part of the colonial period in America society was increasingly forced to do by conscious planned effort what had formerly been done unconsciously, without planning. Schools arose to replace what less formal educative instruments had been doing for over a thousand years.

The new schools were of great variety. The emerging doctrine of equality and the rise of popular government bolstered the long hope for universal elementary education. Some of the new schools were private, chiefly for the children of their benefactors; others were related to churches, under the close control of the minister and other church leaders; others were endowed and independent; still others were charity schools in the "public" realm. Slowly the various types were evolving toward a "common" education for all in the rudiments of learning: reading, writing, a little ciphering, and whatever prevailing religious teaching the society supported. These schools taught the

---

[4] Wilhelm Pauck, "The Ministry in the Time of the Continental Reformation," in *The Ministry in Historical Perspectives*, H. Richard Niebuhr and Daniel D. Williams, eds. (New York: Harper & Row, 1956), pp. 110-48.

vernacular tongue, and provided elementary training for useful citizenship in the emerging nations.

Alongside these developments, the older pattern of classical grammar schools persisted, training the select few in Latin and Greek, graduating them into the academies and the colleges and universities where the leaders of society and church were educated.

In most places in Europe and America the church remained the dominant force in education, whatever the type of school. But as newer forms of schooling arose, the church found its relationship to them shifting. Where the church remained an established religious institution in a state or nation, it taught its faith through whatever common schools the society provided, as in England, in most of the Roman Catholic countries, and in the colony of Massachusetts. When disestablishment occurred in America in the latter years of the eighteenth and early years of the nineteenth century, the church's leaders naturally remained strong influences in education in a society with very few intellectually trained leaders. The course of study continued to be strongly religious in the curriculum of American schools throughout the colonial period, as the widely used *New England Primer,* for instance, indicates. Similarly, the colonial colleges retained a primary religious purpose and orientation, as they sought to train ministers and other leaders.

Growing pluralism in the new world, however, was creating forces that were to remove much of education from the predominant influence of the church. These forces were evident before the Revolution, but the enduring patterns of the American school system developed during the period from 1800 to the Civil War.

## In the Nineteenth Century

During the 1800's the new United States of America developed its characteristic system of schools. Into that development fed various streams from the past. Among these was the Sunday school movement. Born in the charity school movement of eighteenth-century England, this program of schooling on Sunday for children of the streets was quickly copied in the eastern cities of Philadelphia, New York, and Boston. There benevolent societies established schools for the poor, after the British pattern. By 1824 the movement was large enough to form the American Sunday School Union, with headquarters in Philadelphia. From that base the Union moved into the western frontier with extensive programs to establish Sunday schools throughout the Mississippi Valley. In the cities and on the frontier the early Sunday schools provided general education: reading, writing, some ciphering, and some religious training. In so doing they were forerunners to the public schools.

As the five-day-a-week common schools began to emerge, however, the Sunday schools had to shift their purpose to retain a place in the educational system. By 1833 the churches had all been disestablished in the states (following the First Amendment to the Constitution). The public schools could teach only a sort of "common Christianity." Thus the developing denominations needed some agency for particular sectarian teaching alongside the learning their children received in public schools. The Sunday school assumed that function. The search for suitable curriculum materials during this time of shifting purpose showed in the wide diversity of Bible and catechism materials used during the middle third of the century. Thus the public schools and the Sunday schools grew together in what has been called the dual, parallel pattern of American education.[5]

As Roman Catholics and others recognized, in mid–nineteenth-century America "common Christianity" meant prevailing Protestant content and atmosphere. Non-Protestants felt forced to establish private or parochial systems of schooling to keep their children faithful to their particular Christian tradition. The overwhelming Protestant majority, sensing a threat to the new nation from Roman Catholic uniqueness and separation, could not show much sensitivity to the Catholic problem. Thus the Protestants generally supported the public schools as a primary agency for Christian education. They depended upon them to provide what they thought was needed for all citizens: some "book learning" and training in citizenship, plus teaching of moral principles and "common Christianity," usually by means of Bible reading and prayer.

Alongside that "value-laden" agency the Sunday school movement vigorously expanded within Protestantism. In 1872 one of the great enthusiastic conventions adopted the Uniform Lessons, which for almost a century thereafter were to unite most of the major denominations in one pattern of Christian teaching. As the earlier societies declined, the denominations undertook further development of parish Sunday schools, chiefly lay-dominated, largely for children, strongly evangelistic as was most of church life in the period, and staffed by untrained amateur teachers. Under such conditions the Sunday school could hardly be other than a casual operation. Casual, yes, but with the public school teaching morality and "common Christianity," it was sufficient for that day, and for the ensuing century.

In Europe, where most countries were not yet affected by extensive pluralism and the attempt to "separate church and state," the church often continued to enjoy an established position. There the common schools included religious teaching in the ordinary course of study. Observers from Europe were fascinated in the nineteenth century by America's attempt to work out its dual pattern.

In mission lands, where Christianity claimed only a small minority of the people, the new churches tried to establish parallel institutions for particular nurture alongside whatever general education the society maintained. Often in underdeveloped countries the churches and missions provided much of the schooling in the early years until the government could take over. Generally as common schools developed, and as in Europe the churches lost their establishment prerogatives, the necessity for some kind of parallel particular church training became more evident. Dependent upon the common schools for most of education, the churches sought in various ways to nurture their own and extend their influence through Sunday schools and other means.

Meanwhile a somewhat similar development was taking place at the higher levels, as the denominations in America established academies and colleges by

[5] James Hastings Nichols, "Religion and Education in a Free Society," in *Religion in America*, John Cogley, ed. (Cleveland: Meridian Books, 1958), pp. 148-67.

the score to train leaders for church and society. Although largely supported by denominations, these colleges offered a general education to whatever students they could attract. By modern standards the efforts were often pitiful, but throughout much of the nineteenth century the churches seemed to be the most promising institutions capable of offering any substantial higher education.

As the public schools grew, adding high schools after the Civil War, the churches' relationship to common schools at the lower levels grew more and more peripheral. Although at the higher level the trend was slower, with the advent of land-grant colleges in 1862 the great growth of public institutions of higher education began. Thus, before 1900 the church's educational agencies at the parish and elementary level had become clearly adjunct to the public schools, and at the higher levels by 1900 they were moving in that direction.

## The Twentieth Century

Into and during the twentieth century the churches of America fostered a wide variety of other school efforts adjunct to the major school work-week. Almost as early as the Sunday school development came youth work, first the YMCA, then Christian Endeavor, and later, denominational movements. Next came the daily vacation Bible school effort, followed by weekday religious education in released- or dismissed-time patterns. Summer programs expanded to include extensive conference and camp activities, and more recently other types of vacation operations. New graded curricula brought new vigor into the Sunday schools. Early in the century the formation of the Religious Education Association, and, two decades later, the International Council of Religious Education, brought the growing movements together into significant organizations. The very variety of these attempts indicates the churches' continuing search for structures that would fulfill the nurturing task alongside what the public schools provided.

In that long context the significant achievement of the dual pattern can be seen. For well over a century, under new conditions of freedom of religion, the churches of America in their emerging denominational forms maintained a combination of school and nurture operations that helped to attract two thirds of the population into the churches by voluntary decision and to produce evidences of religious commitment impressive in buildings and programs.

However, the chief forms of church education, described above as adjunct to the growing public schools, did not easily fit into the developing denominational structures which were becoming the predominant forms of church life in America. The Sunday school with its lay leadership, amateur teaching, and mixed curriculum, aroused opposition from some church leaders whose traditions emphasized confessional materials and ministerial leadership and teaching. Furthermore, the colleges and the Sunday schools (at the parish level) usually developed quite independently of one another, so that the Protestant system lacked consistency and continuity. The Roman Catholics, with their parochial system, achieved consistency, but at a cost of educational concentration that seemed in retrospect to distort full parish life and worship. The Jews, the minority group, found their identity threatened by American culture and maintained parallel schooling whose intensity reflected their estimate of that threat. Protestantism, more than the others, found its major church educational agency, the Sunday school, adjunct to the traditional church in its denominational form, as well as to the public schools.

But the mid-twentieth century brought changes which threaten the very foundations of that system. As pluralism has become more widespread and radical, the relatively homogeneous culture which could easily foster "common Christianity" through public schools exists in fewer and fewer places. Challenged in the courts in the early 1960's, those twin exercises which had symbolized the Protestant character of that moral and religious training, Bible reading and prayer in the public schools, both fell under Supreme Court decisions. Certain close cooperative patterns of released time weekday religious training were also ruled unconstitutional. Faced with this growing secularism, the Protestant churches found themselves not only in confusion; they were feeling deeper anxiety because they sensed that they no longer commanded a favorable educational strategy. The serious limitations of the casual school effort on Sunday became dramatically evident as the massive public school system upon which this limited effort had depended gradually diminished its religious teaching in the dual pattern arrangement.

During the same mid-twentieth century period the churches saw enrollment in public institutions of higher education pass and then rapidly outdistance enrollment in church and private colleges and universities. For well over a century these church colleges had found their *raison d'etre* in providing general education at the higher level for the majority of those who would go out as leaders in church and society. Now they found themselves in positions distressingly similar to those faced by parish educational programs a century earlier: adjuncts to more massive public institutions of education. The situation challenged church colleges to examine their relationships to the churches and to the world, particularly the academic world, with a fresh depth and vigor. As educational and thought centers of churches, which were being forced after centuries of predominance to redefine themselves as minority institutions, church colleges vigorously sought to discover their significance in the broader mission of the church in the world.

During the same post-World War II decades the Sunday school and other parish patterns of education were undergoing serious reevaluation. For the first time the Roman Catholics openly admitted that parochial schools could be harmful to well-balanced church life and effort, and began to suspect that they were neither as necessary nor as distinctive as the tradition claimed. Protestant denominations, challenged by the massive postwar changes somewhat hidden by the surging religious revival of the 1950's, set out on "new curriculum" efforts for their various church school programs. Led by the Presbyterian Church in the U.S.A. with its "Christian Faith and Life" curriculum in 1948, the denominations produced new programs which ironically, in an age of growing ecumenicity, emphasized the particular traditions of the denomination or church family. Most of the new programs acknowledged the fundamental problem of strategy, but not realizing its seriousness, sought to resolve it by intensifying the efforts by which the churches for over a century had carried out their educational work. The school of the church, overwhelmingly trapped by the one-hour pattern on Sunday morning, with its built-in weakness of amateur teaching, was given new materials, new efforts for leadership training, and serious attempts to extend its time and scope and quality beyond the casual. The home and family, long the object of planned programming since the stable extended family pattern of the Middle Ages had shifted in the new world of urbanization and frontier expansion, received new attention. And the place of worship and liturgy in the nurture of children and adults in the church began to be emphasized again by both Protestants and Roman Catholics.

But the new programs generally failed to halt the disturbing movement away from the church-dominated culture to which Americans had grown accustomed. Critics continued to claim that new forms for church life and nurture were needed. Even the theological seminaries, long the crown and symbol of denominational Christianity, were forced by declining enrollments and rapidly shifting developments in the nature of the ordained ministry of the church to reevaluate their work of training church leaders.

So today the Christian churches of America find themselves in the midst of massive changes in the world within which they live and serve. They sense that they must define their place clearly in order effectively to nurture their young and train their members to maturity adequate to face the complex challenges of today's world. What those forms of education will be like no one today can say with any confidence. Concern for the future comes not only from the fact of change, for which there is precedent, but from the pace and extent of it, for which there is little guidance from history. Christian educators are searching history to understand effective forms of education in other periods when somewhat similar conditions existed, and to gain deeper grasp of how and by what forces the present forms emerged. For the great axles of society are turning more rapidly, and Christian education in America cannot long postpone major changes. In varying degrees churches of other lands face the same problems.

Thus the churches today face a fluid situation in regard to Christian education. Largely convinced that some process of conscious nurture and training must go on, the denominations singly and through the National and World Councils of Churches are searching for patterns which will be effective in the challenging years ahead.

## FOR ADDITIONAL READING

Other brief sketches of the history of Christian education can be found in:

Lotz, Philip H., ed. *Orientation in Religious Education*. Nashville: Abingdon Press, 1950. Pp. 13-25.

Miller, Randolph C. *Education for Christian Living*. 2nd ed. Englewood Cliffs: Prentice-Hall, 1963. Pp. 18-38.

Sloyan, Gerard S., ed. *Shaping the Christian Message*. New York: The Macmillan Company, 1958. Part 1, pp. 1-127.

Taylor, Marvin J., ed. *Religious Education: A Comprehensive Survey*. Nashville: Abingdon Press, 1960. Pp. 11-23.

Useful works of greater length include:

Bailyn, Bernard. *Education in the Forming of American Society.* New York: Vintage Books, 1960.

Butler, J. Donald. *Religious Education: The Foundations and Practice of Nurture.* New York: Harper & Row, 1962.

Kennedy, William Bean. *The Shaping of Protestant Education.* New York: Association Press, 1966.

Lynn, Robert W. *Protestant Strategies in Education.* New York: Association Press, 1964.

McCluskey, Neil G., S.J. *Catholic Viewpoint on Education.* Rev. ed. Garden City: Doubleday & Company, 1962.

Muirhead, Ian A. *Education in the New Testament.* New York: Association Press, 1965.

Sherrill, Lewis J. *The Rise of Christian Education.* New York: The Macmillan Company, 1944.

# Chapter 3

# THEOLOGICAL FOUNDATIONS FOR CHRISTIAN EDUCATION

## *Howard Grimes*

ALL EDUCATION TAKES PLACE WITHIN A CONTEXT, IS BASED ON EXPLICIT OR implicit presuppositions, and includes as one of its purposes the communication of ideas, facts, and information. Christian education is both the organized and the unstructured process by which the Christian community attempts to transmit its faith as both content and personal response. In spite of some efforts in the past to deny or minimize the "givenness" of the faith of the church, we cannot be the church and fail to recognize that it has a family history. That which called the church into being—God's revelation in Israel and supremely in Jesus Christ—is the *raison d'etre* of the church and hence provides the foundation for its teaching ministry as well as its other ministries.

We must recognize, however, that the historical basis for the church does not come to us as pure event. To use the German distinction between two types of history, it is *Geschichte,* or interpreted history, not *Historie,* or mere fact. That is, the Christian faith does not exist apart from interpretation, or theology. Although such interpretation may be unrecognized and unsystematic, it exists for every practicing Christian and in every congregation. Thus, when we speak of the Christian faith or the gospel as one of the givens of Christian teaching, we are really talking about the theological foundations of the teaching-learning transaction.

Christian educators are thus dependent upon the "professional" theologian as well as the church historian and the biblical scholar. The Christian educator, however, should be the best possible theologian, while the systematic theologian should be aware of his responsibility for relating to the human situation and the tasks of the church his systematic efforts to explicate the Christian faith. Thus, one of the urgent and often neglected tasks of the church is for the theologian to enter into effective dialogue with those who are directly involved in the determination of the various ministries of the church, one of which is teaching.

## Theology and Christian Teaching

There are at least three major points at which theology is related to the teaching office of the church. First, as we have seen, the church has a faith to communicate, and this faith must be stated theologically. I am partially thinking of *the* faith, but also of faith as trust, conviction, relationship. Faith as content—story, idea, values, and so on—can be presented in the form of knowledge *about* the Christian faith (that is, more or less objective data). Teaching as witness to one's own faith (trust, conviction, relationship) moves toward knowledge *of* or relationship *to*. The teacher can both talk *about* God and witness to his own relation *to* God. Both types of knowledge, insofar as they are separate—that is, knowledge *about* and knowledge *of*—are parts of the theological content of teaching.

Second, theology affects our understanding of the process of teaching. If we understand the Christian faith in terms of ethical values, we will see that process as the education of character. If we see it as intellectual assent to propositions about God, we will understand the process of teaching as being largely transmission of subject matter. If, however, we understand the Christian faith as crucially a relationship with God as revealed in Jesus Christ, we will seek for a process which encourages this relationship. Whether we believe that teaching can itself lead to the faith relationship or whether we believe it can only prepare for the reception of faith, we will nevertheless structure the process so that it points to the faith relationship.

A third point at which theology affects Christian teaching is methodology. Method and process are closely related, yet not identical. Method grows out of process, and both grow out of theology. Generally, Christian educators still borrow their methods from general education and its cognate disciplines, and consequently this area of our subject is basically an unexplored one.

In this chapter we will be concerned only incidentally with the subject matter to be transmitted. We can only suggest directions for further thought with regard to methodology since this is both a complex and a largely unexplored subject. Therefore, our primary emphasis will be on the relation between theology and the process of Christian nurture and instruction. The areas which are considered are only one person's evaluation of where some of the major issues lie.

## The Context of Teaching—the Church

We have already noted that all teaching occurs in a context, and Christian teaching takes place within the Christian community or church. "Church" must be taken to include its various manifestations: institutional church, Christian family, unconventional structures, and so on. We cannot deal with the question which is often raised concerning the validity of the present institutional church as the church of Jesus Christ, nor can we consider the many problems associated with the family. We can only affirm that if the present structures of Christian community fail to be the church, or if they fail in the future, others must be found to take their place.

The inadequacy of the institutional church *is* a crucial issue for Christian education, however, for only a *community* of faith can effectively communicate the Christian faith. Other agencies can teach about that faith. There is no reason why public schools cannot transmit information about churches and synagogues and their place in history, the Bible and its place in literature, and so on. Increasingly in our world-oriented culture this teaching must also include other world religions.

Teaching about the Christian faith is not faith teaching, however, for faith is communicated only in community. Therefore, it is urgent that Christians in their various church structures evaluate the degree to which they in fact manifest the community of faith. It is further important that we remain open to the possibility of structures of Christian community other than those which now commonly exist.

Roger Shinn has indicated in an earlier chapter[1] that Christianity must be thought of not as a set of abstract beliefs (though it has such beliefs); rather it is the faith of a community which is responding today, in both faith and unfaith, to God's act of self-revelation in Jesus Christ and his continuing revelation as Holy Spirit. Shinn's definition of Christian education, in fact, is centered in the introduction of persons to the Christian community.

This community is both a historic and a dynamic one. Its historic roots go back to Israel's self-consciousness as a called people; they are especially grounded in God's self-revelation in Jesus the Christ. The sense of the church's identification with the old Israel is pointed out in such New Testament passages as Romans 9:25-27, II Corinthians 6:16-18, and Hebrews 8:8-10. In I Peter 2:9-10 the consciousness of the New Testament church as the "called community" is made quite clear. "But you are a chosen race, a royal priesthood, a holy nation, God's own people, that you may declare the wonderful deeds of him who called you out of darkness into his marvelous light. Once you were no people but now you are God's people; once you had not received mercy but now you have received mercy."

The identification of this community with Jesus Christ is made clear through Paul's use of the metaphor "body of Christ" to designate Christians together. I Corinthians 12 is the clearest exposition of this theme, and Romans 12:4-8 echoes it. Colossians 1:18 states quite emphatically, "He [Christ] is the head of the body, the church."

But this was not solely, or even primarily, a matter of past history for Paul, nor should it be for us. The church is a community with its roots in history; it is also a community in which the Spirit (Christ, in Paul's language) is presently at work. This holding in tension of the historic and the contemporary is an insight which is important for the church's teaching ministry, for teaching must never be exclusively concerned with passing on the tradition or with present experience, but with both in relation to one another. It is not enough that one is a member of the family of God in the present; to be a fully participating member he must be aware of his family history.

The recent emphasis on the church as the *whole* people of God and consequently on the ministry of the laity is also of significance for understanding the church's teaching ministry. It is a matter of fact, not theory, that the teaching which the church does cannot be confined to those who are designated as teachers. The whole church does in fact teach, and unless the whole church is conscious of its mission of witness and teaching that mission is obscured or even perverted.

The church teaches, whether for good or ill, through its organized life, through the Christian family, and through other structures. It also teaches

[1] See chap. 1, pp. 11-20.

and witnesses as it is scattered abroad in the world through its individual members. In the past Christian educators have most often been concerned with organized teaching, primarily within the classroom. We are now more aware that if the church is to reach the world it must do so outside the structures which are identified readily as church.

Thus, the ministry of teaching, as it grows out of the nature of the church, is at least threefold, as Roger Shinn has made clear. First, it is responsible for introducing persons, young and old, to Christian community, and this includes the hope that a faith relationship with God will be the result. Second, it is responsible for transmitting the heritage of the community, of making known a systematic formulation of the faith. And third, it must also equip its members to be the church in the world so that they may not only live Christianly in the world but also witness to their faith in deed and word. A fourth responsibility, which we have already noted, grows out of this latter, namely, the work of witness and teaching in the world by those who have been taught within the structure of the church.

Christian teaching, then, is not a detached enterprise concerned with objective data in which the teacher has no personal interest. It is faith teaching, or teaching for commitment, which is the task of the church. Its aim is not only to lead to personal involvement in the community of faith but also to send into the world those who have become so involved to witness to their faith in the various "realms of their calling."

## Revelation and Teaching Process

Although revelation is considered in a separate chapter,[2] it seems appropriate to give brief attention to it here since it is unusually crucial in understanding theological foundations of Christian teaching. This is true for at least two reasons: First, so that it will be clearly seen that Christian teaching does in fact grow out of the "givenness" of the Christian faith, and second, so that the process of teaching can be rooted in the nature of revelation itself.

The importance of the first of these reasons grows out of the prevailing trend in religious education in the 1920's and 1930's toward emphasizing discovery rather than response. "Discovering God in nature" was a prevalent theme, and though this has largely disappeared in contemporary thought, the residue is still with us. At the heart of the Christian faith, however, is the assertion that God takes the initiative in coming to man and that man responds to God's revelation in faith and obedience. This does not eliminate the element of "quest" in teaching, nor does it suggest a single authoritative interpretation of the Christian revelation, as Harrison Elliott feared it did.[3] Interpretations, or theologies, vary, but the centrality of God's action on man's behalf cannot be denied.

Second, if in fact it is God himself who is revealed, not propositions about God, then we have a basic characteristic of Christian teaching inherent within

[2] See chap. 4, pp. 42-49.
[3] *Can Religious Education Be Christian?* (New York: The Macmillan Company, 1940), chap. IV.

35

the Christian faith. As Sara Little has shown, the emphasis on God's self-revelation (personal, not propositional) is that of contemporary theology, growing out of the biblical understanding of revelation.[4] It follows, then, that whatever else Christian teaching may be, it is at its base personal in nature; that is, it is concerned with response to and relation with God and with our fellow men. This does not preclude—in fact, it necessitates—the telling of the story of the Christian community; hence, Christian teaching involves helping the learner become aware of the contents of the Bible, Christian history, and theology. This knowledge serves a more basic end, however, that of preparing for and explaining the nature of encounter with the living God.

## Christian Teaching and a Doctrine of Man

Basic also to understanding the nature of the teaching process is one's view of man. This includes data from the personal and social sciences, and at times Christian education has depended rather too much on these human sciences. I do not mean to suggest that these data are not important, though it is not within the purview of this chapter to discuss them.[5] The Christian educator has much to learn from all those concerned with understanding the human person, and with the fluidity of such thinking no past statements in this area can be considered as either final or adequate. In this brief section, however, we can deal only with a theological approach to man.

Borrowing from nineteenth-century liberal theology, religious educators in the early decades of this century developed a theory of teaching which assumed that man was educable into the good life. One became a Christian "in and through the educational process." The kingdom of God (or the "democracy of God," as George Albert Coe put it [6]) was a human possibility if man could only provide the proper kind of education.

At few points do the various theological positions which have superseded nineteenth-century liberalism agree more than in regard to the nature of man. To be sure they disagree concerning the degree to which man, as rooted in nature, is capable himself of attaining the good life. Some theologians, such as Karl Barth, insist upon a radical doctrine of grace with seemingly little of the divine imprint left in "natural" man. Others, such as the contemporary existentialists, have a radical view of man's freedom with both the necessity and the possibility of decision within a context of grace. Few if any would support the optimism of liberal theology regarding man.

In the early days of neo-Reformation theology many Christian educators interpreted the changed view of man as cutting the nerve of the church's teaching enterprise, and indeed it did, as education was interpreted by many of these men. As a matter of fact, however, it actually makes the teaching of the church more important. If man were essentially educable into goodness, then it is possible that the public schools and character building agencies might perform the task of bringing man to his potential. If, on the other hand, man

---

[4] See chap. 4, pp. 42-43.
[5] See chaps. 5 and 7, pp. 50-59 and 71-84.
[6] *A Social Theory of Religious Education* (New York: Charles Scribner's Sons, 1917).

is separated or alienated from the very ground of his being, i.e., God, then only a radical act of faith in God made possible by God's grace can provide the basis for "the new being."

What, then, is the potential for Christian nurture and instruction? Nurture, as the process of inducting one into Christian practices and attitudes, is supremely the task of the Christian family, though to some degree the congregation can share in the process. By its nature this includes both law and gospel. It includes law, for no one is wise enough to know what is good nor good enough to practice it even when he knows it. Hence, judgment and discipline are a part of nurture as well as grace and love.

If this nurture is effective, it will lead the child to see himself in need of something (or, more precisely, someone) outside himself. However, such nurture, which is largely relational, must be supplemented with a presentation of the Christian faith so that the person *understands* himself as creature in relation to the Creator, as sinner in relation to the gracious, forgiving God. Nurture and instruction are part of the preparation for encounter or relationship—those times when the child, youth, or adult sees himself in need of the grace of God and accepts God's acceptance of himself.

Teaching is not only preparation for encounter: It is also the giving of help in spelling out the meaning of this encounter (or these encounters), and hence instruction and nurture are also follow-up from encounter. Indeed, there is a daily need and hopefully a daily occurrence of encounter, for one is never, in the strict sense of the word, a Christian, only becoming one.

In short, man is understood in his actuality as being separated from God but in his potentiality as being capable of authentic existence (salvation) or relationship with God because of God's gracious act in accepting him and enabling him to have such existence.

## How One Becomes a Christian

A further issue, to which we have already moved in the previous discussion, concerns how one becomes a Christian. I am not concerned at this point with the doctrine of justification by grace through faith, though, of course, this is the background for the concern. Rather, I am interested in the nature of the human response and the relation of Christian teaching to it.

John Baillie in a small book published posthumously[7] has stated the issue with clarity. There are two major ways in which the church has interpreted the beginning of the Christian life. The traditional "catholic" churches have ordinarily thought of it as beginning with the baptism of the infant or the adult, while the churches of the evangelical tradition have insisted on a definite and datable experience of conversion. What he does not note is the relation of this to Christian education, especially in the United States. In the nineteenth century the evangelical tradition predominated and the Sunday school was thought of as preparation for conversion. Although this tradition largely prevails in the sectarian groups in this century, many communions of the

---

[7] *Baptism and Conversion* (New York: Charles Scribner's Sons, 1963).

evangelical tradition have changed their emphasis, under the influence of the religious education of the early decades of this century, and have developed a plan which implicitly (if not explicitly) assumes that a child becomes a Christian through being taught to be one.

It is not within the purview of this chapter to settle this issue, for among other matters it involves an understanding of baptism, one of the points of disagreement in ecumenical discussions. On the basis of current understandings of the nature of Christian education, however, it appears that something of a consensus may be emerging. Regardless of how seriously baptism may be taken as the *beginning* of the Christian life, the prevailing view is that something more than Christian initiation is necessary for the consciously committed Christian to emerge. At the basis of the contemporary emphasis on the renewal of the church is an awareness of the common superficiality of both the understanding and the practice of the Christian life. Encounter and decision, relationship and response are among the words often used to denote the importance and necessity of a self-conscious act on the part of the individual.

In other words, God's initiative in giving himself in gracious love to man calls for a response which involves decision, commitment, and a new life. Although there is no agreement as to whether there should be a "datable" experience, the more common emphasis is on daily renewal. Nurture and teaching, as was indicated in the previous section, are both preparation for and follow up from these times of encounter, decision, and commitment. It is these significant moments—"revelation," to use H. Richard Niebuhr's understanding of the term[8]—which provide meaning for all the other events of our lives. God's grace makes man's decision possible; teaching and nurture give substance and direction as both preparation and explication.

## Theology and Methodology

We have already noted that method in Christian education should be related to one's understanding of the Christian faith. How thoroughly it can be rooted in theology is a question which can be answered only provisionally. By and large recent writing has ignored this relationship, and as a consequence methods continue to be borrowed from general education and cognate disciplines.

Two emphases in recent theological thought appear to be especially relevant to methodology. The first of these is one often associated with the name of Paul Tillich,[9] though it is not exclusively his: namely, the principle of correlation. By this is meant the attempt of theologian and educator to find those points at which the "given" of the Christian faith intersects or correlates with the "given" of the human situation. That is, the questions of life (or "persistent life needs") find their "answers" (or counterpart) in the Christian faith. As Claude Welch has put it, "The theological task and the task of interpretation involves us inescapably in both the language of the church and the language of a contemporary situation. . . . The interpreter or educator who

[8] *The Meaning of Revelation* (New York: The Macmillan Company, 1941).
[9] *Systematic Theology* (Chicago: University of Chicago Press, 1951), I, 59-66.

stands within the Christian community also stands, and must stand, in many other communities if his is to be a genuine interpretation to persons." [10]

There is a much clearer implication here for curriculum than for method or technique. It suggests that the curriculum should be neither "life-centered" nor "Bible-centered" but rather centered on the intersection of the deep needs of life and the Christian faith. Further, subject matter must always point beyond itself to the relation of the person to God and to his fellow men. It does not mean that there will not be content units as such, though it does indicate that in the final analysis content must be seen in relation to man's deepest needs.

What this means for methodology is much less clear. Rather than pointing to any one method as the norm or to even a cluster of related methods it indicates that any method should be ruled out which does not in some degree confront the learner with the Christian faith. What this confrontation involves is still to be determined, however. For example, does play in the block center have a place in kindergarten methodology? Does recreation have a place in the youth ministry? How important is the transmission of content for its own sake? These and other questions are not simply answered, for there are many facets to the total learning process in the context of the church, and it is possible that Christian *koinonia* may emerge more vitally at a time of recreation than in the more obviously "church-centered" activities of a youth group.

Perhaps the questions concerned with the principle of correlation can be partly answered by turning to a second aspect of contemporary theology which is more directly related to method—namely, the emphasis on relationship, encounter, or dialogue. We have seen how revelation is generally taken to be personal encounter—God meeting man in the relationships of man's existence. We have also noted how this points to a kind of teaching-nurture which is concerned with existential encounter, or relationships. This means, then, that methods must be sought which bring learners into a personal relationship with the teacher and with one another, and that these relationships must point beyond themselves, to God. There is a place for the lecture, for the learner must be related to content also, but lecture alone may remain on an impersonal level. Methods which develop interpersonal relationships within the Christian community are especially valuable in implementing this theological emphasis.

It should be repeated that considerably more work needs to be done in both learning theory and teaching methods in the light of the Christian faith and in a Christian context before we have the insights which we need.[11] If we are right that method cannot be separated from either content or context, then this area of research is one which ought to receive extensive attention during the years ahead.

## Conclusion

The struggle for the recognition of the crucial nature of theology in relation to Christian teaching has probably been won. Perhaps we have also to some extent recovered a relevant theology as the *content of what is taught*. We have

[10] "By What Authority?" *Pittsburgh Perspective*, III (June, 1962), 13.
[11] See chap. 5, pp. 50-59.

made considerable progress in relating theology to the *process of teaching*. We have done much less with regard to *theology and methodology*. Here is one of the relatively unexplored areas of the church's teaching ministry.

Nor should it be supposed that the task of determining either content for teaching or the relation of theology to process is a completed one. These are areas of theological thought which require more attention than has previously been given to them. In two of these concerns Rachel Henderlite has recently made helpful contributions, namely, the relationship with Christian teaching of justification through grace by faith, and the role of the Holy Spirit in teaching.[12]

Further, in a time when theological thinking includes such rapid and radical changes, the task of relating the church's ministries to the intellectual life of the church is a never-ending one. Both process philosophy and linguistic philosophy, if they continue to increase in influence, must be brought under purview.[13] I do not mean to imply that the mainstream of the church is likely to follow either of these approaches to thought, nor should it do so with regard to any theological system too much outside the accepted tradition of the church. The Christian educator must be responsive both to the historic tradition of the church and to the currents of contemporary theology, and he should learn from both—Calvin and Bultmann, Wesley and Tillich.

The theological conversation is a continuous task of the church, and the Christian educator ought to be actively engaged in it. The local church teacher should also be sufficiently conversant with the theology of the church that he can do a responsible job of communicating the Christian faith. The burden which the professional Christian educator bears in this conversation is not an easy one, for it involves conversation on the one hand with the biblical scholar, the church historian, and the theologian, and on the other with the specialists in general education and the cognate disciplines. It is one which must be accepted in all seriousness, however, if the church's teaching ministry is to be fulfilled responsibly in the years ahead.

## FOR ADDITIONAL READING

Chamberlin, J. Gordon. *Freedom and Faith*. Philadelphia: The Westminster Press, 1965.

Cully, Iris V. *Imparting the Word*. Philadelphia: The Westminster Press, 1963.

Cully, Kendig Brubaker. *The Search for a Christian Education—Since 1940*. Philadelphia: The Westminster Press, 1965.

Grimes, Howard. *The Church Redemptive*. Nashville: Abingdon Press, 1958.

———. *The Rebirth of the Laity*. Nashville: Abingdon Press, 1962.

Henderlite, Rachel. *Forgiveness and Hope*. Richmond: John Knox Press, 1961.

———. *The Holy Spirit in Christian Education*. Philadelphia: The Westminster Press, 1964.

---

[12] *Forgiveness and Hope* (Richmond: John Knox Press, 1961) and *The Holy Spirit in Christian Education* (Philadelphia: The Westminster Press, 1964).

[13] For a consideration of linguistic philosophy see "Linguistic Philosophy and Christian Education," in *Religious Education*, LX (January-February, 1965), 3-42.

Howe, Reuel L. *Man's Need and God's Action.* New York: The Seabury Press, 1953.

Hunter, David R. *Christian Education as Engagement.* New York: The Seabury Press, 1963.

Little, Sara. *The Role of the Bible in Contemporary Christian Education.* Richmond: John Knox Press, 1961.

Miller, Randolph Crump. *Christian Nurture and the Church.* New York: Charles Scribner's Sons, 1961.

Schreyer, George M. *Christian Education in Theological Focus.* Philadelphia: United Church Press, 1962.

Sherrill, Lewis J. *The Gift of Power.* New York: The Macmillan Company, 1955.

Shinn, Roger L. *The Educational Mission of Our Church.* Philadelphia: United Church Press, 1962.

Slusser, Gerald H. *The Local Church in Transition: Theology, Education, and Ministry.* Philadelphia: The Westminster Press, 1964.

Smart, James D. *The Creed in Christian Teaching.* Philadelphia: The Westminster Press, 1962.

————. *The Teaching Ministry of the Church.* Philadelphia: The Westminster Press, 1954.

# Chapter 4

# REVELATION, THE BIBLE, AND CHRISTIAN EDUCATION

## *Sara Little*

WHAT HAS BEEN THE RESULT IN CHRISTIAN EDUCATION OF THE TWENTIETH-century "rediscovery" of the doctrine of revelation and of the centrality of the Bible to the life of faith? That is the focal question for this essay. Although, admittedly, stating conclusions is always a risk, because conclusions need to be qualified almost before they are made, it does seem fairly safe to say that Christian educators have listened diligently to theological and biblical scholars, the source of the "rediscovery," during the last few decades. The serious listening has eventuated in taking heed, in reflecting the theological renascence, and in undertaking massive reforms in the curriculum of Christian education. A period of assimilation of what has been heard marks the fleeting moment of relative quiet during the mid-1960's. But the future, a new kind of future, already impinges upon the present and raises anew the question about the meaning of revelation and the place of the Bible.

Almost immediately other questions arise, questions which call for interpretation and open the way to deal more adequately with the central area of concern. What has been the occasion for and the nature of the theological renascence? In what specific ways have theoretical formulations of Christian education been influenced? How have these theoretical formulations been utilized or implemented? Are the "results" adequate to the present situation and the emerging future in the church and in the world? An attempt will be made to deal with each of the four questions, in order, in the four sections of this chapter.

## Revelation and the Biblical Witness

From time to time in the movement of ideas and of history there comes a turning point that is clearly discernible. Such was the case with the change signified by the publication of Barth's *Commentary on Romans* in 1918. People debate about whether the turn came because of what has been called a rediscovery of the Reformation understanding of revelation, or whether the rediscovery itself was occasioned by conditions in a world at war, when a liberal theology had almost run its course and was unable to meet the needs of disillusioned men. Actually, the situation was more complex, more factors were at work, than could be suggested by any simple setting forth of alternatives. But the story has been told too often to be recounted here. The important thing to note is that once again Christians were reminded of the uniqueness of their faith as being called forth by a sovereign God who, in his self-disclosure, gave himself, always in mystery, and always in salvation.

When a word drops from the scene or declines in importance, the conclusion may logically be drawn that the reality symbolized by the word is no longer vital to mankind. That observation is applicable to the decline of the concern for revelation in the nineteenth and early twentieth centuries, a period in which the Thomistic understanding of revelation was completely disrupted, as John Baillie has pointed out in *The Idea of Revelation in Recent Thought* (1956). The scientific study of the Bible in higher criticism, the challenge to biblical authority by the authority of religious experience, as well as other factors, contributed to the disruption of the traditional belief that revealed, in distinction from natural, knowledge centered in the words of Scripture. Christianity, as a religion among religions, could be understood by the tools of human reason. This era—in which "modern" religious education was born—was constituted by a revolution in man's perception of himself, the world, and God.

More recently, when the word "revelation" began to appear frequently again in the theological vocabulary, it had a different meaning. The doctrine of revelation, indissolubly linked with the understanding of the Bible, assumed a dominant role in the system of more than one major theologian. This is not to say that all theologians arrived at the same position (imagine putting Barth, Tillich, and Bultmann in the same category!) or that a "new" doctrine of revelation was the sole cause of theological renewal. It is to say, however, that there was and is a general area of agreement, and that much of the theological activity up through the mid-twentieth century can be interpreted from the point of view of the concept of revelation.

The same thing is true with respect to Christian education. When Harrison Elliott, in 1940, raised the question *Can Religious Education Be Christian?* he posed the issue facing religious educators about as strongly and clearly as it was possible to do. If the church seeks to transmit a predetermined body of content, can this rightly be called *education?* Does not the word "education" by definition imply change, openness to new truth, growth? The question is not to be understood solely as an intellectual abstraction. Knowledge of the historical background will have to be assumed here, because the whole matter of the relation of public education to religious education, or of the rise of the Sunday school movement to church education, is as crucial in understanding the present situation as is the one strand of theological thought under consideration. It is true, however, that the answer Christian educators gave to Harrison Elliott—and it was not the answer he desired—centered largely in their appropriation of the idea of revelation. Lewis J. Sherrill, in *The Gift of Power,* spoke for many in addition to himself when he said that the fact of revelation is determinative not only for Christian education but for all the work of the church.

## Consensus and Divergence

By the 1950's a general area of agreement among Christian educators seemed to have arisen, based on affirmation of the necessity for the initiating activity of a transcendent God, revealing himself through history, as recorded in the Bible. That same affirmation was still being made by biblical scholars in the 1960's, according to James Barr.

No single principle is more powerful in the handling of the Bible today than the belief that history is the channel of divine revelation. Thus the formula "revelation through history" is taken to represent the center of biblical thinking, and interpretation of any biblical passage must be related to this historical revelation. The characteristic of extra-biblical religion, it is held, is its timeless or non-historical emphasis, while the centrality of revelation through history marks the biblical religion off clearly from such other religion. These ideas today are not only common, but they enjoy almost unqualified acceptance.[1]

Part of Professor Barr's intent in making this statement was to question it, a point to be considered later. But even in questioning this formula which "has enjoyed such uncontradicted privilege" and served as "a unifying factor in modern theology," [2] he admits that the idea of revelation through history is "a fair expression of a really important element in the Bible," and that it can be taken generally as "the central theme of the Bible, that it forms the main link between the Old and New Testaments, and that its presence and importance clearly marks biblical faith off from other religions." [3]

Around the ideas mentioned by Barr cluster others constituting a part of the consensus. Revelation is dynamic, not static. It is the activity of a living God who discloses himself to his people through historical events. As he enables his people to perceive the meaning in those events, he draws them into a relationship with himself which is simultaneously revelation and salvation. The biblical record witnesses both to event and its meaning, becomes an instrument for understanding and entering into the meaning of God's ongoing activity, and points to the completion of his purposes for mankind beyond history.

The view of biblical history as a revelatory medium, as well as an area for analytical investigation and accumulation of knowledge *about* the Judeo-Christian tradition, drew biblical scholars and theologians together in a common enterprise to be performed in the service of the church. It also sharply differentiated opposing views. Fundamentalism continued to offer its testimony to the power of biblical words, themselves to be viewed as revelation amenable to formulation in propositions which called for assent and served as guides to correct doctrine. Education allied with such a view would logically be a "Bible-centered" education, and would preserve much of the emphasis of the early Sunday school movement, although fundamentalism technically is a twentieth-century movement. It is a rejection of liberalism and a plea for orthodoxy, originating in 1908 when the series entitled *The Fundamentals* began to appear. Similarly, liberalism continued to offer its reminder of value

[1] "Revelation Through History in the Old Testament and in Modern Theology," in *New Theology No. 1*, Martin E. Marty and Dean G. Peerman, eds. (New York: The Macmillan Company, 1964), p. 61. The article was originally published in the April, 1963, issue of *Interpretation: A Journal of Bible and Theology*.

[2] *Ibid.*

[3] *Ibid.*, p. 69.

in a functional or resource use of the Bible, a record of man's experience of God. The opposing views set limits to, and also penetrated and thus influenced, the changing core of Protestantism. In Roman Catholicism growing interest in and openness to Bible study, more than a changing view of revelation, contributed to the development known as "kerygmatic catechetics," in many ways paralleling educational developments stemming from the theological renewal in Protestantism.

What difference did the view of the Bible and of revelation make in the educator's task? The answers are still applicable and the present tense can be used. For one thing, the educator has provided for him a structure for the biblical subject matter to be taught—a story or drama (as distinguished from a system of doctrine, for example), linking the Testaments together and providing a framework for interpretation of particular parts. He has a perspective —that of moving through facts and events to message, meaning, gospel, *kerygma*, to that which is of "ultimate significance." He has an objective— though a better word is hope—that in the movement through and behind the words of the Bible, the student might be confronted by the Word, and, supported by the community of God's people in his response to that Word, might join with them in their enterprise of "faith seeking understanding," and their mission of witness to the world in word and deed.

Patterns of divergence from the background of agreement, related to different churchly traditions, are to be understood in part as efforts to deal responsibly with concern for the appropriation of revelation. As differences are delineated, it must be remembered that contrast is by way of emphasis, rather than of mutually exclusive approaches. Two terms, "content" and "process," are suggestive. They stand as ends of a continuum, with many variations on the line in between. Unless these variations are remembered, the use of the terms may lead to oversimplification. No one writer and no one denomination stands as an exact embodiment of either pole of thought. In general, however, writers such as James Smart and denominations adhering to the Reformed tradition stand closest to the *content* pole; writers such as Randolph C. Miller and the Protestant Episcopal denomination stand closest to the *process* pole.

*Content* is not to be understood as subject matter, but as the dynamic inherent within the subject matter, the living power of truth which imposes itself as such upon the subject matter and forms of Christian education by virtue of its own intrinsic authority. William Temple spoke of the subjective and the objective aspects of revelation. For the *content* pole the objective side is to be stressed. Emphasis is on God's activity in self-disclosure, and on what he reveals of himself. For the *process* pole the subjective side of revelation is more clearly recognized and developed in terms of its significance for Christian education. It stresses the way in which God revealed himself in biblical history, the same way he continues to make himself known. When, biblically, men were led to perceive that God was at work for their salvation, revelation was completed by the perception of the meaning of God's activity in their experience.

Many other concerns of Christian education could be interpreted from the rubric presented here, but consider only two others: How is revelation appropriated? How is the Bible to be used?

How is revelation received and internalized? That is what is meant by the appropriation of revelation. In the *content* pole the important thing is *that to which response is made.* The teacher's role is to clear the way, to guide students to utilize all their faculties (particularly that of reason) to seek understanding of the biblical message. The Holy Spirit may use such human activity to confront man with the living Word. When man responds to him, that response itself is appropriation. The gift of fellowship is the *result* of the appropriation. It provides the context for interpretation, and expresses itself in worship and mission.

In contrast to the key word "response" is the word "participation." The meaning of the biblical revelation is translated into experience and "learned" there as experience is interpreted. Or, stated another way, as men participate in that fellowship when God actively is at work, they are drawn into a saving relationship with him. What happens is that they experience and therefore appropriate the reality of revelation by participating in God's ongoing activity. The church in all its life becomes a matrix within which revelation may be appropriated.

The centrality of the Bible for both positions is obvious. In the first case the Bible is the beginning point. It is uniquely the channel through which God may come to confront men. It has intrinsic, commanding authority. Its relevance is demonstrated as it takes hold of the very being of a person, transforms him, and guides him as he lives out in day-by-day decisions the fact that he is a new being. In the second case the Bible is the only reliable way to interpret the meaning of God's redemptive activity in human experience. Life raises questions (basic questions of meaning and existence, not just superficial questions) and the Bible becomes relevant as it answers them. Thus the Bible has a teaching authority.

The points selected here serve to illustrate the important role the doctrine of revelation has come to play in the contemporary theoretical formulations of Christian education. However, Christian education is best known not by its statements of theory but by what happens week after week in the educational ministry of the church. Are changes apparent on that level?

## Assimilation

The consensus and divergence patterns were derived not just from the writings of Christian educators, but also from a study of official curriculum documents. In other words, they represent what is happening in the working guides set up by educational agencies during a period when almost every major Protestant denomination is at work on improving or revising its curriculum. The chapter on curriculum[4] in this book will offer more details. From the perspective of the particular concern here, it can be said that influence of the idea of revelation is evident on every hand. Sometimes the evidence is in terms of frequent use of certain accepted words, sometimes in the overarching structure of curriculum itself. There is variation all the way from the use of ideas as subject matter for

[4] See chap. 14, pp. 157-68.

subthemes of areas of study to their organic incorporation where they are translated into guidance for learning process.

Even outside denominational efforts the impact of renewed concern with the idea of revelation is evidenced. The new idea is rejected by both the unitarian-universalist group and fundamentalists generally, in favor of maintaining and developing their own distinctive earlier ideas, but in both groups increased activity in education is to be found. For example, the nondenominational literature of several independent publishers, directed toward more conservative churchmen, has appeared with a new format and has been advertised as utilizing the "newest teaching methods," almost as though to imply that it is still possible to be up-to-date and to have the security of an infallible Bible.

In interdenominational affairs much significance is to be attached to the fact that, since 1872, with the inauguration of the Uniform Lessons, provision has been made cooperatively to make the Bible the foundation of Christian education. Although understanding of the nature of the Bible has changed and doctrinal interpretation has varied according to denominational inclinations, it is still the case that the Bible *per se* has been kept in a focal position, as it will be through continued production of the uniform outlines. The changing center of interdenominational cooperation is in the Cooperative Curriculum Project of the National Council of Churches, replacing other earlier curriculum work. What that project will eventually reflect of the consensus mentioned here, in the light of denominational differences, remains to be seen.

In fact, the whole matter of whether the theological renascence will or can penetrate to the minutiae of Christian education affairs has yet to be determined. It is one thing to speak of widespread agreement that Christian education is dependent upon the fact of revelation, but quite another to determine what this means in terms of organization of subject matter, grouping of students for study, teaching methods, and the like. The temptation is always present to falter in the movement from the ideal to the possible, and to acclaim as revolutionary that which is only a pseudorenewal. Indeed, how *are* people led to be aware of God's ongoing activity in the present? How does one concentrate on the unity of the biblical revelation and the centrality of the biblical message without stressing abstract generalizations or propositions rather than the divine self-disclosure rooted in historical events? And if one gives attention to events, to particulars, how does he avoid the much-lamented fragmentation of the Bible? Is concern for character or behavior to be eliminated because of fear of using the Bible moralistically?

Answers to questions such as these continue to be worked on during the 1960's, a period of assimilation in which theories themselves have been affected. A historian will someday enjoy exploring the change in these formulations as influenced by the period of assimilation.

## A Changing Situation

The complicated difficulties of working through theories changing in the process of their implementation are accompanied by other factors, by faint signs on the horizon of the future, which may have something to say to the view of revelation and of the Bible presented here as a working consensus. Hints of these developments are given in relationship to three questions.

First, there is the question as to the climate of the times. Do the ideas of revelation, of an authoritative Bible, of a transcendent God, make sense to man today? Earlier in this century, such ideas could be heard, but doubts are being expressed as to their contemporary relevance. One writer, William Hamilton, noting that "there has been in our time a recovery of what can be called the biblical-Augustinian-Reformed way of speaking about God," [5] states: "A certain idea of revelation is implied in this tradition: the biblical notion that we cannot in ourselves know God, but that he has made himself known to us." [6] He deals with other aspects of the tradition, also, and then goes on to admit that the "contemporary portrait of God is serving well at many points, but some leakage is beginning to be felt." [7] Hamilton, as did Bonhoeffer, has doctrinal questions about "the portrait," as well as concern for the availability of God to suffering mankind. His analyses and "fragments" of theological form are different from the conclusions of a writer such as Paul M. Van Buren, in his *The Secular Meaning of the Gospel*. Contending that communication with man can take place only through the use of language that can be empirically understood, he rules out reference to the category of the supernatural. Others would pose their concern differently. All in all, it may be said that the climate of the times is not so conducive to the continuing ascendancy of the idea of revelation as was once the case—which simply points out that the question of possibility of reception of truth is not totally irrelevant.

Second, there is the question of new developments in scholarly thinking. When mention is made of reception of the truth, one thinks immediately of the growing concern with the hermeneutical question. Heinrich Ott, successor to Karl Barth, states that "the nature of theology as a whole is hermeneutical," and, indeed, that "theology is really hermeneutic." [8] What he means by "hermeneutic" has more to do with the act of understanding and interpreting the Bible than with a technique or theory. In his view of the unity of theology he specifically includes practical theology as a part of the hermeneutical circle and indicates his intention to emphasize that aspect of the theological task. His willingness to use the later Heidegger's philosophical categories, where language is viewed as the "house of being," as the response to being's unveiling itself through man's thinking, marks a new openness to a liaison between theology and philosophy. Gerhard Ebeling and Ernst Fuchs, continuing Bultmann's well-known concern for the problem of communication, place an equal emphasis on the function of words, or the "word-event," though from a different methodological position. They are, indeed, the proponents of what is called "the new hermeneutic." It may well be that the word "hermeneutic" is on the way to replacing the word "revelation" as a key concern in contemporary theology.

[5] *The New Essence of Christianity* (New York: Association Press, 1961), p. 35.
[6] *Ibid.*, p. 36.
[7] *Ibid.*, p. 44.
[8] "What Is Systematic Theology?" in *The Later Heidegger and Theology*, James M. Robinson and John B. Cobb, Jr., eds. (New York: Harper & Row, 1963), p. 78.

If so, the idea of revelation is not abandoned. It is, rather, assumed, as stress is laid on biblical interpretation and on communication.

The understanding of history may also have something to say as to whether the idea of revelation changes. James Barr's assertion about the "formula" of revelation through history was made in order to raise questions. He is not alone in his questioning, and in his conviction that the view of history is significant for every aspect of Christian theology, as well as for the understanding of revelation.

Has the idea of revelation continued to be dominant in the writings of Christian educators themselves? Iris Cully's *Imparting the Word* is the most direct recent treatment of the subject. Other writings either assume the idea, or approach different concerns moving into the forefront of attention.

Third, there is the question of new opportunities facing Christian education today. It is quite conceivable that Christian educators may move toward investigating the idea of *hermeneutic* in relationship to their approach to the Bible. The emphasis on *understanding* suggests that option, as does the openness to the symbolic and poetic modes of thought.

On the other hand, they may be led to see the necessity for new approaches to the Bible through calls arising outside the traditional study curriculum. If religious education finds some new alliance with public education, what will be the place of the Bible? Or as Christians face ethical problems of momentous importance daily, how can they find guidance for fulfilling their responsibilities as free Christian men? The battleground seems to be here, rather than in academic controversy as to the place of the Bible. What would happen if Christian educators were to move toward setting up structures through which biblical relevance might be experienced in the process of ethical decision-making?

Christian education is an elusive, mediating discipline. But whatever the duration of the venture, the stance taken with regard to the meaning of revelation and the use of the Bible will be one major clue as to what Christian education considers itself to be.

## FOR ADDITIONAL READING

Baillie, John. *The Idea of Revelation in Recent Thought*. New York: Columbia University Press, 1956.

Cully, Iris V. *Imparting the Word*. Philadelphia: The Westminster Press, 1963.

Jones, Clifford M. *The Bible Today: For Those Who Teach It*. Philadelphia: Fortress Press, 1964.

Little, Sara. *The Role of the Bible in Contemporary Christian Education*. Richmond: John Knox Press, 1961.

Robinson, James M. and Cobb, John B., eds. *The Later Heidegger and Theology*, Vol. I of *New Frontiers in Theology*. New York: Harper & Row, 1963.

————. *The New Hermeneutic*, Vol. II of *New Frontiers in Theology*. New York: Harper & Row, 1964.

# Chapter 5

# PSYCHOLOGICAL FOUNDATIONS FOR CHRISTIAN EDUCATION

## *Donald E. Miller*

ANY INQUIRY ABOUT THE PSYCHOLOGICAL FOUNDATIONS FOR CHRISTIAN education immediately faces the question of the relationship between the science of psychology and the Christian view of man. A proper answer to this question could in itself take more than the space allotted here, and yet we cannot avoid the question. Let us, therefore, give the briefest possible answer as a way of introducing the presuppositions of this essay.

Contemporary scientific psychologies are by and large empirically rather than theologically oriented. They are inductive from accumulated experience rather than deductive from faith assumptions. Psychology usually tries to give a causal explanation of individual learning rather than a purposive account. These characteristics in themselves are enough to ask whether psychological and theological assumptions about the nature of man are irreconcilably at opposite extremes from one another.

Indeed, they often are, but they need not be for at least several reasons. The first is that faith stands between God's being over against every human experience and God's concrete presence in the midst of human experience. Faith extends beyond the change and variability of human moods, so that every event serves to confirm what faith already secretly knows. At the same time faith is wholly and totally involved in life as a new reality in every new circumstance. The double stance of faith means that empiricism must be taken seriously, but not too seriously. This is only another way of saying that the God who is the origin and destiny of history can be known only from within the very common events of history as its Redeemer.

The second reason is that new empirical information constantly alters the believer's understanding of the Christian faith. Biblical faith is ready to accept every new factual finding with the confidence that God will appear there in some surprisingly new way. He will, nevertheless, be recognizably the God who appeared in Jesus Christ. Faith is in a running dialogue with the scriptural and historical account of its origin, with the community of those who are nourished by it, and with a constant reevaluation of new experience. Faith is its own reality; the gospel is its own criterion of truth, but always within the rich diversity of human experience. The content of faith is constantly up for reconsideration, though the ultimate concern of faith never is.

The third consideration is that every science is to some extent a covert expression of faith assumptions. Science is as much an expression of the spirit of the times as it is a cause of that spirit. To put it another way, empirical psychology is always wholly entangled in the presuppositions and imaginative hunches of the scientist. The psychologist helps to formulate and give expression to the assumptions about human nature that are shared in his time. For example, Japanese psychotherapy aims at eliminating personal impulses toward individuality, while Western psychotherapy aims at the acceptance of individuality. Scientific psychology takes a different shape in a culture that does not share the Western assumptions about human nature.

We can conclude only that a Christian view of man cannot ignore the findings of empirical psychology, but that it should be critical of the faith assumptions of any psychology. Christian education will use the findings of empirical psychology to elucidate the gospel, but never to replace the gospel. In what follows we shall concern ourselves principally with the psychology of learning, the area of psychology that has most direct bearing upon Christian education. Psychologies of learning may be broadly considered under four types: conditioning, perceptual, developmental, and existential theories.

## The Conditioned Response

Conditioning theory is one of the most widely accepted scientific explanations of learning. Conditioned learning occurs whenever an original stimulus is accompanied by a second stimulus so that after some repetition the response to the second stimulus will be elicited by the original stimulus. For example, teachers often condition their students to certain attitudes. If coming to class elicits a joyful response from a child, while the annoyance of the teacher elicits anxiety in the child, soon coming to class will in itself elicit anxiety from the child. Unfortunately, parents and teachers often believe that the child's anxiety causes their own annoyance, when actually the reverse may be true.

Perhaps the most dramatic application of the conditioned response is the development of mechanical teaching devices called teaching machines. A whole new technology is developing around the behavioral engineering of teaching, and it shows every possibility of revolutionizing teaching in many ways. James G. Holland has very succinctly stated seven principles upon which teaching machines operate.[1]

1. Immediate reinforcement must be provided for correct answers. Reinforcement refers to the reward given to a particular response. The machine provides reinforcement by letting the student see the correct answer as soon as he has given his own answer. Laboratory studies indicate that the efficiency of learning is greatly reduced whenever the delay between the student's response and the reinforcement is increased by as much as a few seconds. This fact should sensitize teachers to the importance of immediate reinforcement in the learning situation. Furthermore, the teacher must have a clear idea of what he expects from the student, else he cannot reward the correct response immediately.

2. "Behavior is learned only when it is emitted and reinforced." The machine requires the student to make an open response before it will allow him to go

[1] "Teaching Machines: An Application of Principles from the Laboratory," in *Human Learning*, Arthur W. Staats, ed. (New York: Holt, Rinehart & Winston, 1964).

on to further material. Whether verbal or other skills are desired, the behavior must be acted upon before it may be learned. Teaching that does not allow for the open expression of ideas and activities can hardly be called learning.

3. There must be a gradual progression from simple to complex repertoires. The teaching machine moves through a series of steps, each of which is only slightly different from the one before. The student has the continual experience of succeeding in his learning. Any good teaching will require the careful planning of gradual steps from one level of difficulty to another. If the steps become too difficult, the student will become anxious and rebellious at the process.

4. There must be a gradual withdrawing of stimulus support. At first a learner sees the whole answer before him. Then he is given fewer and fewer clues to the answer until the question itself will elicit the total response.

5. The student's observing and echoic behavior must be controlled. If the student is not constantly alert and actively responding to what is occurring, he cannot learn. The machine requires him actively and regularly to respond to what is being presented to him. The classroom teacher can so easily go on without regard to the echoic behavior of his students, whereas the machine will not go on until the student finishes an item.

6. To establish an abstraction many examples must be provided. Unless a wide variety of examples is given with only one single property in common, the student may very easily learn something other than what is intended. To learn the quality of God's relationship to persons requires a wide variety of very concrete illustrations, such as is contained in the Scriptures.

7. The material should be revised according to the student's particular difficulties. A program for a teaching machine may be shortened where it is too easy and lengthened where it is too difficult. So also the sensitive teacher will adjust his teaching to the ease with which the students are learning.

Any teacher may follow the principles of learning according to conditioning theory. This approach requires one to know exactly what it is that he intends to teach and to consider very carefully the steps by which it may be learned. The preparation of a program for a teaching machine is in itself an extension of the principles of good teaching. Mechanical teaching devices may not be criticized for being less than human, for they are no less human than is a book. There is every reason to think that they can be used in Christian teaching. On the other hand, the teaching machine cannot replace the teacher, for the machine cannot decide the purpose for which it is being used. The teacher is and will remain the principal aid to the learning process.[2]

Conditioning theory places a premium upon knowing what is to be taught. For Christian education the story of God's action in history, as given in Scripture, the history of the church, and in contemporary events makes up the content. The church also teaches an attitude of open, self-giving love, although one might question whether the living reality of God's love in history may be learned by conditioning. The living history of God's love, nonetheless, does come in the midst of learning that occurs in ways described by conditioning theory.

[2] Jerome S. Bruner, *The Process of Education* (Cambridge: Harvard University Press, 1960), pp. 87 ff.

## Perception of Self and World

Perceptual theories portray learning as a change in a person's perception of himself and his world. They are sometimes called Gestalt or field theories. A person's perceptual pattern includes the way he sees the physical and social worlds, including all facts, concepts, beliefs, and expectations.

One of the strongest of personal motives is to find some kind of meaning or patterned consistency in experience. Psychologists have long known that whenever anyone is presented with a jumble of items, he will try to "make sense" of them. Commonly known also is the fact that an incomplete activity is more likely to be remembered than a completed activity. Most persons have had the experience of "recognizing" someone only to find upon second glance that the recognition was an error. The color of the hair, the gait of the walk, or some other characteristic was so familiar that it triggered a false recognition. Each of these instances illustrates the human propensity to "make sense" of experience.

Likes and dislikes are closely related to a pattern of perceptions. Some parts of a person's world as he perceives it will be attractive to him and other parts will carry negative motivation. The way things appear to a person guides his "attractions and aversions to groups and group standards, his feelings in regard to status differences, and his reactions to sources of approval or disapproval." [3] Not only are motives related to the perceptual field, but the same is true of openly expressed behavior. Teaching is a process wherein the student's perception of himself and his world is so changed that his motives and his expressive behavior are altered.

The perceptual psychologists, especially Kurt Lewin, have shown how learning is totally and in every way interwoven in a social context. What a person accepts as reality is to a very high degree determined by what is socially accepted as reality. To believe that experience alone will teach a person is utter naïveté. Consider that modern, commonly accepted views of gravity were wholly unknown for millenia, though men were constantly living within the experience of gravitation. The basic task of education can thus be viewed as one of changing the individual's social perception.

What one learns in a group is governed less by his knowledge about that group than by the sentiments prevailing in the social atmosphere of the group.[4] The group atmosphere may be characterized by such qualities as purposefulness, explicit procedures, flexibility, and high morale, or by purposelessness, unordered urgency, rigidity, and low morale.[5] Learning also takes place as persons within a group take upon themselves certain functional roles and relate to others within these roles. The teacher may take the role of a "good example" or of a "tyrant." The students in turn may take the role of "hero," "seducer," or "scapegoat," to mention a few of the many possibilities.

---

[3] Kurt Lewin, *Resolving Social Conflicts* (New York: Harper & Row, 1948), p. 59.

[4] *Ibid.*, p. 63.

[5] Jesse Ziegler, *Psychology and the Teaching Church* (Nashville: Abingdon Press, 1962), chap. 3.

Important, however, is the fact that any person's activity is to be seen in part as the role he has in the particular group of which he is a member.

The process of education will normally encounter hostility since significant learning of even a few facts may involve the deep reorientation of a person. Genuine learning means that a new self is replacing the old self. Learning cannot occur until hostility has given way to openmindedness, until teacher and students have come to feel as one group with a common set of values. Education occurs only when a new set of values and beliefs has reorganized the person's perception of himself and his world. The acceptance of a new orientation is linked with "the acceptance of a specific group, a particular role, and a definite source of authority as new points of reference." [6]

Perceptual theory has great significance for Christian education. Teachers must know the underlying perceptual pattern that guides the content of their teaching. To discern the way in which God has acted and is acting in the world becomes central to all teaching. If the rudiments of higher mathematics can be taught to kindergarten children, so the rudimentary understanding of God's active presence among men can also be taught to children.

Of perhaps greater significance is the fact that Christian education can never be abstracted from either the group in which it takes place nor from the life of the congregation in which it occurs. To seek only the "cognitive conversion" of the child or adult is a serious mistake. Learning takes place as a process of incorporation or "adoption" of persons into the life of a witnessing community, into a *koinonia*. Only in the interplay between the individual and the group, between the group and the congregation can real learning take place. Learning in this sense is *always* on the edge of conversion.

## The Development of Personality

The principal developmental theory of personality is the psychoanalytic. Learning occurs according to the psychoanalyst within a developing life history that is shaped by an attempt to handle basic and often conflicting needs. Erik Erikson, one of the most creative interpreters of psychoanalytic theory, declares that the growth of personality always follows the epigenetic principle.[7] Each part of the personality has its own proper time for development, nor may development occur until the proper time has come. Personal initiative cannot occur until some degree of trust is present, just as running cannot be learned until walking has begun.

Psychoanalytic theory points out that learning always involves conflicts and crises with authority figures, such as parents and teachers. Interpersonal encounters are decisive for what is learned. They shape the emotional life of the child in a way that becomes the generalized pattern for responding to all persons thereafter. Teaching is always an interpersonal encounter in which deep feelings are involved, whether or not they are openly recognized and ex-

[6] Lewin, *Resolving Social Conflicts*, p. 68.

[7] What follows is dependent upon Erik H. Erikson, "Growth and Crises of the Healthy Personality," *Psychological Issues* (New York: International Universities Press, 1959), Vol. I.

pressed. Learning is a process by which a person "identifies with," or models his behavior after, the teacher.

Erikson has carried the psychoanalytic theory of learning beyond the Freudian psychosexual model to what he calls the "psychosocial" model with its characteristic ego strength. He is willing to discuss purpose, meaning, and virtue, subjects heretofore virtually ignored in psychoanalytic literature.[8] The development of the personality moves through eight stages, each with its characteristic psychosocial modality and ego strength.

The first year of life is one in which the infant receives nourishment and care from a mother who has mixed feelings of tender affection and annoyance toward the child. As the annoyances come and are reconciled, the infant learns a psychosocial attitude somewhere between trust and mistrust. The basic mixture of trust and mistrust becomes the foundation upon which the infant's personality develops. The characteristic ego strength of interpersonal trust is hope, the confidence that external frustrations and inner angry urges will pass away.

The second year of life finds the child with new abilities to bite, walk, grasp, and eliminate. These new capacities run into the parental restriction of proper time and place. The child learns either to accept restrictions put upon him or to feel ashamed of his own urges in the presence of restriction. The mixture of autonomy and shame becomes a fundamental part of his personality pattern. The ego strength or virtue related to his newly developing capacities is that of will. This description of the relation of autonomy and shame is a commentary upon the biblical doctrine that God submitted himself to the destructive urges of man in order that men might regain the autonomy by which they could willingly live within the limitations that he has set.

Imagination is the radically new element during years three to five. Coupled with growing physical and conceptual abilities, imagination allows the child to play endlessly and to be wonderfully entertained by stories. At the same time the child can begin to imagine himself carrying out his aggressive urges and cannot avoid feeling guilty. The child stands between a new capacity for initiative and a developing sense of guilt. The parents' or teacher's caring, confidence, and willingness to accept the expression of guilt feelings is fundamental to the child's selfhood.

During the early school years the child increasingly learns to achieve, although to some extent he finds himself to be inferior. His mixed feelings of competence and inferiority are related to the development of skills and games with his peer group, to growing conceptual abilities in school, and to the role of being a boy or being a girl.

Adolescence is a time of searching for identity mixed with a sense of lostness or identity diffusion. In modern industrial societies youth develop a separate culture from that of adults and act out various social roles among their peers. They test the extent to which they will accept for themselves the identities and values that have been taught to them throughout childhood. Negative identity feelings must be expressed and acted out before the adolescent can feel a sense of fidelity to his own personhood. The youth is being historicized,

[8] *Insight and Responsibility* (New York: W. W. Norton & Company, 1964).

i.e., his own personal history is being joined into the stream of a broader history. Youth is an age when the history of God's activity among men can take on very special significance.

The psychoanalytic account of learning emphasizes the history of interpersonal encounters and crises. The teacher becomes a model for the student not only in what is taught but in his whole style of life. The teacher who is intuitive and responsibly spontaneous will encourage intuitive learning and spontaneity by his very presence. The presence of a faithful teacher speaks with far greater power than his words. Teaching is finally to love and care for the student within the encounters and crises of interpersonal relationships. To teach is to find one's own personal history taken up and expressed by historical and contemporary accounts of God's activity among men. As the life history of the teacher meets the life story of the child, each grows to maturity.

## Existential Engagement

Existential theories of learning focus upon being and nonbeing, meaning and meaninglessness, authenticity and inauthenticity, genuineness and phoniness. While existential theories are not strictly empirical to the same degree as the others already considered, they are making an important impact upon practicing psychologists. The emphasis is upon openness in the interrelationships between person and person, person and social situation, person and meaning. To be closed is to be cut off from relationships with other persons, to destroy social situations, and to be closed to new meaning. Teaching and learning are ways of standing before meanings and events so that new significance and new relationships may arise.

Learning is the revelation of what it means to be gathered together in the name of Christ. Teaching is to allow the truth of Christ to be revealed, for he is the true teacher, and his word is becoming actualized among those who are gathered in his name. Teaching is to converse, await, and act upon his unexpected coming. Robert Boehlke is speaking from an existential theory of learning when he writes, "The concerns of Christian nurture are learned as God creates new selves through the engagement of persons with their field of relationships." [9]

According to the existentialist view, teaching refuses to be dominated by either situations or traditions. Teaching and learning are both unified in their willingness to accept meanings and purposes when they appear. Learning occurs in the moment that truth is encountered. More importance is to be put upon the truth that is actually encountered rather than upon the goals that guide learning. Traditional goals will always guide a learning situation to some extent, but the actual encounter with truth places all goals in question. The specification of goals takes second place to meaning as it actually comes.

The role of the teacher is also understood differently. Whoever is designated as teacher stands with his students as a learner before the truth of God's

[9] *Theories of Learning in Christian Education* (Philadelphia: The Westminster Press, 1962), p. 188.

revelation. Both speaker and listener are under the unexpected power of what is said and done. The one who speaks finds himself speaking to each in his own freedom and to the whole group in its own uniqueness. The one who speaks, whether student or teacher, also finds that he is speaking seriously with himself and listening for the genuine meaning that may be there. The new idea, the imaginative construction, the wonder of interpersonal encounter, these are the truths to which the teacher is tuned. Learning comes not by manipulation, but by sensitive relationships.

The existential theory of learning may break through the traditional class-room situation as well as redefining the meaning of pupil and teacher. To the extent that the truth of Christ is taking shape throughout God's creation, Christians will learn outside the classroom as well as in. Learning means a genuine engagement with life outside the walls of the church. This calls for interracial exchanges, inner-city and suburban exchanges. It calls for new kinds of experimentation in learning. The new structures of urbanized social life must be encountered within the teaching of the church. Secret discipline for mission in the world, to use Bonhoeffer's phrase, may become the center of learning. The existential theory of learning in no case allows simply for business as usual.

The context of learning is the relationship between the church and the world, between the truth of Christ not yet formed and that truth openly expressed. The dynamics of learning occur between the hiddenness of God's activity and the open understanding of that activity. The knowledge learned is the relation between the mighty acts of God recorded in Scripture and his powerful activity in the world today. The attitudes to be learned are love, joy, and hope for the living presence of Jesus Christ in and among those who associate together. The skill of worship is learned by lifting up everyday occurrences to sacramental significance in the presence of a group. Revelation has a centrality in the existentialist theory that is usually lacking in other theories. The depths and mystery of learning are perhaps best described here. The church can hardly afford to ignore this view.

## Psychology and Christian Education

Each of the four major psychological schools treats significant dimensions of learning. Both the strength and the weakness of conditioning theory is that it focuses upon the biological side of man. It rightly values clear objectives and overt, active, and immediate responses between teacher and student. The suggestions for teaching procedure are very useful. Yet, conditioning theory overvalues the control of the learning situation and ignores the social and relational dimensions of learning.

Field theories are quite strong in their portrayal of the way a person perceives himself and his relationship to a group. They correctly point to the importance of both the group life of the class and the congregational life of the church, not to speak of the larger life of the broader community. They also emphasize the importance of the overall pattern of the curriculum. Their weakness lies in their inability to handle personal and general history.

Psychoanalytic theory is superior in its description of the relationship between pupil and teacher, of the developmental history of the student, and of the place of crisis and anxiety in learning. The relationship between personal life history and the history of God's activity among men takes on high significance. Recent developments open the whole discussion of virtue and purpose in a new way. On the other side, the theory still suffers from the use of a great deal of mythological jargon. Nor is the psychoanalytic theory genuinely relational.

Existentialist theory points to the way in which God's truth and God's revelation occurs in the relationships between persons, groups, methods, and events to bring in new meanings in its own way and its own time. God comes to those who are open to the new humanity outside the traditional ways of teaching as well as in them. Existentialist theory is in many ways antithetical to empirical psychologies, but it brings a perspective that cannot be found in them. As no other theory, it allows revelation the central place that it must have in Christian education.

The danger is that a teacher will take a narrow view of learning, ignoring the rich complexity of what is described by the various theories. More work needs to be done to account for empirical evidence about learning in a more adequate way. A unified theory of learning, however, will not completely solve what in the last analysis is a problem of faith assumptions about human nature. This is not to deny the positive value of psychological theories, but to be realistic about their limitations.

The question of human nature is wrapped up in the fact that God comes in ways that break through man's limited understanding of him. The teacher's task is to confess what God is doing in the world and to remain open to his action in the relationships, social events, and meaning that make up the learning situation. The practical task of the church is to celebrate constantly the new life that God is establishing in her midst, to tell the story as her own story, and to participate meaningfully and perceptively in the events in the world through which God is making himself known.

## FOR ADDITIONAL READING

Allport, Gordon W. *Becoming: Basic Considerations for a Psychology of Personality*. New Haven: Yale University Press, 1955.

Boehlke, Robert R. *Theories of Learning in Christian Education*. Philadelphia: The Westminster Press, 1962.

Bruner, Jerome. *The Process of Education*. Cambridge: Harvard University Press, 1960.

Cully, Iris. *The Dynamics of Christian Education*. Philadelphia: The Westminster Press, 1958.

Erikson, Erik. *Insight and Responsibility*. New York: W. W. Norton & Company, 1964.

———. "Identity and the Life Cycle." *Psychological Issues*. New York: International Universities Press, 1959. Vol. I.

Hilgard, Ernest R. *Theories of Learning*. New York: Appleton-Century-Crofts, 1948.

Lewin, Kurt. *Resolving Social Conflicts*, ed. Gertrude Weiss Lewin. New York: Harper & Row, 1948.

Staats, Arthur W., ed. *Human Learning*. New York: Holt, Rinehart & Winston, 1964.

Ziegler, Jesse. *Psychology and the Teaching Church*. Nashville: Abingdon Press, 1962.

————. "Psychology of Religion and Religious Education," in *Religious Education: A Comprehensive Survey*, ed. Marvin J. Taylor. Nashville: Abingdon Press, 1960. Pp. 34-43.

*Chapter 6*

# PHILOSOPHICAL FOUNDATIONS
# FOR CHRISTIAN EDUCATION

## *Marcus J. Priester*

FOR MORE THAN TWO DECADES NOW THERE HAS BEEN A LESS OBVIOUS AND less direct liaison between philosophy and education than that which existed in previous eras. Some of the cause for this may lie in the fact that philosophy as a discipline has been widely varied in its expressions. It has also been over-shadowed in its relation to education by the swift advance of the social and psychological sciences, by the physical sciences and technology, by rapid social change, and by the welter of practical necessities that confront education.

Religious education in the churches was at the same time being subjected to forces similar to those that were confronting general education. In addition, it was also preoccupied with relating the new emphases in theology to its expanding program of teaching and nurture. The new theologies, as represented by such stalwarts as Karl Barth, Emil Brunner, Paul Tillich, Reinhold Niebuhr, H. Richard Niebuhr, Rudolph Bultmann, and others, pressed the church for a critical review of its educational aims, methods, and curricular materials. And along with all of this, the religious education movement was also feeling the impact of the emerging strong confessional interests of the church that accompanied the burgeoning ecumenical movement.

During this period of rethinking and enlargement of its enterprise, the religious education movement has not been devoid of philosophic questions and influences, even though these have been more or less indirect and subtle. Such influences have been felt through the adoption of some of the insights and practices of general education, as well as in the guidance appropriated from psychology and sociology. Theology, too, along with its new emphases, brought fresh methods and insights of philosophic thought. One cannot escape noticing, for example, the influences on contemporary theology of the philosophy as well as the piety of Kierkegaard. Quite as clearly seen is the way in which Bultmann and his followers have used certain categories from Heidegger's philosophy. Likewise one must admit the strains of influence from Hegel, Whitehead, James, Buber, and Dewey, as well as that of the analytical philosophers and others of older historic fame.

This present essay is designed primarily to suggest some of the influential patterns of development in the relationship of philosophy to educational thought and practice.

## Importance of Philosophy for Christian Education

Why should Christian educators be concerned with the relationship between philosophy and education? Is theology, as it interprets the Bible, worship, heritage, and the Christian style of life, not a sufficient guide to the teaching and nurture of people? Most Christian educators today would grant the overarching significance of theology as providing a normative perspective and discipline for education in the churches. In actual practice many other sources of knowledge, apart from reflection upon Christian revelation and tradition, are being sought out and pressed into service in the intellectual activity of theology as well as in the educational ministry of the church. Arguments prevail about the necessity of philosophy for critical thinking and over the precise way in which philosophy helps form theological expression. The plain fact is that theology makes use of the thought and methods of philosophic inquiry in order to carry on its work and to assist it in achieving meaningful communication.

Neither the theologian nor the religious man exists in isolation from the thought-forms and meanings of the culture which it is the prime task of philosophy to examine reflectively. Although philosophy and theology may grant different significance to the content informing their enterprises, both share mutual concerns such as truth, value, ultimacy, knowledge, and the common good. Both examine the bases of belief on which religious convictions are grounded. Both analyze the discernible data of man's experiences, offer help in understanding the patterns of human thought, and illuminate the form of the problems of contemporary man. It is important, therefore, to be aware of the presuppositions and methods of philosophy that form much of the context of theological thinking about Christian education.

As with all branches of human culture, educational activity (including Christian education) is articulated, organized, and executed with the aid of distinctive clusters of concepts functioning in a variety of ways. Philosophy has a perennial interest in the critical examination of the conceptual framework of education. A study of the history of philosophy and education reveals the close relationship of philosophy to the constructive development of the aims of education, the assumptions of the teaching-learning process, and the values to be expressed.[1]

Philosophy seeks to discover proper questions and to strive for appropriate answers about the world and man's relationship to it, formulating the findings and hypotheses into logically consistent and comprehensive structures of thought. Claims about the past, present, and future, the actual and the ideal, the real and the possible, all come within the purview of its search. The philosopher, striving to be an interpreter of the meaning of reality in human existence, analyzes, evaluates, and synthesizes his reflections in the construction of a synoptic view of the range of expressible human experiences.[2] The educator faces the ever-persisting problem of selectivity of ideas and descriptions that are deemed by him to be true and worthy of his commitment. Therefore, any

[1] In reflecting upon the intimate relation between philosophy and education, it is interesting to note that John Dewey defines philosophy simply as a general theory of education. See *Democracy and Education* (New York: The Macmillan Company, 1916), p. 383.

[2] For helpful discussions on the variety of approaches to the discipline of philosophy see, for example, Samuel M. Thompson, *The Nature of Philosophy* (New York: Holt, Rinehart & Winston, 1961); and Elmer Sprague, *What Is Philosophy?* (New York: Oxford University Press, 1961).

valid theory and practice of Christian education must take into account philosophy as well as other disciplines that deal significantly with the human scene.

## Major Types of Philosophy

The most thorough survey of philosophy as it relates to religion and education has been written by J. Donald Butler.[3] He has selected four types of philosophy for comparative study: naturalism, idealism, realism, and pragmatism. Within these categories as they are set forth in representative philosophers, there is to be found a wide range of particular emphases and developments. Caution must always be exercised in attaching a particular label to the work of any individual philosopher. All four types, however, persist in one form or another in philosophic thinking today.

Naturalism, as the word itself implies, is the viewpoint that accepts the world of physical nature as being all there is to reality. The early Greek philosophers sought for an ultimate substance common to all nature—water, air, fire, or atoms in space. It was Aristotle (384-322 B.C.), who shares with Plato the fame of expressing Greek thought at its apogee, who refined naturalism in classical form. He contended that reality consists ultimately of many concrete things such as those we constantly find in the world about us, and that nothing else is real except insofar as it in some way pertains to these things. Aristotle's view

may be said to be the general metaphysical position which best sustains, justifies, and verifies the humanistic ethics. The humanistic theory of man and the naturalistic theory of nature, so to speak, go together logically. . . . However specifically human and distinctive from the rest of nature man is, his life exhibits, though in a peculiarly human form, the generic traits which run through the whole of nature.[4]

Naturalism tends to define religion as purely a phenomenon of nature or of human experience. Man is viewed as a creature of nature, though a significant one to be sure. There is no room in the system for revelation or for God, except as the naturalist speaks of God as the structure of good in nature that makes possible the realization of values. More critical naturalism defines nature as process, a continuous generative force that governs the self and the society of selves. Forms of realism and pragmatism have much in common with the metaphysical views of naturalism and with the dependence upon natural phenomenon through knowledge of the sciences.

Herbert Spencer (1820-1903) turned the idea of evolution made prominent in the biological studies of Charles Darwin into the organizing principle of an all-embracing world view, the ultimate reality of which is energy and force. It should be noted that Spencer applied his theory to education and assumed

[3] *Four Philosophies and Their Practice in Education and Religion* (Rev. ed.; New York: Harper & Row, 1957).

[4] Sterling P. Lamprecht, *Our Philosophical Traditions: A Brief History of Philosophy in Western Civilization* (New York: Appleton-Century-Crofts, 1955), p. 78.

that a study of the sciences is the paramount subject matter.[5] His famous five educational objectives of "complete living" still have a contemporary ring:

1. Self-preservation
2. Securing the necessities of life
3. Care and nurture of children
4. Maintenance of social and political relations
5. Enjoyment of leisure

The chief rival of naturalism through the centuries has been idealism or, more strictly speaking, "ideaism." It roots back to Plato (427?-347 B.C.) and his dialogues. Plato posited an ideal world of forms of which the objects of sense are shadows or images. There are also ideas which are not represented in physical forms such as absolute beauty, goodness, and essence in general. Platonic thought has had great influence on the Christian tradition both from Plato's own writings and from the neoplatonic writings of Plotinus (A.D. 205-70), who reinterpreted Plato to combat the stoicism and skepticism of the third century A.D. A contender against the antithetical worlds of the gnostics, Plotinus rejected dualism in all its forms. He believed that there is but one order of being containing various levels and different kinds of existences. This order depends upon, and owes its being to, a central principle which Plotinus called the One. Through the process of contemplation and the discipline of the virtues, man's soul may rise to a state of mystic union with the One.

The tradition of idealism has centered attention upon the rational powers of the self as it is related to Universal Mind. To be known at all, the whole of reality must in some sense be similar to our ideas of it and to the mind that knows it.[6]

The theism of certain idealists who have written on the subject of the philosophy of education has exerted substantial influence on Christian education. Note the definition of education given by Herman Harrell Horne (1874-1946): "Education is the eternal process of superior adjustment of the physically and mentally developed, free, conscious, human being to God, as manifested in the intellectual, emotional, and volitional environment of man." [7]

In the twentieth century there appeared a type of philosophy known as realism which has its roots in the thought of Aristotle and Aquinas, Locke and Kant. The modern expression of realism came as a rebellion against the theory of knowledge set forth by the proponents of idealism and the metaphysics implied. The idealists emphasize the thinking self or subject; the realists stress the object of thought. Things exist, however, apart from thought. Some realists tend toward naturalism in their metaphysics, while others lean toward idealism. But all are concerned to affirm the reality of external phenomena. Those realists who exhibit a dualism insist that mind exists as something different from

[5] *Education: Intellectual, Moral, and Physical* (New York: D. Appleton and Co., 1880). See the first essay on education, "What Knowledge Is of Most Worth?" These essays first appeared in 1861.

[6] George Berkeley (1685-1753) insisted that the character of the world as we experience it depends so much upon mind that there is no such thing as existing without someone perceiving it.

[7] *The Philosophy of Education* (Rev. ed.; New York: The Macmillan Company, 1927), p. 285.

and superior to matter, or (in terms of Thomas Aquinas) hold that the universe is composed of both form and matter.

In his book *Building a Philosophy of Education* Harry Broudy presents a thoroughly developed statement on the implications of realism for education.[8] He maintains that the authority of education is based upon a distinctively realistic assumption about knowledge, i.e., that education is a science and as such possesses a body of knowledge that guides the profession. Stress is placed on the real need of the self and its forms of selfhood—self-determination, self-realization, and self-integration. The union of these subjective needs is to be found in the objective estimates of the society. The substance and content of what is taught and the processes of forming the pupil are given the emphasis.[9]

In this century in America the philosophic tradition that has been most influential in education is that form of empirical and experimental philosophy characterized by the term "pragmatism." Key figures in the development of this approach are Charles Peirce (1839-1914), William James (1842-1910), and John Dewey (1859-1952). Peirce meant by pragmatism, not a general philosophic position but a logical theory, that the meaning of an idea is the sum of all the practical consequences which might ensue from the truth of that idea. In adopting the pragmatic method James held that theories are instruments and ideas are plans of action—ideas need testing, revamping, and reconstruction. Dewey moved from the absolutism and idealism of the Hegelians to develop his own brand of pragmatism which he himself preferred to call empirical naturalism. Pervading his thinking were his emphases on experience (the interaction of organism with environment), on a dynamic view of all nature in constant flux, and on the pluralistic character of life.[10] Pragmatism is a complex cultural movement that has elements of relativism and utilitarianism but which never yields to becoming materialism or skepticism.

The vast impact of John Dewey's influence upon American education in both the schools and the churches continues to be felt. He labored hard to overcome the inherited dualisms between science and morals, theory and practice, mind and action, learning and living, means and ends. He opposed traditionalism, rigidity, and formalism in both philosophy and education. Dewey's life is associated with the liberal social movements of his time, not the least of which was to help precipitate reforms in the patterns of American education. His accent upon growth as an unending process, upon patterns of interest and activity, upon the school as an embryonic democracy, and upon the necessity of learning through the proper use of the scientific method are still common in the educational marketplace.

[8] (Englewood Cliffs: Prentice-Hall, 1954).

[9] Previous works in realist educational philosophy include J. F. Herbart's *Science of Education*, 1806; and the comprehensive work of Johann Amos Comenius, *The Great Didactic*, 1632. The latter refers to the school as "a true forging place of men." See also John Wild's essay, "Education and Human Society: A Realistic View," in *Modern Philosophies and Education*, Nelson B. Henry, ed. (Chicago: University of Chicago Press, 1955), pp. 37-41.

[10] See particularly John Dewey, *Democracy and Education* (New York: The Macmillan Company, 1916) and *Experience and Nature* (New York: W. W. Norton & Company, 1929).

## Contemporary Trends

A number of the recent developments in philosophy and related disciplines hold promise of challenge and enrichment for our thought in Christian education and theology. Only a few, however, can be selected for special mention here.

One development of current importance to both philosophy and education is the contemporary fascination with language. In 1923 C. K. Ogden and I. A. Richards published their much-quoted study entitled *The Meaning of Meaning,* in which they attempted to make proper distinctions among valid modes of interpretation.[11] A theory of signs was proposed in which the functions of language were grouped in two categories: the referential and the emotive. Studies since have appeared that cover many aspects of language, meanings, and symbolic forms.[12]

The problems of language and meaning are fundamental to a group of thinkers known as the analytic philosophers. This school has an intense interest in the clarification of statements made by philosophers. Much of their early inspiration came from G. E. Moore, Bertrand Russell, and Ludwig Wittgenstein. Linguistic analysis, although it is related historically to the logical positivism of the Vienna circle of the 1920's, is not to be confused with the expression of a somewhat dogmatic spirit that frequently characterized that philosophy.

The current interest in linguistic analysis has placed special focus upon the analysis of questions in order to facilitate the formulation and communication of ideas with clarity and appropriateness. Attention has been given also to the logical analysis of how words and statements function, and to the change in the use of particular words and their meaning in specific social settings.[13] A number of interesting studies of religious language have appeared which are pertinent to the process of teaching religion.[14]

Another area of philosophic concern important for Christian education is the problem of knowledge. What does it mean to *know?* What are the conditions and limitations of knowledge? How can knowledge be validated? Are there various kinds of knowledge, and how are they related? What is the relationship of knowledge to belief and commitment? How do we define the process of knowing?

[11] (New York: Harcourt, Brace & World, 1923).

[12] Ernst Cassirer has published three volumes of his study of the types of symbolic forms and their relationships: *Philosophy of Symbolic Forms* (New Haven: Yale University Press, Vol. I, 1953; Vol. 2, 1955; Vol. 3, 1957). See also Susanne Langer, *Philosophy in a New Key* (Baltimore: Penguin Books, 1948).

[13] Paul M. Van Buren, author of *The Secular Meaning of the Gospel* (New York: The Macmillan Company, 1963), was asked to present an article on the implications for religious education of his linguistic point of view. The result was an interesting symposium, "Linguistic Philosophy and Christian Education," published in *Religious Education,* LX (January-February, 1965).

[14] See in particular the following: Ian T. Ramsey, *Religious Language* (London: SCM Press, 1957); and also his book *Models and Mystery* (London: Oxford University Press, 1964); Frederick Ferré, *Language, Logic, and God* (New York: Harper & Row, 1961); Willem F. Zuurdeeg, *An Analytical Philosophy of Religion* (Nashville: Abingdon Press, 1958); and John Hick, *Faith and Knowledge* (Ithaca, N.Y.: Cornell University Press, 1957).

Proponents of idealism conceive the knower and the object known as belonging to a single independent and coherent system. The primary and controlling aspect of human nature is that man is a rational animal, that his unique property is the ability to reason, that his distinctive quality is in the life of the mind. Man's social and cultural forms are expressions of reason. His arts, his morality, his history, his worship—all are reflections of reason. Reason is of the essence. Critical thinkers have suggested that this view of man suffers from the limitation of the fact that such ideas as rationality, reason, and mind tend to be narrowly construed as referring to processes of logical thinking. Too little weight has been given to the processes of feeling, imagination, human relationships, and other experiences that are not rationally or logically conceived in a strict sense.[15]

Attention has been given, therefore, to a more holistic view of man in order to discover the interrelations and meaning of the variety of human functions. Philip Phenix, for instance, has defined a more comprehensive approach under his concept of "meaning."

This term is intended to express the full range of connotations of reason or mind. Thus, there are different meanings contained in activities of organic adjustment, in perception, in logical thinking, in social organization, in speech, in artistic creation, in self-awareness, in purposive decision, in moral judgment, in the consciousness of time, and in the activity of worship. All these distinctive human functions are varieties of meaning, and all of them together—along with others that might be described— comprise the life of meaning, which is the essence of man.[16]

Phenix goes on to suggest that "the proposed philosophic answer to the question about the nature of man, then, is that humans are beings that discover, create, and express meanings." [17]

A recent critical study of educational philosophy by Robert Ulich presents a theory which the author calls "integralism," stressing the need for a reappraisal of ethical theory in relation to education.

The fundamental energies of our being, which are basic to the organism's self-realization, constitute a whole or an integral, the integrants of which are both "material" and "spiritual" in an inseparable unity and finally lead toward ethical behavior. They permeate the total man without his willing it, as life flows through us without our permission. Moral energy, as well as life energy, is a gift, but not one that we are given "to dig in the earth" and hide, as the "wicked and slothful servant" did, but one that we should use as the "good and faithful servants" used the talents delivered to them by their Lord.[18]

[15] The thought of Michael Polanyi, scientist and philosopher, is an important contribution as he develops the proposition that all knowledge is personal. See his *Personal Knowledge: Towards a Post-Critical Philosophy* (Chicago: University of Chicago Press, 1958). His insights on affirmation, doubt, and commitment are fruitful for consideration by Christian educators.

[16] *Realms of Meaning* (New York: McGraw-Hill Book Company, 1964), p. 21.

[17] *Ibid.* Phenix defines general education as "the process of engendering essential meaning," p. 5.

[18] Robert Ulich, *Philosophy of Education* (New York: American Book Company, 1961), p. 55.

Another trend to be found in twentieth-century thinking is existentialism, a movement that is difficult to describe or to analyze. Those who are termed "existentialists" sometimes reject the designation, and often differ widely with their fellow existentialists. In fact, Walter Kaufman has contended that instead of existentialism being a philosophy it is nothing more than "a label for several widely different revolts against traditional philosophy." [19] The movement goes back to Kierkegaard (1813-55) who rebelled against the Hegelian rationalism prominent in academic circles, against the moribund life of the established church of his own country, and against the tyranny of social conventions around him. Whether or not it be a philosophy, existentialism is a movement that has brought a challenge to the abstractions and *a priori* theories of philosophy. It has injected fresh questions into the ways of viewing reason, knowledge, the self, human relationships, and religious experience. Prominent in the existentialists' concerns are such motifs as the predicament of modern man, especially as he faces the crises of tragedy and death, and the energetic social protests against anything that dehumanizes and depersonalizes man. Their contention is for freedom, individuality, and creativity.

Existentialism has not, and probably will not, developed a complete philosophy of education, but it does have profound implications for the theory and practice of education in the schools and in the church. In George Kneller's *Existentialism and Education* one catches a glimpse of the way existentialism views education.[20] Many of the emphases carry a tone similar to the appeals we hear from John Dewey—the necessity for the development of the individual, the uniqueness of the self, education related to life, and creativity. The goal of education, however, is "man's search for himself" in the midst of the realism of life's drama of tragedy and death.

Aided on the scientific level by various psychological studies of the unconscious, and by clinical research of the psychiatrists, the philosophers of existence are probing for an even more comprehensive conception of what it means to exist or to be. Correspondingly, an existentially oriented social psychology reflected in educational thinking may make inroads into the deeper understanding of human personality. Man no longer—if he ever really was—can be viewed atomistically and individualistically. This dimension of sociality and the confluence of events that form the action and response of the life of men is an awareness and description that gives promise to knowledge of the self in relation with other selves.

## Issues for Christian Education

In the early decades of this century, the religious education movement adopted or adapted the insights and methodology of the "new education" movement. A vigorous liberal theology responded with enthusiasm to help reshape the teaching theories and programs of the churches. In the vanguard was George Albert

[19] *Existentialism from Dostoevsky to Sartre* (Cleveland: Meridian Books, 1956), p. 11.
[20] (New York: Philosophical Library, 1958).

Coe, who gave generous impetus to the social and democratic theories of John Dewey. In breaking the shackles of transmissive and content-centered education, Coe proposed the optimistic anticipation of salvation by education. The aim of religious education, as he defined it, was: "Growth of the young toward and into mature and efficient devotion to the democracy of God, and happy self-realization therein." [21]

When the "new theology" appeared with force, the prevailing assumptions of the social gospel and religious education came under question and were sharply challenged by H. Shelton Smith in 1941 in his *Faith and Nurture*.[22] From Smith's theological vantage point he attacked the naturalism and the easy optimism of the aims of pragmatic education. In his appeal for a theological revision of educational assumptions, he insisted that the insights of the realistic anthropology and biblical interpretation of the new theology be made basic to the perspectives of Christian teaching. Smith himself never followed his critical appraisal to its logical ends to develop full-rounded guidance for education.

Within the context of the attack on the new education and the reconstruction of education in the churches, evidences of the attempt to make theological perspectives normative appeared, and continue to appear, in the writings of Christian educators and in new curricula published by the denominations.[23] However, evidences of intense dialogue with educational theorists of the current day are less obvious. The prevailing mood has been to adopt and adapt, to select those principles, practices, psychologies, and descriptions that could be incorporated or grafted onto the church's current program. In this sense the church has been a utilizer rather than a creator of serious inquiry into the nature and practice of education on the American scene. The absence of such substantial dialogue may be the result of a lack of creativity on the part of church educators and a too timid participation in the educational thinking of the day. The church has much to learn from the thought and practices of education and related disciplines, which it can do only through zealous work and forthright dialogue in a spirit of becoming humility.

The church, however, does have a responsibility to be far more creative from within its own unique vocation in the educational world. Lewis J. Sherrill suggests:

The new philosophy of Christian education must come to the subject of education from within the Jewish-Christian tradition, not from outside it. More specifically, it must draw its inspiration from the peculiar genius of the Christian community and of Christian faith rather than from any form of secular society or secular education. . . . The unique nature of Christian education derives from the unique nature of the

---

[21] *A Social Theory of Religious Education* (New York: Charles Scribner's Sons, 1917), p. 55.

[22] (New York: Charles Scribner's Sons, 1941).

[23] See Randolph Crump Miller, *The Clue to Christian Education* (New York: Charles Scribner's Sons, 1950); James D. Smart, *The Teaching Ministry of the Church* (Philadelphia: The Westminster Press, 1954); Lewis J. Sherrill, *The Gift of Power* (New York: The Macmillan Company, 1955); and D. Campbell Wyckoff, *The Gospel and Christian Education* (Philadelphia: The Westminster Press, 1959).

Christian community and Christian faith. . . . The Christian community as a whole is meant to be the scene of a redemptive ministry to the human self as a whole.[24]

At the same time it is instructive to note that Sherrill himself felt free to be instructed by insights from psychiatry, psychology, existentialism, communication theory, and other human sources of knowledge. It is not to be denied that this learning from other disciplines for the development of critical thinking enriches and instructs the church educator when he allows himself to become convinced of the significance of their contribution.

From the perspective of the 1960's there is a need to assess more carefully the contribution that the experimentalists have made to education and to our culture, whether or not Christian educators can agree with all the presuppositions as formulated. As critics of authoritarian, transmissive, and intellectualistic education, they attempted to blaze new trails. Both their thought-forms and practical intentions need to be studied seriously before any attempt is made to adopt or reject them. Similar words of concern and caution should be said with relation to other current philosophies of education.

There remains the need for a clearly articulated and more systematic philosophy of Christian education that will take into account both theological perspectives and educational foundations. Besides furnishing creative guidance, such critical thinking may help church educators avoid the appeal of educational novelty and fads of passing or questionable significance for their task.

Some of the issues with which the critical study of the philosophy of Christian education will need to wrestle have been mentioned in the course of this essay. The ferment produced by opposing philosophies of education is not a fact to be deplored, but rather it should be received as an encouraging sign of the search for greater understanding of the task of teaching and learning that is going on in our society today. The task of those who undertake such a study will entail a reappraisal of the already existing strands of thinking. It will need to involve a new openness to the understanding of revelation as it relates to man's knowing God, himself, and his neighbors. The means of knowing, the structure of the process of knowing, and the relationships these have with the theories of being, all have within them intellectual tensions that are of special interest to the problems of Christian education today. The approach to a critical study will include the possibilities of richer understandings of Christian experience, growth, conversion, and ethics. Particular theological traditions well may have some unique contributions to make to the educational scene. In the new climate of the ecumenical movement, diversity in theology, philosophy, and culture may prove to be the rich seedbed of fruitful dialogue.

## FOR ADDITIONAL READING

Brubacher, John S., ed. *Modern Philosophies of Education*. 2nd ed. New York: McGraw-Hill Book Company, 1950.

[24] *The Gift of Power*, p. xi.

Butler, J. Donald. *Four Philosophies and Their Practice in Education and Religion*. Rev. ed. New York: Harper & Row, 1957.

Kneller, George F. *Existentialism and Education*. New York: Philosophical Library, 1958.

Lamprecht, Sterling P. *Our Philosophical Traditions: A Brief History of Philosophy in Western Civilization*. New York: Appleton-Century-Crofts, 1955.

Munk, Arthur W. *A Synoptic Philosophy of Education*. Nashville: Abingdon Press, 1965.

Nelson, Henry B., ed. *Modern Philosophies and Education*. The Fifty-Fourth Yearbook of the National Society for the Study of Education, Part I. Chicago: University of Chicago Press, 1955.

Phenix, Philip H. *Realms of Meaning*. New York: McGraw-Hill Book Company, 1964.

Rome, Sydney and Beatrice, eds. *Philosophical Interrogations*. New York: Holt, Rinehart & Winston, 1964.

Scheffler, Israel. *Philosophy and Education*. Boston: Allyn & Bacon, 1958.

Schneider, Herbert W. *A History of American Philosophy*. 2nd ed. New York: Columbia University Press, 1963.

Ulich, Robert. *Philosophy of Education*. New York: American Book Company, 1961.

# Chapter 7

# SOCIOCULTURAL FOUNDATIONS
# FOR CHRISTIAN EDUCATION

## *James E. Loder*

A SOCIOCULTURAL APPROACH TO CHRISTIAN EDUCATION IS THUS FAR UN-precedented. In view of the dearth of studies based on a sociocultural perspective, the intention of this essay will be to make an initial contribution to theoretical thinking about Christian education from the standpoints of sociology, cultural anthropology, and related fields of investigation. To solve the problem of integrating findings from several fields of study the following discussion will employ a model of human action attributable primarily to Talcott Parsons. This model divides all human action into four major categories: biological, psychological, social, and cultural. The basic analytical unit in each category varies, but four which may be taken are the body, the psyche, the group, the symbol. Since this essay is "sociocultural," the analyses made here will be confined primarily to the latter two categories and their interrelationships. However, in all cases it should be understood that factors usually assigned to the other two categories are actively and influentially present.

The rationale behind the approach to be taken to Christian education is that the education of persons in the church and the Christian education of the American public involves at least three types of organizational phenomena, all of which have been subjected to sociocultural analyses. These are the American family, public education, and religion. The basic methodological assumption is that an analysis of these three types of organization, integrated from the theoretical standpoint set forth by Parsons, will yield at least a partial analysis of Christian education as a sociocultural phenomenon in American society.

## Definitions and View of Reality

The first problem to be faced is that of definitions of terms. To be sure, the general problem of this essay cannot in the final analysis be isolated from the much more complex issues (more complex than can be dealt with here) of interrelating the language systems of separate disciplines, but some definitions of terms which are used will at least provide an operational starting point. It should also be acknowledged that underlying sociocultural definition is a particular view of reality. Since this view of reality—often unacknowledged or ignored by social scientists—underlies much of sociocultural thinking, it is necessary that it be suggested at the outset through the definitions which follow.

The key to a first understanding of this reality is that it cannot be known

71

directly through experience; it must always be inferred from experience. In order to make such an inference one must set up what are called "models." A paradigm of the model is the architect's cardboard construction of a skyscraper scaled down in perfect proportion to such an extent that it can sit on a card table. The model enables one to imagine the reality through a likeness which can be contained within one's perceptual experience. The nature of the skyscraper can be inferred from the cardboard model. It should be noted that many details have to be omitted in order to present the model, but again this is the nature of the model: It is not intended to be an exact duplication of reality; it merely represents it in its most significant aspects. These significant aspects are sufficient to permit one to make deductions about reality and act on the basis of the inference. All subsequent terms designate "models" of reality.

One of the most common models used in the social sciences is that of "system." What is usually meant by system is an aggregate unity of activities or events for which a basic analogy is the human organism. The predominant characteristic of the system as a model is its dynamic equilibrium which is established between the events or activities of the system so that there is harmony and integration in their operation. The major implication of this model is that if any one of the several activities within the system is altered, the total system is temporarily in a state of disequilibrium, and it is thereafter engaged in an attempt to restore itself to a new equilibrium which will either incorporate or eliminate the altered activity. Common uses of the term which utilize this meaning are "economic system," "transportation system," "communication system." It is not to be assumed that an understanding of any system, *qua* system, is identical with reality; it is merely a way of understanding certain especially significant relationships from which some inferences can be drawn.

The particular function or expected behavior of an individual or of a unit in any system is called a "role." A basic analogue is, of course, the theatrical role. One's role can never provide a substitute for one's identity, because role exists only within a particular system of functions and expectations. Role only gives one his identification within that particular social system; it does not transfer from one system to the next unless the expectations within the two systems are quite similar.

The next term is "transaction." A familiar, common-sense model which has had pervasive influence in the thought of the Western world is the contents-and-container model. What is true of coffee in a cup has become true for "the contents of the mind." Sociocultural analyses, even though they often capitulate to the common-sense way of saying it, attempt to utilize and think in terms of reality as "transactional." That is, the relation of the whole to the parts or the parts to each other is characterized by interpenetrability which is understood not merely from the objective observer's standpoint, but rather from outside *and* inside, above and below, simultaneously. Thus, the individual is seen as transactional when he takes in food and drink and excretes waste products, or when the male impregnates the female who conceives, gestates, gives birth, and nurses. These are all basically transactional, rather than inside-outside, or even interactional, processes.[1]

Boundaries between systems are viewed as permeable; thus it is by transaction that systems—and the roles within them—are related. For instance, when a personality system transacts with another system, the emerging event is something new. Sometimes the system depends upon transaction as in the consumption and excretion of food products through which the body is ever created anew. In other instances the system is upset to such an extent that the restoration of homeostasis at any level is impossible and the system disintegrates. The consumption of poison is an obvious example.

Transactions at interpersonal, social, and cultural levels are much more complex, but in each sociocultural analysis the aim is to provide a descriptive, analytical statement about the dynamics of the transactions—about what is going on—in any given sociocultural phenomenon. Transactions are always multilevel events: biological, psychological, sociological, and cultural. However, in some instances it is necessary to isolate certain aspects of the total community or society for purposes of analysis. It is this procedure of isolation, analysis, and interpretation which is now to be followed regarding those transactions in the social system which are of some particular interest to Christian education.

## The Family System

The family will be viewed first as a social system transacting with American society at large; then it will be viewed as a cultural system in which its symbolic dimensions will be examined.

The family is not, contrary to what Peter Berger suggests,[2] in an essentially dependent position *vis a vis* society at large. Rather, through the mass media, political and economic factors—to mention a few major influences—the family transacts with the American social order. To be sure, the family is shaped by these influences, but the nuclear and extended family also limits and directs these larger social structures. For instance, it is well known to mass media experts that no opinion can be sold to the public which does not anchor its appeal in the opinions of the primary group being addressed, and for most of America the primary group is either the family of origin or the family of procreation. Moreover, industrial and political nepotism make it possible for families to extend their influence—as well as the income and social status of their sons and daughters—far beyond what the mobile, *laissez-faire*, merit system of American idealism in politics and economics would allow. One need not look to dramatic situations in contemporary American politics, but only to Middletown, U.S.A., to note the pervasive power of the family in-group. This comment recorded by the Lynds is indicative: "Every time there's a good

---

[1] Laura Thompson, *Toward a Science of Mankind* (New York: McGraw-Hill Book Company, 1961), pp. 83-85.

[2] "The Second Children's Crusade," *The Christian Century*, LXXVI (December 2, 1959), 1400.

job in Middletown, who gets it! Somebody's son or relative. That's why Middletown is a tough place for the young fellow to break through in." [3]

To see more precisely what one's family of origin does to influence his adult life in society is to see how the patterns of family life come eventually to have influence upon the national social organization. For instance, the two biological bases for differentiation in the family are sex and age; these aspects of family life supply the grounds for the later development of the individual's pattern of conduct as male or female in society and for the development of his leader-follower self-understanding.[4]

Sex at the psychophysical level supplies the basis for what is called at the psychosocial level the "instrumental-expressive" axis. Women, who are universally more intimately concerned with early child care than are men, tend to be more "expressive." That is, they are concerned primarily with the harmony or solidarity of the family, the relations of the members to each other, and their "emotional" states of tension, or lack of it, in their roles in the family. Men, on the other hand, tend to be "instrumental" in that they are concerned primarily with the relations of the family to the situation external to it. This involves adaptation to the conditions of that situation and the establishment of satisfactory goal relations for the family system in and for the situation. These respective patterns are learned by the child as he develops his identity through initial identification, and eventual transaction, with the parent of the same sex. What one learns from his family about how to conduct himself in a fashion becoming his sexual identity affects all aspects of his conduct in all the roles which he plays in the social system.

Age supplies the biological basis for what is called the "leader-follower" axis. The prolonged period of dependency of the child on the parents is the principal biological basis for the growth of the individual's understanding of what it means to be a follower and by imitation what it means to be a leader. Again, what one learns in his family about how leader-follower relations are conducted extends to every aspect of his social existence, for in all social situations some such differentiation is always present where the group involved has cohesion.

Two important contemporary examples of how family patterns transact with the structure of the national social system can be seen in two studies: one by Bronson, Katten, and Livson; the other by Miller and Swanson. The first [5] suggests that over the last twenty-five years patterns of child rearing have shifted with the father becoming increasingly more affectionate and less authoritarian, and the mother becoming relatively more important as the agent of discipline. There is as a result an equalizing effect as the male and female roles shift. That is, the "expressive-instrumental" differentiation is losing some of its biological mooring. This does not mean that the biological differentiation

---

[3] Robert S. Lynd and Helen M. Lynd, *Middletown in Transition* (New York: Harcourt, Brace and Co., 1937), p. 98.

[4] Talcott Parsons, "The Incest Taboo in Relation to Social Structure and the Socialization of the Child," *British Journal of Sociology*, V (1954), 101-17.

[5] W. C. Bronson, E. S. Katten, and N. Livson, "Patterns of Authority and Affection in Two Generations," *Journal of Abnormal and Social Psychology*, LVIII (1959), 143-52.

will become anachronistic. It merely indicates that new sociological definitions of the male and female roles are emerging on the same biological bases.

In the second study Miller and Swanson[6] have pointed out that with this equalization in the family there is a tendency to promote the equalitarian ideal and the "democratic" family. Clearly, it could be argued that as the female becomes more prominent in establishing the control patterns, the family will tend toward "expressive" methods of arbitration, and family decisions will be made in a harmonious fashion agreeable to all. The upshot of this study is the prediction of the researchers that American society is moving toward a bureaucracy which is more content with "getting along" than with "getting ahead." "Democratic" family life is complementing this movement by producing young men who are "organization" types, successful bureaucrats. This is how the leader-follower pattern ramifies from family patterns to the organization of total society. Of course, as the transaction continues, the entrenchment of bureaucratic structures in the American social system exerts further pressure on the family to continue producing effective bureaucrats.

The cultural aspects of family life in America have been derivative predominantly from the religious heritage of the nation. As a consequence, one must look to western Christianity in general and Puritanism in particular for the major symbols which transact with family life. The Christian view of God's nature and his action in history is based upon a family structure; the Mother and her Child, the Father and his Son are the key relationships which have been celebrated by Christian ritual and practice since the first two centuries A.D. In the Assumption of the Virgin Roman Catholicism has completed the family structure of the Godhead. Protestantism, while it has made less of femininity as an aspect of the Deity, has in part restored the place of women through its emphasis upon the feminine character of the church and, as anthropologist Lloyd Warner has indicated, through the popular ecclesiastical significance "Mother's Day" has achieved since its establishment under secular auspices several years ago.

Moreover, the "God we trust" has appeared not only on our coins, but in the legislature, the Supreme Court, the installation of the chief executive, the public schools, the armed forces—indeed, every institutional aspect of American life is "under God." This God who is principally a cultural derivative of Puritanism, supplies, in a symbolic fashion, the cosmological basis for the sacrosanctity of fatherhood and the family in the modern American version of the "good" life.

According to the principle of transaction, however, the family structure is what preserves these cultural phenomena; i.e., the family-oriented theology of Christianity and the religious heritage of American life. Were family life to change in structure, it is probable that these cultural phenomena would also have to be radically altered if they were to avoid the public museum. But the alternative is also true: A breakdown in the structure of these cultural phenomena contributes decidedly to the weakening of the family structure.

The last point is of especially great concern to a generation preoccupied

[6] D. R. Miller and G. E. Swanson, *The Changing American Parent* (New York: John Wiley & Sons, 1958).

with a "God is dead" theology. To a very large extent we have come of age with regard to symbol systems. As several observers have noted, the word "God" is coming apart at the seams; regardless of how it is put, whether the word is "empty" or "equivocal" or "odd," the entire symbolic significance of theological language has come under question as never before. Sociologically, the so-called end of Christendom—which is usually focused on the problem of language—means that related structures such as the family are being called into question at the level of their ideological roots. In effect our having come of age with regard to symbols ramifies widely throughout society; this maturity has consequences beyond the breakdown of the traditional language structures and the psychological manipulation of language and imagery in mass media hucksterism. This development suggests that existing social structures which have for centuries depended upon theological language for their cultural base must seek new cultural bases or else pass out of existence.

Some of the contemporary efforts to create a new culture for the family have come through the mass media. Harvey Cox's analysis of sex and secularization[7] illustrates well the power of mass media to create contemporary cults which serve as temporary alternative cultures. He points to two such cults: the cult of "The Girl" based upon the various rituals surrounding the selection and promotion of Miss America, and the "Playboy cult" epitomized by Hugh Hefner's *Playboy* magazine. Moreover, Ian Suttie[8] in his analysis of the functions of religion in social organization supplies a basis for asserting that television serves many of the therapeutic functions performed by religion in the more primitive societies. Thus, according to Cox's analysis, the male and female roles are being redefined by the contemporary cults, and, by Suttie's analysis, the symbols of Christianity have lost much of their therapeutic and integrating power—at one time vital to family cohesion—to the medium of television.[9] Transacting with these cultural alternatives the family is being redefined—or undefined—by the interconnected and combined influences of the cults and the mass media.

As to how the family is being redefined, Kimball and McClellan[10] point to some of the key words which characterize it in "family magazines." These include "understanding," "mutuality," "sensitivity," "intuitiveness"—all of which tend to emphasize smooth, unruffled interpersonal relations in the family. It should be noted also that what appears in words in the family magazines appears in pictures on the television screen. Refrigerators, automobiles, cereal, soap, and even cigarettes are presented against a background of smooth, usually fatuously harmonious family relations. It seems evident that material possessions are purchased not for their own sake, but because of their power to promote the kind of family life displayed in words and pictures.

[7] *The Secular City* (New York: The Macmillan Company, 1965), chap. 9.

[8] *The Origins of Love and Hate* (New York: Julian Press, 1952), Chaps. IX and X; see also L. Bogart, *The Age of Television* (New York: Fredrick Ungar, 1956).

[9] For an analysis of the relation between family structure and television viewing see Leon Arons and Mark A. May, eds., *Television and Human Behavior* (New York: Appleton-Century-Crofts, 1963).

[10] Solon T. Kimball and James E. McClellan, *Education and the New America* (New York: Random House, 1963), pp. 252-53.

It might be deduced from the analysis set forth by Kimball and McClellan that the family under feminine leadership is moving into a defensive position *vis a vis* the urbanized, industrialized society of modern America. That is, the family supplies the "withdrawal" dimension in the "rat-race-and-withdrawal" pattern of modern life. As a consequence, family conflict is kept at a minimum in order to look as unlike the "rat race" as possible. It is this goal to which advertisements appeal, upon which the pattern of bureaucracy depends, and toward which the family as a sociocultural phenomenon is moving.

## The Education System

It is possible—and common—to view Christian education as primarily an educational enterprise; so, whatever may be said of public education is in part true of Christian education as well. As with the family, the discussion will take up first the social and then the cultural aspects of education as a sociocultural system in the United States.

A general study of the sociology of education yields, almost without exception, four basic conceptions. First, education in American society is an extension, differentiation, and specialization of the enculturation functions of the family. As such the public schools are partially transformers of society, but preeminently the transmitters of the established social structure. Second, nearly every function of the public school is influenced by the phenomenon of social class. The middle class is the predominant class subdivision of the American social system, and values imposed and striven for in the public schools are biased accordingly. Third, the racial caste system which exists in a given community is inevitably reflected in the public schools. In integrated schools this racial discrimination is usually couched in the punitive imposition of middle-class values upon the Negro, who is, as a rule, the bearer of lower-class characteristics. Where schools are still predominantly segregated, the reflection of social discrimination in education is obvious; each school by its very existence teaches divisive social organization. Fourth, school boards are generally representative not of the local community as a whole, but of the politically influential classes. This may account for such conditions as exist in Massachusetts where nearly one out of five superintendents views his school board as a major block to the effective performance of his professional responsibilities.[11]

The impression left by these four conceptions is that public education is heavily determined by the established social order. Perhaps the education of the public through preschool family experience and the mass media is in fact more significant than public education. As indicated in the foregoing section, children come to the public schools with values, knowledge, and beliefs which they did not learn there. Throughout their school years and after they are subjected to the influence of family patterns, mass media, youth groups, professional organizations, industrial unions, and other organizations which educate them in ways which the public school cannot. As an illustration of this, it is

[11] Robert K. Merton, Leonard Broom, and Leonard S. Cottrell, Jr., eds., *Sociology Today* (New York: Basic Books, 1959), p. 133.

interesting to note Louis Harris' assertion in *Newsweek* (published in the summer of 1964) that the current Negro revolution is preeminently a television revolution, inspired by the expectations Negro citizens have learned from television programs and commercials. It is not, therefore, inspired by learning the ideology of American democracy in the public schools; the schools have had only a partial influence on the revolution.

Yet the contrary emphasis is often made. The schools by John Dewey's declarations and achievements are society's great instrument for shaping itself. Countless agencies, unions, and organizations believe it is so and exert every effort to make sure their vested interests get a favorable hearing. Moreover, nearly all volumes written in education assume at least part of what Dewey assumed: The school not only ratifies what is taking place in the social order, but in fact selects, distills, and reconstructs the present social order for the coming generation. *Education and the New America* by Kimball and McClellan, cited above, is an excellent example of such a treatment.

From the standpoint of transactions between systems, both emphases are valid, but neither to the exclusion of the other. While the Negro revolution in America may have been promoted by the mass media, it is by no means entirely the task of television to imbue American life with the benefits and responsibilities of the revolution. That is, the public schools now become responsible for the institutionalization of the transformation of prejudicial opinions which have emerged from the revolution.

An example of how the schools are transacting with society at large in this regard is supplied by a study performed for the New York State Education Department by Thomas F. Pettigrew and Patrica Pajonas.[12] In essence the study develops ways in which racial prejudice stifles creativity. It then suggests that the institutional conditions which foster creativity be applied to the schools as at least a partial antidote to the prejudicial attitudes which prevail in interaction patterns among persons in the school system. For example, systematically nurturing an interest in complexity rather than simplicity, a recognition and acceptance of personal differences, an unwillingness to submit totally to authority, a trust in one's own personal insight, and an openness to experience—all foster creativity and simultaneously stifle prejudice. New patterns of interaction are emerging for the school as a result of education's transaction with the Negro revolution, which may affect not only racial attitudes but social class bias and even the power of interest groups to control attitudes toward what is learned.

Public schools transact with the social order at large, shaping and being shaped by that society. However, the public schools, unlike the family, have no biological basis for their existence. Thus, the chief check upon vested interests of the economically powerful classes, upon the formative influence of social class and the prevalent disrespect for minority groups, is the culture of the school.

By constitutional decree the culture of the schools cannot be overtly re-

[12] "Social Psychological Considerations of Racially Balanced Schools" (New York State Education Department, 1965). Some of the conclusions are contained in *Harvard Graduate School of Education Association Bulletin*, IX (Winter, 1964-65).

ligious. Rather the major value-bearing symbols of the public schools center around three notions which belong very decidedly to the public as a whole: freedom, equality, and progress. The Gettysburg Address and the pledge of allegiance to the flag—both basic creeds of Americanism—state or imply the primacy and mutual dependence of freedom and equality. In an era of optimism —the late nineteenth and early twentieth century—John Dewey created a philosophy of experimentalism and spearheaded the American progressive movement in education. This movement established for American "collective wisdom" the view that the longevity of democracy—the preservation of the ideals of freedom and equality—depends upon two factors: (a) fostering the experimental spirit of the younger generation; and (b) fostering more adequate social adjustment in order to support the continuity of society and the continuity of the individual with himself. These two factors were the major axes of education for a democracy. The basic conception which Dewey added was optimistic change. The first factor combines change with freedom; the second combines change with equality. However, both factors presupposed an optimism about process or change itself. Thus, one might view the systematic interaction of these three potent verbal symbols as central to the overarching ideology of the public schools.[18]

When the first Sputnik was fired, the culture of the school began to change from "adjustment" to "achievement." Today the ascendant verbal symbol is "excellence." In some respects "education for excellence" is a synonym for the first of Dewey's axes mentioned above, but speaking less conservatively this is a contemporary statement of the transaction which is presently taking place between a burgeoning scientific, technological society and the schools. The emphasis upon "achievement"—some would say "competence"—has moved planful, purposeful, and, if possible, "creative" behavior into the exemplary position, and it points the direction in which the schools are moving.

## The Religious System

Perhaps most commonly, Christian education is viewed as an aspect of a religious system. Because the cultural dimension of the church was discussed to some extent under the section on the family, it will be presupposed here. Emphasis will still be upon religion as a sociocultural phenomenon, but a somewhat briefer treatment is in order.

Religion has been studied widely from sociocultural perspectives as a tension-reducing, pattern-maintaining type of institution. For instance, Kingsley Davis writes:

Religion, then, does four things that help to maintain the dominance of sentiment over organic desire, or group ends over private interest. First it offers, through its system of supernatural belief, an explanation of primary group ends and a justification of their primacy. Second it provides, through its collective ritual, a means for the constant renewal of common sentiments. Third it furnishes, through its sacred objects,

[18] For a fuller discussion of this area see James Loder, *Religion and the Public Schools* (New York: Association Press, 1965), chap. 2.

a concrete reference for the values and a rallying point for all persons who share the same values. Fourth it provides an unlimited and insuperable source of rewards for good conduct, punishments for bad. In these ways religion makes a unique and indispensable contribution to social integration.[14]

In his study of church and sect in Gastonia, North Carolina, Liston Pope demonstrated essentially this same point.[15] Both church and sect contributed to change in the social organization through appropriate tension-reduction (sect) and reinforcement of established patterns of social action (church).

Both Emile Durkheim and Max Weber are interpreted by Parsons as giving to religion a decisive formative influence upon the sociocultural matrix in which it appears. The characteristics of the positions held by Durkheim and Weber need not be stated here.[16] Rather the discussion turns to the more recent study by Gerhard Lenski which avowedly attempts to carry the views of Durkheim and Weber into the modern metropolitan community. Lenski's persuasive study, *The Religious Factor*, was conducted in the Detroit area, and it developed Durkheim's and Weber's views into a theoretical base which was borne out by the findings and conclusions. Lenski writes that goals, values, beliefs, and action patterns, though acquired in one institutional context, frequently manifest themselves in others. Moreover, he says, "What is possible, what is probable, and what is inevitable in any given secular organization is a function, in part, of the characteristics of the individuals who staff them; and this in turn is a function, in part, of the socio-religious groups to which they belong." [17]

One further point which Lenski emphasized, which is of particular importance for this essay, is that in order to understand the power of socioreligious groups it is essential to recognize their capacity to absorb primary groups, usually the family, as subunits in their organizational system. Because of this, the norms of socioreligious groups are constantly reinforced in these intimate and highly formative primary groups.[18]

A theoretical approach to the study of religion which presupposes almost all of the foregoing studies and which attempts to resolve the dilemma presented by these studies of religion has been suggested by Robert Bellah. The dilemma is: to what extent is religion an imaginative creation of corporate man

---

[14] *Human Society* (New York: The Macmillan Company, 1960), p. 529.

[15] *Millhands and Preachers* (New Haven: Yale University Press, 1942).

[16] The reader is referred to the classic statements of their respective positions. Durkheim, *The Elementary Forms of Religious Life*, trans. by Joseph Ward Swain (New York: The Macmillan Company, 1915); and Weber, *The Protestant Ethic and the Spirit of Capitalism* (New York: Charles Scribner's Sons, 1948).

[17] (Garden City: Doubleday and Company, 1961), p. 310.

[18] (a) Some of the significance of the findings of the Lenski study should be modified in view of the study's confinement to the Detroit area. As indicated by Andrew Greeley's volume, *Religion and Careers* (New York: Sheed & Ward, 1963), a national sample can alter the findings concerning the significance of religion in American life. The results suggested by Greeley are generally in support of Kingsley Davis' statement about religion.

(b) The role of the family as described by Lenski is supported by Robert J. Havighurst in *The Educational Mission of the Church* (Philadelphia: The Westminster Press, 1965), especially chap. I.

functioning to meet only the tension-reduction needs of the sociocultural system at large and to what extent is it actually formative of the core value system of a given social order? Bellah begins with the idea that unless individual or societal action has meaning for the actors, the stability of the personality and, consequently, of the society, is threatened. Concrete action derives its meaning from social norms. Beyond the norms, however, is a symbol system—"superordinate meaning system"—which gives meaning and coherence to the norms themselves. For example, the act of voting is supported by social norms which, in turn, derive their meaning from belief in a superordinate system, democracy. The superordinate meaning system becomes "sacred" in character when any threat to it evokes a hostile reaction or when one is willing to die for its preservation. The exception to this general systematic approach to the study of religion is that in some instances persons are primarily committed to the norms and alter the superordinate meaning system so that it functions to maintain the norm. The White Citizens Councils, committed to the norm of segregation, will shift superordinate referents accordingly. Russian ideological leaders and officials, on the other hand, have had no qualms about changing legislation concerning divorce when the prevailing norms began to threaten the superordinate system.[19] Such a hierarchical ordering of the values in a religious system could move sociological analyses of religion beyond institutions per se into the matrix of meaning which comprises the religious life of communities.

## Conclusions

The three sociocultural subsystems—the American family, public education, and religion—have been discussed in terms of their social and cultural transactions with American society at large. Those transactions most relevant to Christian education were selected, and seven aspects of that relevance can now be noted, in conclusion.

1. The foregoing analysis has perforce returned repeatedly to the basic significance of the family subsystem. The public school is an extension of the family's enculturation function; the institutional church depends upon its families for the experiential basis of its language and for the extension of its teaching into the life of the total community. If Christian education is understood as involving the three subsystems analyzed above, then the first conclusion to be drawn is that the sociocultural unit which is most significant for Christian education's concern for shaping human behavior is neither public education nor the church, but the family.

2. The family system is of predominant significance, but its transactions with the other two systems are also of vital importance to Christian education. From the transaction between the achievement-oriented, democratic family and the culture of "excellence" in public education, young persons have emerged who are more planful and purposeful than the previous generation, but also are more aggressive, tense, domineering, and cruel.[20] These sobering conse-

---

[19] Merton, Broom, Cottrell, *Sociology Today*, p. 156.

[20] Urie Bronfenbrenner, "The Changing American Child—A Speculative Analysis," *Journal of Social Issues*, XVII (1961), 6-18.

quences of the single-minded pursuit of "excellence" in a bureaucratic society indicate an aspect of the core value system of the current American society which is of serious concern to and relevance for the Christian education of the public.

The dynamics of change in this regard depend primarily upon a systematic reconsideration of the family as the originating and responsible agent in the education of the "emotions" and upon the incorporation into the public schools of a program which insists that education for "excellence" include responsibility for religious literacy and human—as well as national—values.

3. The transaction between the family system and the institutional church has been discussed extensively above. It needs to be added in this conclusion that many persons belong to the church as to a surrogate family. As a consequence, small-group procedure in Christian education may benefit but will most likely suffer. It is sometimes beneficial for those who need, but do not have a satisfactory family life, to find a pattern of leader-follower differentiation in a small group which has members who are able to maintain both the expressive and the instrumental functions of the group. However, such family-type involvement is usually effective only if the psychological transference of family functions to the group is based upon a satisfactory family life outside the church. It is the real family, not the surrogate family, which is basic to the formation of ideas and behavior patterns. Unfortunately, small groups often lose their instrumental function, become narcissistic and even incestuous; so, they become supportive of the too familiar attempt to pervert small-group functions into satisfactions for basic personal needs appropriate only in an actual family; needs for intimacy, affection, mutuality, and esteem. The institutional church undermines its sociocultural base in its educational methods and in its teachings if it tries to replace the family in fact; it rather sustains itself more effectively when it addresses the real family system as a sociocultural phenomenon whose existence is independent enough of the church to transact with it.

4. The transaction between religious systems and education is also of serious importance to Christian education. In this regard the church, unlike public education, is not an effective socialization institution. This is true partly because the church educates as if it were a closed society within the social system at large, when in fact it is not. Persons are brought up through the church's "school" and "promoted" into the adult society where they "commune" on equal terms alongside adults. The series of actions concerned with communicant education amounts to a "rite of passage" [21] which is empty because it usually does not, in any way that is significant to the young person, pass him from one status to another. The real rite of passage for the young person is his graduation from high school or college, his movement out of his family of origin, and his assumption of adult social responsibility. The charade of education for upcoming communicants in the church is self-destructive because it does not move young persons out of the family of origin but rather into

[21] The "rite of passage" phrase is taken from cultural anthropology and refers to the rites by which a young person is in actuality made an adult member of the tribe into which he was born. Thus, it designates a socialization process.

a different form of dependence upon the family, namely, upon the "family of God" and upon an institution which in turn is dependent upon family structures. The familiar "drop-out" patterns after high school and college are a matter of sociocultural determination; when the real rite of passage is experienced, the charade is completely exposed.

To suggest that, therefore, the "school" in the church should be abandoned is to oversimplify the matter and to misunderstand the multilevel nature of the transaction between the church and various other subsystems such as the family. The "school" clearly serves several purposes other than socialization. For example, although one effect of the "school" is the relief of family conscience regarding religious instruction at the point where it could be most effective, namely, in the family, it would be unrealistic simply to drop this responsibility into every family's lap. The result would be the proliferation of cultic solutions to the consequent problems of intensified parental guilt. Moreover, creative instruction in religious ideas as suggested by Pettigrew for public education could begin to break down some of the social class bias and bondage in which the acculturated church finds itself, and it could thereby relate religious meaning to the actual socialization process of young persons. Abandonment of the "school" in the church forfeits this opportunity.

5. As described above, theological language reflects in large measure the position of the family in society. Consequently, the traditional family of God withdraws to the "depths" (Robinson) or "ground" (Tillich)—or simply dies —as the family of man withdraws from society. As man seeks self-fulfilling achievement in the bureaucratic "technopolis," theology becomes man- and Spirit-centered; and it speaks ethically—and ambiguously—about "a man in the world" (Bonhoeffer) or the "truly human" (Lehmann). Since the form of all language is taken from one's experience with the world, theological language cannot be renewed in a vacuum; and since the basis of that language is the family system, it would seem to be the responsibility of Christian education to reexamine the family, *qua* family, not only as the chief agent for the education of the emotions (conclusion 1 above) but also as the point of departure for the substantive renewal of the meaning of theological language for our time.

6. If, now, the transaction between religion and public education be shifted to the grounds of the public schools, Robert Bellah's functional analysis of religious systems becomes most helpful in avoiding a self-defeating religious program. According to his analysis there exists in America a national religious system for which the "established" religious education program is the public school. The "sacred" is taught to and inculcated in our citizens. Kindergarten children spontaneously observe the hushed, reverent similarity between the pledge of allegiance to the flag and sectarian public prayer. The ritual celebration of national holidays (such as Memorial Day) and of the birthdays of our great forefathers all reinforce our commitment to Americanism and ultimately to a willingness to die in the cause of our nation. The flag is a surrogate cross which stands at the center of our "faith."

The implication of this national religious heritage—based upon Bellah's views —is that prayer and Bible reading in the public school—rather than strengthening the work of the church in society—tend to sanctify the national religious system and contribute not only to the misunderstanding of the separation of church and state, but, more seriously, encourage the loss of the meaning of the Judeo-Christian culture by separating the language from its experiential basis in the family and from its traditional base in a worshiping community.

7. Future sociocultural analyses of Christian education must move more deeply into both dimensions of the phenomenon: first, the Christian education of Christians, which has been found here to be dependent in many irreducible ways upon the family; second, the Christian education of the public, which calls for responsible leadership to interpret and to cope with the new values and meanings which are emerging in the key subsystems of the American social structure. The renewal of Christian education, then, lies in large measure in the renewal of its total self-understanding.

## FOR ADDITIONAL READING

### General

Kneller, George F., ed. *Foundations of Education.* New York: John Wiley & Sons, 1963. Parts II and III.

Lindzey, Gardner. *Handbook of Social Psychology.* Vol. I. Reading, Mass.: Addison-Wesley Publishing Company, 1954.

Merton, Robert K.; Broom, Leonard; and Cottrell, Leonard S., Jr. *Sociology Today.* New York: Basic Books, 1959. Chaps. 5-7.

Parsons, Talcott and Shils, Edward, eds. *Toward a General Theory of Action.* New York: Harper & Row, 1962.

### Family

Erikson, Erik. *Childhood and Society.* Rev. ed. New York: W. W. Norton & Company, 1964.

Parsons, Talcott. *Family Socialization and Interaction Process.* New York: The Free Press of Glencoe, 1955.

Warner, W. Lloyd. *The Family of God.* New Haven: Yale University Press, 1961.

### Education

Havighurst, Robert J. *The Educational Mission of the Church.* Philadelphia: The Westminster Press, 1965.

Kimball, Solon T. and McClellan, James E. *Education and the New America.* New York: Random House, 1963.

Spindler, George D., ed. *Education and Anthropology.* Stanford: Stanford University Press, 1955.

### Religion

Durkheim, Emile. *The Elementary Forms of Religious Life.* Trans. by J. W. Swain. New York: The Macmillan Company, 1915.

Weber, Max. *The Protestant Ethic and the Spirit of Capitalism.* New York: Charles Scribner's Sons, 1948.

Yinger, J. Milton. *Religion, Society and the Individual: An Introduction to the Sociology of Religion.* New York: The Macmillan Company, 1957.

# Chapter 8

# THE DIALOGICAL FOUNDATIONS
# FOR CHRISTIAN EDUCATION

*Reuel L. Howe*

EDUCATION DEPENDS UPON COMMUNICATION. COMMUNICATION IS NOT easily and readily accomplished and, therefore, neither is education. The purpose of communication is to bring about a meeting of meaning between two or more persons which requires dialogue and not monologue. When this meeting of meaning occurs, it is because the meanings of each side have been opened to each other; that is, they have been in dialogue. Since education depends upon communication, and dialogue is essential to communication, dialogue is equally essential to education. The meanings of the teacher and pupil must meet to the edification of both.

Back of the need for meeting of meaning as the object of communication lies man's inevitable search for meaning and the fact that everything has meaning. The search for meaning is pursued both consciously and unconsciously. Primitive, ignorant, and illiterate persons' search is largely unconscious and random, and is expressed more by nonverbal means than verbal. Their verbal expressions of their search for meaning often make it difficult to recognize that they are looking for it. A more skilled and literate person is apt to be more consciously seeking for meaning and is more obviously restless when he is frustrated in finding it. The search for meaning is a resource for the accomplishment of a meeting of meaning.

The search for meaning and the communication that accomplishes a meeting of meaning is supported by the fact that everything has meaning. The task of the teacher is to help the student recognize and respond to meaning in any form or place. We are tempted to say that some things have meaning and others do not. This is untrue. There is no act, event, or thing that either does not have meaning within itself or points to some meaning. If we say that something has no meaning, we can only understand that we do not know what the meaning is. The denial of meaning to anything removes the learner from the possibility of learning.

Also, we can safely assume, I believe, that people bring meaning to every encounter. We may not recognize their meanings; we may not like them, and we may wish that they had brought other meanings, but the fact remains, meaning they bring. But we cannot assume that the meanings people bring to the educational encounter are available to them. One of the tasks of the teacher, therefore, is to help the pupil formulate them, that is, to formulate his questions and insights, on the basis of which he may learn by being met with meanings beyond those he holds. Thus, what he knows and understands is joined to what is known and understood by others.

## Blocks to Communication

The experience of teaching, as in any communication, reveals the existence of blocks that prevent or distort a meeting of meaning. A teacher, for example, who was trying to help a group of laymen understand the nature and practice of Christian love, was told by one of his students that Christian love was a "beautiful idea but it wouldn't work in a rough and tough world." Here the meanings of the teacher did not meet the meanings the student brought to the class which led him to repudiate the teaching. The teacher was concerned with an important truth; the layman was concerned with an important problem. The teacher did not communicate to the student, and the student did not hear the teacher.

What are some of the barriers to communication? First, *language* can be a major barrier. Much biblical and theological language causes difficulty to contemporary men. They neither receive nor convey their own meanings by use of them. Common words such as "love" are not effective instruments, and many of our other specialized religious words are meaningless to thousands of people, including church members. And yet teachers and preachers have been trained to use this language and are baffled when they discover its ineffectiveness for communication. The traditional words, however, are not to be despised or thrown away as some suggest. We have a twofold responsibility in relation to them: first, to explain their original meaning or significance; and second, to help people relate that meaning to the meaning of their lives today. In other words, we need to build bridges between contemporary meaning and traditional symbols of meaning.

*Images* are another barrier to the meeting of meaning. The images which the participants in a communication have of one another or of the subject matter can effectively obstruct the communication. This happens when what the other person says has to filter through what we think he is like and, therefore, what we think he is saying. Thus the communication is distorted, and person is separated from person. The problem is, how do we break through these images so that real communication can occur?

Our *anxieties* are a third barrier that keeps us from speaking to and responding. These can be either personal anxieties or anxieties about the subject matter.

A fourth barrier has to do with our *defensiveness* when anxieties threaten. It is only natural for human beings to feel vulnerable and to act in defense of themselves. Instead of dealing with the relationship or the real issue, we may justify ourselves at the expense of others, or we may blame others for our own failures, thus employing two very common human defenses: rationalization and projection. Or we may withdraw from the situation; or we may begin to talk compulsively and seek to hide from the difficulty by erecting a wall of words.

Another barrier is the *differences* that exist between us: differences of age, sex, education, background, and so on.

Thus the problems of languages, images, anxieties, defenses, and differences all exist as barriers to the meeting of meaning and as blocks to the accomplishment of the purpose of communication. They are, however, only psychological and emotional symptoms of a deeper barrier to communication: the ontological one having to do, naturally, with our concern for being. Every person, because he is both finite and guilty, inevitably lives with some anxiety in relation to known and unknown threats to his being. He looks for guarantees and reassurances that will give him the courage to be. The search for affirmation and reassurance sometimes draws him nearer to his fellows and at other times separates and alienates him from them.

This self-concern not only sets him apart from his brother but makes it difficult for him to communicate with him or to hear his brother's cry in behalf of his own ontological concern. This ontological preoccupation, anxiety, and purpose is a primary block to communication, of which the other barriers are but an expression. Some barriers to communication, therefore, exist in all relationships of men. We should expect their presence and be prepared to act responsibly in relation to them.

## Monologue vs. Dialogue in Education

Many educators are unaware of these barriers and untrained in knowing what to do about them. A part of their inability in relation to barriers stems from their monological conception and practice of communication. Many of them think that communication is accomplished by "telling" people what they ought to know and do. This monological illusion about communication is widely prevalent in the church. Monological Christian education lays a veneer of content over people's meanings, and because there is little interpenetration of meaning between content and experience, the veneer of education "peels away" from the real meanings by which people live. Even a short experience of preaching and teaching quickly frustrates the minister and teacher because they soon realize that telling is not an effective means of communication. In monological communication teachers often suffer from "agenda anxieties" and are so preoccupied with the content of their message, their purposes, that they are blind and deaf to the needs of their students and their search for meaning. Our experience at the Institute for Advanced Pastoral Studies, reinforced by other research in the field of communication, makes clear that monologue fails to accomplish the communication task. Many teachers and ministers, however, resist this insight and even pride themselves on not knowing anything about communication or about how people learn, and offer as their defense their own prejudices based on untested experience. And yet these same teachers are often impatient and frustrated because of the poor showing of their students. Communicators' effectiveness must be judged by the hearers' response as made in their own terms.

Complaints about the theological and religious illiteracy of church people are numerous. The reason for the illiteracy is not that the church's teaching has not been presented to them, but that the church's method of teaching neither pays attention to the meanings the people bring to it nor checks their understanding of it in terms of their ability to communicate it in their own words. When we do not make ourselves responsible and responsive to the patterns of experience and understanding that people bring to a particular learning situation, our communication is doomed to failure. The meaning barriers are usually able to defeat monological communication.

As we have said before, people always bring meaning to every encounter. Earlier reference was made to a teacher's attempt to explain the nature of Christian love which a layman rejected as too "dreamy" a concept to be workable in everyday life. In the discussion that followed he explained that in his job at the bargaining table when agreements between labor and management were being hammered out and relations became strained and tempers short, it was necessary for him to keep the person of his opponents and colleagues in focus. He found that if he did, he was better able to keep the issues clear, that after the ordeal mutual respect and even friendships resulted. He believed that if they worked through the various images they had of one another and the difficulties of communication, some creative solution to their problem would be achieved. Out of the meanings of his own life and in his own words he said the same thing the teacher had said: Keeping people in focus as persons and acting responsibly in relation to them is an act of love of the kind the teacher was talking about. Out of the rigors of one of the most difficult tasks in our culture, a man brings to the hearing of the gospel insights which, if he could hear with them, would prepare him to understand in real depth the relevance of I Corinthians 13 for modern industry. Unfortunately, he could not understand the message in the teacher's terms, and unfortunately the teacher did not take the pains to help him understand the message in his terms, with the result that their meanings did not meet. When brought into dialogue through the discussion, however, the meeting did occur.

## Christian Education as Dialogue

The true concept and principle of communication is dialogue in which there is address and response producing a meeting between the meanings the students bring to the educational encounter and the meanings responsibly presented by the teacher.

It is important at this point to make a distinction between dialogue as principle and as method. The possibilities of communication should not be limited by restricting the method to the dialogical ones such as seminars and discussion groups. Not every educational task can be accomplished by them. We are, instead, speaking in behalf of the *principle* of dialogue which any method may use. A sermon or lecture may be dialogical even though there is only one speaker, but the dialogical lecturer is one who is able to draw his students into an implicit dialogue with him in such a way that the meanings they bring to the occasion are activated by the meanings he brings to them.

Christian education must move from monologue to dialogue. Communication as dialogue is revealed in Scripture as a matter of address and response between God and man, and man and God. Even the concept "Thus saith the Lord" does not mean that God spoke in a way that forbade man's freedom of response, but that he spoke as a participant in the dialogue with man whom he had made free, and that he spoke in response to man's last response to him and in anticipation of his next reply. The Incarnation made the address and response between God and man immediate and personal. In a face to face way it became a dialogue between person and person. The Cross is a symbol of an event in which the barriers to dialogue were accepted as a part of the dialogue: They can be overcome only when there is honest address and response between person and person; when the meanings of one are confronted by the meanings of another in such a way that the being and freedom of each is respected in spite of every negative force.

The Christian teacher has the responsibility not only of preparing himself to speak the truth, but the responsibility also of preparing his students to hear it. The proclamation of the gospel has to be faithful to the meaning of the gospel, but the hearing of the gospel has to be faithful to the meaning of life. Furthermore, the meaning of each must inform the meaning of the other. In other words, the word of man must be in dialogue with the word of God in order to be judged, purified, and transformed. And the word of God must be in dialogue with the word of man because it is the word for man, being born as it was out of the dialogue between God and man.

The kind of teaching that we are talking about is the kind engaged in by the greater teacher, our Lord. The dialogical principle with its employment of correlative thinking lies at the basis of his parables. All of his teaching was dialogical because his life was. Read the pages of the gospel and note how he taught. Notice how he moved in his conversation with the woman at the well from a consideration of the water that quenches physical thirst to the living water, and from a theoretical discussion about religion to a consideration of the kind of life the woman was living. Teaching of this kind calls for correlative thinking. When we are considering doctrine in its propositional form, we should, at the same time, think in terms of the life situation that asks for it. Similarly, if we are studying the meaning of a human situation of any kind, we ought to think also of the ultimate meaning to which it points. The cultivation of correlative thinking is indispensable to the Christian teacher and is one way to practice the imitation of Christ. For thirty years he listened and observed before he spoke, and as a consequence his teaching has a quality that grows out of all that he saw and heard. He really saw and understood men and their behavior. He was able to use the events and things of their life as symbols of their meanings. He used the common things of life such as a penny or a mustard seed to point to the common meanings of life. By them he helped people gather their meanings as preparation for hearing and understanding him. Somehow we have failed to learn and use his principle of communication.

Teachers also often think that their role is to give answers to their students' questions. This "answer-dispenser" image requires that the teacher answer the questions instead of using his understandings and skill to help the students move in the direction of an answer to their own questions. Many of the ministers who study at the Institute complain that their teachers did too much thinking for them. The teachers formulated the questions instead of helping them to do it, and then they proceeded to give the answers instead of supervising the students' working out the answers for themselves. This kind of education weakens a person rather than strengthens him and makes him more dependent rather than more resourceful. The graduates of this kind of education with whom I work are more apt to quote someone else than speak as their own authorities. They would rather that I give them answers to their problems than help them to do their own thinking. Education of this kind creates barriers to communication rather than overcoming them.

The purpose of communication, and therefore of education, is not to give people answers but to help them work out their own relation to a truth. On the other hand, we need to beware of avoiding answers. If a question has been asked, an answer should be formulated either directly or indirectly. We have witnessed in our own time an interesting shift in the teacher's understanding of his role. Some teachers, as a result of the emphasis on the group process of learning, have moved from the old authoritarian role to a new permissive nondirective role, with the result that many teachers now involve their people in an *ad nauseam* formulation of the questions because they think it unorthodox for a teacher to address himself directly to questions. They have a sense of guilt about speaking directly, offering information, and formulating the insights that have come out of the educational endeavor. They have been removed from one horn of the dilemma and impaled on the other. Dialogical teachers should responsibly decide, insofar as they are able, what students need to do in the process of learning, whether to discuss, to formulate questions, to consult authorities, or to formulate their own understandings and answers; or, as teachers, to raise other questions, to formulate the insights that have grown out of the discussion, or speak as authorities out of their own previously acquired knowledge or other competences. I am making the point that in the employment of the dialogical principle teachers should not assume the students' responsibility. They should seek to avoid doing for their students what the students can do for themselves.

Dialogue is necessary not only for teaching subject matter, but also for the development of relationships of trust in which true meeting of person and person is achieved and upon which true education depends. Too often we feel that we are experts and that what we have said should be accepted because we have said it. On the other hand, if we can accept the dialogue, our communication in education will be more successful not only didactically but interpersonally as well.

There are two sources of learning in dialogical education. First, there is the learning that comes from the study of the topic; and second, the learning that comes from the study of the relationship between the student and teacher, between students and students, and the relation of them all to the life of which they are a part.

There is no mystery about the subject matter being a source of learning. It seems to be commonly recognized by everyone. The other source of learning, however, comes as a surprise. Few people consider what happens between men as a curriculum which may be studied and from which learnings may be derived which correlate with the learnings that come from the subject matter. Anything the Christian educator says about God will be spoken in the context of his life with God and expressed in his relation with his neighbor. He believes that the act of communication, and therefore the act of teaching, is both a *description and* an *embodiment* of the truth. In other words, human becoming and identity are founded on the act as well as the content of communication. While I teach about love my teaching must be an act of love. If I would speak of God, then God himself must make his appeal through my speaking about him. There can be no separation of the word and the life, of subject matter and relationship.

The abstraction of biblical, historical, and theological thought from life makes it difficult for us to accept the full religious meaning of contemporary dialogue. What happens now between man and man and man and God is also a part of the curriculum of Christian education. I remember an occasion when, in the course of a seminar for laymen on the meaning of the atonement for modern man, several members of the group became alienated as a result of feelings and opinions expressed during the discussion. When it was observed by a discerning member of the group that the condition of relationship within the group was relevant to the subject of discussion and should receive attention, several other members protested that they ought to stick to the subject, namely, God's atoning work in Christ. Considerable time and effort was required before some of them could see that what was happening between them was a legitimate and relevant part of the conference curriculum. It is much easier to talk about atonement than it is to participate in God's reconciliation in the concreteness and complexity of our human relations.

The dialogue between man and God produced the Bible, and the study of the Bible is concerned with the encounter that took place between God and man. Similarly, the dialogue between God and man produced the formulations of theology, and the study of theology should have as its primary concern the illumination of the relation between God and man. Unfortunately, however, many teachers have been trained to think theologically about theology and religiously about religion, but do not know how to think theologically or religiously about and out of life. Likewise, the dialogue between God and man through the centuries has a history, but the study of that history should give perspective to the contemporary encounter between God and man. Unfortunately, many people who have studied the history of the church have no perspective to bring to the life of the church in their own time.

In a very real sense the contemporary dialogue between God and man is but a continuation of what we call the Scriptures. The word of God and the word of man have to be kept in dialogue. To read contemporary news and comment thoughtfully and not read the Bible meditatively is to be irresponsible as a citizen; and to read the Bible meditatively and not read the news and comment responsibly is to read the Bible irresponsibly. The Bible was born out of the meeting of the news of the day and the word of God. Likewise, the participation in contemporary life needs the illumination of the Bible just as the understandings of the Bible call for participation in the making of contemporary history. Let us never forget that out of the meeting of history and the word of God was born the good news, and the good news will continue to appear in our own time as men live responsibly in the world and to the word of God. What happens, therefore, between man and man in dialogue with the word of God is as much a part of the curriculum of adult education as anything that is delivered to us by the theologians.

## Dialogue and the Purposes of Education

Many think that the purpose of communication is the transmission of knowledge and the securing of agreement to a point of view. Instead, the purpose of dialogue, and therefore of communication, is to help the person participating in it make a responsible decision, whether that decision be a Yes or a No in relation to what is being considered. Such a purpose is consistent with the fact that in dialogue each person is free to make his own response. Communication is successful if either response is made. We worry too much about the No or negative response. It is necessary sometimes to say No before we can say Yes. Surely we see this in the life of children. A No may be a part of the process that leads to saying Yes.

We should also expect that a No to one thing requires a Yes to other things, and that a Yes to one action means a No to possible other ones. One purpose of communication, then, is to help people realize to what they are saying No and to what they are saying Yes.

The word spoken in monologue seeks to be a concluding word. The word spoken in dialogue is always a word of beginning. The word spoken in monologue is helpless in the face of the barriers to communication, but the word spoken in dialogue accepts and uses the barriers as a part of the communication. Similarly the monological word is defeated by a No response whereas the dialogical word accepts the No response as well as the Yes because of the conviction that a responsible No has more meaning and future than an irresponsible Yes.

Another purpose of dialogical education is to help the student realize his creative potential and become a participant-contributor to life around him.

An individual is not only born into a family but into the stream of history. In this flow of event and meaning that has been going on for centuries and will continue long after he has departed, he is a new event having within himself the potentialities of a creative person, and as such he is a potential participant in the shaping of the history of his own time. Whether or not he realizes these potentialities depends in large measure on how he is met. Education is the relationships and processes, formal and informal, that meet the individual and influence his becoming. The objective of education is to select that which is necessary for the individual's education in relation to the powers and potentialities of the individual at that time. Unfortunately, however, educational choices and actions are often made that destroy the individual's potentiality and his power to participate in the life of which he is a part.

One tragedy results from the domination of the pupil by the teacher. The weapons of this domination are many, among them the authority of history, the pressure of tradition, and the absolutism of knowledge which at best can only be partial. The objective of educational domination by parents, teachers, and others is the conformity of the student to the patterns, concepts, and values of the culture. This dominating endeavor impoverishes both the student and the culture. Behind this domination are the needs of the teacher which often corrupt the educational relationship. For example, the teacher's will may be inflated by the authority of his knowledge or the tradition which he represents. Here we have one of the most conspicuous causes of the loss of creativity and power of participation in countless individuals. The corrective of this condition would be the balancing of the authority of the teacher with the authority of the learner—a relationship which requires mutual respect and which is dependent upon the initiative of the teacher.

Tragedies in education also result from a teacher's loneliness, isolation, and longing. He has the human need of being accepted and of achieving. Lack of his acceptance can produce in him a defensive kind of teaching that drives him to serve ulterior purposes. A lack of a sense of achievement can cause him to exploit the educational situation, seduce the student's response, use the pupil as a means of meeting his own needs, or make the pupil a scapegoat for problems he cannot handle himself. The corrective for this condition is the recognition of the need for asceticism in teachers' relations with students, an asceticism that rejoices in the world entrusted to us for our influence but not our interference.

As Martin Buber observes, a teacher cannot choose his students out of his inclination but "finds them there before him." [1] He has equal responsibility for each and all of them regardless of his personal preferences. If he grades them, he must do it by some other criterion than his own personal inclination to "enjoy" selected ones of them. All his judgments of them all, however, must be constantly subject to correction by the address and response of the particular being of his students, "For in the manifold variety of the children the variety of creation is placed before him." [2] The teacher's vocation calls him to a special humility.

The monological relationship and communication in education cannot accept the "manifold variety of children," and is unable to welcome it as a part of the educational situation. The dialogical teacher, however, because of his practice of the inherent principle of inclusiveness, rejoices in variety, makes himself responsible to it, and is enriched by it.

The relation between the individual and the culture is delicate, and if he is to be fulfilled, his life must be one of dialogue. The purpose of education and the teacher is to bring the student into dialogue with the life of which he is a part, help him realize his creative potential, and guide him on his way to becoming a participant-contributor in life in response to the creative spirit.

## FOR ADDITIONAL READING

Buber, Martin. *Between Man and Man.* London: Routledge and Kegan, 1947. Chap. III on Education, pp. 93-103, is particularly useful.

Cantor, Nathaniel. *The Teaching-Learning Process.* New York: Holt, Rinehart & Winston, 1953.

Howe, Reuel L. *The Miracle of Dialogue.* New York: The Seabury Press, 1963.

Hunter, David R. *Christian Education as Engagement.* New York: The Seabury Press, 1963.

MacMurray, John. *Persons in Relation.* New York: Harper & Row, 1961.

[1] *Between Man and Man* (London: Routledge and Kegan, 1947), pp. 94-98.
[2] *Ibid.,* p. 95.

*Chapter 9*

# THE OBJECTIVE
## OF CHRISTIAN EDUCATION

*Randolph Crump Miller*

AN OBJECTIVE IS THE POINT TOWARD WHICH AN ARMY IS ADVANCING. IT IS synonymous with a goal or end. A general objective may provide directives for a total plan of action. To move in this direction, one must have aims, marks, targets, and purposes. The design of an educational process adopts suitable means to specific goals which are stepping-stones to the major objective.

### Reasons for an Objective

An objective exists to guide the educational life of a community. It provides the reason for existence, an understanding of the basis for motivation, and the end toward which the process moves. It is sufficiently broad in its coverage to be relevant to all of the activities of the community, and yet it is specific enough to be a basis for unity. It operates in many ways when it is broken down into particular goals, but it serves in at least three capacities when it remains generalized.

First, it is a guide to all writers and editors of curriculum materials, for it provides an overarching goal. No matter what the details of specific guidance may be, as found in a lesson plan, unit outline, or in resources for the teacher, the objective is a reminder of the direction in which the educational process should move. No matter what kind of imagination a creative writer may have, the objective keeps him from getting too far away from the movement of the learner in the desired direction. Here is to be found the unity which every series of lesson materials must have, in spite of the variety which is essential for effectiveness.

Second, as a teacher works out the specific goal of a unit, the aim for a particular lesson, or the long range plan for the year, the objective provides the orientation needed so that the myriad of particular educational activities may point toward adequate outcomes. Because the objective is general, the teacher has freedom in selecting materials and methods, flexibility in relating suggested lesson plans to the growing edge of the pupils, and imagination in using extra resources and activities. This freedom within a general objective is limited so that it does not become anarchy, for the objective provides the overall control, a sense of direction, and a feeling of security as a framework in which to work.

Third, an objective provides a basis for evaluation. Because it is general, it is helpful as a basis for establishing specific goals that are open to some degree of measurement, observation, or estimates of achievement. Evaluation has admittedly been the most difficult of all practices in Christian education because the results are not open to the normal channels of testing, but if the goals of lesson writers and the aims of the teachers have been sufficiently specific to provide adequate guidance, it is possible through careful analysis to determine whether desired outcomes have occurred.

An objective may not be formulated so that these reasons are fulfilled. An objective needs to meet theological standards, and these have to have enough relevance to provide guidance. An objective needs to be within the realm of possibility in the light of our psychological and social understanding of the nature of the pupils. It needs to be within the teaching possibilities of those responsible for the educational program. It must allow room for the work of God, of the teacher, and of the pupil, with a rationale for each.

## Objectives of 1930

In 1930 Paul H. Vieth published *Objectives in Religious Education*. He had analyzed the writings of ten outstanding leaders in the field, of other educators, and the statements of objectives up to that time. The result was a list of seven objectives (to which an eighth was added later).[1] Vieth caught hold of the climate of thinking to such an extent that no revisions were made until 1958. He reflected both the theological and educational insights of the period, and yet what he proposed had an enduring quality. The International Council of Religious Education adopted them "as a basic document for curriculum work, subject to revision from time to time as further experience may make desirable."[2] The objectives were:

1. Christian religious education seeks to foster in growing persons a consciousness of God as a reality in human experience, and a sense of personal relationship to him.

2. Christian religious education seeks to develop in growing persons such an understanding and appreciation of the personality, life, and teachings of Jesus as will lead to experience of him as Savior and Lord, loyalty to him and his cause, and will manifest itself in daily life and conduct.

3. Christian religious education seeks to foster in growing persons a progressive and continuous development of Christlike character.

4. Christian religious education seeks to develop in growing persons the ability and disposition to participate in and contribute constructively to the building of a social order throughout the world, embodying the ideal of the Fatherhood of God and the brotherhood of man.

5. Christian religious education seeks to develop in growing persons the ability and disposition to participate in the organized society of Christians—the church.

6. Christian religious education seeks to lead growing persons into a Christian interpretation of life and the universe; the ability to see in it God's purpose and plan; a life philosophy built on this interpretation.

7. Christian religious education seeks to effect in growing persons the assimilation of the best religious experience of the race, pre-eminently that recorded in the Bible, as effective guidance to present experience.[3]

[1] (New York: Harper & Brothers, 1930), pp. 70-78.

[2] *Book One: Principles and Objectives of Christian Education* (Chicago: The International Council of Religious Education, 1932), p. 10.

[3] *Ibid.*, pp. 10-15.

In 1940 an additional objective appeared:

"Christian education seeks to develop in growing persons an appreciation of the meaning and importance of the Christian family, and the ability and disposition to participate in and contribute constructively to the life of this primary social group." [4]

The expansion of these objectives illustrates certain theological principles. God reveals himself "in nature, in the Bible, in Jesus Christ, and through the operation of the Holy Spirit in human experience and achievement. . . . God's part in this process is revelation, man's part that of discovery." [5] "Christianity is not simply a religion of growth and development, but also one of redemption." [6] There is emphasis on the church, "which finds its mission in the service it renders." [7] The Bible is "a record of God's search after man and of man's increasing experience of God." [8]

This approach took account of what it was assumed man can do. It recognized that God is not subject to the objectives set by man, but that man can be guided in his search for the meaning of his life. The objectives pointed to what it was believed was being achieved in the lives of growing persons. A program could be set up to achieve these goals.

This point of view was elaborated in the objectives for the age groups. Based on the knowledge of development as it existed then, each age group was carefully studied and the objectives listed in detail. This information was particularly valuable for the writers of closely graded lesson materials and for all teachers and supervisors, as it was sufficiently concrete to be immediately applicable. [9]

## Objectives of 1958

The theological upheaval which hit the seminaries and later the churches led to a study of Christian education in 1944, but the existing objectives were not reformulated in spite of the careful rethinking that resulted from the conference. [10] By 1952, however, the Division of Christian Education of the National Council of Churches was ready to move. Already some of the denominational boards had started on new adventures in creating lesson materials with reformulated objectives. A committee was formed, with Lawrence C. Little as chairman, which worked on the problem over a five-year period. Much background work was done and various drafts were revised before the document was presented for study, after which time it was then commended to the

[4] *Christian Education Today* (Chicago: The International Council of Religious Education, 1940), p. 16.

[5] *Book One: Principles and Objectives of Christian Education*, p. 10.

[6] *Ibid.*, p. 11.

[7] *Ibid.*, p. 14.

[8] *Ibid.*, p. 15.

[9] Three mimeographed works, two of which were over 300 pages, dealt with all the age groups, including adults. They are summarized in *Book One*, pp. 28-61.

[10] See Paul H. Vieth, *The Church and Christian Education* (St. Louis: The Bethany Press, 1947).

churches. No attempt was made to relate the statement to the age groups.[11]

Under one purpose, five general objectives were formed:

The supreme purpose of Christian education is to enable persons to become aware of the seeking love of God as revealed in Jesus Christ and to respond in faith to this love in ways that will help them grow as children of God, live in accordance with the will of God, and sustain a vital relationship to the Christian community.

To achieve this purpose Christian education, under the guidance of the Holy Spirit, endeavors:

To assist persons, at each stage of development, to realize the highest potentialities of the self as divinely created, to commit themselves to Christ, and to grow toward maturity as Christian persons;

To help persons establish and maintain Christian relationships with their families, their churches, and with other individuals and groups, taking responsible roles in society, and seeing in every human being an object of the love of God;

To aid persons in gaining a better understanding and awareness of the natural world as God's creation and accepting the responsibility for conserving its values and using them in the service of God and of mankind;

To lead persons to an increasing understanding and appreciation of the Bible, whereby they may hear and obey the word of God; to help them appreciate and use effectively other elements in the historic Christian heritage;

To enable persons to discover and fulfill responsible roles in the Christian fellowship through faithful participation in the local and world mission of the church.[12]

During the same period another commission was working on an objective for senior high young people. It wrote that objectives "of Christian education are conceived not as a list of tasks to be performed or relationships to be dealt with or areas of content to be covered, but as one end toward which the whole process is directed." [13] Everything that happens is to be determined by the one objective. It is more than all that is aimed at in specific instances, but it permeates every instance of learning and is the basis for evaluation.

The objective of Christian education is to help persons to be aware of God's self-disclosure and seeking love in Jesus Christ and to respond in faith and love—to the end that they may know who they are and what their human situation means, grow as sons of God rooted in the Christian community, live in the Spirit of God in every relationship, fulfill their common discipleship in the world, and abide in the Christian hope.[14]

Under this are five learning tasks:

Listening with growing alertness to the gospel and responding to it in faith and love.
Exploring the whole field of relationships in light of the gospel.
Discovering meaning and value in the field of relationships in light of the gospel.
Personally appropriating that meaning and value.
Assuming personal and social responsibility in light of the gospel.[15]

[11] *The Objectives of Christian Education: A Study Document* (New York: National Council of Churches, 1958).

[12] *Ibid.*, pp. 21-22.

[13] *The Objective of Christian Education for Senior High Young People* (New York: National Council of Churches, 1958), pp. 12-13.

[14] *Ibid.*, p. 14.

[15] *Ibid.*, p. 34.

The two committees met together but could not resolve their differences. A comparison indicates that the objective for youth stresses God's self-disclosure, man's self-knowledge, growth within the church, discipleship in the world, and the Christian hope. The general objectives in the document prepared by Little's committee have a broader scope, with emphasis on the Bible, the mission of the church, and man's action, but the distinctive notes of God's grace and man's response in faith are missing. This difference in theological stance is even clearer in the statement of 1964: "The objective . . . is that all persons be aware of God through his self-disclosure." [16] The word "help" has been eliminated, for it is part of the task rather than of the objective. Thus the objective has no instrumental significance but becomes an overarching hope, and learning takes place through more specific goals and tasks as Christians minister to one another.

The noninstrumental nature of the senior high objective, as amended in 1964, eliminates the "equipping" ministry which is presupposed in the general objectives of the Little committee, for in the latter we are to "assist, help, aid, lead, enable," and in the senior high objective the learner is to "listen, explore, discover, appropriate, assume." The difference is partly between the emphasis on teaching in the one and learning in the latter, but the emphasis on teaching assumes a response by the learner, while the emphasis on learning points to no stimulus unless the learner is to "wait on God."

## Objectives in Lesson Materials

As new lesson materials have been conceived, planned, and written, variations on the objectives have been developed, reflecting theological insights and educational purposes. Among the recent series, the Episcopal Church began the process of developing new materials in 1946; these materials first appeared in 1955. This marked a step in a new direction from the old objectives and from the United Presbyterian materials which first appeared in 1948.

The Episcopal Church took its direction from a statement by Archbishop William Temple:

Knowledge of God can be fully given to man only in a person, never in a doctrine, still less in a formless faith, whatever that might be. . . . There is great use in formulated doctrine, because it points us to that in which many have believed themselves to find the revelation of God. But the life of faith is not the acceptance of doctrine. . . . Faith is not the holding of correct doctrines, but personal fellowship with the living God. . . . What is offered to man's apprehension in any specific Revelation is not truth concerning God but the living God Himself.[17]

This approach led to the emphasis on religious issues in the lives of the learners as the organizing principle of the curriculum. What is important is that God is at work now for the redemption of his people, and the learner

---

[16] *The Church's Educational Ministry: A Curriculum Plan* (St. Louis: The Bethany Press, 1965), p. 8.

[17] *Nature, Man and God* (London: The Macmillan Company, 1934), pp. 321-22.

may be led to know God now as he makes decisions about his own life. The organizing principle is not the subject matter; the religious issues in which God is at work provide it.[18] Theology guides the curriculum, but in the foreground are the grace of God and the faith of man. Within the community the heritage is appropriated because it sheds meaning on life situations.

The United Church of Christ seeks "to introduce persons into the life and mission of the community of Christian faith." "This," says Roger Shinn, "is a humanly possible activity." God may act where he will, and persons remain free to accept or reject him, yet it "offers persons the opportunity for a transforming relationship with God and fellow men." [19] A similar statement is that we are to "surround individuals with the reality of the Christian fellowship, past and present." [20] To achieve this, the themes of God, man, Jesus Christ, and Holy Spirit are used both as content and as guides to the educational process.

The Presbyterian Church, U.S., stresses the covenant relationship, with the hope that those who respond "will seek to live out in the world, both corporately as his people and individually as his servants, the meaning of the covenant obligation." [21] The objective is "that all persons may respond in faith to the call of God in Jesus Christ and be nurtured in the life of fellowship with him, that they may face all of life's relationships and responsibilities as children of God." [22] The church provides the context of education, but only God changes lives. The curriculum not only includes all that the church does but the whole of human life.

The Lutheran Church of America has made available a more detailed analysis of objectives. It begins with a single objective, with a preamble:

> Inasmuch as the Church, as the Body of Christ, seeks to become more effectively that community of believers in which the Holy Spirit calls, gathers, enlightens, and sanctifies individuals in their relationships with God and their fellow men, the church's central educational objective, therefore, shall be—
> To assist the individual in his response and witness to the eternal and incarnate Word of God as he grows within this community of the church toward greater maturity in his Christian life.[23]

This is spelled out in terms of deeper understandings, more wholesome attitudes,

[18] See David R. Hunter, *Christian Education as Engagement* (New York: The Seabury Press, 1963), p. 37.

[19] "Christian Education as Adoption," *Religious Education*, LVII (March-April, 1962), 89; see his *The Educational Mission of Our Church* (Philadelphia: United Church Press, 1962), pp. 20-23.

[20] "A Statement of Educational Principles as Seen in the Light of Christian Theology and Beliefs," Unpublished working paper of United Church of Christ, 1957, p. 8.

[21] Sara Little, "The Covenant Life Curriculum," *Religious Education*, LVI (July-August, 1961), 268.

[22] *Education for Covenant Living* (Richmond: Presbyterian Church in the United States, 1962), p. 25.

[23] W. Kent Gilbert, *As Christians Teach* (Philadelphia: Fortress Press, 1962), pp. 158-60. See *Objectives of Christian Education, The Age Group Objectives of Christian Education,* and *The Functional Objectives of Christian Education* (Philadelphia: Lutheran Church of America, 1957, 1958, 1959).

and more responsible actions, which in turn are related to God, the church, the Bible, others, the world, and the self. In the light of developmental studies these are broken down into "observable learnings which occur in these relationships," and which are to be sought in the home, confirmation class, and other Christian gatherings. There are continual involvements and learnings as the Christian grows toward maturity.

The Methodist Church presents the purpose of Christian education in terms similar to those of the National Council:

Through Christian education the fellowship of believers (the church) seeks to help persons become aware of God's seeking love as shown especially in Jesus Christ and to respond in faith and love to the end that they may develop self-understanding, self-acceptance, and self-fulfillment under God; increasingly identify themselves as sons of God and members of the Christian community; live as Christian disciples in all relations in human society; and abide in the Christian hope.

[Sinful persons are] in need of repentance and saving grace—that is to say, salvation. [And this is] met in the gospel. [We are to use every resource of modern knowledge in order to] help *persons*.[24]

Other denominations, among them the American Baptists, Southern Baptists, Disciples of Christ, and the United Church of Canada, have been revising their materials, and in the course of this have rethought their objectives. The three basic themes of the United Church of Canada, God and his purpose, Jesus Christ and the Christian life, the church and the world, are undergirded by the objective "that persons at each stage of their lives may know God as he is revealed in Jesus Christ, serving him in love through the worship and work, fellowship and witness of the church."[25]

Just as in the case of the National Council, the denominations seem to be moving toward one objective. With the exception of the Lutherans, there is no stress on objectives for age groups, yet we find careful studies of age group characteristics in most of the materials. The objective moves toward a broad base, a "field of relationships in the light of the gospel," which D. Campbell Wyckoff calls "scope."[26] This does not provide any specific guidance. It is true that those responsible for Christian education are to "introduce, help, assist, aid, lead, and enable," which means that there is a ministry of teaching to "equip God's people," but no particular goals are provided in the light of our knowledge of how people develop.

Furthermore, some ideas occur in the denominational statements which introduce difficult concepts. God is at work now, revealed in the religious issues

[24] *Foundations of Christian Teaching in Methodist Churches* (Nashville: The Board of Education of The Methodist Church, 1960), pp. 31-32. *Foundations* was the basis for the current new curriculum. *Design for Methodist Curriculum* (Nashville: General Board of Education of The Methodist Church, 1965) makes use of the noninstrumental objective of the National Council of Churches.

[25] *Focus on the Church School* (May-June, 1964), p. 2.

[26] *Theory and Design of Christian Education Curriculum* (Philadelphia: The Westminster Press, 1961), p. 77. See his chapter on "The Question of Objectives" for an excellent summary statement.

of life. The Christian fellowship can become a reality, in so far as its members are faithful. Maturity is the goal of Christian living. "Self-understanding, self-acceptance, and self-fulfillment under God" may be equated with salvation. These are theological assumptions, and they guide the formation of the objectives, but from some points of view they are open to criticism, just as the noninstrumental statement of the National Council may be criticized from an opposite point of view.

## Some Other Statements

Father Georges Delcuve, editor of *Lumen Vitae,* writes that "the aim of the catechist, of the professor of religion, of the preacher, is to work with grace in the awakening or the increase of that faith which justifies us." [27] This simple statement carries profound meaning, for it points to the priority of God, assumes that man has a share in God's activity, and expects that there will be discernment and strengthened commitment. When Christians work in the service of God, they can "participate in and guide the changes which take place in persons in their relationships with God, with the church, with other persons, with the physical world, and with oneself," as Lewis J. Sherrill wrote.[28]

The new interest in religious language may help in understanding or recasting the objective. If we see that religious language is logically "odd" and that its purpose is to bring about "discernment" or "disclosure," then, as Ian T. Ramsey writes, the primary task is "to teach insight, to evoke disclosures in which we come to ourselves when and as we discern a world which has 'come alive' in some particular situation. . . . The aim of the teacher must be to lead to a vision, and to prepare for a response, in which the grace of God is known and discerned." [29] There is a Christian language, however it may be modified according to modern use, which remains logically "odd," and the church must use it so that it will "come alive" and "evoke a cosmic disclosure, when we 'really understand it for the first time,' though we may have looked at it, and said it a thousand times before." [30] This approach makes a difference in the way we tell our stories, for it moves us from the world of fantasy, possibly through myth, to the world of reality where redemption is a possibility. It leads us into the dialogue between God and man in which God is the chief actor, and this is the biblical priority of all our stories. In this way we may hope that Christian language may become significant and evoke a cosmic disclosure followed by commitment.

[27] "Confirmation at the Age of Reason," in *Shaping the Christian Message,* Gerard S. Sloyan, ed. (New York: The Macmillan Company, 1958), p. 281.

[28] *The Gift of Power* (New York: The Macmillan Company, 1955), p. 82. See Carol C. Rose, "Objectives," in *The Westminster Dictionary of Christian Education,* Kendig Brubaker Cully, ed. (Philadelphia: The Westminster Press, 1963), pp. 475-78.

[29] "Christian Education in the Light of Contemporary Empiricism," *Religious Education,* LVII (March-April, 1962), 95-96.

[30] Ian T. Ramsey, "Discernment, Commitment, and Cosmic Disclosure," *Religious Education,* LX (January-February, 1965), 14.

This language gains its currency in the Christian community, and Christian education is what happens to a person in the Christian community. We need in our objective an adequate doctrine of the church as the agent by which people become the church. We need to recognize the institutional element in learning as well as the influence of community living. We need to see the significance of living in the world under God as ministry.[31]

Religious language "comes alive" in worship, which is the environment setting the tone for Christian nurture, an atmosphere in which the Holy Spirit is uniquely at work. In genuine worship there is a sense of the presence of God, however vaguely conceived, for worship is primarily the adoration of God. One reflects on the experience one has in worship and therefore sees more clearly the meaning of God in his life.

Christian education means telling the story of God's mighty acts in such a way that the listener participates in the dialogue and comes into an engagement with God in his daily life, and therefore he sees the meaning of his life in a new way, and he is reborn daily with Christ as he lives in community as a Christian in the world.[32]

## The Issue

The issue behind these statements of the objectives of Christian education is what man can do. Certainly it is possible to "introduce" persons to the community life of a parish church. It is possible to relate the story of God's acts in the Bible, in history, and in our lives so that the other will listen and respond with his story. He may not be led to discern God in how either story is told, but the objective at least will be clear. On the levels of interpersonal relationships, much is communicated by man's actions. But just as man cannot be coerced or manipulated at the deepest level of his being, so God is not an automaton responding to some kind of push-button learning. When we use the word "God" we do not necessarily evoke his reality, and this may be due to resistance on man's or God's part. Still we seek to lead, help, assist, and enable in the hope that by Christian communication we may evoke a cosmic disclosure which will be followed by commitment or the increase of a previous commitment. Among God's gifts is that of teaching "to equip God's people for work in his service, to the building up of the body of Christ" (Eph. 4:12 NEB).

We can be helped to see the relationship between God's grace, man's faith, and the work we are called to do. An objective must be related to these three elements in order to provide adequate guidance. This is not only a theological exercise, although this may be primary, but it also involves a consideration of the psychological, philosophical, sociocultural, and dialogical foundations of Christian education. Because Christian education is an interdisciplinary area, it

[31] See my *Christian Nurture and the Church* (New York: Charles Scribner's Sons, 1961).

[32] See "From Where I Sit," *Religious Education*, LX (March-April, 1965), 105; "New Thinking in Christian Education," *Concordia Theological Monthly*, XXXVI (February, 1965), 88, and (March, 1965), 144.

looks in many directions for guidance. But because it is a discipline in its own right, it must formulate its own point of view as a basis for creating and using its objectives.

The objectives considered in this chapter reflect this kind of overall thinking, and we have pointed out some of the distinctions that should be noted. Some of these are matters of emphasis, but there are significant distinctions between noninstrumental and instrumental objectives, between assumptions about areas of man's work and God's work, between teaching and learning theories which underlie the formulations (although these are not explicit), and between views of the church and the scope of its educational task. The basis for judging between such issues turns us back to a reconsideration of the chapters on foundations of Christian education.

There is also a pragmatic test of these objectives in the light of the reasons for them. They must be useful to guide us in the formation of lesson materials, to inform teachers in their planning, and to evaluate the impact of the educational program. We need to see clearly what man can do and what God may do, and we have evidence not only from today's knowledge but also from the history of the church to assist us in making this distinction.

## FOR ADDITIONAL READING

Book One: Principles and Objectives of Christian Education. Chicago: The International Council of Religious Education, 1932.

Bower, William Clayton and Hayward, Percy Roy. Protestantism Faces Its Educational Task Together. New York: National Council of Churches, 1950.

Christian Education Today. Chicago: The International Council of Religious Education, 1940.

The Church's Educational Ministry: A Curriculum Plan. St. Louis: The Bethany Press, 1965.

Education for Covenant Living. Richmond: Presbyterian Church in the United States, 1962.

Foundations of Christian Teaching in Methodist Churches. Nashville: The Board of Education of The Methodist Church, 1960.

Gilbert, W. Kent. As Christians Teach. Philadelphia: Fortress Press, 1962.

Hunter, David R. Christian Education as Engagement. New York: The Seabury Press, 1963.

Little, Lawrence C., "The Objectives of Protestant Religious Education," in Religious Education: A Comprehensive Survey, ed. Marvin J. Taylor. Nashville: Abingdon Press, 1960.

Miller, Randolph C. Education for Christian Living. 2d ed. Englewood Cliffs: Prentice-Hall, 1963.

Monks, Gardner. The Church Looks Ahead to the New Curriculum: Specifications. New York: Protestant Episcopal Church, 1948.

The Objective of Christian Education for Senior High Young People. New York: National Council of Churches, 1958.

The Objectives of Christian Education: A Study Document. New York: National Council of Churches, 1958.

Rose, Carol C., "Objectives," in *The Westminster Dictionary of Christian Education*, ed. Kendig B. Cully. Philadelphia: The Westminster Press, 1963. Pp. 475-78.

Shinn, Roger L. *The Educational Mission of Our Church*. Philadelphia: United Church Press, 1962.

Vieth, Paul H. *The Objectives in Religious Education*. New York: Harper & Brothers, 1930.

Weigle, Luther A. "The Aim and Scope of Religious Education," in *Orientation in Religious Education*, ed. Philip Henry Lotz. Nashville: Abingdon Press, 1950. Pp. 87-98.

Wyckoff, D. Campbell. *Theory and Design of Christian Education Curriculum*. Philadelphia: The Westminster Press, 1961.

## Part II

# THE ADMINISTRATION
# OF CHRISTIAN EDUCATION

### Chapter 10

## LOCAL CHURCH STRUCTURE
## AND CHRISTIAN EDUCATION

### Harriet Miller

THE ORGANIZATIONAL STRUCTURES OF THE CHURCH ARE THE CHANNELS OF communication by which those who are the church make visible the image of the church which they hold. These structures either help or hinder the activating of the idea of the church that motivates individuals and groups. When a structure becomes so rigid that its functions are determined by its form, there is need for renewal of purpose within the group. Regardless of its location, i.e., local church or denomination, there is always the movement toward a more adequate organizational plan. Or there is at least an attempt to adjust the structure or destroy part of it when it becomes too rigid.

Ideally, function or purpose should determine the organization. Once a structural plan is developed, however, there is a strong tendency to maintain it. This is true even though the purpose may have been lost or kept static in spite of the changing conditions around the church. This is illustrated in a statement by George Webber: "The institutional forms of the congregation today do not reflect any clear New Testament pattern or even the style of the Reformation, but were formed in the life of a rural and small town America, a century ago." [1] The task of the administrator is to help persons be aware of the adequacy or inadequacy of their image of the church for the present situation and age. He must also help develop the structural forms by which this image may become visible.

By recalling some descriptions of the church that have guided Christians in forming their images, we may be able to discern and examine the structures that we have inherited. F. W. Dillistone in *The Structure of the Divine Society* describes the two traditional views of the church and examines how these have influenced the church at work. The two perceptions of the church are: the

[1] *The Congregation in Mission* (Nashville: Abingdon Press, 1964), p. 35.

*organic* view, based on the natural growth of an organism; and the *covenantal* view, in which encounter, promise, and dialogue are suggested. The first uses the metaphor, the body of Christ. The second is sometimes described as the people of God or the new covenant.

The teaching ministry of the church assists persons in deciding to become a part of the church in training for discipleship and participating in the mission of the church. Dillistone shows that these two traditions have become distorted as the structures develop and are in need of corrective measures in order to renew their purpose and commitment to God.

The main purpose of the church is to help persons become aware of God's activity through Jesus Christ in behalf of all men. The structure of a local church should help individuals not only to perceive God's work but to provide form for an individual and corporate response. If the response is in faith and love, the forms of the church's program will enable individuals to grow in depth and skill of response. Individuals find who they are and sense their part and place in the whole structure. The corporate sense is found in being able to align oneself with a group and participate in corporate decisions and action.

## Organic View of Structure

The church, when called the body of Christ, is being viewed organically. As in a family, all members hold certain affinity in common. The church as the family of God has Jesus Christ as head. Persons are grafted into a growing organism. Each one finds his place and learns to make his contribution. He apprehends the unity of the whole structure by losing himself in the being of Christ. At the same time, as a human being, he is formed by the whole structure. Augustine spoke of this body in a mystical, spiritual sense. The head, Jesus Christ, and the body, the church, together constitute the complete Christ.

The ideal of all parts of the local church working together as an army may also symbolize this view. In each metaphor we see the whole unit acting as one. Aquinas enlarged upon the idea of the body with greater clarity concerning the organizational structure itself. He saw it as a monarchy in which the whole differs from and is greater than its parts. Out of these images grew a hierarchical structure with each person or team of persons finally responsible to the head. This organic view, whether one sees it as a family, a well-organized army, or a monarchy, emphasizes the wholeness and unity of the organism. The imperfections are minimized, and one sees the entire church working at the task.

We see the organism being formed through teaching in our emphasis upon developmental grouping and grading. The sequence of our planned experiences is decided so that each stage of development takes the person farther into the total organization. Policy decisions are made concerning how many groups are needed to cover all the possible age groups. The aim is to fit the person into the area and group which will make possible his best growth. Once the person is located in a group most like himself, it is assumed he will grow in a neat, orderly pattern until he begins to contribute and take a working role in the organization. In this carefully constructed pattern there is the danger that he will be lost in the total group and expected to conform to prescribed patterns of response at a specific time.

This view also assists in developing specialized leaders for designated tasks. The organizational plan requires that each stage of development be filled with a trained, capable person. Those who are being brought into the church need to learn from the best leaders possible. The structure is made in hierarchical form. In the local church the minister or the director is the chief officer or the head. The voting members elect or choose a commission or selected group for policy making. In the organic view in which the concern is on unity and efficiency the leaders would be chosen for their capability and specific talent in an area. Once a person has been trained for a task, there will be a strong tendency to continue the person in this task. The purpose is to keep the inner operations of the church efficient and competent. But this concentration on the inner life of the church may narrow the view of its larger task. A commission on education whose decisions are only concerned with keeping the total program active within the church has lost sight of its true purpose to serve the world.

The monastic movement arose as an extreme view of the body of Christ as an organic unity. To be committed to that view one must renounce possessions, community responsibility, and even family responsibilities. This closed group developed a rigid discipline in order for the individual to be absorbed in the rhythm and structure of the cosmic order.

This structure becomes evident today in churches whose organizational plans are all designed to bring people into the church by completely separating them from nonchurch groups. To overemphasize the difference in dress, conduct, or in desires may defeat the purpose of communication with the world. There is a tendency for sanctity to become irrelevant and withdrawn.

It should be noted, however, that this tendency has been absent in most churches in the last few decades. More churches have adopted the value patterns of the social class which they serve. Sanctity or patterns of discipline required for entrance into the church are rarely enforced in the present day. To be a member of the church requires little in terms of personal commitment, so long as one is willing to be involved in some activity.

Charles Morgan spoke of this shift from the inward view to the outward signs in this way:

> The error is the error, which is the curse of modern civilizations, of judging men and institutions not by what they are inwardly, but by what they do apparently. Priests are promoted because they are active in good works and have the attributes of an efficient civil servant; they are sometimes scorned and passed over as being intellectually aloof if they devote their lives to meditation and the exercises of the spirit.[2]

The emphasis on the outward action of the church suggests a carefully planned structural pattern. The figure of a pyramid best describes this orderly plan for operation. At the top is the person who acts for Christ, the head. The other agencies and parts all are established to work together. In the local church this head is either the minister or the director of Christian education. If the church has only one staff person the educational program will be one part of

---

[2] *Reflections in a Mirror* (London: The Macmillan Company, 1945), p. 149.

his total task. If there is a special staff member for the educational task, he or she will work with the other staff person or persons to maintain a unified plan.

Many churches have established their program with age-group directors, department heads, teachers, or counselors. Other helpers are given specific tasks such as secretary, usher, treasurer, specialized technicians such as music, drama, or craft leaders. Each assignment is dependent on the others for completion. Each requires a special description, yet each is necessary and contributes to the whole plan. The commissions or age-group councils become instruments for interpretation of the specific area of the task.

The advantages of this structure are evident. The total organization is geared to a task as interpreted by and exemplified in the head. There is clarity and certainty of thought. Any ambiguity can be traced either up or down the structure to the most responsible person.

The organization can act with efficiency because the responsibility can be centered or focused upon a specific area. A large part of present-day manuals for church workers are occupied with diagrams, or job descriptions in order to give businesslike efficiency to the implementing of purposes designed for each part of the structure.

Examining this structure from the other side presents certain disadvantages. There is little opportunity for personal freedom or creativity. A person is indoctrinated into previously determined purposes. He is given a job description of his area of the task. He is supervised by a trained person who has responsibility to the total plan. New developments must gain approval through a long chain of command, or they stop the entire enterprise for adjustments.

The strong pressure is toward continuing a pattern that eliminates conflict, yet greatest growth often comes from the resolution of conflicting purposes or methods. New ideas must be examined, and often a new aspect is gained. But this is discouraged by the structural plan that develops in either the monastic or imperial images of the organic tradition.

In summary, local churches that are a part of denominations that stress the organic, body of Christ, view of the church will be organized according to an hierarchical plan in which all the parts are united with the head both mystically and visibly.

The structural plan of the local church will stress:

1) Careful distribution of responsibility according to representative and designated leadership roles;
2) The minister not only as a spiritual leader but the chief educator;
3) Specialization of tasks as needed to enrich the entire program;
4) Comprehensive plan to provide learning opportunities for all age groups, varying needs, and interests;
5) A plan for progressively greater responsibility as one's skills are developed;
6) Continuity because the task goes on when leadership is replaced.

The dangers that are resident in this view are:

1) The loss of individual freedom and creativity;
2) The tendency to make new developments and changes very difficult to attain;

3) Specialization of tasks leading to narrowing of the total purpose;
4) The pressure toward policy decisions being centered in fewer select individuals;
5) The policies become more and more adapted to the social environment;
6) The pressure for balance, harmony, and beauty eliminate many opportunities in conflict and tension which could produce new patterns.

## Covenantal View of Structure

The people of God responding to his call live in encounter and dialogue. The covenantal view focuses in the promise of God as fulfilled in both the law and the gospel. God speaks to man who responds according to his part of the contract. The church is seen as groups of people or as differing individuals responding in various ways to one clear demand for obedience to God. The groups that are formed will be held together by devotion to a sign or symbol, by allegiance to a contract or a book. This view makes strong reference to history since it points back to the ways in which God's promises were revealed to different people. Each time in the history of the church the covenantal view became strong, there was a revival of the study of the biblical record or a renewal of worship forms that centered in God's action toward man.

The covenantal view is interpreted in several patterns. When a heavy emphasis is put on God's unchanging revelation, there may be only limited reference to man's experience of this action. Man's response is often rigidly prescribed. Only those who are chosen to be the people of God may be included in the church. The examples of this are shown in the selected groups who choose to emphasize one particular aspect of human response and make that the law by which they fulfill their contract with God. In these cases the structure is designed to explicate very carefully the conditions, the discipline, and the kind of behavior which is necessary to be a member of this group. This view emphasizes only the narrowed response as represented in a group of very select principles.

Karl Barth's position concerning the church seems to be that the church "exists, where, and in so far as it dares to live by the act of its living Lord." [3] He seems to make the act of God purely arbitrary through Abraham and through Christ. It is hard to see where these acts take human form in the church. Many of Barth's followers fail to put into structure or form any human response shown to God's revelation. Their emphasis is only upon God's work.

The evidence of this view is seen when the structure provides a strong worship program with a large group presentation as the center of the plan. The plan provides for proclamation of God's action, but leaves the response to individual choice. A structure that has few delegated responsibilities or a structure that centers around a few capable "proclaimers" results. The gathered group provides little variation in methods for various age groups, or limited variety of organizational patterns. There is a strong focus on the covenant or

---

[3] F. W. Dillistone, *The Structure of the Divine Society* (Philadelphia: The Westminster Press, 1951), p. 209.

promise to God. It is based on the particular event which established the relationship with God. This is shown either in the person's constant renewal of this commitment or in an elaborate description of the events in which God revealed his purpose to his people. The educational aspects of the program are often neglected.

The attempt to make human experience more demonstrative of the relationship to God makes the church an educator and a disciplinarian in order to help persons fulfill their contract with God. Each society becomes an autonomous unit in which its members determine how they wish to carry out God's commands. The group becomes a free, voluntary society of people who devise their own plan of worship and service.

The strength of this view is in the strong cohesion within the group as persons give themselves completely to the contract. Status within the group is not attained by contribution but by the strength of one's commitment to the cause. The written codes in the biblical record, the established creeds, or constitutions of individual groups become very important.

The persons who have this higher allegiance find they control, dominate, and use the natural world to develop their pattern of response. Instead of adapting to the natural and social structures, the group finds ways to use them for God's purpose. The covenant is maintained by the continuing conversation between the covenanted members. The individual members are encouraged to express differing views in order that the original covenant may be tested.

The church structure in this view is designed to hold together groups who maintain strong unity within each group by open dialogue. The stronger emphasis in this view is on the functions or needs of the groups. Commissions or committees are formed to provide worship, service, fellowship, or study. Within each of these areas of work, there may be provision for age groupings. These committees will be developed according to need and are often dissolved when the function is completed. They are often developed by events in time rather than by a natural growth sequence. This structure allows for more individual and group freedom, but often deters speed of action or decision because of the need for interaction between differing groups.

Each of these local churches in maintaining autonomy of structure finds it harder to relate to a denominational or ecumenical structure. Many local churches become ingrown groups, because of their self-preoccupation and lose their connection with the larger church. A class or group may be satisfied with its own service to God even though oblivious to the larger concerns outside its own group.

These contractual groups who have developed their own terms of response to God's call may find it hard to change. Any change may be a threat to the unity of the group. The members grow most in their encounter with one another in tension and in fellowship as happens in creative relationship within the family. If, however, groups such as the women's or men's groups, the social action committee, or the Christian education commission do not see the larger purpose of the church both locally and generally, they may be motivated by too narrow a purpose.

The pattern of response may also become mechanized within this view. The

110

group may divide itself from those outside the covenant so completely that the changes in the social and economic context are not felt or included in their image of the church's task. If the original purpose of the group was dissatisfaction with the present status, the group may lose its freshness when the limited purpose of reform is achieved. The group needs to see its covenant as larger than individual or specific group relationship to God.

Summarizing the covenantal view and its effect on the patterns of structure, its strengths are:

1) God's direct call comes to particular people at particular times as it came to Abraham and through Jesus. A clear imperative and purpose makes the needed structure clearer.

2) Emphasis upon the event and the present means that structure must be flexible and may need to be created for limited periods and immediate tasks.

3) The structure must provide for conversation about the meaning of covenant between differing groups and individuals in order to keep the purpose fresh and alive.

4) The covenant allows for differences and variety within the larger whole.

The covenantal plan also has possibilities for distortions and dangers to good organization, such as:

1) The contractual view in which God's action seems unchanging may produce a mechanized response on the part of the people. This can best be seen when the church becomes only a school of doctrine in which the principles and plan of operation are based upon rigid interpretation of God's laws. It may come also from an interpretation of the gospel as a constitution for living rather than a dialogical relation between God and the church.

2) The church may become a school for doctrine or a disciplinary action in which persons learn the pattern of response without being involved in the total situation of the church in the world. People who may use the groups only for self-realization or therapy, but never relate to the larger world issues may find self-satisfaction, but become sterile.

3) Losing the sense of covenant to a contract in which the church members only meet the minimum requirements may not be sufficient. Teaching groups that interpret God's action as a bargaining with man as in a contract may lose the whole sense of discipleship which is implied in covenant.

In the covenantal view churches have achieved a strong unity including diversity, as long as good channels of sharing are maintained between the groups. This view allows for more flexibility of program. Changes may be brought about by working with other groups without upsetting the whole plan.

In both the organic and covenantal views of the church the structure may become rigid, but for different reasons. In one case the pattern of growth follows natural lines, and change means going against the comfortable patterns. In the other view the rigidity comes because of a desire to rely upon an interpretation of God's unchanging patterns of action. This view limits God's action to the past rather than accepting the reality of a living encounter.

## The Family of Families

Local church structure to meet the needs of a changing world requires that both views of the church be held in a creative relationship. Both are necessary for the life and growth of any true society. The church is the body of Christ, but it is also the people of the new covenant.

A family has within it at the same time an intimate relationship between its members as they grow into a unit as well as a strong authority in the head of the family. The church must have both the nurturing aspect which comes by being brought into the body of Christ and the demand for discipleship which is emphasized in God's call and promise.

The church provides a time and place for each person to become a participant in the family of God. The home provides the first field of action. The church organization must provide guidance in establishing a home and maintaining an open and loving atmosphere for its members. This assumes that the adult education of the church is planned according to needs as well as according to age. There must be provision to meet specific needs for adults such as being a parent, facing issues of political, economic, social, and moral responsibility, rethinking value scales in terms of discipleship, and finding the center of life in living rather than in daily work.

These groups also provide for the continued nurturing of adults. Adults who continue to grow as persons are more able to accept as their concern those persons whose family does not provide nurture and support. At the adult stage we see the three elements of local church structure in dynamic relation. There is the constant nurturing process that is needed by any person all through life. This is symbolized by the quality of "family." Small groups which are brought into being because of a specific need, task, or issue will stimulate persons to continue growth.

The second aspect of the structure is training. Not only is the educational task to nurture persons in the group, but to train them in the disciplines of Christian living. This phase of the program must provide corporate worship opportunities in order that the individual be reminded regularly of his covenant relationship both to the people of God and to God. There must be study groups in which there is emphasis upon the process of ministry to one another as well as the supporting fellowship referred to as nurture. The training groups are designed to help persons effectively listen and share in a group. The purpose of the training is developing interdependence without losing the sense of self that is being made real in the nurturing process.

The third element is that of discipleship. The term implies both being sent out as in mission and continuing to be nurtured and trained as the demands of mission are felt. The structure of the local church requires a means by which the members become aware of community and world needs. There must also be the opportunity to test out one's actions in mission in a loving, supervised group. The person who serves on the city council needs a sounding board for his ideas in his local church if he is to function as an ambassador for Christ in the world.

Thus, the local church structure must have three functions:

1) The first is to provide nurturing or family opportunities at all ages for all levels of maturing. The most natural structure for this is by chronological or mental age. Some common groupings are:

## CHILDREN'S DIVISION [4]

Nursery—birth through age 3
    or in separate groups according to each year up through 3
Kindergarten—ages 4-5
    or in groups of 4-year-olds and 5-year-olds

| | | |
|---|---|---|
| Primary—grades 1-3 | | Primary—grades 1-2 |
| Junior—grades 4-6 | —or— | Lower Junior—grades 3-4 |
| | | Junior—grades 5-6 |

## YOUTH DIVISION

| | | |
|---|---|---|
| Junior High—grades 7-9 | | Junior High—grades 7-8 |
| Senior High—grades 10-12 | —or— | Middle High—grades 9-10 |
| Young People—post high school | | Senior High—grades 11-12 |
|    through college | | Older Youth—post high school |
| | |    through college |

## ADULT DIVISION

| | | |
|---|---|---|
| Young adults | | Elective study groups |
| Middle Adults | —or— | Vocational groups |
| Older Adults | | Parent groups |
| | | Leadership Training Groups |

The other part of the nurturing process is provided in:
    a) weekday study, art, recreation, and club groups;
    b) child care and parent groups;
    c) fellowship and organizational groups.

If the covenant view is to act as a corrective, there must be opportunity at least from the adolescent period on for groups that provide support and fellowship in which age is not the prime factor. These groups need to be less structured and flexible in their purpose to allow persons to find themselves as changing individuals, yet centering in a self that has integrity.

2) The second function of structure is to provide training opportunities, including:
    a) studying and skill groups which develop the disciplines of Christian living such as prayer, Bible study, witnessing, and serving;
    b) groups in which leadership roles are demonstrated and practiced; and
    c) opportunities to participate in boards and committees whose decisions may indicate the relatedness of the tasks within the church and in the world.

[4] Many larger churches will provide separate groups for each age or grade from three years through junior or even senior high school.

Some training opportunities now being tried are:
  group therapy or personal growth groups;
  training groups for leadership skills;
  book study groups;
  Bible study groups;
  house groups for prayer and communion;
  consultations with leaders; and
  task committees.

3) The third function of organization is to provide opportunities and challenges to full discipleship in:

a) research groups that keep the church members informed of the needs of the community and the world;

b) consultation groups in which persons who are serving Christ in their vocations, in politics, or in service projects may evaluate their efforts in a church group; and

c) corporate experiences of commissioning and choosing representatives to act for the church in specific situations.

Some examples of action groups are:
  survey groups for community action;
  community councils;
  lay academies;
  organizational groups; and
  board and committee sessions.

One of the opportunities for the total group to sense its unity is best offered in congregational worship. This implies that worship in departments or organizations must point toward and prepare for participating in the corporate service of worship.[5]

## Organizations Within the Church

Some groups become organized around a set of purposes with similar organizations throughout the denomination. This pattern follows the organic view in which there is in each church a branch or unit of a denominational organization. These are designed to give larger scope to the work of the church, but the local unit must guard against two tendencies. One temptation is to try to provide all the aspects of Christian growth, i.e., nurture, training, and mission, within each organization, thus becoming a self-contained "little church." The other temptation is to center its total attention on the goals of the denominational organization without sensing responsibility for growth of individuals and local community awareness. These two tendencies may be checked when we help organizations designate a primary purpose and allow the others to be secondary benefits. For example, in the same church the adult Sunday church school class could major in study, while the women's society may emphasize service activities with study as the need dictates. Fellowship may be a secondary purpose in both or fellowship may be provided by a bowling or

[5] See chap. 21, pp. 242-55.

sewing group at another time. The communication between groups is essential if overlap and wasted energy in too many groups are to be avoided.

Instead of trying to cover all aspects of the educational task in each group, a coordinating council should help each group specify major and minor purposes. The coordinating council will need also to evaluate the number, size, and scope of each group to be sure that each of the stages of development (intellectually, socially, and spiritually) is being served. This coordinating council should have representatives from each kind of group and should be able to enlist special help for specific studies or needs. The coordinating council may be called commission on education if it is primarily concerned with the teaching ministry. In some denominations the various national agencies now work together in a program council or interboard committee. The movement toward total church unity is best demonstrated when the functional boards of missions, evangelism, worship, stewardship, etc., are represented with the educational committees in overall curriculum planning. The local-church coordinating council will deal with the beginning and terminating of provisional groups. The council will also need to choose the policies for movement from one group to another.

The tasks of the coordinating group can be described as:

1) The limiting of groups to produce the quality of "family" within the gathered life of the church. Each person needs to be known as a person, yet each must learn the skills of group decision and action.

2) Learning how to deal with those who break the disciplines that are training essentials. Standards for group solidarity must provide acceptance and loving concern as well as competence and efficiency.

3) Providing for opportunities for healing and reconciliation. Each group must learn the use of challenge and reconciliation. The professional staff must be primarily responsible for developing this skill, yet the total group must be aware of the constant work of the Holy Spirit in this task.

## Mission—A Style of Life

The church of the twentieth century lives in an urbanized society, with a call to be the people of God. George Webber speaks of the style of life of today's church as mission. He quotes H. Berkhof as saying—

It cannot be the primary task of the Church to contribute to the general work of supporting, developing and improving human life. This is good and necessary work to which Christians and non-Christians alike are called. . . . The unique task is to be *help of the helpless*. . . . The first task of the Church is to keep her eyes open and to pray God that she may see the really helpless; and to have the courage, not only to take up the new tasks but also (which is perhaps more difficult) to give up forms of help which have lost their witness-character.[6]

This chapter has sought to describe the creative tension present in the local

[6] H. Berkhof, "The Church's Calling to Witness and to Serve," *Ecumenical Review*, X (October, 1957), 29-31, cited in George W. Webber, *The Congregation in Mission* (Nashville: Abingdon Press, 1964), pp. 175-76.

church structure between two traditional images of the church: 1) The church as an organism into which the members are grafted and pruned in order to provide union with the head and constant growth. This gives us a developmental pattern of groups and an organizational plan emphasizing special responsibilities and contributions combined in the entire organization. 2) The church as a covenanted people of God in which differences and divergent groups are brought together by a common promise from God and a response given in a variety of ways.

The congregation must be a family that nurtures and supports; an army that trains and disciplines its members for service; and a mission station that sends out its forces and renews their commitment regularly to serve the world's needs. The organizational structure has both coordination of small groups and larger corporate actions with the professional staff acting as consultants, resource persons, prophets, evaluators, and critics. Whether the local congregation will remain as a parish group or whether it will be dispersed in many smaller groups will be part of the change to which we adapt in the coming years.

The tasks within the parish church become the laboratory for the primary task of "helping the helpless." Every task has two dimensions—that of growth of the individual and that of the challenge to perform a task that contributes to the total purpose. The priority of action as well as strength for the task lies in God. The organizational plan must point beyond itself to the Holy Spirit as teacher and counselor. The local church planning should recognize the presence of Christ as well as the continuing promise of God to his people as shown in the law.

## FOR ADDITIONAL READING

Adams, Rachel Swann. *The Small Church and Christian Education*. Philadelphia: The Westminster Press, 1961.

Dillistone, F. W. *The Structure of the Divine Society*. Philadelphia: The Westminster Press, 1951.

Gable, Lee J. *Christian Nurture Through the Church*. New York: National Council of Churches, 1955.

Grimes, Howard. *The Church Redemptive*. Nashville: Abingdon Press, 1958.

Johnson, Robert Clyde, ed. *The Church and Its Changing Ministry*. Philadelphia: The United Presbyterian Church, 1961.

Miller, Randolph Crump. *Education for Christian Living*. 2nd ed. Englewood Cliffs: Prentice-Hall, 1963.

Vieth, Paul H. *The Church School*. Philadelphia: United Church Press, 1957.

———. "The Local Church Organized for Christian Education," in *Religious Education: A Comprehensive Survey*, ed. Marvin J. Taylor. Nashville: Abingdon Press, 1960. Pp. 247-58.

Webber, George W. *The Congregation in Mission*. Nashville: Abingdon Press, 1964.

# Chapter 11

# THE DIRECTOR OF
# CHRISTIAN EDUCATION

## Gentry A. Shelton

THE VOCATION KNOWN AS "DIRECTOR OF CHRISTIAN EDUCATION" IS AS American as the Declaration of Independence or the 4th of July and as currently new as the twentieth century. The profession has had its beginning, advancement, and rapid development here in the United States. While Christian education is as old as Christianity itself, the "director of Christian education" is remarkably young in terms of the years of the Christian era.

After the separation of church and state in America the church accepted the Sunday school movement as its major teaching arm. The gratifying and almost overwhelming response seemed to indicate that the churches had found an answer to their dilemma and a way to confront children and youth with the teachings of Christ.

As interest and activity increased, the realization of the necessity for trained leadership began to bear fruit. Vanderbilt University organized a department of religious education in 1902, and the Hartford School of Religious Pedagogy was established in 1903. The new type of ministry soon found other schools preparing to train lay workers. The offering of graduate degrees in religious education quickly followed.

The new vocation appeared in 1909 when several larger eastern churches employed directors. By 1915 more than one hundred were employed, and by 1929 approximately three hundred churches were being served. The depression years of the 1930s caused the influence of the profession to decline, but only temporarily. The demand for trained directors has rapidly exceeded the supply. Today, although the opportunity for Christian service is great, not enough youth are in preparation to fill the increasing number of positions.

1965 statistics show almost 11,000 persons currently employed as Christian educators in local churches in the United States. The twentieth century has witnessed the advent and growth of this new ministry—the ministry of Christian education—a flourishing, important church vocation.

## The Task of the Director

In 1930 the director was defined as "a technically trained religious educator employed by a local church to have general charge of the educational aspects of its total program, and standing beside the minister as a professional member of the church staff." [1] The writer identifies the director as "the trained leader

[1] Harry C. Munro, *The Director of Religious Education* (Philadelphia: The Westminster Press, 1930), p. 16.

responsible for the total educational program, or a certain defined segment of the educational program of a church." [2] Wayne M. Lindecker, Jr., asserts that the director is "one specially trained to share in the ministerial function in churches large enough to require more than one minister: to serve in such a church on the ministerial team; to help plan the total staff approach to the work of the church and to serve as a specialist in guiding the ministry of education." [3]

Since the profession is still comparatively new and church groups have had difficulty in knowing and deciding what the director should do—definitive statements are few. Most pamphlets, articles, and brochures avoid direct definitions. Instead, much is written about what a director *should do* or what the director *should* or *should not be*. The 1960 statement that "denominations are just beginning to assume their responsibility for defining the new profession," [4] continues to be accurate today, for the process is still going on and the end is not yet in sight.

### What Is a Director of Christian Education?

1. The director is a minister. It is important that Christian education as a profession be considered fundamentally as a ministry. If not so conceived, little progress will ever be made toward defining or redefining the vocation as a distinct calling within the history and tradition of the church. The director, serving as a trained professional staff member of a church, in the broad concept is a minister, and the work of Christian education in the church is a *ministry to perform*. The director, man or woman, ordained or unordained, assumes the role of a minister by virtue of the responsibilities placed upon him by the employing church and congregation.

Professional leadership in Christian education, for many, can become little more than secular ventures in supervision, administration, group dynamics, pastoral counseling, etc.—but if a profession within the church perspective is fundamentally a *ministry* all of these tasks though creatively informed and assisted by secular views and skills become part of a spiritual ministry. The result, as far as outlook and approach and function are concerned, is vastly different. [5]

2. The director is an educator. The position of the director has been compared with that of the principal in a large public school because the director is the *administrator* of a definitely organized church school with a staff of teachers and other workers using a specific curriculum. A major difference

---

[2] Gentry A. Shelton, "A Study of Directors of Christian Education Among the Churches of Disciples of Christ in the United States" (Unpublished Ed.D. dissertation, University of Kentucky, 1954), p. 4.

[3] "The Status of the Director of Christian Education" (Unpublished lecture delivered to the American Association of Schools of Religious Education, December, 1959).

[4] William F. Case, "The Director of Religious Education," in *Religious Education: A Comprehensive Survey*, Marvin J. Taylor, ed. (Nashville: Abingdon Press, 1960), p. 260.

[5] James B. Miller, "Standards for Evaluating a School of Religious Education" (Unpublished lecture delivered to the American Association of Schools of Religious Education, December, 1963).

between the two lies at the point of the teachers. The school administrator works with teachers who are generally chosen because they have *already been* trained to teach and are paid for their work. The religious educator must set up plans, "aided by the other ministers and laity for the education of his *own teachers*." [6] In addition the church school teacher is a volunteer. The director thus must not only know *how* to teach, he must function as a teacher of teachers. "The director is first, last and always a teacher interpreting by daily living what is meant by the Christian life." [7] This requires an adequate understanding of educational techniques and procedures as well as an educational point of view. "The teaching responsibility is most directly fulfilled through the organized educational program. So the director helps the church develop an understanding of its goal and purpose which in turn determine and control its policies." [8]

The director is concerned with curriculum—the educational plan of the church—the training of leadership, and the development and encouragement of an educational approach for the total life of the congregation. This is necessary if the director is to lead in planning a comprehensive educational program in line with the policies of the church and if the educator is to coordinate the many educational activities of the church into one unified program. As educator, the director interprets the educational objectives and programs to the congregation. Since the Christian education program is concerned with persons, the director should know how to evaluate the life and work of the church in terms of the persons so involved.

The director must possess understanding of *administration* and *organization*. The ability to organize a comprehensive program of Christian education and see that it functions smoothly, efficiently, to the mutual benefit of all concerned is a demanding and continuing task. Although denominational groups have suggested organizational patterns, adaptations must be made. The cliché that "all congregations are different" is truer than one might wish to admit. The good director will use *administration* and *organization* not as necessary evils but as instruments to make the work of the church in Christian education what it should and must be if the ultimate is to be reached.

3. The director is a supervisor. Reduced to its simplest form supervision means that two people grapple with problems hitherto left to one. It suggests that the supervisor does not take over the task of another but helps to inspire and direct the other to greater accomplishments so that work may proceed on a thoroughly understood, cooperative basis. The director as supervisor must systematically and continuously endeavor to improve the quality of the church's total program of education.

The church has long been plagued with the fact that because of limited time and untrained teachers the educational achievement has been less than adequate. Christian teaching must be improved. If the objective of supervision

---

[6] "The Director of Christian Education," *Westminster Dictionary of Christian Education*, (Philadelphia: The Westminster Press, 1963), p. 199.

[7] E. W. Keckley, "The Ministry of Christian Education" (Unpublished manuscript, 1947).

[8] Taylor, *Religious Education*, p. 261.

is to transform the teacher into *his own* most *stimulating* and *exacting* supervisor, the task cannot be neglected.

The director should understand and be able to share the principles of supervision—of helping others—of using methods, skills, techniques, and resources to mutual advantage and above all to the advantage of the Christian community. As supervisor, the director works not only with individual teachers but with groups. In fact, some of the most effective work will be accomplished through groups—departmental groups, boards of Christian education, committees, etc. Through *observation, planning,* and *careful evaluation* after the work has been done, suggestions relevant to improvement can be made. Christian supervision today cannot be overlooked.

### What Does a Director of Christian Education Do?

The 1947 Directors Workshop listed responsibilities of directors, and the list is currently used.[9] The writer's study discovered that primary responsibilities were:

To organize, promote, supervise and administer, with the cooperation of the pastor, a program of Christian Education integrated into the total program of the church, which will meet the needs of all church members. To enlist and train adequate lay leadership, to lead all members into a better understanding and conception of the objective of Christian Education and to use the latest methods to accomplish these objectives. To guide people into a fuller understanding of and closer relationship with God and Christ. To help all persons grow into the fullness of Christian character and to nurture their deepening loyalty through the educational process. To be a consecrated, well-oriented, available, equipped resource person capable of motivating others to give of themselves for service to the Kingdom of God.[10]

Responsibilities considered secondary by directors include: pastoral, secretarial, musical, social and recreational, public relations, audio-visual, editorial, departmental advisory, community and denominational duties.[11]

One director says "that the director is in a sense the 'Conscience' of the educational program," [12] while another writes that the director is "a many splendored thing." [13] The director's scope of work is specifically concerned with the educational task of the church.

### Some Problems Which Must Be Faced

1. Status. The problem of the director's status should be faced realistically and honestly by ministers, directors, and churches. This problem which has

[9] *The Local Church Director of Christian Education* (New York: National Council of Churches, 1952), pp. 4-5.

[10] Shelton, "A Study of Directors of Christian Education Among the Churches of Disciples of Christ in the United States," pp. 138-39.

[11] *Ibid.*, p. 137.

[12] Mary Huey, *If You Want to Be Wanted* (New York: National Council of Churches, 1955).

[13] Louise McComb, *D.C.E.: A Challenging Career in Christian Education* (Richmond: John Knox Press, 1963), p. 23.

plagued the profession for years must be resolved if the continuing ministry is to flourish.

2. Instability. The profession has incurred a measure of instability brought about by all too brief length of service in local churches—the average is only two to three years. Caused by various reasons (securing of pastorates by men, marriage by women, uncertainty on the part of churches as to work of director, etc.), this image needs to be changed.

3. Title. Another problem is that of the director's title. Several have been used:

   a. Director of Christian Education

In recent years this problem has been thoroughly discussed and standards published. It is common knowledge among denominations (although not completely accepted by churches) that the title "Director of Christian Education" should be reserved for persons with adequate training. This includes a bachelor's degree and a master's degree from an accredited educational institution, or a bachelor of divinity degree from an accredited seminary wherein the work includes a concentration or major in Christian education.

A program for certification of directors has been in progress for several years in The Methodist Church and more recently in the Presbyterian Church, U.S., and the United Church of Christ. Methodist directors, to be certified by the church, must possess a baccalaureate degree plus one year of graduate work in Christian education and one year of work in a local church. Since December 31, 1965, the master's degree in Christian education has been required. The United Church requires the bachelor's degree and the master's degree plus one year full-time experience as a local church director and membership in the United Church. The Presbyterian Church, U.S., certifies workers with (1) the master's degree, or (2) the bachelor's degree plus seven years' successful experience, or (3) associates in Christian education with four years of successful experience. All three assume the highest personal qualifications.

   b. Minister of Christian Education

This title applies only to persons who are ordained as ministers by their respective denominations. They must possess a bachelor of divinity degree with a concentration or major in Christian education.

   c. Assistant (or Associate) in Christian Education

This title "should apply to any person employed by a local church to guide educational work, if he has a bachelor's degree from an accredited college, or has been and is actively working toward such a bachelor's degree." [14]

   d. Educational Associate or Assistant

The fourth title is sometimes used to designate workers in Christian education who have no college degree, and who may or may not have had one or two years' college training. While other titles (Program Coordinator, Program Director, etc.) appear from time to time, these several designations are recommended by denominational and interdenominational agencies.

4. Additional Responsibilities. In some churches directors, because of par-

---

[14] W. Randolph Thornton, "If You Want a Director," *The International Journal of Religious Education*, XXXVI (June, 1960), 19.

ticular training and/or ability, are asked to assume other responsibilities such as music, recreation, drama, pastoral assistant, secretary, etc. Such combinations may be necessary in churches not financially able to employ more than one professional staff person in addition to the minister.

Combination work can be satisfactory and helpful, however, only if careful consideration is given by the churches and the directors concerned. Complete understanding of the dual role of the persons must result.

## The Qualifications of a Director

Christian education, as a vocation, is a ministry in Christian service. Consequently basic devotion to Christ and his church must be unquestioned. Equally important is recognized Christian character. Trained and consecrated leadership possessing personal dedication, a depth of faith, and commitment is demanded.

Almost as important is a sincere interest in and ability to work with people. Unless directors possess a genuine love and concern for people and a readiness to accept them as they are, their work will not succeed.

Other personal qualifications include: knowledge of the educative task, attractive Christian personality, ability to work democratically as a member of a team, physical well-being, spiritual and emotional maturity, and commitment to a self-directed program of study and improvement. To these may be added qualities such as neatness, sense of confidence, tact, patience, leadership ability, resourcefulness, sense of humor, cheerfulness, creativity, tolerance, sincerity, and loyalty.

While few possess all of these attributes, everyone possesses some of them and others may be acquired. Of extreme importance are the first two.

### Academic Requirements

The ministry of Christian education demands directors with high academic qualifications so that they may meet the challenge of the present age. The major denominations suggest that directors possess a baccalaureate degree from a four-year accredited college and either a master's degree (M.R.E. or M.A.) or the bachelor of divinity degree with a major in Christian education from an accredited seminary. The difference in the bachelor of divinity and the master's degrees is not only the extra year of seminary study but the fact that denominations require the former for ordination. Studies show that most women seek the master's degree and most men the B.D. degree. More men B.D.'s are ordained than women although in most denominations women with B.D. degrees are not prohibited (by their sex) from ordination if they so desire.

Supervised field work and apprentice or intern training in local church work are highly desirable for persons during their seminary careers.

Certification (discussed above) seeks to improve the quality of Christian education workers in the church and to discourage the untrained workers.

### Continuing Personal Growth

Directors must include in their personal standards the desire for self-improvement. No professional person can remain static in the rapidly moving world and expect to do that which is required by the churches of Jesus Christ today. Christian educators must keep abreast of events since education goes on all the time. The church cannot employ persons who are living in the past. Directors must remember that no one will look over their shoulders and tell them that they must continue to learn—it must be self-motivated.

Self-improvement must include spiritual development. One cannot love God and seek to serve him without seeking to know him. The spiritual life should never be neglected. Periods for private devotion, meditation, prayer, and Bible reading must be included as a regular part of the daily life and habits of directors.

Self-improvement must include mental activity. "A director's workaday world fairly bulges with occasions for mental stimulation." [15] Such stimulation should include not only religious and educational material but also current local and international events. Directors live in the world—not apart from it. Reading, preparation for teaching, attendance at conferences, lectures, special courses, discussions with persons in other fields are readily available methods giving opportunities for directors to be stimulated mentally.

There is no excuse for directors to wither and die on the vine since opportunities for continuing educational experiences are increasing. Every denomination provides numerous conferences, institutes, and workshops (local, regional and national) in order that directors may continue to be involved in the learning process. Each denomination has national denominational directors' fellowships which meet annually and to which all directors of the denomination are invited. The meetings, conversations, and sharing with coworkers who are in the same discipline and who share many common experiences offer continuing inspiration.

At the interdenominational level the directors' section of the Division of Christian Education of the National Council of Churches offers local-church directors expanding opportunities for learning. Meeting annually, this fellowship has enjoyed phenomenal growth from thirty or forty in attendance twenty-five years ago to over eight hundred in 1965. This fellowship would be considered essential for those who desire to continue their professional growth. Participation in regional conferences sponsored by state or city councils of churches, local city fellowship groups, and ecumenical conferences (such as the World Council of Christian Education) will give directors an expanding perspective of the task of Christian education not only in state or region but throughout the world.

Directors must not neglect their own personal lives. Time must be given for family, recreation, hobbies, and other interests which relax and restore the person. Returning to work after moments which refresh gives a new zest and a renewed enthusiasm for the creative task which lies ahead.

Every director should constantly strive toward the goal of Christian maturity—a goal which can never be reached but which beckons one ever onward, ever upward. "Daily, monthly, and yearly, one has the privilege of struggling

[15] McComb, *D.C.E.*, p. 59.

to leave his 'low-vaulted' past and move upward—no matter how slowly—in his private pilgrim's progress." [16]

## The Director and Staff Relations

### The Professional Staff

It is extremely important that there be a clear understanding of the duties and responsibilities of members of a staff. However, the director's relations with the pastor should first be considered. The pastor is usually regarded as the chief executive or minister in charge. Most congregations hold him responsible for all that happens in the church and for the supervision of staff associates. While it is obvious that the director and the pastor should be coworkers with the director the second in command, there should never be boss-servant relationships. Directors should not be employed to do things which ministers do not want to do. Pastors and directors, as coworkers, coservants of the churches that employ them, work together as Christians, interested in the Christian fellowship, striving to share the message of Christ with those whom they guide and who look to them for leadership. They should be regarded as shepherds-of-the-flock, not as shepherd and assistant shepherd. They should be able to converse, have adequate time to talk through problems which each may face, receive mutual guidance and inspiration, and be loyal and uphold one another in the work that they are doing in God's kingdom.

Usually pastors, being older in years and experience than directors, will be able to give wise guidance to the fledglings. A greater degree of compatibility should occur when directors and pastors share something of the same theological position. Difficulties can arise if areas of work are misunderstood, or are not clear, if theological positions are far apart, or if there is fear that one will usurp, directly or indirectly, the position, influence, or image of the other. More unhappy situations have been the result of poor interpersonal relations between pastors and directors than any other problem. This does not have to be—and must not continue to inflict negative influences upon the profession.

"As organizations increase in arithmetic size, their difficulties in administrative cohesion grow in geometric proportion." [17] Many churches in America have found that their growth has made necessary the employment of multiple staffs to guide and direct the work of the congregations. As more professional workers are employed, the more important staff relations become. "The basic working relationship in the administrative team (the multiple staff) is that of sharing, of interdependence, or partnership." [18] Robert Edgar has said, "The key to any multiple ministry leadership is not in the structure, but in the Christian spirit of the ministers." [19] "Already the image of the ministry and

---

[16] *Ibid.*, p. 60.

[17] Ordway Tead, *The Art of Administration* (New York: McGraw-Hill Book Company, 1951), p. 179.

[18] *Team Work or Else* (New York: National Council of Churches, 1961), p. 13.

[19] "A Ten Year Experiment," *Pastoral Psychology*, XIV (March, 1963), 22.

of the pastoral role is being changed by the presence of a large number of multiple staffs." [20] While there must be some recognized authority, there should be a shared relationship resulting in effective ministry. Respect for each member as a Christian, for the abilities and professions of each member, ability to work as a team, dedication to the common task to which each is called, and an abiding spirit of love will make possible relationships among staff which will be constructive, binding, and challenging.

## The Laity of the Church

The responsibility for Christian education in the local church is centered in the board, committee, or commission of Christian education. The board, with the assistance of the director, must define basic principles as well as ways of accomplishing the task of Christian education. Through work with such lay groups the director's philosophy of education will be reflected, and the resulting influence will either permeate the life of the congregation or totally miss the mark. Consequently, it is extremely important for the director to work closely and intimately with the members. The director is the executive secretary of the board, works with the chairman in planning agendas, reports regularly, makes recommendations, and constantly seeks with the board to evaluate and improve the church's educational task.

Probably the most important lay workers with whom directors will be associated are church school superintendents. Such individuals are usually the chief administrative officers of the Sunday church school. Being volunteer workers and serving only part time, these persons can either be influential leaders or contented driftwood. Directors must help superintendents achieve greater comprehension of their task, encourage their growth through reading, sharing of ideas and ideals, personal confrontations, and through mutual respect. Again effective team work is necessary.

Directors in the role of teacher of teachers have a very important relationship to their church's teachers. This demands that they inspire as well as motivate those who fall under their leadership. Christian teaching must constantly be improved and encouraged, and a large portion of time will doubtless be spent in this work. Three separate surveys show that directors prefer the work of teaching teachers over almost all other areas of the task. Liaison must be maintained with the teaching staff and time made available for aid and assistance. Curriculum must be interpreted and suggestions of more desirable and helpful resources shared.

Directors maintain close associations with persons of all ages. They also have an obligation to these persons, for the church serves all ages from the nursery to the golden-years fellowship. Thus, directors must seek to know and understand those with whom they work. Their perspective cannot be limited to one age group. Parents must not be forgotten. Without the help and encouragement of the home the results of Christian teaching may be much less than desired. The home sets the climate which makes Christian teaching effec-

[20] Herman J. Sweet, *The Multiple Staff in the Local Church* (Philadelphia: The Westminster Press, 1963), p. 11.

tive or ineffective. Directors must help parents in their understanding of the church's educational and redemptive task, must encourage their efforts, and provide the guidance they often seek.

The world does *not* move forward on the feet of little children; it rather is largely formed or *de*formed by adults who are responsible for the forming of younger selves before such selves have much of a chance for independent decision. For this reason the church is increasingly coming to see that its program of Christian education must be aimed fundamentally at parents and that any work it may do with children is relatively ineffective unless this is the case.[21]

## The Church's Responsibility to the Director

### Employing or Calling a Director

Since Christian education is an important ministry of the church of Jesus Christ, the director should be employed (or called) by a local congregation just as the pastor is called. In most instances, according to church polity, this will be through proper committee recommendations (the pastor as an ex-officio member) with final approval by the congregation. The way directors are called reflects the importance given by the local churches to their ministry. Directors are sometimes employed by committees or even by individuals, with congregations feeling absolutely no direct responsibility. Since Christian education is a total church task, the calling of the person to direct the work must be the action of the entire church membership. The same procedure should apply to resignations.

### Job Descriptions

In recent years the job description or job analysis has become an important aid to churches as well as directors. While not yet universally accepted, the idea of preparing job analyses is gaining momentum, not only among directors but also churches that employ directors and denominations that place them. Where there are multiple staffs, each member should have a job description, including the pastor. If viewed analytically, the job description can be the basis for some honest probing on the part of congregations and boards of Christian education as they seek to define the work of Christian education. When descriptions are completed and published, many congregations for the first time have some understanding of the nature and scope of the work, as well as a clearer picture of what the extra staff member is really supposed to do.

The job analysis should not be a legalistic, binding agreement but rather a descriptive outline of areas of responsibility which are translated into life through the personality and activity of the director. Descriptions must be flexible and stress the importance of keeping channels of communication open at all times. To directors the job description is an imperative. Every recent study of the profession almost unanimously recommends the use of job descriptions. One major denomination has prepared a description, approved by

[21] Howard Grimes, *The Church Redemptive* (Nashville: Abingdon Press, 1958), p. 92.

its educational staff, which is recommended for use in its churches. The 1960 consultation recommended "that each denomination and/or local congregation prepare a job description that could be used in employing a director, minister, or assistant in Christian education." [22]

## Salary and Working Agreements

Directors should receive a salary commensurate with their years of preparation and service.

It may be possible in some cases to get a person to serve as director at a low salary. To do so is false economy. A church that pays a meager salary is not likely to hold a competent director. If a church pays its director a salary that compares favorably with that of the minister, and with the standard of living in the community, it may expect a teaching program that measures up to other phases of its work.[23]

The Educational Consultation in 1960 carefully considered the salary matter and made this recommendation:

The salary of the Director or minister of Christian Education, whose academic preparation is comparable to the pastor's and who has an acceptable background of experience, should be equivalent to at least a minimum of 65% of the pastor's salary. The beginning salary for the director, or minister of Christian Education just out of seminary, or who is in his first job as a director or minister of Christian education, may be slightly less than the above recommended minimum of 65%, but by the end of the second year of service, the salary should be in an amount equivalent to at least 65% of the pastor's salary at that time. It is recommended that annual increases be considered.[24]

This recommendation has been suggested as a standard so that churches and directors may evaluate themselves. While no pattern can be regarded as mandatory, churches must carefully examine their own actions as they consider the salaries of the professional staff. The problem of salary has always been with the vocation for there have been gross salary inequalities between pastors and directors. Many competent male directors accept pastoral appointments because of inadequate compensation. Churchmen must not react as did one pastor who emphatically stated that the total salaries of his two associates should not exceed the total of his salary. It is interesting to note that women directors still receive somewhat lower salaries than men.

Directors should receive the same consideration as pastors regarding salary increments and supplemental benefits. Directors would thus receive housing allowances, car expense, conference or convention expense, pension or social security benefits, equal vacation periods, moving expenses, and time off for additional study, if such time is granted the pastor. Attendance and work in

[22] Thornton, "If You Want a Director," p. 18.
[23] *The Local Church Director of Christian Education* (New York: National Council of Churches, 1952), p. 16.
[24] Thornton, "If You Want a Director," p. 19.

denominational programs should not be considered as part of the vacation period.

Churches should provide suitable office or study space, secretarial aid, one day off weekly, and remember that directors need time for regular study, prayer, and meditation.

### Responsibilities Beyond the Local Church

Directors cannot live in a vacuum. As residents of local communities they should be active, participating citizens. Not only do directors have leadership talents to offer, communities have benefits to offer directors. "The Director of Christian Education who has made non-church contacts beyond his own congregation and developed interest in the cultural life of the community is far more effective in his official duties than is the twenty-four-hour devotee who allows himself to become known as a church drudge." [25]

Care must be exercised, for it is easy to become community chore boys rushing to do the many volunteer tasks which may be assigned and thus neglect the employed task.

Outside activity must be recognized by churches as a necessary part of the director's total ministry. Encouragement rather than criticism should result.

### Whence and Whither the Profession

All indications point to the fact that the future of the ministry of Christian education is excellent. "The church is coming to a new age. Like it or no, the age of the specialist is here." [26] Directors are going to be needed for a long time. This period of the twentieth century finds a "buyer's" market for directors, since there are always more positions available than there are persons trained to fill them. The status of directors, long a problem, is improving, for the vocation is moving out of the second-class compartment and is more highly considered than at any previous time in history.

The new profession of religious education has experienced a normal growth, has outlined its objectives, erected professional standards, produced an amazing amount of literature, and formed societies and associations for its welfare and advancement. It has, in addition, afforded many persons, . . . of character, ability and personality, a vocational opportunity which was nonexistent a generation ago.[27]

So it may be said: "The best is yet to come."

### FOR ADDITIONAL READING

Grimes, Howard. *The Church Redemptive*. Nashville: Abingdon Press, 1958.
Lotz, P. H. and Crawford, L. W., eds. *Studies in Religious Education*. New York: Abingdon-Cokesbury, 1931.

[25] McComb, *D.C.E.*, p. 64.
[26] Lindecker, "The Status of the Director of Christian Education."
[27] P. H. Lotz and L. W. Crawford, eds., *Studies in Religious Education* (New York: Abingdon-Cokesbury, 1931), p. 46.

McComb, Louise. *D. C. E.: A Challenging Career in Christian Education*. Richmond: John Knox Press, 1963.

Munro, Harry C. *The Director of Religious Education*. Philadelphia: The Westminster Press, 1930.

Sweet, Herman J. *The Multiple Staff in the Local Church*. Philadelphia: The Westminster Press, 1963.

Taylor, Marvin J., ed. *Religious Education: A Comprehensive Survey*. Nashville: Abingdon Press, 1960.

Tead, Ordway. *The Art of Administration*. New York: McGraw-Hill Book Company, 1951.

*Westminster Dictionary of Christian Education*, ed. Kendig B. Cully. Philadelphia: The Westminster Press, 1963.

## Special Studies

Carpenter, Thomas W. "A Survey of Professional Educational Personnel in Churches of the American Baptist Convention." The Commission on the Ministry, the American Baptist Convention, New York, 1956.

Lindecker, Wayne M., Jr. "A Normative Description of the Certified Director of Christian Education in The Methodist Church." An unpublished Ph.D. dissertation, Boston University, 1961.

Shelton, Gentry A. "A Study of Directors of Christian Education Among the Churches of the Disciples of Christ in the United States." An unpublished Ed.D. dissertation, University of Kentucky, 1954.

## Other Resources

Denominational Boards of Christian Education usually provide pamphlets and reports on the office of Director of Christian Education.

The Division of Christian Education of the National Council of the Churches of Christ in the United States of America offers numerous published materials on the work and relationships of the Director of Christian Education.

# Chapter 12

# LEADERSHIP THEORY AND PRACTICE

*David W. Jewell*

ONE OF THE MOST SIGNIFICANT ALTERATIONS IN THE LIFE AND EXPERIENCE of the Christian church flowing from the Reformation is to be found in the implementation of the concept of the priesthood of all believers. While it can be safely said that the full implications of this affirmation have yet to be developed in the church, it is true that herein lies one of the elements giving uniqueness to Protestantism. The educational endeavor of the American church has been to express this idea, as here for a over a century and a half lay men and women have been working in a realm which elsewhere has been almost exclusively the province of the clergy or specialists.

Today we are more self-conscious than ever about the responsibility of each layman for his fellow Christian and for demonstrating his faith to people outside the church. We are finding new or renewed justification for the lay person to participate in the educational ministry of the church—even when the place and usefulness of the traditional form of church education, i.e., the Sunday church school, is under attack. Our concern today is not simply for better trained teachers for church school, but for more effective lay ministries both within and without the church as institution.

It is in light of this changing situation that we need to rethink our conception of Christian leadership. No longer can we operate in terms of laymen helping the ordained clergy do their job. No longer can we justify lay teachers simply because the minister does not have time. We are realizing now that at any time, in any situation, *any* Christian may be called upon to fulfill a leadership role or function. We need to understand, therefore, as completely and honestly as we can, just what it means to be a Christian leader. Thus we have first of all the task of developing a *theory* of leadership, not just a listing of skills required for leadership. We are beginning to recognize that the most practical thing one can have is a good theory. When we know what it is to be a Christian leader, then we can begin to talk meaningfully about how such a leader will operate.

In the development of such a theory or theology of Christian leadership, we will of necessity have to draw on two major sources: theology, or the church's understanding of what being a Christian means; and social science, or the information now available about human relationships and the dynamics of the interchanges between persons in groups of varying sizes.

130

## Leadership Theory

As we view the newer thinking about Christian education, shaped in part by changes in general education and by new theological constructions, we are aware at once that many of the more traditional conceptions of the teacher, the administrator, and the committee chairman need revision. The image, for example, of the teacher as one whose main function is to communicate interestingly certain information or "content material" to a passive group of pupils has been questioned seriously. This questioning is based upon the realization that much of the so-called important information about the faith is meaningless for modern children and youth unless it somehow becomes "alive" for them. The problem is most sharply seen in the metropolitan church where young people are faced early with the harshest "facts of life"; sophisticated in their awareness of these facts, which they find in immediate "existential" contacts, they have little or no verbal or intellectual symbols with which to frame and/or communicate this awareness. What verbal tools they do possess have no point of contact with the traditional language of faith or of the Bible.

A second prod to the questioning of traditional concept is the realization that it is not the specific language of the Bible, the actual words printed in "Das Buch," which is of ultimate significance, but rather that toward which the words point—their larger signification. This insight enables the Christian to discover he may be able to teach the Bible without using any of the usual biblical terminology—in fact, he may be teaching the Bible without using any words at all! More precisely, perhaps, we should say that a person can teach *that which the Bible teaches* without using Bible verses!

The raising of these questions and the understanding which can result from such "second thoughts" push us back now onto an old, old Christian truth about witnessing: Namely, what we are as persons is the most powerful communicator of faith. And this truth suggests that in the area with which we are dealing, Christian leadership, any situation wherein a Christian is given opportunity to demonstrate in him*self* as well as in his words—the thrust of faith—is a situation fraught with possibilities for teaching. Thus leadership is not narrowly confined either to certain structural roles one fills (i.e., chairman, classroom instructor, etc.) or to certain methodological patterns (i.e., discussion leading, recitation, lecture, etc.). A group leader is more than just a convener or chairman. A teacher is more than just a transmitter or lesson planner. Every Christian is constantly placed with other persons in situations in which some form of leadership is possible, and in fulfilling that leadership some teaching-learning is going on.

If we consider, for the moment, only the work of persons within the confines of the church and its program, leaving aside the significant and wide-ranging problem of the ministry of the laity, we are then forced to conclude that every worker in the church, lay and ordained alike, is called to fulfill a leadership role, regardless of the particular task. This is the case whether the worker is in an official leadership position or is simply a member of a church group. And in so concluding that every Christian is a leader we are expressing one facet of the Reformation principle of the priesthood of all believers.

For this reason it is imperative that each of us has a carefully worked out and theologically valid theory of leadership. Because whether we wish it or not we are "leading," and unless we are careful about our leadership much that we communicate, or teach, will be other than that which we most fervently hope to transmit. The principle here is simple: Nothing is taught that is not learned. It is not that we teach either Christianity or nothing, but that we teach either well (that is, teach the content and meaning of faith) or badly (that is, teach ideas, practices, and the like which contradict the *thrust* of faith). Nothing we do is without its consequences; we must be sure that the consequences bear some positive correlation to what we intend. An immediate practical implication of this thrust is one which we shall develop more fully later; namely, that *all* adult education in the church is, at least partially, education in leadership.

## Resources from the Social Sciences

The evolving of a theory of leadership must make use of the research of the social scientist, for he provides much useful information about the nature of leadership, the dynamics of human interaction, and the effect of leadership upon those human interactions. But a word of caution must be interjected here, since it is always a temptation to accept uncritically the insights of science and to build one's theory solely upon these. We need to use this knowledge but to work with it within our theological frame. For example, much of the research in group life and leadership has its *Sitz im Leben* in the industrial setting. What has been discovered there about the relationships among persons is valid for us, but this is not so for some of the values which directed the proposals toward certain goals and ends. How a factory supervisor relates to those under him, and what this does to those employees is significant, but in the church we are not concerned with production figures and reduced costs. But being cautious about our discrimination in use of knowledge from the social scientist is in no way a negative judgment on the researcher; it simply defines the limits which surround our application of his insights.

The literature in group dynamics especially is very rich, as is that from research in the nature of teaching and the meaning of a teacher's self-understanding. To attempt a survey of it in this chapter is impossible. We can only note some of the more significant works and suggest in the reading list places for further exploration.

### Kinds of Leaders

Within the literature there has evolved a consensus regarding leadership within which we can discern roughly four kinds of leaders, each with unique characteristics and with related forms of relationship between the leader and the group. Further, in each case there are certain definite results in terms of the climate within the group and the character of the group's life (including the kinds of relationships which exist among the group members). The four kinds of leadership have been categorized as follows: autocratic, benevolent autocratic, *laissez-faire,* and democratic.[1]

The autocrat is the one who takes upon himself all responsibility for decision-making. He literally drives members to the aims he sets and along paths he establishes. He evidences no real concern for the person of any group member but is interested only in accomplishing the task as he sees it. The results of such leadership are low morale, buck-passing among the members, poor participation, and lack of initiative or imagination. Most members resent the leader and are unwilling to cooperate with one another. When the leader is not present the group tends to disintegrate and movement toward the goal is markedly slowed. The group is dependent upon the leader.

The benevolent autocrat, while he has many of the above characteristics, plays the game differently. He is interested in the group members, wants them to be happy, and praises them as much as he criticizes them. His way of operation, however, is not truly that of a concerned "boss." Rather, he utilizes the technique of evoking loyalty to him as a person. Members are openly evaluated in terms of having fulfilled (or failed to fulfill) what the leader wants. Consequently, the members are told that they have pleased the leader (or displeased him) in a kind of emotional blackmail. Such a leader views any failure as a sign of personal disloyalty to him. The group is apt to be happier under this leadership than under the autocrat, although those who "see through" the leader feel intense dislike for him. There develops within such a group a large degree of dependence upon the leader, and no one tries anything new or suggests other options unless he is certain that the leader will approve. There is a good deal of submissiveness and some lethargy, and when the leader is out of sight group purpose meanders.

Under the *laissez-faire* type of leadership the leader literally abdicates. He tends to hide from the group by involving himself in paper work or other routine tasks. He leaves almost everything to the group, even the making of most of the major decisions, and even here he does not provide much guidance as the group struggles toward clarification and resolution. He tends to provide resources only upon request, seldom interjecting himself or his ideas into the situation. As a result the group will have extremely low morale and will seldom attain much movement toward its goal (which it may not even understand or perceive). Group activity is sloppy with disorganization making for duplication of effort, scapegoating is frequent, and teamwork doesn't exist. In voluntary situations such a group will rapidly disintegrate.

The democratic leader is one who sees his task as that of sharing many of the activities of decision-making, scheduling, and the like with the members. He will also involve the members in many functions which under the autocratic leadership are reserved to the "chief" alone. In a group with this type of leadership morale is strong, as is teamwork. Members display a good deal of initiative and responsibility for what the group is doing. In such a group

---

[1] See, for example, Leland Bradford and Ronald Lippitt, "Building a Democratic Work Group," *Leadership in Action, Selected Readings Series,* II (Washington: National Training Laboratories, N.E.A., 1961), pp. 52-61.

members tend to grow as persons, finding an atmosphere which is conducive to trying one's wings and so to discovering new things about oneself.

The concern for self-discovery has been found to be important in the literature in general education, specifically that about the teacher and his interest in the student's self-understanding. Arthur Jersild, of Teachers College, Columbia University, has been at the forefront of this research. He notes

The teacher's understanding and acceptance of himself is the most important requirement in any effort he makes to help students to know themselves and to gain healthy attitudes of self-acceptance. . . . It has become increasingly clear . . . that self-understanding requires something quite different from the methods, study plans, and skills of a "know-how" sort that are usually emphasized in education. . . . What is needed is a more personal kind of searching, which will enable the teacher to identify his own concerns and to share the concerns of his students.[2]

The insights from these two realms then, social psychology and learning theory, suggest that leadership which hopes to foster the growth of selves requires some growth in self on the part of the leader.[3]

## The Nature of Leadership

It is obvious that democratic leadership has most to commend itself to those who have as their main concerns the development of a cohesive group, the growth of persons, and the attainment of constructive purposes. Therefore, it is necessary to understand some of the elements in group experience which are set free to function by democratic leadership.

The type of leadership which we are here describing tends to understand group experience as consisting of the sharing among the members of most, if not all, of the elements required for both successful completion of a task and the growth of group feeling. In these terms leadership is seen not as an office held by one person, nor as an aspect of a person's character (his possessing charismatic gifts as the "hero" figure), but rather a linking of activities or functions any one of which can be carried out by a member. The established leader (appointed or elected) attempts to provide opportunities for each member to join in leadership functions rather than himself serving as the center and source of all these functions.[4]

The democratically led group gives more of its attention, especially early in its life, to developing among members the awareness that they are free to take on leadership roles and affords some experience of what these roles are and how to execute them. As the members develop skill and insight in participation in leadership, the group draws together more closely as a community and begins also to move more rapidly along the road toward fulfillment of its task. Thus, while such a group appears at first to be doing little about its job—

[2] *When Teachers Face Themselves* (New York: Bureau of Publications, Teachers College, Columbia University, 1955), p. 3.

[3] See chap. 24, pp. 278-91.

[4] For one discussion of these roles see Kenneth Benne and Paul Sheats, "Functional Roles of Group Members," *Group Development, Selected Readings Series,* I (Washington: National Training Laboratories, N.E.A., 1961), pp. 51-59.

whatever it is—before long it becomes far more efficient and productive than a group under any other type of leadership.

### Christian Leadership

We go back now to pick up the earlier thread, the weaving of the data from the social sciences into the theological view of what being a Christian means.

Immediately we can find interlacing points of contact. The gospel calls us to minister; and that ministry is to persons, not to an institution nor to any given set of theological ideas nor to some collection of biblical passages. The ministry is the same whether it takes place in a room full of pupils or around a table with fellow committeemen. We are first of all hoping to serve others that they might grow into more mature persons in a more profound relationship with God.

Christian leadership, then, would seem naturally to follow lines suggested by democratic leadership; for in this we find what one teacher has called a form of leadership like unto the midwife, i.e., one who assists at and helps bring into being something new! Further, because it is Christian leadership, the implication follows directly that it takes place within a particular community with its unique traditions and history, its own outlook on the world and its self-determined ways of living and acting. In short, a Christian leader is not only one who knows how to lead so that others will develop their faith, but he is also one who has himself engaged in and is now engaged in the process of personal and Christian growth. The Christian leader, by definition, is one who has some knowledge of the tools of leadership as well as some involvement in the life of the community and its wisdom. Such leadership requires specifically self-understanding, skills, and knowledge of the faith. The Christian leader in his ministry is both guide and enabler; that is, he can instruct others in the faith, and he can help them realize those talents and potentials inherent in their very being. So led, they are enabled to show the power of faith in their lives by the way they live and function as well as by the way they understand the world and man's experiences in it.

## Christian Leadership Practice[5]

We have now outlined our theory of Christian leadership and as a result have a basis for working out a consistent, educationally sound, and effective structure for leadership development. In attempting to fulfill its responsibility to implement its theory of leadership, a church will begin with an exploration of the specific leadership needs of its program, including both elective and appointive offices.

This audit of the tasks for which leaders are required will demonstrate clearly the variety of jobs and necessitate some itemization of the leadership required. Once such a study is completed, the responsible group (board of education or subcommittee of the official board) can consider what is presently

[5] Other useful material on this same subject can be found in Lee J. Gable, "Selecting and Training the Local Church's Educational Staff," in *Religious Education*, Marvin J. Taylor, ed. (Nashville: Abingdon Press, 1960), pp. 272-80.

going on, both in terms of leadership operative in the situation and in terms of the direction in which training programs must go. The end result of such an analysis should make clear what characteristics are desired and needed in the leadership (remembering that under the term "leader" we are including both teachers and other officers).

These data will make possible an intelligent evaluation of present leadership, i.e., levels of competency for particular tasks now being done among present leaders, and relevancy of present leadership training. It should also suggest some guidelines to be used in the selection of new leaders. What is hopefully obvious here is that persons should be selected in terms of their potential for the task, and not just because they are willing or available. One sure index could clearly be whether or not the candidate is willing to engage in leadership training opportunities, or is presently engaged in them, i.e., adult study groups.

In addition, this preliminary survey will make clear the scope of leadership training opportunities necessary to provide the best training for the persons available for the tasks for which they have been selected. We should not forget in the recruitment and selection process that the invitation to take on a leadership role will have more attraction if it can truthfully be said that the committee has selected that person after deliberation—that he has been selected with an eye to his competency or potential competency for the particular task at hand. Also, it follows from the above, that persons should be placed as carefully in leadership training programs as in leadership roles. In other words, just as leaders need to be selected individually, so also should their participation in training be planned with individual needs in mind.

### Training Programs—Resources

Obviously, we are suggesting that a wide range of leadership training programs needs to be made available, and in effect we are implying that the aims of leadership training programs will be different from time to time and program to program.

We have already noted that Christian leadership involves three dimensions which cannot be separated neatly in practice, although they are differentiated for purposes of discussion and description; the three are: self-growth, knowledge of the content of faith, and skill in leadership (teaching). Some programs for leadership training will be aimed more directly at one or another of these three dimensions while other programs will attempt some combination of two or three.

In many situations the local church does not have available resources to provide the wide scope of leadership training that has been implied above. This often means that an investigation of other sources of help will have to be made. In many communities it may well be possible for churches to cooperate by each providing one or two of the many varieties needed. Such a cooperative endeavor could be embarked upon if each church could discover its own strengths in resource people. Also, a group of local churches might be able to bring in outside trainers where a single church could not. Certainly this type of endeavor is most practicable in relation to leadership training which does not insist on too narrow a concern with one church's tradition. Such community programs would probably be most successful in terms of skill workshops and occasionally in self-growth of teachers. Although in the latter case there might be some divergence in aim, sheerly because in many instances self-growth will (or should) be tied into study of the faith itself, and here traditional differences (not as important as we tend to make them) can be a barrier to cooperative effort.

When the designated aim of the training program is such as to make denominational emphasis significant (as with curriculum workshops or the study of the unique tradition), then once again a local church may find it difficult to provide leadership from within itself or out of its budget. In such a case the place to turn is the district office (or other such small geographic division) of the denomination. Workshops and other types of leadership training opportunities are offered regularly by denominational staff people on a regional or state basis. Local churches should be alert to such services and make every effort, including financial assistance, to ensure that those leaders who will personally benefit from them are in attendance. It is also possible, at least in some denominations, to arrange for state or national staff personnel to provide leadership for programs set up by groupings of local churches.

There are also many other leadership training opportunities on the national scene. The best known example is that of the annual meeting of the Division of Christian Education of the National Council of Churches. Many denominations (as well as the N.C.C.) provide both general and specialized sessions during the summer months which make possible several days of concentrated work on leadership problems and practices. It is a certainty that many churches are not aware of the rich variety of opportunities presently available in this field.

Finally, there are many opportunities offered by departments of Christian education of local and state councils of churches. Often these are exceedingly effective and useful, but too often there is little awareness of them, or support, by local church leaders. It is important for the appropriate people in local churches to be reminded of such opportunities and to be urged to attend.

### Training Programs—Various Types

The types of programs that have been found useful for differing aspects of leadership education are legion. It is such a rich field that to particularize them even for purposes of description is difficult. What we shall do here is first to suggest something of their diversity in terms of aim or "content" and then to consider various forms within which the content might be presented.

First there is that wide range of areas under the general heading of *information-giving*. By this we mean those programs aimed at assisting the leader in growth in his knowledge and/or information of some particular subject area. Programs included here would be those aimed primarily at helping leaders master such fields as: Bible, theology, history, psychology, ethics, and the like.

Second are those programs aimed primarily at instruction in the *skills of teaching-leading*. Under this grouping would fall a large range of concerns which involve one in developing competency in the use and understanding of methods helpful in various leadership situations.

Third would be the training sessions aimed at guiding teachers and leaders in their own *self-understanding* and *personal growth* as persons and as Christians. By this is meant sessions which are so designed and led as to give the participants the opportunity to look at themselves both as individuals and as leaders, so that they might discover something of why they behave or respond as they do and thereby gain some measure of insight into ways in which they might function differently. This type of program is most difficult to plan and lead; it is also likely to be ultimately the most significant type, for leading is basically a matter of the kind of person one is—and only secondarily what he knows and is skillful at.

Earlier in the chapter it was noted that adult education is one form of leadership training. Let us begin here, then, with our consideration of the variety of programs a local church, or group of churches, might engage in to help prepare its leaders.

*Adult study groups* may be of all kinds, although most fall into one of two general forms: the classical type in which the main aim is simply the enjoyable acquisition of knowledge; and the more recent small study group which is concerned with personal involvement and growth through discussion and intimate sharing of ideas and experiences. The former usually provides its members with not only knowledge, when effective, but also the portrayal of leadership as the knowledgeable lecturing and answering of questions. While this is a legitimate assessment, contributing both content and method to leadership education, it may well suggest to some in the class that this encapsulates the "best" image of the leader. While it is true that in some kinds of situations this image of leadership is workable, the danger is that it leaves the impression that it is the only way to lead. Members of such a class need to balance this experience of leadership with some other experiences in which the form of leadership is different. This may be had simply by having the leader of the adult class use a variety of methods, or it may be provided by opening up other educational experiences to the class members. It is here that the other form of adult study groups can be important, for these provide an entirely different approach to study and to human growth. In other words, while adult study groups contribute to learning about leadership they, too, must be viewed in light of the need for more than one experience on the part of the leaders who receive instruction through them.

Concerning the adult groups whose aim is more personal growth through face-to-face confrontation in discussion, it must be said that the contribution to leadership development is more in the realm of self-growth than in acquisition of knowledge, although the latter should be a by-product. However, here, too, we note that not all leadership situations are amenable to the type of experience sought by the small group, and so leaders who participate in these may need yet another educational experience as a balance. After all, there are cases of material which are not "discussable" and situations in which presentation of ideas and information is best accomplished by lecturing.

A specialized form of adult study group, which may be seen in either of the above two types, is the *parents' class*. Here the unique element is that the membership consists of couples who are together by virtue of their common concerns as parents. While this is the organizing principle of the class, it is a mistake to think of this simply as a training ground for parents. It needs to be seen as not only an aid to parents who want help in becoming better parents, but also as an opportunity to help these persons become more mature as individuals. So once again, the Christian educational principle of concern for persons as persons provides a guideline and protection against the improper use of an educational situation.

One of the more common types of leadership education which we often overlook, or do not use most creatively, is *reading*. Many churches boast libraries, but even a cursory glance at the collection suggests its uselessness for educational purposes. The castoffs of well-meaning church members, old novels or outdated books of popular theology, and antiquated dictionaries and commentaries are not really much help in the modern church program. Those responsible for a church library need to select acquisitions with an eye to their contribution to the constructive growth of the readers. Changes in biblical scholarship in the last decade have made many of the older resources, if not useless, at least confusing when placed over against the newer curriculum materials. And any usable library should include an up-to-date collection of pamphlets (which people are more apt to read) and current issues of good magazines on church life and thought (as well as complete back files of the most significant periodicals). The librarian can contribute immensely, not only by keeping the library collection in order, but also by making particular persons aware of material of special interest to them. A new type of material which should be added to our church libraries is the whole range of documents of our time found on records and tapes.

Turning now to the variety of forms for training programs, let us first note that we have already suggested a few. The *lecture* is a legitimate educational method for certain kinds of purposes and should not be discarded. It can contribute much by providing a good deal of material in simple and well-ordered form. It can set forth ideas to stimulate thought and discussion, and it can provoke hearers to action. *Discussion* is also an excellent device for working with groups. While there are some aims and types of groups which cannot be satisfied with discussion alone, or discussion at all, it is still true that discussion does tend to create involvement and thus some degree of personal commitment to the matter at hand. It allows for a kind and depth of clarification which lecture and question-and-answer cannot, and, therefore, it may lead to more change in a person than the simple acquisition of knowledge can effect. Participation in a properly led discussion can also teach group members something about the appropriate way to come to grips with a difficult problem requiring resolution. Such discussion, however, is not to be confused with either the classic "bull session" or "brainstorming." The former is simply an unguided sharing of ideas and opinions, and the latter is a technique for stimulating imagination and collecting a variety of ideas on some particular issue. Both may be useful at appropriate times, but they have to be used with care.

We have mentioned a variety of kinds of meetings, local, community, and national. We need now to consider the various forms which such meetings might take, remembering that they may include within them various methods, including those already mentioned, and may be planned by any one of many different groups.

A *conference* can be an amalgam of many forms, but it is usually distinguished by more emphasis on information-giving and sharing, depending in the main upon presentations by experts from whatever fields of interest are being considered in the particular conference. One is more apt to find in a conference, lectures, audio-visual presentations, and question-and-answer periods, with discussion devoted primarily to clarification of matter presented earlier. In most cases we think of conference delegates as fulfilling a role somewhat more passive than active since their activity rarely helps shape the very nature of what goes on.

A *workshop* is characterized by more active involvement of the persons attending. There is likely still to be great dependence upon visiting experts, but they participate more in terms of resource people who have to work somewhat "off the top of their heads" rather than from prepared lectures. Of course, in a workshop the participants actually do some "work." They will, for example, if the workshop is centered on the creative arts, actually try out certain arts, techniques, and crafts as well as hear related lectures and have discussions about the place and value of the arts in learning. Here the educational principle of direct involvement is applied to the task at hand so that all go home having actually done some of that which is discussed in the more formal part of the program.

An *observation school,* which may be part of a workshop, is a situation in which teachers (leaders) are given the chance to see a competent teacher (leader) in an actual leadership situation with real class (group) members. The observation school can be as simple as taking some teachers to see a class in session in another church or in a local public or parochial school. Care is taken in the selection of the class to be observed, and careful plans are made with the teacher and school officials ahead of time. The observers are also given some instruction in how to behave and what to look for while observing. Usually such an experience is followed by an evaluative discussion of what was seen.

A *demonstration school* is much like the observation school except that the situation is created by a specialist working with a group brought together just for the period of the school. In this case there is greater opportunity for discussion about the session with the teacher-leader both before and after the session (or sessions), so the observers have a chance to gain some insight into the reasons why the teacher-leader does certain things and what she hopes to accomplish with the group. The demonstration school (which may be part

140

of a conference or workshop) is an excellent way to sharpen up experienced teachers and to introduce new teachers to the teaching task.

The *laboratory* situation is a further refinement of the demonstration situation. The significant difference is that it actually presents an opportunity to student teachers to try themselves out within a situation which is carefully structured and surrounded by guides who can help in the planning, teaching, and evaluating of the student's work. The "lab school" situation is a refinement also of the student-teacher experience so prevalent in many teachers colleges. The student-teaching experience usually runs over a long period of time and is likely to have over-all supervision but not the intensive and immediate kind possible in the lab school, for in the latter every moment of the student's teaching is under careful observation. The same type of experience can (ought) also be structured for the committee chairman or congregational moderator. This type of training experience is difficult, and not a little painful. But it is probably the best single approach to leadership training because in the most intense and rich lab school experience the student teacher (leader) not only tries himself out in a real leadership situation, but also learns a good deal about himself as well as his pupils (group). Further, he discovers something about his knowledge of the subject matter, whatever it may be, for he has to prepare a real lesson for real students and the questions from a "live" class can be penetrating, making clear where one has not dug deeply enough or reflected sufficiently.

It is possible to use any of these forms of education for leadership in a local situation, but they are frequently more possible in some cooperative endeavor. However, it is feasible and most effective to make the monthly teachers' meeting a time to introduce on the local level some of the types of experiences coming through conferences, workshops, and the like. Certainly, during this traditional periodic convening of teachers and staff, more should be offered than the hashing over of minor details of church school administration.

There are a few other types of educational experiences for leaders which can be used in the local situation without much, if any, dependence upon outside resources. *Supervision* of teachers by someone with some experience and training (such as a local public school teacher or administrator) can contribute greatly to teacher development. Observation of committee meetings by a businessman who has had training in group procedures can help to improve the quality of meetings throughout the church's life. However, what is involved here is not a task that anyone can do at just any time. It is imperative that the supervisor (observer) first gain the trust of the teacher (leader) with whom he will work. Only then can the supervisory visit be made and the groundwork laid for the evaluative post-session conversation with the teacher (leader) in which strong and weak points are analyzed and insights glimpsed to be remembered for future sessions. A variant of this procedure is to be found in the growing use of *classroom observers* or *co-teachers*. In this type of situation the second person in the classroom is present every time the class meets (this can be done also with committees). The observer may even do some of the teaching, but his primary task is to be the noninvolved eyes and ears of

141

the teacher. One who is not carrying the burden of leading can see and hear more of what goes on than can the responsible leader. After each session this observer can share with the leader insights and suggestions which greatly enrich the leader's understanding and planning for the next session.

## Conclusion

The caliber of the educational life of a church will be determined not by the programs that are available, but by the character of the leadership available. Whether or not any program of education or committee structure will be effective in helping a church fulfill its ministry depends upon what the leaders bring to their particular service. Therefore, it must be emphasized that care in selection and training of leaders may well be the point at which a local church stands or falls in its effectiveness.

We have said above that it is imperative that every church develop a cogent theory, and one such theory has been outlined. We have also described some of the general forms in which a particular theory might be expressed. It needs to be noted that these are suggestive only, not the complete description of all that might be done. Along with the development of a theory, each church should exercise its creativity by experimenting boldly with new forms of training. Our call is to stewardship of whatever talents and opportunities the resources of the congregation and the community provide. We fail if we limit ourselves to the practices of the past, only the tried and true. As the demands and pressures of society change, we must be open to new ways of going about the work which has been set before us. One way in which we can do this is to keep ourselves informed of new experiments as reported in various educational and religious journals and to be responsive to the opportunities and experiences afforded by the workshops and conferences in which we participate.

## FOR ADDITIONAL READING

Adult Education Association of the U.S.A. *Leadership Pamphlets*. Numbers 1, 4, 6, 7, 8, 9, 10, 11, and 14 are most valuable.

Bennett, Thomas R., II. *The Leader and the Process of Change*. New York: Association Press, 1962.

Buchanan, Paul C. *The Leader and Individual Motivation*. New York: Association Press, 1962.

Douglass, Paul F. *The Group Workshop Way in the Church*. New York: Association Press, 1956.

Howe, Reuel L. *The Miracle of Dialogue*. New York: The Seabury Press, 1963.

Jersild, Arthur T. *When Teachers Face Themselves*. New York: Bureau of Publications, Teachers College, Columbia University, 1955.

Lippitt, Gordon L. and Seashore, Edith. *The Leader and Group Effectiveness*. New York: Association Press, 1962.

Maves, Paul B. *Understanding Ourselves as Adults*. Nashville: Abingdon Press, 1959.

National Training Laboratories. *Selected Readings Series*. No. 1: *Group Develop-ment;* no. 2: *Leadership in Action;* no. 3: *Forces in Learning*. Washington: National Education Association, 1961.

Ross, Murray G. and Hendry, Charles E. *New Understandings of Leadership*. New York: Association Press, 1957.

Weschler, Irving W. *The Leader and Creativity*. New York: Association Press, 1962.

Ziegler, Jesse H. *Psychology and the Teaching Church*. Nashville: Abingdon Press, 1962.

# Chapter 13

# RESEARCH AND EVALUATION IN CHRISTIAN EDUCATION

## D. Campbell Wyckoff

RESEARCH IN CHRISTIAN EDUCATION IS A SEARCHING OUT OF FACTS AND relationships through which theory and practice may be better understood. Evaluation is a systematic comparison of some aspect of Christian education practice with the standards that should characterize operations in that area, looking toward the identification of points at which improvement is needed.

So defined, research has a crucial role to play in evaluation in establishing standards, getting at existing situations accurately, and discovering the conditions for improvement. In this practical aspect the role of both research and evaluation is to awaken, inform, correct, and give new direction to Christian education in the home, church, and other community agencies. By the nature of participation and control in the agencies involved, this role is best played in a completely cooperative spirit.

The role of research in Christian education, however, is not confined to helping in evaluation. The process and findings of basic research (theological, biblical, historical, behavioral, and educational) help define Christian education, determine its objective and approaches, formulate its curriculum, and shape its structures, agencies, leadership, and patterns of participation.

## The Field

Thus Christian education research encompasses the field of theological and scientific inquiry in both social and individual aspects of Christian experience, while evaluation puts the results of such inquiry to use in appraisal and decision-making.

The nature of scientific inquiry in religion is, of course, problematical. However, it seems clear that inquiry into individual experience may at least examine and interpret significant exterior data while exploring the possibilities of the inner world. And social inquiry may gather and assess data on religious groups and institutions by seeing the institution in its total social setting, maintaining objectivity in observation, and interpreting the findings cooperatively.

Christian education research and evaluation, to make the matter specific, takes place in a field that includes at least the following:

1. Theological research into the nature of the learner, the nature of the learning process, the implications of theology for education, and the appropriate and necessary means for Christian education.

2. Historical research, making it possible to reassess the work of Christian educators of the past and to get the present into perspective.

3. Research into the nature, history, status, and use of the Bible.

4. Behavioral research, developing empirical findings in religious experience and integrating them into a psychology and sociology for religious teachers and counselors.

5. Research on the relationships between the social order and religious experience (social psychology of religion), and their implications for education and social action.

6. Research in the implications of the community's "secular" life for Christian education.

7. Research and evaluation in religion and Christian education in the home.

8. Research and evaluation in the church's program of Christian education: objectives; functions; professional roles; organizational structures; finance; the church school, including method, curriculum, and administration; and the educational implications of the church's worship, preaching, mission, and social action.

9. Research and evaluation in curriculum: purpose, scope, process, context, personnel, timing, design, sequence, settings, organization, and format.

10. Research and evaluation in leadership education, including the training experiences needed and the conditions for maintaining creativity in leadership.

11. Research and evaluation in religious and Christian education through community agencies: the public school, youth-serving agencies, and the mass media.

12. Research and evaluation in the functions of denominational and inter-denominational structures and agencies in Christian education.

## Background and Status

Research and evaluation in American Christian education was at first a concomitant of the interest in psychology of religion, and tended to wax and wane with that interest. The peak was reached with the publication in 1927 of Goodwin B. Watson's *Experimentation and Measurement in Religious Education,* and in 1928-30 of the Hartshorne and May *Studies in the Nature of Character.*

To the extent that this interest was sustained in the intervening years, it has been through the efforts of Ernest M. Ligon and his Character Research Project. Among other activities C.R.P. has conducted basic research since 1935 in Christian character education and in such areas as individual differences, the home and family, youth work, learning, and experimental design. Ligon has described his position, methods, and findings in *Dimensions of Character* (1956).

A modest revival of concern for the psychology of religious experience is evidenced in the results of the 1961 Research Planning Workshop of the Religious Education Association. The publications of the workshop include *Review of Recent Research Bearing on Religious and Character Formation* (1962) and *Research Plans in the Fields of Religion, Values, and Morality and Their Bearing on Religious and Character Formation* (1962). The Religious

Education Association has taken the lead in trying to spur interest in empirical research in religious education.

Another tangible evidence of revival of interest in this area of research is Lutheran Youth Research, participated in by several midwestern Lutheran denominations. The first published product of Lutheran Youth Research is Merton P. Strommen's *Profiles of Church Youth* (1964), whose most startling finding is the discrepancy between youth's self-perception and the perception of those same youth by their adult church leaders.

Spurred on by developments in American education, religious education had a coming-of-age educationally between World War I and the great depression. Characteristic of the extent and sophistication of interest in research and evaluation in this phase of development were Walter S. Athearn (ed.), *Indiana Survey of Religious Education* (1924) and Ernest J. Chave, *Supervision of Religious Education* (1931). The fruit of this work was put at the church's disposal in Otto Mayer's *Measurement in the Church School* (1932), but the timing of the publication of this booklet doomed it to neglect.

After World War II this aspect of Christian education research took on new life in the denomination-wide Christian education study of the Presbyterian Church in the United States and the Long Range Parish Program of the several cooperating Lutheran bodies that later joined to form the Lutheran Church in America.

As interest in psychological investigation waned in the late 1920's, sociological studies of religion increased and have been sustained up to the present. Summarizing work to that point and setting the standard that prevailed for two decades was H. Paul Douglass and E. deS. Brunner's *The Protestant Church as a Social Institution* (1935). To the sociological investigator, however, Christian education was a side issue and was looked at only in institutional light.

In the late 1950's, however, the concern of sociologists of religion for more than demographic and institutional matters began to become clear. This was evidenced by the broadening range of research undertaken by the Department of Research of the National Council of Churches. For many years the Department had confined itself to the collection of dissertation abstracts, statistics, and data required for policy decisions of units of the National Council, so far as Christian education was concerned. Typical of its later and newer concerns is the Presbyterian National Educational Survey, which the United Presbyterian Church commissioned the Department to undertake on its behalf.

Research and evaluation are costly in time, energy, and funds. They require highly trained workers who not only must have the skill and patience to do their research jobs, but who also can work with practitioners to identify problems, gather data, interpret the data, and get at implications for action. Practitioners, including administrators, have for the last decade been acutely aware of the need for such persons in the decision-making process in Christian education. The result is that there is scarcely a denomination without a new or enlarged research department, manned by trained personnel in research, evaluation, and curriculum development.

## Where Research and Evaluation Fit

As the Christian educator works out his job, a structure of thought emerges, dominated by his definition of the Christian education task and the objective or objectives that he sees as focusing the task. There are learning processes, dynamics of interpersonal influence (including teaching), and ways in which God deals with man and man responds, that he comes to see as keys to implementing the objectives and accomplishing the task. His methods develop from such considerations. Facing the responsibility for setting up a plan by which the church (including the family and other church structures beyond the parish) may fulfill its educational task, the educator shapes up a curriculum and program. The curriculum and program, in turn, require administrative implementation (planning, organization, management, and supervision).

In the supervisory area research and evaluation come into play. Supervision is a matter of setting standards, evaluating, and systematically improving the curriculum and program of Christian education. When the criteria for curriculum and program have been determined, evaluative processes are possible, including appraisal of individual attainment and appraisal of program and process. Here testing, the personal case history, assessment of teaching and group leadership, survey, institutional case studies, and research, all find roles. The appraisal process, in turn, provides information and guidance for systematic improvement through personal supervision, field supervision, leadership education, structural reorganization, and curriculum revision.

## The Process of Research

Research properly begins with a person, a parish, a community, a denomination, or a council of churches that is faced with a problem, must answer a question, or has a concern. Pressing as the problem may be, it often goes unsolved because of lack of precise formulation. The researcher does not invent the problem, though he is able to help in taking a vague and undefined problem area and reducing it to logical series of formulated problems that lend themselves to sequential study. He does not initiate the question, but he is in a position to help in asking it clearly and in planning to answer it, including the finding of ways in which to get pertinent and reliable information on it. He does not produce the concern on which to work, but once the concern is keenly felt, he can assist in analyzing and tackling it.

This basically auxiliary role of research must be kept in mind at all times, both by the researcher himself and by the person or group whose problem, question, or concern is to be dealt with. This is a fundamental principle that states a relationship that must not be violated.

Having stated this principle of research's auxiliary role, however, two misconceptions are to be avoided. The first is that the researcher must wait around for piecework to develop in the form of immediate problems, questions, and concerns that persons and groups need to have worked on. The fact is that the researcher would not be in a position to be of much help in such cases were he not working away constantly on a long-term basis at the identification of the great clusters of problems that the church and its faith inevitably face over and over, and were he not gathering and analyzing great stores of primary data concerning these problems. This is basic research, and it provides a framework of understanding from which any particular problem may be more readily identified and interpreted. Such basic research also helps to provide the experience and skill with the tools of research that may be brought to bear upon particular problems as they arise.

The second misconception is that the contribution of research to the solution of problems is mechanical or merely technical. The researcher may be a statistician; he may know how to manipulate the machines into which raw data are fed and from which refined facts emerge. But he can make his real contribution only if he is accepted as a full participating member of the team that is working at the problem, trying to answer the question, or exploring the concern.

What this means is, on the one hand, that the researcher is not to be expected to devise problems by himself and to work them out in olympian isolation, and, on the other hand, that he is not to be reduced to the status of a mere technician. His proper place is as a contributor to the identification and definition of the problem, question, or concern; to the formulation of hypotheses; to the testing of these hypotheses; and to the interpretation of the findings.

These four steps of contribution are, in fact, a definition of the research task. To understand the role of research, each needs to be examined.

The *first step* in research is the identification of the problem, the articulation of the question, the nailing-down of the concern. A foggy perplexity is impossible to study. Yet that perplexity may be very real and may present itself as desperately needing resolution. The task of the researcher is to ask those questions about it that will eventually yield some logical analysis, some pinpointing of the heart of the question, some focusing of the concern. The researcher knows that the problem has been identified when the reaction is, "Yes, that's it. If we get at these issues, we will have what we need."

The *second step* in research is the formulation of hypotheses. Reduced to its simplest terms, this means the stating of the most astute guesses that can be made as to the solution of the problem, the answer to the question, or the outcome of the concern. These guesses must then be weighed and the most promising selected for testing.

The question may be raised about the value of taking the time and effort to formulate hypotheses in this way. Yet this is the heart of good research. Let a researcher work through to the point where he has a good hypothesis, and he can proceed to test it and arrive at a clear idea of the degree to which it is a valid solution to the problem. Once the degree of validity of a particular hypothesis has been determined, it may be discarded, adopted, or modified intelligently.

What are the alternatives? One alternative is to muddle along without the formulation of hypotheses or the weighing of the hypothetical possibilities. But does not this reduce itself to dependence upon outworn hypotheses and the avoidance of the problems themselves? The other alternative is to act upon the first appealing hypothesis that presents itself. This is a rash, if very common, process by which vast time, energy, and expense are poured into all too often abortive attempts to solve our problems. Sometimes, however, two appealing hypotheses present themselves to two different people at the same time. The attempt to handle them without research leads to some of the worst and most destructive political clashes that the church experiences.

The *third step* in research is the testing of those hypotheses that have been chosen as most promising. Here the researcher is able to bring all his experience and skill to bear upon the problem in the most meaningful way. He must, of course, select the most appropriate research methods. For the testing of certain hypotheses, methods of biblical, theological, or philosophical research may be most appropriate. In connection with hypotheses of a sociological kind, he may conduct social surveys, make case studies, or gather statistical data. The crucial questions he must ask himself are: What data are needed for the testing of this hypothesis? Where are the data? How may they be gathered? How may they be analyzed? How may they be interpreted?

One of the researcher's persistent problems is that of knowing how to stay on the track at this point. A good hypothesis is what he needs. If he can keep his study, analysis, and interpretation trained upon it, he will not wander far afield. The result will be a clear judgment on the hypothesis. He will then know whether the hypothesis is sound. If so, he may be secure in acting and building upon it. If it proves not to be sound, he may be secure in rejecting it. If it proves to be partially sound, he will have some idea of how to modify it so that it may be tested again, possibly with greater success.

Important as it is for the researcher to stick to the point, there are important by-products that may be developed along the way. No research is conducted without producing hints of new problems that might be investigated and promising hypotheses that might be tested. The resourceful researcher will note these, catalog them, and hold them in reserve for later attention.

The *fourth step* in research is the indication of the meaning of the findings. In some kinds of research the researcher himself, having summarized his findings, projects his conclusions. It may be valuable for any researcher to do this. Yet this is a point at which the cooperative character of the enterprise is likely to be most productive.

E. deS. Brunner used to tell his students that after they had the data of community analysis before them, they had to spend hours and days staring at them, rearranging them, dreaming over them, and letting them finally tell what they really meant. An individual may do this. But in the case of Christian education it would be better for many individuals and groups together to do the kind of creative meditation and interpretation that is implied. Here the researcher's strength is indeed in his auxiliary role. In no sense should he withdraw. Neither should he arrogate to himself the sole responsibility for interpretation and determination of the meaning and significance of the findings.

All this, in addition to spelling out the basic process of research in problem-locating and problem-solving, reinforces the earlier point that the researcher and the person or group with the problem will be most productive if they work closely together. The researcher does not stand alone.

## Distinctive Contributions of the Researcher

While it will be readily recognized that the research process, as presented here, is a delineation of the process that would be followed in any careful and intelligent problem-solving situation, there are characteristic contributions that the researcher adds that improve the process and make it more dependable and productive. These characteristic additions from research might be called tools, skills, resources, findings, a "stance," and a theoretical framework. In order to make the picture complete, a word about each is necessary.

The distinctive tools that the researcher brings to the problem-solving process may be illustrated by mentioning such things as logical control, statistical methods, survey techniques, case-study method, testing, sampling, and depth interviewing. These are only illustrations, but they perhaps indicate the types of tools that a researcher has at his disposal for use when he is a part of a problem-solving team.

A researcher's skills are not truly distinctive, except as experience and training have enabled him to develop a degree of proficiency in using them that is not characteristic of the ordinary problem-solver. These skills cluster in the areas of problem identification, problem analysis, and the collection and interpretation of data.

The resources which the researcher has at his command may be illustrated well in our particular field. Interest, personnel, and funds that would not otherwise be available are opened up to us when it becomes clear that we are concerned for tackling our problems in this serious way. A religious body plagued by a problem is not of great interest to universities, foundations, or research bodies. But, when that problem has been pressed to the point of formulation and there is a determination to submit it to research, then there will be genuine interest on the part of universities, foundations, and research bodies. Furthermore, there is a professional sense of participation in a common enterprise among researchers of many different interests that ensures against parochial handling of our problems.

When we speak of the findings that the researcher can make available, we mean those inventories of data that have been gathered by researchers over the years. They consist of the accumulated experience of research in any problem area. The person or group requiring that a problem be solved may become temporarily annoyed at the delay while the researcher makes a careful review of what is already known through research in the problem area under consideration. The value of this procedure proves itself, however, in every case. The tragedy is that so little time has been available for the systematic collection and publication of the research inventories that are so desperately needed.

The "stance" of the researcher is (even though it sounds like a contradiction in terms) one of detached involvement. The researcher probes deeply into the problem area; he identifies himself with it. Yet at the same time he has to be shown. In many ways it is precisely this stance of detached involvement that makes him such a valuable member of the problem-solving team. He could not contribute to the solution of problems were he not involved. He could not make his distinctive contribution were he not skilled in detached observation and reservation of judgment.

Possibly the most significant contribution of the researcher to the solution of problems is his ability to construct and use a theoretical framework within which to operate. To see a problem in the most meaningful context is to have that problem well on the way to definition and possible solution. The theoretical framework to which the researcher should be able to refer the problem ought to be both conceptual and methodological. What is the framework of ideas that can provide this problem with a meaning and a setting? What framework of research method holds promise for this case?

A comment is required on the use of the findings of research. No complaint is more often voiced than this; that time, effort, and expense have produced "research" but that it has not been heeded in decision, policy, and practice. The cooperative role which I have suggested between those who initiate research and the researcher himself should tend to reduce this difficulty. If the problem is identified, analyzed, researched, and the findings interpreted cooperatively, then it is likely that the researcher will not go off on some tangent that will make his work seem irrelevant. The likelihood is also that the findings of research will be taken more seriously by those who have watched and participated in the development of each step in the problem-solving process.

## The Evaluation Cycle

No program of evaluation has been effective until implications for next steps toward improvement have been derived from it. The full cycle in evaluation and appraisal is the recognition of a problem or need, the examination of the existing situation in order to analyze and describe it accurately, the setting of standards or criteria by which to judge the existing situation, comparison of the existing situation with the standards in order to ascertain points at which the standards are met and points at which they are not met, and the identification of implications for improvement and corresponding steps toward improvement. The outcome, without which the process is likely to be somewhat meaningless, is consciously arrived at decisions for change.

## Program Evaluation

The Christian education program of a church is the organized structure by which its responsibility for its teaching mission is fulfilled. This program inevitably involves dynamic interchange among many groups and persons. Realistic appraisal of the program begins by taking this complex interchange into account.

The major parties to the interchange that constitutes the Christian education program of a church are: the church itself, its members and constituents; the denomination and its distinctive character, purpose, mission, program, and standards for the local church; the community in which the particular church is located, its problems, opportunities, and challenges; the curriculum that is in use, its purpose, scope, context, process, and design; the participants in the program with their education, aims, interests, needs, and Christian experience; the parents of the children and youth who are participants in the program, and the homes from which they come; the leadership of the program including teachers, administrators, and other leaders; the buildings and equipment that are available for the program; the personal and financial support of the program; and the organization and management of the program.

In every church all of these are blended into some kind of program of Christian education. The ultimate test of the program itself, of these various elements that make it up, and of the way they are blended, is whether or not in really significant and appropriate ways the objective of Christian education is realized and the purpose and mission of the church fulfilled.

But out of these various elements and their interchange a program is forthcoming. It is for this particular program that accurate description must be sought and applicable standards developed.

The *first step* in program evaluation, then, is the setting of *useful categories* that will allow for complete and comprehensive description of the particular program. A simple set of categories, in terms of which most programs could be described, might be as follows:

The purposes of the program
Lines of responsibility and authority
  The governing body
  The officers and their duties
  Channels for communication between the governing body, the officers, and other leaders and participants in the program
Organization of the participants (recruitment and attendance, grouping and grading)
Organization of the staff (job descriptions, recruitment, tenure, staff relationships)
The curriculum
Building, equipment, and supplies
Finance
Operational services (maintenance, audio-visual, library)
Public relations
The total program for children (Sunday, weekday, vacation)
The total program for youth
The total program for adults (including coordination of educational activities of men's groups, women's groups, young adult groups, and groups of older persons)
Christian education in the home
Cooperative community services
Supervisory services
Leadership education

The *second step* in evaluation is to describe the existing situation in the local Christian education program in each of these categories (or whatever set of categories is really appropriate). The best method for doing this is the conducting of a *survey* through which factual data on each aspect of the program systematically are collected, recorded, and compiled into a "profile" of the program, a self-study or a "case study" of the program of the particular church. Enough data ought to be collected so that the church is sure that the picture is complete and accurate, but not so much that it uses up the time and energy that needs to go into other aspects of the evaluation. There is as a rule, however, a healthy zest injected into the situation when the factual study begins to reveal the situation for what it really is.

The *third step* in evaluation is the setting of *standards*, using exactly the same categories as those used to describe the situation. Thus, there will be standards that indicate what the cooperative community services of the church ought to be in Christian education, with which the actual cooperative community services may be compared, and so on for each category.

Who should set these standards, and how? If the evaluation is being conducted by a committee that has been set up especially to do so, this committee may very well take the initiative in suggesting standards. In doing so, however, the committee should be certain that opinions and suggestions are sought from those capable of and interested in the program as a whole and in its various aspects. Suggested standards should be referred to the proper persons and groups for revision and ratification. In other words, the setting of standards should be a cooperative process from start to finish.

The cooperative setting of standards is a health-giving procedure for the church and its Christian education program, since it gives a real opportunity for rethinking the very basis for the program, and engages all the proper people in it. Furthermore, when standards are set with the cooperation of those who are concerned with them, there is much more chance that the findings of the evaluation will be accepted and used.

The *fourth step* in evaluation is the *comparison* of the situation with the standards. Since by this time, adequate data are in hand in the form of a profile or case study of the program and program standards, and since they are organized in the same categories, the comparison may proceed by taking each of the categories, studying the situation as described, looking at the standards, and noting similarities and differences. The similarities are indicative of the points at which the program is acceptable. The differences are indicative of the points at which need for program change exists. The compilation of both similarities and differences into a comprehensive report will provide the church with an analysis of the "state of health" of its Christian education program. It will also provide a useful list of the needs remaining to be met in and through the program. On the basis of such a list of needs the various persons and groups in Christian education in the church may be engaged in working toward decisions on improvement. The needs ought to be looked at carefully, the possibilities selected, and then recommended to the proper persons or groups or directly implemented.

At this point the process of evaluation has been completed, and it is fulfilled in appropriate action to meet the needs that have been identified systematically. For various groups and various aspects of the program, the process of evaluation may be reactivated from time to time so that up-to-date descriptions of the program will be available, standards will be renewed and changed, and emergent needs identified and met.

## Process Evaluation

The process of Christian education in a local church consists of the actual give and take, the interpersonal exchange, by which the objective is achieved, often in unique and locally characteristic ways. Four aspects of the Christian education process will concern the evaluator in particular.

The *first aspect* to which the evaluator will give his attention is the dynamics of the *teaching-learning process*. What is actually taking place in the interchange in the classroom? With what aims, attitudes, and approaches is the work being undertaken? What is being achieved? How is it being achieved?

The *second aspect* to which the evaluator will give his attention is the dynamics of group process in the more *informal educational situations* in the church. By informal educational situations is meant committee meetings, discussion groups, action groups, recreational occasions, and the like. In what ways are these groups identifying their group purposes? How are they setting themselves to the achievement of those purposes? What is the quality of the give and take in the group? How does the group deal with forces and persons that tend to impede its work?

The *third aspect* to which the evaluator will give his attention is the *curriculum and method* being used. In general, church educational programs follow a curriculum plan that has been devised by the denomination to which they belong. What are the fundamental objectives, principles, and design of that curriculum plan? In what ways is it particularly well suited to the conditions that exist in this local church and community? In what ways does it need to be changed and adjusted to meet conditions in this particular church and community? How does it meet the needs of the people for whom it is intended? How does it have to be changed and adjusted in order to meet their needs more effectively?

In scrutinizing the method of Christian education in the local process, the evaluator will keep in mind that the heart of method is involvement in the life and work of the community of faith in such ways that the person learns and truly grasps the meaning of the Christian faith and the Christian life. What methods are used in the Christian education process locally? In what ways are they modes of involvement in the life and work of the community of faith? Do they truly engage the persons for whom they are intended, each at his own level of ability to respond? Do they, through involvement in the corporate challenge and task, further the achievement of the objective of Christian education?

The *fourth aspect* to which the evaluator will give his attention is the dynamics of planning, organization, management, and supervision. The *administrative processes* of the Christian education program are to be regarded as themselves part of the educational process. The administrator (whether he be the minister, director, superintendent, or custodian) is himself a Christian educator in his relations with his fellow workers and with the learners. What processes, attitudes, and aims are at work in the administrative operations of this church? In what ways do they foster and aid the work of Christian education? In what ways do they hinder the work of Christian education?

For each of these aspects of the Christian education process much the same approach in evaluation may be used as has been suggested for the evaluation of the program. Suitable categories are to be established, data gathered by which the process may be described as it now operates, standards set cooperatively, situation and standard compared, and implications as to needs and next steps for improvement drawn.

As this evaluation proceeds, however, it becomes evident that the differences between program and process bring into play certain new evaluative methods. Two of these are particularly important: self-evaluation and personal supervision.

Self-evaluation is a procedure by which individuals and groups weigh their own performance and achievement. In the Christian education process there are several strategic points at which self-evaluation is useful. It is particularly useful when a meeting or class has finished its work, or when a curriculum unit has been brought to a close. If a group gets bogged down in the midst of its work, self-evaluation is needed. When a group feels that it has "arrived," that sense of achievement well may be scrutinized closely by the group itself. In making its plans for the future a group needs to evaluate where it has come in relation to its purposes. Further, a group may well take the time to evaluate the way it does its work, the role that its leaders play, and the quality of participation of its various members.

Individual self-evaluation is a matter of taking stock of one's achievements and the way one has done one's work, in light of the purposes and goals that one has set out to achieve. The most important thing about any teaching-learning situation is the goal or aim that really motivates the learner. If the learner can be brought to conscious articulation of that aim, evaluation of it, transformation of it in light of the objective of Christian education and the purpose and mission of the church, and self-scrutiny in terms of the transformed goal, he is likely to be motivated for the kind of Christian education process that he really needs. Self-evaluation not only produces this kind of effective motivation; it also makes the individual an effective contributor to planning for and conducting the direction of the whole enterprise. He is no longer content to accept what comes; he is actively critical and constructive of the whole process of which he is a part.

Self-evaluation implies the conscious setting of goals by the individual and the group, the collection of pertinent data about process and achievement, and the rendering of evaluative judgments by the individual or group themselves, leading to determination of changes that are needed and new directions that ought to be followed.

Personal supervision is a method of evaluation and the guidance of improvement by which a skilled person, the supervisor, gives his concentrated attention to helping a particular leader or group through a cycle in the educational process. The supervisor will help the leader or the group make appropriate plans. He will then observe the carrying out of those plans. Finally, he will help the leader or the group evaluate what took place and draw implications from the experience that will enable them to improve the process in the future.

Such a process of evaluation and improvement is, of course, exceedingly demanding upon the persons involved. But it is at the same time probably the most effective way of helping the individual leader or particular group improve the work in which they are engaged. Aims may be tested, plans carefully scrutinized, the style and talents of the leader analyzed, and the abilities and processes of the group examined. Criticisms and suggestions are based upon actual observation of the person or group at work. The most careful follow-up is possible in the postmeeting or postteaching conference.

An analysis of the personnel in process evaluation indicates that the key people are the participant, as he engages in meaningful self-evaluation; the group, as it looks at its aims, its methods, and its accomplishments; the teacher or leader, as he plans, conducts, thinks through, and replans the educational process; and the supervisor, who helps the others by providing another trained mind, spirit, and set of eyes for planning, observation, evaluation, identification of need, and identification of implications for improvement and change.

## A Look Ahead

Research in Christian education needs a strong theological base. Upon such a base a trained staff may work widely with parish and other leaders in Christian education to identify significant problems, develop hypotheses, gather data, test the hypotheses, draw conclusions, and suggest implications. The widespread acceptance of research and its effective use by the church depends upon the working out of such a theological understanding.

The scandal of research is the lack of a comprehensive inventory of research findings, available both to researchers and practitioners. Christian educators need an information retrieval center for consultation on the research that has already been done on the problems they face.

The clearest imperative for evaluation is to do it, and to do it faithfully throughout the whole program. Enough is known about evaluation to clarify our situation and locate our problems in such a way that they may be effectively worked on. A climate can be cultivated for the acceptance of the results of evaluation. This climate would mean a willingness to participate in evaluation and to take action upon the resultant findings.

## FOR ADDITIONAL READING

Cook, Stuart W., ed. *Review of Recent Research Bearing on Religious and Character Formation.* New York: Religious Education Association, 1962.

Gage, N. L., ed. *Handbook of Research on Teaching.* Chicago: Rand McNally, 1963.

Harris, Chester W., ed. *Encyclopedia of Educational Research.* New York: The Macmillan Company, 1960.

Little, Lawrence C. *Bibliography of Doctoral Dissertations on Adults and Adult Education.* Pittsburgh: University of Pittsburgh Press, 1962.

Wyckoff, D. Campbell. *How to Evaluate Your Christian Education Program.* Philadelphia: The Westminster Press, 1962.

## Part III

## PROGRAMS, METHODS, AND MATERIALS
## FOR CHRISTIAN EDUCATION

*Chapter 14*

## THE CURRICULUM
## OF CHRISTIAN EDUCATION

*C. Ellis Nelson*

THE DECADE OF 1960-1970 WILL PROBABLY BE KNOWN IN CHRISTIAN EDUCA-
tion history as the years of curriculum revision. Almost all Protestant denominations in the United States and Canada are involved in producing a new
curriculum, or they are in a cooperative arrangement to produce new teaching
materials. Protestant churches under regional committees sponsored by the
World Council of Christian Education are producing new curricula for use
in Latin America, Africa, and the Far East. Thus, by 1970 most Protestants
around the world will be using new curriculum materials.

### Why New Curriculum?

Why is there such a widespread effort to produce new curriculum? When we
note that it takes eight to ten years of planning and editing for a denomination
to revise its curriculum, we cannot help being sobered by the amount of time,
money, and energy committed to this work. There are three main reasons for a
church's producing a new curriculum.

The first of these is obvious. Every church desires competent instructional
materials, the basic reason for publishing any organized curriculum. Producing
instructional materials means that the church has to arrive at a consensus about
its theology and its attitude toward the social sciences, especially psychology.
This is extremely important because churches without an official creed, such
as the Southern Baptist Convention, have their beliefs formalized only in their
curriculum. Creedal churches seldom modify their historic statements, but
they adjust to current situations through their curriculum revisions. Curriculum is, therefore, the self-image of the church and is the most reliable place
to examine the actual beliefs of a denomination.

As theology changes or changes its emphases, a denomination feels that it should bring its instructional materials in line with the actual belief-situation represented in the denomination; and this feeling sparks most curriculum reform. Recent shifts in theology, which take the human situation and worldly condition as a part of the problem of communication, which stress the corporate aspects of faith in a church setting, and which give the Bible a fresh place of authority, have been the motivating forces for revising curriculum.

A second reason for curriculum revision is to permit response to ecumenical concerns. The ecumenical nature of the Sunday school movement throughout the nineteenth century constitutes an unwritten chapter in American church history. When the Uniform Lessons were developed in 1872, one reason advanced for preparing materials that were to be used by many denominations was that they would be a means of drawing the churches together in a closer fellowship.[1] This history of close cooperation by denominations in the practical work of the church has helped prepare the mind of the church for church unions and other interdenominational activities. The proposed union between the Presbyterian Church, U.S., and the Reformed Church of America is an illustration of how churches that learned to know each other through curriculum activities are now considering closer union. Also, when church union takes place or when it is planned, the churches involved often bring together representatives of each denomination to start a new curriculum. Thus, they shape a new image for their new estate. A new curriculum provides the process whereby leaders learn to know one another and to create a product that "sets" the operating theology of the new church. This unique role of curriculum is demonstrated in the new American Lutheran Church, the Lutheran Church of America, and the United Church of Christ, each of which was formed out of several denominations and each of which created a new curriculum at the time of their mergers.

The third reason for curriculum revision is the need to renew denominational effectiveness. Curriculum building requires not only an appraisal of theology and the social sciences in order to produce instructional material, but it also requires a vast effort to inform local churches about the new materials and a massive program to train local leaders in its use. Seldom does a church say directly that it is developing a new curriculum for this purpose; but when the old curriculum goes stale or when local churches begin to buy and use materials produced by nondenominational publishers, then leaders become aware of the need to renew and refresh their denominational life by means of a new curriculum.

## Definition of Curriculum

The educational process involves the social setting in which education takes place, the teacher, the pupils, the goals, methods used, time available, and many other factors. Curriculum is sometimes thought of as the sum of all the factors that make for education; but for purposes of this chapter, we shall

---

[1] H. Clay Trumbull, *A Model Superintendent* (Philadelphia: John D. Wattles, Publisher, 1880), p. 124.

use the more common and restricted idea of curriculum as the materials that have been planned in advance for use in the local church, most often by a teacher in a classroom setting. From the standpoint of Christian education the broader definition of curriculum as the dynamic interaction of many factors would be our main interest, yet there are so many intangible human elements involved in the broad definition that we cannot hope here to describe curriculum using this definition. Therefore, we shall deal with curriculum in this chapter from the standpoint of what the editors of a denomination planned for use in a local church: for this *can* be studied and analyzed.

There are settings for Christian education other than the local church, such as parochial schools, summer camps, and college courses, and denominations often prepare and supply curriculum materials for these settings. However, we shall further confine this chapter to a discussion of materials prepared for educational agencies sponsored by and in the local church.

The following are major elements in curriculum. By an examination of these elements we can understand the architectural structure of a particular curriculum and can make comparisons between them.

*Objective.* Since curriculum is an effort to arrange educational experience, all curricula will have an objective stated in general terms. The objective provides a way of focusing the various facets of the Christian religion so they can be articulated in a program. These capsule statements are carefully worded to reflect the major goal of the curriculum and to give some indication of the way the purpose is to shape the curriculum.[2]

*Design.* Curriculum is educational architecture, and like any building, it must have a design. The design is an arrangement of materials and experiences—Bible, songs, stories, activities—in order to accomplish the purpose. Design is a statement about how learning situations are to be devised and about the interrelation of various elements such as leader, group, church, parent, and individuals that are used in the educational process. The design also plans for the proper role of the various agencies of education such as the church school, the home, catechetical class, vacation school, and other agencies operated by the local church.

*Organizing Principle.* The organizing principle is the formula by which the design is carried out, so the two are closely related. The organizing principle suggests a starting place for the educational effort. In some cases the organizing principle is the individual, his age level, and his needs in relation to the Christian faith. Other leaders have developed curricula with Christ as the center, or with the church and its concerns as the practical way to take hold of the teaching-learning process in the local church. The organizing principle in the Uniform Lesson series was biblical content arranged for teaching over a seven-year cycle.

*Comprehensiveness.* Since curriculum is the operating theology of the denomination, it is important that the materials be comprehensive. This means that all of the important areas of thought and action must be accounted for in

---

[2] See chap. 9, pp 94-104.

the final curriculum. Often a three-year cycle is planned in order to ensure proper treatment of important areas. The United Church of Canada, for example, plans to rotate its material through annual emphases on God and his purpose, Jesus Christ and the Christian life, and the church and the world, in order to ensure comprehensiveness.

*Balance*. The amount of time allocated to each topic or unit of the curriculum defines its balance. We would expect curriculum to give more time and attention to the life and teaching of Jesus than to a study of the Song of Solomon. Also, we would expect the youth age level to consider topics on boy-girl relationships that might be absent from material designed for older adults.

*Sequence*. Since curriculum is designed for the whole age span, the problem of relating the materials to each succeeding age level is called sequence. There should be some logical movement from one age level to another; and the materials used in one stage should prepare the person for the next stage of development. For example, at the adolescent age level the curriculum can prepare the person for confirmation instruction, even though the confirmation instruction may be handled by an agency or a leader separate from the church school.

*Interpretation*. Every curriculum is an interpretation of the Bible. Since not all of the Bible can be used in any curriculum, the process of selecting passages for use is itself an interpretation of Scripture. More important, however, is the way the passages are interpreted. Some curriculum includes in its purpose the use of the historical-critical method; and from the earliest age level it interprets myth, song, parable, poem, and narrative material from the Bible, not only according to its literary form, but according to its place in the developing story of God's relation to man. Curriculum is also an interpretation of contemporary life, because curriculum is an organized effort to provide meaning for the church's theology in terms that can be readily understood. Although some church school material in the past tended to be moralistic, the newly developed curriculum tends to involve the student in a quest for discovering what is right, rather than telling him what he ought to do. The Seabury Series, for example, is built on the basis of the pupils' having to define the topics to be discussed, based on their experiences, and then relating these generalized human problems to the biblical material.

## Cooperative Curriculum Project

Probably the most important modern curriculum development is the Cooperative Curriculum Project (C.C.P.). This project is a continuation of Protestant cooperation in curriculum that began in 1872 with the Committee on the Uniform Lessons. In the 1950's this committee, continuing the Uniform Lesson Plan and the Committee on Graded Series, undertook the sponsorship of a series of special studies in curriculum over a four-year period by commissioning papers and planning discussion on the following topics: 1) the relationship between theology and psychology in Christian education; 2) the philosophy of curriculum and the biblical message; 3) the scheme of curriculum including objectives, scope, organizing principle, and planning theory; and 4) the learning sequences that should be built into curriculum. At the end of this period of study, sixteen denominations decided to form a cooperative project in order to formulate a curriculum design based on these discussions that they might use within their denominational boards and agencies to plan a parish curriculum.

Begun in 1960, the C.C.P. concluded its formal work in 1964 after a curriculum design was completed. The following denominations worked together in this project: Advent Christian Church, American Baptist Convention, Christian Churches (Disciples of Christ), Church of the Brethren, Church of God (Anderson), Church of the Nazarene, Evangelical United Brethren Church, Methodist Church, Presbyterian Church in Canada, Cumberland Presbyterian Church, Presbyterian Church in the United States, Protestant Episcopal Church, United Church of Canada, Southern Baptist Convention, African Methodist Episcopal, and the Mennonite Church. The wide range of these denominations in size, polity, and creedal affiliation shows the possibility of an ecumenically planned curriculum. Moreover, the total membership of these denominations represents the bulk of American Protestants, so the project has possibility of being the major development in contemporary Protestant curriculum construction. The Methodist Church, for example, with ten million members, has already utilized the basic work of C.C.P. for its newly developed materials for children; and curriculum developments in other cooperating denominations in the future will probably come from work done in C.C.P.

The C.C.P. is unique in its organization. Although administered by the Division of Christian Education of the National Council of Churches, the C.C.P. functions as a joint enterprise in which the denominations not only have invested money but have allocated staff time. Therefore, rather than an "extra" activity, the C.C.P. was an integral part of the cooperating denominations' regular work. Moreover, the C.C.P. was planned to lay the foundation and to erect a framework, leaving each participating denomination free to complete the building to suit its specialized needs or to join with other denominations to prepare a curriculum. The production of printed curriculum ready for local church use was considered to be the task of the denomination. During the planning stage of C.C.P. approximately one hundred and fifty denominational representatives met in various committees with consultants in theology, psychology, sociology, and economics. In order that the curriculum include the whole work of the church from the beginning the committee also included leaders from the fields of evangelism, missions, and social action. It was also determined early in the project that the curriculum should provide for a variety of settings, such as the vacation church school, weekday classes, summer camps, Sunday church school, and for many other kinds of groupings.

The objective of the curriculum is considered to be the same as the objective of the church's educational mission and is stated in these words:

The objective for Christian education is that all persons be aware of God through his self-disclosure, especially his redeeming love as revealed in Jesus Christ, and that they respond in faith and love—to the end that they may know who they are and what their human situation means, grow as sons of God rooted in the Christian com-

AN INTRODUCTION TO CHRISTIAN EDUCATION

munity, live in the spirit of God in every relationship, fulfill their common discipleship in the world, and abide in the Christian hope.[3]

The C.C.P. defines the scope of curriculum as man's relationship to God, to his fellow man, and to the world, and this scope when related to the major facets of the objective defines areas of curriculum. The areas of curriculum are not to be considered as separate from one another but as a way of approaching the overall objective. The areas of curriculum are also related to the lifelong concerns of the learner, so that a finished curriculum can be worked out which treats an area of curriculum at various age levels simultaneously. In other words, if desired, the whole church can be at work in one curriculum area at one time. In order to facilitate this more refined handling of the areas of curriculum, themes have been defined within the areas. A theme is a fairly specific concern that represents a part of the Christian faith as it speaks to a persistent life issue.

The following is a listing of the five curriculum areas and the associated themes:

1. Life in its setting: the meaning and experience of existence. Within this area are the following themes: man discovering and accepting himself, man living in relationship to others, man's relation to the natural order, man's involvement in social forces, man's coping with change and the absolute, man's daily creativity.

2. Revelation: the meaning and experience of God's self-disclosure. Themes related to this area are as follows: God speaks in man's search for meaning beyond himself, the living God seeks man, the gracious God judges and redeems, the sovereign God dwells with man, God speaks to man through the Scriptures, God acts through his church to make himself known, God speaks to man through the natural order.

3. Sonship: the meaning and experience of redemption. The themes within this area are as follows: God's redeeming love for man, man's responding to God's redemptive action, becoming a new person in Christ, growing up in Christ, finding identity in the Christian community, the Christian's hope rests in the triumphant God.

4. Vocation: the meaning and experience of discipleship. The themes within this area are as follows: God's call to responsible decision, call to serve one's neighbors, the stewardship of life and work, discipline in the Christian life, joined in discipleship in the word, toward the kingdom of God.

5. The church: the meaning and experience of Christian community. The themes within this area are as follows: Christians are bound together in God's love, God's continuing action in and through his people, the church permeating society, extending reconciliation and redemption, the church lives by worship, the Christian community mobilizing for mission, preparing and equipping for ministry.[4]

We cannot tell how these principles will work out except as the cooperating denominations develop a finished curriculum for use in a local church. Since this process is just beginning, the full implications of this approach to curriculum will probably not be apparent for another five to seven years.

[3] From *The Church's Educational Ministry: A Curriculum Plan,* published by The Bethany Press, copyrighted 1965, by the Division of Christian Education, of the National Council of the Churches of Christ in the U.S.A., and used by permission.
[4] *Ibid.*

## Brand Name Curriculum

Denominations have often published their own curricula apart from ecumenical ventures, and sometimes several like-minded denominations have formed coalitions to publish curriculum. In each case the purpose has been to achieve a distinctive style of curriculum or to further the special theological or social interests of the sponsoring group. After World War II the first denomination to fabricate a new curriculum was the Presbyterian Church in the U.S.A. (now the United Presbyterian Church in the U.S.A.). This curriculum, called "Christian Faith and Life," was conservative in theology and in its use of the historical-critical method of Bible study. It presented a fresh and interesting curriculum that was widely used by local churches in many denominations. "The Seabury Series" of the early 1950's was the first official curriculum of the Protestant Episcopal Church. It broke new ground by its efforts to develop adult education, leadership education based on "parish life conferences," and materials that took an existential approach to the Christian faith. Today the United Church of Canada, the American Lutheran Church, the Lutheran Church of America, the United Church of Christ, and a group of Presbyterian Churches have all published, or are in the process of publishing, a new curriculum. Let us look at materials from three denominations to see how each has built its new curriculum.

## United Church of Christ

The United Church of Christ has made a deliberate effort to get around the classic problem of religious education, content versus experience, by thinking of Christian education as an effort to "draw individuals into the reality of the Christian fellowship and to nurture them in the Christian faith and mission so that, by accepting with gratitude and obedience God's forgiveness and power for new life, they will be enabled to mature as Christian persons and will become faithful participants in the mission of the church." [5] These are not considered to be three different responses: they are, rather, different ways of looking at how one can respond to the gospel, and they can be considered the principle tasks of all Christians at every stage of development. In order to make the tasks manageable, six themes have been selected that unify biblical and historical material with the experiences pupils are having and with contemporary issues. These themes are: "1. Growing as a Christian; 2. Exploring our Christian heritage; 3. Christian living with one another; 4. Responding to God's love; 5. Belonging to the Christian fellowship; and 6. Living in God's world." [6] The curriculum is prepared for two semesters each year, paralleling the public school semesters, plus one summer unit. One theme is used each term for all age levels, but the themes so overlap that there is no sharp break between semesters. The emphasis within the theme is on living. The theme is not just a

---

[5] Roger L. Shinn, *The Educational Mission of Our Church* (Philadelphia: United Church Press, 1962), p. 151.
[6] *Ibid.*, p. 68.

topic for all ages to talk about on a given Sunday; rather, the church as a living community facing contemporary issues is the model supported by the unifying themes.

The family is seen in this curriculum as both a partner in the religious education of children and as a semi-independent educational enterprise. The curriculum provides suggestions for family cooperation with the church in various activities.[7] The church also is asked to conduct meetings with parents in order to help them become more effective in moral and spiritual nurture of their children, and a special parents' resource book is provided. Yet the curriculum is not written so that parental response is necessary, because some parents will not assume responsibility for their children's religious education.

Although this curriculum is orderly and neatly defined, the view of education that underlies it is not systematic. Rather, this curriculum assumes that good education is a dynamic, changing development within the self. It sees the individual as always undergoing change. Growth is uneven and no attempt is made to regularize or standardize age level problems. Moreover, the individual is considered to be free and capable of rejecting the Christian message and the claims of God on his life. The individual or the pupil is seen not as an abstract man or as a normal person for an age level but as a person who is unique in selfhood and who confronts situations to which he must react. With this understanding, we see the pupil's book not as a textbook in the conventional sense but a resource book that the pupil can use in a variety of ways. The leader's book does not contain dated lesson plans but gives practical and specific plans for developing classroom discussion; the teacher is provided with audio-visual materials that are correlated with the lessons, and many contemporary-style pictures are also available. Thus, the local church leader must take the initiative in planning the actual educational experience for the group he leads.

### Lutheran Church of America

The new curriculum of the Lutheran Church of America started when leaders of four independent Lutheran churches decided they should work together to prepare an educational program.

Early in the discussion the following general objective was formulated:

Inasmuch as the church, as the body of Christ, seeks to become more effectively that community of believers in which the Holy Spirit calls, gathers, enlightens and sanctifies individuals in their relationships with God and their fellow man, the church's central educational objective, therefore shall be—to assist the individual in his response and witness to the eternal and incarnate word of God as he grows within the community of the church toward greater maturity in his Christian life through ever-deepening understanding, more wholesome attitudes, and more responsible patterns of action.[8]

[7] See chap. 25, pp. 292-303.
[8] *The Objectives of Christian Education* (Philadelphia: Lutheran Church of America, 1957), pp. 12-13.

This general objective is considered to become operative for a person as he gains a deeper understanding in his relationship to the church, to the Bible, to his fellow man, to the physical world, and to himself. Simultaneously, the individual is seen as developing more wholesome attitudes and more responsible patterns of action in these same five areas.

Early in the planning of this curriculum it was decided that its organizing principle would be "continual life involvement" related to "continual Christian learning." The continual life involvement assumes that the purely individual aspects of a person's life cannot be treated directly in a curriculum, but that the elements of life that are common at each age level do lend themselves to educational work. The exact formulation of the continual life involvement is related to age levels, but the common problem extends throughout life. For example, in infancy a person begins to possess a self-understanding, yet this self-understanding is a constant problem through life and is especially acute during the adolescent years. Specific continual life involvements have been grouped into three categories: those of a personal nature, those of an impersonal nature, and those of an interpersonal nature. These continual life involvements do not form the substance of the curriculum but are points of readiness and need where the curriculum can take hold. In order to be effectual at the point of involvement, the Lutheran Church of America curriculum has a set of continual Christian learnings that correlate with each specific life involvement so that the Christian point of view is related.

With the correlation of life and gospel the curriculum plan then starts with the child of one year old and for every year through seventeen, then through older youth, young adult, middle adult and older adult, works out in chart form the characteristics of the age in relating the continual life involvement with the continual Christian learning. The integration of all these factors is probably the most comprehensive work of its kind in Protestantism, and it is published in two books, *The Functional Objectives of Christian Education* and *The Age Group Objectives of Christian Education*.

The use of continual life involvement turned out not only to be the key concept of the curriculum design, but also it provided a way to solve one of the most vexing problems of Protestant Christian education, the matter of curriculum material for the various agencies of the church. This Lutheran Church has very few parochial schools, so the coordination of that agency with parish education was not a major problem; but catechetical instruction as a separate agency was widespread, and the other agencies such as youth fellowships, vacation church schools, and various adult groups were all involved in some form of educational work without much coordination. By using the continual life involvement idea, coordination could first be developed throughout the life span, and then the various agencies could pick up different facets of the age-level involvement. Thus, a person in any educational agency of the church would have curriculum materials that were coordinated. Studies showed that the Sunday school was the most widely used agency, so it became the "nuclear" or mainline agency. The traditional catechetical class was broadened to become a weekday school of religion, and each of the many agencies of the parish was given a curriculum to supplement and enrich the other.

## Covenant Life Curriculum

Four churches in the Reformed tradition, who had had experience in joint planning and printing of curriculum, began plans for a new curriculum in the late 1950's. This curriculum, known as the Covenant Life Curriculum, is now appearing and will be in full operation in 1967. The covenant is "the conviction that God has come and continues to come to man, inviting man into everlasting covenant with him." [9] The covenant is simultaneously an affirmation about God's concern for man, man's response to God for his grace, and man's effort to order his whole life under the lordship of Christ and the church. The stated objective is "that all persons may respond in faith to the call of God in Jesus Christ and be nurtured in the life of fellowship with him, that they may face all of life's relationships and responsibilities as children of God." [10]

This approach gives the C.L.C. its uniqueness. Rather than a scientific and systematic age-level analysis, such as the Lutheran Church of America devised, the Covenant Life Curriculum attempts to present "the whole gospel" to "the whole of human life." The gospel is considered the unity of the church. It cannot be subdivided, and it cannot be taught in bits and pieces. Although the full meaning of the gospel cannot be taught at every age level, no part of it will be withheld because of age. Specifically, the curriculum will not teach the humanity of Jesus to little children and then at a later time add the idea of his divinity. Nor will stories of the miracles be withheld in favor of natural theology. The curriculum expects to deal with the whole of life as the Bible does by leading people to examine all aspects of their life in relationship to the gospel.

Such a position immediately raises the question of sequence. If the whole gospel is to be presented (or different meanings of it) at every age level, how will the curriculum materials be graded and progress be made from one age level to another? This is answered by saying that the gospel is communicated at four levels, and each is characteristically the mode of a certain age level. The first level is the nonverbal in which communication is through relationships. The small child or the nonbeliever first learns the gospel by association with people who do believe, by participation in worship, and by an inductive association with religious vocabulary. The second level is the verbal, and this is appropriate for the older child who is busy listening and probing the explanation of the gospel. The third level is that of commitment. At this stage, usually identified as the teenage, the person is seeking an identification of himself with his beliefs, and this becomes the normal time to make a public confession of faith. The fourth stage is that of witnessing to the faith. This is the adult response, when a person not only orders his life in relation to the gospel but also assumes responsibility for developing an ethical response to public problems in light of the gospel.

Although these levels have a general coordination with developmental stages, they are also going on all the time in the community of the church and repre-

[9] *Education for Covenant Living* (Richmond: John Knox Press, 1962), p. 21.
[10] *Ibid.*, p. 25.

sent a model of the process by which one grows in grace. Such a conception gives the local church a major place in Christian education. In fact, the organizing principle in the curriculum is considered to be the local church in its worship, study, and work rather than a certain configuration of content of experience that can be devised for the classroom. For convenience in publishing the materials, three approaches to the Christian life are used: the Bible, the church, and the Christian life. Each approach will become a yearly theme in a three-year cycle.

In practical terms this curriculum gives more attention to adult education than any contemporary curriculum, because adults form and fashion the local church. The home is considered one of the important settings in which education takes place, and materials are provided for the home, to be used in the home, and to be used in the church with parents. Although standard grading is to be used for classroom work, there is a tendency to deemphasize the importance of grading in favor of the normal lifelike ungraded situations of a congregation.

## Trends

Looking at all of the new Protestant curricula that are now in publication or that are planned for the remainder of the 1960's, what are the general trends?

First, biblical and theological experts are now an integral part of the curriculum process along with educators. The idea of a special "Sunday school theology" is completely gone. These biblical and theological experts not only consult about all the aspects of the curriculum development, but they are also writers for major curriculum materials.

Second, field testing of new materials prior to publication is almost universal, and most boards of education now have a permanent staff for research to maintain a constant evaluation of materials and methods in Christian education.

Third, the learner is considered to be the clue to teaching. New materials tend to be carefully graded in order to reach the reader's interest in contemporary language and modes of thought. Many denominations are using "themes" in an attempt to unify biblical and historical content with contemporary human experience.

Fourth, materials are attractively printed with the finest modern art work. The old "bathrobe biblical scene" has disappeared. The old quarterly has also largely disappeared, for most new materials are in book or magazine format, planned for use throughout the year or for a semester, and they are generally conceived as resource books rather than textbooks.

Fifth, more leadership helps are built into the curriculum. Audio-visual materials are often prepared to go with lesson materials, and sometimes a record or filmstrip is packaged with the leaders' guide. Team teaching and various group methods are promoted, along with a stronger effort to get leaders to use more methods that involve the pupils with one another and with the world.

Sixth, all new curricula provide material for all agencies of the church within one logical whole, so that the idea of the Sunday school as a semi-independent agency run by laymen has been completely abandoned.

## FOR ADDITIONAL READING

*The Church's Educational Ministry: A Curriculum Plan.* St. Louis: The Bethany Press, 1965.

*A Guide for Curriculum in Christian Education.* New York: National Council of Churches, 1955.

Wyckoff, D. Campbell. *Theory and Design of Christian Education Curriculum.* Philadelphia: The Westminster Press, 1961.

Contemporary Protestant curriculum planning is being done, as this chapter indicates, by denominations and groups of denominations, and each curriculum is accompanied by books explaining its purpose, design, scope, and theological orientation. If a person wants to study curriculum today, he must write directly to the agencies developing teaching materials. The two interdenominational agencies are as follows: (1) The National Council of the Churches of Christ in the U.S.A., Division of Christian Education, 475 Riverside Drive, New York, New York 10027. Sixteen denominations, named above, have developed the Cooperative Curriculum Project in relation to the National Council of Churches. (2) The World Council of Christian Education and Sunday School Association, 150 Route de Ferney, C.P. Geneva 20, Switzerland, has sponsored curriculum committees to plan materials for use in Latin America, Africa, and East Asia.

Among the denominations that have, or are now developing, a new curriculum are the following:

American Lutheran Church, Division of Parish Education, 422 South 5th Street, Minneapolis, Minn. 55415.

Lutheran Church of America, The Board of Publication, 2900 Queen Lane, Philadelphia, Penn. 19129.

The Methodist Church, The Curriculum Committee of the General Board of Education, 201 Eighth Ave., South, Nashville, Tenn. 37203.

Presbyterian Church, U.S., with which are associated the Reformed Church in America, Moravian Church in America, the Associate Reformed Presbyterian Church and the Cumberland Presbyterian Church. Their "Covenant Life Curriculum" is published at Box 1176, Richmond, Va. 23209.

Protestant Episcopal Church, Department of Christian Education, 815 Second Avenue, New York, N. Y. 10017.

United Church of Canada, Board of Christian Education, 85 St. Clair Avenue East, Toronto 7, Canada.

United Church of Christ, Division of Christian Education, 14 Beacon Street, Boston, Mass. 02208.

United Presbyterian Church, Board of Christian Education, 425 Witherspoon Building, Philadelphia, Penn. 19107.

# Chapter 15

# THE CHRISTIAN EDUCATION
## OF CHILDREN

*Carrie Lou Goddard*

A BRIGHT YOUNG MAN IN HIS SENIOR YEAR OF COLLEGE WAS SHARING THE plans he had for his life with a faculty member. In all sincerity and with no intent to be humorous he said, "After I have my bachelor of divinity degree I want to take some Christian education courses, but I do not intend to study Christian education."

The faculty member looked at the earnest face and wondered, "How does one take a bachelor of divinity degree and courses in Christian education without studying Christian education?" Christian education is a derived discipline and is a combination of Bible, theology, philosophy, psychology, sociology, and education. To study in any one of these areas is to partially study Christian education. To combine them all into one discipline is to create Christian education.

An understanding of Christian education of necessity means some understanding of each of the disciplines from which it is created. It is impossible in one chapter to deal with all of them with any degree of adequacy. Whole libraries have been written on each one of the disciplines of which Christian education is comprised. However, this chapter does intend to deal briefly with some of the major concerns in the area of the Christian education of children. Perhaps the reader will be challenged to pursue the subject to greater depths.[1]

## A Backward Look

The general concept of how the young or immature in the faith are nurtured and made fully participating members of the fellowship of the Christian church has been the subject of much discussion and controversy. Because there have been conflicting points of view as to how it can be most effectively accomplished, the methods used have embraced a wide range of educational practice and psychological understanding. The twentieth century has been a time of thoughtful evaluation of positions relative to the nurture of the young and immature in the faith. An awareness of some of the considerations in the evaluative processes that have been going on will help in attempting to understand and to deal effectively with the present-day situation in Christian education.

Prior to the twentieth century there were several movements which greatly

[1] See chaps. 3-8, pp. 32-93.

affected the happenings of this century relative to Christian education. One of these was the Sunday school movement which, although there were other contributing influences, grew largely from Robert Raikes's establishment of a school on Sunday for children. Out of Raikes's attempts to reform criminals, he came to the conclusion that rehabilitation of those who had made a career of crime was all but impossible. In his endeavor to improve society Raikes decided to shift his energies and to begin with the children. He began his work in Gloucester, England, with "ragamuffins" who were free on Sunday from their labors in the industrial enterprises of the city. Raikes, from the beginning, had remarkable success in this endeavor, and similar schools were started in other cities. This movement eventually became the church school as we know it today. The purpose of the school established by Raikes was moral and social reform—one which is frequently given the school of the church today.

A second movement that has had its influence on twentieth-century Christian education is that of nineteenth-century psychology. This movement began on the continent of Europe, and its consequences have been felt in many parts of the world. Its influence has been markedly felt in Christian education. From Johann Heinrich Pestalozzi's emphasis on a sense-perceptual basis for relationships and concepts came the rationale in religious education that learning takes place through the human experience. For example, love is first and best learned in the mother-child relationship and may then be associated with God. Through this same means the child also learns trust, obedience, and gratitude. The crucial time for the child, according to Pestalozzi, is when he becomes independent of the mother and transfers his dependence to God.

Friedrich Wilhelm August Froebel's strong influence on religious education is the result of his experience with the kindergarten schools which he founded. Froebel's most important idea was an all-pervading principle of unity. To Froebel all is in God and not all is God. Thus, religious education is largely an effort to awaken in the child an awareness that he is one with God. Religious education then became not so much redemptive in character as a reawakening or reminding of a reality that already exists. Froebel, like Pestalozzi, believed in sense perception but added a new dimension to the teaching-learning process with his concept of age levels. This concept divided the years known as childhood into several periods and defined specific learning tasks to be mastered at each level of growth and development.

It is not difficult to find the influence of these two men in Christian education in the twentieth century. The oft-quoted concept of the early part of the twentieth century that "every day in every way we are growing better and better," can be viewed as a perversion of Froebel's idea of all-pervading unity, that since man is one with God an awakening of this reality in him can only lead to man's becoming better and better. The events of this century have led to a reassessment of this concept. But the two most important influences of this psychological movement in Christian education today are: *first*, the sense-perception concept, which has brought the realities of life, experimentation and experience, both personal and group, into the teaching-learning process as a replacement for the verbalism of an earlier period; and *second*, the recognition that there are levels of functioning ability as the individual matures and moves through the years of childhood and that learning is easier, more relevant, and more permanent when there is readiness growing out of need for the particular task of information that is to be mastered.

A student of Christian education once humorously remarked, "Thank God for Horace Bushnell; he means so much to my professors." Although we may smile at this quip, Horace Bushnell did greatly influence the Christian education movement. The main thesis of Bushnell's book, *Christian Nurture*, is "that the child is to grow up a Christian, and never know himself as being otherwise." [2] He enlarges upon this idea by indicating that the child can learn to love that which is good from his earliest years. It is then unnecessary for him to go through the violent conversion experience deemed necessary by the revivalists. However, Bushnell did feel there was some kind of conversion struggle which each child should experience. It is apparent that Bushnell was thinking of the children of religious parents, and the question has often been asked, "But what of those children outside the Christian community?"

It is not difficult to become aware of an acceptance of concepts related to those of Bushnell when one examines the philosophy and practice of Christian education in the church today. In those congregations that practice infant baptism parents and congregation dedicate themselves in the presence of God to see that the child be taught the meaning and purpose of the sacrament and that he be instructed in the principles of faith and the nature of the Christian life. The infant is then considered a "preparatory member" of the congregation. Other congregations, in one way or another, indicate a strong conviction that even the very young must be trained and nurtured in the Christian faith.

Thousands of dollars and multitudinous hours of study and labor go into the preparation of graded curriculum materials to be used by parents and teachers in the guidance and instruction of the young and immature in the faith to the end that they may grow up with the witness of the Christian faith always present. No one can question the fact that a very high percentage of the members in any congregation came into full membership through the process of religious instruction in the home and in the school of the church. But the depth of their faith and the personal struggle through which they have gone in attaining it may be open to question.

A fourth movement that has made an impact on twentieth-century Christian education is the philosophy of John Dewey and progressive education. Dewey's philosophy is both complex and profound, and it is at the risk of oversimplification that two ideas are chosen to illustrate something of his influence on Christian education. *First*, Dewey redefines knowledge and learning. Life, according to Dewey, is episodic; that is, it moves from one situation to another. Certain kinds of knowledge are required for solving the problems of each situation. The learner is confronted with the necessity for analyzing the problems, bringing to bear upon them the knowledge required, and working out satisfactory solutions. From this experience he gathers knowledge and skill which he carries with him to the next episode or situation.

A *second* idea from Dewey's philosophy that has had its effect on Christian

[2] (New Haven: Yale University Press, 1947).

education is a concept of being. Being, for Dewey, is a fluctuating, moving, changing flow. In this philosophy there is nothing that is static or fixed, and no ultimate truths. Life is ever changing, ever moving.

An examination of the unit method of teaching and the teaching skills employed cannot help but make one aware that these sprang from a philosophy that emphasizes confrontation with the problems of life, gathering knowledge, and making decisions. The movement of planned curriculum units in cycles of increasing difficulty points to an acceptance of the idea that knowledge gained at one level is relevant at another and that life is a series of episodes. The second idea, that of being as a fluctuating, moving, changing flow, is more subtle in its influence. Values are seen as relative, teachers speak of "a changing, growing concept of God" and the whole existentialist movement. These illustrations are not meant as negative attitudes but as awarenesses of how a philosophy has been accepted and modified in the light of the understandings and experiences of Christian education.

Christian education in the early part of the twentieth century had accepted parts of ideas and concepts from each of the movements described above. Because Christian education had grown with such rapidity, and in the midst of new developments in the areas of philosophy and psychology, there were distortions and departures from what had been considered basic positions of the church. With the reawakening of an interest in and concern about theology it was quite proper that Christian education be reevaluated and new positions taken.

## A Present-Day Approach

The twentieth century has been a time of theological inquiry that has resulted in new dimensions of thought and insight. The searchlight of new and reawakened theological insights has been turned on Christian education. Christian educators have been forced to reevaluate, rethink, and restate the purpose, content, and method of Christian education.

The earlier assumption of some that Christian character can be created by a carefully made plan practiced diligently by parents in the home and teachers in the school of the church has been modified. The necessity of the learner himself at each level of his development to become actively engaged in the process, struggling with the problems of his own relationship with God and his fellow men in the choices he makes each day, has become increasingly clear. The content is that of the seeking, redeeming love of God as revealed especially in Jesus Christ, in creation, and in the Christian community. The psychological learnings, both of the nineteenth and twentieth centuries, have continued to indicate that human growth and development is gradual, that there are problems to be solved at each level, and the greater the involvement of the individual in solving his own problems, the greater the growth in both ability and knowledge. The educator now looks at the child to discover the level of his development, to ask what are his needs, to ascertain his capacity for meeting and handling them, and to seek ways of making the gospel of Jesus Christ relevant in his life as he deals with the needs and problems of his own human existence. Rather than being the manipulator of a plan or a program, the educator becomes a witness to the power of the gospel and a translator of the faith.

The earlier optimistic view of the nature of man has been reexamined in the light of the history of this century. Man's inhumanity to his own kind, the hate, greed, and ugliness of which human nature is capable have made clear man's need for redemption. Christian education seeks to witness to and to communicate the redeeming love of God as seen in Jesus Christ to boys and girls at their own level of understanding and in the midst of the experiences of their everyday lives. This is an undertaking that is far from easy but nonetheless essential if Christian education is to fulfill its mission. Repentance is interpreted as more than just being sorry for behavior and forgiveness, as more than just checking off a misdemeanor.

Kirk, a very intelligent boy of almost four, dominated the nursery class by grabbing or snatching whatever he wanted from the hands of the other children. Any child who attempted to resist or to protest was the target of Kirk's fists or was shoved to the floor by an onslaught of Kirk's almost-four power-machine. When approached by a teacher, Kirk's face would take on a penitent look, and he would blithely utter the magic phrase, "I'm sorry," and go on his merry, grabbing, snatching, pushing way.

After one particularly trying session one of the teachers took Kirk by the hand after one of his glib "I'm sorry's" and walked out into the hall and into an empty room. The two sat down in the room. The teacher said very little but remained calm, firm, and friendly.

"I said I was sorry," Kirk said after awhile. "Let's go back to the room."

Quietly the teacher looked into his bright intelligent eyes. "But that is not enough," she said.

A few minutes passed and Kirk repeated his sorrow and desire to return to the room with the other children. Again the teacher said, "But just being sorry is not enough."

Then, because Kirk was a bright child, a questioning look crossed his face and he asked, "What is enough?"

"To see that your hands do not grab and snatch the toy that another child is using, or to push someone away," the teacher said quietly.

Kirk was thoughtful as they walked back to the classroom. His human relations improved for the remainder of the class session, but it took many such experiences before Kirk learned to live with his classmates with respect and consideration and that being sorry meant much more than a glib phrase that could erase his inconsiderateness and misbehavior.

Educators, whether they be parents or teachers, must help children understand that more than sorrow is demanded of the individual in repentance before God and that only then does one feel truly forgiven.

Depth Bible study to discern meanings and their relevance for life today has replaced the memorization of a certain number of passages deemed so necessary in earlier religious instruction. Although memorization may well be a part of the instruction in Christian education today, it is done after meanings have been discovered and deemed valuable enough to be committed to memory. The passage is learned for its own value and witness to the learner's spiritual life rather than for the gold star or prize awarded as an external reward.

## The Child in the Midst

The twentieth century has brought a changed point of view toward children. One of the important changes has been that of seeing each child as a growing, developing person in his own right, different from any other that has ever been or ever will be created and with a potential for fulfilling his own calling in life. Earlier attitudes had been to view the child as a miniature adult to be brought into line with the world of his elders or as an animal to be trained.

The later concept of the child as a growing, developing person has led to study and research to determine physical, mental, and social functioning levels, to discover the effects of motivation on abilities, needs, and readiness for learning, to learn the unfolding ability for spiritual relationships and moral judgments. The results of this work have contributed much to the educational philosophy of Christian education and to the building of a curriculum that takes into consideration the whole of a child's life.

It is interesting to note here that many of the major Protestant denominations are either in the process or have just completed a restudy of the curriculum of Christian education as viewed by their own particular interpretation of the faith. These studies have resulted in the production of new curriculum designs[3] which incorporate the learnings of the earlier years of the century and whose aim is to proclaim the revelation of God in Christ and to encourage response in faith and love.

The developments of this century have focused attention on the child. The teacher, or adult world, was once the center, and the child was taught and forced to learn and to do what the adult world thought he should know and do. With the child as the focus, it is his needs, readiness, and ability to conceptualize that determine what from the whole store of life's knowledge, values, and concerns shall be shared. When the realities of life meet him at his own level, the child can face them, learn to handle them, and make the proper responses. He moves from one level of reality to another, having mastered enough of its concerns to have gained skill and confidence for the next.

This shift in focus has meant several readjustments for the adults who are the teachers. One important adjustment is that teaching deals with the realities of life in which the teacher, as well as the child, is involved. No longer are things done with children or are children taught content because they are "good for" boys and girls but because they are concerns of life in which all persons regardless of age are involved and about which decisions and commitments must be made. The activities, content, and concerns of life will be determined by the child's developmental level. For example, the five-year-old will deal with the realities of his world in accordance with his functioning level,

[3] See chap. 14, pp. 157-68.

his needs, and his abilities, but these realities are also concerns for his teacher for they are eternal realities.

The five-year-old is discovering the world in which he lives. He is seeking answers to such questions as, "Who am I in relation to this world of trees, plants, animals, blue sky, rain, and sun? What do I have to do with this world? Who am I in relation to the other persons who are part of my life? How do I relate to them and deal with the problems of socialization?" These are questions with which every age is confronted, so teacher and child are dealing with common problems at different levels of maturity.

Christian education is then viewed as a process that helps each child live each level of his development to its fullest, dealing with his life concerns within a context of Christian concepts and values and guided by the witness of the more mature in the faith. Instead of preparation for life at a later time, it is life today lived to the fullest capacity of the age level and in the presence of God.

## Communicating the Message of Christian Education

Since the whole of life is within the purview of Christian education, so are the means of communicating its message. In every situation, through each experience, the child may come to know something of God, may be aware of some aspect of the life and teachings of Jesus Christ, and he may come to make some response. It may involve a new understanding or insight, the development or practice of an attitude, a decision based on a Christian value or a response of faith, praise, or thanksgiving. Although the child is learning in every aspect of his life and in ways over which there is often no control, there are some specific ways and means of communication available to those concerned about sharing the Christian gospel.

A pert little lass of about six years sat on a bench with an adult friend in the backyard on a summer day. She cast brown eyes upward and scanned a rapidly clouding sky. "We had better go inside," she advised her friend. "I have a feeling in my bones it is going to rain."

No mention of weather had been made between the two on the bench. The environment itself had communicated a message. The conditions were those the child had learned through earlier experiences brought rain. This might be labeled environmental learning.

Every person is sensitive to the environment in which he lives and moves and has his being. We learn from it, we accept as right or wrong that which is commonly present and pattern our thinking, our acceptance, and our practice after it. A child reared in an atmosphere of constant disorder and disrespect for things accepts this as a way of life. The orderly classroom, with work materials in their proper place and ready for use, speaks a silent message of respect for property, for having materials ready and available for everyone, and for a dependable way of life.

Reverence, as well as respect, is learned in nonverbal ways. The beauty of a lovely sanctuary immediately communicates its own message. Attitudes of respect and reverence for personality are more often revealed in the facial

175

expression, the extended hand, and the supporting smile than in the words that are spoken. The words without the silent message of glance or manner may convey an entirely different message. Children are particularly sensitive to the atmosphere of a room, to the expression of approval or disapproval, the genuine concern that is revealed in behavior without comment. The environment, both that of persons and that of things, is a potent factor in communicating any message and particularly so in communicating the message of the Christian gospel.

Cynthia was a three-year-old who, because of circumstances in her own home, had come to live with her grandfather and grandmother. This disruption of the normal routine of her life had made her quite insecure and at times unwilling to let her grandparents get out of her sight.

One day her grandfather brought her to the nursery class. She seemed quite secure this day until she happened to glance out the window in time to see her grandfather's car pull away from the curb and move down the street. Waves of fear and insecurity enveloped the little girl, and she dashed across the room and out into the hall in a frantic attempt to run after her grandfather. One of the teachers caught Cynthia in her arms.

Almost wild with fear and sobbing uncontrollably, Cynthia kept saying, "I want my Granddaddy. I want my Granddaddy."

"I know you do," the teacher said quietly and firmly. "But he is gone now. He will come for you when it is time to go home."

"I want to catch him now," Cynthia sobbed. "I want my Granddaddy."

The teacher held Cynthia's hands and forced the child to look at her face. "I know you want to go and to catch your Granddaddy but it is not safe to be in the street. I love you too much to let you get hurt. Your Granddaddy will come for you when it is time to go home."

The teacher's message slowly penetrated Cynthia's mind. Her sobs grew quieter. "You may sit on my lap for awhile," the teacher said comfortingly.

With a sigh Cynthia snuggled against her teacher's body and leaned her head against the teacher's shoulder. For about ten minutes the little girl sat on the teacher's lap drinking in the feeling of being loved, of being safe, and of being secure; then she climbed down and entered into the activities of the nursery class.

At the end of the class session Cynthia's grandfather came for her. As she left holding happily to his hand, Cynthia looked up at the teacher who had stopped her frantic dash after her grandfather in the early part of the session. "Thank you for your lap," she said shyly.

This incident is an excellent illustration of situational teaching. Children's lives are full of situations involving all kinds of emotions, attitudes, understandings, and actions. The values that are used in making a decision, the concerns that are expressed and the way in which they are communicated, the emotional responses made, are all important factors in dealing with the situations that arise in the daily lives of children. Some of life's most important lessons are learned in these situations. When the decisions that are made and the actions taken are witnesses to the Christian gospel, the child is helped in his understanding of the meaning of Christianity and is given guidance for making his own decisions and commitments.

The role of the adult in situational teaching is not an easy one. He must be as objective as possible in evaluating the situation and in choosing a course of action. He must at the same time be sensitive to the child or children involved. The decisions made need to be communicated to the child in such a way as to secure his cooperation because he comprehends the reasons and is able to accept them. Authoritarian procedures may settle the problem, but it is not likely that children will grow in understanding of reasons or values underlying the decision.

A third means available for communicating the Christian gospel to children is that of planned teaching. Planned teaching may be described as a series of teaching-learning activities under the guidance of a more mature member of the congregation with the desired outcome of growth in some area of the Christian faith. It is for this kind of communication that curriculum materials are produced and leadership training enterprises are held.

The content of the curriculum for teaching that is planned to bring about some response to the faith deals with the Christian heritage. The massive amount of knowledge in this whole area is surveyed carefully by a curriculum committee with each age group in mind. Selections are made of areas of content to be taught to each age group with attention to the general abilities and capacities of those to be taught. The content is then organized into units of study which progress in difficulty from one age group to the next and which are arranged in what is considered to be a proper sequence to encourage and stimulate maximum learning.

Teachers are selected from the congregation to minister through the program of planned teaching sponsored by the church. Teachers chosen for this ministry witness most effectively through their own lives. A teacher who has great knowledge of the Christian heritage and is skilled in the best procedures of teaching will fail if his own life does not witness to the reality and validity of the faith he teaches.

Leadership training enterprises are organized and executed in an effort to educate and train those chosen for the teaching ministry of the church. It is well to remind ourselves that parents are members of this teaching ministry and should be considered when plans are made for training enterprises.

Those responsible for communicating the Christian gospel in a program of planned teaching need help in several areas. One of these areas is that of knowledge of the Christian heritage, including such studies as Bible, church history, and theology. A second concern is that of human growth and development. An understanding of persons and particularly of the age group with which one is to be working is essential for the most effective teaching. The third need is knowledge of, and skill in, the performance of teaching procedures. Laboratory schools, in-service-training programs, and unit planning sessions provide training and experience in these areas.

In planned teaching, just as in environmental and situational teaching, it is the child who does the learning. The most carefully made plans of the best prepared teacher will fall short of the intended goal if the children themselves are not involved in the process. They must be challenged with content which they recognize as relevant to their world and therefore important for them to know and, more important, they must realize that the teacher is involved in the learning for the same reasons they are.

The church—and by this is meant the Body of Christ, not the social institution—exists for the purpose of nurture and service or witness. The three ways of communicating the gospel listed above are means for nurturing the young in the faith.

Worship is an equally integral part of nurture. The adult mind is apt to leap to the service in the sanctuary of the church building when the word "worship" is used. Children's worship is simple, direct, and often very brief. Some of their most worshipful moments are the result of situational teaching and may occur at any time and in any place. Adults who are sensitive to children's moods and expressions are true instruments for children's worship of God.

As children grow and mature, they begin to recall experiences, to associate knowledge, and to be more formal in their worship of God. Here again the teacher needs to be sensitive to that which has had meaning and to guide children in discovering and organizing materials that will enable them to express their feelings and make their response to God.[4]

Christian education is concerned with witnessing as well as learning. Nurture includes instruction that provides knowledge through experience and results in the expression of feelings and commitments in worship. Effective, meaningful nurture inevitably results in witnessing. Even the smallest child can and does witness to the Christian nurture that he has been given.

Five-year-old Sammy was standing at the kitchen door looking out at a beautiful sunset sky. Sammy's mother paused in her preparation of the evening meal to stand beside her son and enjoy the loveliness of the evening sky. "It is very beautiful," she said. "Shall we thank God for creating such beauty?" she asked softly.

Without taking his eyes from the sky Sammy took his mother's hand, "I just have," he said quietly.

This story sums up all that this chapter has attempted to communicate. Christian education of children is concerned with discovering and practicing the best and most effective means of bringing children into the presence of God and helping them express their own feelings in worship and witness.

## FOR ADDITIONAL READING

Cully, Iris V. *Children in the Church*. Philadelphia: The Westminster Press, 1960.

———. *The Dynamics of Christian Education*. Philadelphia: The Westminster Press, 1958.

[4] See chap. 21, pp. 242-55.

DeWolf, L. Harold. *Teaching Our Faith in God*. Nashville: Abingdon Press, 1963.

Hill, Dorothy LaCroix. *Working With Juniors at Church*. Nashville: Abingdon Press, 1955.

Lee, Florence B. *Primary Children in the Church*. Valley Forge: Judson Press, 1961.

Morrison, Eleanor S. and Foster, Virgil E. *Creative Teaching in the Church*. Englewood Cliffs: Prentice-Hall, 1963.

Schreyer, George M. *Christian Education in Theological Focus*. Philadelphia: United Church Press, 1962.

Tobey, Kathrene McLandress. *The Church Plans for Kindergarten Children*. Philadelphia: The Westminster Press, 1959.

Ziegler, Jesse H. *Psychology and the Teaching Church*. Nashville: Abingdon Press, 1962.

# Chapter 16

# THE CHURCH'S
# YOUTH MINISTRY

## *Robert L. Browning*

PARADOXICALLY, AT THE VERY TIME WE ARE EXPERIENCING A CRISIS IN THE church's youth ministry we are beginning to build a theological and educational foundation for this ministry which has genuine promise. It cannot be denied that the church is being perceived as ineffective and "out of touch" by countless youth both inside and outside the community of faith. Yet, matching those who are disenchanted there are many who testify to having found significant growth in their church experiences. Thus, any attempt to generalize about the relevance of the Christian education of our youth will fail to find universal support when individual youth in varying churches are interviewed. Still, thoughtful leaders are deeply concerned about the growing numbers who are not responding to the traditional approaches to youth ministry. The whole field seems to be in flux. Old patterns are being abandoned, often not without resistance from parents and even youth for whom these approaches have had meaning. Feelings of guilt and gnawing defensiveness tend to confuse those who are seeking seriously to reconstruct the church's ministry with youth. Such introspection and honest evaluation, however, have produced a period of solid theological reassessment concerning adequate goals, as well as creative experimentation in respect to curriculum, settings, and methods for youth ministry.

### Present Goals for Youth Ministry
### Are Theologically More Defensible

At the same time youth leaders were cooperatively probing the theological foundations for their work, there arose a strong movement for church renewal in general. A plethora of books and articles appeared which attempted to define more clearly the nature and mission of the church in the world. This quest to clarify the essential nature of the church's life and ministry has been exceedingly fruitful for the endeavor to find theologically more adequate and penetrating goals for the church's youth ministry. Much of this dialogue was conducted ecumenically as well as denominationally. For instance, the Senior High and Junior High Committees of the National Council of Churches have produced unofficial but most helpful materials which reflect the theological and educational direction of the present period of creative thinking.

Clearly, Protestant Christian education for youth had embraced, consciously or unconsciously, goals which were perhaps worthy but often sub-Christian. To provide moral or character education, healthy group activities, and service projects to raise money often became the accepted goals of "youth work" in many of our churches. It was a common experience to hear college chaplains or campus foundation directors lament the fact that entirely too many youth, coming out of active youth programs in our local churches, had little understanding of the distinctive nature of the gospel or very clear commitment to the mission of the church. The Jacob study of college freshmen confirmed this fact. 78 percent of the freshmen said they had a strong need for religious faith in terms of helping them organize their lives and to give them a sense of security. However, they did not want their faith to disturb their private plans for social success and economic achievement. Jacob concluded that privatism was the overwhelming attitude of the students and was a reflection of adult mores. The only exceptions were students in schools where the faculty and administration evidenced a sense of mission and personal involvement in the controversial issues of our time.[1] It seems clear that many of these youth did not understand the demands of the gospel for personal commitment to and involvement in the church as a community of believers, called by God, to extend his love to all peoples. The exceptions suggest a needed model for effective and responsible education.

Increasing awareness of the inadequacies of the Christian education of youth in their early and middle teens called forth the basic studies by the National Council of Churches' Youth Work Committee which resulted in a statement on *The Objective of Christian Education for Senior High Young People*. A Junior High statement is in process but not available at the time of this writing. Starting its work in 1958 the Senior High Committee has published the results of its study in a series of monographs, entitled *We Have This Ministry: A View Toward Youth in the Church's Ministry*.

The first two monographs reveal that a new theological focus for youth ministry is taking shape. It was quickly seen that the objective of Christian education for youth should be the same as the objective of the total church. If the church's purpose is to communicate the good news of the gospel and to be an agent of God's love to all the families on the face of the earth (Gen. 12:1-3), then the objective of Christian education for all age levels, including youth, should be to help persons hear and respond to God's gospel, identify themselves as his children, and commit themselves to be his ministers in the world.

With this understanding in mind the committee formulated the following statement of objective which has been exceedingly influential as a guide for the development of new principles and approaches in many denominations.

The objective for Christian education is that all persons be aware of God through his self-disclosure, especially his redeeming love as revealed in Jesus Christ, and that they respond in faith and love—to the end that they may know who they are and

[1] Philip E. Jacob, *Changing Values in Colleges* (New York: Harper & Brothers, 1957), pp. 18-29.

what their human situation means, grow as sons of God rooted in the Christian community, live in the Spirit of God in every relationship, fulfill their common discipleship in the world, and abide in the Christian hope.[2]

In other words, the gospel is at the heart of our Christian education. The goal of our work with youth is to nurture them in the Christian community so they will hear the gospel and experience its meaning, become aware of God's love in their lives, and respond in faith and love. This objective is to be reached by helping them "explore the whole field of relationships" they are experiencing as adolescents "in the light of the gospel," discover, personally appropriate, and assume responsibility for the meanings and values which become clear to them as they identify themselves with the purpose and mission of the church in the world.

1. This means that youth, employing their natural curiosity, should be encouraged to move out, to explore the worlds of history, nature, persons, and institutions to discern their meaning in light of the gospel. Erik Erikson, Harvard University professor of human development, supports this approach when he says that a crucial developmental need for the middle to late adolescent is to find someone or something in which he can put his faith. However, he states, this quest for a great fidelity must take place in a climate that encourages full inquiry concerning all of the diverse faiths that a human being may appropriate.[3] This means we must encourage our youth to explore freely the diverse meanings and values they are experiencing but always "in light of the gospel" so they will be able to see and compare the Christian faith in relation to alternate commitments.

An attitude of responsible freedom within the Christian community is essential in order for youth to be able to identify who they are in ultimate terms. Youth need to be nurtured in the faith of their parents. But, they also need a climate where they may test this faith, refine it, and relate it to all their wider experiences so it can become their own firsthand faith.

Too often our Christian education of youth has failed at two points: (a) As pastors and leaders, we have not communicated the gospel to our youth. They have not been led "to listen with growing alertness to the gospel" because often we were not sufficiently in touch with their world nor were we clear enough about the gospel, its language and symbols, to be able communicators. (b) We have created a climate which was calculated to be accepting but was actually so amorphous that youth were inclined to conclude that "It doesn't make any difference what people believe so long as they are sincere." [4] Or, we have created the opposite: a climate which rejected honest diversity and dialogue. Both of these deficiencies have caused resentment and disillusionment for inquiring youth who wanted to get hold of something significant and challenging in their church schools or fellowship groups. It is my firm con-

---

[2] *We Have This Ministry: No. 2* (New York: National Council of Churches, 1964), p. 12.

[3] *Youth: Change and Challenge* (New York: Basic Books, 1963), p. 3.

[4] See the findings of the Lutheran Youth Research, reported in Merton P. Strommen, *Profiles of Church Youth* (St. Louis: Concordia Publishing House, 1963), p. 57.

viction that the high "drop out" rate among youth in our Protestant church schools can be attributed heavily to these defeating experiences.

2. A major goal of the Christian education of youth is to create persons who identify themselves as ministers. The word "minister" may be a stumbling block here. However, we have repeatedly failed to design a Christian education around the concept of the church as a ministering community, a universal priesthood of believers, even though it is a central biblical understanding of the church and a cardinal principle of Protestantism.

Without apology we should rejoice in the theologically sound trend to prepare youth to identify themselves as ministers to one another and to younger and older members of the church in order that they may be better able to minister to God's people in their wider world of relationships beyond the community of believers. Youth are now being seen as "full members of the church" in terms of the ministry of concern and trust which they can express from their baptism or dedication on. They are full members of the body of Christ and are not to be considered less important than their elders, although their tasks of necessity may be different in the life of the church. Both youth and adults are to identify themselves as priests to one another and to the world. Both youth and adults are in need of continued training and "preparation" for increased ministry in the world, through personal, community, family, vocational, and political relationships. Youth are to be seen as young laity, young *laos*, young people whom God has called to continue his ministry of reconciliation in the world. In addition to creating a community of lay ministers it should have the salutary effect of giving new integrity to the ordained ministry, in which vocation many more promising youth are urgently needed. There are several experiments in respect to confirmation education which are being conducted in local churches in order to help youth develop their commitment to this personal and social ministry on two or three levels of maturity, climaxing in the senior year of high school rather than in the seventh grade. Several denominations are studying the purpose of confirmation and the problems of timing, relationship to the total Christian nurture of the youth, and his developmental need to engage in honest and deep firsthand questioning and internalization of his faith in middle and late teens rather than early teens when most confirmation classes are held.

Also, many youth lose interest because they have never seen the goal of their continuing participation in Christian education, worship, and service experiences. Acceptable behavior, right belief, fellowship, or biblical and historical knowledge for its own sake are not dynamic or challenging enough goals to motivate youth who are alive to the issues in a complex world. To participate in a ministry which faces divisions, hurts, misunderstandings, and physical or spiritual needs in the real world before them *is* big enough to evoke response from youth who are yearning to give themselves to something worth their total energies.

Youth and adults alike need to be strengthened in the gathered church in worship, study, and mutual caring so they may be prepared to continue Christ's ministry in his scattered church—out in school, community, recreation, family, and vocational relationships. There is evidence that a special training is needed to make the ministry in the scattered church effective. It will not just happen naturally.[5]

## The Church Is Seeking to Look at the World
## Through the Eyes of Youth

This trend is evident for several reasons. For one thing, various studies of adolescent psychology are approaching consensus that the crucial need in our work with youth is to be sensitive to the way they *perceive themselves* and the way they perceive their world. It is helpful to know with Arnold Gesell what the expected developmental behavior of a thirteen-year-old may be in comparison to a fourteen-year-old, but this does not tell us how any one thirteen-year-old sees himself and his relationship to other persons, God, or the church. The crucial need is for adult leaders and parents to be in communication with youth, to listen to their perceptions, so that adults can be in a position to help them "listen to the gospel" at the point of some real struggle they are having with themselves, their physical motivation, their relationship with the opposite sex, or the social pressures on them to act in ways contrary to their previous values.

This approach calls for the creation of an honest community of youth and sensitive, committed, yet open adults. It deemphasizes "programs" and "classes" and emphasizes youth and adults working together on issues that really matter from the youth's perspective. In the quest for meaning and values concerning these issues which are alive for youth, both adults and youth share their honest questions and beliefs so there is a genuine meeting of persons. In this climate both youth and adult leaders grow. Both participate in planning and teaching. Both assume designated and functional leadership roles. Adults give needed guidance and encouragement. They are responsible for being resource persons but not "answer men" to youth. Youth can be heard. They, too, take responsibility for providing resources and ideas. Adults and youth can "listen to the gospel" in relation to the real world and come to affirmations together. In this kind of community, whether in class, small group, weekend retreat, or camp, youth can find themselves. They can identify "who they are and what their human situation means," as they define themselves in relation to adults who are honestly caught in many of the same human predicaments but who have commitments and values which are felt and expressed in community.

Edgar Friedenberg maintains that "adolescence *is* conflict-protracted conflict —between the individual and society." That is, youth must find values and demands in the adult world which they may resist or with which they may identify. American youth, he maintains, have a most difficult time finding strong, honest adults who are committed to values and purposes with which

[5] See David Hunter, *Christian Education as Engagement* (New York: The Seabury Press, 1963), chap. 5, "Engagement Training For Mission," p. 71.

they may identify or over against which they may define new values.[6] It is true that youth find many spineless, pleasure-seeking, irresponsible images of adulthood in our culture with whom to identify. Yet, these images can hardly qualify as adult, and therefore they make it exceedingly difficult for youth to move through the "marginal" land from childhood to adulthood. This point of view buttresses the present trend toward seeing Christian education as a by-product of all the relationships of the people who make up the church family. If the youth are discussing the brotherhood of man in a class in a church which excludes members of other races from worship in its sanctuary, it is not surprising that the youth will learn not to take the gospel or the church too seriously.

Since G. Stanley Hall's research on adolescence and Anna Freud's psycho-analytic view, there have been leaders who have seen the adolescent years, from pubescence to genital maturity, as days of storm and stress, no matter what society does about it. On the other hand there have been those who, like the early Margaret Mead and Ruth Benedict, have seen adolescence as a culturally conditioned period which need not be especially stressful. Such cultural anthropologists have emphasized the possibility of continuity of growth in cultures which are consistent about their values in childhood and adulthood. In our American culture, they say, we have vast areas of life which are taboo to children but which are acceptable and highly valued for adults. In this kind of culture it is easy to see why the adolescent does not know what behavior will gain the approval of adults and free him from his status as a child. There-fore, he is anxious and threatened.

More recently biologically oriented and culturally oriented interpreters have come closer together in their view of the adolescent years. Field theorists, build-ing on the work of Kurt Lewin, and psychoanalytic thinkers such as Erik Erikson, and even the more recent thought of anthropologist Margaret Mead, have agreed on the importance and universality of adjustments caused by biological changes as well as cultural conditioning. A more promising stance is to view adolescents as members of a marginal group, neither children nor adults, but not to classify them too rigidly as a group. Rather, each adolescent's behavior makes sense if it is interpreted in terms of the field of forces at work in his life (physical, social, emotional, and cognitive). Further, it is important to discern very concretely how he perceives himself and his situation, because he will "act out" his self-concept in relation to the demands of society on him.

In American society the period of transition between childhood and adult-hood is vastly prolonged in comparison to primitive cultures. Thus, the adolescent seeks rather long-term security in his own peer group. We have a youth culture, therefore, which is very influential, with its own values, language, and customs. Conformity to this culture is crucial. The church must listen to and be in conversation with this world. Any penetration of the lives of individual youth will be made in relation to these ever-changing values. However, no one adolescent puts together his biological changes, his past values

[6] *The Vanishing Adolescent* (Boston: Beacon Press, 1959), p. 12.

from childhood, his present conditioning from his peer group, and his cultural *ethos,* in the same way as any other adolescent.

This means at least two things for the strategy of the church: (a) We must have many more adults working with youth so we can give much more individual attention to the uniqueness of each person. For too long we have succumbed to the idea that youth should be in charge of their own life, with only a minimum of concerned adults working with them. This has tended to allow the values of the youth culture to pervade the church's ministry with youth without any healthy tension being brought to the thinking and planning by adults who are grounded in the gospel. On the positive side, more adults are needed who will take seriously the honest, imaginative questions and suggestions of youth who are members of a youth culture which is often opposed to the status quo. (b) We will need to build Christian group life of a quality which offers youth genuine alternatives to the pervading standards and which can enter into honest conversation with the dominant youth culture, with a view toward transforming the culture itself. Several of the new experiments have to do with training of teams of youth and adults in cohesive and responsible group participation. Youth and adults are taught the power of shared leadership where members have reached working agreements and are committed to concrete Christian goals in harmony with the nature and mission of the church in the world.

Since the gospel is relevant to all of life,

all subject matter and every experience are appropriate to the purview of Christian education. There are not some topics which are "religious" and therefore suitable for the youth program-curriculum and others which are non-religious and therefore unsuitable or even contaminating. All of life—the whole world—is a proper field for youth to explore for meaning and value in the light of the gospel.[7]

This means we must look at the world the youth actually experience through their eyes and organize our teaching-learning sessions around these real-life issues. In so doing we may see them as religious issues. Fortunately the curriculum resources of most denominations are planned with the hope that teachers and leaders will be able to bring the crucial issues and situations in the youth's society into "meaningful relationship with the givens of the gospel."[8]

## Hypotheses for Future Approaches

In order to achieve a deeper penetration and a greater response on the part of "young laity," some major changes in our expectations and our approach are needed. The following hypotheses are offered as possible guidelines for future approaches to the church's ministry with youth.

[7] *We Have This Ministry: No. 2,* p. 26.
[8] *Ibid.,* p. 28.

*Hypothesis No. 1: Youth, in every socioeconomic situation, are much more serious about their quest for a faith than we may have assumed.*

Remembering our conclusion that the actions of youth make sense when we see them as a "living out" of their perception of themselves and their world, the behavior of the most rebellious adolescent reveals a profound desire to find meaning in life. In a recent study of five hundred youth from both inner-city and suburban communities by the Ecumenical Institute of Chicago it was discovered that "both inner city and the suburban youth were found to possess the qualities of seriousness, underlying openness, anxiety about the future and revolt against unquestioned tradition which characterizes the world of youth today. No fundamental distinction was discovered in their concern for a significant life and for genuine participation in society." [9] While there were very real differences in the perceptions of the two groups, in their feelings about their situations, and in their patterns of escape (disruptiveness for inner-city youth and intellectualization for suburban youth), each pattern was seen to be a genuine attempt to find meaning for life. Similar conclusions have been reached in the research of Block and Niederhoffer on youth gangs and by Norman Kiell in his study of adolescent experiences from varying cultural settings.[10]

If this hypothesis is valid, it would mean that our expectations concerning the basic seriousness of youth are much too low. If we take their perceptions, their faltering attempts to define themselves, with seriousness, perhaps they will take the approach of the church more seriously. Also, it means we need to challenge youth to greater effort, rather than assume they are carefree and careless. Recent attempts to challenge youth to enter covenant relationships for serious study and service seem to be in the right direction. This does not mean these approaches should be "intellectual" or stuffy. It does mean they should deal with real issues and with the meat of the gospel.

Perhaps the creative work of Ross Snyder of the Chicago Theological Seminary has been most responsible for growing numbers of experiments, built on the presupposition that youth want honest discussion about basic values with adults who will participate with them in a mutual "ministry of meanings."

*Hypothesis No. 2: Ministering to others, the life and work of service, is much more highly valued by youth than we have supposed.*

Experiences with young people in work camps, in the Peace Corps, in the three-year missionary programs of various denominations, in the witness of youth in the civil rights struggle give strong and growing evidence that our previous youth ministry has been much too self-centered and self-sufficient. Youth respond to opportunities to participate in the outreach as well as the internal ministry of the church.

Where youth have seen themselves as the church in action, they have moved out in power, often to the surprise of their elders. Some churches have opened opportunities for youth to function in all the facets of the ministry—in

[9] "Youth in the Urban-Suburban Complex," *Image*, Journal of the Ecumenical Institute, a Division of the Church Federation of Chicago, III (Winter, 1965), 16.

[10] *The Universal Experience of Adolescence* (New York: International Universities Press, 1964).

preaching and witnessing; in worship leadership within the gathered church, and in new and relevant settings for the scattered church; in pastoral services to fellow youth and their families, to the elderly, infirmed, dispossessed, handicapped in body or mind; in the multitudinous tasks of administering the outreach of the church; in the prophetic ministry as they face and witness to the Christian way concerning the personal and social problems before them. The church that takes seriously youth's need for meaningful self-giving will build a deeper and more committed fellowship of youth and adults than seems possible without this assumption.

*Hypothesis No. 3: New and more flexible forms and settings of youth ministry are needed in our highly mobile and fluid society.*

Many responsible youth leaders have become increasingly convinced that the traditional Sunday morning classes, Sunday evening youth fellowships, and summer and mid-year institute patterns leave much to be desired. These forms, it is maintained, are the product of an earlier agrarian-oriented Protestantism which no longer describes our urbanized culture. With many family members called upon to work in shops and factories on weekends, and other families being enticed to spend growing hours of leisure away from their homes in quest of recreation and physical renewal, the traditional times and patterns seem not to be evoking interest and commitment from multitudes of youth and their parents.

Leaders who are calling for changes maintain, on theological grounds, that the actual needs and life situations of contemporary youth should be the criteria employed to help define the forms and settings the ministry with youth should take. If the church is really people and not a building or a program, it should seek to communicate God's loving concern for youth where they are, and find patterns of organization appropriate to their needs.

Since many youth find relative meaning in present patterns, it is important to help them and their parents evaluate the strengths and weaknesses of present structures. Where they discover depth and significance in present approaches, they may want to reaffirm and deepen these expressions. Where they discover weaknesses and omissions, they may be more open to the discussion of forms and patterns which may have more power to reach youth not now participants in the life of mutual ministry and mission.

Some of these more flexible forms which are being explored and tested in various denominations are:

(1) More flexible grading and grouping of youth in present classes and fellowships. Denominational leaders are beginning to prepare curriculum materials which are designed to be used flexibly in one, two, or three grade groupings in junior high and senior high, whether these classes meet on Sunday morning, Sunday evening, or during the week. Here again the principle is one of discovering the actual situation and needs of the youth and forming teaching-learning-serving-worshiping groups which evoke the greatest response and deepest commitment. In order to make this flexible approach operational, local churches may select different tracks on which their youth will travel. These tracks will be planned to guarantee maximum comprehensiveness and balance in the curriculum along with increased flexibility and relevance.

(2) *Koinonia* or core group settings. Emphasizing the need of every human being for an honest, accepting, trusting relationship with other persons, youth and adults in countless churches are forming small *koinonia* groups. In this setting any problems youth are experiencing may be explored in the light of the gospel. These small groups emphasize the unity of persons in God's love and the necessity for ministering to one another and to the world. Since Henry Tani's proposal and plan for small group work in 1957, many churches have found renewed life in these intimate groups of youth.[11]

Closely akin to *koinonia* groups are core groups which emphasize "listening evangelism." Trained and sensitive adult leaders meet with youth, in groups of ten to twelve for two hours a week for eight to ten weeks. Youth who have some sense of Christian commitment join youth who are either inactive church members or nonmembers to discuss any problems or concerns they may wish to bring to the group. These groups may meet after school, in the evenings, or on weekends at any place and time most convenient to the members. The focus of the group is on listening to one another discuss ultimately important questions in a nonmanipulative climate.

(3) Weekend settings. Materials and resources are now being prepared for use with Junior High and Senior High youth on four or five weekend retreats per year. Experimentation has revealed that for many youth more depth in personal relationships as well as solid academic study of the Christian faith can take place at a camp, retreat house, or even at the local church from Friday evening to Sunday afternoon than can take place in comparable total time divided into small segments of fifty minutes per week.

(4) School of religion settings. Similarly following the principle of flexibility, it has been discovered that some youth prefer to block out three weeks in the summer to study and discuss, in a much more comprehensive and systematic way, some area of mutual concern in the light of the gospel. In both rural and urban situations youth and adult leaders have met for five nights a week for three weeks. This pattern can provide thirty hours of study in a setting that encourages personal involvement and allows enough time for ideas to be explored more fully and internalized more adequately. Some schools of religion have been held during the day and have granted college credit, as did one in Mansfield, Ohio, offered by the council of churches in conjunction with Heidelberg College.

(5) Weekday settings. Curiously, released-time religious education is declining in many communities at a time when the decisions of the United States Supreme Court sustain the legality of sharing the school day between public and religious educational institutions. Shared-time or dual-school enrollment plans are being proposed as a way to increase the quantity and quality of religious education of our children and youth, while at the same time supporting and improving our free public schools in America.

Religious centers or foundations are being proposed, to be sponsored independently or jointly by Protestants, Roman Catholics, and Jews, adjacent to public schools. In communities where cooperation between churches and

[11] *Ventures in Youth Work* (Philadelphia: Christian Education Press, 1957).

schools can be developed, it appears to be possible for youth to study their respective faiths regularly during the week. Again a more systematic study of biblical, historical, and theological questions is made feasible in a setting related to their general educational experiences.

Wesner Fallaw, professor of religious education at Andover Newton Theological School, has experimented with such a program. He helped to found the Institute of Religious Studies in Newton, Massachusetts, where high school students have studied solid academic courses in religion. The Institute has received the approval of several colleges and universities and has a working relationship with them. The National Council of Churches and several state and local councils of churches are studying similar projects.

(6) Service settings. Youth as full members of Christ's body need to find creative ways and tools for extending and continuing Christ's ministry in the world. If they, like Christ, take the form that most powerfully communicates to persons in need, they will look first at the human needs and then decide on patterns of service.

There is growing interest in finding ways for youth to work within service settings—in work with disadvantaged children, older persons, infirm or crippled persons, lonely and detached persons, hungry or destitute persons. It is hoped that study, prayer, and mutual sharing, can be related significantly to such service settings. In which case these settings could be powerful educational experiences as well as visible expressions of the relevance of the church in our world.

(7) Other experimental settings. With many youth (in lower and to some degree upper socioeconomic strata) out of touch with our organized churches, various patterns need to emerge which will offer means of communication.[12] "Coffee houses" for youth are being employed.[13] Creative projects sponsored ecumenically, employing drama, music, or the arts, have reached otherwise uninvolved youth. Full-length motion picture series which face contemporary youth problems, with discussions following, have reached wider audiences. The assigning of detached workers in inner-city areas to relate spontaneously to youth gangs has been effective in major cities. The sponsoring of tutorials, "study halls," and vocational guidance service has ministered to real needs. The whole area of Christian education out-of-doors is growing rapidly.[14]

*Hypothesis No. 4: There is much more interest on the part of youth in communication and cooperation between youth and adults (including parents) than has been thought.*

Studies and research by several denominations have uncovered substantial support among youth for increased opportunities for communication with their parents and other adults. This has included a desire for regular corporate worship as a family and even for family devotions in the home. Youth also

---

[12] See the longitudinal study of the church's effectiveness with youth from varying socioeconomic levels in Robert J. Havighurst's *Growing Up in River City* (New York: John Wiley & Sons, 1962).

[13] See chap. 17, pp. 193-204.

[14] See chap. 30, pp. 350-59.

desire opportunities to discuss and work together with the adults in the congregation.

If this hypothesis were to be found valid, many more educational, worship, and service experiences could be planned in cooperation with adults. Experiments with youth and adult study groups should be expanded. Youth and parent weekend dialogues on sex and other moral concerns of youth seem to hold real promise. Including youth on the committees and commissions of the church could help youth come alive if adults had higher expectations and evoked genuine participation.

Family worship and study patterns have been found to be effective especially in Episcopal churches and increasingly in churches of other denominations. Here parents and youth worship together, followed by study either together or in separate groups. Separate youth "churches" are declining in number and effectiveness.

*Hypothesis No. 5: While youth are the church in mission, they have special needs which the church must not overlook.* Responsible adults must be sensitive to the needs of youth in their total growth. Many young adolescents are suffering from physical or emotional immaturities, academic problems, or spiritual struggles to which other members of the church must be sensitive, and for which difficulties they must open avenues of help. This means that opportunities for athletic expression are not inconsistent with the church's ministry with youth. It means that social life, parties and recreation often are crucially needed. It means that academic and vocational guidance should be the concern of the church, as is the case with the guidance program of the Presbyterian Church, U. S. It means personal and group counseling should be amply available to youth in their struggles.

To include youth as full participants in the ministry and mission of the church must never indirectly exclude them from receiving needed ministries, however nonreligious they may appear at first glance.

## FOR ADDITIONAL READING

Bowman, Clarice M. *Ways Youth Learn.* New York: Harper & Row, 1952.

Cummings, Oliver De Wolf. *The Youth Fellowship.* Valley Forge: Judson Press, 1956.

Erikson, Erik H. *Childhood and Society.* Rev. ed. New York: W. W. Norton & Company, 1964.

————, ed. *Youth: Change and Challenge.* New York: Basic Books, 1963.

Ferguson, Rowena. *The Church's Ministry with Senior Highs.* Nashville: Graded Press, 1963.

Friedenberg, Edgar Z. *The Vanishing Adolescent.* Boston: Beacon Press, 1959.

Gesell, Arnold; Ilg, Frances L.; and Ames, Louise B. *Youth: The Years From Ten to Sixteen.* New York: Harper & Row, 1956.

Griffiths, Louise. *The Teacher and the Young Teens.* St. Louis: The Bethany Press, 1954.

Havighurst, Robert J. *et al. Growing Up in River City.* New York: John Wiley & Sons, 1962.

Johnson, Eric. *How to Live Through Junior High School.* New York: J. B. Lippincott Co., 1959.

Muuss, Rolf E. *Theories of Adolescence.* New York: Random House, 1962.

Remmers, H. H. and Radler, D. H. *The American Teenager.* Indianapolis: The Bobbs-Merrill Co., 1957.

Roberts, Dorothy M. *Partners with Youth: How Adults and Teen-agers Can Work Together.* New York: Association Press, 1956.

Seidman, Jerome, ed. *The Adolescent: A Book of Readings.* Rev. ed. New York: Holt, Rinehart & Winston, 1960.

Smith, Ernest A. *American Youth Culture: Group Life in Teenage Society.* New York: The Free Press of Glencoe, 1962.

Strang, Ruth. *The Adolescent Views Himself.* New York: McGraw-Hill Book Company, 1957.

Strommen, Merton P. *Profiles of Church Youth.* St. Louis: Concordia Publishing House, 1963.

Tani, Henry N. *Ventures in Youth Work.* Philadelphia: Christian Education Press, 1957.

*We Have This Ministry: A View Toward Youth in the Church's Ministry.* Monographs No. 1 (1963) and No. 2 (1964), published by the National Council of Churches, New York.

Wittenberg, Rudolph M. *Adolescence and Discipline.* New York: Association Press, 1959.

————. *On Call for Youth.* New York: Association Press, 1955.

*The Young Adolescent in the Church: A Guide for Workers with Junior Highs.* Philadelphia: The Westminster Press, 1963.

# Chapter 17

# THE CHURCH'S
# YOUNG ADULT MINISTRY

## Allen J. Moore

THE ERA IN LIFE CALLED YOUNG ADULTHOOD HAS ONLY RECENTLY EMERGED in our society. The breakup of rural social structures and the rise of urban mass culture has led to an increased compartmentalization of life. The specialization of age groupings has been gradually taking place for forty years or more in the educational programs of the church and in the study of human development by behavioral scientists. This has been especially true of young adulthood as the growing complexity of modern urban society has increasingly required a transitional period between youth and adult maturity.

The church's focus on this period of transition is relatively recent. The reason for this lies in part in the nature of the early church youth leagues. Youth work in its early stages of development was broadly conceived, and it included persons of older youth and young adult age. It was not unusual for these leagues, such as Christian Endeavor and Epworth League, to have members up to at least forty years of age. The development of person-centered education, the impact of psychology, and the growth of churches in cities led denominations in the 1930's toward youth programs oriented more to the developmental needs of young people. The upper age limit of these programs was set at twenty-three, and provisions were made in the new youth organizations for older youth and college students who were eighteen years of age and over. This new definition of youth contributed to the rise of denominational programs for young adults, patterned to a large extent after the organizations for youth. Apparently, the majority of the young adults were married and were within the twenty-four to thirty-six age definition adopted by most denominations. But there were programs for single young adults in some of the larger city churches, especially during the 1940's.

A period of life is also defined culturally, as well as by years of age. The events of history and the forces of social change have increasingly pushed persons into early maturity. A world in crisis and a technological revolution, along with the induction of eighteen-year-olds into the armed forces, early marriage and parenthood, urban migration, and radical advances in nutrition, communications, and transportation have all contributed to the speed-up in maturation and the early assumption of adult responsibility by the young. By 1950 church leaders were being confronted with older youth who had more in common with young adults than youth and with persons still in the young-adult age-range who had long completed the developmental tasks of early adulthood.

These factors led the Youth and Adult Committees of the Division of Christian Education of the National Council of Churches to appoint in the early 1950's a research committee to study older youth and young adults.[1] Three strategy conferences were held in order to find out more about the nature of this age group and to learn ways to program more effectively. The underlying issue in these studies was: When does youth work end and young adult work begin? Emerging was the growing conviction that persons in the late teens were more nearly young adult than youth and should be a part of a young adult ministry. Also, it was concluded that this young adult period in life generally did not extend beyond the late twenties.

Building upon the findings and hypotheses of these studies, several major research projects were initiated between 1960 and 1962. Notable were the Young Adult Research Project of the Methodist General Board of Education[2] and the Study of Young Men and Women of the National Council of the Young Men's Christian Association.[3]

Several general conclusions emerged from these projects. The first is that persons the church has categorized as older youth *and* young adults are actually one unit, grouping, or focus of concern, rather than two. Persons in the late teens and twenties are best characterized as transitional, in that they are working out the life issues which will move them from youth to adult maturity. In this process they have specific and unique needs which distinguish them on one hand from youth and on the other hand from more mature adults.

The second is that although there are distinctive psychological needs which create one young adult unit, there are also wide sociological divergences within this unit. Young adults have a variety of life patterns, are found in many social situations, and represent various subcultures. They may be single, married, or divorced; a college student, employed, or unemployable; a sophisticate, conformist, or drifter; or a combination of these with numerous other possible categories.

The third is that age is not always an accurate criterion for describing who is a young adult. Persons enter this period of life and leave it at different ages, and the rate in which they move through the developmental tasks will greatly vary. A sixteen-year-old may be a high school dropout trying to make his way in an adult world of work; an eighteen-year-old girl may be married and pregnant with a second child; and a twenty-six-year-old couple may have completed its family, be established socially and vocationally, and have started to work on questions characteristic of middle adulthood.

The crucial issue still unresolved is the descriptive label for identifying church programs for these persons. Among those used are "Older Youth/ Young Adults," "Young Laity," "Young Churchmen," and "Young Adults." Psychological terms, such as "new adults," "early adulthood," and "the

[1] A mimeographed report was distributed to member denominations. A booklet also was printed, *A Manual for Young Adults* (New York: National Council of Churches, 1960).

[2] Five reports, as well as other documents, have been published. For information write Young Adult Project, General Board of Education, P. O. Box 871, Nashville, Tenn. 37202.

[3] Allen S. Ellsworth, *Young Men, Young Women* (New York: Association Press, 1963).

transitional years" are probably more descriptive of the experiences of the age group but are awkward to use as program labels.

## Set in an Urban World

The young adult period of life is partly a result of urbanization. The urban revolution has led to the breaking down of community, the crumbling of traditions and values, the rapidity of social change, the diversity of adult models, the changing function of the family, and the increased mobility of the young. With few certainties and almost no guidelines, the process of becoming adult has become more difficult, the crises more pronounced, and the time required to complete the tasks more specified.

In rural society there was not a need for a period for testing out alternatives for adult life. The various elements of the society, including the generations, were closely interwoven. With less isolation between age groups, and with fewer alternatives as to life patterns, the movement into the adult world was completed by meeting several formalities. One remained in the family setting until marriage, and a change of residence generally did not take a young family out of familiar surroundings. Whatever pain was involved in growing up, it was greatly reduced by the presence of close, warm relationships of a primary group.

On the other hand, urban life, in spite of its many benefits, is best characterized by a complexity of social patterns which are often unrelated, by an isolation of the generations, and by the loss of primary relationships and an increased contact with secondary groups. Upon graduation or dropping out of high school, the young person is cast adrift from friendship patterns, family relationships, and established ways of life. Before finding adult maturity, most young adults experience much uncertainty and lostness and go through much stress. Fortunately, most persons successfully complete the transition and enrich themselves and others in the process. Unfortunately, there are many who break down in the process or who decide that it is not worth the effort and regress into some kind of permanent adolescence.

The difficulty of becoming adult in a complex society is evidenced by the kinds of young adult problems listed below.

1. The problem of anomie or being detached, disorganized, ungoverned, and uncommitted. Even young adults who make significant commitments to a cause tend to remain aloof from the major social institutions and disconnected from the social processes of life.

2. The problem of poor mental health is characterized by the unusually high level of guilt and anxiety found in many young adults. Studies indicate that depression, guilt, and wishful thinking tend to increase as persons move out of adolescence and become more pronounced as they enter the twenties.

3. Marital problems and divorce are urgent concerns of young adults. The greatest stress in a marriage generally occurs during the first five years, and one half of all divorces involve persons under twenty-nine years of age.

4. Almost every study points to sex as a major problem of young adulthood. Illegitimacy, premarital coitus, and infidelity score high among persons eighteen

to thirty. For example, up to fifty percent of young women and an even higher percentage of young men experience premarital sexual intercourse. Also, other sexual problems of young adults should not be overlooked, such as homosexuality.

5. Crime and delinquency involve a limited number of persons in our society, but this is ever increasing, especially among young adults. This age group makes up the majority of state and federal prisoners and commits the highest rate of hard core crime.

6. The problem of mobility is actually more symptomatic of the problem of rootlessness. It does indicate how difficult it is for society to maintain contact with this transitional group. At least forty percent of the men and women under thirty-five are reported to change residences every year. Also, persons eighteen to twenty-four move twice the average for all ages.

7. The problem of unemployment is still another young adult concern. During the 1960's twenty-six million young people will enter the labor force and will need to compete in a labor market which has more applicants than positions for young workers. The problem will be compounded because of increased automation, inadequate training or lack of skills altogether, and a growing number of high school drop-outs.

8. A neglected problem, by church and society, is the stigma attached to the unmarried young adult especially when social success is measured in terms of marriage. This problem increases for individuals as they move through their twenties, and one study indicates that for young women the rates of sexual promiscuity and premarital pregnancy increase in the late twenties, apparently as a result of the struggle to achieve some compensation for failing to reach the expected state of marriage.

In addition to being a *consequence* of urbanization, the young adult is an important *element* in the metropolis. Young men and women are helping to populate the expanding city. Already two out of three young adults live in cities, and because of birth rate and migration, they are increasing the population of most cities more than any other age group. The post-war baby boom is growing up into young adulthood. During the 1960's persons between the ages of eighteen and twenty-four will increase 64 percent while the entire population increases only 17 percent. Rural areas will show a sharp decrease in this age group while some metropolitan areas will increase over 100 percent. In fact, the young adult population in some cities makes up at least one fourth of the total.

Little evidence exists indicating that rural churches are doing very much to prepare youth for urban migration, and few city churches have learned the secret of contacting and absorbing them into their programs. The result is that urban migration becomes a time of high church drop-out.

The young adult is also symbolic of the new urban man. Needless to say, there is contradictory evidence here because there are those young men and women, like many Protestants with rural backgrounds, who dislike and even fear the city. There are others who cling to a church group not out of any search for new religious orientation but rather out of attempts to shield themselves from the demands of secularization. The church for them becomes a place to hide from a world which demands relations with different cultural and racial backgrounds, contact with other styles and patterns of life, and forces some new decisions regarding social and moral issues.

There is, however, much evidence to suggest that young adulthood has generally become the style of our times. The youthful modern look dominates housing trends, leisure patterns, sexual attitudes and practices, mass advertisement, and fashions ranging from clothes to automobiles. Also, behind this facade are the dispossessed, slums, and a life of poverty. And yet from both the glitter and the decay is emerging the secular urban man—free from religious and metaphysical control and learning to turn away from the *other* world and toward a *present* world that is coming of age. For the church young adults become important because they reflect this turning away from religion and its institutions and symbolize the kinds of questions which urban society is asking. It has been suggested that the young adult world is like a prism through which the whole of modern culture passes and becomes magnified. All the best and all the worst features of the present age come to focus most sharply in the young adult.

Young urbanites from all walks of life are in search of a point of view and a way of life that will be rationally consistent with their understanding of the modern situation. They see the older forms of society breaking away under the strains and stresses of accelerated change. Technical advances have made available to the masses the symbols of culture and the luxuries of life reserved until recently for the very rich. And although there is unemployment and poverty, more young adults than ever before are sharing in the rising prosperity. A ministry to urban and affluent young people will need to recognize that an increasing number either do not take the church seriously or choose to ignore it altogether. The response to this kind of cultural agnosticism and hostility must be formulated from a new understanding of the world rather than reacting out of defensive fear to the threat it represents.

## An Era of Life

A clue to the church's ministry to young adults lies in the nature of the person at this time of life. As Ross Snyder has suggested, this is not just a phase which persons pass through on the way to adulthood.[4] Rather it is an *era:* a time in which certain important events and happenings are taking place within a person. It is a period in one's history in which crucial developmental issues are bursting forth, "itching" to be solved. No relevant ministry can occur until the church learns to see beneath the surface of young adult behavior, some of which may even be deplorable, and to recognize the deeper signs of an intense struggle for meaning and selfhood. Inherent in the very nature of young adulthood are developmental tasks and issues which are of

[4] "The Young Adult," a special issue of *The Chicago Theological Seminary Register*, XLIX (November, 1959).

great religious significance and to which the church must relate the profound insights of the Christian faith.

Psychological constructs contributing to an understanding of the nature of young adulthood are rather limited. In fact, there seem to be only two distinctive theories of this period of life.

One of the first persons to identify this period of life was Robert J. Havighurst.[5] He maintains that "early adulthood" consists of certain developmental tasks which emerge out of the meeting of individual need and societal demands and which must be learned if a person is going to move successfully into middle adulthood. Developmental tasks of early adulthood are: (1) completing or continuing education, (2) selecting a mate, (3) learning to live with a marriage partner, (4) starting a family, (5) rearing children, (6) managing a home, (7) getting started in an occupation, (8) taking on civic responsibility, and (9) finding a congenial social group. Havighurst's distinctive contribution was the identification of society's expectations of persons who had reached the early adult stage of maturation.

A later contribution to the understanding of the nature of young adulthood has come from Erik Erikson. In contrast to Havighurst's emphasis on outward expectations, Erikson has focused on the inner or genetic conflicts inherent in the development of personality. He has been particularly preoccupied with the young adult, as exemplified by his book *Young Man Luther*.[6] Drawing upon psychoanalytic theory and cultural anthropology, Erikson has delineated eight stages of personality development; each of which has inherent a critical psychological conflict or issue which demands resolution. Personality development consists of a ground plan and at its special time of ascendancy, a stage, and its inherent genetic conflict will arise. This does not imply that the other seven conflicts are totally latent as they continue to arise to minor levels of concern at various times in a person's development. For the young adult stage intimacy versus isolation is the chief conflict, but the problems of identity (characteristic of adolescence) and of generativity (characteristic of adulthood) are active and strongly felt.

More recently, the studies of the Methodist Young Adult Research Project and the work of Ross Snyder, who served as consultant to the project, have clarified the developmental questions or issues of the young adult era. Although much additional work is needed, some general observations can be made.

1. *Self-Definition vs. Vagueness.* This relates to the issue of "Who am I?" as a human person, as male or female, and how is this *I* going to be expressed in life. It is the experience of seeking to understand oneself as a person who is distinctive and unique. The task of finding one's personality is not a static experience but is lifelong. It becomes a question in adolescence and continues as a crucial concern for most young adults, partly because of the residue of adolescence and partly because the task of finding one's self takes on adult dimensions. Maturity is a dynamic process by which an individual grows in

---

[5] *Developmental Tasks and Education* (2nd Ed.; New York: David McKay Co., 1952).

[6] (New York: W. W. Norton and Company, 1958). See also *Identity and the Life Cycle* (New York: International Universities Press, 1959), chap. 2.

his capacity to bring integration to his kaleidoscopic existence and to formulate his unique expression or mode of being. To fail at finding a definition of selfhood is to live as a formless *thing* that tends to be fixed and definite. The chief characteristic of the person who does not achieve a grasp of his personality is to lose contact with himself and with much of life itself. For many young adults it becomes easier to assume a synthetic ready-made personality than to struggle to know one's own uniqueness of being.

2. *Belonging vs. Isolation.* Belonging is a deepening encounter of two or more selves. It is the ability to give of oneself as well as to receive another; to create as well as to sustain relationships of depth and meaning. Belonging is more than being with another, but it is what Snyder has called "creating a co-personal world" in which two or more persons know one another and share with each other something of life. For Erikson the crisis here is the psychological struggle for intimacy, psychologically and sexually. The mistake many young adults make is to short-cut the search for belonging with sexual activity. It is true that physical relations do not require a true and mutual psychological intimacy with another person. And yet, sexual relations do not prevent isolation although many persons try to solve the young adult problem of loneliness through sex. To fail at finding relationship results in not only being cut off but in the repudiation and rejection of peers and in the fear of the opposite sex.

3. *Maturity vs. Regression.* Maturity is the dynamic process of growing in one's ability to assume responsibility for the various aspects of human life. Irresponsibility is a mark of the immature life, and, when a person ceases to reach beyond himself, he will find himself shrinking back from life's demands and regressing inwardly. A mark of the mature person is his desire to enter fully into the process of history-making and to assume responsibility for the shape of the future.

4. *Meaning vs. Confusion.* A person really lives only as he is able to find an organized body of meaning that gives significance to life. To fail to find a meaningful reference for life results in confusion, a limited perspective on events, and a deep sense of lostness. To be without meaning is to become a stranger to the universe. For the young adult the task is to find a frame of reference for life, a sense of direction. A system of meanings gives reason for going ahead into adulthood, a claim on conscience, and an interpretive map for understanding one's history. To lose the struggle for a meaningful reference for life leaves the young adult in a kaleidoscopic maze of disorder.

5. *Spontaneity vs. Rigidity.* In this struggle the young adult is learning how to be free from his impulses and from stereotype behaviors. At issue is the ability to accept oneself as a process rather than a static calculator. It is to be alive to the now rather than caught in the dead past. For many young adults rigidity is the stance which they bring to life. They are constantly battling their impulses, referring to codes of conduct, calculating what might be socially expected. To achieve some semblance of spontaneity is to accept and trust one's feelings, to accept and have confidence in one's organism, and to be open to new experiences.

199

## Some Assumptions for Ministry

In the light of the social and psychological situation of young adulthood, the church must learn to shape a ministry. The church's record with the young adult has not been very good, and it has especially failed to make any meaningful contact with those young people who fall outside of typical middle-class patterns—the sophisticates, trade school students, the dispossessed, armed services personnel, and many others. The young adult seems to challenge the church at so many critical points that any serious attempt at ministry forces an evaluation of assumptions and formulation of new ones. Some assumptions which have emerged from the several studies are considered below.

1. The young adult ministry must become one of the major commitments of the church. The lack of effectiveness with this age group is due largely to the marginal attention which young adults have received. They have not occupied the same place of importance as children, youth, and student work. The scope of the ministry requires specialized professional staff, especially trained; program resources; and adequate budgets.

2. Young adults themselves should be involved in setting the direction of the ministry and in its implementation. The ministry is not *for* young adults but is *with* young adults. A latent resource are the young men and women who can be made aware that they have a ministry with their peers and who can be trained for a mission in the world. Young adults are more in contact with other young adults than anyone else.

3. Ministry with young adults must be based upon clear theological formulations, including a concept of the nature and purpose of the church in urban society. Such formulations will assist the church in finding new criteria for evaluating its ministry and will deliver it from a preoccupation with membership, attendance records, and institutional growth. It seems that the mission of the urban church for this age is to make relevant the gospel in relation to human need and to help man experience a growing love for God and neighbor.

4. The ministry will need to be flexible. The church can probably no longer rely on uniform programs developed nationally. Instead, congregations will need help in understanding their unique settings and in knowing how to implement the peculiar ministry to which they seem to be called. Also, the definition as to the *kind* of young adult that a congregation will serve must be flexible. One inner-city congregation was found expending much effort to reach middle-class professional young adults in the suburbs when it had two of the nation's largest trade schools within a block and with which it had done nothing.

5. Much of the church's ministry may be a ministry in dispersion: outside the church building itself. The church will need to go where young adults are and participate in their world. And in all of this the church must maintain, to the best of its understanding, its identity.

6. The church must learn to listen deeply and accurately before it acts or speaks. The right to speak is always earned, and this is especially true for young adults who may no longer be listening. Harry Emerson Fosdick is reported to have said in a sermon that Jesus did not minister to an individual until he had spotted the hurting need. This same kind of sensitivity is needed in the young

adult ministry. Otherwise, the response may be to surface behavior which has led the church into moralism and legalism, resulting in cutting individuals off from the healing love of Christ.

7. The church must learn to come of age and to take a secular posture. This is in contrast to escaping into a world of the past. More than twenty years ago Bonhoeffer understood that the church had difficulty understanding and accepting the city, and he called for the church to break out of its anti-world stance and to love the world—even the secular world of the young adult.

8. The church's response to the world of the young adult rests in its ability to recognize the real life to which all men are called. This is an ontological question and concerns the nature of authentic Christian existence. Most young adults are trying to live life to the fullest. But they fail because they have only the symbols of life. It is the church's role to point the young adult to his real potential as a person and to provide the means by which realization can take place.

9. A ministry to young adults will need to become truly ecumenical. In the first place, young adults have a minimal loyalty to denominations. And in the second place, within the present context of competition, some persons are being overministered while numerous other needs are being neglected. One of the hopeful signs is the willingness of denominations and councils of churches to sit down for study in order to develop a metropolitan strategy for a young adult ministry.

## A Strategy for Ministry

The church's ministry with young adults does not just happen. Sincere interest is not enough. It requires study, experimentation, and continued evaluation. In short, the church in the modern world must formulate a strategy for getting its work done. A strategy includes the collecting of information, setting goals, attempting something, and evaluating the results. Some steps involved in this process are among the following.

The first step is finding a group of persons, including some young adults, who are deeply concerned and who are willing to work as a strategy committee. And the first thing that must be done is to digest the available data on young adults and the church's work with them. A theoretical understanding of the age group is essential.

The next step is to secure an understanding of the particular setting in which ministry is projected and to come to some concept of the most basic needs. A social program may be the last thing a group of busy professional young adults will need. Also, not every congregation is located in a situation that includes young adults. The need may be to send only two or three young people in the neighborhood to another church where an effective ministry is taking place. A strategy grows out of a careful definition of what needs to happen. It also involves identifying the resources required in order to meet the need.

Another step is to identify the larger issues involved in the situation and discover what other agencies might be at work in the area. Many of the needs of young adults involve social, political, and economic issues. The church involvement with young adults may lead it to work for legislation that will provide remedial training for unemployed high school drop-outs. A projected program of the church could result in duplication of social agencies' work. This suggests that the church in urban society no longer has to do all the work and that part of its ministry may be to support that which others are attempting.

In response to certain needs a number of strategies for getting at a young adult ministry have emerged. There seem to be few clear answers, and there is much to be learned. Undoubtedly workers with young adults will continue to utilize the best educational, psychological, sociological, and theological insights for formulating strategies for ministry. Below are examples of some possibilities.

The *orientation of rural youth* for life in the city is a real need which the church must meet. A conference for rural high school seniors, held in the largest city in the region, has had some success. It serves to expose young men and women to the problems as well as the opportunities of the city. Opportunity is provided for them to get involved deeply with young adults and adult leaders from various walks of life. Using a laboratory approach, seniors are given some significant experiences in the areas of housing, employment, recreation, and religion. More especially, time is given to working through in small groups and with adult leaders feelings about the city and the problems which an individual may have as he makes his move.

Loneliness and isolation are generally characteristic of young adults who move into modern apartment complexes. A supervisor of a large number of young women indicates that their chief problem is that of becoming isolated behind the walls of a self-contained apartment. There is certainly evidence that many young adults purposely seek out those apartments which can best protect them from invasion by social groups, including the church. An *apartment ministry* is being tried in several different situations in order to meet this need. The purpose of such a ministry is not to go where one is not wanted, nor to use the apartment as a gimmick for getting additional church members. Rather, a ministry within an apartment complex is an attempt to interpenetrate the young adult world and to be alongside as the church in moments of need. *Chaplains to apartments* provide a minister-in-residence who shares in the normal life of an apartment and who responds as called upon to opportunities for ministry. Often, the swimming pool, coffee hours, and laundry rooms become opportunities to identify oneself as a minister and to establish meaningful relations. Apartment discussion groups give laymen an opportunity to involve friends and neighbors in significant study and fellowship and to help break down isolation and provide the ground out of which belonging can begin to take place.

A *minister in dispersion* in a large city may become a pattern that will have validity. This has been tried with some effectiveness, but the secret seems to be in the man who is selected. It is well known that not all adults are able to communicate with young adults. Many use young adults to live out their own incomplete young adulthood and thus become somewhat less than authentic as an adult Christian. A minister in dispersion is alongside the young adult in the various expressions of life and is a channel of communication with local congregations. He identifies the needs that exist in a city and helps congregations meet these needs; also he becomes a living port of entry for new young adults who are trying to find their way.

Another example of a strategy is the *cluster young adult group*. This is where two or more churches unite in a common ministry with young adults. Such a pattern operates as effectively in rural settings as in city or suburban situations. It recognizes the need for young adults to belong to a group of peers which is large enough to sustain itself and to provide a meeting ground for social relations as well as opportunities for deeper experiences of belonging. It has been well substantiated that the secret of this kind of group, as with most other young adult groups, is the adult leader. This should be a person who is mature, sensitive to others, and who can guarantee by his own life that adulthood is good and is worth striving toward.

A final example is interesting because of its possibilities for all who are involved. Studies have indicated that many local church young adult groups are composed to a large extent of persons who are poorly equipped emotionally, religiously, and socially. In short, they are sometimes referred to as "misfits" who have no place to go other than the church. Often there are no leadership resources in the group, and the entire group may be so weak that maintenance is an effort, if not an impossibility. There are churches which have responded to this situation by recruiting from other churches healthy and well-endowed young adults. Their task is to *infiltrate* the weaker group in order to give it strength and to provide internal resources. This has had some interesting results. First, it has provided leadership and the possibility for a group to meet some of its maintenance and task needs. Second, it has provided some adequate young adult models, and group interaction has led to greater health for some individual young adults. Finally, the young adults entering the situation become involved in a significant experience of mission. They not only learn to give of themselves but also discover that they can receive something from those who are not as well endowed.

## Unanswered Questions

There is much to be learned as the church begins to take seriously its responsibility for young adults. There are many unanswered questions about this period of life, especially regarding what shapes developmental needs take in various subcultures. Almost all that is known about young adults has come from studies of white middle-class persons.

More understanding is needed of the unmarried young adult, including factors contributing to his continued singleness and ways in which the church can help the unmarried find a more meaningful mode of life. Few studies have been made of the sexual needs of the unmarried and how these can be met in a society which is predestined to produce an increasing number of adults who will not marry. Also, a great deal of research is needed regarding the early years of marriage: the kinds of adjustments which are required, factors contributing to marital stress, and the ministry which is required.

Evidence points to the effectiveness of adult leaders who possess a particular quality of personality. Some of these qualities have been identified, but additional studies are needed here. The finding of ways to train such leaders is just as urgent. Related is the hunch that young adults need to assume more leadership roles in the various patterns of ministry. How can they be motivated, and what kind of training is required?

As implied, the young adult ministry is finding it necessary to evolve new patterns and organizational structures. If it is true that young adults are not easily contacted and resist being pulled into church groups, then what kinds of organizations are needed? What shape shall the church take in its relation to this young urban person? Related here is the need to develop a more carefully trained professional staff, some of whom will be called upon to work outside the normal local congregational structure.

Finally, there is need for much work toward developing criteria for evaluating the effectiveness of young adult ministries. How do you measure success with a highly mobile and transitional age group? Apparently, the institutional standards of success are inadequate, but what will take their place as the new measuring rod?

## FOR ADDITIONAL READING

Duvall, Evelyn M. *Family Development*. Rev. ed. Chicago: J. B. Lippincott Co., 1962.

Ellsworth, Allen S. *Young Men, Young Women*. New York: Association Press, 1963.

Erikson, Erik H. *Identity and the Life Cycle*. New York: International Universities Press, 1959.

————. *Young Man Luther*. New York: W. W. Norton & Company, 1958.

Havighurst, Robert J. *Developmental Tasks and Education*. 2nd ed. New York: David McKay Co., 1952.

Sherrill, Lewis J. *The Struggle of the Soul*. New York: The MacMillan Company, 1952.

Stein, Maurice, *et al. Identity and Anxiety*. New York: The Free Press of Glencoe, 1960.

Symonds, Percival M. and Jensen, Arthur R. *From Adolescent to Adult*. New York: Columbia University Press, 1961.

Winter, Gibson. *The New Creation as Metropolis*. New York: The Macmillan Company, 1963.

Webber, George W. *The Congregation in Mission*. Nashville: Abingdon Press, 1964.

For additional information regarding programs for young adults, research reports, and bibliographies, write:

Department of Adult Work, National Council of the Churches of Christ in the U.S.A., 475 Riverside Drive, New York, New York 10027.

Young Adult Research Project, Division of the Local Church, General Board of Education, The Methodist Church, P.O. Box 871, Nashville, Tenn. 37202.

Chapter 18

# ADULT EDUCATION IN THE CHURCH

## William F. Case

THE CHURCH FACES A RADICALLY NEW DAY IN ITS TEACHING MINISTRY WITH adults. The theological demands on the church as it lives in new social structures and under new cultural forces call for a new adult educational ministry. As Bruce Reinhart has pointed out, the church plays only a marginal role in American society, and adult education is only of marginal concern to the church.[1]

## New Demands on Adult Education in the Church

The church and its responsibility for adult education can no longer be marginal if it is to fulfill its role in our world. The prevailing mood of our time, as revealed by artists, writers, and social scientists, is one of pessimism and disorientation. We not only do not know how to reach our goals, we are not at all sure what are our goals. In the face of such a mood, the advisory committee on the main theme of the Second Assembly of the World Council of Churches reminds us, "God summons the Church of Jesus Christ to speak plainly about hope. Jesus Christ is our hope. In all humility and boldness we are bound to tell the good news of hope given to us in him." [2]

At least part of the reason for the feeling of lostness and despair in which the world lives is the change which is so much a part of our lives. Social structures, value systems, educational aims, and economic goals are all in a state of flux and transition. Even the geography of our world is no longer stable. We not only must learn to live with nations whose names we have never heard but perhaps with people who don't even share our planet. No relationship is stable and secure in such a world. Certainly it is not necessary to detail all of the changes with which we must live—changing family patterns, increased leisure, technological revolution, and all the rest are commonplaces of our existence.

But it is a task of the church to remind us that this crisis of change may be characterized quite as much by promise as by threat. Surely if God's way is to be fulfilled and if Jesus Christ is to be Lord of history, there must be change from our present patterns and structures. Perhaps the church has

[1] *The Institutional Nature of Adult Christian Education* (Philadelphia: The Westminster Press, 1962).

[2] Report of the Advisory Commission on the Main Theme of the Second Assembly, "Christ —The Hope of the World." World Council of Churches. *The Christian Hope and the Task of the Church* (New York: Harper & Row, 1954), p. 1.

been irresponsible in its educational ministry with adults if they have not been helped to understand that God may be at work in this change.

There has been a tendency at certain points in the history of the church, not least of all in our time, to identify God as being active only in relationship to individuals on a personal basis. The picture of God, so clearly seen by the prophets, as being active and fulfilling his purposes on the broad stage of history has been largely ignored. The world seemed to be evil, and the church was the body of the saved. Its role was to snatch the individual from this depraved world into its safekeeping.

This is scarcely true to the biblical revelation where God is seen as being active in all of life and history to fulfill his purposes. He called the church into being not to be a refuge from life but to continue his work begun in Jesus Christ of "reconciling the world." God's grace is found in the world as well as in the church. He may be in the change which characterizes our world as well as in the stability of a world that has passed.

Some theologians and social scientists have seen only threats to man in the current technological changes. Yet man has been blessed by having more material goods; fewer persons have starved; more persons have been warm; men, women, and children have had to struggle a little less to keep alive. Surely God is not unconcerned about these blessings—they are the gifts of his grace. As Myron Bloy reminds us, "Technology is not as demonic or enslaving as some romantic theologians seem to think, nor as lacking in intrinsic value as others aver, but it enhances man's freedom, nurtures his humility, and deepens his affirmation of life." [3]

In the face of such a truncated witness the task of the church through all its ministries, including adult education, is formidable. Surely the church is called to a larger responsibility than to perpetuate its own life. The educational ministry with adults has a greater mission than to prepare persons to serve the institution well, to be good churchmen. As Paul Essert of the Institute of Adult Education, Teachers College, Columbia University reminds us,

Why is continuing education of adults a marginal or peripheral concern of the churches? Some authorities say that it is because the church does not understand what Christian adult education is for, and what content is needed to achieve its purposes. Adult education in the churches is too often regarded as an instrument of survival of the institution. As such, it is directed inward toward reinforcement and support of church doctrine rather than outward toward the problems of Christian living in modern society. A continuing-education program of a church that is directed outward would lose its marginality by becoming central to the need of adults to find the workings of God in their daily lives. [4]

John R. Fry has cautioned us, "The Church will not be reformed or transformed by adult education no matter what its exponents claim or expect. The

---

[3] *The Crisis of Cultural Change* (New York: The Seabury Press, 1965), pp. 110-11.
[4] "The Challenge Adults Face," *International Journal of Religious Education*, XLI (January, 1965), 9.

church is not open to its 'future of grace.' . . . It is oriented to its past; its present is filled with the contents furnished by tradition. That is the problem." [5] Of course, no Christian expects the church to be reformed or transformed by anything or anyone but by the act of God. Yet God can work through the channels of the church's ministry in many ways, including its adult ministry, to bring about a reformation of society and a transformation of lives. If he does it will not be because of our cleverness or our diligence but because he has chosen to make himself known to us and because we have been obedient to what he has made known.

In a world so dominated by fast-moving change, an adult must be constantly learning to adapt to and make use of this change. Industry must constantly train its people for new skills. Professional men must be continually studying individually and in groups to keep up with developments in their fields. Someone has said that a doctor who doesn't study is out of date five years after graduation from medical school and after ten years is a fraud. No wonder adult education has become so characteristic of our society. Essert points out, "During 1961 twenty-five million persons, or more than one adult in every five, were engaged in some form of organized class or course or home-study program." [6]

Adults who are growing and changing in every area of their lives cannot be static in their understanding of the Christian faith and its relationship to life and still be faithful "ambassadors for Christ."

### The Direction of Adult Education in the Church

Surely the adult, as has been indicated above, has a deep need to find a sense of direction, of purpose, of meaning in life. As always, the gospel provides the only fully satisfying answer to this need. The church in its adult education is called to help the adult free himself from every dependence save his dependence on God. The church is called to help him find God active in every event of life, to trust life at its deepest level for this reason, and to celebrate with joy God's act completed in Jesus Christ and continued through the Holy Spirit. The church continues to have a crucial ministry to the individual as he faces life, its triumphs and tragedies, its struggles and its successes, its battles and its refreshments, under the providence of God.

But the adult lives in a world of social structures and human relationships that nourish and sustain him and that also batter and frustrate him. These structures and relationships affect and direct him so that he is what he is largely because of these structures and relationships. The church needs to provide understanding and strength for the adult as he deals with these forces.

The adult who is called to be a Christian is called to be a Christian in such a world and to be obedient to God in serving to bring this world under the Lordship of Jesus Christ. He is called to serve in the mission of the church.

[5] *A Hard Look at Adult Christian Education* (Philadelphia: The Westminster Press, 1961), p. 5.
[6] "The Challenge Adults Face," p. 9.

This mission is in and to the world. Consequently, adult Christian education is directed toward witness and service in the world. Worship, study, and fellowship play their part as they strengthen and equip the Christian for witness and service.

The church is increasingly seeing that it is the "people of God" sent by God for a mission and ministry in the world. This mission will not be fulfilled by missionaries or by ministers but by the whole church in mission and ministry. This is the meaning of the priesthood of believers, that every believer is called to be a priest in the church's mission and ministry.

Consequently, adult education in the church is directed toward equipping the saints for a ministry in the world. This ministry is evangelistic—to find and to save the lost, and it is transforming—to transform the kingdoms of this world so that they become the kingdoms of our Christ and of his God.

The church has attempted to formulate its direction in a statement of purpose for Christian education. This statement, adopted by the Commission on General Christian Education of the National Council of Churches, has guided a great many ecumenical enterprises such as the Cooperative Curriculum Project. It has also been widely used by denominations in the direction of their life and work. For instance, the Evangelical United Brethren have adopted it as a statement of purpose for their program council, and it has guided the development of new curricular materials for The Methodist Church. This widely accepted and used statement catches up what has been said about the direction of adult education in the church when it formulates the purpose of Christian education as follows:

The objective for Christian education is that all persons be aware of God through his self-disclosure, especially his redeeming love as revealed in Jesus Christ, and that they respond in faith and love—to the end that they may know who they are and what their human situation means, grow as sons of God rooted in the Christian community, live in the Spirit of God in every relationship, fulfill their common discipleship in the world, and abide in the Christian hope.[7]

## How Adults Learn

It was once thought that it was a waste of time to try to get adults to do any learning. The experience of the past years has clearly demonstrated how false this is. Adults are learning in fields that were not even known when they were children and youth. Every adult must learn constantly to keep abreast of developments in our rapidly changing world. What may be observed by any thinking person has been corroborated by experimentation and research. Carefully developed studies indicate that most adults continue to learn throughout life. In areas where there is some loss of ability to learn with the same speed as was possible at younger ages, this loss is often offset by the wider experience the adult has to draw on and by his greater motivation to learn.

This is not to say that adult learning is exactly the same as learning at

[7] *We Have This Ministry* (New York: National Council of Churches, 1964), p. 12.

earlier stages. Adults are at a different stage on the life span, and they face different experiences and situations. They are also at a different level of maturity so that they bring this level to the learning situation. Their motives for learning may be quite different and, although they may be highly motivated, it will be for different reasons than for children or youth. Adults also have more and different experiences to bring to the learning situation. For these and many other reasons adult learning varies from the learning of children and youth. The person who is concerned with adult learning will need to take these various factors into account in planning for adults.

On the other hand, personality growth and development is an organic process, and the adult is not a different person than he was as a child nor is his process of learning completely broken from any continuity with the earlier process. Personality growth and development take place through the learning process. True learning results in changes in behavior, insights, attitudes, values, ideas, and relationships of the person who is learning.

There are certain things about learning as it applies to adults that are widely accepted. These understandings about which there is emerging consensus may help to guide the education of adults in the church.

1. Adults learn as total persons. Learning is not the response of a particular aspect of one's being but of his whole personality. As a person is an organic whole, he learns as a whole. In dealing with adult learning the physical condition of the learner may condition what is learned. The emotional state of the learner may determine what the adult takes from a learning situation. The adult brings his total past experience to every learning situation and every new situation is affected by all that has gone before.

2. Adults learn most effectively when they are active participants in the learning experience. This means that they should be involved in planning the experience, guiding its progress, activating its outcome, and evaluating the whole experience. Most adults are accustomed to being involved in directing the course of their lives and do not respond well to situations where they are directed by others. Those who are most restricted in directing their own lives may most need the experience of participating more actively in such a process if they are to be able to understand and accept their "freedom in Christ."

3. Adults are strongly affected by the interpersonal relationships that exist in a learning situation. They respond to the other persons in the group in such a way that it makes a great difference in the type and quality of learning that takes place. The group may motivate more and deeper learning or it may block learning almost completely.

4. All experiences of adults provide learnings for them. The church needs to recognize the role that the adult's total experiences play in his learning. The home, work, mass media, community, social group—all these and a host of other influences provide learning that must be recognized and reinforced or mitigated by the church. It is foolish to plan learning experiences for adults in the church apart from learnings that are taking place in all the rest of their lives.

5. Each adult is an individual with unique capacities, abilities, interests, needs, concerns, and opportunities. Since this is true, each adult is a unique learner. Further, he perceives every situation in a unique way. There will, of course, be common perceptions by members of a group, but there will also be unique perceptions by each person in the group. For the persons doing the perceiving this will be the reality of the situation. He will take from the situation that which he perceives as valuable to his needs and interests.

6. The adult tends to take on the values and viewpoints of persons with whom he has significant relationships. This process plays a highly important role in the areas of life with which the church has concern. It is, therefore, of considerable significance that relationships that are capable of playing this role in the life of adults be fostered in the church.

7. Adult learning is not complete until it has emerged in appropriate action. One of the most vital ways of fixing learning is to make it lead to some action. Yet in adult education in the church seldom is any outcome expected nor is any channel provided for action. Learning is surely incomplete in any Christian sense unless it leads to some appropriate action.

8. When an adult has learned effectively, this stimulates further learning and becomes itself motivation for new learning. This is why when a church begins to take seriously its task in adult education it finds each successful experience leading to further and deeper learning.

9. The teacher or stimulator of learning plays a significant role in adult learning. The role of the teacher in adult learning is different from the role with children and youth, but it is no less significant. One of the major tasks facing the church as it fulfills its responsibility for adult education is to discover and help prepare adequate teachers for this important function.

Each of these understandings makes significant contributions to the way by which the church carries on its educational ministry with adults. Together they suggest a major revolution in adult education in the church. Each church and each person working with adults will need to evaluate what is being done in light of these understandings and work to bring about the changes that are suggested by this evaluation.

## Helping Adults Learn

Recently I attended an adult class in a local church. There were about seventy-five members in the class, seated in pews that rose from the front to the back of the balcony in stair-step fashion. The class opened with a prayer and a greeting from the president to which the class responded. There were then a number of songs, ending with the singing of "happy birthday" to class members who had celebrated their birthdays during the week as the celebrants placed their coins in a "piggy bank." One of the class members then led in "devotions" by reading an excerpt from *Guideposts*. The teacher finally began the lesson. He assured the class that he just wanted to share with them his faith, that he didn't want to confuse them with any of the complexities that seemed to bother so many people, that he wasn't a theologian and didn't want to bother them with theological abstractions.

The teacher, a devout and sincere man, then proceeded to expound by biblical proof texting a theology and understanding of the Bible that was completely different from the understanding of the Christian faith that was held by the church, the pastor, or Christian scholars. With the best of intentions he was, nevertheless, undercutting the faith his church professed and was contributing to the confusion of a group of adults undertaking education in the church.

In this situation we have seen a fairly typical adult education experience in a large, wealthy church of one of the major denominations. We have also seen a clear example of many of the crucial weaknesses of adult education in the church. 1) A class so large that few of the members could have any sense of participation and in which there could be no discussion to help discover what was being learned. 2) Too little time for any significant learning. There was a confusion of goals so there was an effort to do everything—worship, fellowship, instruction, even money raising. 3) Inadequate setting and equipment for effective teaching-learning. There was no provision or opportunity for any kind of teaching other than the lecture. There was no possibility of using visual aids, not even a chalkboard. Nor was there any opportunity to use any method that called for any participation on the part of the learners. 4) A totally incompetent teacher in terms of any of the goals that have been set for adult education in the church. He had not been given any help in understanding the nature of the faith, of the persons he taught, nor of the skills necessary to communicate the faith. Yet he was in every way an admirable person, an active churchman, an honest businessman, a devoted family man, and a delight to know.

What does this situation suggest for how we may help adults learn?

1. We need to determine clearly what is the goal of education for adults in the church. For this to be done adequately the adults themselves will need to be involved in this process. It will never become the goal of a group of adults by their being told that this is their goal. They will need to wrestle with the question of what they are trying to accomplish, why they are in the church, what is the mission of the church, what is their role in this mission, and how may they be more effectively prepared for this mission.

Once the adults themselves have really determined the answer to their purpose for being together, they will be more nearly ready to discover the ways by which they may move toward this purpose. Only those things which contribute to the fulfillment of this purpose have any reason for being a part of the adult class.

Adults may need to face the reality of many goals for adult education in the church. Adults will need to worship, to study, to have fellowship, and to serve as a part of their education and growth in the faith. But it is unlikely that any one group at any one time will meet all these needs. This is why there will be many different groupings of adults in the church. Each group will more nearly fulfill its goal if the adults understand and are committed to that goal for that group.

2. Groups will need to be formed or restructured in terms of the particular ends that are to be aimed for. As we have seen, many adult classes are too

large for effective learning to take place. These classes will need to face this and discover what to do about it. Many large classes that have been together for a long time may choose to continue to meet together on Sunday morning to provide stimulation for additional study that will take place during the week. These additional study groups may meet at different times and places—some may meet during the morning in homes, others may meet during lunch hour in a downtown restaurant, and others may meet in the evening. Other large classes may decide that they can't accomplish much in real study, so they may decide to stop meeting during the church school hour and meet only for social events at scheduled times in the evening. They will select a number of different study topics to be elected by members of the group for short term, intensive study during the church school hour.

There is no limit to the creativity of adult groups to find the time and setting for serious study if this is what they want to do. This is why so many adult departments in so many of our churches are involved in all kinds of changes. Adults are recognizing that there is no particular time, no particular place, no particular structure that is always best for adult learning. Rather, new times, places, and structures must be found to better meet the need for adult learning.

3. Adults need to be provided, or to discover, the facilities and resources that will help them in learning. In general, this is not an especially difficult problem. Adults do not need an elaborate setting for good learning to take place. Usually a comfortable room, arranged in an informal way, is about all that is needed. If adults are to participate with a group in learning, they need to be seated so that this is facilitated rather than hindered. Other facilities will be needed from time to time depending on the way learning is being encouraged—at times there will be need for a chalkboard, a map, a film or filmstrip projector, tables to write on, or other equipment.

In the past few years resources for adult learning have greatly increased in both quantity and quality. When the Episcopal Church began its new curriculum development in the 1950's, it prepared a series of six books designed to provide an introduction for adults to the whole range of the Christian heritage and life. These are still being studied on a regular basis in many Episcopal churches. The Methodist Church is developing a study series for adults that over a two-year period will introduce them to the full scope of the Christian faith and life. It is expected that this series will be offered regularly for adult study and will be supplemented by additional study in depth according to the individual's need, interest, and concern. The Presbyterian Church has developed an excellent series of books for adult study called the *Laymen's Theological Library*. Besides these especially prepared series many significant volumes in almost every area of biblical and theological study are available in paperback editions. On almost every problem that adults might wish to study there is authoritative material available at nominal cost. The national board of education of each of the major denominations can provide valuable and varied lists of resources that may be used to enrich adult study.

Of course, the denominations continue to prepare regular study material for use by adult classes. Much of this is greatly improved and would provide excellent resource and stimulation for adult study. There is almost no limit to what is available as resource for adult learning.

4. Adequate teachers need to be discovered and trained to stimulate and facilitate adult learning. Here is undoubtedly the most crucial challenge facing adult education in the church. Although adults are becoming increasingly well-educated in every other area of life, there are still too many persons, both within and without the church, who see no need to become informed about the Christian faith or the meaning of the Christian life.

There is a great need for persons who are adequately informed about the church and its faith and who are also skilled in helping adults learn. This need will be met only if the church accepts this as a major responsibility. Training classes, workshops, seminars, laboratory schools, clinics, and every other kind of training situation needs to be developed and fully exploited.

Teachers need to be helped to see that their role is to help others learn rather than to do the learning themselves. This means stimulating others to learn and providing skills and resources by which they can learn. The teacher of adults doesn't need to have answers to all the questions learners may ask, but he needs to be able to help find these answers—have the skills and resources that makes this possible. If we can develop a new understanding of the role of the adult teacher, we may find more who are willing to undertake the role.

The adult teacher also has to see himself as having a different responsibility. He is not primarily providing information. He is primarily stimulating adults to accept and fulfill a mission. To do this the adult will need information, but the information is not an end in itself. It is a means by which he is stimulated and equipped for his mission.

No single issue is more crucial for the future of the church, from the human side, than this one of discovering and training persons who can stimulate and facilitate adult learning.

5. As an outcome of adult education in the church, adults should be involved in service and witness. Certainly we know that the goal of adult education in the church is never fulfilled unless the adults who participate in it are involved in mission. But also the most powerful stimulus and motivation for learning comes when adults are involved in witness and service in the world. It is here that their faith takes on real meaning and vitality. It is here that it becomes worthwhile to study. The adult who sees his whole life as one of witness and service as a Christian is the adult who knows the need for further enrichment and enlightenment. Of course, this is the role every Christian plays. But it is a part of the educational task to make this self-conscious for each person and also to thrust each person into such service and witness as a part of his education. Every adult learning experience should have adults active in service and witness. Always the question should be: What does the learning demand that we do?

Perhaps the phrase "learning by doing" has been overdone. But the Christian who understands anything of the Christian faith knows that he must be in mission, and as he is in mission he recognizes his constant need for new resources and insight.

6. As we ask how we may help adults learn, we recognize the need to provide organization and structure to implement the process. In many adult groups organization has been overemphasized. However, there is need for sufficient organization to see that certain tasks are fulfilled. If each class is to be responsible for participating in its whole learning process there must be an organization by which this is done. Whether this means a group of officers with traditional titles or whether it means a steering committee makes little difference. But some structure needs to be provided through which the members may channel their interests, ideas, and concerns. There also needs to be some way by which these are then brought into a program that provides teaching-learning opportunities. These are primarily the functions of such an organization, but these functions must be efficiently fulfilled or the group will be frustrated.

In a church there will also need to be an organization that coordinates the activities of the various adult groups. In many churches this takes the form of an adult council made up of representatives from the various adult groups. The council serves this coordinating function, helps eliminate duplication, and may provide some activities for all the adult groups. It may also evaluate the overall program, discover weaknesses in the total program, and provide for ways to strengthen the places that are weak.

## Conclusion

Adult education in a very real sense is the key to the present and the future life of the church and of the world. Adults respond to God's saving will for them and in this response determine the present life of the church. They create the climate and they make the decisions that represent the human response to God's acts. As they respond, the church becomes the community in which children and youth are nurtured and sustained. The quality of the Christian life that is communicated to young people is the quality that is largely created by adults.

Adults are also responsible for the church's mission in the world. As they live in the home, in the world of business and industry, in the world of politics and world affairs, as they live in every relationship of life, they are the church in the world. They make for good or ill the crucial decisions of the world.

No task the church faces as it fulfills the mission given it by its Lord is more decisive than the way it fulfills its ministry to adults.

## FOR ADDITIONAL READING

Association for Supervision and Curriculum Development. *Learning More About Learning*. Washington, D. C.: National Education Association, 1959.

———. *Perceiving, Behaving, Becoming*. Washington, D. C.: National Education Association, 1962.

Bloy, Myron B., Jr. *The Crisis of Cultural Change*. New York: The Seabury Press, 1965.

Clemmons, Robert S. *Dynamics of Christian Adult Education*. Nashville: Abingdon Press, 1958.

Fry, John R. *A Hard Look at Adult Christian Education*. Philadelphia: The Westminster Press, 1961.

Grimes, Howard. *The Rebirth of the Laity*. Nashville: Abingdon Press, 1962.

Howe, Reuel. *Miracle of Dialogue*. New York: The Seabury Press, 1963.

Hunter, David. *Christian Education as Engagement*. New York: The Seabury Press, 1963.

Kidd, J. R. *How Adults Learn*. New York: Association Press, 1959.

Little, Lawrence C., ed. *The Future Course of Christian Adult Education*. Pittsburgh: University of Pittsburgh Press, 1959.

Minor, Harold D. *New Ways for a New Day*. Nashville: Graded Press, 1965.

Raines, Robert. *New Life in the Church*. New York: Harper & Row, 1961.

Reinhart, Bruce. *The Institutional Nature of Adult Christian Education*. Philadelphia: The Westminster Press, 1962.

Winter, Gibson. *The New Creation as Metropolis*. New York: The Macmillan Company, 1963.

# Chapter 19

# TEACHING RESOURCES
# FOR CHRISTIAN LEARNING

## James Blair Miller

TEACHING IN THE CHURCH REQUIRES RESOURCES AND METHODS WHICH A teacher or leader may use in working within a group, but it is essentially more than methodology and even more than the work of a teacher. Teaching can be understood only in the light of the nature and purpose of the church as a community of faith, and it is therefore best seen in the context of a total view of education in the church. Such a total view has been emerging in recent years as a result of the theological renewal which has characterized the life of the church and affected literally every facet of church life. This emerging theory of education in the church has not neglected the contributions of nontheological disciplines, but as one theorist has put it: "Christian education . . . is not secular education with a halo, although the Christian can ignore secular insights only at his peril." [1]

While readers of this book may refer to the earlier sections[2] for a full account of the total view of education which is emerging in contemporary church life, the writer of this chapter must approach the task of teaching as an integral part of the work of the church and therefore develop to some extent a view of education within the church. The title of the chapter may be rephrased somewhat into the question: "How may the church use resources for Christian learning?" Such a question implies that a community of faith (the church) is seeking to participate in changes (learning) that may take place as a person is guided or nurtured in a particular kind of faith and life (Christian). Even in such a brief question, and in the implications inherent in it, some of the fundamental issues of Christian education theory emerge.

### What Is Teaching?

In the rephrasing of the chapter title in the form of the question above there has been implied a dual view of teaching which needs to be clarified. On the one hand, teaching may be defined, as D. Campbell Wyckoff and others have done, as "the guidance of learning." [3] In our rephrasing of the title of this chapter we have assumed that teaching cannot be defined solely in this way, however, and that in addition to seeing it in terms of the learning side of the

---

[1] Randolph C. Miller, *Education for Christian Living* (2nd ed.; Englewood Cliffs: Prentice-Hall, 1963), p. 5.

[2] See especially Part I, chaps. 1-9.

[3] *Theory and Design of Christian Education Curriculum* (Philadelphia: The Westminster Press, 1961), p. 131.

transaction, it must be viewed in terms of the teaching side. Teaching must be seen in terms of the witness of a community (the church) to what has been given to it (a faith to be taught or communicated). If this is to be properly recognized and accounted for in any theory of teaching, the necessary conclusion is that teaching is more than the guidance of learning. Guidance of the learner cannot be conceived, let alone undertaken, apart from something to be learned. The starting point in teaching is to have something worth teaching, just as the beginning point in communication is to possess something which one is eager to communicate. This is not at all to minimize the responsibility of every teacher to guide the learning process but rather to see that process in relation to what is being taught.

In the church teaching starts and centers in the church's witness to what God has done and is doing in Jesus Christ. From this starting point the work of teaching is then able to move to the guidance of learning, or the participation in the responses that persons may make to what is taught. It is important to understand what a vast difference it makes when the determination of how the church may teach is approached in this manner rather than from the starting point that centers in the guidance of learning itself. When one starts with what the church teaches, it is possible to formulate the issues and questions that are important in the process of sharing in the responses that persons are making to the message, and in a real sense it is then the message of the church which determines how teaching may be done.

A number of questions are now possible in the light of this concern to define teaching both in relation to the message and the guidance of learning. Far beyond the earlier question "How may the church use resources for Christian learning?" we may now add such additional questions as: How may a church introduce persons into the life and mission of the community of faith? How may a church hold out to persons God's offer of grace and salvation? How may a church help persons be aware of what God has done to disclose himself and offer himself to them in the good news?

## The Teaching-Learning Process

The answer to such questions as we have raised centers fundamentally in an understanding of the core element or dynamic in any educational venture: the teaching-learning situation. It is possible that a teaching-learning experience or situation may occur without any organization behind it. In other words, many unplanned and unsuspected situations may become genuine learning experiences. However, the major concern here is the teaching-learning situation which is planned. Usually this will be related to an organized and planned experience in a class or a study group within the church, though the actual experience of learning may in a more specific sense arise out of a relationship between the teacher and a pupil. It may also occur in the involvement of persons with the whole range of activities and experiences in the situation or one specific facet within it.

A teaching-learning situation within the church, if it is to be significant

217

and effective from the standpoint of the deepest meaning of what the church is teaching, must bring the person (or learner) into a vital confrontation with the essential message of the church. While this message will in part contain information and knowledge, and will involve understanding and skills important in a Christian community, it is fundamentally not a matter of information about God and his purposes but personal encounter with God. This is because the faith which the church teaches is not so much information as a quality of life—the new person in Christ. The teaching-learning situation in the church is one in which everything is done in such a way that a channel may be provided through which God may speak to the learner and a living response may be made. The continuous and recurring center of teaching, then, is proclamation of what God is doing and the cultivation of deep awareness of God's disclosure of himself and his offer to address each person and win his living relationship to him. This response is one of faith and love, and results not only in a lifelong relationship between man and God but relationships in love between man and man.

This proclamation, which is the center of the teaching-learning process in the church, is found not primarily in the personal experience of the teacher nor even in the faith which is represented in the church but in the Word which has brought about the faith of the teacher and created the church. This Word is more than a written record, but the Scriptures are certainly the focal point in which the Word may be heard. The Bible points to the revelation which is the source of the church's message and bears witness to the events within which God has acted and within which he continues to speak. Most of all, the Bible points beyond itself to God himself, and it is he who breaks through the words to become the living Word in the teaching situation.

The church's task in the teaching-learning situation is to introduce persons to God at work, as revealed through the Bible, and to stimulate them to expose themselves to the truth and the life which the Bible thrusts into their experience. In its teaching-learning situations the church must raise the Bible to the central and crucial place, above all else that is regarded as important to teach. This is very important, not so much because those who are taught must learn to know the Bible as a book and as a body of content (which they must) but, far more than that, because the Bible is "a prompting script for God's dialogue with *this* generation." [4] If this dialogue is to be carried on throughout the life of every person whom the church teaches, then the relationship of the learner to the Bible is a lifelong process. The exact manner in which the Bible may be brought into the experience of those whom the church seeks to teach will vary considerably according to the process of human development and the needs and conditions of human life. The church is ever challenged to help children confront the Bible in ways that will at once take account of their abilities and needs and their hunger and yearning to listen to what God is saying to them in their personal situation. An equally crucial challenge is faced

[4] James Hastings Nichols, *Primer for Protestants* (New York: Association Press, 1947), p. 136.

by the church in relation to adolescents and to adults at the varied stages of maturity.

If proclamation is the center of the teaching-learning situation in the church, then the other side of the situation is at the point of the response of the learner to proclamation. We have already suggested that the response is dialogue and relationship between the person and God as the learner becomes aware of what God is doing and what manner of life he is holding out for those who are responsive to what has been done in Christ. In any attempt to understand what this response on the part of the learner is and how the church may participate in it, or even condition it, the largest meaning of it must be seen. We may assume that learning is change, and that the kinds of change that may take place in persons are varied. Real learning involves somewhat permanent changes in persons, and these changes may center in the acquisition of knowledge, or the deeper understanding of knowledge that may be akin to personal meaning as well as wisdom. Learning may also center in the development of skills of varied types. At deeper levels learning may result in changes in attitudes, changes in relationships with other persons, and definite changes in patterns of behavior.[5]

In church education learning may be seen as the specific application of these varied changes to the unique teaching-learning process which centers in the activity of God through the Word by which persons are confronted in such a way that their whole field of experience is changed. It is hoped that as a result of teaching in the church persons will acquire knowledge of the Bible, of the traditions of the church, and of fundamental beliefs that are part of that tradition. But far beyond that, it is hoped that persons will discover personal meaning within this experience of arriving at knowledge and will even go beyond knowledge as such to the forming in their own life and personality of the attitudes and behavior that are the "fruits of the spirit." In short, the church seeks to participate in the changes in human life that taken together may be characterized as Christian discipleship as understood in the fullest sense rather than in any narrow definition of discipleship.

There is no single theory that in any sense explains adequately the totality of learning or change involved in individual learning experience. In the field of general education it is necessary to classify the various theories of learning in order to make sense of the whole field of human experience in which learning takes place. Learning is complex, not simple. It cannot be accounted for in any one theory as was once believed. Research in the psychology of learning has been accumulating for a half century or more, at first using animals as subjects for experimentation but more recently based on studies of humans. It is apparent that certain habits and skills may be conditioned by the use of simple stimuli and by repetition to the point of establishing firm patterns of reacting. But it is equally apparent that in the long run people do not behave as a *result of* the external forces exerted upon them so

---

[5] Robert R. Boehlke, *Theories of Learning in Christian Education* (Philadelphia: The Westminster Press, 1962), pp. 31-58.

much as a result of the way external forces *seem* to them. In the attempt to understand learning educators today are working toward greater understanding of human perception because they believe that the most powerful factor in human change is the individual's personal discovery of meaning.[6] Most of all, perception cannot be fully understood except in relation to the whole person and the whole field of personal and social reality with which he is involved.

As in general education, church education requires several theories of learning as a basis for accounting for the specific types of changes that are sought in the learning situation. Some teaching in the church is directed toward the development of skills such as the use of the Bible, and this is learning through practice or conditioning. At the almost opposite extreme, some teaching is centered in the creation of attitudes, the influence of behavior and of value assumptions, and this is learning through identification with persons who embody these and with a group which practices them. In a highly practical sense some of the learning experience which the church seeks to provide finds its focus in difficult problems that an individual or group confront, and this is in the direction of the famous Dewey theory of learning through problem solving.

Wyckoff has developed a fundamental conception of the process of teaching and learning in the church on the basis of the theory of perception of meaning. Known as the learning task theory,[7] this view characterizes the process of learning in the church enterprise of teaching as lifelong learning tasks, with specific tasks described as listening to the gospel, exploring the whole field of relationships in the light of it, discovering meaning and value, appropriating what is discovered, and assuming personal and social responsibility as a result. In this theory, all learning in the church stems from the experience of listening to the gospel. Also fundamental to this theory is the assumption that the learning experience is active and conscious, with the individual who is motivated to a genuine awareness of God's redeeming love in Jesus Christ (the gospel) accepting responsibility for his own learning through willingness to explore, discover, appropriate, and assume responsibility.

The approaches that have been suggested and briefly described, primarily focusing on the learner's side of the teaching-learning situation in the church, all converge in a total view of the changes in persons who are involved in responding to the church's message. The thrust of the church's teaching is toward the direct involvement of the person (or learner) in the teaching-learning process. Passive response is at one side, and the premium is placed on stirring each person to accept responsibility for his own learning. This has led some professionals in church education to make their emphasis one of helping learners learn how to learn rather than helping teachers learn how to teach. This viewpoint has genuine merit unless it is overstated, since there is still an important place to be given to the task of helping teachers learn how to teach.

[6] See *Learning More About Learning*, Papers and Reports from the Third ASCD Research Institute, Alexander Frazier, ed. (Washington: The Association for Supervision and Curriculum Development, 1959), especially pp. 5-20. See also chap. 5 above.

[7] *Theory and Design of Christian Education Curriculum*, pp. 131 ff.

## Methodology in Church Teaching

Methodology, in a very practical sense, is simply the way in which the message of the church is handled within a teaching-learning group. Such a group may be part of the traditional church school or of some wider aspect of Christian education in the church. The normal pattern of work in the group will arise out of the nature and purpose of the group itself, and thus the age of the members and the expected role of the teacher or leader will have a direct bearing on the process as well as the methodology. While it is assumed that such a group will have a teacher, or more than one, the actual title for such a person may be either that of teacher or something else. In some groups leadership may be shared with part or even all members of the group, so that persons other than the designated teacher or leader may participate in determining the methodology and even the purpose and content of the learning situation.

The crucial issue in methodology is the wise choice of methods, and such wisdom as is needed for this arises out of an understanding not only of various teaching techniques but also of the needs of persons in a group and the dynamic life of the group itself. In a real sense methods contribute not only to the handling of the subject matter which is to be confronted but also to the ordering of the relationships of persons to one another in the group. In fact, as has already been stated, the substance of what the church is teaching is essentially not only subject matter but also attitudes, skills, relationships between persons, and relationships with God. Teaching procedures that are based on transmission of subject matter or content alone are but one part of the methodology that is needed for church teaching.

Eleanor Morrison and Virgil Foster have helped clarify the choice of methods in an approach which they call "double-strength teaching." [8] This is teaching with double force or strength because it uses both verbal interpretation of the faith and also experience in a group which seeks to embody the faith in its very life as a community. This kind of group is supportive, and is an expression of what Morrison and Foster assume to be the distinctive characteristics of the Christian life. They are: (1) It is an interdependent life; (2) it is a life in which every person is recognized as having infinite worth; (3) it is a life of trust; (4) it is a life of love. In their view these characteristics of the Christian life not only give form to the life and relationships of persons in a group but also demand procedures or methods which are consistent with them. In this light the choice of procedures falls among three types: (1) Each person in any teaching situation becomes involved in a personal sense, and is at every point encouraged to formulate for himself the meaning of what he is doing; (2) the group carries responsibility, and looks to the teacher to help it choose and plan its own activities and develop a responsible group life; (3) The group must evaluate and reflect on what it is doing and what is happening to its members.

[8] *Creative Teaching in the Church* (Englewood Cliffs: Prentice-Hall, 1963), especially pp. 29-49.

The conception of teaching which Morrison and Foster have developed is of special significance, because it represents a whole new approach to the choice of methods in church teaching. It emerges out of the unique character of the very message which the church wants to teach. It also takes seriously the unique character of the group (or community) in which each learner (or responder to the message) is drawn for the experience of teaching and learning. Whereas formerly it was assumed that the choice of methods could be made on the basis of the characteristics of methods themselves, or of the general goals of variety and balance in types of methods, the contemporary teacher using the resources that major church bodies are now producing faces the challenge of choosing methods on the sound basis of the unique nature of the church and its faith. This newer approach does not neglect the concern of educators for active rather than simply passive methods, and makes proper use of what Edgar Dale has so carefully distinguished in his "cone of experience" which identifies the three basic types of experiences as (1) those which involve *doing*, (2) those which involve *observing*, and (3) those which involve *symbolizing*.[9] The *doing* experiences in Dale's view are direct experiences, contrived experiences, and dramatic participation. The *observing* experiences are demonstrations, field trips, exhibits, motion pictures, recordings, and still pictures. The experiences which are basically *symbolizing* experiences are visual symbols and verbal symbols.

## Preparing to Teach

The teacher or group leader in the church is almost unlimited in the choice of methods that may be used in a group situation. So much has been done with so many methods of teaching in recent years that even a listing of the total number of techniques that might be used is extensive. Oscar Rumpf has written solely from the standpoint of audio-visuals of "32 ways to tell a story."[10] Probably no one really knows how many methods of teaching are available and how sharply the lines of differentiation of one from another may be drawn.

In most instances a teacher will be guided by suggestions in printed curriculum materials in the choice of methods, but even so it is important for him to understand the reasons behind the suggestions and to be able to relate the methods that he uses to the needs of individuals, to their life together in a Christian group, and to the faith that is taught. In some respects the use of methods will vary according to the age of the group, so that those who work in groups with children will need somewhat different understanding of methods as contrasted with the situation of teachers who work with teenagers or adults. This can be overdrawn, however, and there is a sense in which basically sound methods are the same no matter what age group is involved, with the differences appearing in the form and adaptation which are made in the light of the capacities and abilities of the age group. Some methods may

[9] *Audio-Visual Methods in Teaching* (New York: The Dryden Press, 1946), pp. 37-52.
[10] *The Use of Audio-Visuals in the Church* (Philadelphia: United Church Press, 1958), p. 24 ff.

be more usable with only one age group, such as storytelling or certain creative activities, but even these have been successfully used with older groups than children with considerable success.

Perhaps it is helpful for the teacher in the church to develop a way of classifying methods in order to understand them better. In this case, the categories which are used for classification help the teacher see the relationship between the method and the theory of Christian education underlying the entire teaching-learning process.

One way to classify methods is to organize them around the progress of a teaching session or even an entire unit. If this is done a rather natural threefold pattern emerges. First, the session (or unit) must be introduced as a whole so that the members of the group may see what is to be learned in its totality and perhaps be motivated to study and work with it. Often this calls for the introduction of a considerable amount of content, or the outlining of a problem, or the listing of a total area of concern as a basis for discussion. To do an adequate job of introducing what is to be learned may require such methods as a lecture, a discussion outline, a panel or speaker, a film or filmstrip, or perhaps a reading assignment for everyone in the group to do or a presentation by the teacher of the substance of a reading book or a block of biblical material that is to be under study in the session or unit. Second, following the introduction, the next general category of method will focus on probing more deeply into the area of study, so that individuals as well as the entire group working together may penetrate more into the details and the depth of the area. For this second stage in the progress of the group such methods as assigned reading and research, reports, special research projects, special speakers or resource persons, and similar techniques will be needed. Thirdly, the integration, summary, and application of what has been studied (and learned) will be the major focus of attention. In some groups an actual listing of "what we have learned" will be important. Group discussion, of course, will be a natural method to use, encouraging forthright and outspoken participation of members of the group. Other methods that are helpful in this stage of the group are the use of tests, the writing of summary statements or definitions of basic ideas or issues, the use of evaluation procedures and forms, and the preparation of reports which in some cases may be shared with other groups. Often a display of the results of a session or unit of study may be a part of such a report, and this may have as much value for the members of the group doing the study as it does for those with whom it may be shared.

Another way to classify methods is on the basis of what some prefer to call a *principal* method or approach. This may be helpful, or it may be dangerous, and becomes the latter if a teacher falls into a pattern that is essentially the repetition of the same method. Traditionally, the teacher in the church (and elsewhere) has assumed but one principal method—transmitting information by verbal means. However, if a teacher once realizes that what the church teaches is not simply a matter of information or content (though it does involve that) and that something far more than verbal techniques will be needed, it is interesting to experiment with the approach that is based upon a principal method. Locke Bowman, writing of his experience with senior highs, advocates a "dialectic approach" [11] to teaching with this age group. He interprets this in the sense of logical disputation or debate, based primarily on the use of searching questions. In his view, as a teacher of older adolescents, this dialectic approach will involve exploring the claims of faith from every angle, looking for inconsistencies and discrepancies, and engaging in debate in a genuine sense. This principal method which has been wrought by one experienced teacher may not be valid with other age groups, and certainly would be inappropriate with children, but has much to commend it.

Iris Cully has stressed *participation* as a principal method or approach to teaching.[12] This approach provides a rich insight into all methods of teaching which include an opportunity for the learner to become personally involved (or to participate) in the events that are focal in religious history and in his own religious experience. Through such personal participation and involvement he faces the necessity for decision and personal response and also for witness to his own faith that has resulted from participation. The arts are fundamental methods in this approach through participation, calling the learner to become involved in the events that are read and studied from the Bible, in religious paintings, in studying great hymns, in reading religious poetry, in participating in religious drama. Even in listening to a story the learner may become a participant in it. The key to this principal method or approach is that by listening and becoming involved the learner may come to the place where he begins to understand these events and other forms from within, even when they are historical events and his involvement is a matter of placing himself in a framework of past history.

Even contemporary events, including activities that are planned and carried out in a church group or class, provide an opportunity for participation. A child can become very engrossed in a point of discussion or conversation, and any learner may at times be caught up in what a speaker is saying or in the impact of a story being told by the teacher.

Still another way to classify or provide categories that help the teacher understand methods of teaching is to organize the varieties of methods in relation to the natural responses that the persons will need to make to the proclaiming of the gospel or message through teaching. These responses include: *hearing* the message, *exploring* the meaning and relevance of the message, *participating* in the life of the community which is seeking to teach and live the message, and *undertaking* or assuming responsibility which will express the message in the midst of life.

## Growing Edges in Church Teaching

Growing edges in teaching in the church today reflect the contemporary developments in theology and in educational theory and practice. They center in

[11] *How to Teach Senior Highs* (Philadelphia: The Westminster Press, 1963), pp. 98 ff.
[12] *Children in the Church* (Philadelphia: The Westminster Press, 1960), pp. 118-42.

experimental approaches to the work of the teacher, revolutionary ways of organizing groups and working within them, and new types of curriculum materials. Heightened use of certain methods of teaching, some of them new in type or in approach to them, also constitutes a growing edge.

Team teaching is perhaps the most significant growing edge in relation to the function of the teacher in the life of a group. In public education this has been done experimentally in a number of school systems, especially in New England, and has involved the formation of teams of three or four teachers, usually a team leader plus two specialists and a beginning teacher. Some of the teams have consisted of specialists in related fields of teaching, and some have been simply a group of cooperating teachers. Usually the team has been assigned to work with 100 to 150 students, and the approach to the task has been on the basis of genuine sharing of the total responsibility for planning as well as actual teaching.

While it is difficult to ascertain how widespread it has been, team teaching in the church has been developed increasingly in recent years. Often it is a husband and wife team with responsibility for a youth class or perhaps as teachers for a preschool or elementary group of children. Sometimes a team of three or four teachers, often women, has taken on responsibility for a two-year span of children (perhaps Junior age). In any case the team approach to teaching has made possible a combining of various skills that normally cannot be handled by a single teacher and has also resulted in group planning and evaluation as well as actual teaching in the group session. Teachers in these teams have been able to participate in a group sense in some of the methods they later use within the group. They have also been able to develop a group relationship, and to avoid the feeling, so common among single teachers, of working alone and apart.

The traditional pattern of forming groups on the basis of age, especially among adults, appears to be breaking down as a newer emphasis on smaller and disciplined groups continues to increase. John Fry[13] has proposed "contract groups" as a basis for adult education in the church, and David Ernsberger[14] has developed a case for "concern groups" as a cornerstone for adult education that may share in the current emphasis on the renewal of the church. Even at younger age levels, broader groupings of children, following somewhat the public school nongraded approach, have been appearing, and this pattern does seem to be becoming more popular.

It has been common knowledge that most of the major Protestant bodies have been or are now in the midst of revolutionary curriculum change, with the end product being totally new curriculum materials.[15] Far out on the growing edge, as yet almost untrod, is the development of programmed instruction materials. Taking their approach from general education, these materials are textbook versions of self-instruction machines which are potentially

[13] *A Hard Look at Adult Christian Education* (Philadelphia: The Westminster Press, 1961).
[14] *Education for Renewal* (Philadelphia: The Westminster Press, 1965), pp. 100-114.
[15] See chap. 14, pp. 157-68.

quite usable for learning content materials. As yet only a few such books are available in the field of church teaching.[16]

Fortunately, methodology in church teaching as a field of study and experimentation has resisted the temptation to follow new "fads" in teaching techniques. However, new methods drawn from other fields of teaching and of education have influenced church teaching in recent years, such as brainstorming, buzz groups, group conversation, and role playing. The latter has been increasing in emphasis and actual use in church situations and is especially adaptable for all age groups and even for family and other broad age-span groupings. Widespread increase in the use of the case-study method in church teaching has been almost a trend in very recent years.[17]

Research and experimentation are needed in all of these growing edges of methodology in church teaching.

## FOR ADDITIONAL READING

Boehlke, Robert R. *Theories of Learning in Christian Education*. Philadelphia: The Westminster Press, 1962.

Bowman, Locke E. *How to Teach Senior Highs*. Philadelphia: The Westminster Press, 1963.

Bergevin, Paul; Morris, Dwight; and Smith, Robert M. *Adult Education Procedures*. New York: The Seabury Press, 1963.

Cully, Iris V. *Children in the Church*. Philadelphia: The Westminster Press, 1960.

Ernsberger, David J. *Education for Renewal*. Philadelphia: The Westminster Press, 1965.

Fallaw, Wesner. *The Case Method in Pastoral and Lay Education*. Philadelphia: The Westminster Press, 1963.

Fry, John R. *A Hard Look at Adult Christian Education*. Philadelphia: The Westminster Press, 1961.

McKinley, John. *Creative Methods for Adult Classes*. St. Louis: The Bethany Press, 1960.

Miller, Randolph C. *Education for Christian Living*. 2nd ed. Englewood Cliffs: Prentice-Hall, 1963.

Morrison, Eleanor and Foster, Virgil. *Creative Teaching in the Church*. Englewood Cliffs: Prentice-Hall, 1963.

Rumpf, Oscar J. *The Use of Audio-Visuals in the Church*. Philadelphia: United Church Press, 1958.

Wyckoff, D. Campbell. *Theory and Design of Christian Education Curriculum*. Philadelphia: The Westminster Press, 1961.

[16] Among those now available are: William C. Tuck, *Step by Step Introduction to the Old Testament* (New York: Association Press, 1963); Hal and Jean Vermes, *Step by Step in Theology*, adapted from Jack Finegan's *First Steps in Theology* (New York: Association Press, 1962); see also William C. Tuck, "The Development of Programmed Materials for Church School Use," *Religious Education*, LIX (July-August, 1964), 338-43.

[17] Wesner Fallaw, *The Case Method in Pastoral and Lay Education* (Philadelphia: The Westminster Press, 1963).

Chapter   20

# The Arts and Christian Education

## Clarice M. Bowman

"The real God is hardly to be reached by a line shorter than each man's longest, which is the line embracing the world that is accessible to him." [1]

As a working concept, think of the arts as connoting man's ways of communicating in visible, audible, or gestural patterns; these, in myriads of combinations, we call music, drama, painting, sculpture, sermon, and such like. Through the arts meanings may be called forth, experienced, reflected upon, and enhanced within both giver and receiver; not in the mind alone, but in the bone marrow. Arts, authentically, come forth from persons where they are, in existential awareness; and they bid for depth-resonance from other persons in their wholeness as selves, not merely for intellectual assent or dissent.

Arts bid for relation. Through senses of seeing, hearing, feeling, understanding, we venture into relationship with life, with the universe around us, with other lives, with the Divine Other. Arts help intensify our experiencing and our communicating and acting with one another, if to such moments of creation or appreciation we bring our full selves in focus—emotion, mentation, conation reverberating in harmony. What we bring forth may strike a spark in another; what he brings forth may strike a spark in us, and even symbolically become representative of larger experience. A rounding out of the circuit of communication occurs. One gives, others catch. Blind Homer stands in his rough cart and Robert Frost stands before microphones at an inauguration. Both speak poetry. And in whatever century listeners' eyes light up in person-response.

In these days when folk songs and games of the cultures and climes of the world are being shared, something back of the rhythms and melodies seems almost familiar, as if one had heard before. A chord of common humanity is struck. A Mexican Indian touches with awed appreciation a Chinese vase of exquisite workmanship from centuries ago. We are created with and for this kinship, this recognition. In *feeling with* is the root of compassion. In *thinking with* the root of conscience, of moralities. Authentic arts are a bridge between persons and peoples of earth. We do not have to use them artificially to try to teach brotherhood; they simply show or unveil this gift of kinship shared by God's created ones.

Religions of all time have used arts to suggest or point to what could never be fully conveyed by definition or creed. Christians believe that God through

[1] Martin Buber, "The Question to the Single One," *The Writings of Martin Buber*, Will Herberg, ed. (Cleveland: Meridian Books, 1961), p. 75.

Christ in the spirit calls to us in the personal depths he has created within us, and bids for our fullhearted response. He is not dependent upon our arts. But we from our side may be helped through arts media to stretch, realize, respond, know, and share with others some glimmerings of what has come to us.

## Christian Education Probing Depths

For Christian education, picture more than a church school classroom. The flock, God's people, is made up of families, of persons of all ages. Called into being as the church body, they meet—sometimes in larger groups, sometimes in smaller, sometimes person with person. The very young, the elderly, and actually all at times of their lives, need special care and guidance. Each in his own way, whether or not he can put his yearnings into words, seeks God-relation, neighbor-love, and self-growth.

Minister and people together ask, seek, knock, wrestle with problems, venture in prayer, move forth decisively from gathered meetings to daily orbits of home, work, and intermeshing networks of relationships in which conviction and courage may be severely tested. How does the church prepare all its people, young and old, for this daily life-witness? We think immediately of core occasions: congregational worship, Sunday and weekday church school sessions, camps, vacation schools, youth fellowships, Bible study groups, and such like. But educative moments come also as officials meet to plan regarding finances, as a visitor goes to call on a needy or unreached family, as a neighbor helps another in bereavement, as youth show leadership in school, as a businessman or politician makes a decision, as women converse over coffee cups, as individuals and groups speak fearlessly in wider social problems to bring Christian convictions to bear as a leaven. Guiding growth Godward, which is what Christian education means, takes place not only in regularly meeting, planned-for times, but in wider arenas.

But let us be clear. Man does not do all the guiding. As said of worship, we affirm also for Christian education, that the Holy Spirit is foremost a teacher—the dove descending. Our humanly devised methods and aids are but preparatory, the aspiration ascending. All our ways and methods, including our use of arts, if seen in the service of the spirit, must be honed to the best possible, and kept ever open for more light.

Arts in Christian education means more than a teacher choosing a picture from a curriculum packet, or putting clay or crayons in children's fingers; more than youth preparing a play for Easter; more than a minister searching for a hymn to fit his sermon theme. Arts are not extras, to be added or not after the lesson. Arts are not alone for experts, or those inclined to certain hobbies. Arts are not only for entertainment.

Arts are integral, organic, in Christian education as in life. They search us out where we live, until we hear God calling, "Adam, where art thou?" Whether or not a picture or song or drama or sermon is aesthetically pleasing to our habit-bound perceptions is not the question. The question is whether through it we are prodded, awakened, even possibly revolted—until we rip off graveclothes of apathy or hate or hardness, and turn in radical openness, vulnerable to the judgment as well as the mercy of God, and resilient to his leading us to share with him in costly compassion.

We ourselves are first persons, then ministering teachers. Is God's creative picture for our lives blossoming into the unique fruition he seeks? And are the methods and arts we dare use in our communicating such as to help, and in no wise hinder, his creative shaping hand in those lives in our care? Suppose we trust mainly in our educational methods, learned perhaps at cost and struggle. Suppose we become carried away by enthusiasm for certain arts. Or, oppositely, suppose we react *against?* Maybe some of the arts appear "way out"—threatening, perhaps? Suppose we refuse to stretch our spirits, or to call those we teach to deeper, more existential encounter. Suppose we find it difficult to disengage ourselves (discocoon!) from types of religious pictures, songs, plays, and the like with which we were brought up. We keep these away from our pupils. Yet they are living in their world of differing perceptions now. Or, as is the case with many of us, we feel a bit timid and awkward; we've long thought of arts as for the skilled, and perhaps we hesitate to open for our pupils channels in which they may do better than we! Or, we may argue, "There isn't time!" for anything but my telling them. Yet this easy way out for us may shut doors forever on the learners' more personal, involved, enriched learning that comes from firsthand entering in. Many go through life having known only secondhand tellings about. Thus we may fail—not simply denominational standards or the hopes of curriculum writers—we fail God's own: lives beside whom we walk in awesome stewardship. And the holy moment of teaching-possibility never comes in quite the same way again.

## Theological Groundings for Using Arts

Praise ("O, sing unto the Lord!") or quiet affirmation ("God is our refuge and strength") well up from lived relation, Spirit-with-spirit knowing. From this authentic realizing we seek to clarify, structure, and systematize. When any theological statement is cut off from this living source, it no longer breathes life. True, it may be reified, even made an end in itself, with its formulations (sounding correct and ordered) learned and repeated with mind and voice. A teacher may count himself to have taught when he hears the sounds come back. Even Scripture may be excised from its organic context and used thus, reduced to mechanical question-answer, fill-blanks, memorize by rote rather than by heart, on pulses.

But the arts, when used authentically (and not merely in a surface-skimming, extraneous way), call us to become *engagé,* to bring our theologies and our methods back to root-sources for correctives of both. Reminding us of the far more that can never be caged in neat systems, they round out both our own personal realizings, and our communicating with one another. Early Christians sang their creeds. The Westminster catechism breaks into art when it exults that man's chief end is "to enjoy him forever." We are called to theologize, but ever to regard our formulations humbly, open to light and growth. Always there is the penumbra of mystery about God and his ways with us. We but apprehend, reach toward—never comprehend, reach around. Arts—as iceberg with seven eighths of fullness beneath surface—point beyond literalistic formulas or linear logic. In asking about theological groundings for our methods of using arts, we seek to trace back of formulations (or current fads or jargon) to roots in the God-relation.

1. *God created and creates.* In him is purpose, plan, and sustaining power; in him is spontaneity, freedom, potential. He is not a prisoner in his universe of laws (man's word, not binding on God, merely descriptive of paltry observations man has to date apprehended). He enters in, makes mighty moves, as the biblical story unfolds, now as then, creatively bringing newness of life and redemptively, renewing.

We are his people, sheep of his pasture. Our chemistry (literally that of dust) is breathed into. Our bodies are but a modicum of solid matter. We are mostly spirit, *ruach.* He endows us with image kinship, freedom for responding voluntarily to him, to others, and to the indescribable wonders and possibilities in the ecology of the universe. In us pulses some echo of his creativity, some running to meet his gifts as children do with winged feet. Some presentness of partnership with him is sensed as we note with awe and thankfulness his gifts of glory and beauty in persons as well as in the world. The junior-high girl said, "God smiles to see my heart enjoy these miracles he gave." But there's a deeper sensing of his creativity as we brood in agony over problems, as we wrestle with angels, as we strive to bring forth in travail what the vision asks; and, particularly as we bow in soul-searching penitence for the evil, hurt, and ugliness in ourselves and our world, his hand probes and prods in judgment yet assuages, forgives, cleanses in mercy, then calls to next steps.

Themes for our creativity, then, as we compose, dance, dramatize, sing, paint, and build are not merely echoes or copyings of sights and sounds, however wondrous, of the physical universe, but primarily God's creating and re-creating, his redeeming and his calling us through Christ to share in creative redemptivities. Cézanne cried, "See the work of God!" The gift of seeing inwardly, of insight, or as the poet Hopkins said, *"inscape,"* precedes any communicating or fashioning-forth into arts.

Man's dramas of life are God's story. Biblical insights show history not as mathematically marked-off lines but as high-peak events of realization, the dayspring from on high visiting his people, his mighty moves shattering their smallness and leading them forth as individuals and as nations.

We ask then, not merely what arts people of Bible times used. It is easy enough to discover what musical instruments were like, why taboos on visual presentations, and such like. But the deeper way, and the more soundly theological and biblical way, is to seek to stand with the Bible ones in the fount-experience from which surged Miriam's song and the psalmist's exultation, "with the loud-sounding cymbals!"

His hand is still " 'round about the mountain"; all man's present lostness and chaos, his horrible degradation so voluminously depicted by contemporary arts, is no match for the creative and powerful God! He still brings "the dearest freshness deep down things," as Gerard Manley Hopkins said. There is still something he might make of us—and even of our world.

2. *We are called to hallow all life.* Life is to be seen whole, not separated into sacred-secular. (*Saeculum* means "of our times," not necessarily nonsacred.) Our compartmentalizing is nonbiblical. Seen holistically, every aspect of life is open before God. There is then no separately sacred art. Every day's work can be our liturgy to the Lord, every breaking of bread (organically relating the economic processes of mankind) a Lord's supper. "The earth is the Lord's and the fullness thereof." Any contempt for the material world, any scorn of the earthy elementals of life, is not in accord with the Christ who spoke of wind and rain, seas and fish, yeast and bread, and who came to break the bread of common life with us all: Emmanuel, God with us, Word made flesh.

This stance of approaching the simplest particulars of life with an artist's eye, teaches thankfulness, and might help heal our greed for material things with healthy frugality. Small things take on wonder: a bit of iridescence from a drop of oil in a mudpuddle. We learn to whittle a bit of wood until our fingers develop an artist's "feel" and ever thereafter, we are live to the patina of well-handled wood. We strum a guitar and become one with peoples of earth who have made themselves stringed instruments. We bake a loaf of yeastbread to golden brown, and look out our window at waving fields of other wheat. We visit a potter, and he lets us reach our hands into the soft clay and feel the shape coming to birth under our fingers. As that which we fashion incarnates something of our idea and vision, we catch insight as to how the incarnational God takes flesh and scorns not even the cattle trough.

This hallowing stance calls into question Paul Tillich's "darkness of matter," and "existence" (being "out-from" God) as sin. Rather, it takes thankfully what comes from God, as raw material of earth and life waiting to be brooded over and consecrated. Only he can make sacramental the offerings we bring of our handwork, our artistries, that the material be used not merely to represent but to convey the spiritual.

3. *Arts can be revelatory.* Pope Pius XII said, "The purpose of all art is to break the narrow boundaries of the finite, and open a window onto the infinite, for the benefit of the spirit of man, yearning in that direction." We cannot decide ahead of time at what moment, and by what methods, a revelatory flash may come. Evelyn Underhill suggested that God in initiative bending, accommodates himself to the little apertures of spirit we hold up to him. Whether we are striving to create something ourselves, a song, a poem, a drama, a painting—or appreciating what others have created—it is as if God takes us by the hand and pulls back the veil a little. From this much that we see we seek more. Real art illuminates. Matisse wrote, "I am not responsible for what I make. God is leading my hand." Monet saw, not just flat fields, but light and shadow playing upon them. Charles Connick as a boy picked up pieces of glass in a window-maker's shop and responded to the wonder of "active light" playing through them; he became in turn a craftsman whose windows are for thousands of worshipers enablers toward revelatory meaning.

Illumination may come gradually. An artist may strive for years to develop skills. Manet scraped the paint off day after day, fifty times or more, seeking improvement over the last. Many a writer, composer, or artist, writhes in agony as "it won't come right!" Some grow in inner vision, inscape, as they perfect skills. Some (and this is one of the serious questions about much art today) become enamored of the forms and skills and succumb to the temptation of letting these become ends in themselves, all. No longer are they media for meaning, save that which the recipient himself may chance to bring.

But the disciplined, revelatory artists of all time have paid costly prices within their own being, as the greater Word struggled to birth through them. Creating is like a prayer. Personal will is suspended. The artist submits to the material lovingly, that he and his medium may be in accord. He is obedient to its laws and to the athleticism of his skills. But this is not enough. Can he give himself to what Jacques Maritain calls "the spiritual character of creativity"? Can he endure the torment of the vision, the agony and the ecstasy of expressing?

We have said above that sacred and secular cannot be pulled asunder in authentic arts, because God gives life whole. What, then, is Christian art? It cannot be narrowly fenced off. A shallow answer visualizes paintings of the Crucifixion or of familiar heads of Christ in repose; or glib playlets for Christmas or Easter. These, *if they deal trivially with great aspects of the faith,* may be near-blasphemously un- or anti-Christian.

On the other hand, we cannot succumb to current fads of quoting whatever writers or other artists might be in the public mind, and eisegeting into their depictions of modern life's lostness what Christians might call sin—or pretending to find in certain characters "Christ-figures," when the originators had no such intention. To be sure, God can use in revelatory ways our feeble efforts beyond what we dream.

But writers, dramatists, musicians, and painters who depict the hurts of our angst-ridden age, are perhaps going the first step toward Christian art, in bearing in their beings the stigmata of a "bent and broken world." But it is possible to stop there, to make a cult of portraying alienation, brokenness, fragmentation. Less talented ones then come along and copy the originators and the fad spirals. For one to strike a positive note, to speak a nourishing message may be to expose to ridicule. For Blake to say in our day as he did in his that he saw the face of God, would be to invite epithets of "shallow liberal, naïve, insensitive to evil," or worse. Yet Blake's writings and paintings may still be revelatory.

But a Christian's cue is not taken from crowd mores, even in arts. He marches to a different drummer. He dedicates his unique skills and arts, and his whole self, praying that God's redemptive love may not only renew him but course through him, burning away egotistic ambition, false pride, fear of standing alone. His vocation from then on is, as Kipling sang, "to draw the Thing as he sees it for the God of things as they are." A Christian is called to share a pain greater than merely that of creating; he shares in the travail of the prophet, even with the divine One who broods in sacrificial love. Authentic art, like love, calls to the most intense level of involvement and to patient nourishing of the seed through slow, invisible growth. Michelangelo tried to avoid the commission to paint the Last Judgment, knowing what it would cost in months and years of travail. His humble comment, when he had finished, was, "I am a poor man of little merit who plods along in the art which God gave me." Yet there is an exultant aspect, too, ectasy balancing the agony, as a child seriously intent on work or play, delivering himself of the inner vision as spontaneously as if it were a song.

Perhaps a clue, then, as to whether a given work of art can be called Christian is *not* whether its subject matter is biblical or of Christ; but rather, whether the artist has been willing to go down with Christ into man's sinfulness and need and be made an instrument of God's forgiving renewal. Handel prayed, and *The Messiah* moved forth through him into glorious ever-revelatory being. The early Rembrandt von Rijn, however many commissions he accepted to paint churchly or religious themes, had not reached the existential depths of laying his talent totally upon God's altar. His later paintings, done while he suffered in poverty and loneliness, whether on obviously religious themes or not, point the way to understandings of man and God. Fra Angelico summed up the touchstone of Christian art when he spoke simply of the artist's calm of life in living with Christ. "When the morality of art is transformed by the numinous, by the holy awe, then the work is religious. When religious art stands under the grace of God in the love of Christ, then [it] . . . is Christian." [2]

## Methodological Insights for Using Arts in Discovery and Devotion

Theology and method should be integral, organic. Christian education is no mere matter of stating theological formulations as goals and then tacking on methods (which usually include some forms of arts). Rather, both trace back to the wellsprings, the God-relation. Learning and worship or discovery and devotion proceed *from the inside, out*. They are not activities learners are put through or caused to listen to, from the outside, in. This is a radically different concept from that on which many teachers and ministers proceed today.

*What does it mean to learn and know?* For centuries since Comenius the Western world has in education and Christian education placed trust in categories and formulations forged by reason. This way of knowing and communicating may be compared to a railroad track, with ties laid in precision step by step. In dealing with the physical world, with things, with "brute fact" (if there can be such a thing), and with *tour de force* reductions of persons to statistics, such procedure has furthered scientific and technical advance.

But the realm of personal spirit, where being meets being and responds to the Divine Being, overarches the puny logic-tracks man lays down, even his

[2] John W. Dixon, Jr., *Nature and Grace in Art* (Chapel Hill: University of North Carolina Press, 1964), p. 200.

proudest forays into matter or space. This fuller "knowing" in the biblical sense of recognizing and responding as persons, this more symphonic truth-realizing can never be reduced to reason's categories. The arts are needed to suggest and attest to vaster realms of the personal, existential. Science cannot prove God. Its tools are appropriate only for hypothesizing, experimenting, measuring, tabulating. God is rather to be *met*. He is no end-point to one of the tortuous syllogisms worked out by man's mentation. God *confronts*. Even the greatest arts are struck dumb before the mystery and majesty of a newborn babe. How much more before the Divine and his ways. As Meister Eckhart reminded, only stillness is full enough.

As ministering teachers of young and old in churches today, we need to be sharply aware of this need for the rounding-out, healing, personal knowing prompted by arts. Our age languishes in sicknesses both personal and endemic, for lack of nourishment of these centers of our being. Eroded by mechanism, driven by feverish scientific endeavor, we are separated from sources in the good earth and from elemental holistic knowings. Other languages clarify by differing verbs the knowing of thing or fact, and the personal, intuitive, spherical knowing from within, which the arts uniquely help nurture. Paul Tournier laments in psychologist's terms how "the rational civilization in which the world has been involved for three centuries suffers from poverty of creative imagination. All that is truly creative in man—intuition, art, spirituality—derives from spherical thought and is foreign to this rational civilization, which therefore characteristically despises it." [3] Paul Tillich speaks of the "falsehood, facade, and aesthetic betrayal" which are the "necessary result" of the loss of vital contact with things. [4]

As ministering teachers, then, we are called to grow open to winds of the Spirit, to leave behind fixations, and let arts restore and heal and lead out our own slumbering creativities from their hiding places. Each minute of life can be fraught with zest and wonder, as, freed from hurry and thing-preoccupation, we become open to the purple in evening shadows, a child's laughter, a warmly assuring voice. Earth is crammed with wonder, each common bush glows aflame. We sense what T. S. Eliot meant in "Burnt Norton" about "The still point of the turning world."

Only out from such inner being and becoming *ourselves*, such growing in discovery and devotion from the inside out, dare we seek to teach and guide others. The late Hulda Niebuhr spoke of the artist as teacher:

He makes no pretense to the detached perspective which the scientist and philosopher need. He is full of wonder and excitement about the things he has seen and heard and felt and understood, and he wants to share the essence of his experience. Perhaps that experience is something as compelling as Isaiah's awe before the inexorable demands of God's holiness, with the desire that his pupil be made sensitive to these demands. The artist is not a dispassionate onlooker, not a coolly logical observer, but

---

[3] *The Healing of Persons* (New York: Harper & Row, 1965), p. 75.
[4] *The Protestant Era* (Chicago: University of Chicago Press, 1948), p. 122.

a participant in an experience. Avowedly his interest, his devotion, his appreciation, or his awe and reverence, are determining factors in his transmission.[5]

Those who would make use of arts in Christian education do not so much need talent or skill as this stance, and understanding of the age-level of children, youth, or adults—and then willingness to venture. Educators visiting in Japan marvelled at the originality in children's exhibitions; they found teachers drawing and painting with the children, sharing the pleasure. Art is catching.

Another aspect is exposure to the great. With young children in homes and church schools we can use bits of great music, maybe a little at a time as listening music, and as our appreciations deepen they will catch the contagion. Through well-told stories of Christian greats, dreams are nurtured in the young (the young these days, despite mass communications, are starving for a vision of greatness!). Dramas vivify Bible scenes, and prophets' words reverberate in lives until they come forth in prophetic words for now. In denominational curricula are carefully chosen pictures from authentic and meaningful portrayals of past centuries and now. Usually a wide spectrum of artists is offered in the total curriculum for all ages, lest learners freeze their concepts on any one type of visualization. Herein is the danger of using such cheap prints of Jesus as are often seen on church school walls. There is no excuse for using unworthy songs with children or youth when curricula include for the younger ones one-line "hymns" and prayer-responses and suggest ways of teaching great hymns that are worship-worthy up through the years.

A teacher opens up the curriculum helps for the next unit (several sessions) with his age-level. He remembers levels of learning, as viewed through the eyes of learners: (1) The level of least vitality, gripping engagement, or memorability is that of "teacher-telling." The learner may listen or not; he is little involved. (2) The next level is that of visualization. Flat pictures, filmstrips or slips, movies or other variations may be used. Or learners may be taken to view some place or someone. Impressions through the eye-gate are dangerously influential and lasting. Yet even here the learner may remain spectator. (3) On the next level, the learner enters in vicariously, perhaps almost in spite of himself. A story which "lives" may cause him to traverse time and space, and reverberate emotionally with the characters in their dilemmas. This is true eminently of drama—real-life drama—not pageants where one is asked to portray an abstraction such as a spirit of loyalty. (4) The level of deepest, most life-changing learnings, is that of direct doing and deciding, the learner expressing from the inside out his own discoveries and devotion. Music, interpretive motion, choral-reading, role-play, creative writing, and many other forms or combinations of arts bid for this full-orbed, firsthand knowing.

The teacher, with curriculum helps in his hand, does not lack for aids: packets with pictures, perhaps filmstrips; music printed and in recordings or for autoharp; helps to make dramatizing easy and vivid; stories; "seed-thoughts"

---

[5] "A Seeming Dilemma in Christian Education," *McCormick Speaking*, VII (October, 1953), 6. (A journal published by McCormick Theological Seminary, Chicago.)

for informal worship moments. A far vaster quantity of biblical material is introduced than in old or uniform lessons, and through arts the learners are led to stand with the biblical people insightfully, and to approach each part in ways appropriate to that writing. The same is true of the story of the church through the centuries, with writings, paintings and sculpture, music, and drama rounding out the factual data. Through their own creative working-out, perhaps in combinations of narrative, acting, frieze-backgrounds, and music, the children relive or represent (make present anew). Such learnings are lived, and go deep for life.

Through arts in curricula of church schools, camps, vacation schools, youth fellowships and the like, there is fearless facing of difficulties, sin, sorrow, catastrophe—more than in old methods and materials that make teaching an easy matter of mostly telling and leave an impression that the Christian life is easy, syrupy. Nursery children enact the story of their turtle, "Mr. Red Ears," dying,[6] and are given a healthy steer in the working-through of grief and a big basic trust in God's good plan for life-death. Kindergarten children talk over "good-bad" wind, rain, sun, snow, and pray in vicarious concern for flood-sufferers and seek ways they can help. Youth create dramas portraying starkly man's sin and need. Freed of pressure to use pious-sounding clichés, they chant in verse-speaking narration their compassionate concern, and beat out new rhythms for liturgical commitment.

Time? The teacher is acutely aware that the usual Sunday church school hour is not enough. Some churches offer after-school weekday sessions. Youth and young adult groups find their own times—goodly blocks of time, where they can work through unhurriedly, whether in Bible study, or discussion of current problems, or play-reading, or dramatizing. Methods such as the arts (and these mentioned are but a hint of what the denominational curricula have written in, with abundant helps on "How") create interest and willingness on the learners' parts to spend time. Can the minister, in his responsibility for training his teachers, plant the spark that will inspire; plan with them at first so as to help them get started using the arts more fully; and offer support and encouragement as needed? Can he see to it that his teachers and leaders, along with youth, have a chance to go to conferences and workshops in drama, music, audio-visuals, and other arts? These are the newer and more promising modes of leadership training; more centers need to be set up or brought close to every local church. For participation in the arts ministers to the healing and wholeness of teachers as *selves*, not just their methods-training.

### Worship Ways

With pre-school children, teacher's calm, low-voiced ways and his or her evident warm joy in being with them communicate—far more eloquently than words ever can—that God loves and cares and can be trusted. The teacher comes close with this individual or that one, sensing a moment of wonder or of tension or question. Jimmy watches an ant struggle with a cooky crumb,

---

[6] United Church of Christ curriculum.

and in his still wonder the teacher senses that it would be fitting and not "too much" for her to speak quietly of how God provides for his creatures. No prayer is said formally, but there is dawning thankfulness: "He cares for me, too." As suggested above, depth-learning and discovery as well as worship come *from the inside, out.* The little child cannot yet conceptualize in words or even think abstractly. He enters fully into this immediate moment, so full of wonder and delight. He *lives* meanings before he is ready to speak the word-labels; and when, at some moment of realization later, the teacher says the word, he knows inside, "Aha!" or "Oh!" With the teacher he responds, "Oh, *thank* you, God!"

Classrooms, then, are *living* rooms. Pictures at the child's eye-level and speaking to his experience-range make the room inviting and a challenge to new thinking. As the children and teacher delve into glorious paints (big brushes, easels or floor with newsprint for younger children, finger-paint, clay, no-roll crayons, *never* designs for them to color in the lines), the teacher sings a "thank-you" song, and the children as they work add ideas. Because interest spans are short, methods change soon, and a circle-moving-song about seasons rests bodies and expresses another kind of glad thankfulness. A difficulty in the play-equipment corner calls forth a facing of the problem then and there, and perhaps a little prayer, "Help me remember not to be so rambunctious next time!"

Through relating worship-moments to ongoing experiences of thought, activity, play, and planning, children (1) sense that we can turn to God at any time, and (2) develop a repertoire of brief songs, Scripture, and other aids. If these have been meaningfully used (and not forced falsely when the children were not ready to mean them from within), then the children are well on their way to growing both in their personal prayer life and in their larger worship meetings. Certain great hymns are taught Primary and Junior children (denominational curricula and albums of hymns will help), and units on worship ways tell of customs, symbols, and other arts in worship, used by people of old and used by churchmen now. The minister should know when these units come, and read them himself that he may more wisely help teachers and growing young. He links his confirmation training with what is already being done.

Because many adult churchmen have never had training in ways of worship, and initiation into backgrounds of customs and arts used, a minister has sacred opportunity to offer special seminars or workshops. Lest he be tempted merely to lecture and leave them uninvolved, let him take to heart the levels of learning listed above for the church school teacher! Adults as well as youth need "sings" when they can enjoy fellowship, folk, and fun songs, and then learn great spirituals and hymns to sing reverently yet fullheartedly. Sometimes youth and adults at camps and outings tend to put religious words to popular tunes; *never* should we treat casually the high and holy. Rather, let us learn from the Welsh hymn-singers, with all ages participating and gathering for Gymanfa Ganu festivals. Some ministers teach a hymn a month, interpreting its background and on consecutive Sundays having organist play, choir sing, then congregation sing. Some ministers offer sermons in series on prayer and worship, and arts that enhance worship. The more the people are helped to enter in fully, the more they will grow—not only in awareness and use of arts in their worship and life—but also in their creative responding to the God who calls us to worship.

From juniors through youth and adulthood opportunity is given for planning and taking part in brief worship times. These can be dull, mere exercises in reading or performing, even though music or drama or other media may be used. The key is in coaching, so that whatever is done or said or sung be no mere program put on but a service to God. Children, youth, and adults can be encouraged to write out and pray their own prayers, offer simple meditations in their own words "from the inside, out." Occasionally, one catches the spark and writes a new hymn or paints a picture for a worship setting. Youth and adults need more nudging along, more prompting to creative expressions.

Verse-speaking choirs, with voices chosen for timbre instead of musical tone, help junior highs learn to speak together, and by contrasts of light-dark-medium voices fitted to Scripture or other writings, or to their own compositions, meanings are freshly experienced. Rhythmic motion can be used by all ages. Historically, probably it was the mother-art out of which all others have grown, involving as it does the instrument of the human body. Children easily become snowflakes falling, or planets orbiting. The teacher does not ask that they imitate him or her, just that each one move as he feels inside. The result is grace, variety, creativity, joy.

Juniors, junior highs, youth, adults may form choirs for interpretive motion, robing themselves unobtrusively (usually in dark colors) and moving barefoot through sequences that they themselves work out, as they think through a hymn or prayer they are interpreting. Insights of different ones may be tried, built upon, and streamlined, until a vital pattern emerges; then rehearsals develop teamwork in the expressing. In camps or other informal gatherings, whole groups (if there is room for individuals to move apart) may enter in, each letting gesture flow from within, as, for example, with the hymn, "There's a wideness in God's mercy like the wideness of the sea."

Choirs and organist need to understand worship meanings and ways their anthems, responses, quiet listening music, and leadership of congregational hymns may enhance worship—or hinder. Music in worship, whether in the congregational service or in brief, informal devotions, is never performance (we should never announce "special music"), but a ministering. Where director or choir is noncooperative, this usually means that tactful training in worship has been lacking, no matter how advanced the musical training. Minister and musicians need to spend time together, to develop mutual insights. They are "yokefellows" in the service.

Bell-ringing choirs are being developed where good bells can be afforded, and where a group (usually of boys) is willing to undergo the severe disciplines of practice individually and together. Their participation (if trained in worship along with the art) can prove inspiring, even a way of exulting in the glory of the Lord.

From simple dramatizing in children's and youth groups in their learning and problem-solving, more intensive drama study and artistry may take place with youth, young adult, and older adult groups. Ones who share this interest may meet across denominational or even faith lines. Plays of gripping message may be read in parts, little or no setting being needed, but lighting adaptations being helpful. Often depth-discussions grow out of such readings. Whether these on any one occasion lead directly to closing prayer or worship, they probably lead the participants to depths of soul-searching preliminary to more honest worship. If the minister participates in such groups, let him do so simply as a fellow human being, all masks and roles laid aside.

Chancel dramas, each with a simple thrust of meaning—no pious phrasing— and clear characterization, may help lead a congregation to soul-searching or prayer. Occasionally in the curricula for children of the denominations a play will be offered in which children of varying ages may participate with youth and adults, woven simply around some one facet of Christian living or churchmanship or Bible, or possibly with a hymn or symbol or other art form as central motif. These are usually planned with practicality for use in small as well as larger churches, instead of an outworn performance-routine of class after class for "Children's Day." Some churches expect some kind of "play" for Christmas and Easter; but often the ones chosen are flimsy, and insufficient time is spent in preparation, amidst the many other calls on time at these seasons. Probably a wiser way of celebrating would be a quiet service of song and meditation with settings of beauty. And in less hurried times of the church year, more vital dramas may be prepared.

Drama workshops, to which youth and adults may be brought for serious training, practice, and creation, are developing leadership and encouraging younger youth to follow drama interests. Drama teams of dedicated youth, giving of their talents and time and traveling widely with a repertoire of great plays, are giving a fresh new witness to the world. Once more drama and painting are coming back into the fold of the church, along with music which never left its worship. Dramas with a powerful message, whether couched in traditional religious language or forms or not, can reach multitudes otherwise unreached by the churches.

Harbingering the liturgical revival, church architecture in recent decades has shown astonishing openness to change. The availability of a wider range of new materials, and new engineering insights have brought forth a new language of church building in our time. Generally, structures have a lithe, clean, resilient look. Sanctuaries square or in the round may emphasize the table for the Lord's Supper as accessible by all on the same level. Or, depending upon denominational traditions and emphasis, other aspects of worship may be made central. Artists are finding new ways of creating windows, sometimes nonpictorial but yet worship-prompting, sometimes weaving in symbols or stylized representations of past or present life. The entire church body, children and youth as well as adults, should participate in the study and planning, as in the story of New York's Riverside Church building, *Living Stone*. Children, youth, and new members coming into the church should be taught regarding symbols, windows, or other aspects of the sanctuary or total building, which might prove helpful to them as they enter and prepare personally to worship.

As more lay people learn of the backgrounds of ways of worship and enter participatively through various arts, congregational worship becomes adventurous—no longer with all parts taken for granted and followed unquestioningly as led by minister. Some ministers have groups of laymen with whom they discuss the order of worship, including sermon plans; constant helpful evaluation means moving out from erstwhile ruts, and risking fresh ways while carrying forward into present and future the authentic customs and media from of old. Some Protestant congregations, understanding but little of their own orders of service, might profit from the "narrated service" custom being used in some Roman Catholic churches.

Does the art of jazz belong in the sanctuary? Has it a true liturgical function? Jazz is authentic art; it arose from existential depths. There were periods in church history when authentic folk music of the times was carried over for worship use. Several rather stirring services have been created experimentally. One would have to grow used to such media until one could cease concentrating on the music as such, and move through it to worship. Too, the question needs to be weighed seriously whether worship (centered in God, our response to his call, not just our own fabrication) does not call for reverence-prompting music, as well as other art forms. Significantly, *plainsong* (associated with the name of Gregory who edited and made widely available this simple yet fervent music) has never been used for other purposes than worship.

Arts festivals bring together outstanding leaders in the various arts, with exhibits of visual arts, dramas, music—possibly with massed choirs from many churches sharing in anthems long rehearsed. Not only churchmen but whole communities are made aware of new trends in arts and the burgeoning richness of religious art being created today. Youth are exposed to greatness through such festivals, and some may be encouraged to choose a life-ministry of music, drama, painting, writing, or other forms. Increasingly, through films and exchanges of arts (including children's projects of exchanging art through the American Friends Service Committee and World Council of Christian Education), churchmen over the world are learning of one another's creative interpretations in new and fresh ways; and the newer approach to Christian missions encourages indigenous art forms—music, architecture, symbols, paintings, dramas. Arts are transhistorical and transcultural. And it was through a song that the idea was given man of "peace on earth, goodwill to men."

## FOR ADDITIONAL READING

Bailey, A. E. *The Arts and Religion.* New York: The Macmillan Company, 1944.

Christ-Janer, Albert and Foley, Mary Mix. *Modern Church Architecture.* New York: McGraw-Hill Book Company, 1962.

Dillenberger, Jane. *Style and Content in Christian Art.* Nashville: Abingdon Press, 1965.

Dixon, John W., Jr. *Nature and Grace in Art*. Chapel Hill: University of North Carolina Press, 1964.

Ehrensperger, Harold. *Religious Drama: Ends and Means*. Nashville: Abingdon Press, 1962.

Eversole, Finley, ed. *The Christian Faith and the Contemporary Arts*. Nashville: Abingdon Press, 1962.

Fleming, D. J. *Christian Symbols in a World Community*. New York: Friendship Press, 1940.

Lovelace, Austin C. and Rice, William C. *Music and Worship in the Church*. Nashville: Abingdon Press, 1960.

May, Rollo, ed. *Symbolism in Religion and Literature*. New York: George Braziller, 1960.

Merritt, Helen. *Guiding Free Expression in Children's Art*. New York: Holt, Rinehart & Winston, 1964.

Mealy, Norman and Margaret. *Sing for Joy*. New York: The Seabury Press, 1961.

Morrison, Eleanor S. and Foster, Virgil. *Creative Teaching in the Church*. Englewood Cliffs: Prentice-Hall, 1963.

Morsch, Vivian S. *The Use of Music in Christian Education*. Philadelphia: The Westminster Press, 1956.

Rest, Friedrich. *Our Christian Symbols*. Philadelphia: Christian Education Press, 1954.

Ritter, R. H. *The Arts of the Church*. Boston: Pilgrim Press, 1947.

Smith, Jean Louise. *Great Art and Children's Worship*. Nashville: Abingdon Press, 1948.

Stirling, Nora. *Family Life Plays*. New York: Association Press, 1961.

Switz, T. M. and Johnston, R., eds. *Great Christian Plays*. New York: The Seabury Press, 1957.

Thomas, E. L. *The Whole World Singing, Songs of Praise and Work and Joy from Many Lands*. New York: Friendship Press, 1950.

Torrance, E. Paul. *Guiding Creative Talent*. Englewood Cliffs: Prentice-Hall, 1962.

Tufts, Nancy Poore. *The Art of Handbell Ringing*. Nashville: Abingdon Press, 1961.

Van der Leeuw, Gerhardus. *Sacred and Profane Beauty*. Preface by Mircea Eliade. Trans. by D. E. Green. New York: Holt, Rinehart & Winston, 1963.

Wilder, Amos. *Theology and Modern Literature*. Cambridge: Harvard University Press, 1958.

# Chapter 21

# WORSHIP IN
# CHRISTIAN EDUCATION

## *Grant S. Shockley*

WITHIN RECENT YEARS REVISED CONCEPTS HAVE EMERGED AND NEW EMPHASES are being stressed in the fields of worship and Christian education. That they are crucially important for any reassessment of the worship experience in relationship to the teaching-learning process has become evident. Currently, the worship experience is being thought of as the essence of the renewal of Christian life. Grimes says that "the first and foremost response of the persons involved in the church is worship." [1]

This unique stance of the individual Christian as a worshiper is also characteristic of recent theological thought regarding the nature of the church. At the pre-Lund meeting of the Faith and Order Commission of the World Council of Churches held in 1952 it was stated in a paper entitled "The Church" that every communion "believes that the church has a vocation to worship God in his holiness and to proclaim the Gospel to every creature." [2] The church is frequently referred to as "a worshiping community" of God's people—gathered for adoration, confession, thanksgiving, petition, illumination and dedication in Christ's name and scattered for his service in the world.

Other developments show that worship is being regarded as "celebration." According to Von Ogden Vogt,[3] and certain writers in the field since his time, "Worship is the celebration of life." It presents man with an incomparable privilege and opportunity to thank God for the victory of Christ over all things and for his continuing grace. Through worship man may continuously acknowledge in nature, life, and history the infinite and eternal "worth-ship" of God and find empowerment to assume the daily responsibilities that are consonant with such acknowledgment. Finally, the emphasis upon worship as "response" focuses attention on the freedom of man under God. It also restates a crucial presupposition of contemporary Christian education; namely, that God has acted, but man must and can respond in faith.

Changes that have taken place in Christian education thinking and that have modified our understanding of the place and function of worship can be illustrated by the meaning of three key terms that are prominent in current Christian education literature: comprehensive learning, situational learning, and socialized or group learning. Currently, Christian education is emphasizing the

---

[1] Howard Grimes, *The Church Redemptive* (Nashville: Abingdon Press, 1958), p. 71.

[2] The Lund Conference, Faith and Order Commission Papers No. 7, p. 13. Quoted by Walter M. Horton, *Christian Theology, An Ecumenical Approach* (New York: Harper & Brothers, 1955), pp. 214-15.

[3] *Modern Worship* (New Haven: Yale University Press, 1927), p. 3.

comprehensive nature of learning. It views the whole church participating through witnessing and sharing the whole gospel with the whole person in the totality of his existence. Articulating this objective in and through an educational process in reference to worship relates worship to every aspect of the life-experience. The term "situational learning" has come to describe another educational approach that has influenced education in worship. This approach holds that learning is more meaningful and productive when it is related to and allowed to emerge from ongoing learning experiences under the guidance of a mature Christian. In group-life research it is being discovered and demonstrated that the dynamics of person-to-person relationships in a learning situation may be employed to facilitate worship experiences. Robert S. Clemmons reports: "As the dynamic process of person-to-person learning advances, there will be many occasions when members feel that they want to express in a total way their experience of the worth of God in their lives" [4]

## The Worship Objective in Christian Education

Through varied settings for worship Christian education attempts to enable all individuals—children, youth, and adults—to recognize in a personal sense the implications of the basic Christian affirmation that Christ is Lord and has a sovereign claim upon the totality of one's being. This claim relates Christ to all of life and is interpreted through his life and teachings and given its truest meaning in the fellowship of his church.

Having recognized the centrality of Christ's lordship in worship it is proper to enunciate some further aims:

to develop in individuals the realization of their capacities to adore and serve God in Christ whose lordship they acknowledge.

to assist individuals in initiating, cultivating, and sustaining a personal relationship to Christ that will allow the offering and receiving of his love and fellowship.

to celebrate continuously to "worth-ship" of God through reverence, mission, and vocation.

to make individuals aware of the availability of God's every resource in meeting their continuing needs.

to guide individuals in their personal responses of obedience with regard for their maturity, experience, and opportunities to act as Christians.[5]

## Worship in the Family

There are some specific ways in which these goals might be implemented in the context of a church program that is concerned with an educative ministry in worship. A natural place to begin is in the home. There are several reasons for this. First, in such a situation parents can be reoriented in faith and worship as they are taught and in turn orient their children. Second, much that young children learn about worship in the home will be *caught* rather

---

[4] *Dynamics of Christian Adult Education* (Nashville: Abingdon Press, 1958), p. 100.

[5] Cf. *The Objectives of Christian Education: A Study Document* (New York: The National Council of Churches, 1958), pp. 21-22.

than *taught*. The general importance that parents assign or fail to assign to their prayer and devotional life will be communicated to home members in non-verbal ways. The surest foundation for the church as a worshiping community is laid in homes where family members worship naturally in and through the daily round of their life situations viewed as "encounter-experiences" with the life and teachings of Christ. Finally, the spiritual life of maturing Christian adults depends in large measure on the direction set through guidance and relationships in the home.

In view of these facts the following may be considered as suggestions: (1) emphasize the importance of family worship in premarriage guidance conversations with engaged couples relating this to pertinent portions of the marriage vows and the establishment of a home that is Christian; (2) provide all newly married couples with a simple plan for their prayer and devotional life with a helpful piece of material such as the booklet, *Your First Week Together* by George and Ruth Brown, and arrange for the dedication of the home or dwelling in which the young couple will live and present them, in the name of the church, a gift of some book such as *The Book of Worship for Church and Home*;[6] (3) prearrange pastoral visits with parents expecting the birth of a child for the purpose of offering brief prayers of thanksgiving in the name of Christ and the church and to arrange for the baptism; (4) give to parents some such booklet or leaflet as provided by the *Guild of the Christ Child: Materials to Supplement Your Parish's Ministry to Pre-School Children Through Families* which contains subsections on: "Family Prayer," "Corporate Worship Is a Must," and "Observing Festivals";[7] (5) introduce the person who will act as the church-home coordinator or visitor who will invite all parents to attend the services of the church and suggest the church's ministry of caring for infants while parents are at church; (6) prepare young parents and others through group experiences of various kinds to exploit the potential in the questions that young and older children ask, thus enabling them to form and express growing religious ideas and concepts which are becoming their basis for faith and worship;[8] (7) develop a church ministry to families that will be helpful in assisting them to initiate family worship, including: grace at meals; creative prayers; quiet times; spontaneous moments of worship at home; morning, noontide and evening (bedtime) prayers and stories; parent-child conversations;[9] Bible verses, hymn stanzas, and worship, as well as litany responses; (8) suggest that the observance of various holidays, saints days,

---

[6] *Your First Week Together* (New York: The Department of Family Life, National Council of Churches, 1946) and *The Book of Worship for Church and Home* (Nashville: The Methodist Publishing House, 1964), pp. 373-74.

[7] (Guild of the Christ Child, Diocese of the Protestant Episcopal Church of Maryland, 105 West Monument Street, Baltimore, Maryland).

[8] Among the helpful books on children's questions are: Marguerite H. Bro, *When Children Ask* (New York: Harper & Brothers, 1956); J. L. and A. G. Fairly, *Using the Bible to Answer Questions Children Ask* (Richmond: John Knox Press, 1958); and Edith F. Hunter, *The Questioning Child and Religion* (Boston: Starr King Press, 1956).

[9] See A. L. and E. W. Gebhard, *Our Family Worships at Home* (Nashville: Abingdon Press, 1958), and Elfrieda and Leon McCauley, *A Book of Family Worship* (New York: Charles Scribner's Sons, 1959).

martyrs days, and the seasons of the church year provide excellent opportunities for family worship times;[10] (9) provide guidance in the preparation and use of family-made, as well as denominational-prepared, devotional material.

## The Church School and Worship

In past years the correlation of worship in the regular worship service with worship in the church school was practically nonexistent. Many church school leaders still think in terms of instruction as the exclusive province of the church school and worship as the sole prerogative of the worship service. As a result of this, many teachers do a poor job of relating worship and learning in the session experience. The current approach to the teaching of worship in Christian education is an integrated approach. The teacher seeks for worship opportunities in ongoing learning experiences. The following discussion of age-level and corporate worship will attempt to illustrate this. Various local churches will need to adapt this approach where it is necessary to assemble various combinations of age-levels for their group worship.

## Children's Worship in the Church

Worship experiences for children should be planned with care. First, the goal of Christian worship—to enable individuals at varying stages of growth to experience God's love and concern and to respond joyfully—must be kept uppermost in the leader's thinking. Second, the teacher should take cognizance of the several features of the developmental profile of these youngest worshipers, noting such things as basic needs, foci of energy, radii of relationships, and areas of difficulty in growing.[11] Third, the child's religious development should be considered in planning worship experiences in relation to the understandings that the teacher has about the child's concept of significant adults, authority, new experience, feelings of adequacy, feelings of security, decision-making, self-worth, wonder and awe, death, other persons, curiosity, sharing, symbols and ritual, and so forth.

Planning worship experiences for two- and three-year-olds in the church requires a close look at this particular age-level. Typically, they are ever-busy, exploring, freedom-seeking little people. Though they are not ready for actual formal group experiences, they do enjoy situations that allow brief interpersonal contacts and parallel play. These times of curious exploration are guided by the teacher who allows the freedom which this necessitates.

Worship opportunities at this age may be found in spontaneous individual and very small group experiences, which moments of awe, wonder, or surprise are rich in spiritual potential. Sharing these times with children, sometimes in

[10] See George M. Gibson, *The Story of the Christian Year* (Nashville: Abingdon Press, 1945); Maymie R. Krythe, *All About American Holidays* (New York: Harper & Brothers, 1962); and Mary R. Newland, *The Year and Our Children* (New York: Image Books, Doubleday and Co., 1964). The latter book has a Roman Catholic orientation but contains excellent material that can be adapted for Protestant use.

[11] Cf. *Planbook for Leaders of Children, 1964-1965* (Nashville: Graded Press), pp. 7-13.

silence, with a Bible verse, a sentence prayer, or in a brief conversation, often fulfills their experience with religious meanings otherwise incommunicable.

The four- and five-year-old continues to be an activist. He is often noisy and talkative as he experiments with words in the process of building a vocabulary. He can be helpful at times and is usually eager to play with other four- and five-year-olds. Curiosity reaches a peak at this age-level. He seems to literally "drink in" the environment through an insatiable sense hunger for detail. The kindergartner is a persistent, if not profound, questioner, asking, "How did God make the world?" As he moves toward five, the questions become more meaningful, serious, and empirical, reflecting both a literal and a practical turn of mind. While he can repeat facts and bits of information, they have little if any meaning for him. Since nursery days, the kindergartner has learned to play in small groups, and he is able to do some self-viewing objectively. He is thus capable of understanding something of his own feelings and the feelings of others. Sharing is still a problem but is increasingly understood in rational rather than purely emotional terms. The kindergartner loves stories and storytelling[12] and usually is fascinated with real life objects and picture books.

What do these characteristics mean in terms of kindergarten worship? The basic approach is still that of seizing spontaneous opportunities and using them to share moments of beauty, wonder, or compassion. Following such experiences or as a part of them, the teacher may gather together the fuller meaning of the experience in a story, song, litany, or sentence prayer. Group-together times are possible with kindergartners. These should be used sparingly but enough to enhance the growing group-feeling at this age. Kindergartners should not be confined in their worship to the interior of the church building. Unusual experiences await them in the out-of-doors where "signs" of fall, winter, spring, and summer can be a background for excellent worship conversation.[13]

Primary boys and girls (ages 6-8) bring still other capabilities and needs to worship times in the church. Having crossed the threshold of an age-level involving family members and primary play groups, they now encounter neighborhood and school groups. These new social experiences pose the problems of peer-group selection and adjustment. Also there are other issues closely related to this, such as adjustment to authority, value-judgement decisions, and some degree of self-discipline.

On a personal level primary children have longer attention spans permitting participation in a somewhat extended worship experience. Toward the end of their first year in elementary public school, they are well oriented to the basic language-art skills (listening, speaking, writing, spelling, reading) and are thus able to employ these skills in worship-learning. Increasingly, schools and churches are providing incidental and formal instruction along with experience in library use. This is now a new resource for the worship leader.

[12] See Jeanette Perkins Brown, *The Storyteller in Religious Education* (Boston: The Pilgrim Press, 1951).

[13] Elizabeth Brown, "Outdoor Experiences Are Not Extras" (Leaflet 951-C), order from Service Department, Methodist Board of Education, P. O. Box 871, Nashville, Tenn., 37202.

While it is the continuing responsibility of the parent and church teacher to exploit significant occasions which have spontaneous worship potential, it is also important to develop children's worship capacity in other directions. In addition to spontaneous experiences, planned or unplanned, teachers will want to help primaries initiate and sustain a personal devotional life. They will also be interested in more meaningful group experiences of worship, climaxing during this age-period in family corporate worship participation. At this age-level boys and girls can work cooperatively in developing worship services. They can write prayers, dramatize Bible stories, plan and execute sharing projects. Seven- and eight-year-olds can read the Bible for themselves. Eight-year-olds may want to paraphrase it or write or tell a parable in a contemporary setting.

Questions are a fruitful source for worship opportunities available to the teacher of primaries. Children at this age are asking questions for the sake of meaning. Many of these can become themes for worship on a personal or group level. Others can be answered through a group-created choral reading.[14]

Juniors (ages 9-11) live in an ever-broadening world of change, ideas, discoveries, and adventures. As they further develop their large muscle skills, they are found outdoors engaging in scouting, camping, and hiking. They are also developing communication tools. The neighborhood group becomes the "gang." Some problems that their parents and church teachers are likely to encounter and which should be considered in giving leadership to this worship are: (1) group identification and status in the group; (2) personal friendships or lack of them; (3) social ostracism due to class distinctions; and (4) feelings of inadequacy and images of authority.

There are other developments that are occurring which should be of interest to worship leaders of this age-group. They are interested in meanings largely for use and application. Dialogue or two-way conversation is now quite possible. Their emerging ability to think abstractly now enables some use of symbolism.[15] A historical sense is now evident, making the study of biblical history more meaningful. They tend to be good readers and are usually easily interested in biography, unusual experience, and challenges.

Specific suggestions which may be developed as activities, experiences, and projects for junior worship must also be considered. These children can develop their own prayers spontaneously or work them out prior to their use.[16] They can compose litanies, find calls to worship, invocations, and responses. Their ability to question and evaluate judgements and form opinions permits more dialogue-conversation than has been possible until now. Rosemary Roorbach feels that this age group can now profit from the study of symbolism in relation to the morning worship service.[17] The junior's yen for the unusual can be captured for Christian learning purposes through reading. Suggestions for in

[14] See H. A. Brown and H. J. Heltman, eds., *Choral Readings from the Bible* (Philadelphia: The Westminster Press, 1954).

[15] See Dorothy B. Fritz, *The Use of Symbolism in Christian Education* (Philadelphia: The Westminster Press, 1961).

[16] See Lois Horton Young, "When Children Pray," *International Journal of Religious Education*, XXXII (February, 1956), 13.

[17] *Teaching Children in the Church* (Nashville: Abingdon Press, 1959), p. 145.

and out of session material include Bible biography, poems, fables, myths, and legends.[18]

## Youth Worship in the Church

Worship forms must speak clearly to guide youth in understanding their predicament in relationship to God's will and their heritage in his grace. Youth worship is not an end in itself. Its principal end is communication with God. Through personal, group, and corporate experiences, its aim is to help youth hear and reply to the gospel after having been in the presence of God and seen themselves as they are, their fellow man as he is, and their world as it is.

*Junior high worship* should have three main objectives: (1) to inspire toward personal devotion; (2) to guide in group experiences of worship; and (3) to provide corporate worship time and skills.

In addition to continuing efforts toward deepening the worship life of these young people in the home, there are the unplanned and planned worship times in the church school. During the morning session of the junior high youth fellowship the alert teacher will sense the propriety for worship occasions growing out of the session material itself. An unforgettable worship can emerge from play-acting a parable, the meaning of which is closely or directly related to a situation or decision being faced by the group. Another junior high worship experience that has unusual potential is the planned service. Groups of junior highs who meet during the week can discuss problems in their group and worship life and then develop more adequate programs with their leader. In the case of a cross-departmental worship service, junior high leaders can provide materials that are understandable and participation roles that are meaningful and interest-engaging. Some materials that can be used with this age group are written prayers, conversation-meditation, pictures, cooperatively developed litanies, music, and art.[19] There are other opportunities available to leaders as they seek to teach how and when worship can be helpful as junior highs grow in Christian faith. Parents can be alerted to some specific junior high worship needs such as: the various types of prayers; the sources of materials for meditation and silent periods as well as prayers that match their sense of guilt; their moods of depression and exaltation; and their need for forgiveness and friendship.[20] Family conversation about prayer with junior highs can be a rewarding experience, as well as can their participation in family devotions and family grace at mealtime.

Junior high activity weeks, held in summer-outdoor or winter-indoor settings, still provide other opportunities for worship-learning. In the case of

---

[18] See *Bible Readings for Boys and Girls* (New York: Thomas Nelson & Sons, 1959), and Mary Ellen Chase, *The Bible and The Common Reader* (New York: The Macmillan Company, 1952).

[19] See L. H. Curry and C. M. Wetzel, *Worship Services Using the Arts* (Philadelphia: The Westminster Press, 1961).

[20] See Oliver De Wolf Cummings, *The Youth Fellowship* (Valley Forge: The Judson Press, 1956), chap. VI, and H. F. Couch and S. S. Barefield, *Devotions For Junior Highs* (Nashville: Abingdon Press, 1960).

a summer-outdoor setting, a nature-occurrence, such as a storm or a sunrise, may easily produce worship possibilities. In the case of other settings, an experience of rejection, a newfound friendship, or a particularly difficult decision may serve to cue the sensitive leader of worship to engage the individuals involved or the group in an act of worship.

Another junior high worship opportunity that should be mentioned is camp worship. In these havens of God's created beauty, worship experiences are possible that are otherwise unavailable. Group devotions, vespers, hymn sings, camp fires, nature hikes, folk-dancing—all of these lead toward unforgettable group experiences and worship experiences if counselors know when to lift up significant feelings, experiences, or insights for moments of sharing and praise.[21]

*Senior high worship* must consider seriously the social environment of youth. The dynamics of youth's personal, interpersonal, and corporate relationships must be reassessed. The key term in this evaluation is "contemporaneity." Youth worship must be pertinent to the problems of youth culture. Senior highs are asking questions about the worthwhileness of continuing in school, the ethics of alcoholic, tobacco, narcotic, and sexual indulgence, the significance of death, and the meaning of life.

Worship forms must make youth aware of God's deathless love and eternal purposes for them. In the words of Cummings, "Youth should feel that they belong to the family of God, . . . that . . . worship voices their own feelings and responses to God, and that God speaks to their hearts and lives in worship." [22]

Some guiding principles to direct this new thrust in a youth ministry will include an understanding on the part of youth that the cultivation of the spiritual life is a "discipline," the acceptance of which implies the practice of the devotional reading of the Bible, prayer, and worship. Spiritual discipline for youth, and adults as well, also implies that the insights of the spiritual life are to be related to the common problems that senior highs face in personal, family, and social relations.[23]

Forms that give body to these new accents include: (1) private worship with renewed meaning; (2) participation in family devotions with deeper responsibilities; (3) group worship experiences before school or possibly weekly early breakfasts followed by devotional periods at church;[24] (4) continued searching for more adequate formats for the weekly meeting of the church youth fellowship groups to allow for more meaningful worship;[25] (5) inter-

[21] See Clarice Bowman, *Worship Ways for Camp* (New York: Association Press, 1955).
[22] *The Youth Fellowship*, p. 114.
[23] See Byron Deshler, "Disciplines of the *Spiritual Life*" (Service Department, Methodist Board of Education, P. O. Box 871, Nashville, Tenn., 37202); Clarice Bowman, *Youth At Prayer: An Elective Unit for Young People* (Nashville: Abingdon Press, 1947) and *Power* (Dayton, Ohio: Christian Youth Publications, published quarterly).
[24] See Janice Bennett, "Lenten Services" and "Weekly Breakfast at Church," *International Journal of Religious Education*, XXXIV (January, 1958), 24, 41.
[25] Warren S. Webb, "A New Structure for an Emerging Ministry with Youth" (unpublished Master's thesis, Northwestern University, 1965). This study reports an action-research which suggests many opportunities for incidental and spontaneous worship experiences for youth.

church, interdenominational, and interfaith exchanges involving worship deputations.

Finally, opportunities for worship abound in youth institutes, assemblies, and camp settings of various kinds. E. S. Morrison and V. E. Foster, in their book *Creative Teaching in the Church,* describe how these can be made to provide unique environments and situations for memorable encounters with God.[26] In the local church attendance upon, and participation in, corporate worship, family corporate worship, and occasional youth emphasis Sunday worship celebrations provide continuing experiences of both growth and reinforcement in perfecting the spiritually disciplined life of youth.

### Adult Worship in the Church

It is often taken for granted that adults know how to initiate and sustain their worship existence. Adults, like children and youth, must be accepted where they are in their worship life and guided into ampler ways of expressing and celebrating God's victorious reign over life and death. This is the assumption that is being made as we discuss the worship life of young adults, middle-aged adults, and adults of riper years.

The key to the development of an effective program of worship among adults in any local church is the discovery of how to be of help to them as they seek to relate their Christian faith to life. As the church becomes more effective in bringing adults to deeper insights and higher reaches for their capacities and as it makes available to them real help in their negotiating their several developmental tasks, worship—personal, group, and corporate—will take on new meaning and greater significance. The task of Christian education in relation to adult worship, then, is clear. It is to work with adults in evolving worship settings and forms that will bring life into Christian focus and initiate a vital and continuous dialogue between who they really are and what they are called to be and to do in the world of today.

Young adult life in our time affords an excellent example of the many opportunities to live the Christian life worshipfully. Amid the uncertainty, instability, mobility, and propaganda that constantly surround them, the gospel is the one thing that can clearly guide and truly renew their lives. The church must seek to make known just how this can be done in their situations. A vital approach to worship can be of help here. These are some suggestions: (1) in small groups on prayer some of the great prayers of the Bible can be read; (2) "prayers that have helped me" can be shared; (3) religious plays can be read as worship experiences; (4) problems and trends in contemporary worship forms can be discussed; (5) hymns can be studied and used as prayers; (6) an elective unit, dealing with the religious value of the arts, can be undertaken;[27] (7) studies of liturgical concepts and practices in various denominations and

[26] (Englewood Cliffs: Prentice-Hall, 1963), p. 118.

[27] See Curry and Wetzel, *Worship Services Using the Arts;* Finley Eversole, ed., *Christian Faith and the Contemporary Arts* (Nashville: Abingdon Press, 1957); Walter L. Nathan, *Art and the Message of the Church* (Philadelphia: The Westminster Press, 1961).

worship in various religions of the world can be studied;[28] (8) services of home dedication can be held; (9) Christian symbolism can be studied; and (10) attendance at corporate worship may be followed by sermon discussions of various types.

Some of the most significant worship experienced by young adults is found in their own group fellowship. Through varied types of programs and services relevant and unique experiences emerge which call forth new forms. There should not be an attempt to mimic a corporate worship experience. Brief, planned services have proved more meaningful with this age group. Some groups devote a session at the beginning of each season of the church year to study and worship pertaining to that season and provide suggestions and resources for the private use of group members.[29] Interpretative reading of the Bible from various translations, letting the group discuss their situational value for today, is done by some groups. Young adult groups which are often interdenominational and interfaith should find exciting freshness in using *The Anchor Bible,* whose contributors are Jewish, Roman Catholic, and Protestant.[30] Finally, young adults could initiate a church library project to build a collection of worship resources and through such a project discuss the lore and meaning of worship.

In any effort to rejuvenate and assist adult worship in the church serious consideration must be given to the need for providing guidance in developing a Christian theological basis for the personal prayer and devotional life of adults.[31] The suggestion is that this be accomplished through small study groups that explore some of the biblical bases and examples of prayer, and then seek to discover, with guidance, the meaning that prayer can have for life today.

Other useful modes and means of initiating and cultivating the personal devotional life of adults include (1) the institution of prayer and personal Christian growth groups in which the members "aspire to relatedness with God both as individuals and as a unit of the kingdom of God";[32] (2) the conducting of schools of prayer, possibly within the scope of a Sunday evening fellowship setting, in which study courses on prayer, methods of prayer, and devotional classes are taught; (3) the sponsoring of a prayer mission under the joint leadership of spiritual life leaders in the church and the committee on education for the purpose of involving the laity in a churchwide venture that would lend support to individual and group efforts toward more effective prayer experience; (4) the organization of prayer vigils around issues emerging

[28] See Geoffrey Parrinder, *Worship in the World's Religions* (New York: Association Press, 1961); Bard Thompson, *Liturgies of the Western Church* (Cleveland: The World Publishing Company, 1961).

[29] See K. B. and I. V. Cully, *Two Seasons, Advent and Lent* (Indianapolis: The Bobbs-Merrill Company, 1954).

[30] (New York: Doubleday & Company). The various biblical books are being published separately; the first appeared in 1964, and the full translation is expected by 1970.

[31] Nels F. S. Ferré, "What Is Prayer?" *International Journal of Religious Education,* XLI (February, 1965), 3-4.

[32] H. W. Freer and F. B. Hall, *Two or Three Together* (New York: Harper & Brothers, 1954), p. 16.

from personal, national, and international concerns and crises; (5) the holding of prayer retreats, preferably away from the church, at which time the congregation participates in actual prayer experiences, guided by group leaders as resource persons; (6) a survey of personal prayer life in the church with the use of some such schedule as the *Personal Prayer Inventory;*[33] the observance of the Universal Week of Prayer, a period set aside during January, a Sunday of which could well offer a sermon on prayer or the devotional life followed by a post-sermon discussion feedback technique.

The final word in this section must be about worship in the adult class. In the past and at the present some adult classes congregate for an assembly-worship and then divide into groups for classes. Other groups have a closing assembly, sometimes with the children's department. The trend seems to be toward the self-contained group experience with only occasional departmental or church-school-wide worship preceded or followed by corporate worship.

A second important question that arises is the relation of adult worship to the class session. Should this come at the beginning of the session or at its conclusion? What type of service should it be? The answers to these questions are not easy. Worship in the adult class, as in any class, should grow out of the issues of Christian faith and life that confront the group through the ministry of teaching-learning process. Such moments of worship will be spontaneous and manifested in flashes of insight, moments of gratitude, and feelings of dependence upon God or empowerment by his spirit. Other worship times can be planned in relation to the theme of the material with sufficient flexibility to allow the addition of a hymn or prayer. In any event, this service is session-related and not envisioned as duplicating the morning worship.

The church's senior adult ministry considers two types of persons—those older persons able to attend and the shut-ins. It is assumed that senior adults, though aged, participate normally in the ongoing life of the church and parish. Hence, this discussion will be confined largely to those who are physically incapable of attending services and activities at the church building.

Any worship ministry to shut-ins should begin by attempting to meet their greatest problem, loneliness. Pastoral and lay visitation to shut-ins secures them in the knowledge that they are not forgotten and that they are still a part of the church. During his visits the pastor will not only reassure by his physical presence, but he will offer Christ's reassurance through the administration of the Sacrament of Holy Communion, the Divine Presence. When laymen visit, they offer the Divine Presence in prayer, helpful conversation, and fellowship.

Adults who are confined to homes may also be aided in developing more meaningful Bible reading and prayer experiences. Local church and denominationally prepared worship materials can be made available for their use. These could include: (1) periodic booklets of devotions; (2) Bible reading programs and plans; (3) reading books about the Bible, such as Edward P. Blair's *Getting to Know the Bible.*[34]

[33] This is available from Tidings, 1908 Grand Avenue, Nashville, Tennessee, 37203.

[34] (Nashville: Abingdon Press, 1956).

In addition to this, shut-ins can be aided in their personal devotional and religious life through a monthly information folder which previews significant offerings for their religious growth. Such information could well be a monthly church bulletin insert for the entire congregation. It could include: (1) notations of devotional columns and articles in newspapers and magazines; (2) meditations and articles in denominational and other religious periodicals; (3) notice of broadcasts; (4) announcements about recordings and tapes of their own church services; (5) church bulletins and newsletters; and (6) selected television viewings and inspirational telephone meditations.

Group worship experiences can be provided for shut-ins. Pastoral prayers should include them, and they in turn should send their prayers to the church. Occasionally, these prayers might find their way into the church bulletin. Prayer chains and prayer vigils can include shut-ins.

A final word has to do with corporate worship experiences. Occasionally they may be brought to the church for such a service or as Maves suggests, a service for older people could be held on Sunday afternoon and sponsored by the council of churches, thus making it possible to draw a larger clientele for such a ministry.[35]

There is also a place for the older adult in the family corporate worship service. Virginia Stafford points out that: "They contribute to the worship experience of the entire church family. . . . More than their influence on others in worship is the fact of the older person's need for worship with God's people." [36]

## Family Corporate Worship

Churches are increasingly aware of the values inherent in family participation in a morning corporate worship service. Graded teaching, learning, and worship in the modern church school have enhanced the educational process, but they have also contributed to the division of the family worshiping together as a unit at the morning service. Randolph C. Miller feels that this is due to the fact that the typical morning service is not constructed with children in mind. "Although some congregations have successfully appealed to families at the major service, in most cases the younger members refuse to participate or attend under pressure." [37]

Also, the practice of scheduling church worship services to meet at the same hour that church school classes meet necessitates the exclusion of one or the other of these experiences. This arrangement conveys the false impression that worship or study is optional. Wayne Lindecker points out that worship and study are complementary. "Persons are the church as they gather for both study and worship." [38]

This "complementary" concept respecting the relation between study and

[35] P. B. Maves and J. L. Cedarleaf, *Older People and the Church* (Nashville: Abingdon Press, 1949), chap. 10.
[36] *Older Adults in the Church* (Nashville: The Methodist Publishing House, 1953), p. 71.
[37] *Education for Christian Living* (2nd. ed., Englewood Cliffs: Prentice-Hall, 1963), p. 263.
[38] "Your Commission on Education," *The Church School*, XVI (September, 1963), 31.

worship, when viewed in terms of education in worship, commends the corporate family worship experience. This important dimension in the worship life of every congregation should be introduced to children during the late preschool years. In such a service symbolic objects, movements and acts of corporate praise, confession, and dedication provide a unique setting for learning by children, youth, and parents. Family corporate worship is designed with families in mind, especially young children. It is usually followed by a second worship service geared to the traditionally adult congregation. If it is intended to be an integral part of the total program of church education, it should be offered weekly or periodically on some regular basis.

Family corporate worship services should be complete; they should not be adulterated in any sense. Modifications are in the interest of the essential teaching motif of the total experience and consideration of the presence of younger children. Such a service may be of thirty to forty-five minutes' duration. How does this service proceed? There are several necessary elements.

*Home Preparation:* Parents prepare their children to gather for worship rather than for "going to church." This approach teaches children that they are the church. When they are "gathered" for worship, they are the worshiping church. When they are "scattered" in worship, they are the serving church.

*Spiritual Preparation:* Parents prepare themselves and their children for the spiritual offering of their lives in worship. This may be done by recognizing those things that hinder fellowship with God and the receiving of forgiveness.

*The Order of Service:* The Scripture lessons, hymns, prayers, responses, and readings have been reviewed in the home, and each family member has some understanding of their message. Mention has been made of the needs which the offering is fulfilling, and the family's envelopes are ready.

*At the Church:* The family enters the pew together, kneels or bows for a moment of silent meditation, thanking God for the privilege of worship and for the church. The church bulletin is scanned. Scripture lessons, readings, and hymns are located and read quietly with younger children.[39]

*The Order of Worship:* The object of family corporate worship is participation by each family member to the full extent of his capacity. This may be enhanced by having families as units lead certain designated acts of worship, such as a call to worship, collect, psalter, or responsive reading. Families as units may also become member-families of a family choir.[40] Further involvement of younger family members can be achieved by the use of brief introductory remarks or "orienting observations" prior to selected acts of worship.[41]

*The Sermon:* Probably the most difficult part of the family corporate

[39] Cf. William H. Genné, "Family Worship in Church" (Leaflet BB 10-1049, Department of Family Life, National Council of Churches, 475 Riverside Drive, New York, N. Y. 10027).

[40] Richard R. Alford, "A Choir of Families," *Music Ministry,* I (April, 1960), 1-2; and Philip R. Dietterich, "Music for the Whole Family," *The Church School,* XVI (March, 1963), 14.

[41] William Sydnor, *How and What the Church Teaches* (New York: Longmans, Green & Company, 1960), pp. 1-13.

worship service is the sermon. Genné reports how one pastor met this difficulty by developing a "family-conversational" sermon style.[42]

*Follow-Up:* Sydnor suggests that following the corporate worship, and in the home, further interpretation can take place. Prayers and Scripture readings may be explained and new hymns sung again. Symbols can be explained and discussed.[43]

*Family Worship Training:* Preparing families to appreciate and accept corporate family worship requires training. Some suggested settings for this are: (1) Sunday evening fellowships; (2) family camps; (3) actually preparing and presenting such a service to inaugurate Family Week.

## FOR ADDITIONAL READING

Abba, Raymond. *Principles of Christian Worship.* New York: Oxford University Press, 1957.

Baxter, Edna M. *Learning to Worship.* Valley Forge: Judson Press, 1965.

Bowman, Clarice. *Resources for Worship.* New York: Association Press, 1961.

Brown, Jeanette P. *More Children's Worship in the Church School.* New York: Harper & Brothers, 1953.

Curry, L. H. and Wetzel, C. M. *Worship Services Using the Fine Arts.* Philadelphia: The Westminster Press, 1961.

Davies, Horton. *Christian Worship.* Nashville: Abingdon Press, 1957.

Fahs, Sophia L. *Worshipping Together With Questioning Minds.* Boston: Beacon Press, 1965.

Fritz, Dorothy B. *The Use of Symbolism in Christian Education.* Philadelphia: The Westminster Press, 1961.

Gibson, George M. *The Story of the Christian Year.* Apex ed. Nashville: Abingdon Press, 1963.

Lovelace, A. C. and Rice, W. C. *Music and Worship in the Church.* Nashville: Abingdon Press, 1960.

Morrison, E. S. and Foster, V. E. *Creative Teaching in the Church.* Englewood Cliffs: Prentice-Hall, 1963.

Morsch, Vivian S. *The Use of Music in Christian Education.* Philadelphia: The Westminster Press, 1956.

Paulsen, Irwin G. *The Church School and Worship.* Nashville: Abingdon Press, 1940.

Thomas, Edith L. *Music in Christian Education.* Nashville: Abingdon Press, 1953.

Towner, Vesta. *Guiding Children in Worship.* Nashville: Abingdon Press, 1946.

Underhill, Evelyn. *Worship.* New York: Harper & Brothers, 1937.

Vogt, Von Ogden. *The Primacy of Worship.* Boston: Starr King Press, 1958.

---

[42] "Family Worship in Church."
[43] *How and What the Church Teaches,* p. 15.

# Chapter 22

# THE CHRISTIAN EDUCATION
# OF EXCEPTIONAL PERSONS

## *Allen E. Kroehler*

EVEN THOUGH THE CHURCH HAS FOR ITS MANY YEARS PIONEERED IN MINISTRY to persons of need, the educational needs of exceptional persons have usually not been met by the church. They are all too often among those invisible persons whose voice is not heard in the public forum and who seldom have a spokesman in high places. But fortunately, the witness of prominent leaders to the need for concerted and powerful action to improve the condition of the handicapped person is now producing results.

Pearl Buck wrote a moving book about her own retarded child at a time when such personal revelation took more courage than it would today. The physical disability of President Franklin Delano Roosevelt launched a series of research programs which continue to make significant discoveries and to effect liberating change. The work begun by the Kennedy family on behalf of mental retardation and related problems has released reservoirs of creativity and resource for this large segment of our population. The education legislation of of the mid-1960's will surely make available leadership and facilities for thousands of handicapped persons for whom communities have not been making adequate provision.

Whether or not handicapping is a tragedy in itself depends upon the responses persons make. A person with handicaps can become a whole person and can make significant contributions to society. As Helen Keller's life illustrates, a handicap can become the stimulus to unusual achievement. The way a person or his family responds to the opportunities and challenges of handicapping can be a triumph of human potential.

Persons are strongly influenced in their becoming and being by what others expect of them. Persons with handicaps are further disadvantaged when nothing is expected of them. All persons tend to perform more adequately and to achieve more successfully in the warm nurture of confidence and trustful expectation.

Churches are beginning to expect more from their handicapped members. They are learning that the whole body functions most productively and healthfully when every member of it is operating at his best. Some churches, trying to discover what is interfering with their wholeness, have found themselves neglecting some of their members.

The church and exceptional persons need each other. The churches are beginning to understand their responsibilities to persons of special need and to develop proposals for effective ministry.

## Who Are They?

### Exceptional Persons

Exceptional persons are those whose needs are not met in routine ways. For some reason, special services or methods are required to help them realize their potential. Exceptionality has become a very specialized term for use in special education. Specialists in education of exceptional persons have found it useful to understand the type of handicapping present in persons and the factors which will determine what nonroutine attention will be required.

Exceptionality falls, for educational purposes, within at least seven broad categories,[1] including twelve types of exceptional persons.

Pupils with intellectual limitations
  (1) the educable and
  (2) the trainable mentally retarded
Pupils with superior intellect
  (3) the gifted
Pupils with behavior problems
  (4) the emotionally disturbed and
  (5) the socially maladjusted
Pupils with
  (6) speech problems
Pupils with impaired hearing
  (7) the deaf and
  (8) the hard of hearing
Pupils with impaired vision
  (9) the blind and
  (10) the partially seeing
Pupils with neurological and nonsensory physical impairments
  (11) the crippled and
  (12) the chronic health cases

It may seem that some of these categories are too narrowly defined, while others include a wide range of variety. The distinction is to be found in the somewhat different equipment, materials, curriculum content, and instructional competence which are required for each. To be sure, there will be local differences which produce changes in the suggested broad categories. The previous educational experiences of a person will also help determine the kind of provision which must be made to meet his present needs. The types of advanced equipment which may be available in some communities might place a child otherwise required to learn Braille in a partially seeing class. Careful attention must be given by local administrators of church school programs for exceptional persons in consultation with the best professional help available to the most appropriate placement of each individual.

### Found in Every Congregation

Every congregation will discover, if it is not now aware, that it has members with exceptional educational needs. The highest percentage of persons

[1] Lloyd M. Dunn, ed., *Exceptional Children in the Schools* (New York: Holt, Rinehart & Winston, 1963).

with special need are those with intellectual limitation. It is generally agreed that three out of every one hundred persons are so limited. Severely retarded persons are sometimes hidden. Stigma and ignorance about the nature and causes of retardation still consign many persons to lives of confinement and despair who could otherwise be helped. Public education about this and other handicapping conditions can be enlightening and re-creative to communities functioning on outmoded concepts. Many congregations will discover relatively simple ways to bring new life to members whose opportunities have been unnecessarily curtailed. A congregation can become, sometimes for the first time, a community of concerned Christians, helping bear one another's burdens in redemptive ways when the overpowering weight of individual and family difficulty is shifted to the entire fellowship. In an age of increasing impersonality, one of the greatest ministries of a parish can be its renewed attention to the needs of its individual members.

### Central to the Gospel

Congregations which have learned the central meaning of the gospel, that God accepts each person without merit, will have begun already to minister to persons with special needs. If they have begun to operate with the recognition that each person is a unique individual and a child of God with a particular mission to fulfill, meeting the needs of exceptional persons will find a natural place in a congregation's life and work. In the Christian fellowship exceptionality is always a matter of degree, not of kind. All persons are exceptional and have special needs. All have gifts and contributions to make. Every class must have a teacher who recognizes that he cannot teach the group unless he teaches the individual and differing members of that group.

### Like Other Persons

Exceptional persons are more like than unlike other persons. Each person is born with a blueprint for growth to maximum potential within him, yet each finds his complete development limited or thwarted at some points. Each person is empowered to accept and conquer developmental barriers or to retreat from challenges which are uniquely his. Everyone depends for survival and wholesome maturation upon acceptance and love from those upon whom he is dependent for his nurture, and all need to live with others in relationships which affirm their value and worth. No one can become whole in isolation. Each needs to learn that he is unique, that no one before has occupied precisely his space in relationship to his time and company, and that the opportunity thus presented him is his alone. Every person must come to have a clear and realistic picture of himself, as he is, with his limitations and potential. Each needs to find an identity, a sense of who he himself is, to know significant being apart from, and in relationship to, other being. He must experience both freedom and discipline to become a self-disciplined person.

These characteristics are true of exceptional persons.

### Exceptional Persons Unintentionally Handicapped

Social and psychological damage is often added to other handicaps persons have. Inadequate or inaccurate diagnosis in early childhood may produce further handicapping or delay useful treatment and care. Misunderstanding about causes and meanings of a child's difficulty has often produced immobilizing fear in parents and prevented their taking appropriate steps to learn the truth. Earlier conclusions about some handicapping have been proven unfounded. Help is available for many once thought hopelessly deficient. Early identification, acceptance, and attention are needed to relieve, eliminate, or significantly reduce many conditions.

Parents and family of newborn infants always need training to meet the escalating responsibilities which they have assumed. Sometimes special insight and care are needed. Occasionally profound personal reorientation is needed by parents when their child turns out to be less than one hundred percent perfect. Rejection and denial by his family can be more damaging to a child than some severe disability with which he must meet life. Overprotection and coddling, as well as mistreatment, can cripple him for life or delay his responsible development. The church offers a fellowship in which reality can be dealt with and where biblical and relational supports can be found by families given the special opportunity and blessing of handicapping.

### Church Not Alone

Nowhere else in the world are there more resources for help to the exceptional person and his family than in the United States. The quality of services to the severely damaged is being steadily improved. While it is still true that many parents dispose of unwanted children in state institutions for the care of handicapped children, state and federal governmental agencies are providing more financial and professional support to meet the overwhelming quantitative need. Programs for prevention and rehabilitation are receiving impetus. The church welcomes and encourages such public and private efforts as help to meet the special, severe needs of persons.

Competent, professional assistance is needed by severely disturbed persons. As a significant contribution the church should acquaint itself with the causes of severe emotional and mental disturbance and begin preventative work. The number of causes of severe mental deficiency is being reduced. For some their lives must be lived out in maximum security and with intensive care. The church can assist in the dissemination of information about the causes of mental retardation, its prevention and reduction. It might concentrate its considerable strength along with other agencies and persons to remove from the environment in which men must live these and other contributory causes—poverty, ignorance, illegitimacy, wretched prenatal care.

Ministry to some persons must be in special facilities outside the church. To some it may be in their homes and by physicians, nurses, therapists, and volunteers. To some it may be in highly specialized schools or machines. To some it may be through special hearing or communication devices.

## What Can Churches Do?

### Church Supports Community Services

For many persons of special need the job of the church will be to support and get others to support community and private services. Sometimes it will be the responsibility of the church or its members to advertise a need and find the resources in the community to fill it. Many times it will be the central responsibility of the church to know where help can be secured and to refer persons to the best help. Whole armies of volunteers are needed to meet the growing needs of persons in our exploding society. The church will help train the young and retrain the retired for such domestic "peace corps" service.

Members of congregations where there are persons with particular special needs will want to acquaint themselves with the best ways of meeting those needs and interpret their special members to everyone else. The pastor should include educational information in his sermons, announcements, newsletters, and visits.

### Community Interpretation

Films and filmstrips for use with classes, church, and community groups are available to help with interpretation. Recommendations can be secured from the national offices listed below in this chapter and from their local branch offices.

### Special Education Needs

Many exceptional persons can participate in the life of a class or group when provided special resources. In one congregation a hard working team of persons regularly transposes the pupil's book and supplementary resources provided by the church school teacher into Braille for a member of the junior class. Other juniors have found it possible to translate maps and even illustrations into bas-relief for their friend. They work closely with another person whose responsibility it is to maintain contact with the John Milton Society and other libraries from which Braille books and talking books can be secured. In one church there is a busy time when two members in wheel chairs get together to produce on large charts the reading material needed for next week's church school class by partially sighted pupils.

In several churches there are regular reading and recording sessions when the reading wishes of some other students are read carefully by fellow classmates onto tape for private listening with increased volume. Opaque and overhead projectors are used creatively. Many churches making new building plans, and some which are remodeling, have recognized the need to include ramps or floor-level classrooms, special hand grips in long hallways, space for wheel chairs, access to bathrooms and drinking fountains for the handicapped, etc.

A project sometimes becomes occupational therapy for the helpers when the homemade toys and equipment needed in the special education class are constructed by a neighborhood youth group and their adult friends from the church. Physical needs of crippled members of a class are added to the list of regular assignments shared by others in the daily routine.

### Churches Meeting Exceptional Needs Together

Ministry to and with exceptional persons is a responsibility of the whole community. United work on their behalf need not wait upon denominational program nor upon church union. Many communities have already found ways of working together which have been rewarding to the participating churches and organizations and conducive to increasing respect and cooperation.

Educational needs ought to be addressed by all responsible and related units in a community together. Educational needs should be seen in the context of the whole life of exceptional persons. The needs met by churches and other interested units may require much more comprehensive understanding than is commonly seen as "educational" or "church school." Churches which seriously address themselves to meeting the special needs of persons will often discover complexities and implications which require cooperative community response.

An unusually effective organization has been developed in suburban Philadelphia by the Main Line Ministerium. They have incorporated their work as the Church Council for the Exceptional Person; they employ an executive director and provide a responsible advisory council to assist him. A board of church representatives includes one lay volunteer from each church, and a board of professional consultants supports the work of the council. Services are now being provided or planned for the intellectually exceptional, those with impaired hearing, those with impaired vision, the crippled person, those with speech handicaps, the emotionally disturbed, the multihandicapped, and the homebound. It is hoped that the council can expand its services to include community church schools for mentally retarded, emotionally disturbed, deaf, blind, crippled, and speech-handicapped persons. Planning is also beginning to provide such services as teacher training sessions, curriculum study and development, seminars for religious leaders, vacation church school, camping, scouting, special equipment, information center and library, community education, parent groups, and interpretation. A women's unit, called Friends of Exceptional Children, undergirds the work of the council.

## Resources

### Steps a Church May Take

Persons called to special ministry with exceptional persons through the church find it useful to include sound study and preparation in their earliest responses.

The congregation and community, both and sometimes together, study the general subject of exceptionality. One book which informs and motivates is *Who Cares?* written by Janette T. Harrington and Muriel S. Webb. It was designed as a study for adults in the Friendship Press resources for "The Church's Mission and Persons of Special Need." Another insightful and informative book for study group use is *The Church and the Exceptional Person* by Charles E. Palmer, published by Abingdon Press.

Use of either of these books can be supplemented with materials available from the many agencies and organizations devoted to exceptional persons. Nearby universities and colleges are ready to recommend the latest textbooks being used in their special education departments and often to provide skilled, professional leadership for such study and planning groups.

Needs of the congregation and community should be studied and evaluated with professional help. How many persons need what kind of class or group experience? Can needs be met in special groups or in regular ones? What is needed which is not now already provided in some way to serve adequately our persons of special need?

Resources of the community are sought out and brought together. How can we help one another? Who has the best resources for meeting which needs? Can governmental and agency leaders help provide the training needed by church school leaders who have exceptional members in their regular groups? By special education groups?

The experiences of other churches and communities will give helpful suggestions for churches just exploring their responsibilities.

### Information Available

A church or community sponsored resource center can develop a library of materials to be used. It may include a wide variety of pamphlets and leaflets from the agencies and organizations working with exceptionality or it may maintain an up-to-date bibliography service and help its users write to the appropriate place for their own copies of the latest available publications.

The National Association for Retarded Children (420 Lexington Ave., New York, N. Y. 10017) publishes selected bibliographies about recreation, religion, religious education, etc. Since they undergo frequent revision, current copies should be requested.

*The International Journal of Religious Education* (published by the National Council of Churches, 475 Riverside Dr., New York, N. Y. 10027) has given sustained attention to the educational needs of exceptional persons in recent years. See the back file of the *I.J.R.E.* for articles and special issues, especially February, 1962, "The Church's Ministry and Persons with Special Need," and February, 1965, "No Two Alike/Leaders of Persons with Special Needs."

The United States Department of Health, Education, and Welfare (Washington, D.C. 20202) publishes many monographs which are useful to parents and leaders. It will send lists and bibliographies on request and make available captioned films for use with deaf and hard of hearing persons.

Catalogs and lists of materials are also available from:

The National Society for the Prevention of Blindness, Inc., 16 East 40th Street, New York, N. Y. 10016

The American Association for Health, Physical Education and Recreation, 1201 16th Street, N. W., Washington, D.C. 20036

The National Association for the Education of Young Children, Room 600, 104 East 25th Street, New York, N. Y. 10010

The National Association for Mental Health, Inc., 10 Columbus Circle, New York, N. Y. 10019

Family Service Association of America, 44 East 23rd Street, New York, N. Y. 10010

Child Study Association of America, 9 East 89th Street, New York, N. Y. 10028

John Milton Society, 475 Riverside Drive, New York, N. Y. 10027

National Society for Crippled Children and Adults, 2023 West Ogden Avenue, Chicago, Ill. 60612

Child Welfare League of America, Inc., 44 East 23rd Street, New York, N. Y. 10010

Public Affairs Committee, 381 Park Avenue, South, New York, N. Y. 10016

American Public Welfare Association, 1313 East 60th Street, Chicago, Ill. 60637

Within the broad category of chronic health cases, individual requests should be addressed to city, county, or state offices of societies for information and referral.

PERIODICALS

Some church-sponsored and other libraries will include periodicals which provide current information for their patrons. Among these are:

*Journal of Rehabilitation,* official publication of the National Rehabilitation Association (1029 Vermont Avenue, Washington, D.C. 20005), serves professional workers in all phases of rehabilitation of handicapped persons.

*Children Limited* is published by the National Association for Retarded Children (420 Lexington Avenue, New York, N. Y. 10017).

*Exceptional Children* is the official journal of the Council for Exceptional Children, N.E.A. (1201 Sixteenth Street, N.W., Washington, D.C. 20036).

Some journals of a general nature contain related and pertinent articles on special education. For example:

*American Education* is published by the United States Office of Education. It may be obtained from the U. S. Government Printing Office, Division of Public Documents (Washington, D.C. 20402).

*Educational Leadership* is the journal of the Association for Supervision and Curriculum Development (1201 Sixteenth Street, N.W., Washington, D.C. 20036).

*The International Journal of Religious Education,* which was noted above, should be included in this list of related periodicals also.

*Young Children* is the journal of the National Association for the Education of Young Children (104 East 25th Street, New York, N. Y. 10010). It has many related and supportive articles.

*Childhood Education,* published by the Association for Childhood Education International (3615 Wisconsin Avenue, N.W., Washington, D.C. 20016) is similarly helpful.

*Children* is another publication of the United States Department of Health, Education, and Welfare and is available from the U.S. Government Printing Office, Division of Public Documents (Washington, D.C. 20402).

Denominational journals frequently include articles and reviews dealing with exceptionality and the church's role.

TECHNICAL JOURNALS

Numerous journals of a technical nature suitable for professional use are also available. For example, The American Speech and Hearing Association (1001 Connecticut Avenue, N.W., Washington, D.C. 20036) publishes three: *The Journal of Speech and Hearing Disorders, The Journal of Speech and Hearing Research,* and *Asha.*

Organizations devoted to particular exceptional needs also often publish materials such as the *Easter Seal Bulletin* and *Rehabilitation Literature* which are services of the National Society for Crippled Children and Adults (2023 West Ogden Avenue, Chicago, Ill. 60612).

Especially useful for locating recent research findings and published resources are the journals which review books and articles, digest and abstract studies and reports, such as:

*Rehabilitation Literature,* available from National Society for Crippled Children and Adults;

*Children,* published by the Department of Health, Education, and Welfare;

and *Exceptional Children,* a National Education Association publication. Addresses for these are noted above.

## Summary and a Look Ahead

### Education for the Exceptional

Education for exceptional persons in the church is not simply a matter of starting a class for them. They are not easily classified. They come in many categories and often in more than one. Unfortunately, since our values communicate conformity and perfection, for the person who is clearly different or unable to perform inconspicuously, psychic damage often accompanies other exceptionality. In congregations organized to function in large groups, the needs of an individual or a small, heterogenous group are not easily met.

Careful evaluation of a community's special education needs is often best done cooperatively with other interested persons and units. Care and educational equipment and staff may best be provided by the cooperating interests of the community. In some instances united concern for special education needs has led to united community attention and to total educational planning.

Churches may find it impossible to meet the Christian education needs of exceptional persons because their broader educational needs are not being met. They may need to provide or convince the community, and particularly the public schools, to provide year-round weekday classes. Churches may also decide that their special education can only be done together.

In many communities planning and training are done together. In some, interchurch or interfaith classes are provided together. In others, parent and family classes unite persons from all participating congregations across faith lines.

### Challenge Christian Education Boards

The needs of exceptional persons in any community are diverse, multiple, and individual. They require planning committees and boards who are aware of them and willing to give persistent attention to their changing needs. They cry for congregations which are real cells of concerned human beings, who value the unvalued and the valueless. They need persons who, standing alongside their families, will devote a significant portion of their lives to meeting the special needs of others. They need integration, insofar as possible, into the normal life and ministry of the church and community.

The teachers of exceptional persons become special people. They must have unusual understanding and adjustment to the human situation. They require special training for the meeting of other than routine needs. They are expected to make creative adaptations of curriculum resources and to meet individuals where they are in development. Their work becomes the embodiment of the words, "I am among you as one who serves," and "that they may have life abundant."

## Integrated and Special Education

Most exceptional persons are members of regular Christian education groups and classes. There the unique needs of special students are met by thoughtful planning, the cooperation of their peers, special equipment or resources, and extra attention from teachers as needed. In most such cases the church school curriculum materials in use in the church are used and creatively adapted to engage and serve the special student.

For some persons of special need, however, separate and different classes must be provided. For some of these, usual curriculum resources may prove inadequate because of age-group inappropriateness, for theological or educational reasons.

Leaders of two such groups have been given suggestions and help in recent publications. Books for special education in the church are becoming more readily available. In 1963 Abingdon Press published *Christian Education for Retarded Children and Youth* by LaDonna Bogardus. In 1964 United Church Press published *Christian Education for Socially Handicapped Children and Youth* by Eleanor Ebersole. The Greater Philadelphia Council of Churches has experimented with church school materials for use with young persons in detention.

Church school curricular resources for groups of mentally retarded children and youth have been prepared. For preschool age retardees the Christian Churches (Disciples of Christ) have begun a publishing program. For institutionalized teenagers the Connecticut Council of Churches has produced several church school courses and has ministries to various other groups.

A comprehensive plan for church school curriculum, related to recent interdenominational planning under the auspices of the National Council of Churches, was developed in June, 1965, to provide for classes of retarded persons.

## National Council of Churches Committee

A Committee for the Christian Education of Exceptional Persons has been providing significant leadership from within the National Council of Churches since 1959. Consultations are held occasionally to assess the educational needs of exceptional persons served by the churches. For a number of years the committee did much of its work in subcommittees related to physically, mentally, emotionally, and socially handicapped persons. Churches interested in improving their educational work with the exceptional persons in their community are advised to write to the National Council of Churches for staff counsel and suggestions.

Many denominations now have staff persons with responsibility for Christian education of exceptional persons from whom churches and interested persons are urged to request help. Important new resources are now becoming available as a result of years of concerted efforts by individuals, agencies, and churches.

# Chapter 23

# CHRISTIAN EDUCATION
# AND THE INNER CITY

## *Letty M. Russell*

THE SHAPE OF CHRISTIAN EDUCATION TODAY EMERGES OUT OF THE PROCESS of dialogue between our faith in Jesus Christ as Lord and our understanding of the world in which we live. The concern of this chapter on "Christian Education and the Inner City" is to enter into this dialogue at the point where the Christian faith meets the inner city with its problems, frustrations, opportunities, and gifts. First, I will try to take a new look at the problems of the inner city; second, at our theology of Christian education. Then, as examples of how our theological and sociological dialogue can point the way to new shapes of Christian education, I will discuss Christian education in the context of the total church life, the peer group as the teacher, and team teaching.

My experience as a Christian educator and clergyman has been largely as a worker in the East Harlem Protestant Parish in New York City. However, experience in other places, such as Cambridge, Mass., Middletown, Conn., and Westfield, N. J., has shown me that the problems discovered in East Harlem also exist in suburbs and towns and that a look at "Christian Education in the Inner City" will help mirror those problems in terms of intensity and scope. Therefore our reflection on this one situation may further illuminate the needs and methods described elsewhere in this book.

## Problems and Opportunities in the Inner City

The term "inner city" in this chapter will be used to describe the forgotten world of poverty which lies at the center of all our large cities. Such slums are the dwellings built as immigrant housing or left behind in the middle-class retreat from the city but now inhabited by minority groups who have neither the power nor the money to break out of the city ghettos. Here all the problems of city life are mirrored at their worst. Here the church as an institution has as much trouble finding "answers" as any other city institution, be it the welfare department, housing authority, or board of education.

The East Harlem community, where I serve as pastor of a Presbyterian Church, is an economic ghetto consisting of tenements, built to house Jewish and Italian immigrants at the end of the nineteenth century, and high-rise city housing projects. The community is interracial, consisting of about 40 percent Negro, 40 percent Puerto Rican, and 20 percent other white groups—predominantly Italian. Some have called this community a "sleeping dragon" because its large population, aroused by the civil rights crisis, could exert tremendous political pressure. However, the community is only now very slowly emerging from its lethargy, helplessness, and despair born of the generations of poverty, prejudice, ignorance, and exploitation which have robbed its inhabitants of the right to live as human beings.[1]

In the inner city there are certain social problems which affect the work of the church in Christian education. First, there are *large numbers of children* ready and eager to come to the programs. For instance, in the seven-block area surrounding the Church of the Ascension which I serve live over 16,000 people. Large numbers of children find themselves with nothing to do and will come to the church to be "entertained" if given half a chance. Second, there is always a *discipline problem*. The families themselves are full of stresses and strains which produce behavior problems. The child seldom receives training in self-discipline either at home or at school. Third, according to middle-class social standards, the life of the children and their families is *amoral*. In communities where the struggle for existence is so real that everyone learns to lie and cheat and steal as a matter of course, the standard of behavior is "what's in it for me?" The kind of "be good" teaching which is found in most Sunday schools is at best ineffective, and more often hypocritical in such a situation. Fourth, the children *lack family encouragement*. It is simply ridiculous to expect the family to be the mainstay of Christian education.[2] The family has a hard time staying together at all. Children are fed and clothed and then left to entertain themselves. Lastly, there is predominantly a *lack of education* among parents and children alike. Parents have not had educational advantages which would enable them to teach their children a love of learning and of ideas. The types of questions which Christian educators often imagine a child might want to discuss in class would never even occur to the parent, let alone the child. And the children also are forced to accept inferior education as they attend ghetto schools which are warped by the woeful inadequacies of outworn, bureaucratic, or irrelevant systems of education.[3] In the East Harlem community children in junior high read on the average of two grades below their grade level. Some cannot read at all, and almost none would take interest in a Christian education curriculum based on reading and discussion.

This is the context of Christian education in the inner city. In the face of such problems the effectiveness of the public schools is very limited, and the effectiveness of most programs of Christian education is nonexistent. With new fervor we speak about "only the grace of God," for it would seem that any program is powerless to overcome the crippling effects of poverty, discrimination, and ignorance.

The inner-city church brings certain practical problems of its own to the task which it faces. Not only does it feel defeated by the community problems but also by its own lack of resources to work in and through these problems.

---

[1] Cf. Michael Harrington, *The Other America* (New York: The Macmillan Company, 1962).

[2] Cf. Letty M. Russell, "The Family and Christian Education in Modern, Urban Society," *Union Seminary Quarterly Review,* XVI (November, 1960), 33-43.

[3] James Conant, *Slums and Suburbs* (New York: McGraw-Hill Book Company, 1961).

Church staffs are usually limited because of lack of funds and lack of vocational opportunities for advancement. Church school teachers are few in number. Most people with natural ability are usually very busy working overtime or on two jobs, and others, who are forced to struggle for existence on welfare because of their many problems, find themselves unable or unwilling to cope with other people's children, and with curriculum outlines they often cannot even read. The church buildings are usually old and inadequate, having either too much or too little space. Physical plants already run-down with neglect and disuse begin to deteriorate rapidly when their doors are opened to large groups of children and youth.

Recently the various denominations have begun to take a new look at the ministry in the inner city. Where men and women are willing to stop and listen to the inner-city community and to live each day in the conviction that Christ is Lord of the inner city as well as the suburb, signs of understanding and new forms of ministry and education have begun to emerge.

The Christian educator who truly desires to make Christian education a living and vital part of a Christian community will do well to follow these four steps: (1) Don't sit down and weep, for a vast world of wonderful people and unknown resources is open to all who would follow Christ out into the world where he lived and died. (2) Live in and with your community. Study and learn about your community and its culture. Listen with an open mind, and love the city and its people with an open heart. You will often find that what you thought was apathy was simply the community's refusal to respond to the middle-class blueprint of church life which you brought with you. Together with the members of the community seek out the real problems which you face. (3) Continue to let your understanding of the Christian faith grow and mature as you struggle with what the gospel message means for this time and place. (4) Turn the problems of the community to advantage by working out patterns of Christian education which are suited to the culture of the inner city where you live and serve.

## Christian Education in the Context of Total Church Life

The shapes of Christian education should take form in a situation of dialogue between theology and sociology. Having considered relevant problems of the city and the inner-city church, it seems important to examine briefly our theological thinking about Christian education so that we can understand the shapes of education which have emerged in my work in East Harlem.

Christian education is the *work of the church in extending Christ's invitation to all men, women, and children to join in God's work of restoring men to their true, created humanity by reconciling them to himself and to one another*. This means that the church invites men, women, and children not only to let the love of Christ work in them to shape their lives by his love, but also to join in Christ's action to bring about reconciliation and wholeness to all of society. In order to extend this invitation the church must make itself continually aware of the way God has revealed himself in the past by thorough study of the biblical record. At the same time it must make itself continually aware of the way God is acting in the events of our own time through careful study of the issues which confront men today. With the eyes of faith to search out God's actions of judgment and reconciliation in the world, the church may be able to point to this activity of God by the integrity of its own life as a Christian family and by its involvement in the work of Christ's healing and reconciliation in its own community.

Thus Christian education involves three dimensions: the work of opening men's eyes to see God's activity, helping them find ways to join in this activity in the world, and pointing to this activity so that others may see and receive the invitation to be partners with God. Nurture or the "equipping of the saints" takes place continually in the light of the invitation to join in God's action both as preparation for and through involvement in that action. Martin Luther has said that no man is ever a Christian—he is only on the way to becoming a Christian. This is why the invitation to join in God's work must be extended over and over, in, with, and during every task which a Christian congregation undertakes. Then it may be continually strengthened in its insight, its faith, and its service to the world in the name of Jesus Christ. The work of extending this invitation is the job of the total church congregation—the job of Christian education.

In the light of this definition of Christian education it becomes clear that a program of Christian education can never be separated from the rest of the life and witness of a congregation except for the purpose of planning and evaluation. A church family is needed to strengthen the weak families where they exist, and to be the Christian family to those who have no other. In such a family the invitation may be heard by those who have been told by society that they are *worthless*. Here they learn that their service is needed, that they indeed can be part of the high calling of Christ's mission. In such a family the invitation may be heard by people who have learned the hard way that you have to look out for yourself and your own because *no one else cares*. Here they find other men and women who really do care—care enough to visit in their homes, care enough to work with their children, care enough to fight for better schools, housing, and government, care enough so that they can begin to dare to believe that God cares. In such a family the invitation may be heard by people who are so *chained by their problems* that the best they can do is sit and wait for each problem to come. Here they find a church family full of the same problems of broken homes, narcotics addiction, delinquency, emotional disturbance, finances, and health. But they find that these people are helping one another bear these burdens. Together they are helping with family and financial problems, helping young people in trouble, finding mental and medical help. And the people who have been chained find their chains growing lighter as they begin to lift the load of others in the services of Jesus Christ. In such a family the invitation may be heard by men and women who have been taught *destructive and self-defeating* habits of life by their culture of poverty. Here they find people living in the same culture who have been able to develop at least the beginning of new habits of Christian living which help them resist the pressures all around them. Extending Christ's invitation to join in God's action of reconciliation is the work of the entire church family because this is where the invitation is heard and lived so that others might also hear and live it.

If the total church is to be the instrument of Christian education, certain principles follow in terms of specific programming. The first is that the church family should involve children and youth as much as possible in its ongoing life of worship and service to the world. Children should be welcomed and encouraged to attend worship, and the worship should contain enough dramatic content and congregational participation so that it is of interest to the children. The same is true for service in the world. Great effort should be made to let the children help make signs for a picket line, or put out flyers for a rally, etc. Youth should be encouraged to overcome their own feelings of defeat, failure, and antagonism toward the world by working actively for civil rights and other community causes. Thus the children and youth, as well as adults, learn by doing and sharing together in Christ's mission.

The second principle is that the study of the mighty acts of God as revealed in the Bible should be planned in such a way that all the different ages and groups in the church are studying the same theme. As people struggle with the same text and its meaning for their life, many new insights are gained. In the East Harlem Protestant Parish the churches follow a *Daily Bible Reading* lectionary which is designed for Bible-study groups and preaching in inner-city churches.[4] Here the same text is studied by staff and Bible-study leaders on Monday, by all the house Bible-study groups on Wednesday, by the children and youth on Sunday, and is the basis for the sermon. Amazing variety is found in interpretations and uses, yet, often just because the word had been listened to so often with such seriousness, God grants new gifts of understanding of his purpose for his world.

When the total church is the instrument of Christian education, a third principle emerges. The minister or pastor of the church must be centrally involved in the planning and execution of educational programs and of the working out of a consistent theology and plan of Christian education in the church family. A church family capable of hearing the invitation of Christ to join in God's action of reconciliation in the world, and/or sharing that invitation with others, grows slowly and develops a pattern of Christian involvement and service in the world through patient years of tender loving care. The minister who views preaching and an adult Bible study class as his share in Christian education has missed the whole point. As long as there is a pastor, the total life of the church cannot be an instrument of education unless the minister sees this and seeks to put it into practice by his direct participation, as well as by cooperating with others who may be hired especially to work in programs of Christian education.

When the total church is the instrument of Christian education, a fourth principle emerges. Christian education is the work of the total church and

---

[4] Letty M. Russell, *Daily Bible Readings, Inner City Parishes,* East Harlem Protestant Parish, 2050 Second Avenue, New York, issued quarterly.

should involve the total budget. No longer does the Christian education item mean a small sum for paper and crayons. The question of how a church raises and distributes its money should be examined in the light of the question of whether it is enabling the church to extend Christ's invitation to join in God's work of reconciliation. Beyond this the budget should recognize that the work of specific programs of education such as Christian action workshops, Bible-study groups, remedial reading clinic, church school, and youth program all deserve an important share of the church funds.

### The Peer Group as the Teacher
### in Work With Children and Youth

Men who live in the inner city are by and large "mass men" whose lives are conditioned by peer groups and by group pressures of society. We have already noted the opportunity which this situation provides in working with adults and children in the context of the total church family life. The importance of the church community in the support it gives to individuals was underscored. Here I would like to emphasize the importance of the peer group in work with children and youth. Children and youth dress, talk, and act like their friends. Wearing heavy rubber rain coats in hot summer weather or sneakers in a blizzard is normal behavior if that happens to be the style. Going places *together* is the only way children and youth are willing to go. The more crowded a candy store, teenage hangout, or church canteen, the more they want to go because "everyone is there." [5]

Any specialized Christian education programming for children and youth should take the peer group and peer-group behavior into account unless it wishes to be ineffective before it even begins. For the peer group, rather than being a negative factor in education, has great possibilities in helping the church face the problems described above. The problem of amorality can be faced only on a large group basis, for the only way it is possible to change the habits and style of inner-city people is to help a group of people change together so that they do not feel that they are alone in what they are doing. If it were the style to study hard and work to get ahead in school, many wonderful things could happen to our children's school records. If it were the style to save money rather than to spend it on show items and food, the financial patterns of at least one group of inner-city children and youth could be altered. If self-love carried with it the desire to share this love with others, the selfish patterns of living could be revolutionized. This, of course, calls for large groups of children and a strong community of leadership which is able to set and maintain a particular style.

The problem of large numbers of children and youth thus already appears to have some advantage if it were not for the difficulty of dealing with a large group in terms of limitations of space, disciplinary control, and teaching staff. But a large group of from fifty to one hundred children and youth can be

[5] *Youth in the Ghetto* (New York: Harlem Youth Opportunities Unlimited, 1964), pp. 370-71.

handled in one or two moderately large rooms. They like to be together. In fact, they like to be crowded. Given some skill in leadership and group dynamics, the problems of discipline tend to decrease rather than increase when a large group of children is together. A pattern can be set for the group by a consistent routine and schedule and the following of certain basic rules of safety and behavior which will be enforced by the majority of the group itself.

One of the most important characteristics of the peer group is that it teaches itself. Children learn from peers the very information which fell on deaf ears when spoken by adults. In teaching a large group the one teacher can help the children share together in their learning in such a way that through dramas, quiz shows, craft projects, questions and answers, they teach one another.

The basic curriculum of a group program has three elements: the church family, fun, and the Bible. Unless this program is part of the life of a *church family* which is constantly seeking to serve Christ and invite others to hear, and constantly seeking to involve the children in its work and witness and family life, it will fail. For children sense hypocrisy very easily. They live with it every day. And the invitation of Christ which is extended to them is no invitation at all unless it is issued from a church community which has integrity in its life and work. Children and youth need their own programs and own peer groups, but these need to be part of a larger church family which cares about them.

*Fun* is also a crucial element in the curriculum, for learning is at its maximum when children are enjoying it and participating in it. This can be seen in our own childhood experiences. Learning by doing is not only helpful to children who cannot read well, but also is essential if it is to be fun for children. An important aspect of this is craft projects which teach the lesson, but at the same time are fun to make and valued possessions. These projects cost more and take more time to prepare but often can be made of discarded materials. Another equally important source of fun and participation is skits on Bible stories or life situations which can be practiced briefly. The children do not have rigidly memorized lines, but "ad lib" and generally enjoy showing off to their peers. Two other sources of joy are singing songs[6] with good rhythm and quiz shows.

Christ's invitation to join in God's action of reconciliation comes to all of us from the Bible, and it is from the Bible that the history of salvation must be learned. As children grow to adulthood, they will be helped to respond to Christ's invitation if the history of salvation is already part of their life and learned and lived out in the church community of which they are a part. In using a biblically centered curriculum, the life situation of the children and youth is not ignored. Now life is viewed from the perspective of God's action in the past and present.

One example of church family, fun, and Bible will help show how these things go together to make a curriculum. In the East Harlem Protestant Parish for thirteen weeks the whole church studied Exodus and the story of

*Alleluia, A Hymnbook for Inner City Parishes,* East Harlem Protestant Parish, 2050 Second Ave., New York, N. Y.

freedom.[7] When it came time for the sixteenth anniversary of the Parish we decided to celebrate with a worship service and a family potluck dinner for two hundred people. The theme of the dinner became "Sixteen Years in the Wilderness." Decorations, music, etc., were arranged accordingly. The youth who had also studied Exodus collected all the skits they had done into one long drama of freedom, complete with Moses in a baby carriage, a bush equipped with a burning blowtorch, a cardboard sea, and Miriam's dancers. Everyone enjoyed the play immensely, even when the bush nearly burned up, and the youth had a chance to make a real contribution to their church family. The children were thoroughly involved, for they had also studied Exodus and most of the scenery had been made by them. The next day two four-year-olds who had attended the festivities were overheard talking together. One child dressed in a green bathrobe said to the one in a red bathrobe, "Will you let my people go?" The red-robed boy replied, "Yes," to which the child in green said with great disgust, "You're not supposed to say that!"

## Team Teaching and Training
## in the Peer Group Approach

For many years one of the most serious problems faced by inner-city churches in their programs of Christian education has been the lack of trained teachers. One solution to which many inner-city churches have turned is the use of seminary students. Students need field-work jobs for experience and to earn money, and they are usually noble enough to give at least a year to the "slum children." In addition it gives them an opportunity to practice teach in a most difficult situation. It is very important to help train seminary students, but the fact is that their inexperience, coupled with a complete lack of understanding of the values and behavior patterns of urban society, and their own desire to teach great theological thoughts which will really "make a difference to the child," makes them useless as teachers except as part of a team approach where they are not left to sink or swim by themselves. They have even more difficulty with discipline than parents because they have been taught to be kind, they do not understand the children, and above all they want to be liked and accepted by their children.

One possible answer to the shortage of teachers is to recognize that the church has aggravated this problem out of all proportion by thinking that all teaching and all teachers have to fit a certain middle-class pattern. We have assumed that each teacher must learn to be punctual and regular; skilled at discipline; and trained to read, digest, and teach a written curriculum. The result is a great cry that curriculums for the white middle-class suburbs are no good in the inner city. Instead of making the teachers over into poor copies of middle-class, college educated teachers, why not uncover and utilize the strengths they do in fact possess? The staff of one such program at the Church of the Ascension consisted of myself as leader, another minister as disciplinarian,

[7] Russell, *Daily Bible Readings.*

the church custodian, the church secretary, parents, and youth assistants.[8]

The peer-group method of teaching with large groups of children affords many opportunities to play to the strengths of the inner-city teacher. It permits the teacher to work with the children so that he can make use of his knowledge and experience of the children's culture in relating to them without having to assume a pseudo-role. In the program emphasis is always put on ways children with leadership ability can form the teaching core both informally through group participation, skits, etc., and formally when they are selected to work as assistant teachers in a particular program. The best teachers for youth are youth or young adults who are slightly older. These are the ones who set the patterns every day on the streets and who can communicate best with those whom they teach. This also gives the younger teachers valuable experience in their responsibility to serve others as a part of the church family. Lastly, peer-group teaching makes it possible for a teacher to be a valuable part of a Christian education program even if he cannot read a lesson plan.

In peer-group teaching "in-service training" for the teachers is the best method. First, this form of teaching takes place in the context of the total church life as the teacher. Those who come forward to teach are already being nurtured and sustained in other parts of the church family life. The lessons which are taught to children and youth are the same themes that the teacher meets through his entire church life. He has the opportunity to explore its meaning in house Bible-study groups and to share insights gained in the teaching program with his house group. He knows that questions raised concerning the meaning of a particular text will often receive attention in the sermon. The interaction of thought and experience around one theme gives to the teacher a foundation of training which continues week after week.

Second, a teacher can begin to serve right away with no training or skill at all. Because he is part of a team, he can find the job best suited to his ability and knowledge, be it taking attendance, making kool-ade, preparing crafts, or simply sitting with the children and joining them in singing, discussing, and working together. The teacher is free to learn new skills and greater self-confidence as he enters into new areas of teaching, such as planning, leading worship, coaching and acting, running visual-aid equipment, etc. He learns more quickly if given help and encouragement because he has others who are doing it with him and does not have to sink or swim by himself.

Third, because the emphasis is largely on helping the peer group teach itself, any older person who cares about the children and enjoys being and working with them will bring to the peer-group program what it needs most—encouragement of the children to participate in and enjoy the program and a "leaven" of adult responsibility in the larger group which will free the children from the need to misbehave. In a peer-group program ten adult or youth teachers working and participating and sitting with the children will be suffi-

[8] Letty M. Russell, "Equipping the Little Saints, An Emerging Pattern of Christian Education," *Adult Teacher*, Board of Education of The Methodist Church, Nashville, Tenn., January-February, 1962.

cient to maintain the order needed with only occasional assistance from the trouble shooter and the person directing the program.

It is possible to run a peer-group program with little or no group planning. One person can plan the entire program, and the teachers can be prepared the half hour before the program begins. Although adult leaders in the inner city are very shy about performing in front of a group or leading a group, some will come to join with the children, youth, and young adults who love to show off and perform in front of the group in skits and panels, etc. Others who never worked with children before will learn to help a small group put on a program for the larger group. Children love to see their teachers making fools of themselves in a play or funny program. The teachers themselves can plan "take-offs" on the children or simply enter into a game such as Truth or Consequences with the children in which they have to sit on a child's lap or hop around the room once.

Team planning and teaching does not need to ignore the value of small groups and individual attention. It merely puts them in a larger framework. In fact, the group approach is not fully adequate unless the teachers do give children individual attention. A child needs to know that someone in particular cares about him, knows his name, knows when he is absent, and wants to help him with his work. Children naturally relate to a particular teacher and tend to seek that teacher out even if they are not assigned to that teacher's table. To aid in this individual concern it is advisable to assign the teachers to particular age groups. Then they are able to develop personal contacts by working more closely with certain children; taking them on trips, entertaining them in their homes, planning skits together, helping them with crafts, and visiting their families. Such personal interest increases the enjoyment and the feeling of worth and importance of both the child and the teacher. Team teaching and planning will help children and teachers alike develop a spirit of cooperation as they work together to make their own program a success. They become a family within a church family which has a particular job to do and enjoys doing it together.

## Conclusion

The approach to Christian education as a work of the total church family, which is best carried out in children and youth programs by peer-group teaching, is one way of reflecting on the work of the church in the light of some of the problems found in inner-city communities. The comments and suggestions come out of my experience in the Church of the Ascension and are not designed as a blueprint for any other church. Rather they are an attempt to point the way for churches to rethink the work to which God has called them and to listen to what the voice of the inner-city community is saying through its problems. Each church must have its own program of Christian education, but that program should reflect an understanding of the theology which is informing the total life of that church and an understanding of the needs of the community which it serves.

## FOR ADDITIONAL READING

### On the Church and the City

Clark, Kenneth. *Dark Ghetto*. New York: Harper & Row, 1965.

Conant, James. *Slums and Suburbs*. New York: McGraw–Hill Book Company, 1961.

Cox, Harvey. *The Secular City*. New York: The Macmillan Company, 1965.

Harrington, Michael. *The Other America*. New York: The Macmillan Company, 1962.

Lomax, Louis. *The Negro Revolt*. New York: Signet Books, 1963.

Michonneau, Abbé. *Revolution in a City Parish*. Westminster, Md.: Newman Press, 1950.

Webber, George W. *The Congregation in Mission*. Nashville: Abingdon Press, 1964.

———. *God's Colony in Man's World*. Nashville: Abingdon Press, 1960.

Williams, Colin W. *What in the World?* New York: National Council of Churches, 1964.

———. *Where in the World?* New York: National Council of Churches, 1963.

Winter, Gibson. *The New Creation as Metropolis*. New York: The Macmillan Company, 1963.

### Pamphlets and Periodicals on Education in the City Church

*The City—God's Gift to the Church*. Available from the Division of Evangelism, The United Presbyterian Church in the U.S.A.

*Church in Metropolis*. A useful periodical available from the Episcopal Church Center, 815 Second Avenue, New York. See especially #4.

*Renewal*. Published by the Chicago City Missionary Society, 19 S. LaSalle St., Chicago, Ill.

### Curriculum Resources

*Alleluia, A Hymnbook for Inner City Churches*. Available from the East Harlem Protestant Parish, 2050 Second Avenue, New York.

Archibald, Helen. *The Good News*. A Curriculum for Released Time in City Churches. Available from Chicago City Missionary Society, 19 S. LaSalle Street, Chicago, Ill.

Ebersole, Eleanor. *Christian Education for Socially Handicapped Children and Youth*. Philadelphia: United Church Press, 1964.

Russell, Letty M. *Daily Bible Readings, Inner City Parishes*. Issued quarterly by the East Harlem Protestant Parish, 2050 Second Avenue, New York.

———. *Church Membership*. Also available from the East Harlem Protestant Parish.

White, Edward. *Negro History in the Churches*. Available from The United Presbyterian Church, Room 8, 746 Fullerton Avenue, Chicago, Ill.

*Chapter 24*

# GROUP THEORY
# AND CHRISTIAN EDUCATION

## *Ross Snyder*

RELIGION IS THE CREATION OR REVITALIZATION OF A PEOPLE, NOT JUST AN individual. *A people* is a threefold complex—a thrust of history-making, a constellation of symbols that catch the meaning of life's events and give direction, and the warm immediacies of interpersonal relationships through which the daily good of life is secured. The *Christian* religion is a *change* religion, whose essence is transformation, leaps into new existence, the break-through of New Time. Thus, Christianity is mocked by merely individualistic forms, by conventional Christians who do not intend to risk or change or deeply relate to their fellow man. It is also mocked by people for whom life consists of dutiful attempts to obey commandments rather than to find freedom to be for man and for God, and those who are numbed by Bonhoeffer's declaration, "Only in the midst of the world is Christ, Christ."

As we increasingly move toward authentic modes of Christian existence, lively ideas and events that could be labeled "group" and "a people" happen to us. This might become most clearly manifest, if I endeavored to describe the journey a Christian educator has taken in this direction.

The group concern and intuition of a Christian educator begin with the archfather in his field, Horace Bushnell. A century ago Bushnell tried to shake the church of his time into new vitality with a new mode of nurture. "All society is organic . . . and there is a spirit in each of these organisms, peculiar to itself and more or less hostile, more or less favorable to religious character, and to some extent, at least, sovereign over the individual man." [1] The fight still goes on to establish that there is such a thing as "group." And that climate (the prevailing mode of relating and being) is a determining actuality in every group!

In talking to parents (and it applies equally to teachers and leaders of any group), Bushnell laid down this policy:

You must take them into your feeling, as a loving and joyous element . . . cherish and encourage good, and live a better life into the spirits of your children. . . . What, then, are they daily deriving from you, but that which you yourselves reveal . . . ? [2]

First of all, they [parents] should rather seek to teach a feeling than a doctrine; [3]

---

[1] *Christian Nurture* (New Haven: Yale University Press, 1947), p. 22.

[2] *Ibid.*, pp. 45, 46, 50.

[3] *Ibid.*, p. 39.

And, since Bushnell is usually misrepresented (and since an educator is trained in developmental theory), the educator must take seriously the real Bushnell:

The growth of Christian virtue is no vegetable process. . . . It involves a struggle with evil. . . . The soul becomes established in holy virtue, as a free exercise, only as it is passed round the corner of fall and redemption, ascending thus unto God through a double experience, in which it learns the bitterness of evil and the worth of good. . . .[4]

The educator then comes to John Dewey. Dewey helps us see that education is for the purpose of building a civilization, for the purpose of constantly revitalizing a society so that dry rot will not set in. Citizens need to learn how to build worlds. George Albert Coe, owing much to Dewey, wrote a provocative book after World War I on *What Ails Our Youth?* What ails them, Coe asserted, is that they are kept away from the fundamental issues and growing edges of civilization. They are told to remain idle and disengaged, theirs merely to *prepare,* not to *act* as moral agents or prophetic Christians.

Society-as-it-functions is the fundamental educator. For Dewey the religious quality of life was a person's willingness to try to insert something better into some sequence of history-making, and the courageous handling of the consequences. Without such risk in actual event no *religious* education could be taking place. Educating merely for the sake of educating or training is barren of religious significance.

Dewey also pointed to "conjunct, communicated experience" as the nuclear function which produces society. "Experience" means *a length of encounter* with some objective reality which comes at us in such a way that we sense "This is something that I have to deal with. My name is on it. Fate and destiny hit *me.*" "Conjunct" means that I am joined together with others in and by this length of "having to do with." "Communicated" means that good talk and communion is part of the experience. It is not filled experience unless we make available to each how it is experienced by each; that is, what the meaning and interpretation is for us. Also: What does it lead to? What reconstruction and further equipping of ourselves is called for?

Dewey was of the generation of Sapir, the anthropologist, who saw that every society must be constantly renewed by face-to-face communication. He had as a colleague, George Herbert Mead, and Dewey believed with him that both mind and society were created by the emergence of *significant symbol*. People must experience together, symbolize it, and interchange talk until finally a central symbol (word and deed) emerges in everybody's mind. And everyone who has been within the experience now knows that this has happened. Even further, they know that this word-deed symbol dependably calls out similar behavior in everyone. Thus, the group can move on in courage and trust—rather than in uncertainty, indecision, and fear of traitorship within.

Where there is no "home-grown" emergence of significant symbol, there is

[4] *Ibid.,* p. 15.

no group! Significant symbol cannot be *given* to a group, nor is it identical with newly acquired jargon. It has to come out of encounter, honest inter-communication, and creative hunch. This insight has never been adequately or seriously understood in the work of the local church, not even in group dynamics.

In this same era Josiah Royce evolved his understanding of *the religious* as loyalty to the Beloved Community, a community inclusive of all men, a community of memory and hope, existing through time. This was his way of symbolizing the kingdom of God, for men inside and outside church language. Royce further saw the need of atoning work. Men did become traitors to the Beloved Community—not only alienated and estranged from it, but active agents of evil against it. How shall this be dealt with? Someone from the community must go out to the traitor, "go through hell" with the traitor, and by suffering *with* him bring off at-one-ment. Such a transformed traitor might then be capable of more good than ever before in his life. So Royce unfolded the phrase, "He descended into hell."

For long years Christians have been afraid of conflict. It is supposed to be bad; church is to be a place of peace and harmony. Mary Follett, in her book *Creative Experience,* pushed Dewey a bit further and helped us understand that the beginning of creation is conflict. If we are to have a creative society, it will be one in which differences clash, where people do not all believe the same thing, where something new is constantly battling what is. Keep your eye on creativeness and upon how to handle conflict, so that it may be the beginning of some new creation. People who differ from us are to be seen as *co-creators,* rather than antagonists.

### Lewin and the New Era of Group: A Science, an Art, an Agent of Social Change, as Well as a Philosophy

Kurt Lewin marks the beginning of a new era in group theory. His contribution is not in contradiction to what had been said, but it is a new leap and a new precision. Escaping from Nazi Germany, Lewin had a burning enthusiasm for democratic civilization. He was glad to be part of a nation distinguished by voluntary groups, a nation that observed "the grammar of assent" rather than coercion, that believed in people. He also believed that the psychologist's function was not primarily to *describe* what was happening, and then determine society's direction by social statistics. But rather, it was to change society in the direction of expressing the preferred values of a democracy. This meant conceptualizing working models which might be called "the genus democracy" and then mobilizing a science of the field processes involved. He was interested in action research, and the time was late. He could not, with integrity, be an *observer* of the human scene. He must participate with all the intelligence and drive he could summon to help bring off humane civilization.

With such investment, with a few difference-making, explosive ideas about what a group really is, and some progress toward constructing a science of the necessary group processes, Lewin now *empowered* what heretofore had been largely a viewpoint. *Group life and leadership could be learned.* Change agents could be trained. "Groupness" was not a matter of hormone balance, or custom, or something you were hopelessly born with or without. Vivid experiments could be tried in group life. A field of study and venture was thus defined.

First of all, he knew that he had a value-system and some philosophy of desirable civilization. This was symbolized for him by democracy. Democracy, at the level of the nuclear group, meant that all members had understanding of the life or death world in which they were situated, their group's goal, and the paths by which one could get there. Some areas of decision-making and spontaneity were to be reserved to each member, for responsibility and creative imagination cannot be totally preempted by others, else a *human* being spoils.

As a Gestaltist, he was concerned about *meaningful wholes.* For him the group was a reality, not a figment of the imagination. Each person's reference group is a social ground on which the individual stands. And when we are confused as to our group belongingness, our behavior is restless, timid, over-aggressive, hypercritical of one's self and others. Some examples are the "migrating" adolescent, the Jew who is "between," the Negro—anyone commonly thought of as "marginal man," but in Lewin's imagery seen as man standing on quaggy swamp. Only by anchoring his conduct in something as large, substantial, and superindividual as the culture of a group can the individual stabilize his beliefs and stand up to the day-by-day fluctuations of his faith and behavior. Therefore, for Lewin all permanent learning is acceptance of *new belonging,* or the creation of a new social "meaningful whole." Thus, conversion of a group was easier than the conversion of individuals one by one. What makes a group a meaningful whole is not the likeness of everybody to one another, but *common fate.* With this principle Lewin cut through all superficial ideas that a group consists of people being pleasant to one another, and he placed "group" in the discourse of destiny.

Meaningful wholes had further educational implications. A person accepts not just this idea and then another idea. Learning occurs only at the moment he accepts the new values *as a whole,* as a working system. One learns a *culture,* not isolated bits. He learns a *pattern* of meanings and the social inventions that are necessary to express that value system. He learns simultaneously the ways of perceiving, valuing, thinking, and acting that together are the new culture. Or he learns none of them at all. As a phenomenologist, Lewin knew he had to study how the acting agent felt and saw his *life space.* Life space was the constellation (as perceived by the *agent*) of the forces determining his fate as of that moment, and as arranged by that person's goal in the situation.

So, all change in a person is rooted in changing perception (feeling-seeing) of life space, changing the person-in-group's perception of his social, history-making environment. This is not primarily an intellectualistic effort but a reworking of his perception of what is *significant* in his life space and his possible locomotion within it; i.e., a reworking of his valuings.

However, change in cognitive structures is important in any reeducation.

But they must be cognitive structures based on perception of life space. Ideas and hypotheses are constructive acts of the mind. Cognitive structure is a few elemental ideas, arranged in pattern, that have explanatory power, and create consequences. But the whole person (the meaningful whole!) is awakened and mobilized only in *action totals*. So, for Lewin only *event* finally educates. Explaining and giving advice accomplish little change. Only placing one's self *in situation*—encounter, confrontation, risk—finally brings off change of the all of a person. Thus, all learning of the new involves three dimensions—reworking of valuings and feelings, acquiring new cognitive structures of life space, mobilizing new behaviors in situation. These are all held together by accepting a new membership.

To summarize, Lewin proposed and designed an *educational* way of bringing about new society and a new person. He was trying to devise an alternative to coercion and raw power as the means of social change. *Persons* need to choose new values and new society as *an act of freedom*. For such policy and enterprise the small group is the necessary invention.

### Phenomenology

Prior to intellectual cognition, within the person there is an *activity of organizing experiences and worlds,* the activity of perception. The perceived world is the foundation of all meaningful action and all rationality. So, a large part of any theory of group life will be a theory of perception. In particular, person-perception becomes central. Snygg and Combs helped many people understand that a person must behave in terms of how *he* perceives the situation. Merleau-Ponty is a present originating source for a much more developed understanding of the primacy of perception.

In Merleau-Ponty's thought man is not a victim of determining environment. He is not "naturally" caused but is a "bodied" consciousness. His consciousness is not primarily an observer's consciousness but an involved participant's consciousness. Each man organizes a world order in which he lives. He is a *constituting* agent, polarizing out of the whole world a *habitat* in which he exists and which he saturates with his meanings. Thus, in any group interaction we are dealing with this polarized world and the "intentional arc" which organizes and humanizes it. We are not dealing with this or that idea, this or that act, this or that emotion. Such perceiving—giving meaning and ordering a world out of multiplicity—is *precognitive*. It is not to be confused with the Freudian *unconscious*—regarded as repressed impulse—or even with *preconscious*, but it is simply a *precognitive* seeing and organizing of life-death territory in which one situates one's self. This is what perception is, and what is meant by "phenomenal world." Man inheres in his phenomenal world. And consciousness is a relation with the world "out there," a directedness of attention toward something.

Relative to other people and the human world, healthy consciousness is always *inter*subjectivity, *co*existence, *inter*world. To become man we must learn to think in terms of reciprocity, i.e., two polarities both freely constituting worlds and both receiving each other. Both must be active. For only as an existence becomes aware of itself, grasps itself, and expresses its own meaning is there aliveness. Meaning is the clue to follow. Man is given to himself as something to understand. And this he cannot do without understanding a world which completes him as a system. Only at the moment of understanding another person are we born, and simultaneously by that act of understanding is he born as human existence.

Phenomenology is ontological. It is driven by an intense hunger to discover *"What* is this with which I am dealing? *What* am I?"* But this does not mean *classifying* the situation I am in, with textbook categories taught me or formed by the impulse of my wishful thinking or resentful prejudices. Instead, the policy is to ask anew, "What is the *present* situation *in and of itself?* How do I discover its *formative meaning?"* Comprehending the *dynamic essence* is my mind's task, not cutting up people and situations and throwing them into slots.

Formative meaning is accessible to me only in the individual experiences in which it appears to me. So I must *possess my own immediate significant experience in this particular here and now* and "manufacture" it into insight. It begins with diving into the "lived moment," but it does not stop with the beginning act of perception. For I must not be *enclosed* by any one experience. It should improve my power to penetrate into the depth of other lived moments, each giving me constantly more insight into *what constitutes* a person, a society, a world.

So, for the educator member of a group, "the phenomenological" is both theory and incorporated style of life. If we would allow him to articulate his prevailing stream of consciousness, it would go something like this—

"I struggle to participate understandingly in what I am living through,
    to be inside it—
experience it from within—
document reality;

get down to the architectonics—
not limit myself to surfaces;

strip my life down to the essentials—
not get it all cluttered up;

be capable of originating,
because I am conscious of
    the essential nucleus—
    the intention—
    the meaning of human acts.
"My escape from Egypt is escape from *external* time,
    where I am being flooded along—
        helplessly,
        hopelessly,
        numbly,
        obediently,
        softly,
        squashingly.
"I intend to be aware the first time around.

"I intend to have a life world organized and partly made by me, tinctured with my decisions and tone. I am a subject, who intends intersubjectivity."

## Existential

A group can all too easily degenerate into a soft society of dependent people and arrested development. Existential thrust within each person is necessary, accompanied by some common understanding and sanction of what this means. Existential thrust first of all means that I intend to *live;* to be burgeoning energy, potential on its way to significant form; to experience creation's joyful cry, "I am"; to be a unique person and particularity, caring deeply about some things. Existential thrust suggests that I am a freedom invoking other freedoms, open hands, ears, eyes, mouth—rather than closing fingers. I risk significant encounter rather than surface relationship, communication rather than prattle.

Existential thrust is the movement to become authentic, to incarnate vividly the truth I am meant to be, live out of troth. For I know truth only to the degree that I participate in it. A *spectator* can never *know.* And what group could trust an individual whom it perceives as *pretense*—not striving for authenticity? We simply are not credible on any other basis. Existential thrust means "here in this place and *now.*" I either exist or am a nothingness—*now.* I *exist* only when seething potential boils up and takes form. I exist only in some *present* length of relationship. I exist only in the moment of exploding imagination and furious thinking. I exist only *in the midst of* a decision event. I exist only *in this experience* of inserting something better into some sequence of my society's events. I exist only as I am sensitive to the possibility of the kingdom of God in the "now" situation. "Only in the midst of the world is Christ, Christ."

Existential thrust means resoluteness and zest in helping establish a unit of humanity of at least five people—a network of thoughtful people, who care about one another, are in honest communication with one another, each responsive to the lure of God to become more than he now is. Existential thrust also means doing something about the strange mixture of good and not-so-good pretense and reality, which we are and of which every historical event is a complex. In each group there is this ambiguous actuality of each particular person. From *time to time* the *most important business* of a group is the purification, restoration, and enlivening of the personal. It is always a necessary function simultaneous with other action. For a person filled with resentment disinherits himself from the enterprise, even to the point of opting out of the present tasks of his civilization. A person whose innerpersonal region has become eroded cannot be truthfully warm toward others, nor creatively productive. A member who has lost contact with his own center, either temporarily estranged or habitually duplicitous in all encounter situations, is a menace. A person living on a starvation diet of respect from others needs filling. A person who does not have frequent enough experiences of being an authority on something in some situation (he really knows, has competence, can give necessary rationale, has in his hands some responsible decision) spoils over a period of time. He becomes weak, except in hatred of himself and others.

Again and again every person needs to do "conscience work," for he violates other persons and tries to evade the resulting guilt. He is hit hard by the constant contrast between his expectancies and what actually happens and he actually is. And he is situated within a group that has a semipublic opinion of him and what he actually is and does. Never to face these is to live—as most of us do—subterranean and anxious.

Less and less we believe that the individual's "private conscience work" alone is adequate, or even with the participation of just one other person as therapist. In many situations the participation of the whole group who was part and cause of the original situation is required. Particularly is this true of corrupted and fear-governed communication in a group. There is no such thing as the *individual self, there is only self-in-world*: self-intermeshed-with-primary group-for-me. So group conscience work is always a proper agenda.

The point here is not that therapy is the sole purpose of groups, though that is true of some. But, rather, that healing or wounding is going on all the time, and we must be aware of the need for special effort in dealing with these internal-but-also-corporate events. We are developing persons at the same time we are getting jobs done. And members expect, particularly of the leader (the president, the chairman), open access to significant persons and creative fidelity from them to their *growth as person,* a consummation devoutly to be prized when found in a pastor!

Groups are concerned with cocreation, both of an enterprise in the world and of personal existence. And that involves some common understanding and competencies possessed by everybody and by the group-as-functioning in "How do we invoke and move toward becoming whole persons in this group? How do we enlarge the horizon within which we work, and intensify meaning?"

## Therapeutic Experience and Theory

There is one professional group whose full time is devoted to transforming, and so group theory will constantly appropriate its hard-won insights. Conversely, with the coming of group therapy and family group therapy, group theory enters into therapeutic practice.

Freud, among many other insights, gave us the expectancy that people do get mad and angry, frightened and anxious. And to handle conflict and anxiety states is a normal part of productive group life. He cued us to ask, when an individual or group became unproductive, "Where is the suppressed hostility?" For Freud the father figure was quite important in any group. First of all, people do have to find an authority who is strong enough to guarantee "a household." Members need to know accurately what his values and intentions are and have some fascination toward them. Through identification, the leader's life and standards become interiorized, become Ego. Then the members must cease being sheep, must slay their dependency, and become authorities themselves. More recently, Erikson has proposed the concept of adult guarantor as more generally and wholesomely applicable. Reality-testing was another major contribution to group theory. Reality testing is a habit of finding out *what really exists* in other people and group event, rather than projecting one's own wishful thinking and perceptions, as if the whole group enterprise was merely an extension of one's own biography.

Carl Rogers has been another source of much group theory. From the very beginning, we are to refuse to preempt decision and policy-making from other people. Regardless of what occurs, we are all *subjects,* not objects. (The remark has been made that Rogers is more "I-Thou" than Buber.) Diagnosing the "sickness" of other members, rather than meeting their personal reality in each moment, is profanation. In an authentic group there are no observers, only participants. Leadership functions are taken by any member whenever he seems to be especially relevant. The group is self-propelling and self-guiding, instead of being "run" by a teacher or leader.

Each is called to be honestly himself, and through this freedom both he and others are brought into authentic existence. There is one person whose openness and transformation he is responsible for—and that person is himself. He *invokes,* rather than attacks, others. Without each person being authentically present, the conditions for a productive group do not exist. His presence depends upon two related matters. His feeling and picture of himself are determinative. It is his dynamic and his guide. It is also where he is most vulnerable, so he spends much energy guarding its preciousness and trying to organize into it the flood of new experiencings with all their conflictful choas. He is an ambivalent mixture of a whole range of feeling and desiring. By symbolizing all the components, he may clarify and order these significant feelings. Another person, who tries to understand him in his complexity, may catch in his total communication of voice, words, gesture, and acts more of his self-situation than he is aware of or has digested. And by putting this into symbol (at the same time respecting him), the other may help him purify and integrate a *full* consciousness. And he is present in the group to the degree that he is so received, understood, and symbolized by others. Much of the conversation of a Rogers group will, therefore, be of this nature.

In recent therapies meanings and responsibility are being emphasized. From experiences in concentration camp, and also professionally, Viktor Frankl is convinced that awareness of responsibility to some loved one, some cause, some god, is what holds life together. So the therapist (or group member) helps such interpretation of the meaning of events and situations. Existential psychiatry, as originated in Binswanger, sees that the project of our one life on earth is the establishment of a *life world,* rather than an abstract self. Glasser has developed what he calls "reality therapy." As for many other psychiatrists, the basic enabling of all transformation is that at least one other person genuinely cares about you, and you care about him. But from there on, he surrounds the person with the expectation that *he* will be responsible for his integration into the reality of society, will be in charge of learning how to fulfill his need to love and be loved, to feel he is worthwhile to himself and to others. Primary group life is obviously central in these more recent therapies and in present expansion of the treatment of family groups, instead of working only with individuals.

## Role Theory

Sociological thought on the group uses the concept of role as a major tool, and it now seems to fit our developing thought. Just what is meant by "role" is complex. The very term often leads to very inauthentic existence, for its first meaning is "a part or character *assumed by an actor in a play.*" That leads to such horrible consequences that we ought not use the word.

But in its functional sense role points to the fact that in any *system* of interactions, certain *processes* do have to go on, and somebody has to perform them. In normal organization in our society responsibility for these functions (or at least responsibility to see that they are performed) is located in certain positions in the social structure. The person in that position becomes gate-keeper, executive, and target of our expectations that these processes will go on. Continuing trouble lies in the fact that if these are seen as the sole possession and responsibility of the president, the boss, the teacher, or the leader, then everybody else withdraws and becomes incapable of initiating or investing themselves. The leader then becomes arrogant, lonely, alienated, or driven. On the other hand, some primary group theory has forgotten that responsibility for seeing that certain functions are performed must be defined (contemporary parents may be suffering from lack of this). So what to do?

For the intentional primary group, we can define the processes necessary for this kind of group life. And these can be understood well enough by all members that all can perform them as needed. This we have to do if a local congregation is to have any existence as *Christian community.* Positions and employed staff will still be needed, but what they are about will be redefined. "The equipping of the saints" will be pointed up. The church does not belong to the minister, nor is he saddled with all its ministering. Ministering belongs to *the people of God.*

This whole essay has been spelling out what we all need to know about the necessary processes of authentic group life. And it might well be the basis of teaching for all adults and all confirmation classes. But certain processes can be summarized as *basic ministry* which underlie all ministries of the church. Regardless of the location or form of Christian enterprise, these we all need to be able to do with some competence. And they are fullness of life for us:

—becoming manifest, encountering, confronting

—understanding and receiving other persons

—invoking authenticity

—interpreting events, culturing experiences and felt significances into meanings. Continuing the Great Conversation

—inserting something better into history-making somewhere; a group matching itself against some human need, risking engagement

## Where Are We Going With Intentional Primary Groups?

A thoughtful pastor of a local congregation has written,

I see less and less point to groups that meet simply to study. How easy it is to study for a year without being called to decision, involvement, risk. Our study and "missions" can be an escape from the new existence to which we are called. We must increasingly help groups to the point of *being* in their own corporate life the message they proclaim. Very few of us have the exciting experience of being the church in the primitive sense of being the reconciled and reconciling community. It seems to me that every group in the church—the official boards, too—should seek to discover what it means to be the church in microcosm.

If we were to summarize, in a sort of confession of sin, the failures of the contemporary church to take very seriously the theory and practice of the intentional primary group, we would highlight the following:

1. *We (church people) have not taken seriously the educational theory involved. In fact, we avoid transforming persons and changing life. We do not believe, nor are we interested in, Lewin or any other of the theorists mentioned.*

By many denominational headquarters group theory and practice is regarded as esoteric. They might admit that perhaps it has some clues on how to get things agreed to—and it can be learned in a one day's conference! But it is not of the *nature* of the Christian church nor anything on which the future of the church depends. Therefore, group life movements have to be outside the official structures of the churches, and these are where the vital ones are. On the whole, local congregations are the "mere rope of sand" that John Wesley found the churches of his time to be. And we place all our educational bets on Sunday instruction. Further, the congregation still believes that the eleven o'clock preaching service is transforming them and the world. (Do they *really* believe that it is change-producing?) And sooner or later, their pastor is lassoed by their conventional Christianity and is no more a threat. Yet wistful adults keep on hoping they can have significant encounter with their pastor and one another. So we are looking for new modes of ministry and new "common fate" groups through which the reality *church* may occur. Whatever the form, these new ministries will need basic theory and skills.

Most seminary classes remain quasi-traditional, specializing in eighteenth- and nineteenth-century teaching-learning methods. But the new theories are being actualized in some classes. Almost all seminary graduates today will have some competencies, though at a meager performance level, and a few catch phrases of theory. Some will have vital group experience in their seminary community.

2. *Communication in our churches is corrupted, abstract, one-way.*

Protestantism has been trapped by the symbol "word." Words are thought to *contain* meaning, rather than *evoke it in the hearer.* Christianity is often thought of as verbal propositions to which people give assent. Church consists of proclaiming words to nicely dressed people sitting in straight rows. Dialogue is *not* a Christian folkway with us.[5] This is starkly revealed in the current arrogance of white Christians. They do not intend to enter into "communion communication" with Negroes.

3. *We have been trying to give training in group methods to people who had no fiery desire to do something. Nor have we convincingly demonstrated that our methods really empower.*

[5] For another discussion, see chap. 8, pp. 85-93.

Some leaders have been overconcerned with training in group dynamics. It is harder and more complicated than we thought, and we have tried to do too many transformations at once. Actually, no one knows how to bring off training that is also transformation, particularly for large numbers of people. Interest in training laboratories in group life has tapered off, rather than expanded. New interest in communication for pastors is an open possibility. We have yet to unify "person-centered" and "task-centered" in the same group, which is finally what the church has to do.

4. *Group life leaders have tended to underrate and neglect significant symbol, meanings, and ideology as the dynamics and cohesiveness of group life.*

In a proper concern to escape from just teaching people a new set of slogans, while their total behavior remains pretty much the same, we have failed to "build the mind of the church." A religious group is a *relating, interpreting, ministering*-to-the-world enterprise. Some church groups have concentrated on working over immediate personal experiences and relationships. These are healing, redemptive groups. Likewise there is place in the church for small "task forces" free to go ahead and do. But interpreting and teaching are also necessary. All three must be put together if we are to have a healthy and continually growing "system of persons."

And at the top level group theory has remained quite undeveloped. Rather than working widely in the range of sources of group theory, most have settled down near their entrance into just one little ghetto of thought. The present essay tries to indicate some of the major areas to be studied. It would seem that in the future we might profit most from further developments in communications theory, in existential philosophy and psychology, phenomenology, anthropology, and group therapy. And we must work on religious interpretation.

5. *The intentional primary group has not had an adequate theological rationale or sustaining myth.*

The left wing of the Reformation, Wesley's Class Meeting, the Pilgrim covenant—all combined with Paul's vision of the organic nature of early Christian fellowship and a renewed doctrine of the Holy Spirit, could have provided historical myth. Without this a revitalization movement never gets off the ground! But this has not yet come. Christian theologians have been derelict, and those who have some taste of group life have been irresponsible, in failing to bring about needed theological reconstruction for the present day. For example, the definition of the church as the place where the word is preached and heard and the sacraments rightly administered must die and rise again in the form of the church suggested by passages such as Col. 3:15; Eph. 4:16, 25; I Cor. 13:13.

Group life cannot be healthy without a return to prophetic religion, including the conviction that God speaks to us through concrete events; that ethic and conscience are not a-religious; that we must take seriously God's continuous creation. It also depends upon a recovery of the doctrine of the Holy Spirit, developed in modern understanding. Bonhoeffer's rejection of sacred versus profane and his living toward a "worldly" Christianity are the present most potent originators of needed thought. Obsession with death and sin is no longer the organizer of Christian existence. Christianity is a thrust to *actualize* life and relationship with all people.

Actually, for some time the whole intellectual-cultural climate has been hostile to group life. Our literature for decades has been written by the alienated, by those who sense man as a horrible mess, and hold that the proper attitude is to cut one's self off. "Hell is people." And all too many biblical theologians have delighted in such literature. Counselors and mass communications have taught youth that they are a new generation, and anyone who is not in violent rebellion against the adult generation, is a "square." Hopefully, the climate has some change in it, and possibility may be around the corner. Somehow we all have to rally to bring off the new world!

6. *We have also been derelict in not integrating religious celebration into group theory and practice.*

Religious celebration is one of the distinctive and potent behaviors we have to offer man. We are obviously entering a time of new invention of folk worship forms more inherent in face-to-face encounter and bearing one another's burdens. This will be more than the present prayer cells. But what it is, is yet to emerge. It will be a people who together offer daily to God the toil and creation of that day. The Roman Catholic Liturgical Reform is actualizing such direction. In contrast, Protestants are trying to find vitality by going backward into history and long printed services.

7. *Finally, it is wealth of religious experience, and convincing report of it, that makes us "members one of another." And this we not only have too little of, we are ashamed of it.*

Religion is a revitalization movement of a people. So we began this survey. An explosion of new vitality comes from strong experiencing of that love, warmth, and destiny which is welling within us from the Creator. Until such experiencing assumes epidemic proportions, small groups will limp along.

## FOR ADDITIONAL READING

### Educators

Bushnell, Horace. *Christian Nurture.* New Haven: Yale University Press, 1947.

Dewey, John. *Democracy and Education.* New York: The Macmillan Company, 1916.

Mead, George Herbert. *George Herbert Mead on Social Psychology.* 2nd ed. Anselm Strauss, ed. Chicago: University of Chicago Press, 1964. Part II.

Royce, Josiah. *The Problem of Christianity.* New York: The Macmillan Company, 1913. I, 254-323.

### Lewin

Lewin, Kurt. *Resolving Social Conflicts,* ed. Gertrude Weiss Lewin. New York: Harper & Row, 1948.

## Phenomenology

Merleau-Ponty, Maurice. *Primacy of Perception*, ed. James M. Edie, tr. by William Cobb, *et al.* Evanston: Northwestern University Press, 1964.

Thévenaz, Pierre. *What Is Phenomenology? And Other Essays.* ed. James M. Edie. Chicago: Quadrangle Books, 1962.

## Existentialism

Buber, Martin. *I and Thou.* New York: Charles Scribner's Sons, 1958.

Heidegger, Martin. *Being and Time.* New York: Harper & Row, 1962. Pp. 149-210; 275-78; 334-96.

Kierkegaard, Sören. *Training in Christianity.* Tr. by Walter Lowrie. Princeton: Princeton University Press, 1944.

————. *Purity of Heart.* New York: Harper & Row, 1956.

May, Rollo, *et al.*, eds. *Existence.* New York: Basic Books, 1958. Chaps. 1-3; 6-7.

## Role Theory

Lindzey, Gardner. *Handbook of Social Psychology.* Vol. I; *Theory and Method.* Reading, Mass.: Addison-Wesley Publishing Co., 1954. Chap. 6.

## Anthropology

Lewis, Oscar. *Five Families: Mexican Case Studies in the Culture of Poverty.* New York: Basic Books, 1959.

Redfield, Robert. *The Little Community.* Chicago: University of Chicago Press, 1955.

## Recent Therapy

Glasser, William. *Reality Therapy.* New York: Harper & Row, 1965.

Satir, Virginia M. *Conjoint Family Therapy.* Palo Alto, Calif.: Science & Behavior Books, 1964.

## Part IV

# AGENCIES AND
# ORGANIZATIONS

Chapter 25

## THE HOME AND
## CHRISTIAN EDUCATION

*John Charles Wynn*

PROTESTANT CHRISTIANS, IN CONTRAST TO ROMAN CATHOLICS AND TO JEWS, must admit to certain disadvantages in their religious education of families. The Jews carefully preserve a valued tradition of family rituals underscoring their age-old conviction that the family is the basic unit within Israel. The Roman Catholics derive their doctrine of the family with its several teachings about religion in the home, sexuality, and marital relations from their dogma that marriage is a sacrament. But Protestants, unable to draw upon either the support of family unity or upon a sacramental concept of matrimony, must turn elsewhere for their educational philosophy of work with families. More individualistic than either of the other faiths, Protestants tend to found their family educational efforts upon an interpretation of biblical theology, plus current indications of program needs within the churches. This peculiar amalgam of the theological and the pragmatic leads both to creativity and to inconsistencies.

Ever since World War II the North American continent has been experiencing an era of familism. Sometimes dubbed "togetherness," this vogue has permeated the social values of a generation and has come in particular to characterize suburban living.[1] Moreover, it has informed churches and denominations with program features that include family nights, parent organizations, and home services of worship, to name but a few. Emphasis within parishes upon the family has been criticized both for its neglect of the atypical household where there are unmarried or childless adults and also for its potential idolatry of the home.[2] At the same time this pervasive interest in

---

[1] For documentation see Gibson Winter, *The Suburban Captivity of the Churches* (Garden City: Doubleday & Company, 1961).

[2] See for example the writer's chapter "The Family of God" in *Pastoral Preaching*, Charles F. Kemp, ed. (St. Louis: The Bethany Press, 1963), pp. 185 ff.

family integrity has inspired new and comprehensive efforts in curriculum publishing, in pastoral care, and in novel educational ventures.

Increased interest in the family shown by many denominations has also caused some sober thinking about the limited influence of the family in contemporary culture. Exaggerated slogans—e.g. "The family that prays together stays together" or "The hand that rocks the cradle rules the world" —have had to be tempered by unhappy data that disprove them. The immense influence of the nuclear family upon children has been well attested by psychoanalysts, by anthropologists, and by religious educators. That such influence can be witnessed, traced, and documented cannot be denied; but its limitations are notable when compared to the permeating influences brought upon members of the family by society, by economics, and by the political state. Of the several institutions and structures in society that bear on the home and on individuals, it is unlikely that the church could be characterized as among the most powerful.

As the world continues in the midst of rapid social change, the family-as-institution is undergoing dismaying changes as well. Sexual roles have been altered remarkably in the past two decades in that economically independent women bear a different attitude toward their wifely and motherly tasks; and few fathers any longer make very serious claims to being head of the house. Vocational developments have brought a new and extended leisure. Medical advancements have made possible both longer life and larger population. An affluent society and a less restrictive sexual ethic have altered cultural mores. And all of these have affected the family in dramatic variety of positive and negative ways. Positively they have offered increased freedom, made us more aware of family life, and have quickened us to the need of family stability. Under these circumstances, studies of marriage and of the family have grown profuse. (By contrast, only thirty-five years ago a survey that was a progenitor of this volume was Lotz and Crawford's *Studies in Religious Education*;[3] yet for all its variegated chapters written by the church educators of that day, not one of them refers to the family, and the index reveals no references to "family," "home," "marriage," or "sex.") In the generation that was to follow that publication the family came to receive wide attention from sociologists, psychologists, educationists, and religionists. Negatively it can be noted that the family is under heavy fire from several sides from the ethical relativists, from the divorce trends, and from the sexual revolution. It would be a mistake to assume that the stalwart institution of the family is going down under these challenges. But the impact has been sufficient to cause concern and to attract considerable attention from the helping professions who have come to the aid of the family.

## The Sexual Crisis and Sex Education

Although the term "sexual revolution," as used above, is inaccurate for today's preoccupation with sexuality in our society, enough of a sexual crisis exists

[3] Philip Henry Lotz and L. W. Crawford, eds., *Studies in Religious Education* (Nashville: Cokesbury Press, 1931).

to make it appear revolutionary if compared to the puritanical standards of yesteryear. The advent of numerous problems in regard to sexual ethics has forced this subject to the fore of family education among the churches. The so-called new morality—with its emphasis upon love rather than law, freedom rather than fixity, and persons rather than principles—has made impressive inroads, along with the new secular theology, into current thinking about Christian ethics. At the same time a stepped-up ethical relativism has been gaining strength in North American society and has profoundly affected sexual behavior. The combination of these factors has made sex education the most urgent of the several elements within family education today.

Sex education with reproduction education has long been a component of Protestant church curriculum, but never before has it been as forthright and as persistent as now. With the virtual disappearance of older deterrents to sexual experimentation, Christian moralists have been faced with a new challenge. That is, they can no longer rely on scare techniques (threats of conception, of venereal infection, or of discovery) to clinch their arguments on behalf of chastity. The fact that these highly moralistic, quasi-pragmatic arguments had always made bad theology seemed unimportant to former Christian educators. But now that effective contraception, miraculous antibiotics, and automotive privacy have reduced these traditional threats to pale cautions, more valid reasons are being found for Christian ethical behavior. In the candor this subject now enjoys, it is possible to deal factually with the problems and factors of sexual conduct as never before. And churches are everywhere taking advantage of this openness with courses for young people, adult-youth forums, sermon series, and study groups organized around puzzling sexual questions. There was a time, only a decade ago, when such courses would emphasize the joys of sexual love and acknowledge the goodness of God in his creation of sexuality. But in a "sex-saturated society" it has become unnecessary to emphasize sexual love as joy, a point that may very well have been overdone. Instead, the obligation for the Christian to exercise his responsible freedom in fidelity is the emphasis needed now. And this is no easy topic to handle; for churchly teaching has been unaccustomed to mention of freedom in this one department of ethics even though freedom is emphasized in all others.

Impressive and startling adjustments are taking place in the sexual mores of Western culture. Nonmarital coitus is known to be increasing, as a number of responsible studies demonstrate.[4] Society's attitudes have liberalized toward the availability of contraception, the treatment of homosexuality, the practice of artificial insemination, the rationale for therapeutic abortion, and the remarriage of divorced persons.

It would be remarkable if the churches were unaffected by so great an impact; and they have indeed been shaken. The contextual ethic, advanced both by secular theologians and by moral philosophers, has prompted a demand for response to ethical decision in the midst of the total context rather than

[4] Ira Reiss, *Premarital Sexual Standards in America* (New York: The Free Press of Glencoe, 1960).

too simply on the basis of absolute imperatives. Under heavy fire because their teaching coincides with that of the moral relativists in some spots, the contextual ethical group is making a serious attempt to understand the freedom implicit in the gospel of Christ in relation to human events. These include international relations, war and peace, social justice and racial relations, business and commerce, as well as sex and family matters.

Complicated questions of sexual behavior have become the agenda for many a troubled consultation in contemporary ecclesiastical and educational circles. Two North American Conferences on Church and Family (1961 and 1966) have so far been called to work specifically on such questions. Likewise, several conferences on sexual ethics have been convened by the World Council of Churches for representatives of Western churches. Administrators and faculties of secondary schools and universities are compelled to give increasing attention to the permissiveness that an open society has pressed upon its youth. Deep concern is expressed by many of these leaders as they face astonishingly difficult problems which our Victorian forebears once thought settled.

An interesting footnote to the church's dilemma is that churchmen no longer agree that theological teachings about sexuality are derived from the Christian doctrine of marriage. Formerly this was widely taken for granted, so that once the marital foundations were understood, it was comparatively simple to explain sexual ethics as a derivative of the doctrine. However, a group of modern theologians, among whom are Fr. Leclerq and Helmut Thielicke,[5] have challenged this assumption with a phenomenological rebuttal. Contrary-wise they argue that our understanding of Christian marriage is really to be formulated from our understanding of what sexuality means in God's order of creation. This seemingly obscure argument is already having its impact upon the way that curricular and program materials are written, as well as upon the sermons we hear from the pulpits of the nation. That this argument must also infect our deeply ingrained convictions about romantic love may be less clear; but it is necessary that we begin to understand something of its import in this question. The Western world's penchant for romanticizing love bears both beauty and pathos. Newer appreciation of such *eros* has found support from Denis de Rougemont, C. S. Lewis, Wallace Denton, and W. P. Wylie.[6] The rich meaning that romance can bring to marriage and to family life is seen as a stabilizing force within a democratic society where most persons have considerable choice in dating and mating. But the romantic illusion that sometimes hounds *eros* also brings problems: the occasional assumption that meaningful marriage can be built on love at first sight, or that a marriage must be broken because one spouse has fallen in love with some new person. Such problems as these have been docketed for prior attention in up-to-date studies of theology and of pastoral care.

[5] Thielicke, *The Ethics of Sex* (New York: Harper & Row, 1964).

[6] Wallace Denton, *What's Happening to Our Families?* (Philadelphia: The Westminster Press, 1963); and W. P. Wylie, *The Pattern of Love* (London: Longman's, Green & Company, 1958).

## Theological Clues and Theological Problems

Recent decades (as noted in Part I of this volume) have witnessed a careful review of biblical theology in relation to the whole of Christian education. Theological inspiration has offered both clues and problems to the particular concern of family education. And what H. Shelton Smith did for Christian education in general with his shaking *Faith and Nurture*,[7] Derrick Sherwin Bailey was to accomplish in particular for family education with his significant *The Mystery of Love and Marriage*. For it was Canon Bailey who awakened the church to implicit biblical doctrines that added up to a theology of sexual intercourse. His forthright work reminded readers that Christianity has other than pragmatic bases for its standards of sexual conduct, marital fidelity, romantic love, and family living. As a key to his system he lifts out the concept of one-flesh (*henosis*) from the Bible and demonstrates how this idea impinges upon family education.

But if theology offers support, it also offers problems. The family life of Jesus, despite all the useful homiletical references found in this relationship, can hardly be cited to buttress modern yearnings for togetherness. From the nativity stories that testify to his unusual conception and birth to his mature years of celibacy, the family life of Jesus was unusual not only by our standards but also even for his own times. His estrangement from his own family (Matt. 12:46-50), his sharp sayings about family relationships and hostilities ("They will be divided, father against son and son against father" Luke 12:53), and his unconditional demands for discipleship that took priority over marriage and family loyalties: All these prevent the Christian from too easy an assumption of family solidarity based on New Testament standards.

The New Testament, in fact, tends both to support and also to deemphasize some of the tenets the Israelite family had taken for granted. Much of New Testament thought is positive toward the family, supporting chastity, fidelity, and monogamy. The "tables of duties" emphasize mutuality in loving relationships of parents and children (Col. 3:18 ff.). The Gospels remind us of our obligation to care for the elderly. Respect for fathers in that patriarchal society comes through in a number of instances (Matt. 7:9, Luke 15:11 ff.), and a deep empathy for mothers can be detected in concern for their labor pains (John 16:21) or their housewifely chores (Luke 15:8 ff.).

Yet much of the New Testament also fails to affirm the family. We are assured that we have no real home on earth, but that instead we are pilgrims en route to another home in a city whose builder is God (Heb. 11). In that city there will be no betrothal nor marriage, and no conventional family life (Mark 12:25). And while the Christian makes his pilgrimage through earth, he is to treat even the most intimate of family relationships—as of secondary importance to the kingdom of God and its righteousness—e.g. to live with a wife as if having none (I Cor. 7:29). Both sex and family are to be subsumed far under God's sovereignty.

No less difficult for the church is the contention of many a theologian

---

[7] H. Shelton Smith, *Faith and Nurture* (New York: Charles Scribner's Sons, 1941).

that there is normatively no such group as a Christian family. There are Christians *in* families;[8] or there are sociological entities and substructures that can be designated as families related to the rolls of a church. But theologically speaking, it is difficult to demonstrate that a family is to become Christian in the identical sense that a person can, i.e. by salvation, or that church families represent the unit of Christendom in any manner similar to that of the family unit in Israel. The romanticizing of this incongruous Jewish example goes on in denominational magazine and lesson series as well as in the pulpit. But it is difficult to document.

Enlarging ecumenical interests of recent years have enriched family education in several ways. Open dialogue with representatives of Judaism and Catholicism has allowed for a less threatening consideration of interfaith marriages, has aided in understanding differing standards of planned parenthood, and has revealed a breadth of commonalty in many areas, e.g. parent education, premarital guidance, and even worship customs within the family. More than this, the ecumenical "thaw" has promoted serious research and inquiry among Protestant leaders who are compelled to reexamine their own doctrines and reevaluate their cultural suppositions as a result of challenge. Subsequently searching questions are being asked about contraception and population problems, about the church's attitudes toward divorce and remarriage, about sterilization and about therapeutic abortion.

If, as we have contended, Protestants cannot found their theological convictions about family life on the same principles used by the other faiths, we still are not without theological foundations. (1) First of all, the sovereignty of God, that foremost doctrine that stems from John Calvin's contribution to the Reformation, stands as a cornerstone to family theology. This teaching emphasizes the standard under which all human relationships must be ordered (including the covenant of marriage) and from which they are to be derived. (2) The doctrine of the priesthood of all believers has direct relevance to the family wherein each member has a responsibility and right not only to make his own decisions about faith and practice but also to carry this principle into other spheres of democratic family living. It is this doctrine in particular that gives Protestantism its strikingly individualistic bias that sometimes militates against family unity. (3) The doctrine of the church as the body of Christ stands as a third important tenet for the ordering of family theology. For this fellowship is actually considered to consist of the family of God (Eph. 2:19), and it makes possible the understanding of the scattered church as existing in the homes of Christian people wherever they live. Moreover, the Reformation doctrine of the church, which had breached the former wall between the church and secular society, lifted marriage to a new respect and freed it from the sacrilizing ecclesiastical domination it had known previously.

It is from theology that the church deduces both her ethical systems and her educational curricula. These are pronounced in the pulpit, taught in the classroom, and propounded in seminary. And they are forced to face the challenge of change in an ever-changing world.

[8] Roy W. Fairchild, *Christians in Families* (Richmond: Covenant Life Curriculum Press, 1964).

## A Changing World and Its Changing Families

"Everything changes" declared Heraclitus, the pre-Socratic Grecian philosopher; but modern man cannot help suspecting that today's changes are far more rapid and profound than they must have been in ancient Greece. The church, long resistant to change (a conservatism that is at once a strength and a weakness), has begun to adapt her ways to some demands of twentieth-century life with its explosion of knowledge, its increased mobility, and its newly automated civilization. With these social changes the family has been changing also, prompting subsequent alterations in still other areas.

Innovations in the roles of men and of women, for instance, (indeed this is also a part of the sexual crisis) have been rapid in this generation. Ever since World War II when working women, having become accustomed to their wage scale, refused to return to kitchen captivity, women's roles have been shifting markedly. Their interests, their activities, their very clothing are all in sharp contrast to their grandmother's day. Woman has meanwhile awakened, as Cynthia Wedel reminds us,[9] to talents and freedoms she never knew she had, and which would have been unthinkable a few generations ago. With all this she remains still burdened by customs within a man-dominated society—and not least in that prejudiced institution, the church, where some confusion persists as to whether women may be ordained as clergy, whether they may assume roles of leadership, and (to tell the truth) whether they are certain about their own goals.

And in the meantime men's roles have been changing so that they too now have multiple tasks: bread-winning, household chores, laundering, baby care, and socializing their children. They also show signs of bewilderment. There is no doubt that new roles are being worked through for both men and women,[10] a process, however, that finds the churches less often in the front than at the rear of the procession.

But changes that affect family living are rife. The movement into an increasingly automated and industrial society has altered family and church considerably. No longer a producing but now a consuming unit, the home has had to consider not how many "hands" children represent, but how many "mouths." The move toward an urbanized culture has complicated home life even while offering new convenience and ease. The speed-up of living and the corresponding increase of leisure, paradoxical as this combination appears, have brought to some families a new sense of unity and to others a threat of breakdown. An open society, with its anonymity and its occasionally wild permissiveness, has accelerated the decline of many family values and has doubtless led to a wider acceptance of divorce. The meaninglessness of many lives in the midst of this rapidly changing world has hardly been alleviated by the uneasy and sporadic truce among nations in these recent years, by the bureaucratic inroads of government upon home life, and the sometimes

[9] Cynthia Wedel, "Sexuality in Society: Roles of Men and of Women" in *Sex, Family, and Society in Theological Focus*, J. C. Wynn, ed. (New York: Association Press, 1966).

[10] See Margaret Mead, *Male and Female* (New York: William Morrow & Company, 1949), Part IV.

heartless and often awkward expectations made upon church families by the ecclesiastical institution. Meaninglessness gets expressed in a search for faith, but also sometimes in marital strife and in delinquent behavior.

Another changed attitude, that toward divorce and remarriage, has startled society in recent years. The remarkable part of this is not, as some critics contend, that the church merely reflects societal mores, but instead that the church has rediscovered its theological base for consideration of the failed marriage and the doctrine of forgiveness.

The ever-high divorce rate (which surprisingly evidently duplicates a condition extant in Jesus' day) has deeply concerned the church. Despite the barely comforting statistic that church members divorce less often than all others in the population, divorce has made a resounding impact upon the churches and even to some extent within the ministry itself. The major denominations, forced to restudy their attitude toward those whose marriages have failed, have gradually ameliorated their attitude toward divorce and subsequent remarriage. Some now recognize divorce and remarriage by regulatory, some by definitive, and some by advisory decrees; but all of them show greater tendency toward understanding and forgiveness and less tendency to search out the guiltier party in a divorce action.[11] This move toward a dynamic rather than a legalistic interpretation of divorce and remarriage is one of the more encouraging current changes in family education.

## Parent Education and Family Nurture

Patterns of home-church cooperation are nothing if not heterogeneous. Currently one denomination is attempting to regulate all families through an agreed syllabus and curriculum for church and family, while a sister denomination is quietly giving up all but a vestige of its family features in church school curriculum. Another denomination concentrates on getting families to worship together in the Sunday service, and still another is content with sending home leaflets and letters to parents.

Researchers have discovered that home curriculum materials are observed more in the breach than in the reading. One survey[12] reports that six out of ten active church members had seldom or never opened the parents' materials that came into their homes. The same survey found, however, that certain parents were more likely to be among the minority who did read such literature thoroughly and who did learn from it. These tended to be persons enrolled in adult education, parents who were teaching classes in the church school, and parents whose pastor prompted them to read the parental literature.

Family education in the churches has traditionally emphasized worship practices in the home, albeit with only moderate success. One denomination has learned that less than one family among twenty ever reads from the Bible

[11] Refer to James G. Emerson, Jr., "Marriage and Remarriage: Questions About Forgiveness," in *Sex, Family, and Society in Theological Focus*, J. C. Wynn, ed.

[12] Roy W. Fairchild and J. C. Wynn, *Families in the Church: A Protestant Survey* (New York: Association Press, 1961), pp. 187-88.

or conducts any worship other than perfunctory grace at meals. Despite a greater obligation for the home to inculcate the reading of the Bible and religious instruction, now that the public school more than ever is relinquishing any such practices, few homes follow the ancient (and rural) practice of family prayers.

Meanwhile fathers and mothers, puzzled by their vocation as parents, continue to seek counsel wherever they can find it. The PTA at school, the newspaper columns, the "coffee klatsch"—all assist in interpreting parental roles. However a confused, yes fearful, generation of parents has been showing need of help in understanding themselves, their children, and their times. The churches that meet such needs find a readiness among parents to study developmental stages in family life: the growth of children from babyhood through the preschool years, into primary grades and the latency period, and on into their teens. The reciprocal development required of the parents themselves is abetted by the group sharing that takes place in these sessions.

Change has also come into the consideration of nurture and curriculum development in relation to the family. Horace Bushnell (1802-76) could conceivably be considered the father of family education in Protestant churches, for it was he who awakened a nation to the immense influence that parents have on their impressionable children. But Bushnell's precocious and stimulating concepts of Christian nurture[13] have been called into question in our day. The questions have arisen from grim experience and from the research data cited above.[14] Denominational programs designed to center church school curricula in home participation have come acropper at the point of parental indifference. And serious queries have arisen from educators as to whether parents can actually be teachers to their children, whether the unconscious but powerful education of home life can be geared to church programming, and whether practical means exist to make such a program work in any wide sense. Bushnell's insights into the unconscious and exemplary influence of parents are not to be doubted (numerous data support him there). But whether this insight can be programmed by churches has come to be held in grave doubt.

Churches can, however, aid parents to understand something of the self-system and the ego-structure of their children. To understand the self as the custodian of awareness, to see the need for a child to develop autonomy and interpersonal competence (even at the price of some negativism toward Mother!), to allow for an expectation of anticipated behavior problems: these constitute Christian education in process.

Beset by the demand for the education of parents, and aware that numerous programs are necessary for varieties of parents, parishes are devising a spate of plans that include classes for parents, mothers' clubs, cooperative nursery schools, family nights at church, couples' clubs, family vacation church schools, and numerous other measures.[15] Because families differ so widely it is now

[13] *Christian Nurture* (New Haven: Yale University Press, 1947).

[14] Fairchild and Wynn, *Families in the Church*, p. 237.

[15] See Wesner Fallaw, "The Role of the Home in Religious Nurture," in *Religious Education: A Comprehensive Survey*, Marvin J. Taylor, ed. (Nashville: Abingdon Press, 1960), pp. 143-51.

realized that different parents require varying approaches at different stages in their lives. This has inspired the diversification in parent education and some ingenuity in parish programming.

## Pastoral Care and Preaching

True as it is for all of Christian education, it is especially true for family education that some of the most far-reaching work is accomplished by the pastor in his pulpit and pastoral ministry. The sermons he preaches about religion in the home, sexual ethics, marriage, parents and children, or the entire gamut of human relationships serve effectively as family education.

His pastoral care program may be the most important family education that the church has to offer. There no longer can be any question about whether the pastor will be a family counselor. The only possible question that remains is how well he can do his counseling. In family counseling he has a brace of strong aids in his knowledge of spiritual resources that strengthen family life and in his reliance upon the church fellowship as a support to family members. He himself must have come to terms with his own marital status, be he single or married, in order to carry on this work; and it will help his cause materially if he has a knowledge of the family dynamics that operate within this most intimate of all human relations. He has immense advantages in his family ministry because he has such direct access to the homes of his members, can draw upon the resources of their faith, and can work with the aspirations and ideals of his people.

Pastors educated in the past twenty-five years have taken seminary courses that enable them to understand psychology and interpersonal relationships. Many of them in addition have had clinical training and social work supervision. They have been instructed in the ways of pastoral care through the common ventures of family life: occasions of birth and death, of marriage and vocation, of child rearing and family adjustments. To each of these developmental stages the pastor learns how to bring the resources of pastoral care and of family education. Through such experience the pastor has become so accepted as a counselor to families that many parishioners will not consult a psychiatrist or other counselor unless first referred by him.

But family education draws not only upon psychology, but also upon theology, sociology, and anthropology. The family is touched by a myriad of social forces of which the church is only one. Therefore church leaders do well to join hands with some of the nearly five hundred national agencies that serve families. A splendid advantage in such organizations is that most of them are represented in local congregations by church members. Many churches can draw upon the helping professions for assistance in family education and for therapy. In addition, there are professional persons in nearly every church: physicians, attorneys, teachers, nurses, social workers, and a host of others. Yet experience indicates that although these professionals are numerous enough, they are seldom called upon to assist in family services in the parish. Their participation in such ministry, when it can occur, is an outstanding example of the priesthood of all believers at work. The pity is that less than half of the nation's clergy report any referrals to such persons in their ministry to families.

Gradually some of the former professional jealousy between the clergy and social workers is being erased. Some clergymen now study social case work and some few gain social work degrees. Here and there churches are employing social workers on their staffs. Closer working ties are developing at last between the clergy and the multidisciplinary professions that also serve families, resulting in a mutual respect for specialties and talents of one another.

## Further Study and Research

Much of family education is unsystematic; and the newness of the discipline may be responsible for its open-ended situation. Many aspects of family education remain to be discovered, to be studied, and to be researched.

Churches need urgently to understand the dynamics of child rearing in the Christian faith. At present we depend upon an amalgam of experience, folkways, and mental health teachings. If we knew this field better, we would be able to improve our methods of teaching parents, of relating to the changing homes of today, and of writing curriculum studies.

We need better empirical studies than now are available to understand the correlations between sexual behavior and Christian faith, between divorce and religious practice, between marital relations and religious patterns. Before-and-after studies are long overdue in premarital and in postnuptial education, with new patterns of family life worship, and in all types of mixed marriages.

New challenges to the home now require new understanding of church families. What are the changing roles of parents in regard to their self-images, to their understanding of parenthood, to their methods of child rearing, to their concept of psychosexual definition? What types of families can the church expect to work with in future years as the old middle-class monopoly of Protestantism is broken? What helps are there for grandparent education? For those confused by the sexual crisis of modern society? For the parent who must serve both as father and as mother after widowhood or separation?

Decisions confront the churches also in regard to the education of inner-city families whose home patterns differ widely from the suburban and rural ethos to which Protestant churches are more accustomed. They will need to work out curriculum aids for unusual families: those with exceptional or retarded children, new approaches for the families with rebellious adolescents or broken relationships, and new methods of outreach to the unmotivated or hostile parent.

In a post-Protestant era the churches find themselves struggling with enormous ignorance of the faith, with immense loneliness even in families, with emotional problems, and with severed communication in marriages. In the face of such challenges as these, family education and family ministry merge into one.

## FOR ADDITIONAL READING

Bailey, Derrick S. *The Mystery of Love and Marriage*. New York: Harper & Row, 1952.

Denton, Wallace. *What's Happening to Our Families?* Philadelphia: The Westminster Press, 1963.

Duvall, Evelyn and Sylvanus. *Sex Ways: In Fact and Faith.* New York: Association Press, 1961.

Fairchild, Roy W. *Christians in Families.* Richmond: Covenant Life Curriculum Press, 1965.

Genné, Elizabeth and William. *Foundations for Christian Family Policy.* New York: National Council of Churches, 1961.

Hulme, William. *Pastoral Care of Families.* Nashville: Abingdon Press, 1962.

Schur, Edwin M. *The Family and the Sexual Revolution.* Bloomington: Indiana University Press, 1964.

Thielicke, Helmut. *The Ethics of Sex.* New York: Harper & Row, 1964.

Wynn, J. C., ed. *Sex, Family, and Society in Theological Focus.* New York: Association Press, 1966.

# Chapter 26

# INTER- AND NONDENOMINATIONAL AGENCIES AND CHRISTIAN EDUCATION

## *Marvin J. Taylor*

THE OVERWHELMING MAJORITY OF CHRISTIAN EDUCATION PROGRAMS OCCUR in the local churches of the United States. Of course, there are exceptions; such as, summer camping, campus ministries, etc., as described in other chapters of this volume. But their comparative infrequency, as well as the relatively fewer numbers of persons reached, serves further to illustrate the primacy of the local parish in Christian nurture.

This fact of programming must not be misunderstood, however. It does not imply that interest and work in Christian education are confined solely to the individual congregation. Every denomination maintains, under one name or another, a national board of education which is ordinarily charged with responsibility for devising and recommending program patterns and producing the leadership development and curriculum materials needed for their implementation in the churches. Often these staffs of educators are quite well trained and thoroughly professional in the discharge of their duties. Thus, while any program proposed will probably be carried out in a local church, the entire denomination has usually established the program and supports the local leadership with a wide variety of services and publications. The extent of this influence is perhaps best illustrated by the fact that on any given Sunday most teachers of a particular age-group within a denomination will have read the same teacher guidebooks in preparation for the same teaching-learning experiences. There is usually this kind of unity within a denomination. To be sure, the degree of effective implementation will vary widely, but there has been much national planning and guidance.

It must not be presumed from this description, however, that there is no uniformity or coordination beyond the individual denomination. For there are numerous other agencies, both inter- and nondenominational, holding major interest in the work of Christian education. It is the purpose of this chapter to survey the contributions which the more important ones make to the programs carried on in local churches.

## Local and State Councils of Churches

Cooperative concern for Christian education has a long history in American Protestantism. As noted in chapter 2,[1] "Sunday school unions" can be traced back to the late eighteenth century in the major Eastern cities. State unions

---

[1] See above, pp. 26-27.

quickly followed, and in 1824 national coordination culminated in the American Sunday School Union. Today the cooperative local and state functions in Christian education are being performed by the many local and state councils of churches. In August, 1964, the latest date for which statistics are available, there were 340 councils—state and local—with *paid* staff,[2] to which must be added numerous others operating with volunteer personnel.

A local council of churches is a creature of the local congregations within its geographical area. It has been organized in response to the desire of these Christians to demonstrate their unity and to work together on some common tasks. Thus, city councils are formed by official actions of local church boards upon which they are dependent for financial support. While in a sense each council is autonomous, i.e., no other council (state or national) has authority over it, it is functionally responsible to its constituting churches. The basic needs which the churches felt, the goals which they set, will provide the guidelines for the council structure and program. It represents the churches as their organization.

In the field of Christian education local councils have inherited many functions from their predecessors in the Sunday school movement. In fact, especially in the East, the education department of many city councils was formerly the county (or city) Sunday (or Sabbath) school association which merged with other local Protestant bodies to form a single entity—the city council of churches. Their educational programs bear many of the familiar titles: leadership development; children's, youth, and adult work; audio-visual education; vacation church school; weekday religious education; Protestant scouting; Christian higher education; etc. Not all of these will be found in every council, of course. Each must first determine what its constituency desires and needs; programming then can follow. For example, if several churches, or groups of churches, plan to use the interdenominational Cooperative Publication Association's vacation church school curriculum, the council can perform a most useful service for the churches. Laboratory schools, where printed materials may be introduced and their use demonstrated, can be held for prospective teachers; workshops for administrators may be offered; and other similar guidance provided. On the other hand, if different denominational curriculums are selected, there is little that a council's education department can do. Leadership development then becomes the task of the various denominations.

In recent years city councils have been undergoing searching and often painful self-analysis. Churches are no less prone than other organizations to perpetuate indefinitely any function once adopted, even when the circumstances which called it into existence no longer remain. Christian education functions have been equally guilty. For example, at the turn of the century and in the following decades large-scale, city-wide leadership schools were quite common, often with hundreds of persons participating. But there were few, and often no, denominational schools in existence then. Today the conditions are reversed.

[2] Benson Y. Landis, ed., *Yearbook of American Churches* (New York: National Council of Churches, 1965), p. 111.

Every denomination is engaged the year around in regional leadership training programs for its churches, and they are directly competitive with the councils' long-established schools. This illustrates the rethinking which has been forced on councils. As their constituent churches' needs change, so council programs must be altered. At the present many councils are performing far fewer Christian education functions than was true twenty or thirty years ago. This is *not* a sign of council weakness; rather, it reflects the ability of council leadership and staff to engage in meaningful self-analysis and shift both focus and program to meet new needs and abandon those which are now met by other organizations. In these periods of self-study councils often find it possible to pioneer for the churches in new areas. The Christian education of exceptional persons, particularly retarded children, is one area of great need in which some councils are doing excellent experimental work.[3] At the present time regional agencies of the denominations are much more active in Christian education than ever before, and this has inevitably influenced the kind of contribution which a council of churches is called upon to make to its members.

Much of the foregoing description is also accurate for the state councils of churches. Their clientele is, of course, different, being composed of state denominational units, i.e., conferences, synods, etc., rather than local churches. But their functions are very similar. Just as the local churches of a city have need to do some things together, so also at the state level. This is particularly true when Protestantism needs to speak with a united voice to the state government in matters pertaining to religion and public education, church-state relations, and similar concerns. The shift in direction noted above for local councils in Christian education programming is also characteristic of most state councils. The once-famous state Sunday school conventions, largely promotional in nature and attracting thousands of enthusiasts, are much less in evidence today, their usefulness having been outlived. In their place are dozens, and often hundreds, of more effective local programs sponsored often by denominations but also frequently by the state council of churches. It must be noted again that this is not a criticism of the state councils. Circumstances have radically changed, and programs must conform to needs.

## The National Council of Churches

Few persons in local churches, often including the ministers, realize the valuable role played by the National Council of Churches (N.C.C.) in the support of their local program. The most obvious example of this support is in the realm of curriculum materials. Since 1872 uniform lessons have been structured on outlines developed by the N.C.C.'s predecessors, the International Sunday School Association and the International Council of Religious Education.[4] In 1908 graded outlines were added to these services, and until recently the great majority of denominations have constructed almost all of their curriculum publications on one or both of these foundations. Thus, the church

[3] See chap. 22, pp. 256-67.
[4] See chaps. 2, 14, and 27.

school materials which most local churches have used each Sunday have had their origin in the work of the Council.

The Council was organized in 1950 through a merger of numerous individual interdenominational agencies. Up to this date each of these separate bodies had served the churches only in some single area of cooperative work; i.e., missions, Christian education, higher education, etc. The new Council was created to unite and coordinate all Protestant and Orthodox endeavors. Currently the Council is organized in four functional divisions (Christian Life and Mission, Christian Education, Overseas Ministries, and Christian Unity) with some supporting units (Planning and Program, Communication, and Administration).

The Division of Christian Education itself was created in 1950 as the result of a merger. The former International Council of Religious Education, the Missionary Education Movement, the National Protestant Council on Higher Education, the Interseminary Movement, as well as some of the student Christian organizations (which affiliated with the Division as "related movements"), are now incorporated in the Division. The by-laws of the Council, which have been frequently amended since 1950, now charge the Division of Christian Education with responsibility to:

a) Develop, initiate, and where suitable carry out programs to extend the use of the Bible.
b) Develop and conduct cooperative study, research, experimentation, and programs to assist the churches in:
i. Their total educational task, in the home, local church, and community, including programs of parish education for all ages, weekday church schools, leadership training, cooperative Christian education endeavors, and the development of standards and objectives for Christian education.
ii. Their responsibility to strengthen marriage and family life through programs of education, counseling, and guidance, and through advocacy of adequate laws and sound public policies.
iii. Their enlistment and education of pastors, for both parish and special ministries, and of layworkers in church-related occupations; and the promotion and development of continuing education and clinical training programs for parish and institutional ministries.
iv. Their responsibility to assist all Christians in selecting and preparing for a vocation, emphasizing that all are called to repentance, faith, and to mission and service in and to the world.
c) Prepare, provide for publication, and promote the use of special educational books and other materials in support of annual thematic and special program emphases.
d) Assist the churches in their concerns for all of higher education and academic scholarship; foster relations between the churches and colleges, universities and theological seminaries, including their administrators, faculties, and students; and develop and promote campus programs and projects.[5]

The governing body of the Division is a Program Board composed of official representatives of the member denominations, councils of churches, affiliated

[5] By-laws of the National Council of the Churches of Christ in the United States of America (approved by the General Board, June 1, 1964; effective January 1, 1965), Part VI, paragraph 2d(2).

agencies, related movements, and other participating bodies. This program board fulfills the duties outlined above through a series of standing committees (chiefly with administrative functions) and four major departments (Educational Development; Education for Mission; Higher Education; and Ministry, Vocation, and Pastoral Services). These departments are organized into commissions, committees, etc. for the accomplishment of their assigned functions, as follows:

*Department of Educational Development*
    Commission on Children's Education
    Commission on Youth Education
    Commission on Adult Education
    Commission on Marriage and Family Life
    Commission on Administration and Leadership
    Commission on Curriculum Development
    Commission on the Church and Public Education
    Commission on Educational Media
    *The International Journal of Religious Education*
*Department of Education for Mission*
    Committee on Children's Work
    Committee on Youth Work
    Committee on Adult Work
    Committee on Special Mission Education Resources
    Production Department
    Order Fulfillment Department
*Department of Higher Education*
    Issues in Higher Education
    Legislation and Public Policy
    Communication
    Theological Study and Teaching
    Faculty Interests
    National Staff for Campus Christian Life
    Fay Campbell Lectureship
    Acting Editorial Board for *The Christian Scholar*
    *Christian Scholar* Study Committee
    Advisory Committee on Educational Opportunities
    Committee on Church-Related Colleges Founded for Negroes
*Department of Ministry, Vocation, and Pastoral Services*
    Committee on Church Ministries
    Committee on Vocation
    Committee on Pastoral Services

Perhaps one of the best-known services of the Division has been the Revised Standard Version of the Bible. The work in preparation for this translation was begun in the 1930's under the auspices of the International Council of Religious Education, and the first stage of completion was reached with the publication of the New Testament in 1946. Six years later, in 1952, the full Bible became available with the completion of the Old Testament. Subsequently a Revised Standard Version of the Apocrypha has appeared. A Roman Catholic Edition of the R.S.V. New Testament was published in mid-1965, and a Catholic adaptation of the Old Testament, including the deuterocanonical books, is anticipated in the future. Since 1950 the I.C.R.E.'s interest in Bible translation has been incorporated into the Division's program. The Revised Standard Bible Committee is in charge of the basic text, and general policies are recommended by the R.S.V. Bible Policies Committee. Through contracts made with the Division six publishers are now authorized to issue the R.S.V. Bible.

In the field of curriculum development the most significant recent achievement has been the Cooperative Curriculum Project. Growing out of a study which was initially sponsored by the uniform lessons committee in the 1950's, sixteen denominations worked together in the C.C.P. between 1960 and 1964. The purpose of the project was the formulation of a curriculum design which might be of significant use to the denominations in their future planning of curriculum.[6] It is, of course, much too early to assess the value of this endeavor, but the project itself is clear illustration of the kind of cooperative enterprise which the numerous denominations can undertake through the central coordinating facilities of the Council's Division of Christian Education.

As Gerald E. Knoff, the Council's Associate General Secretary for Christian Education has written, "One will never understand the Division of Christian Education unless he understands it as a thoroughly representative agent of the educational forces of the Protestant and Orthodox churches of the United States and Canada. . . . It is not a free-wheeling agency with the freedom which independence makes possible." [7] Just as local and state councils function within boundaries set by the expectations and desires of their membership, so the National Council. As has been noted, its very structures are designed to foster this type of program. The Commission on Children's Work of the Department of Educational Development, as an example, brings together children's work specialists from many denominations. Within the framework of this commission they are able to communicate with one another, share problems and experiences, engage in research, and in various other ways carry forward their common duties in a cooperative manner. The numerous other committees and commissions of the Division provide similar opportunities for the specialists in their areas of educational work. The publication program of the Division is designed to support these endeavors by making available to the churches at large the results of their labors. The Associated Sections of the Division bring together professional Christian education personnel in annual meetings for similar purposes, often the sole opportunity for interdenominational contact available to these persons.

In summary, the Division's goal is to provide a structural framework whereby the denominations can do together those things which they cannot do separately. It has no program which is its own, apart from, or set over

---

[6] For full details on the Cooperative Curriculum Project, see chap. 14, pp. 160-62.

[7] "Christian Education and the National Council of Churches," in *Religious Education: A Comprehensive Survey*, Marvin J. Taylor, ed. (Nashville: Abingdon Press, 1960), p. 346.

against the denominations. The Council's program is established through its representative procedures; and once established, it is the program of the member denominations as well. To observers this is often a slow, cumbersome process. Nothing happens rapidly, and to the uninvolved observer, during those interim periods in which proposals are being evaluated, it sometimes appears as if nothing at all is ever accomplished! But, despite these lengthy and complicated procedures, decisions are ultimately made and programs of significance are actually launched. When one does emerge, it is the product of many individuals' and agencies' careful study. This is the manner by which the Division best serves the interests of the churches.

## World Council of Christian Education

International cooperative interest in Christian education dates back to the late nineteenth century. In 1889 the first World Sunday School Convention was held in London under the joint auspices of the International Sunday School Association (the United States and Canada) and the National Sunday School Union (England and Wales). Subsequent meetings occurred every few years, and at the World Convention of 1907 held in Rome the World Sunday School Association was formed. Its administrative functions were divided between British and North American committees, and the work of the W.S.S.A. was chiefly the support of the Christian education aspect of the total task of world evangelism. Recognizing the fact that Christian education is a much broader enterprise than Sunday school work, in 1947 the Association changed its name to the World Council of Christian Education, adding "and Sunday School Association" in 1950. From 1947 to 1954 the work of W.C.C.E.S.S.A. was done primarily through British and North American Administrative Committees, with a World Office being established in 1954. In 1965 the Board of Managers acted to unify the administration of the Council in Geneva, Switzerland, where the major program staff will be located. A series of regional committees have been organized around the world, and much of the Council's work will now be done through and in cooperation with them. Membership in W.C.C.E.S.S.A. is composed of national Christian councils, councils of churches, councils of Christian education, and other equivalent bodies, including denominational boards of education.

The Council cooperates closely with the World Council of Churches in its work around the world. Since 1948 when the latter was organized, the World Youth Projects activity has been a jointly sponsored program. Both also carry on individual functions, including the well-known ecumenical work camps, the organization of youth groups, and the devising of suitable program materials. A Joint Commission with W.C.C. on the nature and meaning of education was established recently and held its first meeting in 1964.

Early in its history W.S.S.A. looked forward to the establishment of a single, uniform Christian education curriculum for worldwide Christendom. But it soon became evident that cultural differences made this impossible, even in the United States and England. Despite their relatively similar heritages, they were unable to use the same lessons. Today W.C.C.E.S.S.A. recognizes the crucial importance of indigenously produced materials, and the Council lends its services and support to various areas of the world which are engaged in such work. Nine indigenous curricula in Asia, Africa, Latin America, the Near East, and the South Pacific have been major concerns. Its "Christian Education Guide" on "The Preparation of Curriculum Materials" has been particularly useful, as is the quarterly journal, *World Christian Education*. This latter publication serves as a vehicle for sharing ideas, information, and experiences among Christian education workers around the world.

Another major emphasis of W.C.C.E.S.S.A. is in leadership development. In many underdeveloped lands the majority of schools were Christian schools operated as day schools by the churches. Often they were isolated from congregational life, having an independent existence. Thus, many churches offered no direct Christian education programs, leaving this phase of Christian work to the schools. With the coming of freedom and independence, many of these newer nations assumed control of these schools, and they have become secular in nature. This has left a considerable Christian education void. Today the churches are finding serious need for training leadership to institute new programs of congregation-sponsored Christian education, and the Council is participating in this work in a wide variety of ways. Through all of these methods the W.C.C.E.S.S.A. fulfills its objective of supporting Christian education's growth through the world.

## Religious Education Association

One of the oldest and the most significant of the nondenominational organizations is The Religious Education Association. Established in 1903 as a Protestant movement, through the years the Association has gradually altered its membership patterns. Today it is a genuinely multifaith society with individual members from Judaism, Roman Catholicism, and Protestantism. Since membership is open only to individuals, not organizations, each represents only himself in the Association. In a very real sense R.E.A. was started as a protest movement. Protestant Sunday schools were largely evangelistic in nature, and they tended to ignore almost completely scholarly research and insight in both theology and education. Biblical scholarship had added much to man's understanding of the Scriptures, as had educators to the knowledge of pupils and of learning. But the Sunday schools were run by volunteer lay people who generally knew very little of these areas of knowledge and often were antagonistic. The Association promised to be both scientific and pioneering, always searching for new understanding and for better methods and philosophies of religious nurture. One of its early calls was for a trained profession of religious educators who would work full-time in churches, denominational boards of education, and nationally in the organizations responsible for educational programs. R.E.A.'s pressure for such leadership was one of the factors producing the thoroughly professional International Council of Religious Education in 1922.

Another early proclamation of the Association concerned the breadth or comprehensiveness of religious education. In 1903 religious education and

Sunday school work were deemed to be coextensive. R.E.A. insisted that this was an inadequate definition, and it established departments to deal with religious education in universities and colleges, seminaries, public schools, private schools, Y.M. and Y.W.C.A.'s, the home, summer camps, and other such agencies. Its insistence included the need for coordination among all of these educational institutions, a concern unrecognized by the International Sunday School Association and not finally implemented by the churches until the I.C.R.E. was created in the 1920's. Of such has been R.E.A.'s pioneering spirit.

The decades of the 1930's and 1940's were critical years for the Association. The economic depression forced many professional religious educators to seek work in other fields, and the membership of R.E.A. dwindled. During some of these years only its journal, *Religious Education* (which was founded in 1906), remained active. But following World War II the need for a vital Association was obvious to many religious educators, and a concentrated effort at revitalization was undertaken. With generous financial support from foundations it opened offices in New York City, employed a General Secretary and office staff, and began to regain a strong, professionally responsible membership from all three faith groups.

In the mid-1960's the Association pursues its current program in a number of ways. (1) The journal, *Religious Education,* issued bi-monthly, enjoys wide respect as the most substantial publication in the field. It regularly carries significant symposia and articles on all issues confronting churches and synagogues in religious education, and its contributors are usually among the recognized experts from Judaism and Christianity. (2) Periodically the Association holds national conventions on urgent religious and moral issues of the day. The 50th Anniversary Convention was held in Pittsburgh in the fall of 1953, followed by others in 1957 and 1962. Another is planned for 1966. The conventions regularly attract several hundred persons from all three faiths; including religious, professional, and academic leaders. (3) Through its standing committees, particularly Higher Education and Research, there is continued pioneering work being done. The field of research illustrates this quite clearly. Recognizing that research in religious education had lagged far behind that being done in the social sciences, the Association received financial support from a major foundation to assist research efforts. An extended research training seminar was held, with prominent social science consultants assisting, and substantial grants continue to be available for religious education personnel who wish to enhance their skill as researchers. In 1964 the Association added to its staff a Director of Research who will coordinate this program for the improvement of the quality of religious programs in churches and synagogues. (4) In the fall of 1965 R.E.A. began an active promotion of local chapters in cities and counties across the nation. With the addition of an Associate General Secretary to the staff, this became a major concern of the Association. Most cities do possess ample existing organizations *within* faith groups for communication and mutual sharing among religious educators, but few have any local equivalent to the national R.E.A. membership pattern. Since religious education must take place at the local level if it is to be significant at all, this emphasis in the Association's work will be a valuable adjunct to the current efforts of synagogues and churches. These are some of the chief ways that The Religious Education Association seeks to strengthen interfaith work in religious education in America.

## The Church and Youth-Serving Agencies

A major blind spot in the planning and programming with youth in many churches is a tendency to view this in isolation from its context. Churches and their leaders often act and think imperialistically, at least implying that they alone have the right to the young person's free, out-of-school hours. This ignores the fact that there are scores of youth-serving organizations which exist alongside the churches with goals that are thoroughly compatible with the church's objectives. Failing to understand this, churchmen frequently view these agencies as competitors rather than allies in the effort to provide children and youth with the opportunity to "realize their full potential for a creative life in freedom and dignity."

Many of these agencies have no explicit religious goals, yet the values inherent in their work should be recognized and appreciated by the churches. But others are formally committed to religious perspectives, and their relationship with Christian education can and should be strengthened. Five of these agencies originated largely within the Protestant tradition, and their work is clearly complementary. These are Camp Fire Girls, Boy Scouts, Girl Scouts, Young Men's Christian Association, and Young Women's Christian Association. The Camp Fire Girls and both of the Scouting groups have provision for local-church sponsorship, and the program of the Y's in many communities is also carried out in relation to and cooperation with church leaders. But despite these provisions, the isolation from one another and consequent sense of competition noted above tends to continue.

The first significant efforts at coordination were begun at the national level with the establishment of the Committee on Church and Agency Relationships in Work with Children and Youth. Holding membership on the Committee are official representatives from the five agencies, National Council of Churches personnel, and some denominational educational leaders. The Committee has issued various materials designed to assist in community coordination, including a *Church-Agency Relationships* manual. The *International Journal of Religious Education* contains occasional articles on this topic, and one special issue of the journal (September, 1958) was devoted entirely to the work of the agencies and churches.

A major effort of the national Committee during the decade of the 1960's has been work in local communities. In several metropolitan areas church-agency conferences have been arranged, often providing the first opportunity that leaders have had to become acquainted and converse about their respective tasks. For example, in one Eastern city an *ad hoc* committee worked for several months arranging an all-day conference. About 150 persons from all five agencies and local churches were present. The basic program structures of each were presented, and neighborhood-community conversation groups were included. From this one-day experience several community church-agency coordinating committees emerged. The ongoing product of this work has been a new sense of total community involvement and support for work with children and youth and a corresponding diminution in the feeling of frustration which results from a false sense of isolation from and competition with others who are engaged in similar activities with the same youth.

The need for this coordination has been well stated by Ralph N. Mould:

> Leaders of other programs for children and youth need to be informed about the agency groups. Often there appear ways that leaders can correlate and supplement one another's efforts, and avoid conflicts in ideas and scheduling. It is not enough that leaders simply clear schedules with each other. The place of the club program in the whole life of the members will be sensed by the boys and girls most meaningfully if the leaders have discussed basic philosophy and goals together. There must come into being a deep awareness that the leaders are all on one team, working for the full development of the children and youth.[8]

## In Conclusion

In this chapter we have explored some of the major organizations beyond the local church whose work is of importance to Christian education. It should be noted, however, that not all of Protestantism is served by these councils and agencies. Some branches of American Protestantism, particularly those which are theologically quite conservative, for one reason or another decline to be affiliated with the various councils of churches. Many of this latter group do maintain rather loose working ties—without formal membership in the National Council of Churches—with the Division of Christian Education and use its curriculum resources and other services. Others choose to work cooperatively through the National Sunday School Association and the National Association of Evangelicals. The reader's attention is called to the full discussion of these agencies in chapter 27.

All of these interdenominational and nondenominational agencies for Christion education exist for only one purpose. They seek to support, strengthen, and improve the quality of nurture in the Christian life which is available to persons. As such, they merit the understanding and interest of every leader whose responsibilities in the church are related to Christian education in any way.

### FOR ADDITIONAL READING

Bower, William C. and Hayward, Percy R. *Protestantism Faces Its Educational Task Together*. New York: National Council of Churches, 1950.

Chappel, Nelson. "The World Council of Christian Education and the World Council of Churches," in *Religious Education: A Comprehensive Survey*, ed. Marvin J. Taylor. Nashville: Abingdon Press, 1960. Pp. 350-58.

---

[8] "Top Drawer Leadership Needed," *International Journal of Religious Education*, XXXV (September, 1958), 9.

Hakes, J. Edward, ed. *An Introduction to Evangelical Christian Education.* Chicago: Moody Press, 1964.

Knoff, Gerald E. "Christian Education and the National Council of Churches," in *Religious Education: A Comprehensive Survey,* ed. Marvin J. Taylor. Pp. 338-49.

Wornom, Herman E. "The Religious Education Association," *Religious Education,* LVIII (September-October, 1963), 443-52.

## Chapter 27

# EVANGELICAL CHRISTIAN EDUCATION AND THE PROTESTANT DAY-SCHOOL MOVEMENT

## J. Edward Hakes

"WHEN I USE A WORD," HUMPTY-DUMPTY SAYS TO ALICE IN *Through the Looking Glass,* "it means just what I choose it to mean—neither more nor less." So it is with the term "evangelical." According to the most recent edition of the *Yearbook of American Churches,* at least twenty-three differing Protestant communions have incorporated the word into their denominational names. A religious lexicographer says that "the term has meanings, some of which are vague." [1] Therefore, without doing violence to language, it seems permissible to use the term "evangelical" throughout this presentation as referring to that sector of American Protestantism which is either affiliated with or in substantial agreement with the doctrinal position and/or the cooperative program of the National Association of Evangelicals.

The NAE, founded in 1942, [2] is a fellowship of evangelicals rather than a council of churches. It unites thirty-four denominations, hundreds of local churches from thirty additional denominations, and many individuals, on the basis of its statement of faith. Membership now exceeds two million, and the organization claims to serve a constituency of more than ten million through its commissions and affiliated service agencies.

Direct involvement in the field of Christian education is through its Education Commission, which is one of the Association's eleven commissions, and through the National Association of Christian Schools, the National Sunday School Association, and the North American Association of Bible Institutes and Bible Colleges which are among the organization's five official affiliates. There are, however, other educational organizations which, although not organically related to the NAE, function within, or at least in significantly close proximity to, its framework.

### Basic Theological Tenets

If there is one factor above all others which tends to unite evangelicals, it is their common acceptance of historically orthodox Christian doctrine. Whatever else one may find in the literature of their organizations and institutions,

[1] Vergilius Ferm, *A Protestant Dictionary* (New York: Philosophical Library, 1951), p. 90.
[2] The story of the Association's beginnings and early history is told in James DeForest Murch's *Cooperation Without Compromise* (Grand Rapids: Wm. B. Eerdmans Publishing Co., 1956).

a detailed setting forth of theological beliefs is always prominently present. Adherence to a conservative creed is looked upon as a prime essential.

The theological concepts which evangelicals tend to hold in common have been embodied in the Statement of Faith of the NAE:

(1) We believe the Bible to be the inspired, the only infallible, authoritative Word of God.

(2) We believe that there is one God, eternally existent in three Persons: Father, Son, and Holy Spirit.

(3) We believe in the deity of our Lord Jesus Christ, in His virgin birth, in His sinless life, in His miracles, in His vicarious and atoning death through His shed blood, in His bodily resurrection, in His ascension to the right hand of the Father and in His personal return in power and glory.

(4) We believe that for the salvation of lost and sinful man regeneration by the Holy Spirit is absolutely essential.

(5) We believe in the present ministry of the Holy Spirit by whose indwelling the Christian is enabled to live a godly life.

(6) We believe in the resurrection of both the saved and the lost; they that are saved unto the resurrection of life and they that are lost unto the resurrection of damnation.

(7) We believe in the spiritual unity of believers in our Lord Jesus Christ.[3]

It is impossible to understand evangelicals and their approach to any undertaking, including Christian education, without recognizing how seriously they take their beliefs. Unequivocal affirmation of an orthodox creedal statement is the characteristic which all evangelical educators have in common.

## Unique Educational Outlook

Since evangelicals believe that in Christian nurture "one's philosophy is influenced by his theology," [4] it is not surprising that evangelical educational philosophies differ from those of Christian educators who operate within other theological frames of reference. Thus, a peculiarly evangelical way of looking at education has emerged which is appropriate to evangelical beliefs.

The very *aims* which the educative process is to achieve are affected, for example. It is only within the framework of distinctively evangelical ideas about sin and salvation that "the first aim of Christian education must be defined in terms of evangelism." [5] Anything less than bringing the learner to an acceptance of Jesus Christ as Lord and Savior would be a serious dereliction of duty for the educator who holds to evangelical convictions about the state of man apart from Christ. Not only does evangelism demonstrate Christian compassion for the lost, but genuine spiritual nurture is impossible without the initiation of spiritual life through the divine miracle of regeneration.

To portray evangelicals as insisting that evangelism is the sole aim of Chris-

[3] *Constitution of the National Association of Evangelicals*, pp. 1, 2.

[4] C. B. Eavey, "Aims and Objectives of Christian Education," in *An Introduction to Evangelical Christian Education*, J. Edward Hakes, ed. (Chicago: Moody Press, 1964), p. 51.

[5] Frank E. Gaebelein, *Christian Education in a Democracy* (New York: Oxford University Press, 1951), p. 30.

tian education, however, is to caricature them. While the individual's response to the gospel is primary and paramount, "the second function of Christian education is that of nurture. . . . Those who are born again into the family of God must be nourished that they may grow." [6] The ultimate goal "is the man of God perfected in character and conduct until he is like Christ." [7]

The *curriculum* by which such objects are to be achieved is also affected. Because evangelicals hold the Bible to be the written Word of God, it naturally follows that it should be "the core of the curriculum." [8] It is of the highest importance that the eternal truths of God set forth in propositional form in the canonical Scriptures should be learned.

Yet the mere knowledge of Bible content is not the whole story. As Eavey says, "Subject matter is never an end in itself but always a means to an end; it is the basis for activity through which the pupil may grow and develop." [9] Although there may have been a day when the Bible was used as a textbook, selected contents of which were merely to be memorized, today it is considered by evangelicals to be an essential and irreplaceable source of dynamic life-changing truths concerning God, which, along with other means, is used to direct pupil experience along the path of continuing spiritual maturation.

The concept of the *learning process* is influenced as well. Evangelicals hold that man was made in the image of his Creator and therefore is able to think God's thoughts after God. Admittedly, the *imago Dei* has been seriously impaired by the Fall, but, although "we see through a glass darkly," we still can, nevertheless, see. On this basis the learner is capable of receiving and comprehending divine revelation.

But he is not left altogether on his own in this. God himself is directly involved in the dynamics of learning. The Holy Spirit is the ultimate Teacher. Personal interaction of an I-Thou kind occurs. The evangelical Christian educator is confident that he can rely upon such supernatural activity apart from which no real learning of divinely given truth can take place. [10]

## Organizations Active in Evangelical Christian Education

Evangelicals utilize a full complement of educational agencies, including church schools, Sunday evening youth groups, weekday clubs, vacation Bible schools, camps and conferences. Where the size of the congregation warrants it, they employ directors of Christian education. As far as structure is concerned, they resemble the typical Protestant church in the learning opportunities provided for their constituencies.

Certain organizations, however, which function in the field of Christian

---

[6] *Ibid.*, p. 31.

[7] Eavey, "Aims and Objectives of Christian Education," p. 56.

[8] Peter P. Person, *An Introduction to Christian Education* (Grand Rapids: Baker Book House, 1958), p. 72.

[9] "Aims and Objectives of Christian Education," p. 61.

[10] On the basis of his understanding of biblical statements such as I Cor. 2:14.

education, have become prominently identified with the evangelical cause. Representative of these are the following.

## National Sunday School Association

An affiliate of the NAE, the National Sunday School Association was formed in Chicago during May, 1945, by one hundred publishers' representatives and educational leaders from the evangelical ranks. Meeting at the call of the NAE's Church School Commission, they had as a purpose to create a new system of Uniform Sunday School Lessons which would be acceptable to evangelicals. The first national convention was held in the Moody Church, Chicago, in the fall of 1946 with 4,000 in attendance from thirty-five states and two Canadian provinces.[11]

Although a Uniform Lesson series was adopted at the 1946 convention, it never gained widespread popularity because of the prevailing preference among evangelicals for graded curricular materials. Much more significant and far-reaching in its effect was the organizing of the NSSA itself with its dedication to "revitalizing the Sunday schools of America." [12] As the Simpsons, both leaders in the movement, have described it:

Its efforts to accomplish this objective have resulted in the organization of fifty Sunday school associations on local, state and regional levels. Special emphases are observed annually, such as National Youth Week, March to Sunday School in March, National Family Week, and National Sunday School Week. Six commissions have been activated to expedite development in the total field of Christian education: Youth Commission, Research Commission, Camp Commission, Commission for Denominational Secretaries, Publishers Commission, and the National Association of Directors of Christian Education. Much instructional and promotional literature has been produced. Annual conventions, emphasizing inspiration and instruction, have attracted representation from ninety-one denominations.[13]

Since 1955 twin national conventions have been held annually, one in the eastern section of the United States and the other in the western. Attendance at these gatherings has increased steadily, and an infectious enthusiasm prevails which, when carried back home to the local churches, has undoubtedly contributed to the phenomenal numerical growth of the evangelical church schools.

## Evangelical Teacher Training Association

Operating as an independent and nondenominational organization, the Evangelical Teacher Training Association provides preparation for leadership roles in evangelical Christian education for both professionals and lay people. It began in 1930 when Clarence H. Benson and James M. Gray, both of the Moody Bible Institute, invited representatives from five sister institutions to meet in Chicago

---

[11] Elmo H. Warkentin, "The History of 'Revitalizing the Sunday Schools of America' Through the National Sunday School Association" (unpublished Master's thesis, Wheaton College, 1958), p. 74.

[12] Edward D. Simpson and Frances F. Simpson, "The Sunday School," in Hakes, An Introduction to Evangelical Christian Education, p. 299.

[13] Ibid.

for the purpose of forming an evangelical counterpart to the Standard Leadership Training Curriculum of the International Council of Religious Education. Currently the active membership is composed of approximately one hundred institutions of higher learning, including about twenty in Canada and three overseas. In addition, there is an affiliate membership of forty local community schools of adult Christian education.

The ETTA provides three courses of study: (1) the Standard Training Course, offered only in its active member schools, which requires a minimum of 180 class hours of Bible and 252 class hours of Christian education and which leads to the granting of the Teachers Diploma, the Association's highest award; (2) the Advanced Certificate Course, offered by its affiliate member schools, which requires a total of 144 class hours—36 in Bible survey and the remainder in ETTA-prepared courses in child study, pedagogy, Sunday school success, the missionary enterprise, Sunday school evangelism, Bible doctrine, vacation Bible school, and biblical introduction—and which leads to the awarding of the Advanced Teachers Certificate; and (3) the Preliminary Certificate Course, given by local churches and community classes, which requires 72 class hours of study—36 in Bible survey and the rest in child study, pedagogy, and Sunday school success—and which leads to the granting of the Preliminary Teachers Certificate. All textbooks are prepared by the ETTA and are revised periodically.

### Christian Service Brigade and Pioneer Girls

Christian Service Brigade, an organization for boys which functions along lines comparable to the Boy Scouts, but with a strong emphasis on the Bible, began in a Glen Ellyn, Illinois, church in 1937. It now has over two thousand chartered units in more than twelve hundred churches. The Battalion, for boys 12-18, offers two programs: (1) Adventure Trails, for boys 12-14 with graduated ranks of Observer, Explorer, Trailblazer, and Guide; and (2) Frontier Trails, for boys 15-18 with options in seven fields—Airman, Craftsman, Landsman, Mariner, Sportsman, Technician, and Woodsman—wherein, by completing the requirements in any one area, a boy is eligible to work toward becoming a Herald of Christ, the highest recognition in Brigade achievement. The Stockade, for boys 8-11, also has two programs: (1) Builder, for boys 8-9, with achievement units called Blockhouses; and (2) Sentinel, for boys 10-11, with achievement units called Stations.

Besides regular weekly meetings, the Brigade operates numerous summer camps, sponsors regional conferences for adult and peer group leaders, and publishes two periodicals: *Venture,* a monthly magazine for boys; and *Brigade Leader* for the men who work with local units. Distinctive uniforms and attractive guidebooks, *Brigade Trails* and *Stockaders Log,* round out a program for growth through activity which is being sponsored by evangelical churches in all but three states of the country.

Pioneer Girls, a sister organization to the Brigade although not organically joined to it, was begun by Betty Whitaker, a college student, in 1939. Over fifteen hundred churches now have adopted its program and more than eighty thousand girls are enrolled. Members are grouped into three divisions: (1)

Pilgrims, for third through sixth grades; (2) Colonists, for seventh through ninth grades; and (3) Explorers, for tenth through twelfth grades. Achievement programs are provided in several fields, including nature lore, woodcraft, sports, cooking, photography, and community service, as well as in missions and Bible exploration.

Augmenting the activities of the local church units, there are more than twenty summer camps, the magazine *Trails*, and an involvement in foreign missions which has sent seven missionaries overseas, supported by the contributions of the members, and has created thirteen affiliated organizations in as many other countries. Specially designed uniforms, insignia articles, and handbooks serve as identifying symbols for the members.

### The Independent Publishers

A phenomenon peculiar to evangelical Christian education is the extraordinary growth of nondenominational publishers of curricular materials who have identified themselves with the evangelical movement. Several of these are prominent.

Scripture Press, begun in 1933 under the influence of Clarence H. Benson, has developed a comprehensive line of materials designed to cover every aspect of a church's educational need, under the name of the Total Church Program. Best known among its many publications are its All-Bible Graded Sunday School Lessons which are departmentally graded; its Training Hour Youth Program for Sunday evening youth groups; and its take-home Sunday school papers, *Bible Time* for four- and five-year-olds, *Primary Days* for six- to eight-year-olds, *Counsellor* for junior high age, *Teen Power* for high school age, and *Power for Living* for adults. Its teaching materials have been translated into six different languages.

Gospel Light Publications, founded in 1933 by Henrietta Mears, teacher of the college-age class in the First Presbyterian Church, Hollywood, California, serves a large part of the evangelical constituency with its "Living Word" Total Bible Teaching Plan materials. These are closely graded for pupils from age six to seventeen and departmentally graded for nursery, kindergarten, and adults. It publishes the Sunday school magazine *Teach* and the take-home papers *Tell-Me-Time* for kindergarten, *Story Treats* for primaries, *Adventure* for juniors, *Teen* for junior high and high school students, and *Light* for adults.

David C. Cook Publishing Company, founded in 1875, has for several generations published lesson outlines and commentaries based on the International Series. Recently it introduced its own Bible-in-Life Curriculum designed to cover the entire Bible every three years. It is departmentally graded, except for the primary and junior departments where the six-year span in the pupil's life is divided into three two-year periods. Accompanying these materials is the magazine *Leader* for Sunday school workers. Among other publications is the take-home paper *Sunday Pix,* done in a comic paper format, published in twenty-five languages and distributed in seventy-five countries, which has proved popular with boys and girls conditioned to the newspaper comic strips.

The American Sunday School Union, founded in 1817 and assuming its name and present structure in 1824, still issues its familiar single-sheet brief treatment of the International Sunday School Lesson Outlines, along with student workbooks for primary, junior, and intermediate ages. *The Sunday School World,* a magazine for teachers, and *The Sunday School Missionary,* which reports ASSU activities carried on by its 150 missionaries, both appear quarterly. The Union materials are used chiefly in the small rural Sunday schools.

The Christian Workers Service Bureau established in 1953, specializes in the production of materials for Sunday evening youth groups. On a subscription basis it offers churches materials based on the in-group leadership principle for the junior, junior high, and high school levels. Its junior-age program of Jet Cadets in particular is used in many evangelical churches.

### Denominational Programs

Where evangelical homogeneity exists within a denomination, the member churches tend to use the programs and materials of their own denominational publishing houses. Several of the larger NAE-affiliated denominations, such as the Assemblies of God and the Free Methodist Church, have developed curricula and materials which are thoroughly evangelical and which also promote their own denominational distinctives.

In addition, the Southern Baptist Convention and the Lutheran Church—Missouri Synod, although not connected with the NAE, have both developed comprehensive denominationally oriented curricula with a full complement of curricular materials. These two groups represent some of the best efforts in evangelical Christian education today. Their strong emphases on church-sponsored learning explains to a large extent their impressive numerical growth records and their denominational solidarity.

### Evangelical Day Schools

#### Rationale for a Separate School System

An increasing number of evangelicals, although willing as citizens to support the American institution of the free, tax-supported, compulsory public school, prefer to send their own children to Christian day schools. The fact that during the last seven years the number of schools of the Lutheran Church—Missouri Synod increased by approximately 20 percent, those affiliated with the National Union of Christian Schools by almost 45 percent, and those belonging to the National Association of Christian Schools by almost 100 percent, while the total enrollment of students in schools of all three groups increased during the same period by about 35 percent [14] indicates a significant trend among evangelicals toward providing complete educational opportunities for their children in schools operated under their own auspices.

The rationale for the existence of the evangelical-sponsored day schools has both a negative and a positive aspect. On the negative side, there is a growing

[14] The increase in public school enrollment for the same period was 27 percent. (See Kenneth A. Simon and W. Vance Grant, *Digest of Educational Statistics* [Washington: U.S. Department of Health, Education and Welfare, 1964] p. 6).

dissatisfaction with what appears to evangelicals to be a secularized public school system. The NAE committee on the philosophy and practice of Christian education reported, among its conclusions, that "as far as the philosophy of public education goes, secular naturalism is in the saddle." [15] Gordon H. Clark speaks for many of his fellow evangelicals when he claims that "the school system that ignores God teaches its pupils to ignore God, and this is not neutrality; it is the worst form of antagonism, for it judges God to be unimportant and irrelevant in human affairs." [16] Even attempts to provide religious instruction through such arrangements as released time are deemed to be unsuitable.[17] The decisions of the United States Supreme Court in the *Abington School District vs. Schempp* and *Murray vs. Curlett* cases completed the secularization process in the public schools, as far as many evangelicals are concerned.

On the positive side, a number of evangelicals feel that a distinctly Christian world-and-life view must permeate all education if it is to be pleasing to God. As the NAE committee stated, "revealed truth is not something to be added to education just to give it a coating of Christianity, but is rather the river bed in which educational experiences flow." [18] "A Christian philosophy of education," insists Clark, "must be elaborated against the background of a theistic world-view and on the basis of such pertinent principles and norms as are found in the Scriptures." [19] Arthur M. Ahlschwede, a spokesman for the Lutheran Church—Missouri Synod, points out that the Christian world-and-life view allows no distinction between the strictly "secular" and the strictly "sacred" and therefore makes necessary a kind of education that can be offered only through church-related day schools.[20] Thus, the argument runs that, given a unique view of life, this must of necessity lead to a compatible educational philosophy, and this, in turn, requires a school other than the public school which, by its own admission, cannot subscribe to such a philosophy.

### Organization

Most Protestant day schools operate under one of three different types of sponsorship. The identity of the controlling group provides the clue in classifying them.

The *parochial* school is controlled by the church or parish. The local congregation owns the facilities, sets the policies, and, through its appointed administrators, governs the conduct of everyday school affairs. In some churches the congregation delegates responsibility to a board which then assumes full authority for supervising the school.

The *parent-society* school is controlled by an organization composed of the parents of the students enrolled in the school. Often the members of the society come from different churches in the community in which the school is situated,

---

[15] Gaebelein, *Christian Education in a Democracy*, p. 23.
[16] *A Christian Philosophy of Education* (Grand Rapids: Wm. B. Eerdmans Publishing Co., 1946), p. 80.
[17] Gaebelein, *Christian Education in a Democracy*, p. 85.
[18] *Ibid.*, p. 283.
[19] *A Christian Philosophy of Education*, p. 164.
[20] "The Protestant Schools," *Phi Delta Kappan*, XLV (December, 1963), 136.

## Extent of the Movement

The extent to which the Protestant day school has grown is indicated in the following tables.

| | Elementary Schools 1964-1965[22] | | | Secondary Schools 1964-1965 | | |
|---|---|---|---|---|---|---|
| | Schools | Teachers | Enrollment | Schools | Teachers | Enrollment |
| **Baptist** | | | | | | |
| Los Angeles Baptist City Mission Society | 28 | 187 | 4,679 | 2 | — | 307 |
| Southern Baptist Convention | 44 | — | — | 12 | 237 | 3,479 |
| General Conference of Seventh-Day Adventists | 1,041 | 2,677 | 48,327 | 80 | 1,221 | 15,100 |
| General Council of Assemblies of God | 17 | 107 | 1,926 | 4 | 57 | 405 |
| **Lutheran** | | | | | | |
| American Lutheran Church | 57 | 273 | 6,351 | 3 | 36 | 534 |
| Church of the Lutheran Confession | 8 | 17 | 439 | 2 | 8 | 90 |
| Evangelical Lutheran Synod (Norwegian) | 12 | 14 | 278 | — | — | — |
| Lutheran Church in America | 16 | 89 | 1,830 | — | — | — |
| Lutheran Church—Missouri Synod | 1,381 | 6,132 | 160,630 | 32 | 558 | 12,328 |
| Synod of Evangelical Lutheran Churches | 2 | 7 | 188 | — | — | — |
| Wisconsin Evangelical Lutheran Synod | 227 | 879 | 24,457 | 13 | 186 | 3,499 |
| Mennonites | 244 | 389 | 10,061 | 12 | 179 | 2,140 |
| National Association of Christian Schools | 183 | 1,549 | 24,089 | 83 | 508 | 9,608 |
| National Union of Christian Schools | 236 | 1,747 | 46,738 | 32 | 490 | 10,253 |
| Protestant Episcopal Church | 236 | 2,220 | 20,157 | 110 | 2,730 | 28,300 |
| | 3,732 | 16,287 | 350,150 | 385 | 6,210 | 86,043 |

The strong trend toward establishing these day schools will no doubt continue and may indeed be accelerated during the next decade.

[22] These statistics are provided by the Board of Parish Education, The Lutheran Church—Missouri Synod.

although they do not officially represent their congregations. Those evangelicals who assign primary responsibility for the child's education to the home tend to prefer this kind of sponsorship.

The *private* school is controlled by a board of trustees, usually self-perpetuating, and frequently enrolls boarding students. Such a school is especially popular with evangelicals who either have no Christian day school available in their own community or who have both the financial ability and desire to send their children to a school where they can receive a college-preparatory education.

Many of these day schools have denominational affiliation. The Lutheran Church—Missouri Synod and the General Conference of Seventh-Day Adventists have sponsored schools for many years and are in positions of leadership, having built up impressive networks of schools. Other Lutheran communions—especially the Wisconsin Evangelical Lutheran Synod—also operate a large number of schools. The Mennonites and Protestant Episcopal Church are the only other denominations which are significantly involved in the day-school movement.

Those schools which are not associated with a denomination are usually affiliated with either the National Union of Christian Schools which was organized in 1920 or the National Association of Christian Schools which was created by the NAE in 1947. These two organizations hold in common many ideas about education and might have been joined together were it not for the rather exclusive Calvinistic position of the Union.[21]

## Problems to be Resolved

### Evangelical Education in General

a. *Development of a comprehensive philosophy.* Evangelicals have stopped short of spelling out fully their distinctive educational viewpoint. As a result many who are engaged in the evangelical Christian education program tend to operate according to pragmatic standards which evaluate success by attendance figures rather than by other more educationally defensible criteria.

b. *Creation of adequate aims and objectives.* Evangelism and Christian nurture are the broad aims to which evangelicals are committed, but there is need for elaborating what is involved in nurture and growth and for stating developmental progress in terms of changes in the learners' behavior. An adequate statement of both comprehensive and specific aims, comparable to what has been done by the National Council of Churches' Division of Christian Education, is needed by evangelicals.

c. *Wider acquaintance with learning theory.* Too few evangelicals have reckoned seriously with modern learning theory in order to devise curricula which are psychologically sound. There may be a tendency to forget that, although it is true that God is at work in the learning process, he may prefer that the student learn by those methods consistent with the way in which God himself has created the student.

[21] Gaebelein, *Christian Education in a Democracy,* p. 106.

d. *Preparation of professionals*. There is a scarcity of prepared professionals to serve as directors of Christian education in local evangelical churches. Although several evangelical colleges and seminaries offer adequate preparation in this field, the failure to give recognition and status to the profession and the practice of hiring directors of Christian education to serve as church handymen inhibit the process whereby competent personnel are attracted into the work.

e. *Training of lay personnel*. Too frequently the Christian education staff of the local evangelical church is composed of conscientious lay people whose zeal, no matter how admirable, cannot compensate for their lack of knowledge. While a few churches require that their workers receive some sort of training in preparation for their voluntary service, most churches are content to use well-intentioned, but unprepared, people.

### The Day-School Movement in Particular

a. *Formulation of a unique educational philosophy*. The Lutheran and Christian Reformed Churches have outdistanced other Protestant groups in developing a philosophy of Christian education for their day schools.[23] Too many of the others have been content merely to set forth their creedal affirmations without constructing a corresponding philosophy of education.

b. *Statement of aims and objectives*. An examination of the catalogs of the day schools reveals, in many cases, a failure to make explicit any aims and objectives which differ from those to which the public schools are committed. Some schools seem to promise students only that an education not significantly different from that offered in the local public school will be afforded them in a "safe" atmosphere in which standards of conduct approved by their own subculture are enforced. It is difficult to tell to what extent some of these schools are accomplishing their objectives, since they do not indicate what these objectives are.

c. *Upholding academic freedom*. Whether a teacher is able to follow the truth wherever it may lead him in these schools, despite the belief that all truth is of God, is open to serious question. The introduction of original ideas or of novel methods may not meet with the approval of a constituency which tends to be more or less traditional and is anxious to preserve continuity of a religious heritage.

d. *Evaluating results*. Disconcerting to the proponents of the day schools have been the findings of a series of empirical studies, made during the last few years, which tend to show that when other variables are kept constant, such as the influence of the family, there are no statistically significant differences between the graduates from the Protestant day schools and their evangelical counterparts who have attended the public schools.[24] The burden of proof now

[23] See, e.g., Donald Oppewal, *The Roots of the Calvinistic Day School Movement* (Grand Rapids: Calvin College, 1963) and William A. Kramer, *Lutheran Schools*, Information Bulletin on Christian Education, No. 301 (St. Louis: Board of Parish Education, Lutheran Church—Missouri Synod, 1964).

[24] S. M. Elam, "What Do Parochial Schools Accomplish?" *Phi Delta Kappan*, XLV (December, 1963), 121-22. Several doctoral dissertations have conclusions which agree with Elam's.

seems to belong to the Protestant day-school educators to demonstrate that the education they offer does make a difference.

e. *Staffing*. While most administrators and teachers in the Protestant day schools are serving sacrificially, there seems to be a continual turnover in personnel caused by a pay scale which cannot compete with the public schools. This brings to pass a considerable exodus, often participated in reluctantly by those who would prefer to invest their professional lives in Christian education but who find it impossible to care for their families on severely restricted incomes.

f. *Financing*. Education is expensive in our day, and, while the public schools enjoy vast resources from local taxes, church-sponsored schools are handicapped by being limited to tuition fees and sometimes a small share in congregational budgets for their income. Parents, already supporting the public schools by taxes, cannot be expected to contribute more than they are now paying. With no additional supplementary sources of income in sight, this serious problem will probably worsen rather than improve.

g. *Equipment*. The contrast between the modern facilities of the typical public school and the Protestant day school is painfully obvious. Important educational opportunities have to be either curtailed or eliminated in the church schools. This is particularly true in science and language laboratories where modern equipment has become so expensive.

### Conclusion

Evangelicals are deeply committed to Christian education in all of its phases. They can point with justifiable pride to encouraging signs of success. Enrollments in many church programs are increasing substantially. New educational buildings, or the expansion of facilities, have become necessary in many places. Competent leadership is emerging within the movement. Cooperative enterprises, especially the conventions, are alerting the constituency to the yet unreached potential of the churches through their educational programs. The future looks bright indeed.

### FOR ADDITIONAL READING

Clark, Gordon H. *A Christian Philosophy of Education*. Grand Rapids: Wm. B. Eerdmans Publishing Co., 1946.

Cully, Kendig B., ed. *The Westminster Dictionary of Christian Education*. Philadelphia: The Westminster Press, 1963.

Gaebelein, Frank E. *Christian Education in a Democracy*. New York: Oxford University Press, 1951.

Hakes, J. Edward, ed. *An Introduction to Evangelical Christian Education*. Chicago: Moody Press, 1964.

Little, Lawrence C. *Foundations for a Philosophy of Christian Education*. Nashville: Abingdon Press, 1962.

Murch, James DeForest. *Cooperation Without Compromise*. Grand Rapids: Wm. B. Eerdmans Publishing Co., 1956.

Oppewal, Donald. *The Roots of the Calvinistic Day School Movement.* Grand Rapids: Calvin College, 1963.

Person, Peter P. *An Introduction to Christian Education.* Grand Rapids: Baker Book House, 1958.

Rice, Edwin Wilbur. *The Sunday-School Movement, 1780-1917, and the American Sunday-School Union, 1817-1917.* Philadelphia: Union Press, 1917.

Taylor, Marvin J., ed. *Religious Education: A Comprehensive Survey.* Nashville: Abingdon Press, 1960.

Warkentin, Elmo H. "The History of 'Revitalizing the Sunday Schools of America' Through the National Sunday School Association." Unpublished Master's thesis, Wheaton College, 1958.

# Chapter 28

# THE PUBLIC SCHOOLS AND THE STUDY OF RELIGION

## Robert W. Lynn

THE PUBLIC SCHOOL IS A CRUCIBLE OF CONFLICT. HERE, AS PERHAPS NOWHERE else in our national life, one can see the American people at work in hammering out their commitments on the major domestic problems of this decade. The problems now confronting the public school educator constitute a working agenda of the social and political issues that must be attended to in the coming years. To cite a few of the high priority items on that list: the nightmarish complexities of *de facto* segregation, the crisis involved in financing the spiraling cost of local government, the running argument between the "states'-righters" and those who favor federal initiative, etc.

Somewhat further down the agenda comes the problem of religion in education. Nowadays few observers would claim that this issue is as crucial as, for example, the desegregation of urban neighborhood schools. Nevertheless, it does have an importance all its own. For one thing it can be powerfully disruptive of the civic peace. Even more important, the quarrel over religion involves a formidable challenge—Will the educators and the church leaders be mature enough to allow the public school to be the crucible of understanding as well as of controversy?

Our intent in this chapter is to explore the meaning of this quarrel and its implied challenge to Americans of all faiths and persuasions.

### A Turning Point

In the past, as public controversies go, the argument over the place of religion in the schools has been something of a low-grade affair. All too often it was marked by a show of empty-minded partisanship, occasional lapses in clarity on the part of the courts, and (despite some efforts to the contrary) an unwillingness by both churchmen and school officials to deal with the central issues.

A case in point is the furor which resulted from some recent United States Supreme Court decisions. In 1962 the high Court declared that the Regents' prayer, a short invocation for use in New York State classrooms, was unconstitutional.[1] One year later, in the midst of continuing protest against the Regents' Prayer decision, the Court ruled that the practice of Bible reading and the recitation of the Lord's Prayer in the public school were likewise unconstitu-

[1] *Engel vs. Vitale, 370 U.S. 421 (1962).*

tional.[2] The more restrained character of the 1963 decision did little to assuage the Court's opponents. In the spring of 1964, for example, Congress was beset by the supporters of the "Becker Amendment," a proposal for ensuring the legitimacy of religious ceremonies in the schools. This measure generated considerable interest across the country. According to one Washington observer: "Although the newspapers have devoted more space to the long civil-rights debate in the Senate, the volume of Congressional mail might lead one to believe that the school-prayer issue is by far the most important matter being discussed on Capitol Hill this spring." [3]

And so the battle continues. Amidst the din of ill-tempered rhetoric and confusion, it is sometimes difficult to hear the Court's case. The core of its argument centers in two affirmations: (1) The role of the state in these matters is strictly limited. The state is not competent to initiate or sanction worship activities; nor can it promote the cause of any one view of man or prescribe any official religious image for its people.[4] Daniel Callahan's capsule summary of recent history expresses accurately the Court's understanding: "In the past America had a 'neutral' state—favorable to religion. We now have a state which is becoming truly neutral—favorable neither to belief or unbelief." [5] (2) Conversely, the public school is free to engage in the study of religion. The most powerful word spoken along these lines came from Justice Tom Clark. In writing for the majority in the 1963 decision Justice Clark issued an indirect invitation for such an educational development.

It might well be said that one's education is not complete without a study of comparative religion or the history of religion and its relationship to the advancement of civilization. It certainly may be said that the Bible is worthy of study for its literary and historic qualities. Nothing we have said here indicates that such study of the Bible or of religion, when presented objectively as part of a secular program of education, may not be effected consistent with the First Amendment.[6]

Actually there was little new or novel in the Court's dictum. Over the last thirty years a variety of religious leaders have pled the same cause. In the 1930's a small band of Protestant educators, worried about the seeming "secularization" of the American mind, began to stress the option of teaching *about* religion, i.e., an "objective" approach in contrast to the coercive advocacy of doctrines and beliefs—the teaching *of* religion. So, for instance, F. Ernest Johnson suggested that "the same frank approach be made to a study of the churches [and religious beliefs] as is now made to the study of the industries, the press, the government and the cultural activities of 'our town.' " [7] The issue at stake,

---

[2] *Abington School District vs. Schempp* and *Murray vs. Curlett*, 374 U.S. 203 (1963).

[3] Robert S. Gallagher, "God's Little Helpers," *The Reporter*, XXX (June 4, 1964), 24.

[4] For some cogent theological reflections on this theme, see the essay by D. L. Munby, *The Idea of a Secular Society and Its Significance for Christians* (New York: Oxford University Press, 1963), pp. 30-32.

[5] "The New Pluralism: From Nostalgia to Reality," *The Commonweal*, LXXVIII (Sept. 6, 1963), 528.

[6] *374 U.S. 203*, p. 225.

[7] *The Social Gospel Re-Examined* (New York: Harper & Brothers, 1940), p. 187.

he implied, was not any alleged fracturing of the principle of separation of church and state, but rather the educational integrity of the public school.

This point of view was elaborated more fully in the 1940's when a committee for the American Council on Education published the influential report, *The Relation of Religion to Education: The Basic Principles*. The authors of this document cut close to the heart of the problem. While expressing traditional allegiance to the progressive slogan—"We teach the child *how* to think, not *what* to think"—they also commented on the inevitable "double character" of the educational enterprise. Education "must equip the young not only to *pass* on the culture but to pass *on* the culture. Only an appreciative understanding of tradition makes possible a critical appraisal of it." [8] But what about the dangers of indoctrination and controversial subject matter in the public school classroom? Here the committee appealed to the example of the social studies program. "Indeed, all social education in the new pattern has this double character: it avoids partisanship on issues which divide the community, but it impels the citizen, young or old, to action upon conviction. Thus, he becomes the author of his own partisanship." [9]

Well said. Yet the question remained—Can it be done? Up until a few years ago the most candid response to that query would have been "Difficult, if not impossible." Surely the experiences of the 1950's did not encourage the ardent supporters of teaching about religion. During this decade there were a number of earnest attempts to improve the public school teacher's training in religion; none of these efforts were attended by conspicuous success. Likewise the lack of understanding between faith groups represented a constant hazard. By way of illustration one can recount the following story. In a midwestern city in the middle 1950's a public school administrator (inspired, in part, by the report of the American Council on Education) enlisted the help of local clergymen. He asked them to draw up a syllabus on the heritage of Western civilization for junior high students. One of the predictable stumbling blocks was the interpretation of the work of Martin Luther. Beyond the simplest biographical data, they were able to agree only upon the supposed fact that the reformer was the father of the modern public school! This was the dubious result of a process in which religious communities act as "veto" groups, each canceling out the other's point of view.

What of the future? Doubtless the same story will be repeated in the years to come. But there are at least a few hopeful omens of an impending turning point in this controversy. One sign of change is the unexpected vigor of a re-

---

[8] (American Council on Education Studies. Series I, Reports of Committees and Conferences) XI (April, 1947), 13.

[9] *Ibid.*, p. 14. Such a conclusion, however, did not dispel the worry of those educators who feared that the school was being used in an effort to shore up the dwindling power of religion in America. There was reason for concern. Thus F. Ernest Johnson drew fire from several critics when he said that religious "freedom can be realized only when the education of the young makes them intelligent about religion and predisposes them toward a positive appraisal of its resources." (*The Social Gospel Re-Examined*, p. 183). Intelligent awareness is always a proper educational goal. Yet, does it follow that the school should *predispose* American youth toward a *positive* appraisal of its resources?

cent report issued by the American Association of School Administrators (AASA), *Religion in the Public Schools*.[10] The AASA commission spoke to and, in an unofficial way, for one of the most powerful professional organizations in the field. If nothing else, this sober and helpful guide might persuade a skittish school administrator that there is a way through the thicket of problems surrounding religion in public education. Second, the ecumenical spirit, engendered by the late Pope John XXIII and Vatican Council II, provides a more temperate climate of opinion. For the first time, as Michael Novak recently wrote, "it may at last be possible for Protestant, Catholic, Jewish, and secular scholars to sit down and prepare pilot textbooks explaining conjointly the history and purposes of their various world-views." [11] Such an event could mark the beginning of a new phase in an old controversy.

But that turning point is not yet. Its arrival depends in large part upon our willingness to think freshly about some of the difficulties that lie ahead.

## A Second Look

One of our needs is to probe beneath the conventional distinction between the "teaching of religion" and the "teaching about religion." Three decades ago, this comparison was a useful tool of thought in clearing the way for further discussion of the study of religion in the public schools. Unfortunately that discussion was not forthcoming except in scattered instances. Since the publication of the American Council on Education committee's report in 1947, there have been only a few attempts to refine and test this formulation. Instead, it has become a part of the conventional wisdom of our time—incorporated into the thinking of the Supreme Court,[12] widely praised by men of different persuasions as "the" answer to a complex problem—and hence largely exempt from critical scrutiny.

In the meantime a host of questions have gone untended. Where, for instance, is that dividing line between these two types of teaching? How does one locate the elusive boundary between so-called "objective" instruction and "sectarian indoctrination"? Furthermore, what is the precise meaning of "objective"— fair, balanced, safely inoffensive, or what? And does this distinction contribute to the making of good educational policy?

The last of these queries needs to be pressed sharply. Those spokesmen who appeal to the difference between the "teaching of religion" and the "teaching about religion" are often prompted by a fear of coercive and biased instruction in the classroom. Consequently, they tend to emphasize too absolute a distinction between objective and normative teaching. George R. LaNoue's statement is representative of other thinking in this vein:

[10] (Washington, D. C., 1964).

[11] "Religion in the Public Schools: Catholic Children Can at Least Lose Their Faith," *The New Republic*, CXLVIII (April 13, 1963), 18.

[12] In Justice Arthur Goldberg's concurring opinion in the 1963 decision of the Supreme Court, he said: "And it seems clear to me from the opinion in the present and past cases that the Court would recognize the propriety . . . of teaching *about* religion, as distinguished from the teaching *of* religion, in the public schools" (374 U.S. 203, p. 306).

Public school teaching, as is stated in the teacher manuals of any public system, must strive towards a balanced, neutral presentation of religious questions. Descriptive or empirical teaching about religion is acceptable but teaching supported by public funds must avoid normative teaching or teaching for commitment.[13]

What if the same argument were applied to other areas of controversy in the curriculum—such as politics, economics, or history? It would convert education into a dreary succession of "on the one hand . . . on the other hand" courses. There are already enough timid school administrators and teachers who drift toward this bland way of treating lively issues. Why reinforce their anxiety about exploring the heights and depths of contemporary life?

But, the reader might object, any other approach would veer dangerously close to indoctrination. There is no intent here to minimize the threat of abusing academic freedom. In the past that threat has been felt in far too many classrooms. It still lingers in some sections of the country. Yet now the critical problem is not simply the presence of "normative teaching"; *it is also the absence of a sense of the alternatives among diverse world views.* In this connection the stricture of Paul Goodman against the public schools ought to be taken seriously. Recently he wrote that the American high school course is "more and more tightly standardized, scheduled and graded. . . . Rival worldviews, whether folk, traditional, sectarian or artistically and philosophically heretical, are less and less available; the exposure to the one world-view is always more intense and swamping." [14] "Suppose," Mr. Goodman went on, "a young fellow happens to become disaffected from this 'reality.' He is not likely to know of other possibilities of philosophy, political dissent, religious faith." [15]

How, then, can that "young fellow" become critically aware of these "other possibilities"? That question should be of more fundamental concern to the churches than their usual preoccupation with religion in education. Indeed, the study of religion is part of a larger issue: How do we stimulate the school to induct American youngsters into the true diversity of the public experience, past and present? If this conclusion is valid, then the problems inherent in the study of religion are, *in substance,* no different from those encountered in any other disciplined inquiry into controversial subject matter. In all of these explorations the same preconditions must be met at the outset—or else it is better not to begin at all. Some of these initial requirements are as follows: (1) the competence of the teacher in employing the academic disciplines that are appropriate to the material under consideration (for example, in the study of biblical literature such competence would surely entail familiarity with the findings of historical criticism); (2) the freedom of both student and teacher to express ultimate commitments wherever such a statement would more fully explain their interpretation of the material under class discussion; (3) the freedom to accept or reject one another's commitment. (The exercise of this liberty is partly dependent upon two factors—whether one is in a majority or minority

---

[13] *Public Funds for Parochial Schools?* (New York: Published for the Department of Religious Liberty, National Council of Churches, 1963), p. 36.

[14] Cited by Michael Novak, "Religion in the Public Schools," p. 16.

[15] *Ibid.*

group within the class and the school; second, whether or not one has the age and maturity to disagree freely with the opinions of his peers and mentors.)

This perspective upon the study of religion makes good educational sense. It also throws into sharper relief the magnitude of the difficulties ahead. Obviously, one of the obstacles is the scarcity of competent teachers in any field—and particularly so in this touchy area. But even more depressing to contemplate are the restrictions upon the practice of competence in controversial subjects.

By and large, the American school is intimidated and fearful in its handling of controversy. As Edgar Z. Friedenberg has observed:

When a specific conflict arises, the school almost automatically seeks to *mediate* rather than to clarify. It assesses the power of conflicting interests, works out a compromise among them and keeps its name out of the papers. . . . *The Merchant of Venice* is omitted from the reading list in favor of something just as good in which all the Jewish characters are pleasant. . . .

They fear that the American Legion or a Catholic action group will object to the implications of other passages, and they also fear that they themselves will be called censors; so rather than suppress a work, they set up committees to *edit* it and forestall any possible objections.[16]

Yet the schoolmen are partially justified in adopting these techniques. These are the tactics of survival. The position of the public school administrator exposes one to all manner of pressure from such watchful censors as the American Legion, a "Catholic action group," or—let us confess—a group of Protestants. Although American Protestants do not ordinarily think of themselves as "censors," they have sometimes engaged in activities that can only be described by that word. Fundamentalists, for example, have figured prominently in the occasional failures of the public school to deal forthrightly with the scientific views of the origin of man.[17] Even liberal Protestantism has a spotty record as a defender of academic freedom in the elementary and secondary school.

In short, any satisfactory study of religion in the public schools will require something new from schoolmen and churchmen alike: from the teachers and administrators, a newfound appetite for working with controversial material; from the churches and synagogues, more restraint upon "special interest" expectations[18] and a greater willingness to provide scholarly assistance whenever asked. And from both sides a recognition of the underlying issues will be needed. For what should be of concern to all of us is the freedom of the school to transcend its community. The health and vitality of an educational enter-

---

[16] *The Vanishing Adolescent* (Boston: The Beacon Press, 1959), pp. 46, 51.

[17] "From the standpoint of religion and education, the successful attempts of Christians . . . to exclude the presentation of scientific facts and hypotheses about the origin of man and of the world, are far more significant than the Bible-prayer issue" [Marion J. Rice, "Constitutional Issues Concerning Religion and Education" (An unpublished talk at the Atlanta Institution on Public Education and Religion, October 22, 1964: mimeographed), p. 1.]

[18] Some Protestants and Roman Catholics entertain the covert hope that public school courses in religion will somehow blunt the thrust of the secularization of American life. As a matter of fact, it is not clear whether these course offerings would help or hinder the cause of the churches. In either event such an expectation engenders unfair pressure upon the public school.

prise depends upon its ability to treat controversy without fear of reprisal or counterattacks.

Therefore, the test of the churches' maturity in this matter of the study of religion is: Do their attitudes and actions here encourage public schoolmen to deal with controversy *wherever it may be found* in the curriculum? Someday, one can hope, Protestants will be just as concerned about protecting the rights of an English teacher to interpret J. D. Salinger's *Catcher in the Rye* as they are about the scope of his freedom in speaking explicitly of the religious convictions of John Milton. Both are skirmishes in a larger battle—the fight to preserve and extend the school's capacity to reflect critically and responsibly upon the full range of human experience.

### Religious Holidays in the Schools

The same battle is being joined on other terrain. One can point, for instance, to the vexing conflict over religious holidays in the public schools.

In the last few years some Christians, already confused and ruffled by the court's ban on Bible-reading and prayers, have become intransigent at any hint of reducing traditional holiday practices in the schools. In these circles there has been an apparent readiness to complain about the "militant secularism" of Jewish leaders, a predisposition toward an aggressive defense of the status quo. The Jewish community, meanwhile, continues to protest against the nagging reminders of the Protestant-dominated public school of bygone years. This mixture of majority impatience and minority discontent enflames needless and often ugly community strife.

The problems embedded in this conflict are quite complex. Consider, for a moment, the argument over Christmas carols. Here one confronts a tangle of cultural and religious meanings that is extremely hard to unravel. Many Christians, Protestants and Roman Catholics, do not consciously recognize these songs to be a form of confession of faith. But if, due to repetition, they forget to notice what they are affirming, they should not blame the non-Christian who is sensitive to the thrust of their confession.

The plight of the Jewish child amidst these culturally approved forms of an alien confession was vividly illustrated by an exchange between two Christians. In trying to explain to an irate mother why some Jews oppose the singing of those "lovely songs," a Protestant said, "Would you allow our children to sing, 'Jesus is *not* the Son of God'? Well, that is the dilemma of the Jewish mother when we sing carols in the public schools that say 'Jesus *is* the Son of God.'" [19]

One possible resolution of these dilemmas has been advanced by the "de-religionizers," those in our time who hope to make the public schools antiseptically clean of all traces of religious language and activities. Their proposal, in brief, is radical surgery: no more holiday decorations in the classrooms, a ban upon the compulsory singing of religious songs, and an elimina-

[19] Eugene J. Lipman and Albert Vorspan, *A Tale of Ten Cities: The Triple Ghetto in American Religious Life* (New York: Union of American Hebrew Congregations, 1962), p. 224.

tion of religious themes in school assemblies. But what remains after surgery? All too often the dereligionized school assembly at Christmas turns out to be a mélange of carefully denuded musical numbers, the Christmas tree, and Santa Claus. On these occasions one observes a relentless bias toward the bland. One example of this tendency comes out of the experience of a New Jersey community. In 1963, *before* the local superintendent of schools had become apprehensive about the possible implications of the Supreme Court's rulings, the high school glee club's medley of songs in the Christmas pageant included "Away in the Manger," the "Hallelujah Chorus" from *The Messiah,* and "The First Noel." One year later the glee club restricted itself to "Winter Wonderland," "Have a Merry Christmas," selections from "Babes in Toyland," and "Snow White and the Seven Dwarfs." The aftermath of these surgical operations must be considered. What is left—and celebrated—is often the worst of the holiday season.

A saner policy is hinted at in a recent church-state report of The United Presbyterian Church, U.S.A. One guideline laid down in this document is that "Religious holidays be acknowledged and explained, but never celebrated religiously, by public schools or their administrators when acting in an official capacity." [20] Some such distinction between compulsory celebration and interpretation must be worked out. The major religious holidays can be important occasions for understanding one another's inner history. For if, as Michael Novak said several years ago, "the holidays, Jewish and Christian, which impinge upon the school year pass without classroom discussion, education has a remoteness and abstraction from concrete reality which dodges the demands of understanding." [21]

This policy, of course, would raise a variety of issues, all of which deserve further thought. To wit: Can there be understanding of another's faith without some measure of participation in the great occasions of his life in faith? When does that kind of participation amount to an unwarranted coercion of the conscience? How do we mediate between what is permissible to the conscience and what is necessary for an introduction to the diverse riches of a pluralistic society? These questions stand astride our future; their resolution will require a new depth of maturity of both schoolmen and churchmen.[22]

## Time: Shared and Released

Another test of maturity becomes visible in the renewed interest in shared time.[23] Once again, after nearly forty years, there is considerable talk about this option in educational strategy.

[20] *Relations Between Church and State in the United States of America:* Adopted by the 175th General Assembly (Philadelphia: Office of the General Assembly, The United Presbyterian Church, U.S.A., 1963), p. 7.

[21] "Catholic Education and the Idea of Dissent," *The Commonweal,* LXXVI (April 27, 1962), 107.

[22] For some sensible suggestions about procedures of negotiations in this area, see Lipman and Vorspan, *A Tale of Ten Cities,* pp. 242-43.

[23] There are many other possible descriptive phrases that have been applied to this plan: split time, reserved time, dual school enrollment. For further information, see Research

In the early decades of this century a small band of educators began discussing the possibilities of a plan that would allow Protestant children to study some subjects in the public school and others in a church-sponsored day school.[24] In this scheme the wall of separation between church and state was—in effect—drawn down the middle of the curriculum. Thus the church school would be responsible for instruction in the so-called "value-oriented" disciplines of literature, history, and religion, while the public school would remain in charge of the more "neutral" subjects.

For a variety of reasons these first ventures in shared time collapsed. Most Protestant educators—if they thought along these lines at all—preferred the less ambitious alternative of released time, an arrangement whereby the public school agreed to release one hour of the children's time each week for religious instruction. In the 1920's the drive for this kind of weekday religious education gained momentum. And then came the depression of the 1930's; almost inevitably the weekday school, as the newest effort of the Protestant educators, was among the first programs to feel the whiplash of economic retrenchment. The growth of the movement in the succeeding years was perceptibly slower.

The 1940's brought fresh troubles to an already faltering institution. In 1948 the Supreme Court ruled in favor of Mrs. Vashti McCollum, an "avowed atheist" who protested that the released-time program in Champaign, Illinois, violated the First Amendment. The Court's ruling in the Zorach Case of 1952 clarified the legal status of the program; such an arrangement was permissible, the Court inferred, if it did not involve the use of school buildings.

These decisions seemed to mark a further shift in the fortunes of the released-time programs. "With the McCollum decision," Leo Pfeffer has written, ". . . the Catholic Church became the most ardent advocate of the released-time plan." [25] He continued:

More and more Catholic school systems began to participate in it. What was originally a pan-Protestant device quickly became a predominantly Catholic instrument, particularly in large urban areas. . . . It is not too much to say that the released-time plan depends for its existence on Catholic support and that if the Catholic Church returned to its previous position of indifference and non-cooperation, the program would soon collapse.[26]

The same basic plot is unfolding anew in the current explorations of shared time. The future of shared time, once a "pan-Protestant device" for broadening the institutional base of church education, now depends largely upon Roman Catholic initiative and participation. Protestant churchmen have shown little interest in moving in this direction. For the most part they seem content to recommend it to Catholics as a way out of the present crisis of the parochial

---

Report 1964-R10, *Shared-Time Program: An Exploratory Study* (Research Division, National Education Association, 1964), p. 5.

[24] The foremost spokesman for this group was Walter S. Athearn. See his volume, *Religious Education and American Democracy* (Boston: The Pilgrim Press, 1917).

[25] *Creeds in Competition: A Creative Force in American Culture* (New York: Harper & Brothers, 1958), p. 70.

[26] *Ibid.*

school. Many Catholics agree. Beset by skyrocketing educational costs and a growing school population, American Catholicism will at least give shared time a fair trial in the coming years.

The prospect of that development prompts these two concerns: the first involves Protestant and Roman Catholic, Jew and Christian, believer and unbeliever. The proponents of shared time are inclined to advocate it without thinking clearly about its wisdom as an educational policy. (Its legality is not in question; there is little doubt among legal experts on that score *if* the Supreme Court maintains its present direction of judicial reasoning.) Countless problems come to mind *once one sees shared time in relation to other policy problems*. There is space here to mention just one line of inquiry: How would the enactment of shared time affect the process of desegregation in the public schools? Could it not be used by some as a means of filling up empty classrooms in a "white" neighborhood school, thereby minimizing contacts between racial groups? These queries need to be pressed lest shared time become a smoke screen for other motivations that are not so well intended.

The second concern is the particular responsibility of the non-Catholic. Both Protestants and Jews can be of some help in developing community backing for shared-time programs. It is relatively easy for national church bodies to go on record in favor of shared time—as, indeed, a number of Protestant groups have already done. It is quite another matter, however, to work out a feasible plan amidst the crosscurrents of local feelings and religious prejudices. In this setting the non-Catholic's political support could make the difference between success and failure. Here, in short, is another test of our maturity.

But even if Protestants do not participate directly in shared-time programs, they might well reconsider their casual disregard of that "old reliable," the released-time plan. In recent years a few Protestant educators have been doing exactly that. Instead of viewing the released-time program as a supplement to the Sunday church school, they have asked, why not look upon it as complementary to the work of the public school from Monday to Friday? [27] This change in perspective opens up new possibilities and also (it must be admitted) additional difficulties.

The possibilities are manifold. For example, a high school student might study some of the theological interpretations of American history while he is taking the same subject in school. Or the church-sponsored program might offer work in some field that is not covered adequately in the public school curriculum. In any event, the stress would be upon the coordination of instruction, and hence a broader interpretation of the human experience than is now possible in most American communities.

The difficulties built into this proposal are equally impressive. The accelerating rate of change in the public school's curriculum and teaching procedures makes it a task of forbidding complexity. Such an intricate dovetailing of two

---

[27] For some thoughtful comments along this line see the article by David R. Hunter, "Complete Education Includes Religion," *International Journal of Religious Education*, XL (June, 1964), 9.

educational programs would require the churches to devote money, skill, and energy on an unprecedented scale. Would it be forthcoming?

In the course of this chapter we have come across a bewildering array of questions. None of them is subject to quick solution; a few will probably never be resolved. But even so, our way of accepting—or evading—their presence in our common life will provide an answer to the most intriguing question of all: Are Americans ready at last to come of age in dealing with an old quarrel and its new challenge—religion in education?

## FOR ADDITIONAL READING

American Council on Education. *The Relation of Religion to Public Education: The Basic Principles*. American Council on Education Studies. Series I, Reports of Committees and Conferences, Vol. XI (April, 1947).

Fund for the Republic. *Religion and Free Society*. Contributions by William Lee Miller, *et al*. New York: Fund for the Republic, 1958.

——————. *Religion and the Schools*. Contributions by Robert Gordis, *et al*. New York: Fund for the Republic, 1959.

Religious Education Association, "Symposium: Religion in the Public Schools," *Religious Education*, LIX (November-December, 1964), 443-79.

——————. "Symposium: Shared Time," *Religious Education*, LVII (January-February, 1962), 5-37.

*Chapter 29*

# THE CAMPUS
# MINISTRIES

## John E. Cantelon

THE MIDDLE DECADES OF THE TWENTIETH CENTURY HAVE SEEN THE FRUITION of two profound cultural and academic movements which have altered both the form and direction of the campus ministries for years to come. The first of these changes may be described as the coming to maturity of a gradually developing shift in the cultural milieu of the campus. For some time observers have been describing the college generation as "beat," "waiting," "silent," or "uncommitted." Those engaged professionally in the campus ministry use the expression "privatistic" to characterize the inverted withdrawal of student interest from the broader context of the world and its social problems to a personal concern for limited values and private pleasures. The profile of the American college student of the 1950's drawn by Philip Jacob, Nevitt Sanford, and R. J. Kaufmann portrayed a student generation without any strong commitments—religious, philosophical, or political.[1] It was a generation with many opinions but with few convictions, and it generally failed to recognize the importance of the transition from the one to the other.

This naïve, individualistic kind of popular existentialism was challenged and modified in the last five years by two political developments. The first was the effect of the student sit-ins in the South upon Northern white college students —at first principally on the east coast and in the Midwest. And more recently, the Free Speech Movement, with its genesis at Berkeley, Calif., represents a second wave of awakening student commitment and action.

It is not the case of the privatistic existentialism of the 50's being completely replaced by a well-organized, responsible movement of students simply affirming traditional social and democratic values and goals. The anti-institutionalism of the FSM reveals that individualistic and existentialist attitudes still prevail. But the 1960's are witnessing a new kind of campus existentialism—far less personally isolated and pleasure-seeking, and one that is politically oriented and socially judgmental. This new student attitude differs from the liberal crusading affirmations of the young radicals of the 1930's and evokes but limited commitment to proximate goals. It cannot be described as traditionally idealistic. The FSM ethos is a curious blend of political maturity and sophistication verging on the cynical, united with an idealistic naïveté about society in general and the institution of the University of California in particular. This ethos

[1] Cf. "The Careful Young Men: Tomorrow's Leaders Analyzed by Today's Teachers," *The Nation*, CLXXXIV (March 9, 1957); Philip E. Jacob, *Changing Values in College* (New York: Harper & Row, 1957); and Nevitt Sanford, "Is College Education Wasted on Women?" *Ladies Home Journal*, LXXIV (May, 1957).

represents a new and unstable factor with which the religious organizations must deal. That religionists are not traditionally well-adapted to capitalize upon this student outlook scarcely needs to be noted. Religion, in the mind of most students, is burdened with two almost fatal characteristics. First, it manifests itself in an institutionalized form of the church that is almost as odious in student eyes as the structures of the university. And secondly, its commitments are so total and—traditionally—so *a*political as to appear irrelevant to the politically aware but cautious student generation. The great asset that the campus ministry possesses lies in the respect and confidence which students have personally in the professional campus ministers and the faculty teaching in the field of religion. Most of these men and women have, by patient struggle with student apathy and administrative hesitancy, won a respected place in their campus communities. They have been willing to exercise the often unpopular role of academic gadfly and have brought to bear on the problems that beset modern higher education some of the best wisdom of the Judeo-Christian tradition.

A second major change which has become obvious in the mid-1960's is one that has long concerned professional educators—the inundation of the colleges and universities by unprecedented numbers of students. The postwar baby crop has grown up and is now clamoring at the gates of institutions of higher learning all over the country. What is more, this challenge of numbers has been compounded because of certain trends within higher education itself. Perhaps the most widely recognized term used to describe these trends has been the growth of the "multiversity." This kind of education is characterized by a multiplicity of educational goals and the lack of any single coherent educational aim. The university no longer attempts to turn out, as it did in the past, either a renaissance man, a democratic citizen, or a professional specialist—but all of these and more. Thus, specialization has grown apace, and there has developed an increasing emphasis upon graduate education. This has had a profound effect upon the entire institution. Undergraduate education is looked upon as only preparatory to graduate work. The best teachers are siphoned off into research and graduate instruction. At the same time the university acts more and more like a business corporation, producing consequent feelings of depersonalization which have helped to produce widespread student unrest.

College and university administrators have attempted to respond to this problem largely through new curriculum experimentation which permits greater depth concentration in a smaller range of subjects, hopefully inculcating research techniques and independent study patterns. This is designed both to prepare the way for graduate work and to wean the student from overdependence upon the faculty. Most of these curricular changes are too new to be evaluated in terms of their eventual impact. But it must be recognized that no modification of courses or schedules can solve the dilemmas presented by the logistical problems of increasing student numbers and a proportional decrease in faculty size, the diversity of educational goals, and the spreading technology of an increasingly automated society.

Awakened student concern, centering in political and social issues and expressed in terms of rejection of the depersonalization of the multiversity, presages a disturbed next decade in American higher education. What is happening in the campus ministries certainly must be set in the light of the background of these developments.

Although continuing to be established on new campuses and functioning almost everywhere with imaginative programming, the campus ministries of the "Y's" and the denominations must be described as experiencing a leveling-off period in the last few years. Far fewer denominational campus centers are being projected or built; fewer new campus pastorates are being established. The confident projections of the 1950's on the part of those responsible for the campus ministry have just not materialized. There are a number of reasons for this. In the society at large there has been a decline proportionate to the population growth in all the religious indicators—church membership, church attendance, contributions, and construction. The postwar religious revival, largely centered in the suburbs, has ceased, and a new period of retrenchment appears to have set in. Since the campus ministries are not financially self-sufficient but rather dependent upon denominational support, it is natural that they should suffer from a falling off of denominational revenue. One reason for the decline has been the failure of the campus ministry to produce statistics that are satisfying to denominational leadership. There has been no religious revival on the American campus to compare with that of the postwar suburban revival. Students have enrolled in courses in religion in unprecedented numbers, but they have not joined the campus religious organizations in any comparative degree. Thus, in one area the budget allotted by a major denomination for the campus ministry has recently been cut in two, while another large Protestant denomination no longer pretends to provide the staff it once did, i.e., a professional campus worker on every campus with four hundred or more preference students.[2]

The established interdenominational and nondenominational programs, such as the "Y's" and Christian Associations, have suffered the most. They began to feel this financial pressure some years earlier when the various churches began soliciting their congregations and members for the support of the specifically denominational programs. But in these last years the denominational ministries themselves have begun to experience financial scarcity. Their response has not been to return to the "Y" as a vehicle of cooperative ministry, largely because of the churches' feelings that the "Y's" have no solid theological foundation. They have tended either to "go it alone" or to band together in new interdenominational groupings to meet the challenge of expanding campuses and dwindling resources. The United Campus Christian Fellowship, representing the United Presbyterians, the United Church of Christ, the Disciples of Christ, the Evangelical United Brethren, and others represents an ecumenical response prompted, in part, by economic pressures.

[2] A frequently lost-sight-of reason for this diminishing financial support of the churches is the fact that a proportionately small income-producing age group is having to support an unprecedentedly large number of young children and retired people. Thus, the middle-age range of church members does not have the resources to give to church finances and to keep them growing at the rate it once did.

Lest it be assumed that economic factors alone are significant, it should be noted that the impetus for ecumenical cooperative campus ministries also has proceeded from an increasing awareness that most Protestants share a common understanding of the role of the church within the university. What Willem Visser 't Hooft has termed a growing Protestant consensus on the mission of the church has enabled many religious traditions to pool their resources in this specialized ministry. No longer do most campus pastors view their task as simply a holding operation—keeping the denomination in the minds and experience of students so that they will return to its parishes after graduation and take up the supportive role of the laity. While there is no one theology or philosophy of the campus ministry—but rather a diversity of these, as we shall presently note —all of them currently in vogue in the major denominations reject denominational nurture as an insufficient *raison d'etre* for the campus ministry.

This leveling off of new development has also been reflected in the teaching of religion on the college campus. Few new departments of religion have been established, although the existing ones have been expanding their course offerings.[3]

Like the number of college chaplaincies, the departments of religion in the mid-1960's are stable but not increasing at a significant rate. Many new departments were established in the 1940's and 50's, and these expanded rapidly to accommodate increasing enrollments in courses in the field of religion. Few departments of religion have been established at state institutions because, thus far, the legal problems of the separation of church and state have frustrated such efforts.[4] Students still are willing to explore religion academically, although they continue to avoid the institutional commitment which is inherent in the Western religious tradition. The uninformed skepticism of the 20's and 30's is being replaced by a better informed skepticism. This may make the task of the churches in the colleges all the more difficult in the future. But virtually no one on the campus contests the claim that the study of our religious heritage is indispensable in gaining a balanced knowledge of Western culture. Thus, the next five years may well see some solutions to the legal questions and a resultant increase in the number of courses being taught in the subject matter of religion.[5]

[3] A denominational survey taken in 1957-58 of over a hundred campuses indicated only three where new departments of religion were contemplated and only six where expansion was thought to be imminent. There is a concerted attempt being made to introduce courses in religion in some state colleges and universities. In California courses in Bible are offered at the University of California at Los Angeles, and Paul Tillich, at the University of California, Santa Barbara, initiated a department for the study of religious institutions. These may be regarded as trial balloons for the introduction of courses in religion throughout the state system in California.

[4] It is usually noted that there are more ordained persons with a Ph.D. degree who wish to teach religion than there are places for them in institutions of higher learning. This seems to be true except when a particular department of religion starts looking for an outstanding replacement!

[5] There is still a question as to the most suitable form of organization of religious instruction, whether it is to be in separate departments of religion or in conjunction with other departments such as philosophy, history, and sociology. Arguments may be presented for both forms of organization.

One of the enormously vexing problems of the campus ministry is its growing alienation from the institutional and parish life of its supporting ecclesiastical structures. The expectations of these two groups differ, and therefore their evaluation of the campus ministry is largely divergent.

For the most part local congregations are persuaded to support their denominational campus ministries in order to serve their own preference students, providing them with pastoral counseling and sacramental care. Denominational executives (except those specifically related to the campus ministry) and the parish clergy are quick to point to the small numbers of students active in religious organizations—especially at a time when student numbers are increasing astronomically. Campus pastors respond that student numbers are increasing at the greatest rates within commuting universities where the mobility of students makes any organizational life or ministry exceedingly difficult. They also note that if they had the budget and staff that a parish serving the same number of students had, they would be able to make as good a proportional showing.[6]

Campus pastors also state that they understand the campus ministry not so much in terms of nurture to the church's young but in terms of bringing together the campus community of Christians in order to make them aware of their shared responsibility to witness to Christ in the whole life of the university.

Perhaps the real root of the alienation between the campus and the parish ministries lies, at least in part, in the growing dissatisfaction of many clergy with parish life and their increasing desire to escape into various specializations —teaching, the chaplaincy, and the campus ministry. Misunderstanding also arises because some campus pastors seem to evidence an anti-institutionalism which has brought the campus ministries close to the sentiment of those leading sit-ins and FSM's. But it is an attitude which, unfortunately, separates the campus ministry from its supporting congregations, ecclesiastical structures, and also from the administration of the colleges and universities in which it works. A pessimistic prediction would be that the professional campus pastor might find himself *persona non grata*, both in the organized church and on the campus. If this were to occur, the effectiveness of the ministry in higher education would, of course, be greatly reduced.

One form of the campus ministry which might have been predicted to have expanded greatly in this period, but which has not, is the "Faith and Life Community" type of campus.[7] Limitation of finances, in part, explains why this type of ministry did not expand. For although it has continued to provide the most thoroughgoing theological education to laity, it is the most expensive kind of campus ministry enterprise. Earlier critiques of this strategy—e.g., that it tends to establish a Christian ghetto, that it avoids the mission frontier of

---

[6] A campus serving 2,000 preference students of a particular denomination has a total budget of some $17,000; whereas a parish serving 2,000 members would probably have a budget in the range of $150,000-$175,000.

[7] The Faith and Life Community is widely known to have been begun at the University of Texas at Austin under the leadership of the Rev. Jack Lewis. It is a residential community characterized by a concentrated study in the field of theology.

the church in the midst of the university—may be overcome by relatively simple techniques.[8] A few modifications of the Faith and Life Community are operating on or near several campuses, but the most significant impact the movement has made has been through its graduates, now present in many academic communities, and also in its conception of a disciplined study program which forms a part of almost all denominational and interdenominational programs.

A perennial factor which must be taken into account in understanding the American campus ministry is the lack in the United States of any American Student Christian Movement.[9] This lack of a tradition of an ecumenical campus ministry such as has existed on the European continent, in Great Britain, and in Canada, has meant that the campus ministries have had to develop cooperative programs largely on the local or regional level. The university would seem the logical place for putting into effect, even on an experimental basis, the united ministry being projected on the national scale. But the lack of an American SCM has made this possible only to the limited degree of the UCCF. The dependence of the campus ministry upon the denominations for support and the inability or unwillingness on the part of some of the denominations—Methodist, Lutheran, Episcopal—to join the UCCF have prevented the growth of a strategy to which most college and university administrations are most responsive. The effect of the divisions of Protestantism upon the campus ministry is one of the most unfortunate obstacles it faces in attempting to carry out its mission in higher education.

It can scarcely be overemphasized that the campus ministry is a highly diversified one and by no means dominated by a single official theology. Differences in denominational theology and in the ethos of the various campuses account for the pluralistic approaches of the varying forms of the campus ministry. Denominational ties, publications, and the professional campus ministry organization make for some degree of sharing ideas and program techniques. There is also a good deal of imitation of the programs developed on prestige campuses by those ministering in less prestigious situations. This kind of diversity is reflected, but to a far lesser degree, in the courses taught in religion. This is because curricula tend to follow more standardized patterns and reflect far less variety than is represented by, say, a campus coffeehouse ministry, one emphasizing the relationship between jazz and theology, etc.

At present there are at least three differing theological trends discernible within the Protestant campus ministry. At some colleges and universities, one of these may dominate the scene. At others all will be present, one or more being sponsored by the denominational ministries, or the chaplain's office.

The *first* of these diverse theologies represented in the campus ministry may

[8] E.g., one may accept students for only one year residence, excluding freshmen, and insist that each member take part in some campus organization. [The internal quarrel at Austin which was temporarily disturbing was not a significant factor in limiting the spread of this kind of approach to the campus ministry.]

[9] E.g., the excellent program of the Life and Mission Movement of the World Student Christian Federation has had very little impact upon the local American campus, largely because of the lack of an adequate ecumenical instrument for carrying it out.

be termed the search for a new secularity. This search on the part of those engaged in the campus ministry was prompted by two factors; first, the rejection of religiousness by the university community. This, coupled with its vigorous and unapologetic secularism, has forced campus Christians into a new evaluation of what is meant by the secular. Secondly, there is the growing theological interest in the phenomenon of the secular as represented by the theology of Dietrich Bonhoeffer. It is the intellectual heritage of this German martyr, centering chiefly on his two frustratingly enigmatic concepts of "the World come of age" and of a "religionless Christianity," that occupies the attention of many chaplains, campus pastors, and faculties in departments of religion. Our concern here is not to trace the intellectual ramifications of these ideas so much as to stress the impact of this search for a meaningful secularity as it expresses itself in the strategy and programming of the campus ministry.

Bonhoeffer's theology has provided a foundation for a growing rapport and cooperation between the campus ministry and secular forces at work within the university. Humanists and agnostics now find themselves in the company of Christians who do not require of them theistic affirmations as they work together in various human relations councils, free speech movements, American Association of University Professors, or campus branches of the American Civil Liberties Union.

The tendency of these emphases has been toward political awareness and activity. But they also have a strong artistic interest. Programs in the area of art—a new twist on the old "religious questions in nonreligious guise" type of programming—now characterize many aspects of the campus ministry.[10]

A *second* theological trend in the campus ministry may be described as a theological concentration on the morphology of higher education and the social and academic value of religious commitment. The thought of Paul Tillich is more in evidence here than is that of Bonhoeffer. Tillich's conception of culture as expressing the form of religious commitment in a community has stimulated widespread sociological and religious analysis of every facet of contemporary culture—particularly as it is manifested in the university. Those pursuing this type of concern have become involved in studying the forces that influence the direction being taken by higher education in the United States. It is illustrative that the Center for Christian Faith and Higher Education established in 1960 at Michigan State University has increasingly turned its attention from such initial problems as it was given—the training of faculty to supplement the services of the campus ministry—to the exploration of the nature of the university and the impact of specialization and automation in the field of higher education.[11] This emphasis has, perhaps, been more survey and analysis-oriented and somewhat less politically concerned than those following the

---

[10] This emphasis has a powerful organ in the Methodist campus magazine *motive*.

[11] The Danforth Study of the Campus Ministry now being completed under the leadership of Kenneth Underwood reflects much of this concern, as does this Foundation's farsighted support of a program dealing with the depersonalization of students in the large urban universities.

Bonhoefferian approach. It also has had far greater graduate school faculty and administrative appreciation and participation.

A *third* theological trend has been prompted by the new ecumenical emphasis which has received such stimulus from Pope John XXIII and Vatican Council II. The Protestant theology which has been more congenial to this new openness toward Rome has been the more conservative theology identified with Karl Barth. This is a much smaller movement than the first, which in terms of numbers of campuses is the greatest current campus ministry emphasis, and even smaller than the second, the size of which has been limited by the specialized nature of its professional involvement. There is, however, an increasing degree of contact between Protestant and Roman Catholic faculty and students.[12] Some parts of the country are more advanced in this form of ecumenical exploration than others. In some locales the ecumenical outreach is extended to Jewish groups with the common exploration of such issues as the legitimacy of Christian missions to the Jews, etc. This trend has developed a fair degree of student response, although frequently it finds itself subject to the old ecumenical dilemma—that those most interested in ecumenical relations have the least to contribute to them.[13] The first two of these theological trends (Bonhoefferian—secularist, Tillichian—sociological, and Barthian—ecumenical) are, of course, compatible with each other, although the third—at least at present—seems less so. Indeed, evidence of all three is frequently to be found on many large campuses.

Whatever trend or trends are represented in a particular campus ministry, there tend to be certain points of common agreement. Among campus pastors there is a generally recognized necessity for a Protestant doctrine of creation to provide a basis for work within the university. Many Protestants are increasingly aware that there exists no adequate Protestant equivalent to the Roman Catholic doctrine of natural law. Faculty, chaplains, and campus pastors know that the almost exclusively soteriological emphasis of Protestant theology constitutes a serious handicap in dealing with the full range of life represented within the university. The continuing exploration as to the positive meaning of the secular constitutes one attempt to deal with this basic issue. There is also a growing theological agreement among Protestant groups that Christ is the Lord over the whole world, that God is at work in the university beyond the structures of the church. There is, in addition, a generally expressed willingness on the part of those engaged in the campus ministry to cut loose from the traditional ecclesiastical forms and structures. There is also increasing commitment on the local level to new kinds of ecumenical growth and experimentation.

It is certain that continued building upon this agreement and the pursuit of these different trends will eventuate in new forms, strategies, and programs in the campus ministry in the next few years. Indeed, some predictions about the future may be made, with a recognition that the fluidity of the situation

---

[12] *Cf. Ecumenical Exchange*, No. 1, The Kansas City Newman Foundation, May, 1963.

[13] A study of the religious traditions other than those in which the student himself was reared has always continued to be popular in terms of academic coursework.

among the churches and in higher education may direct the course of the campus ministry into unpredicted channels.

It would appear safe to predict that economic factors alone will continue to force a greater degree of ecumenical work. When these economical stringencies are combined with the increasing disposition to work together on the basis of theological agreement, the factors making for a change in the old denominational foundation pattern will be seen to be irresistible. The old pattern of denominational centers will probably persist only on the large residential campuses. And even there it is safe to predict that increasing Protestant cooperation will prevail, the differing denominational centers undertaking specialized cooperative ministries: for example, the Baptists, because of the location of their center, conducting a cooperative ministry among married students; the Episcopalians with graduate students, etc. At most new campuses the trend will be toward a shared ministry housed in a modest ecumenical or interfaith center and staffed cooperatively by fewer, but hopefully better-trained, professional clergy.

There would also appear to be developing a greater degree of denominational selectivity in the strategy of the campus ministry. Denominations will no longer seek to provide staff at every new junior college or state university. The junior colleges, for example, may well be almost the exclusive locus of YMCA and YWCA work. But greater use of professional staff may be concentrated in a few key centers which set the educational pattern for a whole region, such as Ann Arbor or Berkeley. An increase of Christian Faith and Higher Education centers patterned after the German Evangelical Academy may constitute a more significant involvement in the total enterprise of higher education than the older pattern of placing a campus pastor at each of the colleges with given numbers of preference statistics.

The role of the nontheological specialist will also be increasingly important in the university ministry of the future. This is true because neither theology nor philosophy any longer provides the *lingua franca* of higher education. Thus, the faculty and graduate assistants' role in the campus program will be of increasing importance. The campus pastor will continue to be called upon to introduce the Christians on the campus to one another—faculty to student, administrator to research scientist—and to help them face together their Christian vocation and responsibility in that place. This means that the campus pastor, while theologically articulate, might well be himself a specialist in another field. It may be increasingly important that he be trained in some academic discipline in addition to theology so that, within a collegiate type of ministry, there may be those representing the church who can speak to the diverse specializations within the multiversity.

A further development may be predicted—indeed, without it the campus ministry may well not survive. That development should be an increased relationship between the campus ministry and the other specialized church ministries—particularly those in the urban situation. Our modern American colleges and universities differ increasingly from those of the Western tradition because they exist without walls. The contemporary university is open to the world in a unique way. As the church recognizes increasingly its responsibility in an urban culture, it may hopefully find within the university and the ministry it conducts there an indispensable resource for meeting the challenge of witness within the city. It is this response which may bring about a reconciliation between the institutional church and the specialized campus ministry. This would, of course, be dependent upon the facing up to the immensity of the urban task on the part of the church and on the campus ministry being able to abandon its narrow ivory-towered existence for service to the total community.[14]

The church's campus ministry from the beginning has been and must continue to be one of the most significant aspects of its total mission to the world. It is widely recognized that the civilization of the future will be increasingly one dominated by university-trained men and women. If the Christian religion is going to make a meaningful contribution to the culture of tomorrow, it will be because it has been encountered by students today as a vital, relevant, and intellectually respectable movement. It is therefore imperative that the American churches continue to invest heavily in the campus ministry. For it is on the campus that the best thought of the church and the world come together. That the dialogue which ensues between them there may be as fruitful as possible is the continuing task of the faculty member teaching religion, of the college chaplain, and the denominational university pastors.

## FOR ADDITIONAL READING

Cantelon, John E. *A Protestant Approach to the Campus Ministry*. Philadelphia: The Westminster Press, 1964.

Fuller, R. Buckminster, "Notes on the Future," *Saturday Review*, XLVII (August 29, 1964).

Hazelton, Roger. *New Accents in Contemporary Theology*. New York: Harper & Row, 1960.

Miller, Alexander. *Faith and Learning*. New York: Association Press, 1960.

Phenix, Philip H. *Education and the Common Good: A Moral Philosophy of the Curriculum*. New York: Harper & Row, 1961.

Williams, George. *Wilderness and Paradise in Christian Thought*. New York: Harper & Row, 1962.

[14] Little has been made in this chapter of the formal teaching aspect of the campus ministry. In no way has this been because the teaching of religion is underrated. But recent changes in the total campus ministry have been far greater in the fields of denominational campus religious organizations and chaplaincies. In what we have traditionally known as foundation work, everything seems to be "up for grabs," and even the future is problematic. The same is not true of the formal course instruction in the field of religion. The picture there is much more stable and the future much more assured. That increased imagination will be exercised in course offerings and the kind of instruction presented is safe to assume. Cf. Robert Michaelsen, "Religious Education in Public Higher Education Institutions," in *Religious Education: A Comprehensive Survey*, Marvin J. Taylor, ed. (Nashville: Abingdon Press, 1960), chap. 28; Nels F. S. Ferré, *Searchlights on Contemporary Theology* (New York: Harper & Brothers, 1961), Section V on "Theology in Education"; and Alexander Miller, *Faith and Learning* (New York: Association Press, 1960), chap. 5 on "Teaching Religion and Teaching the Christian Faith."

# Chapter 30

# CHRISTIAN TEACHING
# IN THE SUMMERTIME

## William Clifton Moore

PERHAPS THE TWO MOST CRITICAL PROBLEMS FACING A CONGREGATION IN carrying out a significant Christian education program are adequate leadership and sufficient time. Many congregations have found that both of these problems can be dealt with constructively through more extensive use of the time in the summer when potential leaders as well as children, youth, and families have more time at their disposal.

Many adults have fewer other community responsibilities and less work pressures in the summer, giving more opportunity for involvement in leadership preparation and participation. Families have more choice of activities and many choose "vacations with a purpose" as they take part in summer camps and conferences under the auspices of the church. For boys and girls the summer constitutes the largest block of time when they can choose their own activities. Some are involved in organized activities for part—or even most—of the summer, but for the majority of America's children the summer provides more leisure than they can use constructively or happily—as any mother who has heard the words, "What can I do now, Mother?" can testify. While increasingly in our society many youth work during the summer, there is both need and time for constructive learning experiences during these months. The average young person growing up in our country has ten to twelve summers that are relatively free.

This available time in the summer for constructive use on the part of so many is one of the church's most valuable resources for Christian teaching and learning. There are large blocks of time and opportunity for concentration and even full-time involvement in planned and guided learning experiences. These usually take one of four patterns: vacation church schools, conferences, institutes, or camps. While these patterns are distinctive from one another and from other patterns of Christian education activities, they do not stand in isolation from the church's teaching ministry.

## Relation to Year-Round Program

Christian education in the summertime is an integral part of the year-round educational ministry of the church. While vacation church schools, conferences, institutes, and camps use different approaches and methods, they, too, help achieve the basic objectives of Christian education. They try in their unique ways "to help persons, at each stage of development, to realize the highest potentialities of the self as divinely created, to commit themselves to Christ, and to grow toward maturity as Christian persons." Specific age-group needs and objectives are taken into account, and in general denominational planning the curricula for summertime activities are coordinated with curricula for the rest of the year. In seeking to make its teaching ministry as effective as possible, a congregation will carefully plan its total year-round program, making as effective use as possible of the availability of teachers and learners in the summertime for varied experiences in vacation schools, conferences, institutes, and camps.

## Vacation Church Schools

The vacation church school as a means of Christian education had its beginning near the turn of this century, and it spread rapidly across major denominations and among nondenominational religious agencies. It has been estimated that as many as five million children between the ages of four and fourteen are enrolled in these schools in a typical summer. While the vacation church school is usually the extension of learning experiences for children who are enrolled in the regular Sunday church school, it often reaches children who for one reason or another do not receive regular religious instruction during the rest of the year. Sometimes it is conducted as a missionary enterprise in rural or urban areas where there are unusually large numbers of unchurched children—housing projects, migrant workers camps, isolated rural areas, etc. A vacation church school may be conducted by a local church, by two or more parishes of the same denomination, by several churches on an interdenominational community-wide basis, or it may be sponsored by a nondenominational agency.

The typical time schedule for a school consists of a two and a half to three hour session on weekdays during summer vacation for a two to six week period. Patterns of community activities—such as work responsibilities in rural areas—often help determine the best time in the summer for the school. Generally a good time to begin is the second or third week of school vacation. In many communities planning with other agencies is done to avoid conflicts of programs. While typically the schools are in session in the mornings, sometimes the afternoons are better because of other family responsibilities or community activities, or because of the availability of leadership personnel. And a few schools have experimented with evening schedules.

Schools are closely graded or group graded depending on the number of children and teachers involved. Classes generally begin with kindergarten and go through junior high age—although frequently summer Christian education activity for junior high has taken other forms.

In general the vacation church school is distinguished by its leisurely, informal pace, by its use of more creative and experimental methods, by its involvement of students in individual and group activities, by its variety of experiences, and by its joyous atmosphere. There is time for developing conditions for learning and guiding persons and groups in their learning activities. Projects, field trips, dramatizations, play activities, use of outdoor resources, music, group discussions, role-playing and the like are possible to a much larger degree than in the limited Sunday morning sessions. Indeed, many teachers believe they can accomplish more in a two-week vacation school than in a whole year of Sunday church school sessions. Additional advantages inhere in the day-to-day continuity, in the opportunity for teachers to experiment and grow as they try out teaching methods, and in the practice of Christian relationships and social responsibility as groups work and play together over longer periods of time.

In the vacation school more space, indoors and out, is available for activities, and informal school—rather than church—dress makes possible greater variety of meaningful children's activities, helping make the experience one of fun and anticipation. Regular attendance is rarely a problem in a well-planned and guided vacation school.

There is a large variety of curriculum units prepared especially for use in vacation church schools. One series is planned and published cooperatively by denominations working in the National Council of Churches and is coordinated with the general curriculum outline used by these cooperating denominations. Other series are developed by separate denominations and coordinated with their particular Christian education programs. Still other materials are published by nondenominational publishers, but their use requires careful scrutiny to make sure they are compatible not only with the year-round curriculum pattern but also with its theological and educational stance.

In general the curriculum units give guidance for worship, use of the Bible, creative activities, and play in terms of the specific aims of the particular unit. Many of the units are devoted to Bible study, while others deal with the church and with problems of personal Christian growth and living relevant to the particular age group.

Usually the leadership staff is made up of volunteers, although quite often the director is an employed educator who trains the staff as well as directs the school. Regular church school teachers have much to contribute to the staff and at the same time may gain a great deal in knowledge and experience. The vacation school may be a very valuable in-service training experience for potential and apprentice teachers. Indeed, many vacation schools are held in connection with laboratory or observation schools where the children's classes are conducted by expert lead teachers who then meet with teachers-in-training for an analysis and discussion of the teaching-learning experience.

Special attention is also given to preschool staff training. Vacation church school institutes sponsored by denominations and councils of churches for training workers in local schools are in reach of almost every community. In addition members of each school staff plan and prepare together for their particular responsibilities.

Vacation church schools are a major way in which interdenominational cooperation takes place. On the local level denominations cooperate in the schools and in the training of personnel. On a wider scale there is cooperation in the development of general principles, procedures, and curriculum materials, as well as the training of workers.

An alternative to the vacation church school program for junior and senior high youth is a "Youth Activities Week" usually with varied activities each evening and sometime with service projects during the daytime.

Thus, the vacation church school program—with its variation for youth—is, in terms of its potentialities for significantly involving pupils in Christian growth and teachers in improvement of their personal competence, one of the most effective ways in which the church carries out its teaching ministry.

## Conferences and Institutes

The summertime also furnishes opportunity for many kinds of conferences and institutes as a part of the total Christian education program. While vacation church schools are primarily for children and are held in the local community, conferences and institutes are for youth and adults and are usually held at camps, conference centers, or college campuses. Those attending come from many churches and communities. Most conferences and institutes are held on a denominational basis, although there are notable exceptions—especially those sponsored by divisions of the National Council of Churches, by state and local councils, and by certain nondenominational agencies.

Conferences and institutes developed as important parts of the youth movements which mushroomed in many denominations in the latter part of the last century. They were many times parallel to and in conflict with the established camp meetings because their avowed purpose was to be chiefly schools for face-to-face drill in methods of Christian service rather than gatherings for evangelistic preaching.

In the early part of this century many large conference and assembly grounds sprang up across the country drawing people from wide geographic areas. Some are still in operation with widely varied programs, but the original pattern, represented by such centers as Lake Chautauqua, New York; Lake Geneva, Wisconsin; and Lakeside, Ohio, reached its peak in the late 1920's or early 1930's. Emerging philosophies of education and newer means of transportation brought about changes in the conference and institute patterns. Smaller, less elaborate centers were developed in reach of more people, more diversified program aims were pursued, and sponsorship was assumed by smaller geographical units within denominations. By 1939 The Methodist Church alone had more than three hundred conference and institute sites.

Summer conferences and institutes still play a significant role in Protestant Christian education, especially among senior high youth and adults. However, in recent years there has been a noticeable trend toward more conference-type programs with the original objectives of the institute being achieved in other ways.

The purpose of the institute is to train persons in specific areas, usually related to the objectives and program of the sponsoring agency. Persons—youth and adults—come to institutes to learn the meaning of the organization and its program, and how to carry them out effectively in the local church. There is a certain amount of emphasis on personal enrichment in the program, but by and large the focus is on training for specific responsibilities to be carried out back home.

The program of the institute is highly structured and consists primarily of class sessions in an academic setting, "interest" groups for considering special concerns or hobbies, and general programs for worship and inspiration, with "free time" for recreational activities. Until recently little attempt was made to coordinate these activities into a single whole, and little attention was given to the role of group living in the overall learning experience. Usually the class sessions tend to be largely lecture, and the leadership in all activities adult-centered. Very often the institute functions with large numbers both in total attendance and class size.

The institute pattern, with its highly academic approach, resources, and setting, is quite effective in achieving certain objectives related particularly to communication of information about organization, program, and the like. But very often these values are offset by concomitant learnings which are inherent in the structure—some of which are avoided in the kindred type of pattern known as the summer conference, which follows a different educational philosophy.

The summer conference, although sometimes called a camp, an institute, or an assembly, is distinguished by its program, its style of leadership, and its involvement of participants, rather than by the place where it is held. The place is merely a matter of accommodation for living and activities. It may be a camp, a college campus, a retreat center, or a resort hotel.

The primary purpose of the conference is personal enrichment and growth in Christian understanding and commitment, although there may be some aspects of training for specific responsibilities built into the program. When the conference is called an assembly, it usually includes delegated representation, and business meetings of the regional youth organization are held—perhaps with election of officers—during the conference.

The summer conference is supposedly designed so that all activities and experiences fit into a unified whole. It is planned for maximum involvement of those attending. One does not register for certain activities but participates in everything that occurs. The usual pattern is to have a general theme relevant to the needs and interests of those attending with all experiences designed to contribute to making the theme meaningful. There are times for private, small group, and general worship experiences; for inspirational addresses on the theme, followed by small-group discussions; for work projects and interest groups; for recreational activities that help achieve the aims of the conference; for evening programs of drama, audio-visual, and other special presentations; and there is a time for leisurely conversation and consultation with leaders.

Emphasis is placed on the small discussion groups and the involvement of every person in the total experience. Attention is given to the quality of community life with mealtime and time in living quarters important parts of the total learning. Experience has shown that when behavior problems develop they generally are due to a lack of meaningful involvement in a program the youth consider their own. When this happens they develop a sub-rosa program that *is* their own, and it usually runs counter to the conference program!

Another distinctive feature of a summer youth conference is the involvement of youth in planning the conference and in carrying out some of the leadership roles in the conference. It is not something put on by a group of adults for a group of youth. Youth themselves, with effective adult guidance, share in the responsibility for all that goes on—for it is assumed that this is the best way to help youth grow in Christian maturity and develop as effective leaders.

Adult leadership for summer youth institutes and conferences is usually volunteer and is made up mostly of ministers with a few laymen who work with youth in local churches. Some ministers by their training and customary leadership roles are more at home in the institute than in the conference. Here personal involvement with individual youth is less likely and responsibilities are specific and at stated times.

The conference pattern requires leadership that is committed to the informal, personal approach and to involvement in the total program. It requires flexibility and a certain amount of spontaneity, as well as a particular way of working with persons.

Adult leaders are usually chosen for leadership in institutes or in conferences in the light of their interests and the way in which they work most effectively with persons. Even so, there is need for preparing the leaders for their responsibilities—especially in the conference setting. The basic educational philosophy and its implications must be explored, the theme discussed, possible teaching-learning situations considered, and individual responsibilities planned and assigned. General preparation of leaders may be done in mid-winter sessions attended by persons who will work in many institutes and conferences. But each institute or conference staff will meet once or twice before its session begins in order to prepare for its own specific experience. In one or both of these preparation sessions youth leadership will also be involved.

Neither a minister nor his congregation should consider his involvement in a conference or institute as an added extra chore in his already crowded pastoral responsibilities, for they are integral parts of the church's teaching ministry and of the pastor's ministry to persons.

## Outdoor Christian Education

One of the more recent developments in Christian education has been the use of the out-of-doors and experiences in the out-of-doors as resources for Christian teaching. Some of these resources are available to the teacher in the local church in the form of field trips and the like, but widest use is made of them in the variety of organized camping programs carried on by local churches, by educational agencies of the denominations, and by interdenominational and nondenominational groups.

Camp grounds for use by religious groups have been a part of the American scene since the camp-meeting days of the early frontier. But, by and large, their purpose was to provide inexpensive accommodations for large gatherings for the same kinds of religious services and programs that could just as well have taken place in the middle of any city where sufficient facilities were available. No significant use of the out-of-doors was made.

Camping as an organized program for the achievement of religious educational objectives is an innovation of the second quarter of this century. In the view of some prominent Christian educators historians in the future will rank this as a milestone in the life of the church comparable to the beginning of the Sunday school movement in the eighteenth century.

The organized camping movement, made up of a variety of camps sponsored by youth-serving agencies and individuals, had its beginning before the turn of the century. As early as 1880 a pastor and his parish in Rhode Island sponsored a camping program. But the church was late in entering the field of camping to any large extent. Not until "experience centered" education gained wide acceptance by Christian educators were the real possibilities in this type of program for achieving Christian education objectives recognized.

The camping movement in general has had phenomenal growth in the middle half of this century, but the most notable development has been that of camping under the auspices of the church and the public school. Indeed, there has been a marked shift in emphasis in the whole field of camping from outdoor recreation and physical fitness to more specific educational goals having to do with personality growth, including its spiritual dimensions.

### The Out-of-Doors as a Resource for Christian Teaching

Outdoor Christian education is not merely traditional Christian education carried on in the out-of-doors. It is distinguished by the fact that maximum use is made of the resources in the out-of-doors for teaching-learning experiences. This does not mean "nature study." It does mean making use of God's world of nature to help persons understand him and his creative activity, and to help in bringing them into close relationship with him and with one another. It is in meaningful experiences in the out-of-doors that persons come truly to understand what the psalmists are saying to us about God as Creator and Sustainer of the universe. It is here that the wonder and awe so integrally a part of worship, and the at-homeness in God's world so necessary to faith, may be found.

In the out-of-doors campers, who are ordinarily surrounded by a world of man-made things, can discover the world God made. They can be awakened not only to their responsibility of stewardship in God's creation but learn how to work with him in his ever-unfolding purposes for the world of nature and of man.

Organized camping programs, in addition, make possible continuity of experience in a controlled environment—a laboratory of Christian living—where the campers may not only discover the wonder of God's creative work in the natural world but also the meaning of the teachings of Jesus in the elemental experiences of learning to live together in an intentional Christian community. In a variety of experiences and relationships the ability to live together as Christians is tested and interpreted in the light of the gospel.

### The Nature of the Camping Experience

Camping is a particular kind of experience in the out-of-doors. It takes many forms and is made possible through varied types of programs. Characteristic of all of them are informality, simple living, flexibility, and maximum involvement of persons. Campers participate to the limit of their abilities in planning and carrying out the living-learning experiences. Situations that arise in interpersonal relations, as well as chance discoveries in the natural world, become settings for possible significant learnings.

Leaders in the camping experience are guides—more mature persons leading the less mature in the ways of Christian living in a small community in God's great out-of-doors. But they, too, are on an adventure of discovery. Each camp group is a new group of unique persons having new experiences and unique responses to old experiences. Thus, the leader with his resources of knowledge, experience, and setting must help his campers discover and understand significant truths related to particular situations, as well as solutions to problems that arise. Formal lectures give way to informal conversation and dialogue. Worship is more likely to grow out of an immediate experience of thanksgiving, wonder, and awe, or out of a particular sense of need, than from a formal service—although corporate worship is one of the elements in the camp as a Christian community. The Bible is used as a living and relevant resource for understanding, guiding, and enriching individual and group experiences. The existential nature of the camping experience opens uniquely the way for God's self-disclosure in the Scriptures to become real to individuals. The camping experience, then, is determined largely by the kind of guidance given—by the leader's basic approach to the understanding of God and how God works in the world of nature and of persons, by his understanding of how persons learn, and by his ability to relate ordinary experiences to specific goals.

## Types of Outdoor Christian Education

Camping as outdoor Christian education takes many forms. Day camping is a rapidly growing program especially at the local church level for younger children. Campers spend the day in outdoor experiences similar to those in residence camps but return home for the night and usually the evening meal and breakfast. Day camping has the advantage of requiring few facilities and little expense, and it is accessible to more campers and more leadership. The setting is usually a wooded area or farm in easy reach of the church.

Resident camps are perhaps the most common camping experiences for boys and girls in the age groups nine to eleven and twelve to fourteen. They are occasionally sponsored by local churches but most often are under the auspices of denominational or nondenominational agencies. Church camps pioneered in coeducational camping, and in the typical church camp boys and girls of a particular age group participate together in the camping experience. They are housed in separate cabin or tent areas, with about six campers and a counselor in a living unit. Meals and all other activities outside the living area are performed together. Camp sessions typically last from one to two weeks— but in some types of camps they may run several weeks. The optimum number of campers for younger boys and girls is considered to be sixty, and for older boys and girls seventy-five.

Resident camps are of two general types: centralized and decentralized. In the former, campers and staff live in permanent facilities and eat in a common dining hall. Activities in the camp program are planned and carried out for the whole camp under the direction of a camp director, with the help of specialists in certain areas—some of whom may be cabin counselors. Usually the day-to-day program follows a fairly consistent pattern.

In the decentralized camp permanent facilities may also be used, but the activities are planned and carried out in small groups and day-to-day experiences and the time schedule may be quite varied. Usually a cabin of boys and a cabin of girls, with their counselors, constitutes a "family" group which is responsible for all its experiences, some of which may be shared with other groups or with the whole camp. Each group usually develops its own "home in the wood" as a center of activities away from the permanent facilities where they may prepare some of their own meals and have "sleep-outs."

Rustic or pioneer camping is another more advanced form of decentralized camping with all living, meal preparation, and most other activities carried out by the small groups in their own campsites with temporary shelters and other facilities. Usually experienced junior high and senior high campers are involved in this type of camping which gives maximum opportunity for initiative, imagination, participation, and use of the out-of-doors.

Family camping is growing rapidly as a part of summertime Christian education. Families occupy permanent cabin facilities in a resident camp and eat in the dining hall, or provide their own camping equipment and prepare their own meals. The program is family centered and loosely structured in order to encourage families to live and learn together.

Older youth and young adults find in travel camps, canoe trips, and pack trips on mountain trails excellent means for realizing Christian values and for involvement in significant Christian learning experiences in small groups in the out-of-doors.

## Leadership and Emerging Problems

Leadership in church camping is usually volunteer. However, most camps provide a paid service staff, and some camps employ a few program resource persons to augment the volunteer staff. Both volunteer and employed personnel must have genuine interest in and skills for the out-of-doors as well as the ability to work effectively with small groups in informal learning situations. Most camping programs include training for their current and prospective leadership.

In the field of church camping major denominations have, under the National Council of Churches, worked together in developing basic principles and resource materials, and in training leadership. In 1951 a program was initiated with the Outdoor Education Association for the development of philosophy and leadership for decentralized church camping.

Church camping is integrally related to the general camping movement and to the American Camping Association through the Committee on Camps and

Conferences of the National Council of Churches and through the participation of church camp leaders in the leadership of the American Camping Association and its regional sections. Conservative, evangelical church camping is represented in the general camping movement by the nondenominational Christian Camp and Conference Association, Inc., and Roman Catholic Camps are related to general camping through the Catholic Camping Association.

The rapid growth of summertime Christian education, particularly in the camping field, has created major problems, especially in the areas of adequate leadership, sufficient facilities, and needed basic theory relating means to ends. Often more attention has been given to learning camping skills than to how they can be used for achieving the objectives of Christian education. Not enough attention has been given to such things as the role of the Holy Spirit in the small group experiences, and the use of the resources of the Christian faith in the everyday camp experiences. Even so, enough progress has been made to warrant confidence in the validity and the potentialities of these kinds of learning experiences so as to include them among the most significant ways for carrying out the teaching ministry of the church.

## FOR ADDITIONAL READING

Bowman, Clarice M. *Spiritual Values in Camping.* New York: Association Press, 1954.

Butt, Elsie Miller. *The Vacation School in Christian Education.* Nashville: Abingdon Press, 1957.

Doty, Richard S. *The Character Dimension of Camping.* New York: Association Press, 1960.

Ensign, John and Ruth. *Camping Together as Christians.* Richmond: John Knox Press, 1958.

Freeberg, W. H. and Taylor, L. E. *Philosophy of Outdoor Education.* Minneapolis: Burgess Publishing Co., 1961.

National Council of Churches Series: *Let's Go Exploring; Let the Bible Speak Outdoors; Let's Find Outdoor Opportunities for Worship; Let's Teach Through Group Relations.* New York: National Council of Churches.

Todd, Pauline H. and Floyd. *Camping for Christian Youth: A Guide to Methods and Principles for Evangelical Camps.* New York: Harper & Row, 1963.

*Chapter 31*

# Religious Education in the Roman Catholic Church

*Neil G. McCluskey*

It has only been in recent years that Roman Catholics have in numbers been reappraising the separate religiously oriented school and school system. What is it? How did it come about? Is it achieving its goals? Is it any longer a necessity?

Going into the year 1966, the Roman Catholic school system looks impressive. During the last school year enrollment in the 13,208 elementary and secondary schools was in excess of 5.6 million and had recruited the services of 172,900 teachers—in a proportion of one lay teacher to two religious (i.e., priest, Sister, or Brother) teachers.

These figures are even more significant when it is realized that the Catholic schools provide for a large share of the school-going population in many eastern and midwestern cities: in Dubuque, 61 percent; in Manchester, N. H., 52 percent; in Pittsburgh, 42 percent; in Philadelphia, 39 percent; in Buffalo, 38 percent; in New Orleans, Chicago, and Milwaukee, 33 percent; in Cleveland and New York, 26 percent; in St. Louis, 25 percent; and in Detroit, 23 percent.

The average Protestant or non-Catholic is certainly aware of, probably puzzled over, and possibly resentful of this phenomenon. He may occasionally have asked himself why Catholic schools exist on this massive scale. Do Catholics have such a different idea of the nature of education that they feel compelled to withdraw from the common community effort and to establish separate schools for their children? Part of the answer is to be found in the traditional understanding of education, but perhaps most of the answer is explained in the evolution of the American public school and its failure to provide for what Catholics consider a total education.

## The Rationale for a Separate School

Religious education is an ambiguous phrase, and out of ambiguity has grown misunderstanding and confusion about the aims of Roman Catholic education. In a restricted sense religious education can be understood as that systematic instruction in the beliefs and practices of an institutionalized religion whose objective is understanding.[1] However, since the sponsoring group undertakes religious education in order to build commitment among its members, loyalty

---

[1] Religious education in this sense is still not the same as theology. The science of theology is not taught for religious commitment but is a strict academic discipline resulting from the schematic application of the principles of philosophy and history to revealed religious truths.

and service to the ideals of the group are also valid objectives of this kind of education. When the objectives of understanding and commitment are combined, religious education is more properly religious formation.

The Catholic school, however, is intended to be much more than a catechetical institution. In fact, if its primary function were simply to teach the catechism, there would be no need for separate Catholic schools, and there would be no convincing reason why Catholic children should not attend the public schools. One could rightly claim this as the principal task of the school if there were no other way of formally presenting religious doctrine to children save by means of separate schools.

But there have always been other ways of supplementing secular education with religious instruction: by classes in the church hall before or after school hours, by parental instruction, by home visits of a special teacher, by instructions at daily Mass, by released-time and dismissed-time programs. Almost any of these substitutes, or a combination, could be a sufficient and certainly a less costly method of formally teaching religious truth. The teaching of the formulas of the Catholic faith, therefore, cannot be either the exclusive or even the primary function of the Catholic school, let alone its reason for existence.

By making his church the gateway to eternal life, Christ has endowed his religious society with some authority over the education of the baptized. He established his church precisely to provide, largely through religious instruction and training, the means to learn the supernatural truths he has revealed and the practices of the Christian religion he has made obligatory.

The teaching authority conferred by Christ upon the church does not lessen the right and duty of the parents in what concerns the religious formation of the child. In fact, the family into which man is born has the primary right and obligation to educate. This right is prior to the rights of both civil and ecclesiastical society because it is based on the natural relation of parents to their offspring. However, the family right in education is not an absolute and despotic one, but is, in the words of Pope Pius XI, "dependent on the natural and divine law, and therefore subject alike to the authority and jurisdiction of the Church, and to the vigilance and administrative care of the State in view of the common good." [2] In ideal, the rights of parent, church, and state work in harmony for the benefit of the individual.

What are the principal benefits that a Catholic parent and pastor find in education within a separate school? They can be grouped around these four points.

1. The child learns systematically and thoroughly about his religion. He obtains a formal knowledge of the truths of Christian revelation, including the existence and nature of God, Christ's incarnation and redemption, Christ's church and the workings of the Holy Spirit within it, the history of the chosen people and of the church.

2. He enjoys regular opportunities, direct and indirect, for the deepening of his sense of religious dedication. He has ready access to the Mass and sacraments;

[2] Encyclical Letter, "The Christian Education of Youth" (*Divini Illius Magistri*), 1929.

he learns to live a fuller life of prayer; he acquires a practical knowledge and love of the church's liturgical life.

3. The child learns an ordering of knowledge in an atmosphere in which the spiritual and the supernatural hold the primacy in the hierarchy of temporal and eternal values. He learns that his faith is not something apart but is related to the whole texture of life.

4. He acquires a "Catholic" attitude or outlook on life based upon the firm knowledge of his duties and privileges as a follower of Christ; he gains pride and love in—and loyalty to—his Christian heritage.

These four categories cannot, however, be treated as if they were independent of one another. They are closely related, for each is an aspect of Christian growth, each fuses with and reinforces the others. The result is Christian education in all its dimensions—than which no loftier or more perfect educational ideal has ever been conceived. It goes without saying that the religiously related school by itself cannot achieve this ideal but that the school can only build on what the home has already done and continues to do.

Let us look more closely at the four points.

Knowledge is not faith, but since faith is an intellectual virtue, the two go together. A solid grasp of the truths of belief and an awareness of one's motives for assenting are the natural foundation of faith. So systematic instruction is called for. A person learns religion in somewhat the same way that he acquires a language. If he is fortunate enough to be raised in the country where the tongue is spoken, he will normally have a better grasp of the language than would be possible even through intense self-instruction or private tutoring or enrollment in some special class. It always happens that residence in a country facilitates the acquisition of a second language. Here is the learner's great advantage when he is instructed in a Catholic school. He gets a more complete and systematic instruction in the formal truths of the Catholic religion, and he is "in the new country" where the atmosphere reinforces and hastens the process of learning.

Though formal religion classes are only a small portion of the day's instructional total, religion has an indirect influence that enters into many areas of the curriculum. Religious ideas and subjects receive proportionate treatment in other courses when they are germane to the subject. This would be especially true in literature, history, and social studies. It is axiomatic that we receive new knowledge through the filter of what already has been absorbed. If a man believes that humankind is nothing more than a freak accident of the impersonal forces of nature, his evaluation of man's story upon earth will differ markedly from that of a believer in the God of Genesis.

A thorough religious formation comes about through the joint efforts of home, school, and parish. Hence the liturgical life of the church into which the child is initiated is lived in all three spheres of influence. The late Pius XI's encyclical letter on "The Christian Education of Youth" speaks of the educational environment of the church as embracing "the sacraments, divinely efficacious means of grace, the sacred ritual, so wonderfully instructive and the material fabric of her churches, whose liturgy and art have an immense educational value." Ordinarily the parish school is situated beside the church, and this proximity makes for close cooperation in religious education and formation. During his parochial school days a Catholic youngster is closer to the liturgy than at any other period in his life. From September to June he acquires a familiarity in his daily living with the saints and seasons of the church. Along with his knowledge of the heroes of the profane world, the youngster meets the great men and women of the church world. He observes Advent in preparation for Christ's birthday at Christmas and the season of Lent in preparation for Christ's resurrection at Easter. The boys learn to assist at Mass and other liturgical functions, and the girls learn to sing the sacred chants and music that accompany these ceremonies.

The most distinctive, certainly the most important, benefit of education within a Catholic school is the ordering of knowledge in an atmosphere wherein spiritual and supernatural realities are properly ordered in the total scheme of things. A Catholic philosophy of education is rooted in the reality of the supernatural and its primacy in the hierarchy of values. The goals, ideals, and values of the order of nature—important and worthy of pursuit as these may be—must remain subordinate in Catholic eyes to those of the supernatural order. Adam's fall from God's friendship and the supernatural order planned for him have given rise in Adam's descendants to an antagonism between the natural and supernatural orders, felt particularly within man himself.

There are noses that wrinkle in tolerant amusement at talk of the fall of man as if it were a medieval tale, totally irrelevant to the large questions in education. Yet two distinguished philosophers of education as far apart as the Lutheran Friedrich Foerster and the agnostic Bertrand Russell have agreed that, in the last analysis, all theories of education are dependent on the views taken of the dogma of original sin. After all, it does make considerable difference what an educator thinks of the nature of the educand.

The Catholic school shares with the home and church the responsibility of teaching the child that his chief significance comes from the fact that he is created by God and is destined for life with God in eternity. In a modern society where the old religiously based value system is under constant attack the young follower of Christ requires the powerful integrating force of religion. The role of the Catholic school is not the simple one of teaching a set of formulas but in a thousand imperceptible ways to impart an attitude toward life as a whole. It is Catholicism as a culture, not as a conflicting creed, which is at odds with the spirit of the modern world and in a sense makes Catholics a people apart. Christian or Christ-centered culture is the supreme integrating principle from which proceeds all activity within a truly Catholic school.

It was Justice Robert H. Jackson of the U.S. Supreme Court who inadvertently cited the reason that above all justifies the existence of a separate Catholic school, when he wrote in his dissent in the Everson case: "Our public school, if not a product of Protestantism, at least is more consistent with it than with the Catholic culture and scheme of values." [3]

[3] *Everson vs. Board of Education, 330 U.S. 1 (1947).*

## The Rights of Parents, Church, and State in Education

One of the finest formulations of the core philosophy of Catholic education is that contained in the encyclical letter of the late Pope Pius XI, "The Christian Education of Youth." The Catholic idea of education begins with the reality of the supernatural order as revealed through, and in the person of, Jesus Christ the Savior. The Catholic belief that man is a creature of God destined to share in the divine life answers the two questions upon which every philosophy of education is built: What is man? What is his purpose? Man's sharing in the divine life commences at the moment of baptism, when sanctifying grace and the virtues of faith, hope, and charity—man's supernatural faculties, as it were—are infused into his soul. That life, which begins on earth through faith, is to be perfected in a beatific union with God in glory hereafter. For a believer this truth explains the ultimate purpose and final objective of education—not excluding, obviously, more immediate goals in education. For a believer this conviction likewise provides the theological integrating principle and the basis of sanctions in the moral order.

Needless to mention, Catholics hold no monopoly on these things. There are millions of American Protestants who are as deeply committed to these truths as are any Catholics. Yet neither Catholic nor Protestant family can count upon the public school as an ally in helping pass on to their children even as primary a truth as the existence of a personal God or the reality of the supernatural order. In the inevitable process of acquiring a more secular and profane orientation, American society has watched this basic philosophy of Christian education being replaced by an allegedly neutral philosophy of secularism.

In our modern industrialized and urbanized society we have grown accustomed to the shadow of the state over our lives. It could be argued that, given the conditions of modern life, an individual member of a family in the twentieth century has had to surrender certain areas of life to minute state regulation. Yet even seventy-five years ago, the attitude of American society toward control of education differed largely from today's. In 1965 we simply assume that the state has the right to establish and operate schools, but this assumption, at least on a universal scale, is something that arrived on the social scene rather late.

When at the national gathering of the N.E.A. in St. Paul in 1890 Archbishop John Ireland voiced his own conviction that the question of the state's rights in education had been settled, many people, including certain of his episcopal confreres, would have stood in sharp disagreement. It was not at all settled, according to Bishop Bernard McQuaid of Rochester, N. Y., who insisted: "The Catholic is unwilling to transfer the responsibility of the education of his children to the State. His conscience informs him that the State is an incompetent agent to fulfil his parental duties." [4]

This was not an exclusively Catholic view. McQuaid could quote in his

---

[4] *The Public School Question* (Boston: Duffy and Co., 1876), p. 9. McQuaid was the highly articulate leader of the episcopal opposition to Ireland.

favor the authority of Herbert Spencer, who had written: "In the same way that our definition of state duty forbids the State to administer religion or charity, so likewise does it forbid the State to administer education." [5]

An eminent historian of this period has pointed out that up to the time of the struggle by Archbishop John Hughes and the Catholic community of New York for tax support of Catholic schools,

Catholics and non-Catholics had been in essential agreement regarding parental responsibility for the education of children. But with the common school awakening, the gradual disappearance of religious teaching and atmosphere from the public schools, and the new conception that their work was primarily secular and designed to fit the youth of the land for the duties of citizenship, the older idea that education was a parental responsibility gave way to the belief that it was an enterprise of the State.[6]

The attitude of Catholics (and many others) during the nineteenth century that the state could only be a substitute for parents delinquent in the duty of educating the child must be understood against a backdrop of revolutionary social changes in Europe. No change was more dramatic than the state's encroachment on the regulation of marriage. From time immemorial the church had possessed sole jurisdiction over the bond of matrimony. Though marriage was at the same time a contract and a sacrament, both were regulated by the church. The jurisdiction of the state extended exclusively to the civil aspects of the marital union, e.g., inheritances, dowries, legitimacy of succession, etc. In the last quarter of the eighteenth century, however, the secularization of marriage was partially or wholly effected in all the principal countries of Europe. The authority of the church was brushed aside, and the principle was articulated that the secular power has the sole competence in regulating marriage contracts. In fact, during the 1790's the leadership of the French Revolution organized a complete republican liturgy to replace the sacramental ceremonies of marriage, and under Robespierre's urging, the Convention passed a law to establish a Feast of Conjugal Fidelity, upon which marital unions were to be solemnly entered into.

Perhaps the independent school has already performed—and is performing —a considerable service to American society simply by preserving a link to an earlier era when the state's hand rested less heavy on education, and parents were more aware of their freedom to choose the kind of school they wanted for their children. Despite the assumption of some people, the state-established secular school has no prior claim on the allegiance of all citizens, and no parent

---

[5] *Ibid.*, p. 7. The British philosopher had enormous influence on nineteenth-century education.

[6] Merle Curti, *The Social Ideas of American Educators* (Paterson, N. J.: Pageant Books, 1959), p. 349. Whenever the occasion has offered itself, the United States Supreme Court has reaffirmed the principle that "the child is not the mere creature of the State" (*Pierce vs. Society of Sisters*, 1925) and that "the custody, care and nurture of the child reside first in the parents" (*Prince vs. Massachusetts*, 1944). The Universal Declaration of Human Rights, adopted by the General Assembly of the United Nations (Dec. 10, 1948), proclaims the same principle: "Parents have a prior right to choose the kind of education that shall be given to their children" (Article 26, par. 3).

is in the slightest degree "disloyal" when he exercises his natural right to patronize his own school. If there is a primacy of spiritual values over the purely secular, there is a valid choice of a religious over a secular school—at least this was the tradition of Western civilization.

## Some Historical Considerations

The history of the Catholic school in America is part of the larger history of a church which was predominantly immigrant, attempting to survive and adapt in a generally hostile environment. Throughout the nineteenth century the Catholic community remained pretty much outside the principal cultural and political currents.

As young America settled down, after winning independence, and began to grow into a nation, the Catholic community faced a painful dilemma. As their Protestant neighbors, they, too, were eager to send their children to the common schools but—they could not. They appreciated that schooling was the necessary means to share in the American dream, but the common schools had not been designed with Roman Catholic children in mind. The "public" schools, for whose support Catholic citizens were equally taxed, smacked strongly of Protestantism, with their Protestant books, hymns, prayers and, above all, the Protestant Bible.[7] Catholics sought to alleviate their plight in a double way: Catholic pupils should be excused from classroom reading of the Protestant Bible and related devotional practices; school taxes paid by Catholic citizens should be used, in whole or in part, to educate their children in church schools.

No legal redress was to be found in the matter of Bible reading. On the contrary, powerful legal support for the religious status quo in the public schools was supplied by an 1854 ruling of the Supreme Court of Maine (*Donahue vs. Richards*), authorizing school officials to require the reading of the King James Version of the Bible. This precedent was not successfully challenged until near the close of the century.

Catholic efforts to obtain a share of the school tax fund for separate schools likewise failed. In 1840 the Catholic community of New York put its petition before the Board of Aldermen of the city. Speaking of his fellow citizens, the spokesman informed the Board that as Catholics:

They bear, and are willing to bear, their portion of every common burden; and feel themselves entitled to a participation in every common benefit. This participation, they regret to say, has been denied them for years back, in reference to Common School Education in the city of New York, except on conditions with which their conscience, and, as they believe their duty to God, did not, and do not leave them at liberty to comply.[8]

[7] In retrospect it is hard to understand the ferocious tension that plagued the question of what version of the Bible should be read in the public school unless it be remembered that the King James or the Douay Version was a *symbol*.

[8] The complete text of the document, "Petition of the Catholics of New York for a Portion of the Common-School Fund" may be found in *Roman Catholic Education in America*, Neil G. McCluskey, ed. (New York: Teachers College, Columbia University, 1964), pp. 65-77.

The immediate outcome of this agitation was that the common schools of New York were shortly taken over by the state from the private group calling itself the Public School Society. Though this move did not come to terms with the still unresolved question of parental rights in education, it was the first major step toward the inevitable secularization of the schools. The pattern of no tax funds for denominationally controlled schools was established—and with minor exceptions has endured down to the present day.

So it came about that since the Catholic youngster was not made to feel at home in the public school, he went to his own school, wherever feasible. Following the failure of the 1840 effort to have the New York City parochial schools share in common tax moneys, the Catholic communities nationally began to expend their interest and energy almost exclusively on Catholic parochial and private schools. One immediate result was that the public schools became semi-Protestant domain.

But basic dilemmas seldom disappear. In opposing Catholic influence in the public schools, other Americans of strong religious conviction were forced to stand by and watch helplessly while all religious influence disappeared and a totally secular philosophy moved in. By tradition the American people have regarded their schools as the most practical means of transmitting to children the public philosophy which undergirds our society. They have insisted that the school assume a large share of the responsibility for developing the child's character or, in more modern terms, for inculcating moral and spiritual values. Yet the history of the public schools is plainer on no other point than that this mandate, however questionably realizable in the past, can no longer be discharged.

In the 1840's when Horace Mann was giving shape to the prototype of the American public school, this task was relatively simple. Then character formation could be based upon the morality and inspiration of the Christian Bible. Provided the public school did not favor any single sect in the community, the public school could inculcate the generally agreed upon moral and religious truths of all Protestants, as found in the Bible. While a substantial Protestant homogeneity endured, the compromise worked. When non-Protestant groups were sufficiently numerous to make their protests heard effectively, it collapsed.

It was not long, moreover, before important voices in the educational world were heard to the effect that by its very nature the school is completely secular and hence lacking competence in the area of religious education. This position was not based on any hostility toward religion or religious education. It simply argued that in method, spirit, and content, secular truth is of necessity antagonistic to the acquisition of religious truth, so that the two cannot be well taught under the same school roof. (In effect, this position also furnished reasonable grounds for denying a share of public funds to religious schools.)

Moreover, proponents of this philosophy took frank cognizance of the religious fragmentation of American society. On this point they could quote no less an authority than Bishop John Lancaster Spalding, a prominent spokesman for the Catholic hierarchy: "I am willing to assume and to accept as a fact that our theological differences make it impossible to introduce the teaching of any religious creed into the public school. I take the system as it is,—that is, as a system of secular education." [9] But let it also be remembered that when men of Spalding's day used the term "secular," they intended far more than the same word means today. Then moral and spiritual values were universally assumed to have roots in a religious value system. This included belief in the existence of a Creator, who was the source of the justice and the rights defined in America's first great political documents.

The naturalist philosophies propounded in the present century have been largely responsible for emptying the concept of "secular" of its theistic-natural law content. Today the values of secular scientism have generally replaced the moral and spiritual values of the Judeo-Christian tradition as the foundation for character education in the public school. To state this is not, however, to be unmindful of the central problem, namely, the limitations inherent in the idea of one *common* school serving a religiously pluralistic society.[10]

### The 1884 Baltimore Council and Catholic Education

It was only after the Civil War that popular education began to take wide hold. In 1880 public school enrollment hit one million for the first time. Twenty years later, it soared to 15 million, and in 1920, to 21 million. In the aftermath of the Third Plenary Council of Baltimore (1884), Catholic school enrollment began a similar rise. In 1900 there were 854,523 children in Catholic schools; in 1920, this figure had reached 1.8 million. The 1964-65 enrollment was in excess of 5.6 million. Yet this achievement has not been without a price.

Social conditions had forced the American Catholic bishops in 1884 to propose what has been held up ever since as an ideal of Catholic education: "Every Catholic child in a Catholic school." Today, more than eighty years later, despite heroic exertion, the ideal remains as distant as it has always been —at least one half the Catholic school-going population remains outside a Catholic elementary or secondary school. Catholic leadership is more and more realizing that new approaches, new emphases, new methods are demanded in order to continue achieving the perennial goals of Catholic education. In retrospect one can list four less than beneficent outcomes of the drive since 1884 for universal Catholic education in this country: (1) clerical domination of the schools; (2) overcommitment to the elementary schools; (3) confusion of the academic mandate and the pastoral charge; (4) substitution of the school for the family and church as the primary agent in the religious formation of the child.

It was inevitable that from earliest times the conduct of Catholic education

[9] *Means and Ends of Education* (Chicago: A. C. McClurg & Co., 1895), p. 141. No Catholic leader of the last century commanded the respect or wielded the influence of Bishop Spalding of Peoria (1840-1916).

[10] A complete treatment of this question may be found in the author's *Public Schools and Moral Education: The Influence of Horace Mann, William Torrey Harris, and John Dewey* (New York: Columbia University Press, 1958).

in America was almost exclusively the task of the clergy and the religious orders. From the financial point of view there was no alternative. There simply was an insufficiency of funds even for the modest salaries that generally accrue to teachers. Moreover, there was a rich tradition of clerical and religious activity in education. Teaching groups, such as the Brothers of the Christian Schools, the Jesuits, and the Religious of the Sacred Heart, had achieved eminence in their European schools. Quite naturally then, congregations of teaching nuns and Brothers were invited to America. Dozens of native American congregations of teaching Sisters were founded by bishops, and the services of these dedicated teachers made it possible to open schools on an unprecedented scale.

Since 1945, however, two factors have intervened which have altered the pattern of expansion. The demand for teachers has outrun the supply of vocations, and the more demanding standards of teacher preparation have lengthened the period of training. Though the mainstay of the Catholic elementary and secondary school remains the teaching nun, each year sees an increasing share of the burden borne by lay teachers. In 1964-65 on the elementary school level there were 76,750 religious and 42,000 lay teachers; on the secondary level there were 36,050 religious and 18,100 lay teachers. Yet twenty years ago there were only 2,768 lay teachers in the grade schools and 3,752 in the high schools. It seems a safe prediction to say that the key to future development and expansion of the Catholic school lies in the hands of the lay teacher.

Educators and psychologists will never resolve the argument whether the earlier or later years are more important in the child's formation, but it should be beyond argument that today the secondary schools and the college play a much more dominant role in the young person's life than does the elementary school. Oddly enough, Catholic emphasis remains on the elementary pattern of education, just as it did back in 1884 when the Third Plenary Council of Baltimore legislated on the point. Many Catholic leaders regret the present over-commitment of the Catholic Church in the United States to the elementary school.

Social and educational patterns in this country have changed drastically in eighty years. In 1880 the average American completed less than three full years of schooling; today he completes ten years and six months. Eighty years ago about 10 percent of the eligible secondary-school population were attending high school while today it is an estimated 93 percent. Adjustment to these drastic changes in the American school pattern demands boldness and experimentation. Thus far only a few Catholic dioceses have begun to make either the adjustments or the experiments. Parenthetically it should be here remarked that the preoccupation with elementary education partly explains the plight of many Catholic colleges and universities. The building and staffing of elementary schools on a massive scale has diverted the resources of the Catholic community so that vital support is wanting for the colleges. It still comes as a start to most non-Catholic people to learn that Catholic colleges and universities (with a handful of exceptions) receive practically no financial support from the dioceses.

The third negative result of the 1884 Baltimore commitment to universal education has been diminishing in recent years. This is the confusion of the academic mandate and the pastoral charge. Put in its simplest terms, it is an effort to explain the rationale of the Catholic school by saying that it exists "to save souls." But it is just as true then to say that the purpose of any other Catholic-sponsored activity—youth clubs, summer camps, hospitals, veterans organizations, singing groups—is "to save souls." The saving of souls is too general an explanation of the school's purpose and does not indicate its specific objective, that distinctive something which puts the school in one category and takes it out of all other categories. Since the saving of souls is the purpose of all these activities, it can only describe the school's ultimate purpose, a purpose it necessarily shares in the absolute order with every human undertaking.

A related objection and one common among those outside the Catholic communion, is that in conducting schools the Catholic Church is simply trying to proselytize. For what other reason would the army of priests, Sisters, and Brothers be engaged in school work except to make good Catholics?

This objection grows out of a failure to see the difference between the purpose of the work itself and the purpose or *motive* of the worker. Education is education and a school is a school, regardless of the motivation of those operating it. One could argue similarly that because the state wants loyal and dedicated citizens to emerge from its schools, this motivation distorts the nature of a state school. Not at all. The school retains its nature and fundamental purpose despite the reasons the church or state may have for engaging in educational work. However, failure to distinguish between the agent's motive and the intrinsic formality of the work itself leads to two different attitudes, both, in the final analysis, irrational.

In the first case, there results the contrived dilemma wherein one is asked to choose flag or cross, fatherland or faith, Caesar or God—which may be facile rhetoric but is poor reasoning. This is the basis of the sometimes heard challenge to Catholics that they choose between loyalty to the public school dedicated to producing Americans and allegiance to the parochial school dedicated to producing Catholics. The traditional philosophy of Christian education sees no real antagonism between the twin ideals of dedicated citizenry and religious commitment. They are compatible and complementary.

In the second case, the saving-of-souls approach becomes for some well-meaning people justification for academic policies and practices that fall far below the sound and scholarly standards of the educational world. Fortunately, horrendous examples of this sort of thing are becoming difficult to find, but whenever they are found, they provide potent ammunition for hostile critics of Christian education.

A fourth, and perhaps the most serious, drawback resulting from the Baltimore legislation is the reversal of the roles of school and family-church in the education of the child. So often it is the case that families feel absolved of all responsibility for the religious formation of their children once they have entrusted them to the parochial school. Parents who argue, "Leave it to the good Sisters!" often send their children to school almost religiously illiterate.

In many homes there is no concerted effort to supplement or complement the religious teaching of the school.

Bad as this situation is it can be somewhat remedied, but what should be said of the millions of Catholic children who never get to a Catholic school? Many parents do little for them and expect somehow that the parish church will find a way. In some parishes the education program of the Confraternity of Christian Doctrine is doing a thorough job, but hampered by lack of funds and personnel—the money and teachers are all in the parochial school—the results fall far short of the promise.

## In Conclusion

Eighty years after Baltimore the question is fairly raised: Has the separate Catholic school been successful? Does it make a significant difference? In other words, do twelve years of Catholic elementary and secondary schooling produce a better Catholic? Are the products of a full Catholic education truly different in their attitudes toward the broad social, political, and moral issues of modern America? Initial studies produced by Fichter, Rossi, Greeley, and the Carnegie Study based at the University of Notre Dame are inconclusive.[11] Perhaps the results of separate Catholic education are so completely in the realm of the intangible, and perhaps the simultaneous operation of factors such as family life, individual temperament, creedal friendships, and especially the working of God's grace on the soul will make the quest for a scientifically sociological answer pointless.

The reexamination of the value of Christian education within a separate school along with mounting pressures to provide better religious education and formation for the one half of the Catholic school-going population outside Catholic schools have given additional impetus to the catechetical movement. A crisp alertness is perceptible on a number of seminary, university, and college campuses which have pioneered new approaches to the sharing of ancient gospel treasures. Yet, as is so often the case, the excitingly new is in reality the presentation to a new culture and a new generation of what has for centuries captivated the minds and hearts of mankind. Scripture and dogma studies have achieved a place of academic distinction on the campuses of a growing number of institutions. Religious and lay teachers of religion courses in the grade schools are now much better prepared. The part-time courses of instruction offered to youngsters not in Catholic schools are increasingly better taught by the corps of volunteer teachers banded together in the Confraternity of Christian Doctrine. The good news of Christ's message is being heard in the contemporary world.

The theory of the separate religious school is an ideal which has well served

[11] Joseph H. Fichter, *Parochial School: A Sociological Study* (Notre Dame: University of Notre Dame Press, 1958); Peter H. and Alice S. Rossi, "Background and Consequences of Parochial School Education," *Harvard Educational Review*, XXVII (Summer, 1957), 195; Andrew M. Greeley, *Religion and Career* (New York: Sheed & Ward, 1963); "The Parochial Schools Today," *Carnegie Corporation of New York Quarterly*, XXIII (April, 1965).

the Catholic community in the United States. Without it, the American Catholic Church could never have made the contributions to society which it has. Whatever structural modifications the Catholic school system may undergo in the decades ahead, there is one certainty: it will remain; it will try to perform its task even better. Granted the religious and ethical disunities that divide Americans, perhaps a providential role is presently being played by those Catholic youngsters who are outside the separate Catholic school. They may be serving as a bridge—bringing to the Catholic community a greater sense of common social and civic objectives and to the non-Catholic community an important kind of Christian witness.

## FOR ADDITIONAL READING

Hofinger, Johannes, S.J. *The Art of Teaching Christian Doctrine: The Good News and Its Proclamation.* Notre Dame: University of Notre Dame Press, 1957.

Perhaps the most single influential book on the development of modern catechetics by one of the important pioneers in the movement.

———— and Stone, Theodore C., eds. *Pastoral Catechetics.* New York: Herder & Herder, 1964.

Essays by leaders in the modern movement essential for anyone wishing to follow the catechetical *aggiornamento* in American Catholicism.

McCluskey, Neil G., S.J. *Catholic Viewpoint on Education.* Rev. ed. Garden City: Doubleday and Company, 1962.

A concise presentation in popular form of the history and underlying philosophy of Catholic education in the United States.

McGannon, J. Barry, S.J.; Cooke, Bernard J., S.J.; and Klubertanz, George P., S.J., eds. *Christian Wisdom and Christian Formation.* New York: Sheed & Ward, 1964.

A series of papers prepared for a national workshop of Jesuit educators on the place of philosophy and theology in the modern American college.

Sloyan, Gerard S., ed. *Shaping the Christian Message.* New York: The Macmillan Company, 1958.

The first in the series of essay collections which brought the best in European thought to American shores and helped to trigger the revolution in American Catholic catechetics.

# Chapter 32

# JEWISH RELIGIOUS
# EDUCATION

## *Alexander M. Schindler*

BECAUSE IT IS ONE OF THE OLDEST RELIGIONS OF MANKIND—ITS ADHERENTS scattered throughout the world, their faith challenged by many varied winds of thought—Judaism, understandably enough, is not a simple faith. It is, rather, a complex system of life and thought, embracing many points of view and distinctive only in its totality, in the singular integration of diverse details.

The American religious Jewish community reflects these variations. Its principal divisions into Orthodoxy, Conservatism, Reform, and Reconstructionism do not begin to delineate the ideological differences which obtain. Each branch itself encompasses a spectrum of views so that a lucid exposition of their general and educational philosophies cannot readily be offered.

To bring some order to seeming chaos, we will begin our presentation with a brief summary of Judaism's traditional view of education, as it flows from its fundamental theological assumptions. Then we will point to the historical, sociological changes which compelled the Jewish community to modify and to enlarge its traditional approach. Lastly, we will examine the dominant strains of contemporary Jewish religious thought—liberalism and fundamentalism— in the effort to understand their divergent programs of religious instruction.

### Judaism's View of Education

Central to Judaism's philosophy of education is its concept of man, which holds his nature to be a blending of body and soul, of matter and of spirit. Man is made of the dust, yet there is something in him which has its source in the divine and enables him to achieve communion with it. Because he was fashioned in the image of God, he can encounter God, if only he seek him. "Man is not cut off and isolated from the universe, but a part of it. Somehow he can reach out and understand it. Man may be limited and small, but he can grow toward God, because something in him corresponds to God." [1] The realization of this potentiality within him, the attainment of communion with the divine, constitutes man's essential task; it is the infinite duty which has been laid on finite human life.

Education is a principal means for life's fulfillment; "a man needs to study so that he may become himself." [2] The unlearned man can never be pious;

[1] Eugene B. Borowitz, "A Jewish View of Education," in *Philosophies of Education*, Philip H. Phenix, ed. (New York: John Wiley & Sons, 1961), p. 87.
[2] *Ibid.*, p. 88.

he may will to find God, but he does not know the way; he perceives the design, but he lacks the tools and has failed to master the craft. Learning is the key to the universe; man becomes God-like, holy as God is holy, only as he grows in the knowledge of God's world and word.

Education is a means, not the end. Though prizing knowledge above all earthly possessions, Judaism ascribes no worth to study for study's sake alone. "He who has knowledge of the Torah but no fear of God, is like the keeper of the treasury who has the inner keys, but not the outer keys. He cannot enter." [3] The goal of learning is the refinement of a sensitivity to the divine; the beginning and the end of wisdom is the fear of heaven.

Judaism's conception of human nature is unitary. Its dualism, such as it is, is not rigidly drawn. It speaks of body and of soul but sees them bound in indissoluble union. Certainly the body is not burdened with all sin, nor is the soul given credit for all virtue.

To what may this be compared? To a king who owned a beautiful orchard which contained splendid figs. Now, he appointed two watchmen therein, one lame and the other blind. One day, the lame man said to the blind: "I see beautiful figs in the orchard. Come and take me upon thy shoulder that we may procure and eat them." So the lame bestrode the blind, procured and ate them. Some time after, the owner of the orchard came and inquired of them, "Where are those beautiful figs?" The lame man replied, "Have I then feet to walk with?" The blind man replied, "Have I then eyes to see with?" What did the king do? He placed the lame upon the blind and judged them together. So will the Holy One, blessed be He, return the soul to the body and judge them as one. [4]

Man is not a loose federation of two or even three separate states—body, mind, spirit—but, rather, is he a composite of these correlative principles of being.

The implication of this conception for the understanding of education's task is clear. Its function is all encompassing. It cannot be divided in any manner or restricted in any fashion. One cannot refine the competence of the mind while oblivious to the needs and potentialities of the body or blind to the values and the final purposes which are born of man's spirit. The development of the total man is education's concern; *all* life is its proper province.

Judaism's reluctance to ascribe a final duality to human nature extends to the nature of man's universe. Here, too, no artificial divisions are made, no realms sequestered from the horizons of inquiry which a man can properly pursue. "There is no not-holy, there is only that which has not been hallowed, which has not yet been redeemed to its holiness." [5]

The study of nature is not inimical to the pursuit of the religious life; it is a pillar on which the life of faith rests; God can be known only through its free and unrestricted service. [6] The student of science ought never be hindered in his quest by theological presupposition; the "Torah is not a code which com-

[3] Babylonian Talmud, "Sabbath," 31b.
[4] Babylonian Talmud, "Sanhedrin," 91 a-b.
[5] Martin Buber, *Hasidism* (New York: Philosophical Library, 1948), p. 135.
[6] Moses Maimonides, *The Guide of the Perplexed*, Part I, chap. 55.

pels us to believe in falsehoods." [7] A contradiction between the teachings of Judaism and the findings of science can only be apparent, never real, and calls for the careful reevaluation of both. Either may be at fault—tradition misunderstood or scientific method poorly applied—and if the conclusions of science prove correct, tradition must yield the point and modify its understanding of the Word.

Thus, nothing which serves to expand the adventurous horizon of man's mind should be excluded from consideration in the lifelong educative process. The science, the wisdom, the skills of the world are as significant to man as are the teachings of tradition. Man needs them all in order to fulfill the purpose inherent in life.

That purpose must be served. If it is not, knowledge—whatever be its kind —is vain; "the end of the matter; all has been heard. Fear God, and keep his commandments; for this is the whole duty of man." [8]

## Faith Tempered by Experience

Such, in brief, is Judaism's conception of education: Study is a never-ending task in life, a vital means for its fulfillment; all realms of knowledge, not just the religious disciplines, are encompassed by this mandate; and all learning must be made to serve the ends of faith, this end alone, the principal object of being—to help the I encounter the Eternal Thou.

Two aspects of this traditional view merit the emphasis of repetition, and of more careful analysis.

The first relates to the much embracing scope of the subject matter which Jewish tradition designated as the proper object of study. No disjoining of the educative process was countenanced or even envisaged; no effort was made to compartmentalize education into well-defined, only thinly related segments labeled "secular" and "sacred." Tradition did not conceive "religious education" to be a discipline apart; *all* education was held sacred and seen to serve religious ends.

The second aspect of tradition's view which merits closer scrutiny is its conception of study as a religious obligation. "Thou shalt learn" and "thou shalt teach" are oft recurring commandments in the religious literature of the Jew; young and old were enjoined to heed them faithfully. And their observance was seen not so much a *means* for the achievement of the religious life, but rather, as its *fulfillment*.

In this regard also, then, traditional Judaism did not really concern itself with "religious education"—at least not in the current meaning of the term. For when we speak of religious education today, we speak of a program of study which seeks to implant and to nurture the commitment to faith. Traditional Judaism *assumed* the devotion to faith and urged the pursuit of Torah as its lofty expression. In its view study was not a preparation for religion

---

[7] Levi ben Gerson (Gersonides) quoted by W. Gunther Plaut, *Judaism and the Scientific Spirit* (New York: Union of American Hebrew Congregations, 1962), p. 6.

[8] Eccl. 12:13.

but its exercise and practice, on a par with prayer and deeds of righteousness.[9]

The modern day has seen a modification of Juadism's traditional approach to learning, precisely in these two respects. Today's American Jews see the worth of separating secular and sacred study, and they recognize the nurturing of the religious spirit to be a critical goal of the synagogue study program.

These alterations are the consequence of changes in the Jewish environment; they are the product of a people's faith reshaped on the anvil of its experience. The acceptance of education's departmentalization into secular and sacred areas of study is attributable directly to the experience of American Jews whose recent history witnessed their migration from central Europe to America. In the lands of their origin Jews were made to suffer severely. Their existence was in continuous jeopardy, their religious life seriously circumscribed. Invariably, their persecution was most relentless in lands where church and state were bound in official union. By the time Jews came to these shores in substantial numbers, the alliance of Protestant dissent and secular humanism had yielded its richest fruit; the principle of religious freedom was well established and the concept of voluntariness in matters of faith had become a cornerstone of American law. Here Jews found safety; here they found freedom in a measure rarely matched in the two thousand years of their wandering. The sharp and comforting contrast between the old and the new was strikingly manifested in the realm of public education. In Europe only a handful of Jewish children were granted admission to government-established schools; the lucky few who were chosen had to make a high payment for their privilege; they were subjected to stinging indignities, insulted and assaulted, to remind them of their inferiority, to make them appreciate the gracious gift bestowed. Not in America! Here, the American Jewish immigrant found governmental schools whose doors were opened wide to welcome his children, whose teachers and administrators accorded them treatment fully equal to that extended to all other students. Thus it was that the American Jews became willing to isolate religious instruction from general education, limiting the scope of the former by withholding the latter from its immediate concerns.

The enlargement of religious education's function to include the task of preparing the Jew for Judaism is also attributable to pervasive changes in the Jewish environment, in this instance, changes which were experienced by the Christian community as well. I refer to the rise of secularism, to the transformation of the Western world from a believing world to a world which ceased to believe. In the older world the religious commitment of Jewish children could well be assumed. Religion was all about them; they breathed it wherever they went. Their parents lived the religious life; their teachers were religious Jews and so were their friends. They lived in a believing community and within that community they believed. Their education, therefore, their study of Torah and of Talmud, was not meant to introduce them to a life of

[9] Many didactic passages are included in the Jewish prayer book and recited during worship. Conversely, study sessions traditionally begin and conclude with prayer. Solomon B. Freehof offers an excellent discussion of this problem. See his article on "Jewish Learning and Religious Education" in The Jewish Teacher, XXXIII (December, 1964), 10-12.

faith. It was, rather, its expression, a magnificent manifestation of the faith with which they were born, which they absorbed so naturally from the environment in which they moved. Not so, in the newer, nonreligious world! Here doubt, not faith, was in the air which their children breathed, and as a consequence they had to be taught to believe, taught to know and to do and to feel as believing Jews do.

Herein does modern Jewish education differ from the Jewish education of an earlier age: it is now, more directly, an education *for* Judaism.

## The Faith of a People

One other function of Jewish religious education requires consideration: its communal emphasis, its embodiment of the will to be Jewish. Judaism cannot be defined in the narrow sense which the term "religion" in its ordinary usage implies. It represents something more than that, for Jews feel bound to one another not only by the bonds of a common faith, but also by the bonds of kinship and of a common historic experience which spans some twenty centuries. The Jewish religion both draws upon and feeds this sense of peoplehood; the liturgy of the Jews almost always employs the plural pronoun "we" and not the singular "I"; Jewish festivals are not just representations in rite of profoundly religious ideas, but they also portray in colorful, dramatic pageantry the history of the Jewish people. Jewish education reflects this broader understanding of Judaism. It transmits not just a sense of awe but a sense of belonging as well. It seeks not only the continuity of faith, but also the survival of the community which brought that faith to be.

In this realm, too, changes in the Jewish environment have had their impact on Jewish education. In the older world, with its closed Jewish community, devotion to the Jewish people did not have to be engendered. The sense of *belonging* was born of a state of physical *being*. Jews lived in a Jewish world, and they were comfortable in it. And while it is true that they were not allowed to leave that world, it is equally true that they really did not want to leave it, for during the Middle Ages and the Dark Ages, the cultural and intellectual life of gentile Europe was hardly equal to the spiritual life of the ghetto. But once the ghetto restrictions were lifted and the general level of education rose, two strong external forces hindering assimilation were removed, and the disappearance of the Jewish people became a serious possibility. Inner forces had to be provided to counteract this threat, and thus it became Jewish education's task not only to transmit the heritage of the past, but also to instill in the Jewish child, by every means possible, the willingness to be Jewish, the determination to share the destiny of his people.

## The Goals of Jewish Religious Education

This, then, is the confluence of inner and outer forces, the interaction of Jewish theology and Jewish history, which provides modern Jewish religious education with its purposes. The traditional view of education, which flows from Jewish theology, still obtains: Study is a religious obligation, its pursuit a mandate of faith. But superimposed on this central sacred function are the tasks which Jewish experience makes mandatory: The implanting of faith and the instilling of a sense of devotion to the Jewish people.

The educational efforts of *all* contemporary religious movements on the American Jewish scene reflect these purposes. Such variations as there are, are variations of emphasis and not of total concern.

Here, by way of summary, are the aims of religious education articulated by the Reform Jewish community; the goals formulated by the other branches of American Judaism do not diverge from it to any substantial degree:

1. To inspire our children with a positive and abiding faith in the Jewish religion.
2. To stimulate their sense of community with and responsibility toward fellow Jews in all parts of the world, with deep concern for the State of Israel and its people.
3. To guide them in self-identification with the Jewish people of the past, emulating its heroes, aspiring to its ideals, and devoted to its continuance.
4. To provide them with happy, interesting and inspiring experiences in the practice of Judaism in the home, the school, the synagogue, and the community, and in the appreciation of Jewish art, music, and literature.
5. To prepare them to utilize the religious faith, ethical standards, and traditional insights of Judaism in meeting their personal problems.
6. To inculcate in them the universal ideal of Israel's prophets and sages, leading them towards involvement in service for freedom, brotherhood and peace.
7. The curriculum which attempts to achieve these aims must begin with the actual experiences of our children, but must add many important elements of the Jewish heritage which are not present in the experience of the average Jewish child in America. The study of Hebrew is an indispensable element in the achievement of this purpose and must play an important part in our course of study. Above all, our purpose must be to stimulate a process of continuing learning which extends beyond the prescribed program of the religious school and lasts as long as life itself.[10]

The subjects chosen for instruction in the Jewish religious school seek to fulfill these general aims. Among them are history and Hebrew, Bible and post-biblical literature, festival observances and life-cycle rites, personal and social ethics, Jewish religious thought, and comparative religion. Some subjects are taught at an early age, others only later—to adolescents and adults—following the guidelines provided by modern educational theory. Some subjects are taught directly, others only by indirection, as, for instance, the God-belief which is not taught as a subject among other subjects, but rather as a theme to be set forth on every level of the school, in every class, whatever be its subject.

In the realm of subject matter, too, we find a consensus among the persuasions of American Jewry. The subjects taught in the various religious schools are substantially the same. Only differences in emphasis obtain. And there are, of course, substantial variations in the manner in which individual subject matter is treated.

[10] From *The Curriculum of the Jewish Religious School* of the Commission on Jewish Education of the Union of American Hebrew Congregations and the Central Conference of American Rabbis (New York, 1964), p. 11.

## The Major Movements of American Judaism

To understand these variations, we must know something concerning the varying philosophies of Judaism which divide the American Jewish community. Four major religious movements can be perceived on the contemporary Jewish scene.[11] Orthodoxy, Conservatism, and Reform Judaism are institutionally divided; each movement has its own seminary, its own conference of rabbis, its own national congregational body. The fourth—Reconstructionism —draws its adherents from amongst the laymen and rabbis of Conservative and Reform Judaism.

The differences between Orthodoxy and Reform will readily be understood by the non-Jewish reader, for they parallel essentially the differences between fundamentalism and liberalism in Christianity. The crucial point of divergence between them is their answer to the question "What is Torah?"—what is the Pentateuch, what are the Five Books of Moses? Orthodoxy reveres the Torah as literal revelation, as the Spoken Word, given voice by God himself to Moses on Mt. Sinai. Not only was the *written* Torah given then—so affirms Orthodoxy—the *oral* law was revealed as well, all traditional interpretations of the written law, these too were given by God to Moses and then passed on by Moses, orally, along with the written law, to future generations. When seen and understood in this light, subsequent scriptural commentaries of whatever age are not innovations, but merely rediscoveries of an ancient truth; Judaism is not a changing, evolving faith; it has remained the same since Sinai, and must remain the same forever. Reform Judaism, on the other hand, sees the Torah not as literal revelation, but rather as inspired literature—inspired by God, but written by men who strove to know him. And subsequent interpretation, the oral law, is not just rediscovery of ancient truth. It represents a new development, the manifestations of an ever-changing, living faith, a faith reshaped by men.

Closely related to this first basic difference in principle is a second which flows from the first and involves religious practice. Holding the entire Torah to be revealed, the Orthodox Jew regards its ritual provisions also divine in origin, as sacred as every other mandate of Scripture and hence inviolate. Reform Judaism, on the other hand, regards all ritual laws as man-made; in truth, it views them of lesser consequence than the ethical injunctions of Scripture, as means to an end and not the end itself. Thus, Reform Judaism countenances the alteration of religious forms to make them conform to the changing ethical and aesthetic sensibilities of newer times.

Conservative Judaism does not lend itself to such ready categorization, particularly because its leaders eschew the task of formulating a philosophy of

[11] It should be noted, however, that not all American Jews define their Jewishness in religious terms. Some see it as a happenstance of birth—no more. Others stress the bond of nationhood which binds them to their fellow Jew. Still others emphasize the cultural component of Judaism to the exclusion of its religious motifs. For the purposes of this essay, only the religious movements of American Jewish life have been considered. In any event, the vast majority of Jewish children—some 90 percent of the half million currently enrolled—attend congregational schools.

Judaism as a matter of principle. They aver—with some justification, it must be said—that Judaism is not essentially a creedal faith, that it is, rather, a way of life, that what the Jew does is of infinitely greater significance than what he says he believes. The range of religious opinion and practice within Conservative Judaism is wide, running the gamut from fundamentalism to liberalism. Generally speaking, the critical approach to Scripture is accepted, at least intellectually. But changes in traditional observance are resisted: Modifications are countenanced only when changing conditions compel them.

Reconstructionism affirms the liberal interpretation of Scripture. As a matter of fact, it offers a new theology, religious naturalism, proposing to "reconstruct" all fundamental categories of Judaism to make them acceptable to the modern Jew. Above all, Reconstructionism teaches that Judaism is not just a religion, but rather a "religious civilization," an organic complex of literature, language, folkways, religious outlook, group aspirations, ethical values, and aesthetic judgments. It accepts a diversity in Jewish religious thought, even while it fosters a respect for traditional observances.

The foregoing descriptions of varying religious trends in contemporary Jewish life, brief though they may be, should nonetheless suffice to indicate the diverging emphases which their educational programs take. Orthodox Jews, affirming a supernaturally revealed religion, seek to give their children primarily a knowledge of Judaism's sacred texts and to implant in them the habit of religious practice. Reform Jews, valuing the ethical mandate of faith above its ritual prescriptions, underscore Jewish personal and social values in their teaching; in their Bible study, just as one instance, the prophets are given greater weight in time and emphasis than is Leviticus. Conservative Judaism's educational effort is more akin to the program of Reform than it is to that of Orthodoxy, albeit the Conservative effort places somewhat greater weight on the teaching of Hebrew. Reconstructionism, understandably, takes the broadest possible approach to Jewish education, calling for the inclusion in its program of study not just of the purely religious but also of the religio-cultural components of the "Jewish civilization."

## Programs and Problems

In the light of these understandings we can now delineate the concrete programs of Jewish religious schools.

Nearly 600,000 children are enrolled throughout the country in all types of Jewish schools: congregational and non-congregational, elementary and secondary, full-time and part-time.[12] Over half of the enrollees attend one-day-a-week schools receiving some two and a half hours of instruction on Sabbath or Sunday mornings. Forty percent of the students attend weekday-afternoon schools meeting two or more times a week for an average weekly program of

[12] All statistics cited here are taken from the pages of the *American Jewish Yearbook*. See Uriah Z. Engelman's report on "Jewish Education" in LXIV (1963), 151-65.

seven hours of instruction. Less than 10 percent of the enrollees attend full-time day schools. Boys and girls alike receive Jewish education, although boys predominate in the enrollment of the more intensive schools. In the weekend program, the distribution between boys and girls is about even.

Schools under Reform auspices have the largest enrollment, followed by Conservative and Orthodox schools; however, fully half of the afternoon schools are sponsored by the Conservative movement and 85 percent of the day-school enrollment is Orthodox. Reform Judaism sponsors no day schools, although a number of Reform congregants send their children to full-time schools under Conservative or Orthodox auspices.

The trend is definitely toward greater intensification. The percentage of enrollment in the more extensive programs increases from year to year. Reform Judaism, for instance, is making a concerted effort to gain general acceptance of the three-day-a-week system; thus its curriculum states: "It is understood that the aims listed herewith cannot be fulfilled in the one-day-a-week school. As requirements increase, they will necessitate the pursuit of additional studies and activities in more intensive schools—in two- and three-day-a-week schools, to say the least." [13]

The primary and elementary grades still claim the greatest support in registration, although the secondary education program shows signs of growth. Some congregations begin their religious education effort on the nursery grade level; nearly all have programs of instruction for adults. Invariably, the formal program of the religious school is supplemented by the informal education effort of congregational auxiliaries—brotherhoods, sisterhoods, and youth groups—and by summer camp programs.

Next to the problem of time—how to find the additional hours required to teach what should be taught to each Jewish child—the most serious problem confronting Jewish education is the problem of teacher procurement. Since Jewish education is still, in the main, part-time education, it draws not full, but part-time teachers, and part-time teachers are not sufficient for the need; they often lack the fuller qualifications—the knowledge or the commitment—which are required.

Yet teachers are the essential factor in education, indispensable for the fulfillment of its purposes. This is true for all education. It is particularly true in the realm of Jewish education—indeed, of religious education generally—because it is the task of the religious school, as we have seen, not merely to transmit a body of knowledge, but to develop character and attitude, to implant, and to nurture faith. These qualities of the soul cannot be contained in a course or conveyed by techniques however refined. They cannot be ordered into a curriculum or taught from a text. These essential qualities are aspects of all subject matter, not just one of its parts. They emerge not from a course, but from a teacher. They do not flow from a curriculum, but only from a human soul.

[13] *The Curriculum of the Jewish Religious School,* p. 11.

## An Ignorant Man Cannot Be Religious

Hopefully, what has been said suffices to introduce the reader to Jewish religious education. Much more could be said, of course, but at least an inroad has been made.[14]

Undoubtedly, the purposes and programs of Jewish education parallel those of Christian education. If there is a singular Jewish theme, it is its traditional conception of education as a supreme religious duty, as the fulfillment of the divine command.

Torah is the brightest star in the firmament of Judaism's values; its study outranks even prayer in significance. The house of learning is more important than the synagogue. Others may exalt the man of simple, childlike faith; Judaism insists that "the boorish man cannot be a fearer of sin, nor the ignorant man truly pious." [15]

The importance of study in the view of Judaism is nowhere more dramatically expressed than in the Talmudic dictum which holds that when a child, his father, and his teacher are held in captivity, "the teacher must be rescued even before the parent." To which another Talmudic sage rejoined: "Children are not to be excused from school, even for the purpose of participation in the building of the (Messianic) Temple." [16]

## FOR ADDITIONAL READING

Cohen, Jack J. *Jewish Education in a Democratic Society.* New York: The Reconstructionist Press, 1964.

Engelman, U. Z. *Trends and Developments in Jewish Education.* New York: American Association for Jewish Education, 1957.

Gamoran, Emanuel. *Changing Conceptions in Jewish Education.* New York: The Macmillan Company, 1924.

Hertz, Richard G. *The Education of the Jewish Child.* New York: The Union of American Hebrew Congregations, 1953.

Ruffman, Louis. *The Curriculum Outline for the Congregational School.* New York: United Synagogue of America, 1959.

Schindler, Alexander M. and the Commission on Jewish Education. *The Curriculum for the Jewish Religious School.* New York: The Union of American Hebrew Congregations, 1963.

---

[14] For another description of Jewish educational patterns, see Judah Pilch, "Jewish Religious Education," in *Religious Education: A Comprehensive Survey,* Marvin J. Taylor, ed. (Nashville: Abingdon Press, 1960), pp. 382-95.

[15] Mishnah, Aboth 2:6.

[16] Babylonian Talmud, "Sabbath," 119b.

# A Selected Bibliography:
## Since 1959
### (see *Religious Education: A Comprehensive Survey* for earlier volumes)

## *Compiled by Marvin J. Taylor*

The writer of Ecclesiastes was surely correct—there is no end to the making of books, especially in Christian education! Since the bibliography for *Religious Education: A Comprehensive Survey* was compiled in 1959, there have appeared no less than six hundred volumes worthy of consideration for this new listing. Hence, the word "selected" is an important part of the title.

The several factors which have guided these choices are:

1. The outline used is a virtual duplication of the earlier volume. This was done deliberately. It will enable the reader who desires a more comprehensive list on a given topic to combine the 1959 and 1966 lists. Such a combination should make available most of the important books on the subject.

2. Only a very few pre-1959 volumes have been included, usually because of the absence of a more recent replacement. Thus, many superior books had to be omitted, and the reader's attention is called to this fact.

3. The selections have been made from recommendations submitted by the contributors and my own familiarity with the current Christian education literature.

4. Since breadth of usefulness has been a major goal, few distinctly denominational books are included. Doubtless this criterion ruled against many fine volumes, but it was impossible to include all. Each reader will want to add his own denomination's publications to each of the categories.

5. While the basic outline is not new, several new sections have been added (evidence of the fact that the field of Christian education itself is changing). The reader's attention is called particularly to *The Laity, the Renewal of the Church, and Christian Education; Language, the Christian Faith, and Communication; Programmed Instruction;* and *The Christian Education of the Exceptional Person.*

## I. The Nature, Principles, and History
## of Christian Education

### 1. *Nature, Philosophy, and Principles of Christianity and Christian Education*

Butler, J. Donald. *Religious Education.* New York: Harper & Row, 1962.

Byrne, Herbert W. *A Christian Approach to Education*. Grand Rapids: Zondervan Publishing House, 1961.

Chamberlin, J. Gordon. *Freedom and Faith*. Philadelphia: The Westminster Press, 1965.

Cully, Iris V. *The Dynamics of Christian Education*. Philadelphia: The Westminster Press, 1958.

Cully, Kendig Brubaker, ed. *The Westminster Dictionary of Christian Education*. Philadelphia: The Westminster Press, 1963.

DeWolf, L. Harold. *Teaching Our Faith in God*. Nashville: Abingdon Press, 1963.

Fallaw, Wesner. *Church Education for Tomorrow*. Philadelphia: The Westminster Press, 1960.

Ferré, Nels F. S. *Searchlights on Contemporary Theology*. New York: Harper & Row, 1961.

Fuller, Edmund, ed. *The Christian Idea of Education, Part II: Schools and Scholarship*. New Haven: Yale University Press, 1962.

Gilkey, Langdon. *How the Church Can Minister to the World Without Losing Itself*. New York: Harper & Row, 1964.

Glen, J. Stanley. *The Recovery of the Teaching Ministry*. Philadelphia: The Westminster Press, 1960.

Grimes, Howard. *The Church Redemptive*. Nashville: Abingdon Press, 1958.

Hakes, J. Edward, ed. *An Introduction to Evangelical Christian Education*. Chicago: Moody Press, 1964.

Havighurst, Robert J. *The Educational Mission of the Church*. Philadelphia: The Westminster Press, 1965.

Hazelton, Roger. *New Accents in Contemporary Theology*. New York: Harper & Row, 1960.

Henderlite, Rachel. *Forgiveness and Hope*. Richmond: John Knox Press, 1961.

———. *The Holy Spirit in Christian Education*. Philadelphia: The Westminster Press, 1964.

Hunter, David R. *Christian Education as Engagement*. New York: The Seabury Press, 1963.

Johnson, Robert C., ed. *The Church and Its Changing Ministry*. Philadelphia: The United Presbyterian Church, 1961.

Koulomzin, Sophie S. *Lectures in Orthodox Religious Education*. New York: St. Vladimir's Seminary Press, 1961.

Little, Lawrence C. *Foundations for a Philosophy of Christian Education*. Nashville: Abingdon Press, 1962.

Lotz, P. H., ed. *Orientation in Religious Education*. Nashville: Abingdon Press, 1950.

Lynn, Robert W. *Protestant Strategies in Education*. New York: Association Press, 1964.

McCluskey, Neil G., S.J. *Catholic Viewpoint on Education*. Rev. ed. Garden City: Doubleday & Company, 1962.

Micks, Marianne H. *Introduction to Theology*. New York: The Seabury Press, 1964.

Miller, Randolph Crump. *Christian Nurture and the Church*. New York: Charles Scribner's Sons, 1961.

———. *Education for Christian Living*. 2nd ed. Englewood Cliffs: Prentice-Hall, 1963.

Niblett, W. R., ed. *Moral Education in a Changing Society*. New York: Humanities Press, 1963.

Ranck, J. Allen. *Education for Mission*. New York: Friendship Press, 1961.

Schreyer, George M. *Christian Education in Theological Focus*. Philadelphia: United Church Press, 1962.

Sherrill, Lewis J. *The Gift of Power.* New York: The Macmillan Company, 1955.

Shinn, Roger L. *The Educational Mission of Our Church.* Philadelphia: United Church Press, 1962.

Sloyan, Gerard S., ed. *Modern Catechetics: Message and Method in Religious Formation.* New York: The Macmillan Company, 1963.

Slusser, Gerald H. *The Local Church in Transition: Theology, Education, and Ministry.* Philadelphia: The Westminster Press, 1964.

Smart, James D. *The Creed in Christian Teaching.* Philadelphia: The Westminster Press, 1962.

———. *The Teaching Ministry of the Church.* Philadelphia: The Westminster Press, 1954.

Stewart, D. G. *Christian Education and Evangelism.* Philadelphia: The Westminster Press, 1963.

Taylor, Marvin J., ed. *Religious Education: A Comprehensive Survey.* Nashville: Abingdon Press, 1960.

———. *Religious and Moral Education.* New York: The Center for Applied Research in Education, 1965.

## 2. *The History of Christian Education*

Bailyn, Bernard. *Education in the Forming of American Society.* New York: Vintage Books, 1960.

Barclay, William. *Train Up a Child: Educational Ideals in the Ancient World.* Philadelphia: The Westminster Press, 1960.

Bowen, Cawthon A. *Child and Church.* Nashville: Abingdon Press, 1960.

Castle, E. B. *Moral Education in Christian Times.* New York: The Macmillan Company, 1958.

Cully, Kendig Brubaker, ed. *Basic Writings in Christian Education.* Philadelphia: The Westminster Press, 1960.

———. *The Search for a Christian Education—Since 1940.* Philadelphia: The Westminster Press, 1965.

Dendy, Marshall C. *Changing Patterns in Christian Education.* Richmond: John Knox Press, 1964.

Eavey, C. B. *History of Christian Education.* Chicago: Moody Press, 1964.

Gross, Richard E., ed. *Heritage of American Education.* Boston: Allyn & Bacon, 1962.

Henderson, Robert W. *The Teaching Office in the Reformed Tradition.* Philadelphia: The Westminster Press, 1962.

Kennedy, William B. *The Shaping of Protestant Education.* New York: Association Press, 1966.

Kevane, Eugene. *Augustine the Educator.* Westminster, Md.: The Newman Press, 1964.

Knowles, Malcolm S. *The Adult Education Movement in the United States.* New York: Holt, Rinehart & Winston, 1962.

McCluskey, Neil G., S.J. *Public Schools and Moral Education.* New York: Columbia University Press, 1958.

Muirhead, Ian A. *Education in the New Testament.* New York: Association Press, 1965.

Sherrill, Lewis J. *The Rise of Christian Education.* New York: The Macmillan Company, 1944.

Sloyan, Gerard S., ed. *Shaping the Christian Message.* New York: The Macmillan Company, 1958.

### 3. The Laity, the Renewal of the Church, and Christian Education

Ayres, Francis O. *The Ministry of the Laity*. Philadelphia: The Westminster Press, 1962.

Bloesch, Donald G. *Centers of Christian Renewal*. Philadelphia: United Church Press, 1964.

Bloy, Myron H., Jr. *The Crisis of Cultural Change*. New York: The Seabury Press, 1965.

Casteel, John L. *Renewal in Retreats*. New York: Association Press, 1959.

Ernsberger, David J. *Education for Renewal*. Philadelphia: The Westminster Press, 1965.

Gable, Lee J. *Church and World Encounter*. Philadelphia: United Church Press, 1964.

Gibbs, Mark and Morton, T. Ralph. *God's Frozen People*. Philadelphia: The Westminster Press, 1965.

Grimes, Howard. *The Rebirth of the Laity*. Nashville: Abingdon Press, 1962.

Kraemer, Hendrik. *A Theology of the Laity*. Philadelphia: The Westminster Press, 1959.

Raines, Robert A. *New Life in the Church*. New York: Harper & Row, 1961.

———. *Reshaping the Christian Life*. New York: Harper & Row, 1964.

Webber, George W. *The Congregation in Mission*. Nashville: Abingdon Press, 1964.

———. *God's Colony in Man's World*. Nashville: Abingdon Press, 1960.

Williams, Colin W. *What in the World?* New York: National Council of Churches, 1964.

———. *Where in the World?* New York: National Council of Churches, 1963.

### 4. Language, the Christian Faith, and Communication

Bendall, Kent and Ferré, Frederick. *Exploring the Logic of Faith*. New York: Association Press, 1962.

Cully, Iris V. and Kendig Brubaker. *An Introductory Theological Wordbook*. Philadelphia: The Westminster Press, 1964.

DeWire, Harry A. *The Christian as Communicator*. Philadelphia: The Westminster Press, 1960.

Ferré, Frederick. *Language, Logic, and God*. New York: Harper & Row, 1961.

Hordern, William. *Speaking of God: The Nature and Purpose of Theological Language*. New York: The Macmillan Company, 1964.

Laeuchli, Samuel. *The Language of Faith*. Nashville: Abingdon Press, 1962.

May, Rollo, ed. *Symbolism in Religion and Literature*. New York: George Braziller, 1960.

Moreau, Jules L. *Language and Religious Language*. Philadelphia: The Westminster Press, 1960.

Nida, Eugene A. *Message and Mission: The Communication of the Christian Faith*. New York: Harper & Row, 1960.

Perrow, Maxwell D. *Effective Christian Communication*. Richmond: John Knox Press, 1962.

Ramsey, Ian T. *Religious Language*. New York: The Macmillan Company, 1963.

## II. Religious Growth and the Learning-Teaching Process

### 1. Moral and Religious Growth

Allport, Gordon W. *Becoming: Basic Considerations for a Psychology of Personality*. New Haven: Yale University Press, 1955.

## A SELECTED BIBLIOGRAPHY

Blair, Glenn M. and Jones, R. S. *Psychology of Adolescence for Teachers*. New York: The Macmillan Company, 1964.

Chaplin, Dora P. *Children and Religion*. Rev. ed. New York: Charles Scribner's Sons, 1961.

Conover, C. Eugene. *Moral Education in Family, School, and Church*. Philadelphia: The Westminster Press, 1962.

Crow, Lester D. and Alice. *Adolescent Development and Adjustment*. 2nd ed. New York: McGraw-Hill Book Company, 1965.

Doniger, Simon, ed. *Becoming the Complete Adult*. New York: Association Press, 1962.

Erikson, Erik, ed. *The Challenge of Youth*. Garden City: Doubleday & Company, 1965.

————. *Childhood and Society*. Rev. ed. New York: W. W. Norton & Company, 1964.

————. *Insight and Responsibility*. New York: W. W. Norton & Company, 1964.

Estvan, Frank J. and Elizabeth. *The Child's World: His Social Perception*. New York: G. P. Putnam's Sons, 1959.

Farnham, Marynia. *The Adolescent*. New York: Collier Books, 1962.

Friedenberg, Edgar Z. *The Vanishing Adolescent*. Boston: Beacon Press, 1959.

Gallagher, J. Roswell and Harris, Herbert I. *Emotional Problems of Adolescents*. Rev. ed. New York: Oxford University Press, 1964.

Gesell, Arnold; Ilg, Frances L.; and Ames, Louise B. *Youth: The Years from Ten to Sixteen*. New York: Harper & Row, 1956.

Goldman, Ronald. *Religious Thinking from Childhood to Adolescence*. London: Routledge and Kegan Paul, 1964.

Goodenough, Erwin R. *The Psychology of Religious Experiences*. New York: Basic Books, 1965.

Goodykoontz, Harry G. *The Persons We Teach*. Philadelphia: The Westminster Press, 1965.

Havighurst, Robert J. *et al. Growing Up in River City*. New York: John Wiley & Sons, 1962.

Jaarsma, Cornelius. *Human Development, Learning and Teaching: A Christian Approach to Educational Psychology*. Grand Rapids: Wm. B. Eerdmans Publishing Co., 1961.

Kuhlen, Raymond G. *Psychological Backgrounds of Adult Education*. Boston: Center for the Study of Liberal Education, 1963.

Langdon, Grace and Stout, I. W. *Teaching Moral and Spiritual Values: A Parents' Guide to Developing Character*. New York: The John Day Company, 1962.

Lee, R. S. *Your Growing Child and Religion*. New York: The Macmillan Company, 1963.

MacMurray, John. *Persons in Relation*. New York: Harper & Row, 1961.

Miller, Randolph Crump. *Your Child's Religion*. Garden City: Doubleday & Company, 1962.

Peck, Robert F. and Havighurst, Robert J. *The Psychology of Character Development*. New York: John Wiley & Sons, 1960.

Piaget, Jean *et al. The Moral Judgment of the Child*. Tr. by Marjorie Gabain. New York: The Free Press of Glencoe, 1965.

Pressey, Sidney L. and Kuhlen, Raymond G. *Psychological Development Through the Life Span*. New York: Harper & Row, 1957.

Sherrill, Lewis J. *The Struggle of the Soul*. New York: The Macmillan Company, 1952.

Stein, Edward V. *The Stranger Inside You*. Philadelphia: The Westminster Press, 1965.

Strommen, Merton P. *Profiles of Church Youth*. St. Louis: Concordia Publishing House, 1963.

Strunk, Orlo, Jr. *Mature Religion.* Nashville: Abingdon Press, 1965.

————. *Religion: A Psychological Interpretation.* Nashville: Abingdon Press, 1962.

Tournier, Paul. *The Whole Person in a Broken World.* Tr. by John and Helen Doberstein. New York: Harper & Row, 1964.

Vogel, Arthur A. *The Christian Person.* New York: The Seabury Press, 1963.

Ziegler, Jesse H. *Psychology and the Teaching Church.* Nashville: Abingdon Press, 1962.

### 2. The Learning Process

Association for Supervision and Curriculum Development. *Human Variability and Learning.* Washington: National Education Association, 1961.

————. *Learning More About Learning.* Washington: National Education Association, 1959.

————. *Perceiving, Behaving, Becoming.* Washington: National Education Association, 1962.

Boehlke, Robert R. *Theories of Learning in Christian Education.* Philadelphia: The Westminster Press, 1962.

Bruner, Jerome. *The Process of Education.* Cambridge: Harvard University Press, 1960.

Cantor, Nathaniel. *The Teaching-Learning Process.* New York: Holt, Rinehart & Winston, 1953.

Clayton, Thomas E. *Teaching and Learning: A Psychological Perspective.* Englewood Cliffs: Prentice-Hall, 1965.

Crow, Lester D. and Alice, eds. *Readings in Human Learning.* New York: David McKay Company, 1962.

Harris, Theodore L. and Schwahn, Wilson E., eds. *Selected Readings on the Learning Process.* New York: Oxford University Press, 1961.

Hilgard, Ernest R. *Theories of Learning.* New York: Appleton-Century-Crofts, 1948.

Kidd, J. R. *How Adults Learn.* New York: Association Press, 1959.

Little, Sara. *Learning Together in the Christian Fellowship.* Richmond: John Knox Press, 1956.

Prescott, Daniel. *The Child in the Educative Process.* New York: McGraw-Hill Book Company, 1957.

Staats, Arthur W., ed. *Human Learning.* New York: Holt, Rinehart & Winston, 1964.

Stephens, John M. *The Psychology of Classroom Learning.* New York: Holt, Rinehart & Winston, 1965.

Stinnette, Charles R., Jr. *Learning in Theological Perspective.* New York: Association Press, 1965.

Townsend, Edward A. and Burke, Paul J. *Learning for Teachers.* New York: The Macmillan Company, 1962.

Travers, Robert M. W. *Essentials of Learning: An Overview for Students of Education.* New York: The Macmillan Company, 1963.

### 3. The Teaching Process

Brubacher, John S., ed. *An Eclectic Philosophy of Education: A Book of Readings.* 2nd ed. Englewood Cliffs: Prentice-Hall, 1962.

Cully, Kendig Brubaker. *The Teaching Church.* Philadelphia: United Church Press, 1963.

Kneller, George F., ed. *Foundations of Education.* New York: John Wiley & Sons, 1963.

Phenix, Philip H. *Education and the Common Good: A Moral Philosophy of the Curriculum.* New York: Harper & Row, 1961.

————, ed. *Philosophies of Education.* New York: John Wiley & Sons, 1961.

## A SELECTED BIBLIOGRAPHY

Thelen, Herbert A. *Education and the Human Quest.* New York: Harper & Row, 1960.

Walker, Wanda. *A Philosophy of Education.* New York: Philosophical Library, 1964.

Wynne, John P. *Theories of Education: An Introduction to the Foundations of Education.* New York: Harper & Row, 1963.

### 4. Group Work and Group Dynamics

Bonner, Hubert. *Group Dynamics: Principles and Applications.* New York: The Ronald Press Company, 1959.

Douglass, Paul F. *The Group Workshop Way in the Church.* New York: Association Press, 1956.

Elliott, Grace L. *How to Help Groups Make Decisions.* New York: Association Press, 1959.

Howe, Reuel L. *Herein Is Love.* Valley Forge: Judson Press, 1961.

——. *The Miracle of Dialogue.* New York: The Seabury Press, 1963.

Kemp, C. Gratton, ed. *Perspectives on the Group Process.* Boston: Houghton Mifflin Company, 1964.

Knowles, Malcolm and Hulda. *Introduction to Group Dynamics.* New York: Association Press, 1959.

Miles, Matthew B. *Learning to Work in Groups.* New York: Teachers College, Columbia University, 1959.

National Training Laboratories. *Selected Readings Series.* No. 1, *Group Development;* No. 2, *Leadership in Action;* No. 3, *Forces in Learning.* Washington: National Education Association, 1961.

### 5. Leadership Development

Bennett, Thomas R., II. *The Leader and the Process of Change.* New York: Association Press, 1962.

Buchanan, Paul C. *The Leader and Individual Motivation.* New York: Association Press, 1962.

Goodykoontz, Harry G. and Betty L. *Training to Teach.* Philadelphia: The Westminster Press, 1961.

Hendry, Charles E. and Ross, Murray G. *New Understandings of Leadership.* New York: Association Press, 1957.

Lippitt, Gordon L. and Seashore, Edith. *The Leader and Group Effectiveness.* New York: Association Press, 1962.

Weschler, Irving W. *The Leader and Creativity.* New York: Association Press, 1962.

### 6. Programmed Instruction

Foundation for Research on Human Behavior. *Programmed Learning: A Critical Evaluation.* ed. John L. Hughes. Chicago: Aldine Publishing Co., 1962.

Fry, Edward B. *Teaching Machines and Programmed Instruction.* New York: McGraw-Hill Book Company, 1963.

Lumsdaine, A. A. and Glaser, Robert. *Teaching Machines and Programmed Learning.* Washington: National Education Association, 1960.

Margulies, Stuart and Eigen, Lewis D. *Applied Programed Instruction.* New York: John Wiley & Sons, 1962.

Thomas, C. A. et al. *Programmed Learning in Perspective: A Guide to Program Writing.* Chicago: Educational Methods, 1965.

Tuck, William. *Step-by-Step Introduction to the Old Testament.* New York: Association Press, 1963.

Vermes, Hal and Jean. *Step by Step in Theology.* New York: Association Press, 1962.

## III. The Home, the Church, and Christian Education

### 1. *The Church and the Home*

Barrett, Thomas van Braam. *The Christian Family.* New York: Morehouse-Gorham Company, 1958.

Brown, Leslie and Winifred. *The Christian Family.* New York: Association Press, 1960.

Chamberlin, J. Gordon. *Parents and Religion: A Preface to Christian Education.* Philadelphia: The Westminster Press, 1961.

Channels, Vera. *The Layman Builds a Christian Home.* St. Louis: The Bethany Press, 1959.

Colacci, Mario. *Christian Marriage Today.* Minneapolis: Augsburg Publishing House, 1958.

Crook, Roger H. *The Changing American Family.* St. Louis: The Bethany Press, 1960.

Denton, Wallace. *What's Happening to Our Families?* Philadelphia: The Westminster Press, 1963.

Dowdy, R. E. and Harriett. *The Church Is Families.* Valley Forge: Judson Press, 1965.

Duvall, Evelyn M. *Family Development.* Rev. ed. Chicago: J. B. Lippincott, 1962.

Fairchild, Roy W. *Christians in Families.* Richmond: Covenant Life Curriculum Press, 1965.

Fairchild, Roy W. and Wynn, John Charles. *Families in the Church: A Protestant Survey.* New York: Association Press, 1961.

Genné, Elizabeth and William. *Foundations for Christian Family Policy.* New York: National Council of Churches, 1961.

Hulme, William. *Pastoral Care of Families.* Nashville: Abingdon Press, 1962.

Kawin, Ethel. *Parenthood in a Free Nation.* 3 Vols. No. 1, *Basic Concepts for Parents;* No. 2, *Early and Middle Childhood,* rev. ed.; No. 3, *Later Childhood and Adolescence.* New York: The Macmillan Company, 1963.

Larrick, Nancy. *A Parent's Guide to Children's Reading.* Rev. ed. New York: Doubleday & Company, 1964.

Ligon, Ernest and Smith, Leona. *The Marriage Climate.* St. Louis: The Bethany Press, 1963.

McDonnell, Lois E. *The Home and the Church.* Nashville: Abingdon Press, 1961.

Sherrill, Helen H. *Christian Parenthood: A Lifetime Guide.* Richmond: John Knox Press, 1964.

Taylor, Florence M. *Your Children's Faith: A Guide for Parents.* Toronto: Doubleday Canada, 1964.

### 2. *Sex, Sex Education, and Preparation for Marriage*

Bailey, Sherwin. *Sexual Ethics: A Christian View.* New York: The Macmillan Company, 1963.

Batten, Charles E. and McLean, Donald E. *Fit to Be Tied.* New York: The Seabury Press, 1959.

Bibby, Cyril. *How Life Is Handed On.* Rev. ed. New York: Collier Books, 1964.

Bowman, Henry A. *A Christian Interpretation of Marriage.* Philadelphia: The Westminster Press, 1959.

Child Study Association of America. *What to Tell Your Children About Sex.* Rev. ed. New York: Meredith Press, 1964.

Duvall, Evelyn M. *Love and the Facts of Life.* New York: Association Press, 1963.

—— and Duvall, Sylvanus. *Sense and Nonsense About Sex.* New York: Association Press, 1962.

———— and Hill, Reuben. *When You Marry*. Rev. ed. New York: Association Press, 1962.

Ellzey, W. Clark. *Preparing Your Children for Marriage*. New York: Association Press, 1964.

Feucht, Oscar E. *et al.*, eds. *Sex and the Church*. St. Louis: Concordia Publishing House, 1960.

Piper, Otto. *The Biblical View of Sex and Marriage*. New York: Charles Scribner's Sons, 1960.

Schur, Edwin M. *The Family and the Sexual Revolution*. Bloomington: Indiana University Press, 1964.

Thielicke, Helmut. *The Ethics of Sex*. New York: Harper & Row, 1964.

Wynn, J. C., ed. *Sex, Family, and Society in Theological Focus*. New York: Association Press, 1966.

## IV. Organization and Administration of Christian Education

### 1. *Organization in the Local Church*

Adams, Rachel Swann. *The Small Church and Christian Education*. Philadelphia: The Westminster Press, 1961.

Bower, Robert K. *Administering Christian Education*. Grand Rapids: Wm. B. Eerdmans Publishing Co., 1964.

Cober, Kenneth L. *The Church's Teaching Ministry*. Valley Forge: Judson Press, 1964.

Council of National Organizations for Adult Education. *Probing Volunteer-Staff Relations*. New York: Association Press, 1963.

Hoiland, Richard, ed. *Planning Christian Education in the Local Church*. Rev. ed. Valley Forge: Judson Press, 1952.

Howse, W. L. *The Church Staff and Its Work*. Nashville: Broadman Press, 1959.

Keckley, Weldon. *The Church School Superintendent*. St. Louis: The Bethany Press, 1963.

Lindgren, Alvin J. *Foundations for Purposeful Church Administration*. Nashville: Abingdon Press, 1965.

McComb, Louise. *D.C.E.: A Challenging Career in Christian Education*. Richmond: John Knox Press, 1963.

Person, Peter P. *The Minister in Christian Education*. Grand Rapids: Baker Book House, 1960.

Sweet, Herman J. *The Multiple Staff in the Local Church*. Philadelphia: The Westminster Press, 1963.

Towner, Walter. *Guiding a Church School*. Nashville: Abingdon Press, 1963.

Wyckoff, D. Campbell. *How to Evaluate Your Christian Education Program*. Philadelphia: The Westminster Press, 1962.

### 2. *Religion in Public and Private Schools*

Blanshard, Paul. *Religion and the Schools*. Boston: Beacon Press, 1963.

Boles, Donald E. *The Bible, Religion, and the Public Schools*. 2nd ed. Ames: Iowa State University Press, 1963.

Brickman, William W. and Lehrer, Stanley, eds. *Religion, Government, and Education*. New York: The Society for the Advancement of Education, 1961.

Brothers, Joan. *Church and School: A Study of the Impact of Education on Religion*. Liverpool: Liverpool University Press, 1964.

Commission on Religion in the Public Schools. *Religion in the Public Schools.* Washington: American Association of School Administrators, 1964.

Dierenfield, Richard B. *Religion in American Public Schools.* Washington: Public Affairs Press, 1962.

Drinan, Robert F. *Religion, the Courts, and Public Policy.* New York: McGraw-Hill Book Company, 1963.

Krause, Victor, ed. *Lutheran Elementary Schools in Action.* St. Louis: Concordia Publishing House, 1963.

Loder, James E. *Religion and the Public Schools.* New York: Association Press, 1965.

Oaks, Dallin H., ed. *The Wall Between Church and State.* Chicago: University of Chicago Press, 1963.

Phenix, Philip H. *Religious Concerns in Contemporary Education: A Study of Reciprocal Relations.* New York: Teachers College, Columbia University, 1959.

Robinson, James H. *et al.* Education for Decision. New York: The Seabury Press, 1962.

Tussman, Joseph, ed. *The Supreme Court on Church and State.* New York: Oxford University Press, 1961.

Wainwright, Joseph A. *School and Church, Partners in Christian Education: Some Suggestions for Common Action.* New York: Oxford University Press, 1963.

Ward, Leo R. *Religion in All the Schools.* Notre Dame, Ind.: Fides Publishers, 1960.

Whittemore, Lewis Bliss. *The Church and Secular Education.* New York: The Seabury Press, 1960.

### 3. Camping and Christian Education

Beker, Jerry. *Training Camp Counselors in Human Relations.* New York: Association Press, 1962.

Bone, Maurice D. *et al.* Site Selection and Development. Philadelphia: United Church Press, 1965.

Doty, Richard S. *The Character Dimension of Camping.* New York: Association Press, 1960.

Genné, Elizabeth and William. *Church Family Camps and Conferences.* Philadelphia: United Church Press, 1962.

Messinger, C. F. *Church Camping for Junior Highs.* Philadelphia: The Westminster Press, 1960.

Mitchell, Grace L. *Fundamentals of Day Camping.* New York: Association Press, 1961.

Musselman, Virginia W. *The Day Camp Program Book.* New York: Association Press, 1963.

Patterson, Doris T. *Your Family Goes Camping.* Nashville: Abingdon Press, 1959.

Todd, Pauline H. and Floyd. *Camping for Christian Youth: A Guide to Methods and Principles for Evangelical Camps.* New York: Harper & Row, 1963.

### 4. Religion and Higher Education

Baly, Denis. *Academic Illusion.* New York: The Seabury Press, 1961.

Buttrick, George A. *Biblical Thought and the Secular University.* Baton Rouge: Louisiana State University Press, 1960.

Cantelon, John E. *A Protestant Approach to the Campus Ministry.* Philadelphia: The Westminster Press, 1964.

Chamberlin, J. Gordon. *Churches and the Campus.* Philadelphia: The Westminster Press, 1963.

Ditmanson, Harold H.; Hong, Howard V.; and Quanbeck, Warren A. *Christian Faith and the Liberal Arts*. Minneapolis: Augsburg Publishing House, 1960.

Earnshaw, George L., ed. *The Campus Ministry*. Valley Forge: Judson Press, 1964.

McCoy, Charles S. and McCarter, Neely. *The Gospel on Campus*. Richmond: John Knox Press, 1959.

Miller, Alexander. *Faith and Learning*. New York: Association Press, 1960.

Pelikan, Jaroslav J. *et al. Religion and the University*. Toronto: University of Toronto Press, 1964.

Wicke, Myron F. *The Church-Related College*. New York: The Center for Applied Research in Education, 1964.

Williams, George. *Wilderness and Paradise in Christian Thought*. New York: Harper & Row, 1962.

Witmer, S. A. *The Bible College Story: Education with Dimension*. New York: Channel Press, 1962.

### 5. Building and Equipment

Association for Childhood Education. *Equipment and Supplies*. Rev. ed. New York: The Association for Childhood Education, 1964.

Atkinson, C. Harry. *Building and Equipping for Christian Education*. Rev. ed. New York: The National Council of Churches, 1963.

White, James F. *Protestant Worship and Church Architecture*. New York: Oxford University Press, 1964.

## V. Curriculum for Christian Education

*The Church's Educational Ministry: A Curriculum Plan*. St. Louis: The Bethany Press, 1965.

*A Guide for Curriculum in Christian Education*. New York: The National Council of Churches, 1955.

*The Objective of Christian Education for Senior High Young People*. New York: National Council of Churches, 1958.

*The Objectives of Christian Education: A Study Document*. New York: National Council of Churches, 1958.

Olson, Bernhard E. *Faith and Prejudice: Intergroup Problems in Protestant Curricula*. New Haven: Yale University Press, 1962.

Wyckoff, D. Campbell. *Theory and Design of Christian Education Curriculum*. Philadelphia: The Westminster Press, 1961.

## VI. Methods in Christian Education

### 1. General Considerations of Method

Chaplin, Dora P. *The Privilege of Teaching*. New York: Morehouse-Barlow Co., 1962.

Fallaw, Wesner. *The Case Method in Pastoral and Lay Education*. Philadelphia: The Westminster Press, 1963.

Gilbert, W. Kent. *As Christians Teach*. Philadelphia: Fortress Press, 1963.

Klein, Alan F. *How to Use Role Playing Effectively*. New York: Association Press, 1959.

Morrison, Eleanor S. and Foster, Virgil E. *Creative Teaching in the Church*. Englewood Cliffs: Prentice-Hall, 1963.

Swain, Dorothy G. *Teach Me to Teach*. Valley Forge: Judson Press, 1964.

Van Caster, Marcel, S.J. *The Structure of Catechetics*. New York: Herder and Herder, 1965.

## 2. Age-Group Methods
### (a) Children

Adair, Thelma and Adams, Rachel S. *When We Teach 4's and 5's.* Philadelphia: Geneva Press, 1963.

Barnouw, Elsa and Swan, Arthur. *Adventures with Children in Nursery School and Kindergarten.* New York: Thomas Y. Crowell Company, 1959.

Carlson, Jessie B. *Toddlers at Church.* St. Louis: The Bethany Press, 1961.

Cully, Iris V. *Children in the Church.* Philadelphia: The Westminster Press, 1960.

Fritz, Dorothy B. *The Child and the Christian Faith.* Richmond: John Knox Press, 1964.

Goddard, Carrie Lou. *The Child and His Nurture.* Nashville: Abingdon Press, 1962.

Heinz, Mamie W. *Growing and Learning in the Kindergarten.* Richmond: John Knox Press, 1959.

Heron, Frances Dunlop. *Jay Bain, Junior Boy.* Nashville: Abingdon Press, 1963.

Huey, J. Frances. *Teaching Primary Children.* New York: Holt, Rinehart & Winston, 1965.

Hunter, Edith F. *Conversations with Children.* Boston: Beacon Press, 1962.

Keiser, Armilda B. *Here's How and When.* Rev. ed. New York: Friendship Press, 1960.

Lee, Florence B. *Primary Children in the Church.* Valley Forge: Judson Press, 1961.

McCutchan, Marjorie M. *The Church Guides Children's Work.* Richmond: John Knox Press, 1963.

Newberry, Josephine. *Nursery-Kindergarten Weekday Education in the Church.* Richmond: John Knox Press, 1960.

Priester, Gertrude. *Teaching Primary Children in the Church.* Philadelphia: Geneva Press, 1964.

Reeves, Katherine. *When We Teach 3's.* Philadelphia: Geneva Press, 1963.

Roorbach, Rosemary. *Teaching Children in the Church.* Nashville: Abingdon Press, 1959.

Rudolph, Mary B. *The Church Teaching Children Grades One Through Six.* Richmond: John Knox Press, 1964.

Sundquist, Ralph R., Jr. *Whom God Chooses: The Child in the Church.* Philadelphia: Geneva Press, 1964.

Tobey, Kathrene McLandress. *The Church Plans for Kindergarten Children.* Philadelphia: The Westminster Press, 1959.

### (b) Youth

Association for Supervision and Curriculum Development. *Juvenile Delinquency: Research, Theory and Comment.* Washington: National Education Association, 1960.

Bier, William C., S.J., ed. *The Adolescent: His Search for Understanding.* New York: Fordham University Press, 1963.

Bowman, Locke E., Jr. *How to Teach Senior Highs.* Philadelphia: The Westminster Press, 1963.

Erikson, Erik H., ed. *Youth: Change and Challenge.* New York: Basic Books, 1963.

Ferguson, Rowena. *The Church's Ministry with Senior Highs.* Nashville: Graded Press, 1963.

Frellick, Francis I. *Helping Youth in Conflict.* Englewood Cliffs: Prentice-Hall, 1965.

Garrison, Karl C. *Before You Teach Teenagers.* Philadelphia: Lutheran Church Press, 1962.

Roberts, Dorothy M. *Leading Teen-Age Groups.* New York: Association Press, 1963.

# A SELECTED BIBLIOGRAPHY

Smith, Barbara. *How to Teach Junior Highs.* Philadelphia: The Westminster Press, 1965.

*We Have This Ministry.* No. 1 (1963), No. 2 (1964). New York: National Council of Churches.

Wittenberg, Rudolph M. *Adolescence and Discipline.* New York: Association Press, 1959.

Wycoff, Mary E. *Encounter with Early Teens.* Philadelphia: The Westminster Press, 1965.

*The Young Adolescent in the Church.* Philadelphia: Geneva Press, 1963.

## (c) *Adults*

Bergevin, Paul; Morris, Dwight; and Smith, Robert M. *Adult Education Procedures.* New York: The Seabury Press, 1963.

Clemmons, Robert S. *Young Adults in the Church.* Nashville: Abingdon Press, 1959.

Culver, Elsie Thomas. *New Church Programs with the Aging.* New York: Association Press, 1961.

Dees, Norman, ed. *Approaches to Adult Teaching.* New York: Pergamon Press, 1965.

Department of Adult Work. *A Manual for Young Adults.* New York: National Council of Churches, 1961.

Ellsworth, Allen S. *Young Men, Young Women.* New York: Association Press, 1963.

Ernsberger, David J. *A Philosophy of Adult Christian Education.* Philadelphia: The Westminster Press, 1959.

Fry, John R. *A Hard Look at Adult Christian Education.* Philadelphia: The Westminster Press, 1961.

Gray, Robert M. and Moberg, David O. *The Church and the Older Person.* Grand Rapids: Wm. B. Eerdmans Publishing Co., 1962.

Hanson, Joseph John. *Our Church Plans for Adults.* Valley Forge: Judson Press, 1962.

Houle, Cyril O. *Continuing Your Education.* New York: McGraw-Hill Book Company, 1964.

————. *The Inquiring Mind: A Study of the Adult Who Continues to Learn.* Madison: University of Wisconsin Press, 1961.

Hugen, M. D. *The Church's Ministry to the Older Unmarried.* Grand Rapids: Wm. B. Eerdmans Publishing Co., 1959.

Khoobyar, Helen. *Facing Adult Problems in Christian Education.* Philadelphia: The Westminster Press, 1963.

Kidd, J. R., ed. *Adult Education.* Toronto: University of Toronto Press, 1960.

Knowles, Malcolm S., ed. *Handbook of Adult Education in the United States.* Chicago: The Adult Education Association, 1960.

Little, Lawrence C., ed. *Wider Horizons in Christian Adult Education.* Pittsburgh: University of Pittsburgh Press, 1962.

Maves, Paul B. *Understanding Ourselves as Adults.* Nashville: Abingdon Press, 1959.

McKinley, John. *Creative Methods for Adult Classes.* St. Louis: The Bethany Press, 1960.

Reinhart, Bruce. *The Institutional Nature of Adult Christian Education.* Philadelphia: The Westminster Press, 1962.

Rismiller, Arthur P. *Older Members in the Congregation.* Minneapolis: Augsburg Publishing House, 1964.

Saffen, Wayne. *Young Married Couples in the Church.* St. Louis: Concordia Publishing House, 1964.

Verner, Coolie and Booth, Alan. *Adult Education.* New York: The Center for Applied Research in Education, 1964.

### 3. *The Use of the Bible in Christian Education*

Baxter, Edna M. *Teaching the New Testament.* Philadelphia: United Church Press, 1960.

Cully, Iris V. *Imparting the Word: The Bible in Christian Education.* Philadelphia: The Westminster Press, 1963.

Dentan, Robert C. *The Design of the Scriptures.* New York: McGraw-Hill Book Company, 1960.

Dietrich, Suzanne de. *God's Unfolding Purpose: A Guide to the Study of the Bible.* Tr. by Robert McAfee Brown. Philadelphia: The Westminster Press, 1960.

Heim, Ralph D. *Youth's Companion to the Bible.* Philadelphia: Fortress Press, 1959.

Hunter, A. M. *Teaching and Preaching the New Testament.* Philadelphia: The Westminster Press, 1963.

*The Interpreter's Dictionary of the Bible.* 4 vol. Nashville: Abingdon Press, 1962.

Jones, Clifford M. *The Bible Today: For Those Who Teach It.* Philadelphia: Fortress Press, 1964.

Koenig, Robert E. *The Use of the Bible with Adults.* Philadelphia: United Church Press, 1959.

Lace, O. Jessie. *Teaching the New Testament.* New York: The Seabury Press, 1961.

Laymon, Charles M. *The Use of the Bible in Teaching Youth.* Nashville: Abingdon Press, 1962.

Little, Sara. *The Role of the Bible in Contemporary Christian Education.* Richmond: John Knox Press, 1961.

Robertson, Edwin H. *The Bible in the Local Church.* New York: Association Press, 1963.

Robinson, James M. and Cobb, John B., eds. *The New Hermeneutic.* New York: Harper & Row, 1964.

Rolston, Holmes. *The Bible in Christian Teaching.* Richmond: John Knox Press, 1962.

Smart, James D. *The Interpretation of Scripture.* Philadelphia: The Westminster Press, 1961.

Smither, Ethel L. *Children and the Bible.* Nashville: Abingdon Press, 1960.

### 4. *The Arts and Christian Education*

Dillenberger, Jane. *Style and Content in Christian Art.* Nashville: Abingdon Press, 1965.

Dixon, John W., Jr. *Nature and Grace in Art.* Chapel Hill: University of North Carolina Press, 1964.

Eversole, Finley, ed. *Christian Faith and the Contemporary Arts.* Nashville: Abingdon Press, 1962.

Fritz, Dorothy B. *The Use of Symbolism in Christian Education.* Philadelphia: The Westminster Press, 1961.

Glendenning, Frank J. *The Church and the Arts.* Naperville, Ill.: Alec R. Allenson, 1960.

McClinton, Katherine Morrison. *Christian Church Art Through the Ages.* New York: The Macmillan Company, 1962.

Merritt, Helen. *Guiding Free Expression in Children's Art.* New York: Holt, Rinehart & Winston, 1964.

Nathan, Walter L. *Art and the Message of the Church.* Philadelphia: The Westminster Press, 1961.

Rice, D. Talbot. *The Beginnings of Christian Art*. Nashville: Abingdon Press, 1958.

Taylor, Margaret Fisk. *Time for Wonder*. Philadelphia: United Church Press, 1961.

Vogt, Von Ogden. *Art and Religion*. Boston: Beacon Press, 1960.

### 5. Drama and Christian Education

Bachman, John W. and Browne, E. Martin, eds. *Better Plays for Today's Churches*. New York: Association Press, 1964.

Brandt, Alvin G. *Drama Handbook for Churches*. New York: The Seabury Press, 1964.

Ehrensperger, Harold. *Religious Drama: Ends and Means*. Nashville: Abingdon Press, 1962.

Heltman, Harry J. and Brown, Helen A., eds. *Choral Readings for Junior Worship and Inspiration*. Philadelphia: The Westminster Press, 1957.

————. *Choral Readings for Teen-Age Worship and Inspiration*. Philadelphia: The Westminster Press, 1959.

Johnson, Albert. *Drama: Technique and Philosophy*. Valley Forge: Judson Press, 1963.

Kerr, James S. *The Key to Good Church Drama*. Minneapolis: Augsburg Publishing House, 1965.

Stirling, Nora. *Family Life Plays*. New York: Association Press, 1961.

### 6. Audio-Visual Materials and Techniques and Christian Education

*Audio-Visual Resource Guide*. A cumulative index published biennially. New York: National Council of Churches.

DeKieffer, Robert E. *Audio-Visual Instruction*. New York: The Center for Applied Research in Education, 1965.

Harrell, John. *Teaching Is Communicating: An Audio-Visual Handbook for Church Use*. New York: The Seabury Press, 1965.

Kinder, James S. *Using Audio-Visual Materials in Education*. Cincinnati: American Book Company, 1965.

Wittich, Walter A. and Schuller, C. F. *Audio-Visual Materials: Their Nature and Use*. New York: Harper & Row, 1962.

### 7. Music and Christian Education

Lovelace, Austin C. and Rice, William C. *Music and Worship in the Church*. Nashville: Abingdon Press, 1960.

Mealy, Norman and Margaret. *Sing for Joy*. New York: The Seabury Press, 1961.

Morsch, Vivian S. *The Use of Music in Christian Education*. Philadelphia: The Westminster Press, 1956.

Tufts, Nancy Poore. *The Art of Handbell Ringing*. Nashville: Abingdon Press, 1961.

### 8. The Christian Education of the Exceptional Person

Babcock, Fern S. *Ministries of Mercy*. New York: Friendship Press, 1962.

Barbe, Walter B. *The Exceptional Child*. New York: The Center for Applied Research in Education, 1963.

Bogardus, LaDonna. *Christian Education for Retarded Children and Youth*. Nashville: Abingdon Press, 1963.

Carlson, Bernice Wells and Ginglend, David R. *Play Activities for the Retarded Child*. Nashville: Abingdon Press, 1961.

Cruickshank, William M. and Johnson, G. Orville, eds. *Education of Exceptional Children and Youth*. Englewood Cliffs: Prentice-Hall, 1958.

Ebersole, Eleanor. *Christian Education for Socially Handicapped Children and Youth.* Philadelphia: United Church Press, 1964.

Ginglend, David R. and Stiles, Winifred E. *Music Activities for Retarded Children.* Nashville: Abingdon Press, 1965.

Harrington, Janette T. and Webb, Muriel S. *Who Cares?* New York: Friendship Press, 1962.

Palmer, Charles E. *The Church and the Exceptional Person.* Nashville: Abingdon Press, 1961.

Petersen, Sigurd D. *Retarded Children: God's Children.* Philadelphia: The Westminster Press, 1960.

## VII. Prayer and Worship

### 1. *The Nature of Prayer and Worship*

Abba, Raymond. *Principles of Christian Worship.* New York: Oxford University Press, 1957.

Davis, Henry G. *Why We Worship.* Philadelphia: Muhlenberg Press, 1961.

Fauth, Robert T. *When We Worship.* Philadelphia: United Church Press, 1961.

Shepherd, Massey H., Jr. *Worship in Scripture and Tradition.* New York: Oxford University Press, 1963.

Vogt, Von Ogden. *The Primacy of Worship.* Boston: Starr King Press, 1958.

### 2. *Prayer and Worship in Christian Education*

Bailey, J. Martin and Betty Jane. *Worship with Youth.* Philadelphia: United Church Press, 1962.

Baxter, Edna M. *Learning to Worship.* Valley Forge: Judson Press, 1965.

Bowman, Clarice M. *Resources for Worship.* New York: Association Press, 1961.

Couch, Helen F. and Barefield, Sam S. *Worship Sourcebook for Youth.* Nashville: Abingdon Press, 1962.

Curry, L. H. and Wetzel, C. M. *Worship Services Using the Fine Arts.* Philadelphia: The Westminster Press, 1961.

Fahs, Sophia Lyon. *Worshipping Together with Questioning Minds.* Boston: Beacon Press, 1965.

Lee, Florence *et al. When Children Worship.* Valley Forge: Judson Press, 1963.

MacInnes, Gordon A. *A Guide to Worship in Camp and Conference.* Philadelphia: The Westminster Press, 1963.

McGavran, Grace. *Learning How Children Worship.* St. Louis: The Bethany Press, 1964.

Shepherd, Massey H., Jr. *Liturgy and Education.* New York: The Seabury Press, 1965.

# BIOGRAPHICAL INDEX
## OF CONTRIBUTORS

BOWMAN, Clarice M.
Methodist. Duke University, A.B., A.M.; Director of Christian Education, Plymouth Congregational Church, New Haven, Conn. and Wesley Memorial Methodist Church, High Point, N. C.; Staff Member, Methodist Board of Education; Assistant Professor, High Point College; Jonathan Fisher Professor of Christian Education, Bangor Theological Seminary, 1961 to present. Publications: *Guiding Intermediates* (1943); coauthor, *Power Through Prayer* (1947); *Restoring Worship* (1951); *Ways Youth Learn* (1952); *Spiritual Values in Camping* (1954); *Worship Ways for Camp* (1955); *Resources for Worship* (1961); *The Living Art of Worship* (1964).

BROWNING, Robert L.
Methodist. Missouri Valley College, A.B. (1945); Union Theological Seminary (N.Y.), B.D. (1948); Ohio State University, Ph.D. (1960); Minister of Education, Old Stone Church, Meadville, Pa., 1946-51, Community Church, Mt. Vernon, N. Y., 1951-53, and North Broadway Methodist Church, Columbus, Ohio, 1953-59; Associate Professor, The Methodist Theological School in Ohio, 1959 to present.

CANTELON, John Edward
United Presbyterian. Reed College, B.A. (1948); Oxford University, D. Phil. (1951); Pastor, Fairmount Presbyterian Church, Eugene, Ore., 1952-53; University Pastor, 1953-55, and Associate Director of the Christian Association, 1955-57, at the University of Pennsylvania; Staff Member, United Presbyterian Board of Christian Education, 1957-60; Chaplain and Associate Professor, University of Southern California, 1960 to present. Publications: *A Protestant Approach to the Campus Ministry* (1964).

CASE, William F.
Methodist. Ohio Wesleyan University, A.B. (1940); Boston University School of Theology, S.T.B. (1945); Columbia University, M.A. (1948); Columbia University and Union Theological Seminary, Ed.D. (1953); Assistant Professor, Baldwin-Wallace College, 1946-48; Professor, Garrett Theological Seminary, 1949-59; Dean and Professor, Saint Paul School of Theology Methodist, 1959 to present. Publications: Contributor to *Religious Education: A Comprehensive Survey* (1960).

GODDARD, Carrie Lou

Methodist. Maryville College, A.B. (1933); University of Tennessee, M.Ed. (1948); Teacher in Public Schools, Blount County and Maryville, Tenn., 1933-43; Elementary School, the University of Tennessee, 1943-44; Holston Conference Board of Education, 1944-47; Supervising Teacher, Blount County, Tenn., Public Schools, 1947-48; Virginia Conference Board of Education, 1948-54; Associate Professor, Scarritt College for Christian Workers, 1954 to present. Publications: Vacation Church School Texts: *Let's Go to Church* (1947), *God, the Creator* (1965), and *Bible Lands and Times* (1965); Missionary Education Text: *Along a Congo Path* (1959); Children's Reading Books: *Jesus Goes to Church* (1954), and *Cynthia at Church* (1962); Others: *The Child and His Nurture* (1962).

GRIMES, Howard

Methodist. The University of Texas, B.A. (1936); Southern Methodist University, B.D. (1940); Union Theological Seminary (N.Y.), S.T.M. (1941); Columbia University, Ph.D. (1949); Public School Teacher, Cookville, Tex., 1936-37; Associate Pastor, First Methodist Church, Houston, Tex., 1941-42 and 1945-47; Chaplain, the United States Army, 1942-45; Assistant, Associate, and Professor, Perkins School of Theology, Southern Methodist University, 1949 to present. Publications: *The Church Redemptive* (1958); *The Rebirth of the Laity* (1961); *Realms of Our Calling* (1965).

HAKES, J. Edward

Baptist. Wheaton College, B.A. (1937); Eastern Baptist Theological Seminary, B.D. (1941); Western Baptist Bible College, D.D. (1957); Pastor at First Baptist Church, Beacon, N. Y., 1940-42; First Baptist Church, Gallipolis, Ohio, 1942-48; Bethel Baptist Church, Kalamazoo, Mich., 1948-54; President, Grand Rapids Baptist Theological Seminary, 1954-58; Faculty of Wheaton College (Wheaton, Ill.), 1958 to present. Publications: editor of *An Introduction to Evangelical Christian Education* (1964).

HOWE, Reuel L.

Protestant Episcopal. Whitman College, B.A. (1927); Philadelphia Divinity School, S.T.B. (1930), S.T.M. (1931), and S.T.D. (1941); Whitman College, D.D. (1960); Chicago Theological Seminary, D.D. (1960); Vicar, St. Stephen's Church, Elsmere, N. Y., 1931-37; Faculty Member, Philadelphia Divinity School, 1937-44; Protestant Episcopal Theological Seminary, 1944-57; Director, Institute for Advanced Pastoral Studies, Bloomfield Hills, Mich., 1957 to present. Publications: *Man's Need and God's Action* (1953); *The Creative Years* (1959); *Herein Is Love* (1961); *The Miracle of Dialogue* (1963).

JEWELL, David W.

United Church of Christ. Carleton College, B.A. (1948); Union Theological Seminary (N.Y.), B.D. (1951); Teachers College, Columbia University, Ed.D. (1957); Instructor, Mount Hermon School for Boys, 1951-53; Minister of Christian Education, Pocantico Hills, 1954-55; Instructor, Union Theological Seminary (N.Y.), 1955-57; Associate Professor, Bangor Theological Seminary, 1957-61; Associate Professor and Director, Schauffler Division of Christian Education, Oberlin Graduate School of Theology, 1961 to present.

KENNEDY, William Bean

Presbyterian Church, U.S. Wofford College, A.B. (1947); Duke University, M.A. (1948); Union Theological Seminary (Va.), B.D. (1954); Yale University, Ph.D. (1957); Teacher, Spartanburg, S. C., 1948-49; Instructor, Emory at Oxford, Oxford, Ga., 1949-51; Assistant and Associate Professor, Union Theological Seminary (Va.), 1957-65; Associate Secretary of Education, Board of Christian

Education, Presbyterian Church, U.S., 1965 to present. Publications: *Into Covenant Life* (1963, 1964); *The Shaping of Protestant Education* (1966).

KROEHLER, Allen E.

United Church of Christ. Gustavus Adolphus College, B.A. (1950); Eden Theological Seminary, B.D. (1954); Pastor, Mt. Hope United Church of Christ, Whittier, Calif., 1954-58; Director of Children's Work, Board of Christian Education and Publication, Evangelical and Reformed Church, 1958-61; Program Secretary, United Church Board for Homeland Ministries, 1961-64; Director, Laboratory for Leadership and Learning, Lancaster Theological Seminary, 1964 to present.

LITTLE, Sara

Presbyterian Church, U.S. Queens College (N.C.), B.A. (1939); Presbyterian School of Christian Education, M.R.E. (1944); Yale University, Ph.D. (1958); Assistant Regional Director of Christian Education, Synod of North Carolina, 1944-50; Professor, Presbyterian School of Christian Education, 1951 to present. Publications: *Learning Together in the Christian Fellowship* (1956); *The Role of the Bible in Contemporary Christian Education* (1961); *The Language of the Christian Community* (1965).

LODER, James E.

United Presbyterian. Carleton College, A.B. (1953); Princeton Theological Seminary, B.D. (1957); Harvard Divinity School, Th.M. (1958); Menninger Foundation, Theological Fellow (1961-62); Harvard University, Ph.D. (1962); Research Assistant, Harvard University Project in Religion and Mental Health, 1958-60; Assistant Professor, Princeton Theological Seminary, 1962 to present. Publications: *Religion and the Public Schools* (1965).

LYNN, Robert Wood

United Presbyterian. Princeton University, A.B. (1948); Yale University, B.D. (1952); Union Theological Seminary (N.Y.), Th.D. (1962); Assistant Minister, Montview Presbyterian Church, Denver, Colo., 1952-54 and 1956-59; Assistant, Associate, and Professor, Union Theological Seminary (N.Y.), 1959 to present; Dean of the Auburn Program at Union Theological Seminary (N.Y.), 1965 to present. Publications: *Protestant Strategies in Education* (1964).

McCLUSKEY, Neil Gerard, S.J.

Roman Catholic. Gonzaga University, A.B. (1944); M.A. (1945); Alma College, S.T.L. (1952); Columbia University, Ph.D. (1957); Instructor, Bellarmine High School, Tacoma, Wash., 1945-48; Assistant Professor, Seattle University, 1955; Education Editor, *America*, 1955-61; Associate Professor and Dean of the School of Education, Gonzaga University, 1960-64; Director, Gonzaga-in-Florence, Gonzaga University, 1964; Academic Vice President, Gonzaga University, 1964 to present. Publications: *Public Schools and Moral Education* (1958); *Catholic Viewpoint on Education* (1959, rev. ed., 1962); *Catholic Education in the United States: A Documentary Study* (1964).

MILLER, Donald E.

Church of the Brethren. University of Chicago, M.A. (1952); Bethany Theological Seminary, B.D. (1958); Harvard University, Ph.D. (1962); Associate Professor, Bethany Theological Seminary, 1961 to present.

MILLER, Harriet L.

Evangelical United Brethren. North Central College, B.A. (1946); University of Minnesota, M.A. (1957); Elementary Public School Teacher, Minn., 1936-44; Director of Christian Education, Oakland Avenue Church, 1946-48, and Minnesota Council of Churches, 1948-50; Field Worker, the Minnesota Conference,

Evangelical United Brethren Church, 1950-53; Director of Christian Education, St. Paul, Minn., Council of Churches, 1953-56; Associate Professor, United Theological Seminary, 1956 to present.

MILLER, James Blair

Christian Churches (Disciples of Christ). Bethany College (W.Va.), A.B. (1938); Yale Divinity School, B.D. (1941); Indiana University, Ed.D. (1955); Minister, The Christian Church, Plymouth, Pa., 1941-44, and Bethany Memorial Church, Bethany, W.Va., 1944-51; Instructor, Bethany College (W.Va.), 1944-51; Professor, Christian Theological Seminary, 1951 to present. Publications: *Our Church's Story* (1961).

MILLER, Randolph Crump

Protestant Episcopal. Pomona College, B.A. (1931); Yale University, Ph.D. (1936); Pacific School of Religion, D.D. (1952); Church Divinity School of the Pacific, S.T.D. (1952); Episcopal Theological School, D.D. (1961); Instructor, Assistant, Associate, and Professor, Church Divinity School of the Pacific, 1936-52; Professor of Christian Education on the Luther A. Weigle Fund, Yale University, 1952-63; Horace Bushnell Professor of Christian Nurture, Yale University, 1963 to present; Editor, *Religious Education* journal, since 1958. Publications: *What We Can Believe* (1941); *A Guide for Church School Teachers* (1943, rev. ed., 1947); *Religion Makes Sense* (1950); *The Clue to Christian Education* (1950); *A Symphony of the Christian Year* (1954); *Education for Christian Living* (1956, rev. ed., 1963); *Biblical Theology and Christian Education* (1956); *Be Not Anxious* (1957); *I Remember Jesus* (1958); *Christian Nurture and the Church* (1961); *Your Child's Religion* (1962); *Youth Considers Parents As People* (1965).

MOORE, Allen Joe

Methodist. Southwestern University (Tex.), A.B. (1949); Baylor University, M.A. (1950); Perkins School of Theology, Southern Methodist University, B.D. (1953); Boston University, Ph.D. (1963); Minister, First Methodist Church, Kennedale, Tex., 1950-54 and First Methodist Church, Moody, Tex., 1954-56; Minister of Education and Counseling, Chestnut Street Congregational Church, Worcester, Mass., 1956-57; Coordinating Director of the Wesley Foundation and Professor of Religion, North Texas State University, 1957-58; Staff Member, Methodist Board of Education, 1958-63; Assistant and Associate Professor, Dean of Students, The School of Theology at Claremont, 1963 to present. Publications: *Toward Understanding Older Youth—Young Adults* (1962); coauthor, *The Transitional Years* (1964).

MOORE, William Clifton

Methodist. Lambuth College, A.B. (1936); Emory University, B.D. (1940); Boston University, Ph.D. (1954); Pastor in the Memphis Methodist Conference, 1939-43; Staff Member, Memphis Conference Board of Education, 1943-46; Staff Member, Methodist Board of Education, 1946-48; Executive Secretary, Idaho Conference Board of Education, 1948-51; Pastor, New England Southern Methodist Conference, 1951-52; Instructor and Professor, Boston University School of Theology, 1952 to present. Publications: *You and Your Creator* (1960).

NELSON, Carl Ellis

Presbyterian, U.S. Austin College, Sherman, Tex., B.A. (1937); Austin Presbyterian Theological Seminary, B.D. (1940); University of Texas, M.A. (1944); Columbia University, Ph.D. (1955); Minister to Students, University Presbyterian Church, Austin, Tex., 1940-43; Instructor, University of Texas and

Austin Presbyterian Theological Seminary, 1943-45; Staff Member, Presbyterian, U.S., Board of Christian Education, 1945-48; Professor, Austin Presbyterian Theological Seminary, 1948-57; Professor, Union Theological Seminary (N.Y.), 1957-60; Skinner and McAlpin Professor of Practical Theology, Union Theological Seminary (N.Y.), 1960 to present. Publications: Contributor to *Religious Education: A Comprehensive Survey* (1960); *Love and Law* (1963).

PRIESTER, Marcus J.
United Presbyterian. Grove City College, B.A. (1939), D.D. (1959); Western Theological Seminary, S.T.B. (1942), S.T.M. (1945); University of Toronto, Th.D. (1963); Pastor, Woodlawn Presbyterian Church, Aliquippa, Pa., 1940-44; Director, Westminster Foundation, New England, 1946-50; Staff Member, Board of Christian Education, Presbyterian Church, U.S.A., 1950-59; Professor, McCormick Theological Seminary, 1959 to present.

RUSSELL, Letty M.
United Presbyterian. Wellesley College, B.A. (1951); Harvard University, B.D. (1958); Elementary Teacher, Middletown, Conn., 1951-52; Director of Christian Education, East Harlem Protestant Parish, New York City, 1952-55; Minister, Church of the Ascension, East Harlem Protestant Parish, New York City, 1958 to present.

SCHINDLER, Rabbi Alexander M.
Reform Judaism. City College, New York, B.S.S. (1950); Hebrew Union College, B.H.L.-Rabbi (1953); Rabbi, Temple Emanuel, Worcester, Mass., 1953-59; Director, New England Council of the Union of American Hebrew Congregations, 1959-63; National Director of Education, the Union of American Hebrew Congregations, 1963 to present. Publications: *From Discrimination to Extermination* (1950).

SHELTON, Gentry A.
Christian Churches (Disciples of Christ). Transylvania College, A.B. (1933); College of the Bible, M.A. (1935); University of Kentucky, Ed.D. (1954); Instructor, Transylvania College, 1934-35; Minister, Athens, Ky. Christian Church, 1934-35; Minister of Education and Music, Central Christian Church, Lexington, Ky., 1935-55; Professor, Brite Divinity School, Texas Christian University, 1955 to present. Publications: *A Study of Young Peoples Conferences in Kentucky* (1935); *A Study of Directors of Christian Education in Churches of the Disciples of Christ in the United States* (1954).

SHINN, Roger L.
United Church of Christ. Heidelberg College, A.B. (1938), D.Litt. (1963); Union Theological Seminary (N.Y.), B.D. (1941); Columbia University, Ph.D. (1951); Mission House Theological Seminary, D.D. (1960); Franklin and Marshall College, D.D. (1963); Instructor, Union Theological Seminary (N.Y.), 1947-49; Associate Professor and Professor, Heidelberg College, 1949-54; Professor, Vanderbilt University Divinity School, 1954-59; Professor, Union Theological Seminary (N.Y.), 1959-60; William E. Dodge, Jr. Professor of Applied Christianity, Union Theological Seminary (N.Y.), 1960 to present. Publications: *Beyond This Darkness* (1946); *Christianity and the Problem of History* (1953); *The Sermon on the Mount* (1954, rev. ed., 1962); *Life, Death, and Destiny* (1957); *The Existentialist Posture* (1959); *The Educational Mission of Our Church* (1962); *Moments of Truth* (1964); editor, *The Search for Identity: Essays on American Character* (1964); *Tangled World* (1965).

SHOCKLEY, Grant S.

Methodist. Lincoln University (Pa.), A.B. (1942); Drew University, B.D. (1945); Columbia University, M.A. (1946), Ed.D. (1952); Associate Minister, St. Mark's Methodist Church, New York City, 1942-46; Associate Professor, Clark College, Atlanta, Ga., 1946-49; Professor, Gammon Theological Seminary, 1949-51; Minister, Whatcoat Memorial Methodist Church, Dover, Del., 1951-53, and the Janes Memorial Methodist Church, Brooklyn, N. Y., 1953-59; Professor, Garrett Theological Seminary, 1959 to present.

SNYDER, Ross

United Presbyterian. Ohio State University, B.S.; Boston University School of Religious Education, M.R.E.; Teachers College, Columbia University, Ed.D.; Director of Religious Education, Prospect Presbyterian Church, Maplewood, N. J.; Minister of Education, Winnetka Congregational Church, Winnetka, Ill.; Professor, Chicago Theological Seminary, 1940 to present. Publications: coauthor, *Religious Radio* (1948); *Ministry With Youth* (1965).

TAYLOR, Marvin J.

Methodist. Olivet Nazarene College, B.Th. (1943); McCormick Theological Seminary, B.D. (1946); University of Chicago, A.M. (1949); University of Pittsburgh, Ph.D. (1954); Assistant Professor, Olivet Nazarene College, 1948-54; Minister of Christian Education, Mount Lebanon Methodist Church, Pittsburgh, Pa., 1954-56; Assistant and Associate Professor, University of Pittsburgh, 1956-62; Associate Professor, Saint Paul School of Theology Methodist, 1962 to present. Publications: editor, *Religious Education: A Comprehensive Survey* (1960); *Religious and Moral Education* (1965).

WYCKOFF, D. Campbell

United Presbyterian. New York University, B.S. (1939); A.M. (1941); Ph.D. (1948); Teacher and Community Worker in Alpine, Tenn. for the Presbyterian Board of National Missions, 1939-41; Staff Member, Greater New York Federation of Churches, 1941-42; Staff Member, Presbyterian Board of National Missions, 1942-47; Assistant, Associate, and Professor, New York University, 1947-54; Thomas W. Synnott Professor of Christian Education, Princeton Theological Seminary, 1954 to present. Publications: *The Task of Christian Education* (1955); *In One Spirit: Senior Highs and Missions* (1958); *The Gospel and Christian Education* (1959); *For Every Person* (1959); Contributor to *Religious Education: A Comprehensive Survey* (1960); *Theory and Design of Christian Education Curriculum* (1961); *How to Evaluate Your Christian Education Program* (1962); *The Great Belonging* (1962).

WYNN, John Charles

United Presbyterian. The College of Wooster, B.A. (1941); Yale University Divinity School, B.D. (1944); Davis and Elkins College, D.D. (1958); Columbia University, M.A. (1963), Ed.D. (1964); Associate Pastor, First Presbyterian Church, Evanston, Ill., 1944-47; Pastor, First Presbyterian Church, El Dorado, Kan., 1947-50; Staff Member, Presbyterian Board of Christian Education, 1950-59; Professor, Colgate Rochester Divinity School, 1959 to present. Publications: *How Christian Parents Face Family Problems* (1955); editor, *Sermons on Marriage and Family Life* (1956); *Pastoral Ministry to Families* (1957); coauthor, *Families in the Church: A Protestant Survey* (1961); editor, *Sex, Family, and Society in Theological Focus* (1966).

# INDEX

adoption, Christian education as, 12, 17

adults and Christian education, 18, 140, 205-15; current need for new patterns, 205-7; goals, 207-8; learning skills, 208-10; ministry to, 210-15; study groups, 138

Advent Christian Church, 161

African Methodist Episcopal Church, 161

Ahlschwede, Arthur M., 323

Alcuin, 23

American Association for Health, Physical Education and Recreation, 262

American Association of School Administrators, 332

American Association of University Professors, 346

American Baptist Convention, 100, 161

American Camping Association, 358-59

American Civil Liberties Union, 346

American Council on Education, 331, 332

American Legion, 334

American Lutheran Church, 158, 163, 324

American Public Welfare Association, 263

American Speech and Hearing Association, 263-64

American Sunday School Union, 26, 305, 321-22

*Anchor Bible*, 251

Aquinas, 63, 64, 106

Aristole, 62, 63

arts and Christian education, 227-41; methods, 233-36; theological basis, 229-33; worship and, 236-40

Assemblies of God, 322, 324

Association for Childhood Education International, 263

Association for Supervision and Curriculum Development, 263

Athearn, Walter S., 146

audio-visuals 222

Augustine, 19, 106

Bailey, Derrick S., 296

Baillie, John, 37, 43

Bailyn, Bernard, 21, 25

Baltimore Councils and Catholic education, 368-70

Barr, James, 44, 49

Barth, Karl, 36, 42, 43, 48, 60, 109, 347

Becker Amendment, 330

Bellah, Robert, 80-81, 83

Benedict, Ruth, 185

Benson, Clarence H., 319, 321

Berger, Peter, 73

Berkhof, H., 115

Bible and Christian education, 14, 17, 18, 38-39, 42-49, 131-32, 160, 173-74, 218, 235, 271

Blair, Edward P., 252

Bloy, Myron, 206

Boehlke, Robert, 56

Bogardus, La Donna, 265

Bonhoeffer, Dietrich, 48, 57, 83, 201, 289, 346, 347

Bowman, Clarice M., 227-41, 399

Bowman, Locke E., Jr., 224

Boy Scouts, 313-14, 320

Bronson, W. C., 74

Broudy, Harry, 64